A scholarly and rigorous exploration into what drives consumer behaviour in relation to brands – provocatively dissected and evaluated by some of the most forward-thinking academics and practitioners in advertising and brand marketing today. Prepare to rethink your long-cherished assumptions!

Hayes Roth, *Adjunct Professor of Marketing at City College of New York and founder of HA Roth Consulting LLC, USA*

This thoughtful and provocative collection is just the catalyst needed to move brand relationship marketing to the next level. Mixing pioneering theory with practical insights, the authors speak to both the real challenges facing marketers and growth officers today, and the new frontiers that they will soon have to confront: static vs. dynamic brand identities, personal vs. social brand interactions, and beneficial vs. nuanced brand relationships, to name just a few. A must-read for serious brand builders.

Lara L. Lee, *SVP Customer Experience Design, Lowe's Companies, Inc., USA*

For anyone looking to strengthen the bond between their brand and target audience, this is a timely and deeply fascinating compendium. It contains the latest thinking from the best and the brightest about brands, consumers, and the lives they share. Every chapter is rich in insights and inspiration; in particular, the articles on loyalty, social media, and the brand-driven organization have expanded my thinking about how to connect more powerfully with our customers.

David Snead, *Vice President, Marketing, Brand and Customer Experience, New York Philharmonic, USA*

This book is one of the most valuable sources of new research. It includes deeply insightful articles and source material for those who wish to create, build and strengthen brand relationships in today's era of digital Darwinism.

Erich Joachimsthaler, *CEO of Vivaldi Partners Group, USA*

Strong Brands, Strong Relationships breathes new life into marketing! It makes a strong case that the value of brands is in the human relationship, promising a more scientifically grounded, yet authentic future for marketing.

Stephen X. Springfield, *Sr. Vice President, Sentient Decision Science, USA*

STRONG BRANDS, STRONG RELATIONSHIPS

From the editorial team of the ground-breaking *Consumer-Brand Relationships: Theory and Practice* comes this new volume. *Strong Brands, Strong Relationships* is a collection of innovative research and management insights that build upon the foundations of the first book, but take the study of brand relationships outside of traditional realms by applying new theoretical frameworks and considering new contexts. The result is an expanded and better-informed account of people's relationships with brands and a demonstration of the important and timely implications of this evolving sub-discipline.

A range of different brand relationship environments are explored in the collection, including: online digital spaces, consumer collectives, global brands, luxury brands, branding in terrorist organizations, and the brand relationships of men and transient consumers. This book attends to relationship endings as well as their beginnings, providing a full life-cycle perspective. While the first volume focused on positive relationship benefits, this collection explores dysfunctional dynamics, adversarial and politically-charged relationships, and those that are harmful to well-being. Evocative constructs are leveraged, including secrets, betrayals, anthropomorphism, lying, infidelity, retaliation, and bereavement. The curated collection provides both a deeper theoretical understanding of brand relationship phenomena and ideas for practical application from experiments and execution in commercial practice.

Strong Brands, Strong Relationships will be the perfect read for marketing faculty and graduate students interested in branding dynamics, as well as managers responsible for stewarding brands.

Susan Fournier is Questrom Professor of Management and Professor of Marketing at Boston University, USA.

Michael Breazeale is an Assistant Professor of Marketing at Mississippi State University, USA.

Jill Avery is a Senior Lecturer at Harvard Business School, Harvard University USA.

STRONG BRANDS, STRONG RELATIONSHIPS

Edited by Susan Fournier, Michael Breazeale, and Jill Avery

Routledge
Taylor & Francis Group

LONDON AND NEW YORK

First published 2015
by Routledge
2 Park Square, Milton Park, Abingdon, Oxon OX14 4RN

and by Routledge
711 Third Avenue, New York, NY 10017

Routledge is an imprint of the Taylor & Francis Group, an informa business

British Library Cataloguing in Publication Data
A catalogue record for this book is available from the British Library

Library of Congress Cataloging in Publication Data
Fournier, Susan.
Strong brands strong relationships / Susan Fournier, Michael Breazeale and Jill Avery.
pages cm
Includes bibliographical references and index.
1. Brand name products. 2. Brand loyalty. 3. Branding (Marketing) 4. Consumer behavior. I. Breazeale, Michael, 1964- II. Avery, Jill. III. Title.
HD69.B87F69 2015
658.8'27—dc23
2014048783

ISBN: 978-1-138-78682-0 (hbk)
ISBN: 978-1-138-78683-7 (pbk)
ISBN: 978-1-315-76707-9 (ebk)

Typeset in Bembo
by FiSH Books Ltd, Enfield

CONTENTS

FIGURES

TABLES

NOTES ON CONTRIBUTORS

Dr David Aaker, the vice-chairman of Prophet Brand Strategy and professor emeritus of marketing strategy at the Berkeley-Haas School of Business, is the winner of four career awards for contributions to the practice and science of marketing. He has published over 100 articles and 16 books that have sold well over one million copies and include *Strategic Market Management; Building Strong Brands; Brand Leadership* (co-authored with Erich Joachimsthaler); *Brand Portfolio Strategy; Spanning Silos; Brand Relevance*; and *Aaker on Branding*. Named as one of the top five most important marketing/business gurus in 2007, he has won awards for the best article in the *California Management Review* and (twice) in the *Journal of Marketing*. A recognized authority on brand strategy, he has been an active consultant and speaker. A columnist for the American Marketing Association's *Marketing News*, he regularly blogs at LinkedIn and davidaaker.com.

Dr Pankaj Aggarwal is an associate professor of marketing at the University of Toronto. He received his PhD from the Graduate School of Business, University of Chicago in 2002 and his doctoral dissertation on consumer-brand relationships won the Marketing Science Institute's Alden G. Clayton Award for best dissertation in 2000. His primary research interest is in studying "brands-as-people," specifically conducting research on consumer-brand relationships and brand anthropomorphism. He also studies issues related to culture, time, and money. His research has been published in leading marketing and psychology journals such as the *Journal of Consumer Research, Journal of Marketing Research, Psychological Science*, and *Journal of Consumer Psychology*, and he serves on the editorial boards of the *Journal of Consumer Research* and the *Journal of Consumer Psychology*. Prior to entering academia, he was vice-president at J. Walter Thompson Advertising, heading its New Delhi office.

Dr Chris Allen is the Arthur Beerman Professor of Marketing at the University of Cincinnati, now in his third decade at the school. He served as MBA program director from 1994 through 1996 and associate dean for graduate programs from 2009 to 2011. He was a scholar-in-residence with the corporate new ventures group at Procter & Gamble in 1997 and then served three years as program administrator for P&G's Marketing Innovation Research Fund – a funding source for dissertation research. He is a recipient of the college's EXCEL Award for teaching excellence. His primary teaching contributions are in the areas of marketing management and branding strategy. He has published numerous articles in the premier marketing and consumer behavior journals and is co-author of a leading text entitled *Advertising and Integrated Brand Promotion*, now in its seventh edition. Previously, he was a faculty member in the Kellogg School of Management at Northwestern, and in the School of Management at the University of Massachusetts, Amherst. He received his PhD in marketing and consumer psychology from Ohio State.

Dr Zeynep Arsel is Associate Professor and Concordia University Research Chair in Consumption and Markets at John Molson School of Business. She is also a distinguished visiting professor at Aalto University. She is the recipient of 2011 Petro Canada Young Innovator Award, and 2012 Sidney J. Levy Award. Her research was published in the *Journal of Consumer Research* and *Journal of Marketing*. She is on the editorial board of the *Journal of Consumer Research* and *Consumption Markets and Culture*. Her work has been funded by the Social Sciences and Humanities Research Council; the Quebec Fund for Research, Society, and Culture; Association for Consumer Research; Marketing Science Institute, and was featured in mass media outlets including the *Wall Street Journal, Harper's Magazine, Globe and Mail, WIRED, Psychology Today, Montreal Gazette, Vancouver Sun, Ottawa Citizen, Canada.com, Le Devoir, L'Actualité, La Presse*, and countless blogs.

Dr Søren Askegaard is educated in social sciences with an MA, majoring in sociology (Odense University, 1986), a post-graduate diploma in political and social communication (Université de Paris 1 Panthéon-Sorbonne, 1988) and a PhD in marketing (Odense University, 1993). He is currently a full professor of consumption studies at the University of Southern Denmark. He has been heavily involved in European doctoral education of consumer culture theory and is the initiator and current director of the university's program in Market and Management Anthropology (MMA). His research focuses on consumer culture, where he has been particularly interested in issues such as the interplay of globalisms and localisms, the ideology of health and morality of the body, and marketplace seduction. His work has appeared in, among others, the *Journal of Consumer Research, Marketing Theory, Journal of Consumer Culture, International Business Review, Psychology and Marketing, Journal of Consumer Behaviour*, and *Consumption Markets and Culture*, as well as in numerous anthologies. He was an associate editor at the *Journal of Consumer Research* from 2008–14 and serves on boards of a number of other journals.

Dr Jill Avery is a senior lecturer at Harvard Business School where she teaches Marketing; Branding + Different; and Field Immersion Experiences for Leadership Development. Her research focuses on brand management and customer relationship management issues. Her research on online brand communities won the Harvard Business School Wyss award for excellence in doctoral research and a Marketing Science Institute Best Paper award. Her work has been published in *Journal of Consumer Research, Journal of Marketing Research, Journal of Marketing, International Journal of Research in Marketing, Harvard Business Review, MIT Sloan Management Review, Business Horizons, Journal for the Advancement of Marketing Education*, and *European Business Review*. She has written a series of teaching cases on branding that are available from Harvard Business School Publishing. Prior to her academic career, she spent nine years managing brands for Gillette, Braun, Samuel Adams, and AT&T, and spent three years on the agency side of the business, as an account executive managing consumer promotions for Pepsi, General Foods, Bristol-Myers, and Citibank. She received a DBA in marketing from Harvard Business School, an MBA in marketing and finance from the Wharton School, and a BA in English and art history from the University of Pennsylvania.

Dr James R. Bettman is the Burlington Industries Professor at the Fuqua School of Business and professor of psychology and neuroscience at Duke University. His BA (mathematics–economics) and PhD (administrative sciences) are from Yale University. He directs the doctoral program at the Fuqua School and has been the chair/co-chair for 39 marketing doctoral students. His research focuses on consumer choice, adaptive decision making, effects of emotion, and construction of identity. His publications include two books, a monograph, and over 120 research papers. He is an editorial board member for the *Journal of Consumer Research* and *Journal of Consumer Psychology* and an associate editor for the *Journal of Marketing Research*. He has been co-editor of the *Journal of Consumer Research*, president of the Association for Consumer Research, and is a fellow of the American Psychological Association, the American Psychological Society, and the Association for Consumer Research.

Dr Barbara Bickart is an associate professor of marketing and department chair at the School of Management at Boston University. Her research examines how the context of communication influences consumers' inference and judgment processes. Current projects explore how consumers create connections (e.g., emotional affinity, shared experiences) in the context of both consumer-to-consumer and business-to-consumer communication and how such connections influence the interpretation, perceived value, and persuasive impact of a message. Her work has appeared in a number of journals including the *Journal of Marketing Research, Journal of Consumer Research, Journal of Consumer Psychology, Journal of Interactive Marketing*, and *Journal of Advertising*. She is currently an associate editor at the *Journal of Public Policy and Marketing*.

Dr Max Blackston is a partner in BlackBar Consulting and a brand strategist, market researcher, and consumer psychologist with a long track record of innovation in the consumer sciences. He was one of the first in the field to successfully operationalize models of consumers' decision processes, and first to conceptualize a theory of consumer-brand relationships. He has always worked in an operational business framework and has had substantial experience in all of the marketing disciplines. He headed up Research International companies in England and Italy, and was Senior Vice President, Head of Planning and Research at Oglivy & Mather. He was European Marketing Director for Soda Club, predecessor of home-carbonation company, Soda Stream, and a consultant to BrandAsset Valuator at Young & Rubicam. He has made considerable contributions to the marketing sciences, through journal articles, conference papers, book chapters, and white papers. His work covers areas as diverse as micro-behavioral modeling, setting up single location telephone interviewing for multinational research, implementing the account planning process in an advertising agency, and building consumer-brand relationships. His seminal paper on consumer-brand relationships, presented at the 1993 UK Market Research Society Annual Conference, won the "Best Paper" Award, as did his 1995 ESOMAR paper on using cognitive response analysis for advertising pre-testing.

Dr Michael Breazeale is an assistant professor of marketing at Mississippi State University. His primary areas of research encompass consumer-brand connections, retail atmospherics, the consumptions of experiences, and emotional branding. He has published articles in *Journal of Retailing*, *International Journal of Market Research*, *Marketing Management Journal*, and *Journal of Business Research*, and has made numerous conference presentations relating to his research. He has won multiple awards for both teaching and research, and serves as reviewer for several top marketing journals. He is also one of Social Media Marketing Magazine's Top 100 Marketing Professors on Twitter and a 2012 Top Web Savvy Professor according to Best Universities Online. He has performed consulting duties with clients as diverse as Millward Brown Optimor and the US Military, and is co-editor of the book, *Consumer-Brand Relationships: Theory and Practice* with Susan Fournier and Marc Fetscherin (Taylor and Francis, 2012).

Dr Frédéric Brunel is a consumer researcher dedicated to informing two main domains: consumer relationships and product design, including consumption communities on and off-line, word-of-mouth dynamics, customer relationship management and aesthetic response styles and skill sets. His scholarly work resides at the intersection of social-psychology and cultural studies and focuses comprehensively on culture, group/community and personality/gender levels of analyses. He has published in the *Journal of Consumer Research*, *Journal of Consumer Psychology*, *Journal of the Academy of Marketing Science*, *Journal of Advertising*, *Journal of Advertising Research*, *Business Strategy Review*, *Journal of Marketing Communications*, *Marketing Theory*, *Journal of Creative Management*, and *Psychology and Marketing*. His research has also appeared in book chapters, managerial articles and conference proceedings. His work is used by some of the largest corporations and he is regularly quoted and interviewed in a wide array of print, radio, TV, and electronic media outlets. He has taught at all levels: undergraduate, MBA, doctoral, and executive programs. He has been a leader in the design and implementation of integrated cross-functional curricula. He has extensive international teaching experience, including Europe, Latin America, and Asia. Over the years, his commitment to higher education has been recognized through several research, teaching, and service awards.

Matt Carcieri is a brand strategist at The Jim Stengel Company, where he specializes in purpose, positioning, and organizational alignment. He spent 15 years at Procter & Gamble and held management roles on Pringles®, Folgers®, and Pantene®. Following that, he led strategic best practices for P&G and served as the in-house expert on branding. He has consulted with over 30 brands – both inside and outside P&G – to develop and activate their purpose, equity, positioning, and marketing strategies. In addition to his work in consumer-packaged goods, Matt has consulted for clients in the fields of media, technology, prestige, hospitality, retail, and higher education. He holds an MBA from Georgetown University's McDonough School of Business and a BA in international relations from the American University. He is a regular guest lecturer at the University of Cincinnati.

Dr John Deighton is the Harold M. Brierley Professor of Business Administration at Harvard Business School. He has been editor of the *Journal of Consumer Research*, and founding co-editor of the *Journal of Interactive Marketing*, has served as the Executive Director of the Marketing Science Institute, and is a Director of the Berkman Center for Internet and Society at Harvard University. He tweets at HBSmktg. He has been course head of Harvard's first year MBA Marketing course and has taught the elective MBA course in Digital Marketing Strategy, executive education programs in digital marketing, and marketing strategy in China. He has been a visiting scholar at the University of Tokyo, Duke's Fuqua School of Business, the Judge School, Cambridge University, and the Saïd School, Oxford University.

Dr John Desmond is a reader at the University of St Andrews in the UK. He is broadly interested in issues relating to organization, marketing, and consumption. His general interest in marginalia is partly sated by exploring of questions of morality in relation to what is hidden in exchange processes. This interest in marginalia most recently expressed itself in a series of projects that explore the continuing relevance of psychoanalysis to explanation in marketing and consumer research. Preliminary results from his next project, which is based on a study of obituaries, suggest that marketing is more marginal to societal interests than some might think. His research has been published in *Psychology and Marketing, European Journal of Marketing, Consumption, Markets and Culture*, and *Journal of Business Research*, among other journals. He also authored a textbook, *Consuming Behaviour,* and recently published a book on Freudian theory, *Psychoanalytic Accounts of Consuming Desire: Hearts of Darkness*.

Beth Leavenworth DuFault is a doctoral student in the marketing department at the University of Arizona. She holds a BA in sociology (Departmental Honors) from the University of California, Los Angeles, with an emphasis in applied mathematics and cultural sociology. Her research program focuses on understanding communities as fluid entities and how consumers resolve their consumer behavior and social practices that are consequently in tension. She is particularly interested in why, when, and how communities emerge; why, when, and how consumers leave and/or stay in them; and the ways in which consumption and the marketplace are used by consumers to navigate these evolving life spaces. To this end, she uses a wide range of methodologies and theoretical lenses to study how consumers create, join, experience, and leave community. Her focus on community has led to research projects that examine marketing phenomena such as market formation, innovation, brand relationships, brand communities and subcultures, defection and deconsumption, and servicescape experiences. Her work has been published in the *Journal of Consumer Research* and *Journal of Marketing for Higher Education*.

Dr Giana M. Eckhardt is a professor of marketing at Royal Holloway, University of London. She was formerly on the faculty at Suffolk University, Boston and the Australian Graduate School of Management, Sydney and was visiting faculty at China Europe International Business School in Shanghai. She received her BS in marketing from the University of Connecticut and her PhD in marketing from the University of Minnesota. She has published widely in the field of consumer culture theory, in particular on issues related to consumer behavior in Asia, branding, globalization, consumer ethics, and access based consumption. She has published over 20 articles in journals such as *Harvard Business Review* and *Journal of Consumer Research*. She is co-author of *The Myth of the Ethical Consumer* (Cambridge University Press). She is a past co-chair of the Consumer Culture Theory conference, is on the editorial review board of *Consumption, Markets and Culture*, and has guest edited special issues of *Qualitative Market Research* and *Journal of Macromarketing*. Her research has won awards from the Sheth Foundation and the Marketing Science Institute, and been featured in outlets such as *The Economist, The Atlantic, Scientific American*, and on *National Public Radio*. She has received research grants from the Australian Research Council and the Marketing Science Institute, and has worked closely with companies such as McKinsey in Asia and Dunkin' Brands in China. She has presented her work at top institutions and conferences around the world, including at the United Nations CSR Global Forum.

Dr Jennifer Edson Escalas is an associate professor at the Owen Graduate School of Management at Vanderbilt University. Her BAs (Spanish and linguistics, economics) and MBA are from UCLA, while her PhD (business administration) is from Duke University. Her research examines consumers' self-brand connections and applies the concept of narrative processing to study how advertising affects consumers. She has published in the *Journal of Consumer Research, Journal of Consumer Psychology, Journal of Advertising*, and *Journal of Public Policy and Marketing*. She is an associate editor for the *Journal of Consumer Research*, and serves as webmaster for the Society for Consumer Psychology.

Dr Gavan Fitzsimons is the R. David Thomas Professor of Marketing and Psychology at Duke University's Fuqua School of Business. His research focuses on understanding the ways in which consumers may be influenced without their conscious knowledge or awareness by marketers and marketing researchers, often without any intent on the part of the marketer. His work has been published in numerous academic journals such as the *Journal of Consumer Research, Journal of Consumer Psychology, Journal of Marketing Research, Marketing Science, Management Science, Organizational Behavior and Human Decision Processes, Journal of Personality and Social Psychology*, and *Psychological Science*. His ideas have also been featured in many popular press outlets such as *National Public Radio, CNN, MSNBC, New York Times, Wall Street Journal, Psychology Today, Oprah Magazine*, and *Time Magazine*, amongst many others. He is co-director of the Duke-Ipsos Center for Shopper Insights.

Dr Susan Fournier is Questrom Professor of Management and Faculty Director of the MBA Program at Boston University. Her research explores the creation and capture of value through branding and brand relationships. Current projects explore the links between brand strategy and shareholder value, management of corporeal person-brands, attachment style effects on relationship quality, brand relationship measurement systems, and brand relationship development processes. Her work has been recognized with seven awards, including the Long-Term Contribution Award in Consumer Research. She is an Editorial Board member of the *Journal of Consumer Research, Journal of Marketing, Marketing Theory, Journal of Business-to-Business Marketing*, Senior Consulting Editor for the *Journal of Brand Management*, Senior Advisory Board Member of the *Journal of Product and Brand Management*, and At-Large Director of the *Association for Consumer Research*. She previously served on the faculties of Harvard Business School and Dartmouth. She maintains a range of consulting assignments to inform her teaching and research, including a partnership with GfK Research to commercialize her brand relationship frameworks. Her PhD is from the University of Florida.

Belle Frank is Executive Vice President, Global Director of Strategy & Research for Young & Rubicam and has vast experience across many consumer categories. She currently oversees Y&R wellness strategic initiatives. She is recognized in the industry as having great expertise in communications research. In her 30+ years with the agency, she has worked on nearly all of its client accounts. Beginning in 1993, she was part of the small team assigned to develop the agency's BrandAsset®

Valuator (BAV) model. She has a BA in French from Tufts and holds a master's from the Harvard School of Education in human development and the effects of communication. She teaches in the City University of New York Masters in branding and integrated communications and is an active member of the Advertising Research Foundation. She is the author of *The Advertising On-Ramp*, a book that speaks to the new generation of marketing communications talent, and lectures frequently about it. She co-authored several pieces published in *Admap* including "Reinventing Qualitative Research" and "Brand Strategies for an Economic Downturn." She received an Advertising Women of New York, Trailblazing Working Mother of the Year Award in 2007.

Dr Mike Friedman is an associate professor of marketing at the Louvain School of Management, Catholic University of Louvain, Belgium. He holds a PhD in social psychology from Texas A&M University. His research interests include consumer behavior, brands and branding, and research methodology.

Dr Miranda Goode is an assistant professor of marketing at the Ivey Business School and holds the StarTech Professorship in Customer Insights. Her research focuses on factors that influence consumer learning and evaluation. Her first stream of research investigates how aesthetic form and function influence predictions about innovative product performance. Hundreds of new products enter the marketplace each year, and her research provides insight into factors that may contribute to their understanding. She also examines factors that influence how consumers learn about and form preferences for special experiences, such as once-in-a-lifetime trips, with a focus on how prior emotional knowledge and analogy may enhance learning. Her work has been published in the *Journal of Marketing Research, Journal of Consumer Psychology, Science*, and *Current Directions in Psychological Science* and has been featured in numerous media outlets worldwide including the *New York Times, Boston Globe, The Star Tribune, CBC Radio*, and TV.

Dr Renée Richardson Gosline is the Zenon Zannetos 1955 Career Development Assistant Professor of Marketing in the management science group at the MIT Sloan School of Management. She is also a member of MIT's Initiative on the Digital Economy. She has been named one of the World's Top 40 Professors under 40 by *Poets and Quants*, and an "Iron Professor" by the MIT MBA students. Her expertise includes consumer behavior, technology, and branding. Her research topics include the impact of social media on decision-making, brand counterfeiting, and consumer-brand relationships. To address these issues rigorously, she employs both experimental and qualitative methodology. Her research has been featured in academic journals and international business press. Prior to academia, she was a marketing practitioner at LVMH Moët Hennessy and Leo Burnett. She received her undergraduate and graduate education at Harvard University, including a doctorate from Harvard Business School.

Mackenzie Harms is a doctoral student in industrial and organizational psychology at the University of Nebraska Omaha. She is also the lead graduate student on a project funded by the Department of Homeland Security Science and Technology that investigates violent extremist organizations. She plans to continue her research program after graduate school, with goals to pursue a career in the security or intelligence fields.

Dr Wayne D. Hoyer holds the James L. Bayless/William S. Farish Fund Chair for Free Enterprise and is chairman of the department of marketing in the McCombs School of Business at the University of Texas at Austin. He received his PhD from Purdue University. His major area of study is consumer psychology and his research interests include consumer information processing and decision making, cause-related marketing, branding (including brand personality and brand sabotage), and advertising information processing (including miscomprehension, and humor). He has published over 100 articles in academic journals such as the *Journal of Consumer Research, Journal of Marketing Research, Journal of Marketing, Journal of the Academy of Marketing Science, Journal of Retailing,* and other marketing and psychology forums. His 1998 article on assortment perceptions (with Susan Broniarczyk and Leigh McAlister) won the 2003 O'Dell Award from the American Marketing Association. He is co-author of a textbook on consumer behavior with Deborah MacInnis and Rik Pieters (now in the 6th edition).

Li Huang is a doctoral student of marketing at the Darla Moore School of Business, University of South Carolina. She received her bachelor's degree in China and master's degrees in Hong Kong. Her research interests include, but are not limited to, social influence on consumer behavior, brand anthropomorphism, and consumer brand relationships. Her research has appeared in top marketing journals such as the *Journal of Consumer Research*. Prior to joining academia, she worked in the advertising industry.

Dr Deborah Roedder John is the Curtis L. Carlson Chair in Marketing at the Carlson School of Management, University of Minnesota. She is known for her work in consumer branding, including research on brand dilution, cultural influences on brand extensions, and brand measurement. Her current projects examine how consumer feelings and behaviors are influenced by the brands they use. Her work has appeared in the *Journal of Consumer Research, Journal of Marketing Research, Journal of Marketing*, and *Journal of Consumer Psychology*, and has received coverage in media outlets such as *Business Week, New York Times, MSN, Time*, and *AOL News*. She currently serves as a member of the editorial boards of the *Journal of Consumer Research, Journal of Marketing Research, Journal of Consumer Psychology*, and *Journal of Public Policy & Marketing*, and is past-president of the Association for Consumer Research. Her consulting activities include providing strategic guidance for branding issues and serving as an expert witness in trademark and brand dilution litigation. She holds a PhD in marketing from the Kellogg Graduate School of Management at Northwestern University.

Dr Patrick J. Kaufmann is Everett W. Lord Distinguished Faculty Scholar and Professor of Marketing at Boston University. He received a BA in economics from Georgetown University in 1968, a JD from Boston College Law School in 1974, an MBA from Wharton in 1980, and a PhD in marketing from Northwestern University in 1985. He has served on the faculties of Harvard Business School and Georgia State University. His research focuses on channels of distribution and franchising. He serves on the editorial boards of the *Journal of Retailing* and the *Journal of Public Policy & Marketing*, and is past chair of the International Society of Franchising.

Mandeep Kaur Ghuman is an associate professor at University Business School, Guru Nanak Dev University, India. She received her PhD (as UGC Research Fellow) in brand management in August 2014. Her research interests include brand management, consumer behavior, and cross cultural consumer research. She holds a master's degree in business administration from Guru Nanak Dev University, India. She is also a 2012–13 Fulbright-Nehru Doctoral and Professional Research Fellow. During her nine-month fellowship period, she conducted research at the Moore School of Business, University of South Carolina.

Dr Anat Keinan is an associate professor of business administration in the marketing unit at Harvard Business School. She received her PhD in marketing, with distinction, from Columbia Business School. Her research interests include branding, luxury marketing, symbolic consumption, consumer self-control, regret, and the consumption of experiences. She is the winner of the 2011 *Journal of Consumer Research* Ferber Award for her dissertation paper "Productivity Orientation and the Consumption of Collectable Experiences," which introduces the notion of an "experiential CV." Her work has been chosen by the *New York Times* as one of the "Best Ideas of 2006," and as a finalist for the *Journal of Consumer Research* 2009 Best Paper Award. Her research on consumer behavior has been published in the leading marketing, psychology, and managerial journals, and featured in hundreds of media outlets, including *National Public Radio, CNN, FOX, CBS, NBC, ABC, Wall Street Journal, The New Yorker, Scientific American, Business Week, Financial Times, Forbes, TIME, Boston Globe, Washington Post, Slate Magazine, Wired Magazine, Associated Press*, and *United Press International*. She was named a Marketing Science Institute Young Scholar in 2013, and serves on the editorial review board of the *Journal of Consumer Research*. At Harvard Business School, she teaches a new elective MBA course on luxury marketing.

Mansur Khamitov is a doctoral student in marketing at Ivey Business School, Western University (Canada). His research focuses on branding looking at such issues as transgressions, the role of interpersonal influences, and methodological challenges in the context of consumer-brand relationships. Prior to joining the doctoral program, he worked as a brand manager at Procter & Gamble and as a senior product manager at Polpharma in Kazakhstan where he was in charge of such brands as Oral-B, Blend-A-Med (Crest), Camay, Safeguard, and Trichopol. He received his bachelor's degree in public administration and financial management and an MBA in marketing from Kimep University.

Dr Molan Kim is an assistant professor of marketing at the State University of New York at New Paltz. She received a PhD in marketing from the University of Georgia, and a BBA and MS in marketing from Korea University. Her primary areas of research encompass customer relationship management, consumer-to-consumer interaction, online brand community, social media strategy, and computer-aided content analysis.

Dr Soyean Kim is an assistant professor of marketing at the Department of International Studies at Kyung Hee University. She holds a PhD in marketing from Boston University, an MBA in marketing from Columbia Business School, and a BBA in business administration from Yonsei University. Her research interests include online trust, social media, online impression management, self-presentation, self-disclosure, online word-of-mouth, interpersonal persuasion, customer relationship management, and public policy in marketing.

Dr Dannie Kjeldgaard is a professor of marketing at the University of Southern Denmark. Before joining academia, he worked for four years in a London-based public relations consultancy. Published in numerous international journals and books, his work primarily analyzes change processes of market-based glocalization in diverse market domains such as place branding, branding, media and identity construction, global consumer segments, body culture, gender, ethnicity, and qualitative methodology. His research is published in the *Journal of Consumer Research, Journal of Consumer Behavior, Consumption, Markets and Culture, Marketing Theory, Journal of Macromarketing*, and in several anthologies.

Dr Robert V. Kozinets has authored and co-authored over 100 pieces of research, many of them about the intersection of technology, media, brands, and consumer collectivities. His publications include book chapters, research dictionary entries, articles in the world's top marketing journals, a consumer behavior textbook, and three books: *Consumer Tribes* (2007), *Netnography* (2010), and *Qualitative Consumer and Marketing Research* (2013). Currently, he is an associate editor of the *Journal of Consumer Research* and the *Journal of Retailing*, and an academic trustee of the Marketing Science Institute. He is a professor of marketing at York University's Schulich School of Business, where he is also chair of the marketing department.

Dr Harley Krohmer is a professor of marketing, chair of the marketing department, and executive director of the Institute of Marketing and Management of the

University of Bern, the capital university of Switzerland. He is also Dean of the Faculty of Economics and Social Sciences of the University of Bern. He earned his master's degree in business administration and a PhD in management economics at the Koblenz School of Corporate Management (Germany). He completed his habilitation in management economics at the University of Mannheim (Germany). He has published in, among others, the *Journal of Marketing, Journal of Marketing Research*, and the *Strategic Management Journal*. His research focus is on marketing strategy, marketing implementation, price- and brand-management, and luxury marketing. He is president of the board of Brandinvest, a Swiss consulting firm that focuses on investments in brands and the creation of luxury brands.

Aliette Lambert is a doctoral candidate at the University of Edinburgh. Her research interests are broadly related to consumer culture, identity, and gender. She received a Principal's Career Development Scholarship from the University of Edinburgh to fund her doctoral studies on the role of consumer culture and brands in the evolving identity projects of young women. Prior to beginning her doctoral work, she completed a Master's of Research degree at the University of St Andrews, graduating at the top of her class. She published her master's work on narcissism and consumer-brand relationships in *Psychology and Marketing*, and has presented at various conferences, including the Consumer Culture Theory Conference 2014 in which her paper was selected for publication. In addition to her academic experience, she has two years of experience in the financial services industry and extensive experience in the retail sector, from which her interest in consumer culture emerged.

Dr Benjamin Lawrence is an assistant professor at the Cornell School of Hotel Administration. Lawrence earned a PhD in management (marketing) from the Boston University School of Management, an MBA from Mays Business School at Texas A&M University, and a bachelor's degree from the Cornell School of Hotel Administration. His primary research interest involves channels of distribution with a focus on relationships within the context of franchising. He also studies consumers' food and beverage consumption experiences and purchasing behavior. His work has been published in the *Journal of Advertising, Journal of Marketing Channels, Journal of Operations Management, Journal of Retailing, Journal of Small Business Management,* and *Service Science.*

Edward Lebar is a 40-year veteran of marketing and a founding partner of BlackBar Consulting, a firm focused on building consumer-brand relationships, improving pricing power, and raising market valuation multiples by listening to and exploring consumer-brand relationships. He was founder and CEO of BrandAsset® Consulting and built with others the BrandAsset® Valuator model. He returned to Young & Rubicam in 1995 to help grow BrandAsset® Valuator into the largest brand model and database in the world and to guide the development of all BAV joint ventures and alliances. Under his leadership, the BAV analytic group developed many proprietary products including BrandResonance®, BAV Archetypes, as well as multiple methods for valuing brands. He has co-authored pieces in academic journals and his 2008 book, *The Brand Bubble*, was voted third best business book by Amazon. His experience includes working with clients such as Proctor & Gamble, Kraft, AOL & Time Warner, Kodak, Verizon, Microsoft, Yahoo!, the *New York Times*, and *Wall Street Journal*. He holds advanced degrees in economics from New York University and the University of Denver, and a BA from Syracuse University.

Dr Katherine Lemon holds the Accenture Professorship at Boston College's Carroll School of Management and is the chair of the marketing department. Her research focuses on customer management, customer equity, and the dynamics of customer-firm relationships, and appears in leading marketing journals including the *Journal of Marketing, Journal of Marketing Research, Marketing Science, Management Science*, and the *Journal of Service Research*. She received the Early Career Contributions to Marketing Strategy Research Award, the Elsevier Research Scholar of the Year Award, and has received several best article awards for her research, including the 2009 Sheth Foundation/*Journal of Marketing* Award, given each year to the article that has made long-term contributions to the theory and practice of marketing. She is the immediate past editor of the *Journal of Service Research*. Her book, *Driving Customer Equity: How Customer Lifetime Value is Reshaping Corporate Strategy*, received the first annual American Marketing Association Foundation AMA-Berry Book Prize. She received her PhD from the University of California, Berkeley.

Dr Gina Scott Ligon is an organizational psychologist who applies leadership and innovation theory to examine the performance of violent extremist organizations. Her research can be categorized into the broad topics of high level talent management and individual differences in both productive and disruptive organizations. Another theme is the development of measurement techniques to assess extreme behaviors in laboratory and applied settings in unconventional settings. She has published over 30 peer-reviewed manuscripts in *Advances in Human Resources, Dynamics of Asymmetric Conflict, The Creativity Research Journal*, and other organizational behavior outlets. In 2009, she won the Best Paper Award from The Center for Creative Leadership for her publication, "The Development of Outstanding Leadership" in the *Leadership Quarterly Journal*. She is the only management faculty member of the National Consortium for Studies of Terrorism and Responses to Terrorism (START) and director of research and development for University of Nebraska Omaha's Center for Collaboration Science.

Dr Lara Lobschat is an assistant professor of marketing at the University of Groningen. She received her PhD from the University of Cologne in 2013 and her primary research interests include branding and communication effects in multichannel environments, online advertising effectiveness, the effects of social media (marketing), and the application of econometric methods. She has made numerous conference presentations and her work has been published in the *Journal of Service Research* and *Long Range Planning*.

Dr Christopher R. Long is primary data analyst at Quantifid. He received his PhD from the University of Massachusetts and then worked as a post-doctoral research associate at Université Catholique de Louvain, Belgium. From 2004 to 2014 he worked as an assistant professor and then associate professor at Ouachita Baptist University, where he founded the OBU Brand Lab and collaborated with researchers in psychology, marketing, and information science. In 2009, he was a visiting professor at New York advertising agency DraftFCB. His primary research areas include exploring similarities between consumers' brand relationships and interpersonal relationships, as well as understanding the effects of brand deprivation, the role of social networking (on- and off-line) in consumer-brand relationships, and consumer-celebrity relationships. He has published in leading journals in psychology and communications and has presented his research at numerous conferences. His work has been cited by a range of popular publications, from the *Boston Globe* to *Fast Company* to the Israeli business newspaper *Calcalist*.

Dr Marius K. Luedicke is a senior lecturer in marketing at Cass Business School, City University London. Previously, he was the founding director of the Swarovski Brand Research Laboratory at the University of Innsbruck. His research explores the dynamics of consumer culture and branding with a particular focus on moralism and conflict. His work has been published in journals such as *Consumption Markets and Culture*, *Psychology & Marketing*, and the *Journal of Consumer Research*, of which he is an editorial review board member. His research has been cited in international media such as the *New York Times*, *Huffington Post*, and *Wired*.

Dr Deborah MacInnis is the Charles L. and Ramona I. Hilliard Professor of Business Administration and Professor of Marketing at the Marshall School of Business, University of Southern California. Her research interests center on the areas of branding and emotions. She has studied strategic brand positioning, brand extension strategies, and how and why consumers develop emotional attachments to brands, and factors that impact consumers' perceptions of having been betrayed by brands. Her work also examines the role of emotions (e.g., hope, pride, anger, guilt) in consumer decision making. She has published over 60 academic papers in some of the field's leading academic journals. She is recipient of the Alpha Kappa Psi and Maynard Awards for the papers that make the greatest contribution to marketing thought in the *Journal of Marketing*, and the Long-Term Contribution Award from the *Review of Marketing Research*. She is the co-author of a leading textbook on consumer behavior and has served as president of the Association for Consumer Research. She has also served as associate editor and then co-editor of the *Journal of Consumer Research*. She has been an associate editor for the *Journal of*

Consumer Psychology and is currently theory development editor at the *Journal of Marketing*.

Dr Thomas J. Madden was a professor of marketing at the Moore School of Business, University of South Carolina from 1986 until his death in 2014. His research appeared in the leading marketing journals. His research on branding, along with his co-authors, received the Paul E. Green Award for the best paper in the *Journal of Marketing Research* and the Sheth Award for the best paper in the *Journal of the Academy of Marketing Science*. His most recent research focused on the use of value-based marketing strategies and the impact of brand equity on shareholder value. He also co-authored three textbooks on marketing management and marketing research. He participated in consulting engagements with companies such as Colonial Life, Enodis, Land Rover North America, Stouffers, South Carolina Business One Stop, The Sales Factory, US Department of Agriculture, Xerox, and Zeneca. He conducted executive development programs for companies such as Enodis, Gulf Stream, Medical University of South Carolina, Milliken Company, Raychem, South Carolina Electric & Gas, Torrington, Wienerberger, and Xerox. He earned his BS at the University of Bridgeport, Connecticut; his MBA at California State University, Fresno; and his PhD at the University of Massachusetts, Amherst, where he served as an assistant professor of marketing from 1981–86.

Dr James H. McAlexander is currently a professor of marketing in the College of Business and director of the Close to the Customer Project at Oregon State University. He has been a member of the faculty at OSU for more than 20 years. Prior to his academic career, he worked for the Federal Aviation Administration as an air traffic controller. He has established an international reputation for his research in brand community. This work began in the early 1990s with ethnographic research with owners of Harley-Davidson motorcycles and Jeep branded vehicles (published in the *Journal of Consumer Research* and the *Journal of Marketing*). Most recently, he has been examining the ways in which participation in these communities evolve over time. He has consulted and conducted research for such prominent firms and brands as Harley-Davidson, Isuzu, Yamaha, Jeep, Kodak, Nissan, Beltronics, Chrysler, Toyota, Infiniti, Kellogg's, Saturn, and Cadillac. Most recently he has adapted the model of brand community integration for applications that assist advancement professionals in non-profit organizations and explored the dynamic issues and challenges associated with fostering and building brand communities. He has an undergraduate degree in political science, and completed the PhD in marketing at the University of Utah.

Dr Ann L. McGill is a professor of behavioral science and marketing at the University of Chicago, Booth School of Business, joining the school as a faculty member in 1997. She served as the Deputy Dean for the full-time MBA programs at Chicago Booth from 2001 to 2003. She received her doctorate from the

University of Chicago in 1997, subsequently holding positions at New York University and Northwestern University. She has also been a visiting professor at the Graduate School of Business Stanford University, Sasin Graduate Institute of Business Administration (Thailand), and INSEAD. She is the 2005 recipient of the McKinsey Award for Excellence in Teaching and the 2006 recipient of the Provost's Teaching Award. Her research focuses on consumer and manager decision making with special emphasis on product and brand anthropomorphism, causal reasoning, shared consumption, imagery, and freedom of choice. From 2005 to 2009, she served as associate editor, and from 2009 to 2014, she served as editor for the *Journal of Consumer Research*.

Dr Martin Mende is an assistant professor of marketing at Florida State University. His research focuses on relationship marketing, attachment theory, services marketing, transformative service research, specifically examining topics such as conspicuous consumption, psychology of money, and financial decision making. His research has appeared in the *Journal of Marketing Research, Marketing Letters, Journal of Service Research*, and *Journal of Business Research*. He holds a PhD in marketing from Arizona State University. Prior to attending Arizona State University, he earned a doctoral degree in services management from Catholic University of Eichstätt-Ingolstadt, Germany.

Dr Neeru Paharia is an assistant professor at Georgetown University's McDonough School of Business. She conducts research on judgment and decision making, consumer behavior, signaling through brands, social media, political consumption, moral psychology, and digital marketing. Prior to joining the Georgetown faculty, she served as the research director for the Edmond J. Safra Center for Ethics at Harvard University. She also spent three years on the founding team at Creative Commons serving as assistant and executive director, after working at McKinsey as an associate consultant. She has co-founded several community-oriented social networking sites in education, research, and music including Peer 2 Peer University (p2pu.org), Acawiki.org, and ccmixter.org. Her work has been published in the *Journal of Consumer Research* and *Organizational Behavior and Human Decision Processes*, and she has authored several book chapters. She holds a doctorate in marketing from Harvard Business School, an MS in public policy and management from Carnegie Mellon University, and a BA in economics from the University of California.

Dr Seema Pai is an assistant professor of marketing at Boston University. She holds a PhD in marketing from the University of Southern California, and an MBA in marketing from the Indian Institute of Management, Lucknow.

Dr Elisabeth A. Pichler-Luedicke is a senior consultant at the Institute of Brand Logic, a strategy consultancy for brand-oriented companies. She has worked on a broad range of branding issues with clients from diverse industries, ranging from construction through retail to fashion. Previously, she was an assistant professor of marketing at the University of Innsbruck, where she had also completed her doctorate in marketing. Her research has been published in *Advances in Consumer Research* and the *Journal of Marketing Management*.

Dr Erin G. Pleggenkuhle-Miles is an assistant professor in the marketing and management department at the University of Nebraska Omaha. Her research focuses on how institutional and environmental factors influence firm strategy. The main premise of her research focuses on how economic environment conditions as well as community relationships influence firm decisions and strategies, with particular interest in entrepreneurial firms. She also studies how firm relationships impact technology and innovation strategies. Her research has been published in academic journals such as *Research Policy* and *Management Decision*. She acts as an ad hoc consultant for several start-up firms and sits on the board of directors for Plegg's Inc.

Dr Linda L. Price (BA, MBA University of Wyoming, PhD University of Texas at Austin) is the Underwood Family Professor of Marketing in the Eller College of Management, University of Arizona. She has received many marketing honors and awards including the 2013 College of Business Distinguished Alumni Award from University of Wyoming and the 2013 Academy of Marketing Science Cutco/Vector Distinguished Educator Award for Lifetime Contributions to Marketing Scholarship. She currently serves as president of the Association for Consumer Research, as well as serving on the American Marketing Association Council, the Sheth Foundation, and the Advisory Board for the *Journal of Consumer Research*. Her theory and research is published in leading marketing and social science journals including the *Journal of Marketing, Journal of the Academy of Marketing Science* and *Journal of Consumer Research*, and combines qualitative and quantitative methodologies to examine consumer identity and adaptation, social influence and network interactions, and how consumers' emotions and imaginations enrich, distinguish, and give agency to their lives. Her research has been and is currently funded by a variety of agencies including USDA and Marketing Science Institute. She has published books, chapters, and over 70 articles that have collectively garnered over 7,000 citations.

Dr Martin S. Roth is Dean and Professor of Management and Marketing at the Barney School of Business, University of Hartford. His areas of expertise include global corporate and marketing strategy, branding, and customer value. His research has been published in the leading marketing and management journals, including the *Journal of Marketing Research, Journal of International Business Studies, Journal of Consumer Research, Journal of International Marketing, Journal of Advertising, Journal of Advertising Research, Journal of World Business, Marketing Management, Journal of Health Care Marketing, American Journal of Managed Care, Journal of Public Policy and Marketing*, and *Journal of Professional Pricing*. His articles and video interviews have appeared in the *Wall Street Journal*. His *CountryManager* international marketing simulation game is used in over 120 schools worldwide. He has spoken on a variety of marketing and global management topics at industry and academic meetings throughout the Americas and Europe. Prior to his academic career he held a number of marketing research and retail management positions. He earned his doctorate and MBA from the Katz Graduate School of Business, University of Pittsburgh.

Dr Cristel Antonia Russell is an associate professor of marketing at American University, Washington, DC. A graduate of the University of Arizona, she has held positions around the world, from San Diego State University to the University of Auckland and has taught in France, Hong Kong, and Taiwan. A leading researcher on the dynamics of entertainment consumption, she has adopted multiple methods of inquiry to document how and why people connect with TV characters, re-watch TV episodes, or are influenced by embedded messages within the content of their favorite programs. She is best known for her work on the influence of television on youth, especially in the area of product placement. Her publications addressing how brands placed in the content of entertainment programs affect consumers' attention, attitudes, and behaviors span business and health journals such as the *Journal of Consumer Research, Journal of Advertising, Journal of Studies on Alcohol* and *Drugs,* and *Addiction*. She has received funding for her research on the nature and impact on youth of alcohol messages in television series through grants from the United States' National Institute of Health and France's Institut National du Cancer. She speaks at public policy, health and prevention research conferences and at advertising and entertainment academic conferences internationally and is a member of several editorial review boards.

Dr Hope Jensen Schau is the Associate Dean, MBA Programs, an associate professor of marketing, and holds the Gary M. Munsinger Chair in Entrepreneurship and Innovation at the Eller College of Management, University of Arizona. She earned her PhD, MA, and MBA from the University of California, Irvine, and her BS from California State Long Beach. She has published well-cited research on the impact of technology on marketplace relationships, branding, identity-salient consumption practices, and collaborative value creation. An award-winning instructor, she teaches marketing management, managing marketing communications, and social media marketing strategy in the Eller MBA programs. She is a popular visiting scholar at institutions across the globe, including the University of Melbourne (Australia), the University of Hawaii, the University of Auckland (New Zealand), and Fundação Getúlio Vargas (Brazil). Her work has appeared in the *Journal of Marketing, Journal of Consumer Research, Journal of Retailing, Journal of Advertising*, and the *Journal of Public Policy and Marketing*, among others. She serves on the editorial review boards of the *Journal of Consumer Research* and *Consumption Markets and Culture*.

Dr Jonathan Schroeder is the William A. Kern Professor in Communications at Rochester Institute of Technology. He has a BA in Psychology from the University of Michigan and an MA and PhD in Social Psychology from the University of California, Berkeley, and did postdoctoral work at Rhode Island School of Design. He has published widely on branding, communication, consumer research, and identity. He is the author of *Visual Consumption* (Routledge, 2002); co-author of *From Chinese Brand Culture to Global Brands* (Palgrave Macmillan, 2013), editor of *Conversations on Consumption* (Routledge, 2013) and co-editor of *Brand Culture* (Routledge, 2006) and the *Routledge Companion to Visual Organization* (Routledge, 2013). He is editor in chief of the interdisciplinary journal *Consumption Markets & Culture*, and serves on the editorial boards of the journals *Advertising and Society Review, Critical Studies in Fashion and Beauty, European Journal of Marketing, International Journal of Indian Culture and Business Management, Journal of Business Research, Journal of Consumer Research, Journal of Historical Research in Marketing, Journal of Macromarketing, Marketing Theory* and *Visual Methodologies*. He is a founding member of the International Network of Visual Studies in Organization.

Dr Maura L. Scott is an assistant professor of marketing at Florida State University (PhD Arizona State University). Her research interests include over-consumption behavior, goal setting, self-regulation, and transformative consumer research. Her research has been published in leading marketing journals including the *Journal of Consumer Research, Journal of Marketing Research, Journal of Public Policy & Marketing, Journal of Consumer Psychology, Journal of Advertising*, and *Journal of Business Research*. Her research has won the *Journal of Public Policy & Marketing* Kinnear Best Paper Award and an honorable mention for the *Journal of Consumer Research* Robert Ferber Award. She serves on the editorial review boards for the *Journal of Consumer Research* and the *Journal of Public Policy & Marketing*. She has taught consumer behavior, marketing principles, marketing management, and marketing strategy. Her industry background includes marketing positions at 3M Company, Dial Corporation, and Motorola.

Scott Stewart is an account manager in the foodservice department at The NPD Group. He obtained his BBA from Trent University and MSc in marketing from the John Molson School of Business. He was awarded the Joseph-Armand Bombardier Canadian Graduate Scholarship from the Social Sciences and Humanities Research Council (SSHRC) for his MSc thesis research on identity branding. His research interests are based on understanding the social nature of consumers' relationships with brands, and the role other consumers play in the identity value one derives from a brand.

Dr Scott A. Thompson is an assistant professor of marketing at the University of Georgia. He received his PhD from Arizona State University. His primary areas of research include new product adoption, consumer communities, consumer-brand connections, and word of mouth behavior. His research has been published in leading marketing journals including the *Journal of Marketing, Journal of the Academy of Marketing Science, Marketing Letters*, and the *Journal of Interactive Marketing*.

Dr Matthew Thomson is the R.A. Barford Professor in Marketing at Ivey Business School, Western University (London, Canada) and the director of Ivey's PhD program. He completed his doctorate at the University of Southern California's Marshall School of Business (marketing) and also earned degrees from Indiana University, Bloomington (MBA) and McGill University (BA). Before becoming an academic, he worked for the Information, Privacy and Ethics Commissioner of Alberta.

Chip Walker is the EVP, Director of Brand Planning & Innovation at Y&R New York and BAV Consulting, where he leads the Agency's strategic function. He has a proven track record developing marketing, brand, communications, and digital strategy for a wide array of major brands. He has led the strategic function at creative agencies (BBDO, Y&R), a marketing services agency (Wunderman) and at a digital and social agency (StrawberryFrog), giving him a unique multi-disciplinary skill-set. He has also led strategy across the Y&R companies (ad, media, digital, multi-cultural, etc.) for clients such as AT&T. Innovation and leadership have been cornerstones of his career. He worked closely with John Gerzema in conceptualizing and executing the editorial vision for the *New York Times* best-selling book, *The Athena Doctrine: How Women (And The Men Who Think Like Them) Will Rule the Future*. He is a frequent commentator on consumer culture and trends. His ideas and predications about topics ranging from global youth to baby boomers regularly appear in US and international broadcast and print media such as the *New York Times, CNBC, Forbes* and *Business Week*. He holds a BA in philosophy and an MBA in marketing from Vanderbilt University.

Jing Wan is a doctoral student in marketing at the Rotman School of Management, University of Toronto. She received her Bachelor of Science in psychology from the University of Toronto. Her doctoral dissertation combines her interest in moral judgments and the psychology of money and time. She also works on projects related to anthropomorphism, embodied cognition, and prosocial behaviors.

Dr John Wittenbraker is the Global Director of Innovation, Brand & Customer Experience at GfK, where he has a dual role, directing innovation efforts in GfK's Global Innovation and Digital and Global Brand and Customer Experience teams. His responsibilities include collaborations with academics, research institutes, and other businesses to identify, develop, and commercialize new methodologies and tools for understanding consumer experience. Current topics of focus include: biometric/neurometric measurement, social media analysis, application of social theory to brand management, and digital/connected life. Prior to that, he was managing director of GfK Custom Research North America, Corporate

Innovation and also responsible for GfK's Research Center for Excellence (marketing science, online strategies, and sampling). He has also served as the managing director of the North American Brand and Communications business. Trained as a social and quantitative psychologist, he has developed advanced models, analytic systems, and methodologies to support marketing and brand management decisions. He has had broad experience across multiple sectors, including packaged goods, financial services, telecommunications, automotive, retail, and consumer services. Prior to GfK, he was a Partner with ARBOR, Inc., a Philadelphia-based marketing research and consulting firm. He has a PhD from the University of North Carolina, Chapel Hill and an AB from Wabash College.

Dr Sukki Yoon is an associate professor of marketing at Bryant University. In the past, he was an assistant professor at Cleveland State University and a visiting professor at Grey Worldwide, a leading advertising agency in New York City. He has also been a visiting scholar and a visiting professor at several US and Korean universities including Harvard, Sookmyung, Dongguk, and UNIST. He has published and served on the editorial boards of many international journals. He has consulted at a number of firms and government agencies in the US and Korea. He has also written columns on marketing and advertising in major newspapers and magazines. As a basic and applied researcher, his work spans diverse topics. Some of his studies focus on the fundamental questions of consumer behavior: why and how people react to various marketing communications. Other studies address issues that enhance managerial decisions. Trained as an experimentalist, his approach is to use empirical observations, analyzing data collected in laboratory and field settings.

Helen Zeitoun is the Global Head of Brand and Customer Experience at GfK, leading with a specific thought leadership objective to bridge customer experience with brand experience in the context of customer centricity and of digital and social media strategies. She is steering and implementing scientific and techno-logical developments into the whole GfK offering with innovative and integrated tools, metrics, systems, and expertise, and bringing it to life for clients. She is a member of the global executive committee of GfK Consumer Experiences. She has been with GfK for 20+ years, with different responsibilities including president of GfK France on the custom research business, chairman of the GfK Western Europe Board, and board sponsor for Segmentation and Innovation. Prior to GfK, she was a consultant at TNS in charge of semiometry and did modeling for the National Parks for a Canadian-based consulting company (part of SECOR). She has served as president of the academic French Marketing Association (AFM), as vice president of the IREP (equivalent to Advertising Research Foundation in France), member of the SYNTEC council (association of marketing research agencies), and as French Representative of ESOMAR. Trained as a social and quantitative psychologist in the French Rouen Business School, she graduated with honors with an MBA in marketing sciences from Laval University, Canada.

She has been publishing in ranked academic reviews such as *RAM, DM* and the *Journal of Consumer Marketing* and has taught numerous courses in French universities, MBA programs, and business schools.

FOREWORD

Kevin Lane Keller

Relationships are vital to the success and happiness of our everyday life. Figuratively, relationships come in all shapes, sizes, colors, textures, and dimensions. They are complex, hard-to-define, and constantly changing. Relationships know no boundaries and can be found in all walks of life.

In marketing, researchers have studied the role of relationships on a variety of fronts, such as customer service settings, channel management, and employee engagement, to name just a few. Understanding how these relationships should be managed has become a strategic priority for many top firms. In studying these relationships, there has been an increased realization of the many different types of costs and benefits that are involved in creating, maintaining, and nurturing relationships.

Perhaps one of the most active areas of all these studies in recent years is consumer-brand relationships. Researchers in this area have adopted a multitude of concepts, theories, and methods to better illuminate the full richness and diversity of the topic. They have productively brought different disciplinary bases and different managerial orientations to their studies. Nowhere is that more evident than in this expansive collection of research, *Strong Brands, Strong Relationships*. The assembled authors represent some of the brightest minds in the field and, not surprisingly, they break important new ground on a number of fronts. One of the strengths in this volume is how it introduces thoughtful new conceptual material, while also offering rich practical insights.

By reading and studying these works, a much more complete and nuanced view of brand relationships is possible. The strengths and weaknesses of consumer-brand relationships are explored, and different types of relationships in different types of settings are examined, all in depth. The chapters consider such important topics as the role of identities and self-expressions, humanizing and anthropomorphizing brands, the emergence of online branding, threats to and the endings of relationships, and organizational and metrics issues.

In a foreword to the first volume in this series, *Consumer-Brand Relationships: Insights for Theory and Practice*, I wrote: "Together, the chapters offer a stimulating and challenging treatment of the topic and will be a valuable addition to any brand scholar or marketing practitioner." I say, multiply that by two for this second volume. It has raised the stakes in the study of consumer-brand relationships. Careful readers will be enlightened and richly rewarded for their investment.

Kevin Lane Keller
E.B. Osborn Professor of Marketing,
Tuck School of Business, Dartmouth College

ACKNOWLEDGEMENTS

The editors of this book are particularly grateful for the institutional support provided by Boston University, Mississippi State University and Harvard Business School and the research assistance provided by Zarah Sikora, Caitlin Dutkiewicz, and Jennifer Stevens. We would also like to thank Nicola Cupit and Amy Laurens at Taylor & Francis for their guidance and patience as this idea became a reality.

All of the chapters in the book were double blind reviewed, and we are grateful to the reviewers who put numerous hours of their time into improving the submissions and the overall quality of the book. The reviewers are: Pankaj Aggarwal (University of Toronto), Chris Allen (University of Cincinnati), Zeynep Arsel (Concordia University), Søren Askegaard (University of Southern Denmark), Jill Avery (Harvard Business School), James R. Bettman (Duke University), Max Blackston (BlackBar Consulting), Michael Breazeale (Mississippi State University), Matt Carcieri (The Jim Stengel Company), John Desmond (University of St Andrews), Beth Leavenworth Dufault (University of Arizona), Giana M. Eckhardt (University of London), Jennifer Edson Escalas (Vanderbilt University), Belle Frank (Young & Rubicam), Mike Friedman (Louvain School of Management), Miranda Goode (Ivey Business School), Renée Richardson Gosline (MIT Sloan School of Management), Mandeep Kaur Ghuman (Guru Nanak Dev University), Li Huang (University of South Carolina), Patrick J. Kaufmann (Boston University), Mansur Khamitov (Ivey Business School), Dannie Kjeldgaard (Syddansk University), Molan Kim (State University of New York at New Paltz), Aliette Lambert (The University of Edinburgh), Benjamin Lawrence (Cornell University), Edward Lebar (BlackBar Consulting), Katherine N. Lemon (Boston College), Christopher Long (Quantifid), Marius Luedicke (City University London), Thomas J. Madden (University of South Carolina), James H. McAlexander (Oregon State University), Martin Mende (Florida State University), Martin S. Roth (University of Hartford), Cristel Antonia Russell (American University), Hope Jensen Schau (University of

Arizona), Maura L. Scott (Florida State University), Scott Stewart (The NPD Group, Canada), Scott A. Thompson (University of Georgia), Matthew Thomson (Ivey Business School), Chip Walker (Young & Rubicam), Jing Wan (University of Toronto), Sukki Yoon (Bryant University).

INTRODUCTION

Strengthening our understanding of the importance of brands to consumers, firms, and society at large

Michael Breazeale, Susan Fournier, and Jill Avery

To the uninitiated brand enthusiast, the title of this chapter may seem a bit overreaching and self-important. To the more seasoned brand researcher, though, it hints at something that most readers of this book probably understand: brands are *not* the answers to all of life's problems, but the concepts that drive strong brand relationships have implications for almost every aspect of contemporary life. Still need convincing? Read on.

In our first book, *Consumer-Brand Relationships: Theory and Practice*, we delivered a collection of essays from some of the pioneers and emerging voices of brand relationship research. That work explored the psychological and cultural landscape of consumer-brand relationships, delivered insights on theory and state-of-the-art practices, and provided readers with insights into the successful creation and stewardship of consumers' relationships with brands. Topics included mainstays such as consumer-brand identity dynamics, brand loyalty, and brand love, and contemplated variations in brand relationality. Throughout that book, the authors described important work that remained undone and provided insights demonstrating just how far-reaching brand relationship research actually is.

Building upon the foundations of that first book, the editors of this volume recognized the importance of broadening the scope of brand research to consider a broader context of brand relationships as well as the more general branding issues that shape them. In the new volume, we include relationships outside of traditional realms, new theoretical paradigms, and the possible negative ramifications of brands on the lives of consumers. We sought out academic researchers and practitioners who were pushing the boundaries of brand research to illuminate some of the corners – dark and otherwise – where truly interesting and important discoveries often lie. In so doing, we uncovered eight themes that we believe will allow readers to advance not only their *own* understandings of brand relationships, but also to advance brand relationship theory and practice for the marketing discipline.

The first theme we explore in Part I is the way that contexts shape brand meaning, by highlighting the importance of understanding the specific situations that inform consumers' relationships with brands, as well as the way circumstances influence the meaning that consumers take from their relationships. In Part II, we focus more deeply on the processes that allow brands to integrate into consumers' lives and their sense of self. Part III considers consumers' propensity to humanize the brands they love and explores the implications of such activity for marketers.

We shift our attention in Part IV to the adaptation of brand relationships to the online realm, considering the increased capability of consumers to build relationships, not only with brands, but also with each other. Part V examines the factors that damage formerly strong brand relationships and explicates some of the negative consequences of relationship endings. The next two sections embrace branding as a managerial discipline and focus on strategy. In Part VI, we analyze brand strategy as employed by successful businesses, in one case considering terrorist organizations as the context of application. Part VII enables managerial application through metrics for measuring brand relationship antecedents and outcomes. We close the volume with Part VIII which focuses less on existing state-of-the-art brand relationship thought and more on the future of this domain.

Part I: How contexts shape brand meaning

Chapters in this section examine the networks in which brand relationships are situated to advance our understanding of the importance of context. Through unpacking the various relationships between consumers and brands, and among brands and their competitors, the authors demonstrate the relevance of every player in the complex game of interaction between consumers and brands.

Chapter 1, by Linda L. Price, provides an overarching context that situates the role of brands in people's contemporary lives. Price reports research that considers what is learned about the role of brands in consumers' lives by foregrounding their *other* loyalties and relationships – the people and projects that truly claim a big share of their hearts. Asking customers what they truly care about provides a significantly different understanding of how brands are situated in a network of important relationships and loyalties, with important implications for managing and measuring brand loyalty.

In Chapter 2, Neeru Paharia, Jill Avery, and Anat Keinan explore how consumers' assessments of brands are dependent upon brands' relationships with their competitors. Through a series of experiments, they demonstrate that the competitive context in which a brand operates can affect consumers' purchase interest and purchase frequency. They show that brand positioning that communicates that brands are in direct competition with each other elicits size effects; consumers like small brands more when they compete with big brands, and like big brands less when they compete with small brands. They further explore the relationship between brand size and competition, showing that while large brands are punished for being a competitive aggressor, small brands are rewarded when they compete aggressively.

Chapter 3, by Dannie Kjeldgaard, Søren Askegaard, and Giana M. Eckhardt, takes a global perspective to show that brands leverage cultural mythologies relating to the global mindset as well as local mythologies that tap strategic contexts far beyond country of origin. The authors demonstrate how global and local cultural capital are deployed in varying ways through a case study of the Carlsberg beer brand, finding that Carlsberg leverages a spectrum of cultural myths in alternate marketplaces by positioning itself as a local, Danish brand in some markets and a cosmopolitan, global brand in others. Importantly, contrary to global branding theory that emphasizes consistency, the analysis suggests that one uniform brand positioning used around the world is not necessarily the most desirable course of action, given that the nature of consumers' relationships to brands varies in different contexts.

Part II: Brands, identities, and self-expression

This section includes chapters that focus on the self-expressive properties of brand relationships. While this phenomenon stands as a mainstay in branding theory, the authors take highly innovative approaches to its examination. From the underexplored male brand relationship, to relationships formed by lonely consumers or those with a compromised sense of self, these chapters describe bonds that form with unique consumer subsets, while providing insights generalizable to other consumer populations. The final chapter in this section takes a less positive approach to the consumer-brand identity connection and considers what it means to brands and consumers when the relationship is degrading to the consumer.

Chapter 4 by Aliette Lambert and John Desmond tackles the underexplored territory of men's brand relations, answering questions about the existence and nature of male consumer-brand relationships. In studying the construct, the authors discuss both the socio-historical background of masculinity in relation to products, and current literature that addresses male consumption practices and brand relationships. They argue that, like women, men do have purposive relationships with brands and use products to perform aspects of identity that are important to them, such as gender.

Chapter 5 is based on the fundamental proposition that consumers appropriate brand symbolism to construct and communicate their self-identities, forming self-brand connections as a result. Jennifer Edson Escalas and James R. Bettman claim that consumers with compromised self-identities are more likely to engage in the process of using brands to search for meaning and provide self-definition than consumers with more stable self-identities. Their study looks at how consumers in a compromised self-identity state appropriate symbolic brand meaning that comes from celebrity endorsements to construct and communicate their self-concepts.

In Chapter 6, Christopher Long, Sukki Yoon, and Mike Friedman discuss the fact that loneliness has not been a major focus of marketing research. To address that gap, they integrate findings from research in consumer behavior and psychology, as well as new results from the authors' own work. Strategies for how marketers may better support relationships between lonely consumers and their brands are presented.

In Chapter 7, Zeynep Arsel and Scott Stewart focus on the complex situation created when individuals use brands for self-expression and when the brand gestalt incorporates meanings that are disparaging to the consumer. We know that when brand meanings are identity enhancing, the brand serves its identity purpose: people benefit from using the brand as a favorable resource for identity projects and as a desirable social signal. However, if brands are identity-degrading or stigmatizing, these meanings could actually hurt the identity goals of the brand owners. The authors investigate this latter situation, probing the various ways individuals relate to brands with which they have a strong relationship, despite perceiving them as identity degrading.

Part III: Humanizing and anthropomorphizing brands

The focus of this section is on brand anthropomorphism: the process whereby brands are animated and made human-like. Anthropomorphism stands as a cornerstone of brand relationship theory and practice as it is the starting point whereby brands are entertained as relationship partners. Chapters in this section consider the consumer tendency to anthropomorphize brands and provide several viewpoints about the reasons for this phenomenon and its various cultural contexts. The authors challenge long-held assumptions, while suggesting that consumer motivations to humanize brands may be just as important as the outcomes of the tendency. Might this practice eventually lead to a future when brands become so humanized that they take on lives of their own?

In Chapter 8, Jing Wan and Pankaj Aggarwal suggest that although the notion of consumer-brand relationships implicitly assumes that brands are like humans, most prior research on brand relationships does not overtly recognize the notion of anthropomorphism. This chapter first reviews the literature on anthropomorphism and then examines how explicitly incorporating this construct, particularly the motivations behind *why* people anthropomorphize, can shed deeper insights onto consumer-brand relationships.

Chapter 9 by Mandeep Kaur Ghuman, Li Huang, Thomas J. Madden, and Martin S. Roth also tackles the foundational theory of anthropomorphism, but suggests that the tendency to anthropomorphize is not equally shared by all people. Their research empirically investigates the link between the anthropomorphizing tendency and the strength of consumer-brand relationships across different cultural contexts. The authors predict that, due to cultural variances in the acquisition and accessibility of human and nonhuman knowledge, and the varying pace of modern industrialization, the anthropomorphizing tendency should vary across cultures. They also suggest that this propensity would further affect the degree of brand anthropomorphism and how people build relationships with the brands they humanize.

Robert V. Kozinets pushes anthropomorphism to its limits and describes a post-human future of brands in Chapter 10. In this new reality, he urges that we must no longer think of brands as linked to products or to physical matter, explaining that brands have become unbound from the material in exactly the same way that minds have become unbound from brains. Drawing upon the science fictional prognostications of luminaries such as William Gibson, the author proposes that we can foretell a human future where brands are at least as real as the people who use them, and human-brand relationships become an interesting interplay between the real and the virtual.

Part IV: #BrandsOnline

This section addresses the evolving nature of brand relationships made possible by the proliferation of social media. From a broad view of the nuances of consumer behavior in this format, to an explanation of the way that information is transmitted in online networks, and a discussion of the challenges marketers face when they try to join in the conversation, these authors illuminate the digital space as it relates to brand relationships.

In Chapter 11, Renée Richardson Gosline describes the relative paucity of work that links the consumer-brand relationship perspective to the modern consumer's intimate relationship with digital media. The author begins to redress this gap with experiments that measure the changes in consumer-brand relationships based on a relationship hierarchy, from "dislike" to "friend." The chapter focuses on key aspects of consumer behavior in the digital space: consumer-to-consumer communication, customization, and information discovery, and demonstrates that social media can enable identity work, and are most effective in strengthening brand relationships when consumers are able to enhance their digital extended selves.

Chapter 12 by Barbara Bickart, Soyean Kim, Seema Pai, and Frédéric Brunel examines the role of secrets and secret sharing in web-mediated relationships. The authors review the secret-sharing literature and conduct online observation and interviews with influence agents (e.g., bloggers) to develop a typology of how secrets are used in web-mediated relationships – specifically, relationships between an influence agent and their audience. They then explore how different types of secrets and varied facets of secret sharing affect relationships in the online setting.

Molan Kim and Scott A. Thompson suggest in Chapter 13 that marketers' roles are being transformed with the rise of social media. The authors demonstrate how consumers are increasingly interacting in brand-consumer collective environments, including brand and product enthusiast communities. Finding themselves on the outside of these interactions looking in, marketers are struggling with the question of how, when, and whether they should attempt to interact in these collectives. This chapter examines the Customer-to-Customer Relationship Management (CCRM) strategies that marketers employ to build relationships in these environments and the outcomes produced.

Part V: Relationship threats and endings

This section delves inside the underexplored process of relationship dissolution and endings. Whether firm-initiated or consumer-initiated, the processes that accompany relationship endings in the consumer-brand domain represent unique challenges for marketers and for brand researchers. The authors in this section take on that challenge and uncover many of the underlying mechanisms that inform the process. By evaluating the relationship ending from both sides, this research allows a more holistic view than has ever been presented in one place.

Chapter 14 by Marius K. Luedicke and Elisabeth A. Pichler-Luedicke examines what happens to a company's existing consumer-brand relationships when a newly-emerging customer segment becomes attractive to the company. As the company begins to target and attract new customers, existing relationships feel the strain. The authors specifically describe a case in which a company's long-standing relationships with existing customers are threatened when those loyalists interpret the company's alleged flirting with new customer segments as an act of unfaithfulness. Analysis provides insights into the intricate relationships between consumer-brand marriages, immigrant consumption, and multicultural marketing to inform the practice of expanding established brands.

In Chapter 15, Miranda Goode, Mansur Khamitov, and Matthew Thomson look at possible precipitators of relationship termination and explore the situation in which consumers who have developed committed brand relationships sometimes continue to buy options that compete directly with these relationship partners, an activity they suggest can be understood as a form of cheating. Using data from three studies, the authors assess whether so-called triadic brand relationships – those that implicate an interpersonal third party – can safeguard against cheating and protect the brand.

The act of firing customers is a blatant firm-initiated relationship ending and this process is put under the lens in Chapter 16 by Martin Mende, Maura L. Scott, Katherine N. Lemon, and Scott A. Thompson. Although Firm-Initiated Relationship Ending (FIRE) is increasingly common, marketing research has not examined how consumers respond to FIRE, especially in terms of consumer-perceived firm integrity and the motivations for the firing act. Leveraging attribution and social exclusion theories, the authors empirically examine consumers' responses to (non-)deceptive firm-initiated relationship ending strategies. This chapter explores consumers' responses based on which party (firm vs. customer) *caused* the dissolution, and which party the firm *blames* for the action (firm vs. customer).

In Chapter 17, James H. McAlexander and Beth Leavenworth DuFault offer an exploration of the process of consumers leaving brand communities of their own will. The authors suggest that the messy process that consumers experience as they terminate relationships has been overly simplified in the consumer behavior and brand management literatures. They describe a potentially decades-long process that can be iterative, chaotic, and challenging. To better capture the lived experience of these consumers, they introduce a theoretic construct that they term the "Leaving Loop."

In the final chapter of this section, Chapter 18, Cristel Antonia Russell and Hope Jensen Schau draw theoretically from loss and grief research and empirically from consumer narratives to unfold a theory of consumption bereavement that captures consumers' experiences following the market withdrawal of a favorite brand. The authors demonstrate that consumers' history with a given brand impacts their responses to the product's withdrawal and shows the types of products and services most likely to yield strong reactions when withdrawn.

Part VI: Building the brand-driven organization

This section moves us from explorations of branding at the consumer level to the organizational level, where we examine relationships within business-to-business (B2B) channels and what it means to be a brand-driven organization overall. Chapters probe internal strategies that can be employed in various types of organizations centered on the brand, and include organizations as diverse as Motorola and Al Qaeda. The importance of brand meaning is a common theme of these chapters. Diversity across cases and organizations allows for generalization of findings and demonstrates the universality of solid brand relationship theories and ideas.

In Chapter 19, Chris Allen and Matt Carcieri argue that radical transparency and the growing influence of the millennial generation have altered the branding landscape. The authors propose that with the new landscape comes the rise of the culture-based brand – where firms orchestrate internal culture to affect brand meaning, branding from the inside out, and creating deep meaning for brand advocates through shared values. They present qualitative research conducted with three firms that emphasize brand building from the inside out. Their stories illuminate the scenarios where culture-based branding is most applicable and identify practices that foster success with this approach.

Chapter 20 by Michael Breazeale, Erin G. Pleggenkuhle-Miles, Gina Scott Ligon, and Mackenzie Harms looks at branding implications for a different kind of organization: violent extremist organizations. Previous research in the business sector has indicated that a favorable reputation is critical to an organization's economic benefits, performance, and success. The authors explain that despite obvious differences in organizational goals, violent extremist organizations share many structural similarities with business organizations (such as formalization, centralization, and hierarchy) that contribute to their overall performance. They apply Rindova and colleagues' research on celebrity organizations led by charismatic CEOs and existing work on brand relationships to examine the effects of group dynamics and norms on the notoriety of terrorist organizations. Implications for more traditional organizations are also drawn.

Benjamin Lawrence and Patrick J. Kaufmann examine in Chapter 21 the formation and maintenance of business-based brand communities in the context of channels of distribution. Their work examines brand-driven relationships between dealers, some of which take on communal characteristics, and the organizational structures that bound such relations (e.g., collectives), topics that have received little attention in the brand relationship literature. The authors discuss the prevalence of such relationships in channel settings that include multi-level marketing organizations such as independent franchisee/dealer associations, e.g., the Association of Kentucky Fried Chicken Franchisees. Their insights lead to a renewed sensitivity to brand relationships within channel groups.

In Chapter 22, Wayne D. Hoyer, Harley Krohmer, and Lara Lobschat study the Swiss luxury industry to understand the importance of aligning the internal and external brand when building strong brand relationships. According to the authors, brand personality has implications for the understanding of brand effects as well as the firm's performance in the marketplace. They combine managerial and consumer perspectives to focus on the implementation of an intended brand personality by comparing the intention of managers (i.e., the *intended* brand personality) with the perception of consumers (i.e., the *perceived* or *realized* brand personality) and discuss the managerial challenges of implementing an intended brand personality.

Part VII: Systems and metrics for measuring brand relationships

Despite a strong theory base, effective brand relationship practice requires appropriate metrics if it is to be effective. Measurement of brand relationship constructs presents challenges to both marketing academics and managers. In this section, three sets of highly respected practitioners tackle the subject by presenting cutting edge techniques for unpacking the subtleties of brand relationships, while providing insights regarding the nuances of brand relationships that make their measurement so difficult. The common theme of these chapters is that the complex nature of brand relationships necessitates the use of multiple methods to accurately capture the full richness of consumer-brand relationships.

In Chapter 23, Chip Walker and Belle Frank from Young & Rubicam claim that the bar has been raised high for brand measurement, as researchers and practitioners have learned that it is critical to understand what consumers *aren't* saying in order to gain deeper understanding of their relationships with brands. This chapter details results from a new study, analyzed in the context of the BrandAsset Valuator. The study employs two very different research approaches: traditional survey research to assess what people think consciously, and indirect questioning, employing an approach called the Implicit Association Test, to reveal unconscious motivations.

Chapter 24, by John Wittenbraker and Helen Zeitoun, shows how key concepts and tools of basic research on consumer-brand relationships have been validated and commercialized for use in global brand tracking and strategy consulting. Based on fundamental R&D in four countries on over 250 brands, and supplemented by a global database of over 2,000 brands, the authors demonstrate how the use of human relationship metaphors can provide rich insight into the emotional and social side of brands.

In Chapter 25, Max Blackston and Edward Lebar offer another brand measurement system based not on human metaphors but on five universal brand relationships they identified using a rigorous statistical process across multiple product categories and brands. The authors' relationship metrics combine consumers' brand perceptions and brand experiences, explicating a dialogue between brand and consumer going on inside the consumer's mind. Unlike most research that elicits and measures only one side of the dialogue (the one that reflects consumers' attitudes toward the brand), this approach explores the second side of this dialogue – how consumers extrapolate the brand's attitudes towards them from their interactions with the brand. The method asks the consumer not only what they think of the brand, but what the brand thinks of them. The result is a rich diagnostic brand relationship system with strong validation evidence.

Part VIII: Contemplating the futures of branding

This section represents a departure not only from the format found in the rest of the book, but also the typical concluding chapter of volumes such as this one. The nine short essays presented here were collected by the editors from some of the most prolific and cutting-edge researchers in the brand relationship domain. Each was asked to discuss in short form one key issue that they think is particularly relevant to the advancement of branding theory and practice. The diversity of the accumulated thought pieces demonstrates the complexity of the domain, yet the similarity of some of the emerging themes suggests that there are most certainly some actionable ideas that can drive the future of branding research.

Conclusion

This chapter began with the suggestion that brands and brand research have implications so far-reaching that they just might impact every aspect of our lives. A stroll through the topics explored in this book should demonstrate that this claim is not so farfetched. The authors represented herein explore subject populations that include nearly every walk of life. From Swiss luxury consumers to supporters of violent extremist organizations, the volume considers the richness of consumers' experiences. Additionally, practical and actionable advice is provided for both researchers and managers. Readers of this volume should walk away with a better understanding of the domain that is brand relationships and with a renewed passion for exploring the other domains impacted by the study of brands and the relationships that form around them. We hope that this work gives readers a greater sense of the true strength of brands and the necessity of creating strong brand relationships.

PART I

How contexts shape brand meaning

1

LOYALTY AND BRANDS IN CONSUMERS' ASSEMBLED LIVES

Linda L. Price

> Brands cohere into systems that consumers create not only to aid in living but also give meaning to their lives. Put simply consumers do not choose brands, they choose lives.
>
> *(Fournier 1998: 366–367)*

This volume is a testament to the continued interest in understanding the multifarious ways brands insert and are inserted into consumers' assembled lives. Since Fournier's seminal paper (1998) we have learned a great deal about the diversity of consumer-brand relationships (Aaker *et al.* 2004; Alba and Lutz 2013; Coupland 2005; Fournier 2009; Fournier and Alvarez 2013; Fournier *et al.* 2012; Keller 2012; Parmentier and Fischer 2015), as well as the wide-ranging ways that brands and brandscapes shape other relationships (Fournier and Avery 2011; Fournier and Lee 2009; Holt 2002; Martin and Schouten 2014; Muniz and O'Guinn 2001; Wood and Ball 2013). Together, this and other research highlights the embedded and complex quality of brand loyalty (Coulter *et al.* 2003; Fournier and Yao 1997; Mittal and Kamakura 2001; McAlexander *et al.* 2003; Oliver 1999). Moreover, research suggests that enduring brand loyalties emerge from and are strategically linked to important aspects of consumers' life-worlds (Bhattacharya and Sen 2003; Fournier 1998; Moore *et al.* 2002).

The purpose of this chapter is to propose a new perspective on consumer-brand relationships drawing on assemblage theory (Deleuze and Guattari 1987; Epp and Price 2010; 2015; Epp *et al.* 2014; Price 2013). Assemblage theory is still relatively new to consumer and brand research, but holds great promise for understanding complex, dynamic relations among consumers and brands (Canniford and Shankar 2013; Epp *et al.* 2014; Giesler 2012; Lury 2009). The perspective of this chapter differs from the bulk of prior consumer-brand research in two important ways.

First, rather than focus on a dyadic consumer-brand relationship or a focal brand community, I focus on how brand relations are situated in dynamic webs of hetero-geneous relations that comprise a consumer's life-world. In particular, I highlight the interplay of brands and loyalties as consumers traverse within and between key assemblages, territories, and milieus that comprise their lives (Price and Epp 2015; Epp *et al.* 2014; Wiley *et al.* 2010; Wise 2000).

Second, consistent with an assemblage perspective, I stress the way that agency is distributed (Bennett 2005; Price and Epp 2015; Hill, Canniford and Mol 2014). Agency among people, brands, and other heterogeneous actors is constantly reconfigured in response to changed relations and arrangements. In this view, consumers don't exactly "choose their lives," as Fournier (1998) described. Instead, the relations that consumers get bound up in create obligations, habits, refrains, and trajectories – it is the relations themselves that exert agency (Deleuze and Guattari 1987; DeLanda 2006). For example, "Facebook, by organizing heterogeneous relations in a specific way, constitutes a productive force: it makes new relations possible," (Bucher 2013: 481). As relations and arrangements change, brands can insert themselves in unanticipated ways, creating new meanings and opportunities (Epp *et al.* 2014; Giesler 2012; Thomas *et al.* 2013).

In what follows, I briefly outline what I mean by consumers' milieus, assemblages, and territories, and then how brands and loyalties are bound up in these systems of relations and arrangements. Then, drawing on data that directly explores consumers' assembled lives, I illustrate (1) consumers' lived experience of relations and loyalties across multiple assemblages, and (2) brands' relational capabilities within these webs of relations. I conclude by proposing that there may be opportunities for brand managers to increase long-term customer value and share of wallet by focusing on a brand's relational capabilities in complex webs of dynamic and ever-changing consumer milieus and relations.

Imagining consumers' assembled lives

> I got to try and think. Um, yeah, loyalty is important. However, you have the relationship because you are loyal and you are loyal because of the relationship. The two things go hand in hand.
>
> *(M, Married, 4 children, #38)*

> The biggest problem that I have with all these relationships is being able to attend all of the events, meetings, and social activities surrounding these relationships. Both my husband and I work, and our children are very involved in many activities. My husband and I many times must "divide and conquer," which makes me feel like I am short-changing some of my relationships.
>
> *(F, Married, 3 children, #23)*

These two quotes from informants describing their lived experience of loyalties suggest that relations, obligations, and loyalties are inextricably bound together (Coleman 1988; DeLanda 2006; Keller 2007). Figure 1.1 is a necessarily simplistic

FIGURE 1.1 Assembling life and loyalties

representation of the consumer's fuzzy, often intersecting, dynamic, and unique constellation of assemblages that are built up of relations that coalesce and territorialize from the surrounding social, technological, and geographical milieus that are also in constant motion. It is within this complex web of relations that consumers experience loyalties.

Assemblages

Assemblages are dynamic compositions of heterogeneous elements that, in their synthesis, form a distinctive consistency and expression or collective identity (Price 2013; Price and Epp 2015). Consumers get and choose to be entangled in relations of heterogeneous elements that sustain as assemblages, but, at the same time, include diverse logics and priorities. Families, homes, workplaces, churches, and social, brand, and consumption communities are examples of consumer assemblages, each built up in complex webs of not always harmonious relations (Epp and Price 2010; Epp *et al.* 2014; Thomas *et al.* 2013; Wise 2000). Within each of these assemblages, people, pets, plants, practices, and things pull in different directions with varying capacities to relate (Epp and Price 2011). Moreover, processes of reassembling, disassembling, dispersion, and transformation are constant. New possibilities form from new and altered relations, capacities, and arrangements that create what

Deleuze and Guattari (1987) term "lines of flight," or trajectories for transformation. That is, assemblages are always becoming. For example, in prior work, I talk about how a new brand such as a Wii game can enter family and home assemblages and change relationships among people, other brands, practices, and spaces (Epp and Price 2010). More recently, I illustrate how when geographical relations change, families try to reassemble practices through technology across time and distance. In this process, some brands are displaced while others are replaced, and still others are foregrounded in new relational webs (Epp *et al.* 2014).

One important aspect of assemblage theory is that it embraces a view of agency driven by the interplay of all elements rather than focusing only on human actors (Bennett 2010). This is an agency "both of sums and of distinctive parts" (McFarlane 2009: 566). Materiality and brands are important actors that seep into and reach across these and other assemblages in unexpected ways that implicate consumers' relationships and loyalties. By examining how brands are situated in a web of relations, we can better understand how lines of loyalty are drawn and why. That is, we can better understand how and where brands contribute to consumers' assembled lives. Rather than asking whether consumers are loyal to a brand, we can look to see how brands are situated in consumers' relations of loyalty.

Territories

As assemblages of heterogeneous actors gather around a collective identity, they carve a specific territory for the elements out of the surrounding milieu. This territory is contingent, unstable, partial, and situated (McFarlane 2009; Wiley *et al.* 2010). Territories are constantly destabilized by changing assemblage relations and relations with surrounding milieus. For instance, family dinner is an important practice in many home and family territories, yet the surrounding technology milieu, as well as other assemblages, such as soccer and work, often displace or change family dinner in ways that destabilize these territories (Epp and Price 2012). Nonetheless, families recruit creative responses, sometimes involving changed relations with brands, in order to reassert territory against competing forces (Cross and Gilly 2014; Epp and Velagaleti 2014; Price and DuFault 2014).

Territories, rather than being thought of as spaces, are an expression of the practices, habits, and norms that give an assemblage its particular character. For example, the home assemblage may typically conjure up a geographical location, but the expression and, hence, territory of a home is not bound to a particular geography. Territories are more about how relations of organic and non-organic elements are configured and circulate "rather than simply their topographical setting and location" (Allen 2011: 156; Callon and Law 2004). The expression of home as a territory can be decoupled from geography and replicated across time and over distances (Bardhi *et al.* 2012; Wise 2000). Territories are ways that assemblages mark themselves as distinct from the surrounding milieu. In addition, territories are built up from aspects or portions of milieus (Deleuze and Guattari 1987: 314; Wise 2000).

Milieus

Milieus are that rich canvas of our life-worlds. As life is experienced we form relations (seeing, smelling, tasting, sensing) with a vast array of elements that constitute an area of influence: a milieu that is constantly shifting. Territories are constantly borrowing from the milieu and are also vulnerable to intrusions (Deleuze and Guattari 1987; Wise 2000: 298). The concept of milieu is not easily distilled into some set of organized relations. Nonetheless, for the purposes of our discussion we can usefully focus on social, technological, and geographical milieus (Wiley *et al.* 2010). The social milieu is "the population with which we are potentially connected;" the technological milieu is "the infrastructures, technologies, and media that surround us;" and the geographical milieu is the "landscapes through which we move and the available technologies of mobility" (Wiley *et al.* 2010: 345). What elements of the milieu get pulled into the fuzzy territories of the assemblages can play a critical role in how relations form, take hold, endure, and also change or are disrupted (McFarlane and Anderson 2011). For example, in recent research, I illustrate how the technology milieu of families has a dramatic impact on whether and how co-located practices get reassembled when families are geographically dispersed (Epp *et al.* 2014).

Assembling loyalties

Despite a plethora of research on brand loyalty, there is relatively little interrogation of what loyalty means and the forms that it takes in people's lives (Keller 2007). Assemblage theory has been applied to virtually every domain of life from topics as various as nature, disease, politics, history, and organizations, but is relatively silent on the topic of loyalties (Buchanan and Thoburn 2008). Based on this brief introduction to assemblage theory, I posit that loyalties are implicated in assemblage theory in two important and different ways.

First, loyalties are bound up in the habits, practices, and norms that make up assemblage territories (Wise 2000). It is not just loyalty to a person or idea, it is loyalty in a particular relational form: how I will be loyal and what loyalty means in this relational context. Keller (2007) talks about several different prominent expressions of loyalty, such as loyalty in concern (what a parent might feel for a child), but also loyalty in advocacy, ritual, identification, and belief. However, Keller (2007) acknowledges that it is a lot more complicated than this. For example, we may believe, based on attachment and behavior, that a consumer is loyal to a brand, but, of course, the consumer may instead express a loyalty of concern to a child through use of the brand, or loyalty to a belief such as fair labor practices through use of the brand, or loyalty to an assemblage practice or ritual such as Thanksgiving in which a brand is embedded (Wallendorf and Arnould 1991). Habits and practices are the carriers of loyalties – to stay loyal to the territory of the assemblage is to embrace its habits and practices that are the making of family, work, home, church, etc. In fact, we can think of loyalty as particular relational practices or performances. However, consistent with assemblage theory, practices and habits are not just repetitions, but resourceful reinventions around the particulars of the relational capacities; each event is unique and mapped to the relatedness and particulars of component parts (Epp *et al*. 2014; Price and Epp 2015). Thus, making dinner as a loyalty practice within the family assemblage may be stretched to include take-out and different arrangements such as on the couch, in the family room, and over a movie (Epp and Price 2012).

Second, loyalties themselves constitute an important consumer assemblage. Consumers' life worlds are structured by these various expressions of loyalty. The elements that comprise this loyalty assemblage are heterogeneous, with diverse logics and varying relational capacities. Brands can be recruited from the milieu as partners in relational expressions of loyalty. Hence, loyalties as an assemblage built up from the consumer's life-world suggest a different view of loyalty: one that is far less dyadic and one in which the consumer is far less in charge as the primary actor.

Overview of informants and data

Data is compiled from informant interviews on the lived experience of loyalties with attention to the role of brands in consumers' assembled lives. The goal was to examine the lived experience of informants' loyalty relations and how these are embedded within their relational networks and milieu of their lives (Thompson *et al*. 1989). It includes a set of 84 semi-structured long interviews (30–60 minutes) that focused on loyalty, the meaning of loyalty, and whether and how services and brands play a role. This data was collected in a medium-sized Midwest community. Also included are another ten depth interviews with accompanying observations of the consumers' daily life that interrogated more closely the role of brands and services in consumer expressions of loyalty. This data was collected in a large Southwestern community.

Because I was interested in people's multiple expressions of loyalty, the first data collection concentrated primarily on men and women who work full time, often in professional roles with one or more children. Informants were overwhelmingly married, 58 percent women, ranging in age from 21 to over 64, with children in the home. Only about 7 percent of informants' unaided responses to questions about loyalties included a brand or service provider as an important loyalty (i.e., primarily childcare and healthcare providers). In the second set of interviews, I relaxed this requirement and convenience sampled people about their various lived loyalties with more concerted probing on whether and how brands have a role in these lived loyalties. This sample included six women and four men, all married, with children, and are aged from their mid 30s to late 40s.

All interviews and observation notes were audiotaped, transcribed, scrutinized by hand, and analyzed with the aid of a computer-based text analysis package NVivo. In the findings section, I use an interview number and some informant details to protect informants' identities. For the ten depth interviews and observations, I use pseudonyms to protect participants' identities. A more detailed profile of the informants is available from the author on request. Data analysis proceeded iteratively, using a "constant comparative method" consistent with a discovery-oriented approach (Glaser and Strauss 1967).

For the purposes of this analysis, I focus on two important findings that emerged across the two data sets and resonate with the assemblage perspective provided in this chapter. The first is to explore consumers' lived experience of relations and loyalties across multiple assemblages, and the second is to further interrogate brands' relational capabilities within webs of assembled relations.

Findings

Consumers' lived experience of loyalties

Informants experience their lives as a tangle of heterogeneous loyalties with diverse logics. Kaylee, who is 45 years old and married with an 11-year-old daughter, was interviewed in her office while sitting on a giant ball that is supposed to help with posture while eating lunch (Yokahomo Rice Bowl).

> I have to juggle professional obligations with family and my Alumni Association obligations almost every day. So, a most recent example would be my parents are visiting, there's a dinner that I need to go to on Friday night for the Alumni Association and I had to prioritize between spending time with my parents or going to this dinner. And, it also requires that I leave work early to be there, at this event, early enough. So having to make choices about spending time with family or meeting my community obligations is something I do all the time.

The tug and pull of obligations to various assemblages is a prominent part of all informants' lives. Kaylee continues to talk about how she is torn between work and her daughter's basketball games, as well as between cleaning her house for her parents' visit and doing something with her daughter, noting, "I had not spent a lot of time doing anything really fun with her for the last couple weekends." Rocks and Ropes with her daughter and then grocery shopping trumped cleaning the house. This type of narrative of loyalty relations embedded in various assemblages is replicated across nearly every informant.

Two elements of informants' narratives of their lives are noteworthy. First, loyalty expressions, or practices of loyalty, dominate consumers' lives, and, second, these heterogeneous loyalty relations are in complex, not always harmonious interplay with each other. For example, we think of home and family assemblages as overlapping and harmonious, but here we see that they compete for attention and against what are also viewed as obligations to other family members (see also, Dion *et al.* 2014). Kaylee, like a majority of our informants, asserts that she puts family first, but goes on to note, "but every now and then you have to juggle those [priorities] around and one has to take, if you always put your family first, you would never do anything outside of your home."

This tangle of loyalties builds out from our informants to the loyalties embedded in all their surrounding relations. A young homemaker with four children aged between 1 and 10 describes this tangled web of embedded loyalties:

> There was a women's retreat this weekend at the church that I have always gone to in the past years, and [husband] had something going on that weekend and the kids all had soccer games and basketball games, and it was a hard decision to not go to that [retreat] but for the interest of the family I stayed home so that [husband] wouldn't have to watch the kids instead of going on his trip with the kids he works with (at Campus Life Ministries) and it's important that we keep some continuity in our kids' lives instead of always taking them to grandma's when we have to do something.
>
> *(#3)*

The kids' loyalties to soccer and basketball, the husband's loyalty to Campus Life Ministries, and the wife's loyalty to church are all the bundled up with expressions of loyalty, such as going to the games (even though they were very hot and not what she preferred), letting her husband prioritize his loyalty, and making sure Grandma is not "always taking" the children.

Others describe loyalty practices with their children in terms of what can be outsourced and what can't. Samantha is married with two young sons (6 years and 8 months), and a tenured professor at a major university. She feels the tug of yard work and house cleaning and happily outsources as much as she can, but describes her limits (see Barnhart *et al.* 2014; Epp and Velagaleti 2014):

> I won't do things that I've seen my other colleagues do, like I won't hire someone to pick up my kids at school. I think there is a lot of valuable time I spend with them, one, interacting with the teachers and talking with them about how the day went and debriefing and even on the way home, I help my son do his homework on the way home and we talk and we have great conversations, so there are limits to how much I outsource.

For Samantha, particular rituals such as picking her kids up from school are central loyalty practices. She and her husband "try to develop good eating habits for our son," but "Papa John's is on speed dial for Friday night when we are so exhausted". However, because Friday movie night is also an important family practice, Samantha has her own loyalty performance: "And the one thing I do cook is my own popcorn … My son and husband love my popcorn, so I'll make a big batch of popcorn, so that's important. That's our idea of fun."

Throughout the interviews informants describe not just different relational priorities (such as family first), but differing relational capacities that influence their loyalty performances. For example, Rebecca is in her mid-30s with three children between 9 months and 10 years old. She and her husband relocated to the Southwest to be closer to Rebecca's family, which meant moving away from her husband's family in the Southeast. Rebecca's mother is flexible and easy-going and helps with the children two days a week. However, reflecting on how she juggles demands, she observes, "Say, my dad. I love my dad. Pops is a needy guy, but we fill Pops' needs last because he has got many of them."

Informants also describe many failed loyalty performances. A working professional mother of two daughters describes:

> Yesterday was my friends' birthday at work and I felt obligated to satisfy that relationship and meet for lunch. And, on the other hand, a long time ago I had promised my daughters that we would go to the opening day at the zoo. And so I woke up thinking, I can do this first, and I had to do some other errands that needed to be run … when I got to the office it was much later than I had anticipated … I failed. I didn't leave the office by 11:30 and I had promised my daughters and they get priority and so I failed to go out to lunch with my friends.

A striking feature of informants' narratives is how many of them are "yesterday," "this week," "tomorrow," coupled with "all the time." The lived experience of loyalty is pervasive, fraught with tensions as the territories of different assemblages clash, and often filled with ambivalent emotions of one successful loyalty performance against another failed one. By carefully following these consumers and loyalty practices across their assembled lives, a different picture of loyalty emerges, one that at first glance seems to have little, if anything, to do with brands. Across the data, the dyadic relationship between a consumer and brand is the weakest and least represented of all loyalty relationships.

Nonetheless, as is already apparent from some of the examples above, when we focus on consumers' loyalty practices across their assembled complex relational lives, brands are active and transformative elements. For example, Kaylee who took her daughter to Rocks and Ropes, observes how important this was because "my relationship with her got special attention and time." Numerous informants mentioned the partnering role of brands and technologies in loyalty practices that are central to their assembled lives.

Brands' relational capabilities within webs of assembled relations

> Probably the biggest difference in my purchasing since our marriage is in the grocery department. Now I have to buy the types of food that she likes to eat. Well, [wife] wants me to eat healthier so instead of eating Lucky Charms or Toaster Strudels for breakfast, we eat Cheerios or wheat toast. For lunch, instead of eating at Runza or Burger King, we eat Subway or a garden fresh salad, and for dinner, we eat chicken or pasta instead of pizza or cheeseburgers.
> *(Male, late 20s, married, 1 child #50)*

In this section, I highlight the special roles that brands do play in consumers' loyalty practices. Accommodation is an important loyalty practice that frequently implicates brands. An interesting finding that deserves more systematic attention is that in families where one member is brand loyal and another "could care less," the non-brand loyal person accommodates the brand loyal person rather than the other way around. For example, one of our informants observes, "My husband will only drink Coke. That means no matter what the price is or if anything else is cheaper we have to buy Coke" (F, late 30s, 4 children, manager #6).

Samantha who has Papa John's Pizza on speed dial notes that she doesn't care about the pizza brand, but her husband prefers it and her son loves pizza. In other variants of accommodation as a loyalty practice, a brand is used to avoid problems or to mediate differences. For example, tensions among family members may be mediated by brands that have strong relational capacity for unifying across differences: for example, family members who don't agree about politics are able to agree on a movie (see also Price and DuFault 2014; Price and Epp 2015). Interestingly, brands that unify across differences may be everyone's less preferred alternative, because what's important is the ability of the brand to reassert territory for an important assemblage such as family, work, friends, and so on. Many opportunities exist for brand managers to examine loyalty practices of accommodation. In almost all of these cases, consumers would reflect that the purchase is solely because of the relationship.

Not surprisingly, brands as relational bribes, rewards, or gifts are also evidenced in our informants' loyalty practices. What is important about many of these narratives is the way that they are knitted across multiple loyalties and assemblages. For example, Rebecca describes how she navigates the tensions between her children and their piano teacher: "If they do a really good job at piano lessons – I have to bribe them cause they don't like to practice, but if their piano teacher says they did a superior job, they can get a Frappuccino on the way home."

An elementary teacher in her mid 40s with 4 children describes another example: "Yesterday for example, I came home from work, just changed real fast, took Pete to his baseball practice. In between I had to go grocery shopping. While doing that I felt bad about having little [youngest son] sitting home by himself, so I bought him some new headphones." (#17)

This example highlights one important way consumers manage their loyalty assemblage: they toggle or cycle among their loyalties, sometimes implicating brands. Because brands have high relational capacity to "close the gap," they frequently stand-in when other resources have been fully depleted. As one informant describes:

> Some nights I have to miss my boys' sporting events and I hate that, so I find myself taking them to Toys R Us or McDonalds to make up for it. Then if the boys get something you have to get the girls something too, so it is a never- ending cycle.
>
> *(F, late 30s, Manager, married, 4 children #6)*

Two especially important ways that brands are powerful and transformative in consumers' webs of loyalty relations and practices are: first, helping consumers move back and forth between assembled loyalties; and second, enabling consumers to service multiple loyalties simultaneously.

Technologies such as cell phones, notebook computers, and laptops are pervasive as "life-savers," helping consumers to multi-task across assembled loyalties. Often, but not always, these helpers are tagged with a favorite brand.

> I learned a long time ago that keeping one calendar for everything, work, church, home, is so important because if you have multiple calendars things get lost and fall through the cracks and my Dell is my life. And the people that are close to me and around me know that my Dell is my life and it's not just my work life it's my everything.
>
> *(Rachel, early 40s, married, 2 daughters)*

An interesting aspect of this and many other informant narratives is the way that constellations of brand properties create powerful relational capacities consumers draw on in their everyday lives. Although technologies are the most prominent example in this category, other services also surface. For example, a home meal assembly service owner describes how a group of close friends meet meal preparation needs for family but also escape for fun together:

> There's a group of ladies that come in once a month, there are four or five of them "Lucy's party," they say. They come in and tell their husbands that these meals take them four hours to do and they quickly finish their dinners spending an hour and a half there, leave their dinners in the refrigerators and then take off and have drinks and dinner, and then call their husbands on the way out to let them know that they're on their way home, so they trick them into having this free time, their little treat time.

In my data, cultural norms that privilege the family assemblage frequently displace friendship networks. This is an example of how the pull of a friendship loyalty practice is enabled by a brand that helps navigate the assemblages of home, family, and friends.

In prior work, I describe how spaces and objects are recruited to help families integrate across the heterogeneous goals and relations that exist within families (Epp and Price 2011). That theme is also widely evident in this data. However, brands are also used to integrate across multiple assemblages beyond the family, especially helping to integrate across personal projects, work, family, and home. A simple example is Suzie's use of a Turbo Cooker crockpot (mother of 2, married, late 30s). Not only does this help meet the loyalty practice of a home-cooked meal despite the pressures of a full-time job, but it involves the whole family in food preparation, which strengthens and stabilizes the territories of family and home. Target was mentioned by several informants as a brand that helps them navigate their multiple assemblage loyalties including school, church, home, family, work, and individual identity projects. For example, Terri is a nurse with three children between 2–6 years old. Late in the interview when probed on brands that feel closely tied to *her identity*, she responds: "Target. I love that place. It dresses my kids, it feeds my kids, it dresses me. You know I'm a Mom and I'm getting my figure back and I can't justify paying a great deal of money for clothes. I'm the last person that I shop for. So my fashion is La Target."

For Terri her identity *is* her bundle of relational loyalties – she is a Mom – and Target is linked to her through that identity. Early in the interview, Terri describes several examples of how loyalties to multiple assemblages complicate her life, noting:

> Everyday I am the mother, that's what I do. For an example, if I have to work, my husband has to work, and if we don't have daycare, then it is me that stays home. Since he is a professor, he can't cancel his classes and stay home. It is me who has to set aside my work in order to make sure we have childcare.

Across informants, the dyadic relationship of consumers with brands is far less pronounced than the roles brands play in loyalty practices that shape the territories of key consumer assemblages such as home, family, work, and volunteer organizations. Even when asked to describe brands close to their personal identity, their assembled lives are often foregrounded in their choices.

Conclusion

As a plethora of other research shows, brands remain an important aspect of individual identity, and consumers form direct dyadic attachments with brands for many reasons. This research, rather than asking whether consumers are loyal to a brand, looked at how brands are situated in consumers' relations of loyalty. Assemblage theory offers one promising line of flight for understanding how loyalties assemble and how the habits and practices of multiple assemblages built up from the surrounding milieus of everyday life implicate brands, not directly, but indirectly through their relational capacity within complex webs of significant ties.

An examination of consumers' lived experience of loyalty in their complex, assembled relational lives suggests that a fruitful avenue for future research is to examine the nuanced ways brands insert themselves and are inserted into other loyalty relations and practices. I find that informants experience their lives as a tangle of heterogeneous loyalties with diverse logics, and the tug and pull of obligations to various assemblages is a prominent part of their lives. Practices of loyalty emerge as a significant way of thinking about loyalty relations in consumers' lives and some loyalty practices are viewed as more central than others. Brands help consumers with practices of loyalty within particular assemblages, but also help consumers integrate, toggle, and cycle across these heterogeneous assemblages. Brand managers, instead of primarily or only examining consumer loyalty to their brand, might instead ask how the brand can be helpful to consumers' in their most important loyalty practices. I hope my framework and findings will encourage brand managers to move beyond a myopic focus on a dyadic relationship between the firm and its customers to ask how they can better partner with consumers in the loyalty practices and relations that matter most to them.

Acknowledgements

With special thanks to Avinash Malshe.

References

Aaker, J., S. Fournier, and S. Adam Brasel (2004) "When Good Brands Do Bad", *Journal of Consumer Research*, 31 (1): 1–16.

Alba, J.W. and R.J. Lutz (2013) "Broadening (and Narrowing) the Scope of Brand Relationships", *Journal of Consumer Psychology*, 23 (2): 265–268.

Allen, J. (2011) "Powerful Assemblages", *Area*, 43 (2): 154–157.

Bardhi, F., G.M. Eckhardt, and E.J. Arnould (2012) "Liquid Relationship to Possessions", *Journal of Consumer Research*, 39 (October): 510–529.

Barnhart, M., A.D.uff, and J. Cotte (2014) "Like a Member of the Family: Outsourcing Family to Professional Caregivers", *Journal of Marketing Management*, 30 (15–16): 1680–1702.

Bennett, J. (2005), "The Agency of Assemblages and the North American Blackout", *Public Culture*, 17 (3): 445–465.

Bennett, J. (2010) *Vibrant Matter: A Political Ecology of Things*. Durham, NC: Duke University Press.

Bhattacharya, C.B. and S. Sen (2003) "Consumer-Company Identification: A Framework for Understanding Consumers' Relationships with Companies", *Journal of Marketing*, 67 (April): 76–88.

Buchanan, I. and N. Thoburn (2008) *Deleuze and Politics*. Edinburgh: Edinburgh University Press.

Bucher, T. (2013) "The Friendship Assemblage: Investigating Programmed Sociality on Facebook", *Television New Media*, 14 (6): 479–493.

Callon, M. and Law, J. (2004) "Absence-Presence, Circulation, and Encountering in Complex Space", *Environment and Planning D: Society and Space*, 22 (3): 3–11.

Canniford, R. and A. Shankar (2013) "Purifying Practices: How Consumers Assemble Romantic Experiences of Nature", *Journal of Consumer Research*, 39 (5): 1051–1069.

Coleman, J.S. (1988) "Social Capital in the Creation of Human Capital", *American Journal of Sociology*, Supplement: Organizations and Institutions; Sociological and Economic Approaches to the Analysis of Social Structure, 94: S95–S120.

Coulter, R.A., L.L. Price, and L. Feick (2003) "Origins of Product Involvement and Brand Commitment", *Journal of Consumer Research*, 20 (September): 151–169.

Coupland, J.C. (2005) "Invisible Brands: An Ethnography of Households and the Brands in their Kitchen Pantries", *Journal of Consumer Research*, 32 (1): 106–118.

Cross, S. and M. Gilly (2014) "Cultural Competence and Cultural Compensatory Mechanisms in Binational Households", *Journal of Marketing*, 78 (May): 121–139.

DeLanda, M. (2006) *New Philosophy of Society: Assemblage Theory and Social Complexity*. New York: Continuum Books.

Deleuze, G. and F. Guattari (1987) *A Thousand Plateaus: Capitalism and Schizophrenia*. Minneapolis, MN: University of Minnesota Press.

Dion, D., O. Sabri, and V. Guillard (2014) "Home Sweet Messy Home: Managing Symbolic Pollution", *Journal of Consumer Research*, 41 (October): 565–589.

Epp, A.M. and L.L. Price (2010) "The Storied Life of Singularized Objects: Forces of Agency and Transformation", *Journal of Consumer Research*, 36 (5): 820–37.

Epp, A.M. and L.L. Price (2011) "Designing Solutions around Customer Network Identity Goals", *Journal of Marketing*, 75 (March): 36–54.

Epp, A.M. and L.L. Price (2012) "Family Time in Consumer Culture: Implications for Transformative Public Policy", *Transformative Consumer Research*, eds C. Pechmann and J. Ozanne. New York: Routledge: 599–622.

Epp, A.M. and S. Velagaleti (2014) "Outsourcing Parenthood: How Families Manage Care Assemblages Using Paid Commercial Services", *Journal of Consumer Research*, 41 (December): 911–935.

Epp, A.M, H.J. Schau, and L.L. Price (2014) "The Role of Brands and Mediating Technologies in Assembling Long-Distance Family Practices", *Journal of Marketing*, 78 (May): 81–101.

Fournier, S. (1998) "Consumers and Their Brands: Developing Relationship Theory in Consumer Research", *Journal of Consumer Research*, 24 (4): 343–373.

Fournier, S. (2009) "Lessons Learned about Consumers' Relationships with their Brands", *Handbook of Brand Relationships,* eds D.J. MacInnis, C.W. Park, and J.R. Priester. Armonk, NY: M.E. Sharpe: 5–23.

Fournier, S. and C. Alvarez (2013) "Relating Badly To Brands", *Journal of Consumer Psychology*, 23 (2): 253–264.

Fournier, S. and J. Avery (2011) "The Uninvited Brand", *Business Horizons*, Special Issue on Web 2.0, Consumer-Generated Content, and Social Media, 54: 193–207.

Fournier, S. and L. Lee (2009) "Getting Brand Communities Right", *Harvard Business Review*, April: 105–111.

Fournier, S. and J. Yao (1997) "Reviving Brand Loyalty: A Reconceptualization within the Framework of Consumer–Brand Relationships", *International Journal of Research in Marketing*, 14 (5): 451–472.

Fournier, S., M. Breazeale and M. Fetscherin (2012) *Consumer-Brand Relationships: Insights for Theory and Practice*, London: Routledge/Taylor & Francis.

Giesler, M. (2012) "How Doppelganger Brand Images Influence the Market Creation Process: Longitudinal Insights from the Rise of Botox Cosmetic", *Journal of Marketing*, 76 (6): 55–68.

Glaser, B.G. and A.L. Strauss (1967) *The Discovery of Grounded Theory: Strategies for Qualitative Research*, Hawthorne, NY: Aldine Publishing Company.

Hill, T., R. Canniford, and J. Mol (2014) "Non-representational Marketing Theory", *Marketing Theory*, 14 (4): 377–394.

Holt, D.B. (2002) "Why Do Brands Cause Trouble? A Dialectical Theory of Consumer Culture and Branding", *Journal of Consumer Research*, 29 (June): 70–90.

Keller, K.L. (2012) "Understanding the Richness of Brand Relationships: Research Dialogue on Brands as Intentional Agents", *Journal of Consumer Psychology*, 22: 186–190.

Keller, S. (2007) *Limits to Loyalty*, Cambridge: Cambridge University Press.

Lury, C. (2009) "Brand as Assemblage: Assembling Culture", *Journal of Cultural Economy*, 2 (1–2): 67–82.

Martin, D.M. and J.W. Schouten (2014) "Consumption-Driven Market Emergence", *Journal of Consumer Research*, 40: 855–870.

McAlexander, J.H., S.K. Kim, and S.D. Roberts (2003) "Loyalty: The Influences of

Satisfaction and Brand Community Integration", *Journal of Marketing Theory and Practice*, 11 (Fall): 1–11.

McFarlane, C. (2009) "Translocal Assemblages: Space, Power and Social Movements", *Geoforum*, 40 (4): 561–567.

McFarlane, C. and B. Anderson (2011) "Thinking with Assemblage", *Area*, 43 (2): 162–164.

Mittal, V. and W.A. Kamakura (2001) "Satisfaction, Repurchase Intent, and Repurchase Behavior: Investigating the Moderating Effect of Customer Characteristics", *Journal of Marketing Research*, 38 (February): 131–142.

Moore, E.S., W.L. Wilkie, and R.J. Lutz (2002) "Passing the Torch: Intergenerational Influences as a Source of Brand Equity", *Journal of Marketing*, 66 (April): 17–37.

Muniz, A.M. Jr. and T.C. O'Guinn (2001) "Brand Community", *Journal of Consumer Research*, 27 (March): 412–432.

Oliver, R. (1999) "Whence Consumer Loyalty?", *Journal of Marketing*, 63 (4): 33–44.

Parmentier, M.A. and E. Fischer (2015) "Things Fall Apart: The Dynamics of Brand Audience Dissipation", *Journal of Consumer Research*, 41 (5): 1228–1251.

Price, L.L. (2013) "Family Stuff", *The Routledge Companion to Identity and Consumption*, eds A.A. Ruvio and R.W. Belk. New York: Routledge: 302–312.

Price, L.L. and B. DuFault (2014) "Consumption and the Open-Ended Project of Becoming Family", Presented at *Consumer Culture Theory Conference*, Helsinki, Finland, June 2014.

Price, L.L. and A.M. Epp (2015) "The Heterogeneous and Open-Ended Project of Assembling Family", *Assembling Consumption*, eds R. Canniford and D. Bajde. New York: Routledge, forthcoming.

Thomas, T.C., L.L. Price, and H.J. Schau (2013) "When Differences Unite: Resource Dependence in Heterogeneous Consumption Communities", *Journal of Consumer Research*, 39 (5, February): 1010–1033.

Thompson, C.J., W.B. Locander, and H.R. Pollio (1989) "Putting Consumer Experience Back into Consumer Research: The Philosophy and Method of Existential-Phenomenology", *Journal of Consumer Research*, 16 (2, September): 133–146.

Wallendorf, M. and E.J. Arnould (1991) "'We Gather Together': Consumption Rituals of Thanksgiving Day", *Journal of Consumer Research*, 18 (June): 13–31.

Wiley, S.B., D.M. Sutko, and T.M. Becerra (2010) "Assembling Social Space", *The Communication Review*, 13 (4): 340–372.

Wise, J.M. (2000) "Home, Territory and Identity," *Cultural Studies*, 14 (2): 295–310.

Wood, D.M. and K. Ball (2013) "Brandscapes of Control? Surveillance, Marketing and the Co-Construction of Subjectivity and Space in Neo-Liberal Capitalism", *Marketing Theory*, 13 (1): 47–67.

2

FRAMING THE GAME

How brands' relationships with their competitors affect consumer preference

Neeru Paharia, Jill Avery, and Anat Keinan

A prominent narrative in contemporary consumer culture is one in which "category killer" brands like Amazon, Starbucks, Home Depot, and Wal-Mart are forcing mom and pop independent bookstores, coffee shops, hardware stores, and retailers out of business. The narrative tells us that consumers are switching their preferences from small, local businesses to big box retailers (Hosein and Hughes 2006; Spector 2005). Therefore, when big brands move in next door to small, independent businesses, sales for the small brands are expected to decrease.

However, despite their success, many category killer brands have attracted the ire of political activists who organize against them. In many instances, consumers have rallied around small, independent brands and boycotted big brands. This activity suggests that consumers may be willing to forgo the oftentimes lower prices and the broader assortment of goods offered by category killer brands to express their political will in the marketplace and protect small, independent brands from aggressive competition.

In this chapter, we explore the effect of competitive framing, positioning brands in competition with one another, and show that small brands can paradoxically benefit from having large competitors. We explore the effects of competition in the marketplace and show how changing the competitive framing of the market situation positively and negatively affects consumers' support for the brands within it.

In a series of three experiments, we illustrate that the perceived competitive context in which a brand operates and the perceived competitiveness of each brand in that context can affect consumers' purchase intention and frequency. Using diverse competitive framing scenarios, in which a focal brand is positioned either alone or in direct competition with another brand, as well as positioned either in balanced competition with a firm similar in size to them or in imbalanced competition with a firm larger or smaller than them, we examine how the competitive context affects consumers' responses. We find that the effect of competitive framing depends upon the presence of salient competition and the perceived balance of that competition. Consumers increase their preference for small, independent brands and decrease their preference for large, national brands when the two types of brands are framed as directly competing against one another.

We argue the effect of competitive framing is mediated by the consumers' politicization of the purchase episode and their resulting feelings of purchase activism, defined as a heightened desire to communicate one's political opinions and to impact the marketplace through purchasing. When the market is presented as a competition, consumers reframe the purchase situation, moving from assessing it in economic terms, in which they attempt to maximize the economic utility they receive from the product by obtaining the most value for the lowest cost, to viewing it in politicized terms. We also show that competitive aggression plays an important role. In unbalanced competition, large brands are punished for being a competitive aggressor, while small brands are rewarded when they aggressively compete.

The chapter is organized as follows. First, we discuss the phenomenon of politicized consumption and develop a typology to categorize this phenomenon. Next, we focus on a specific context in which consumption becomes politicized – when brands compete. Then, we present a series of hypotheses which propose and explain positive and negative consumer responses to brands in competitive settings. Through a series of three experiments, we uncover the mediating process that drives these effects and consumers' feelings of purchase activism, as well as show how competitive balance and competitive aggression moderate consumers' responses. Our results highlight how brands, both big and small, can frame a competitive context that works to their advantage to increase purchase interest and frequency.

Conceptual foundations

Politicized consumption

One of the critiques of contemporary consumer culture stems from a portrait painted of today's consumers as self-interested and materialistic utility maximizers, constantly seeking fulfillment through goods, and ignorant of the negative effects of their consumption on themselves, their neighbors, and the world around them (Klein 2000; Schor 1998). These are passive and materialistic consumers, opting out of community involvement and political participation in favor of the pursuit of material goods and market-driven experiences. However, interestingly, along with the rise of this negative stereotype, an alternative consumption narrative has come into favor: ethical consumerism or critical consumption. Consumers have long utilized their purchasing power to convey their beliefs and make a difference in the marketplace (Micheletti 2003). Consumers today are using their consumption to exercise their citizenship, express their values, and look behind the products they are purchasing to understand their effects on people, animals, small businesses, and the environment. Across product categories, consumers indicate that they are increasingly willing to pay more for products and services that support ideas that are important to them (Tan 2007).

We define this behavior as *politicized consumption*, consumption that has a political character or meaning beyond the economic exchange, in which, through one's purchasing actions, one can express one's opinions, values, and political positions to participate in enacting social change (Micheletti 2003; Micheletti *et al.* 2006). Unlike economically focused consumption in which consumers attempt to maximize the economic utility they receive from the product by obtaining the most value for the lowest cost, during consumption episodes that are perceived as politicized, consumers look for their purchasing choices to be driven by their moral beliefs, embody the ideals they live by, support what they believe in, and help make a difference in the world. Consumers experience a sense of enchantment from politicized consumption (Thompson and Coskuner-Balli 2007), using it to relieve guilt about their purchasing (Devinney *et al.* 2010), and relishing it for its ability to grant cultural capital in today's hypercompetitive consumer culture (Heath and Potter 2004), indicating that politicized consumption has important meaning to consumers.

Consumers have moved away from conventional political actions which are viewed as ineffective, such as picketing and joining political parties, and have moved towards other political actions, such as boycotting (refusing to buy the goods of a company) and "buycotting" (supportive buying of the goods of a company) to make a difference in their communities and world (Inglehart and Baker 2000). Consumers view purchasing "polit-brands" (O'Guinn and Muniz 2005; O'Guinn and Muniz 2004), brands that reflect an alternative political agenda in contrast to that of the big, corporate, mainstream brands, as a way to fight against the cultural hegemony perpetuated by the perceived marketing machine (Adorno and Horkheimer 1944; Firat and Venkatesh 1995; Thompson *et al.* 2006). Today, purchasing as a rebellious act has become a mainstream consumer practice, driving contemporary consumer culture and advertising and marketing practice (Heath and Potter 2004; Holt 2002; O'Guinn and Muniz 2004). Brands advertise concepts like local, organic, fair trade, not tested on animals, and made in the USA to appeal to consumers' political, social, and moral convictions.

We began our research by developing a typology to categorize behavior related to politicized consumption. Based on a review of related concepts and consumer-facing organizations (e.g., "buying influence," "ethical consumerism," "cause spending," "ethical consumer"), a review of related marketing and political science literature, and an analysis of the open-ended responses generated by our particulars in the scale development samples, we created a politicized consumption typology. There was a considerable variety in the types of purchases respondents reported. Most of the purchases could be grouped into six major categories (summarized in Table 2.1 with examples of respondent responses).

The present research focuses on the "supporting businesses" category. In our

TABLE 2.1 Politicized consumption typology

Politicized Consumption Category	Related Issues	Branding Examples	Examples Generated by Respondents
Protecting the environment/ sustainability	Climate Change, Pollution and Toxics, Habitats and Resources	Patagonia	• Lush Cosmetics. They refuse to work with any company that has negative environmental impacts.
		Stonyfield Farm	• I purchased Reynolds Recycled Aluminum Foil because I like being green and they are the only ones that offer this.
		The organic movement	• I chose to buy Stonyfield milk because it is organic. I like to support brands that use environmentally sound practices and don't use pesticides.
			• I bought SunChips because they had compostable bags.
		Toyota Prius	• I purchase used books from an online bookstore that offers options to pay a little more for shipping 'Eco-friendly' and an option to pay a small fee to offset the carbon emissions of the freight of your order.
		Scott Paper	• I choose to purchase Scott paper products because they practice environmentally sustainable growth in the way in which they manage their woodlands.
			• I bought a Toyota Prius. I care about the environment.

TABLE 2.1 continued

Politicized Consumption Category	Related Issues	Branding Examples	Examples Generated by Respondents
Protecting people	Human Rights, Workers' Rights – pay/working conditions, fair-trade, diversity.	American Apparel	• I choose not to purchase from Nike because of how they treat their overseas help and exploit the work force, I chose to purchase from Saucony instead because they value the work force and observe fair work environment.
		Pura Vida Coffee	• I buy from charity stores when it helps employ people from off the streets trying to get job training or donates funds to charities.
		Saucony	• American Apparel. The clothing is not made in awful sweatshops.
		Equal Exchange	• After hearing about how certain clothing companies treated their workers, I decided not to visit the store to make further purchases.
		Fair Trade Certified	• I do not buy from Wal-Mart's clothing section because of their possible sweatshop conditions.
			• I have tried to purchase clothing that is manufactured in a country where workers are getting a fair wage. I have also purchased items over time from Haiti via a fair market place group who forward art for purchase.
Protecting animals	Animal Testing, Animal Welfare and Rights, Factory Farming	Body Shop	• I buy Clinique products, since they do not test on animals.
		Clinique	• I try to buy meat that is not factory farmed because I believe that animals should not be factory farmed.
		Burt's Bees	• I almost always buy from Ben and Jerry's because their treatment of their animals and manufacturing practices seem to be better than those of many of their competitors.
			• I bought Burt's Bees products the other week because I know for certain they're not tested on animals.
			• I don't buy Tyson meat. The way they treat these animals and the farmers is morally upsetting to me.
			• I don't buy from fur companies because I don't wear animal furs.
			• I choose not to buy a stuffed animal from Ringling Brother's circus brand because of the way they mistreat the animals in their shows.
			• Only purchase StarKist Tuna. It is dolphin safe whereas many other brands aren't.

TABLE 2.1 continued

Politicized Consumption Category	Related Issues	Branding Examples	Examples Generated by Respondents
Supporting/ opposing a social or religious position	Gay rights, Christian businesses	Chick-fil-A	• C28.com is a Christian clothing company and I buy shirts from there because I am a Christian.
		Subaru	• I try to shop at Target stores because they bankrolled anti-gay marriage ads.
		Target	• I bought something expensive from the Apple store and it was about 5 miles from my house. They had the same item at Target which is less than half a mile from the house, but I do not like the nature of their political contributions to anti-Gay politicians. It used to be my favorite store.
			• Once I bought an Android phone because they have a progressive phone company that cares about rights and are concerned about Sarah Palin and stuff.
			• I don't shop at Abercrombie and Fitch because of their history with racial profiling in their hiring practices.
			• I try not to buy Coors brands because the owners have been involved in white supremacist movements.
			• I decided not to buy Pepsi because it supported Planned Parenthood.
			• I don't buy Tommy Hilfiger because he stated that his clothes weren't made for black people.
			• I purchase Hunts ketchup and stopped purchasing Heinz because the values of Heinz are incompatible with the values of America as indicated by Mrs Kerry (wife of John Kerry) who owns the company.
			• I stopped buying Nestle products because the company was pushing mothers in developing countries to use infant formula rather than breast feed their infants … I bought comparable products from other companies.

TABLE 2.1 continued

Politicized Consumption Category	Related Issues	Branding Examples	Examples Generated by Respondents
Supporting a non-profit cause	Corporate philanthropy, CSR, cause-related marketing	Yoplait's Save Lids to Save Lives Product RED Tom's	• I bought a bottle of Evian water over Dasani because a part of Evian's profits were going to breast cancer. • I bought a bracelet from the Invisible Children organization because part of the proceeds went to impoverished women in Africa. • I buy shoes from Tom's (who donates a pair for every pair purchased to a needy person) because 1) I like the brand's shoes, and 2) because of the charitable cause it contributes to. • (Product) RED t-shirts, iPods or laptops, donating large portions of profit to fight AIDS in Africa. • I purchase grocery items that have the box tops for education on them because it helps out my local schools. • Bought a Coke because I know Coca-Cola contributes to all kinds of charities and good causes. • Fresh Step kitty litter which donates a portion of their profits to ASPCA.

TABLE 2.1 continued

Politicized Consumption Category	Related Issues	Branding Examples	Examples Generated by Respondents
Supporting businesses	Competitive context, small, independent businesses, underdog brands, locally owned / operated, domestic (vs. imported), globalization concerns	Local coffee shop vs. Starbucks Apple vs. Microsoft The local-vore movement Made in the USA	• In-N-Out because they use all ingredients from my home state California – supports the economy of my state • Instead of going to Subway, I went and supported the local sub shop down the street. • I bought ice cream at a local ice cream store in my neighborhood because everyone thought the big time one was better just because it was bigger. • I guess I buy less Blue Moon after I figured out it was produced by Coors. • Bought from Costco instead of Wal-Mart because Wal-Mart cheats their providers by forcing them to sell for prices they cannot afford. • I buy from Berryline, a locally owned and operated frozen yogurt place, instead of the larger national chains that may be closer because I choose to support local small business. • I buy food from farmers' market vendors so I can support family farms rather than large corporate farms. • I often spend a little more money to make purchases from small local businesses rather than their big-box counterparts. I like that my purchases are adding back to our local economy, rather than supporting mega-rich CEOs or paying to outsource American jobs. • I purchased Dollar Tree glassware because it is made in the USA ... for the good of our country's economy.

experimental studies, we specifically examine how framing brands in competition politicizes the consumption situation and gives the purchase political meaning. Political meanings in this particular area are concerned with anti-globalization, the loss of independent storefronts, unfair business practices, and the loss of competition due to dominant category killers. For example, one respondent said, "I bought lunch at a small restaurant in a small town in Minnesota to help the economy there rather than hit up the Wendy's down the road," while another respondent said, "I buy Pabst Blue Ribbon because it stands against bland, mega corporation beers."

Contrary to the common perception that ethical consumption is predominantly a liberal left phenomenon (Micheletti 2003; Micheletti *et al.* 2006), many of our respondents reported politicized consumption that was decidedly conservative in tone. This result suggests that all politics matter in consumption, regardless of whether they are liberal or conservative leaning. As Devinney, Auger, and Eckhardt (2010) uncover, ethical consumption is not driven by universal moral beliefs, but rather by individual value judgments that lead to much diversity of opinion about which brands are considered ethical and which are not. People who believe in a political idea or agenda are likely to politicize consumption episodes that evoke ideas related to their political leanings. Next, we discuss how framing brands in competition politicizes the consumption episode.

Framing brands in competition

How and why do brands' relationships with each other affect consumers' responses to them? Unlike prior research, which mainly highlights the dual relationship between consumers and brands (Aggarwal 2004; Fournier 1998), or the common effects of interconnected consumers in brand communities (McAlexander *et al.* 2002; Muniz and O'Guinn 2001), in this chapter we explore a networked understanding of brands by observing how consumers assess and connect with brands not as singular entities, but as part of a competitive landscape. This research aligns with current work in the field of branding, reflecting the consumer culture theory tradition that has examined the relationship between big, national brands and local, independent competitors (Thompson and Arsel 2004).

We believe that a consumer's assessment of and purchase preference for a brand relies not only on consumer-firm interactions, but also on the brand's place in the web of entangled brand relationships. We suggest a "framing the game effect": that a competitive framework can be mobilized to raise brand value by restructuring how consumers judge brands and by reshaping their brand preferences.

We propose that framing the game as a competition changes the process by which consumers evaluate and choose brands. When brands compete, consumers are forced to acknowledge that a game is being played, a game with winners and losers. Consumers can choose a side to support, and this choice adds political meaning to the purchase. Through their purchase, they not only receive a physical product, but they help shape the outcome of the competitive game, helping one brand and hurting another. Specifically, we propose that, when brands are framed in competition with one another, consumers perceive the purchase situation as politicized, which shifts their reliance on attributes associated with economic purchasing(such as price), to attributes associated with politicized purchasing (such as viewpoints, values, ideals, and morals). In politicized consumption situations, consumers are likely to act not only in their self- interest, but also in the interest of greater social, cultural, and political causes. Politicized consumption raises the stakes for consumers, making them look beyond their own immediate gratification and letting them see the social and political ramifications of their purchase, while enabling them to also participate in the struggle (Thompson *et al.* 2006). When the game is framed as a competition, consumers shift from being pure price/quality maximizers to being political agents, and, in doing so, shift their preferences for brands based on how well each brand delivers against their political agendas. As Harrison, Newholm, and Shaw point out in their discussion of the ethical consumer, "Ethical consumers are not, therefore, ignoring price and quality, but applying some additional (and sometimes prior) criteria in the decision making process" (2005: 2).

We also examine whether competitive framing is of differential value to small, independent versus big, national chain brands by exploring how the balance of the competition matters. In the politicized world of consumption, big, category-killer brands such as Starbucks, Home Depot, Amazon, and Wal-Mart often bear the brunt of consumers' criticism while small, independently owned brands reap their accolades (Holt 2002; Thompson and Arsel 2004). Consumers have been shown to prefer underdog brands (Paharia *et al.* 2011) and to revel in schadenfreude when big brands falter (Avery *et al.* 2010), the so-called "tall poppy syndrome." We propose that positioning brands in competition with each other raises the salience of the politicized nature of consumption for consumers and makes attributes related to politicized consumption, such as the competitive balance in the relationship between the two brands, more prominent in the choice situation. Thus, purchase activism is more likely to occur in imbalanced competition, when a small brand and large brand compete, and consumers are likely to "buycott" the small brand and boycott the large brand. In balanced competitions, when a small brand competes with another small brand or when a large brand competes with another large brand, politicization of the consumption episode is less likely to occur.

We propose that framing the game in which a brand is competing can lead to different brand outcomes, despite the fact that the features and benefits of the underlying product remain the same. We, therefore, hypothesize:

> *H1:* Framing a brand as competing against another brand in the marketplace will change consumers' purchase interest in a focal brand and its competitive brand such that:
>
> *H1a:* Consumers will increase their purchase interest in small, independent brands when they perceive them in imbalanced competition with

large, national brands than when they do not perceive them as having direct competition, or when they perceive them as competing in balanced competition with other small, independent brands.

H1b: Consumers will decrease their purchase interest for large, national brands when they perceive them in imbalanced competition with small, independent brands than when they do not perceive them as having direct competition, or when they perceive them as competing in balanced competition with other large, national brands.

H2: Consumers' feelings of purchase activism will mediate the effect of competitive framing on purchase intent.

In addition, we test different ways of framing the game, altering the structure of the competitive game in which the brands jointly operate and the competitiveness of each brand in that game in order to identify moderating conditions for the framing the game effect. In particular, we test how competitive aggression, strategic choices made by firms that are perceived by consumers as overly offensive moves, such as moving in across the street from a competitor or starting a price war, affects brand preference.

H3: Competitive aggression will moderate the results hypothesized in H1a and H1b, such that consumers will increase (decrease) their purchase intent in small (large) brands when the brand is perceived as a competitive aggressor.

In conclusion, we suggest that "framing the game" as a competition significantly modifies the way consumers judge and select brands, steering them to favor local brands over national brands, punishing large brands for competing aggressively but celebrating small brands when they do the same. "Framing the game" politicizes the purchase situation, changing both the way consumers view rival brands and the way they see themselves as citizens for change.

Research methodology and discussion of findings

Study 1: Framing the game as a competition

In this study, we explored how consumer preference for small, independent brands and large, national brands shifts when the brands are viewed in isolation versus when they are viewed as competing against each other, testing H1a and H1b.

Procedure

One hundred and sixty-one participants recruited from a lab at a large US university were randomly assigned to one of three between-subjects conditions that manipulated competitive framings. In two conditions, participants were asked to assess a single ice cream brand: either a small, independent shop (*small independent alone*) or a large, national chain (*large national alone*) in isolation. In the third condition, participants were asked to assess both a small, independent shop versus a large, national chain in direct competition. In the *small independent alone* condition, participants read the scenario with the text in parenthesis and in the *large national alone* condition, participants read the text in brackets. Participants read:

> Imagine you are in the mood for a treat. There is a (small independent ice cream shop) [large national ice cream chain] in your neighborhood that has 30 flavors, frozen yogurt, and a variety of toppings.

In the *competition* condition, participants were told,

> Imagine you are in the mood for a treat. There is a small independent ice cream shop in your neighborhood that has 30 flavors, frozen yogurt, and a variety of toppings. There is also a large national ice cream chain that also has 30 flavors, frozen yogurt, and a similar variety of toppings. They are located across the street and are in direct competition with each other.

Participants then answered a question about their expected purchase frequency, "How often would you go to the independent [national] ice cream shop?" (1 = not often; 7 = very often). In the *competition* condition, participants were asked about their expected purchase frequency for both the independent and the national ice cream shop respectively.

Results

We first compared the results of the *small independent alone* and *large national alone* conditions with a t-test. Participants indicated no significant difference between these two conditions in their expected purchase frequency (3.72 vs. 3.77, *NS*). We then analyzed the results of the *competition* condition where participants evaluated the small, independent ice cream shop and the large, national chain together using a repeated measures analysis. As expected, participants indicated that they would more often go to the small, independent shop than the large, national chain (4.55 vs. 2.98; $F(1, 46) = 17.54, p < 0.001$).

We then conducted a t-test with competitive framing as the independent variable (*small independent alone* versus *competition*) and frequency of purchase for the small independent ice cream shop as the dependent variable. As expected, participants in the *competition* condition indicated they would go to the small, independent shop significantly more often than those in the *small independent alone* condition (4.55 vs. 3.72; $t(99) = 2.48, p < 0.02$). We then conducted a t-test with competitive framing as the independent variable (*large national alone* versus *competition*) and frequency of purchase for the large, national chain as the dependent variable. As expected, participants in the *competition* condition indicated they would

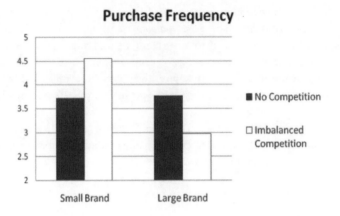

FIGURE 2.1 Framing the game as a competition

go to the large, national chain significantly less than those in the *large national alone* condition (2.98 vs. 3.77; $t(101) = 2.38, p < 0.02$).

Study 2: Testing the mediating effect of feelings of purchase efficacy

Study 2 builds upon Study 1 in three important ways. Rather than portraying the brands in isolation in the alone conditions, we portray them as competing against an equal competitor – to control for the presence of competition. Second, we test the mediating process of feelings of purchase activism. Finally, rather than use purchase frequency as the dependent measure, we use purchase intention.

Procedure

One hundred and forty-seven participants recruited from a lab at a large US university were randomly assigned to one of three between-subjects conditions that manipulated the competitive framing of the marketplace (*1. politicized competition:* small independent versus large national; *2. small independent competition:* small independent versus small independent; and *3. large national competition:* large national versus large national). Participants were asked to assess two ice cream brands in competition. In the *politicized competition* condition, participants read the same manipulation used in Study 1 from the *competition* condition. In the *small independent competition* condition, participants read about two small, independent ice cream shops in competition, and, in the *large national competition* condition, about two large national chains in competition. Participants were asked, after reading the respective purchase scenarios, to indicate their purchase likelihood on a seven-point scale (1 = not likely; 7 = very likely). To test the mediating process, participants then answered items on the feelings of purchase activism scale developed by Paharia, Avery, and Keinan (2014).

Results

The purchase activism items were collapsed into a scale with a Cronbach's alpha of 0.90. We first conducted a *t*-test between the *small independent competition* and the *large national competition* conditions. Participants indicated no difference in the likelihood that they would go to the small, independent shop or large, national chain when they were competing against a similar competitor (4.3 vs. 4.28; $t(96)$ = 0.08, *NS*). In the *politicized competition* condition, participants indicated that they would be more likely to go to the small, independent shop than to the large, national chain (5.73 vs. 3.61; $F(1, 48)$ = 42.9, $p < 0.001$). We then conducted a *t*-test with competitive framing as the independent variable (*small independent competition* versus *politicized competition*) and purchase likelihood of the small, independent brand as the dependent variable. Participants indicated that they were significantly more likely to go to the small, independent shop in the *politicized competition* condition than in the *small independent competition* condition (5.73 vs. 4.3; $t(92)$ = 6.12, $p < 0.001$). We then performed a *t*-test between the *politicized competition* and *large national competition* conditions. Participants indicated they would go to the large, national chain significantly less often in the *politicized competition* condition than in the *large national competition* condition (3.61 vs. 4.28; $t(100)$ = 2.37, $p < 0.03$).

Similar t-tests and analyses using the feelings of purchase activism as the dependent variable yielded higher ratings in the *politicized competition* condition than in the *small independent competition* condition (3.4 vs. 2.49; $t(92)$ = 3.07, p = 0.003), and higher ratings in the *politicized competition* condition than in the *large national competition* condition (3.4 vs. 2.36; $t(100)$ = 3.59, p = 0.001), indicating that competition between the small, independent and large, national establishments increased consumers' political activism, as compared to both the *small independent* and the *large national competition* conditions.

Following Zhao, Lynch, and Chen (2010), we tested whether the political activism scale mediated the effect of competitive framing (*small independent competition* coded as –1, *politicized competition* as 1) on purchase likelihood for the small, independent brand. We utilized a bootstrap procedure to construct bias-corrected confidence intervals based on 5,000 resamples. The size of the indirect effect was 0.15, and the 95 percent bias–corrected confidence interval excluded zero (0.056, 0.284). Using the same procedures, we then tested whether the political activism scale mediated the effect of competitive framing (*politicized competition* coded as 1, *large national competition* as –1) on purchase likelihood for the large national brand. The size of the indirect effect was –0.17, and the 95 percent bias-corrected confidence interval excluded zero (–0.35, –0.06). Political activism thus mediated the effect of competitive framing on purchase likelihood, for both support of the small, independent brand, and opposition of the large, national brand.

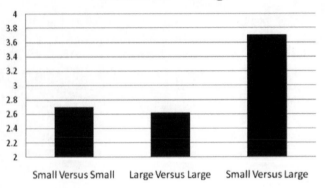

FIGURE 2.2 Mediating effects of consumers' feelings of purchase efficacy

Consistent with H1a, Studies 1 and 2 show both purchase intention and purchase frequency are significantly higher for a local, independent brand when it is framed as competing with a large, national brand, than when it is considered on its own or promoted as in balanced competition. Consistent with H1b, purchase intention and purchase frequency for a big, national brand are significantly lower when it is framed as competing with a small independent brand than when it is considered on its own, or framed as in balanced competition. Consistent with H2, Study 2 shows that feelings of purchase activism mediate the effect. Accordingly, it is not competition per se that elicits the framing the game effect, but rather a specific type of politicized competition that triggers support of small, local brands, and opposition of large, national brands.

Study 3: The moderating effects of competitive aggression

In Study 3, our goal was to amplify the effect by increasing competitive aggression, consistent with H3. More specifically, we manipulated whether a small or a large brand was moving across the street from an established competitor. This manipulation represents an example of competitive aggression, the market invasion of a newcomer into the territory of an incumbent. Unlike Studies 1 and 2, in which we used hypothetical brands, in Study 3, we used a real brand, Starbucks, as our large, national competitor, and introduced a new product category, coffee.

Procedure

Sixty-six participants recruited from a lab at a large US university were randomly assigned to one of two competitive conditions that manipulated competitive framing. Participants were asked to assess two coffee shops in direct competition, Starbucks and a small, independent coffee shop called Joe's Java. The between-subjects text varied which brand was the aggressor between conditions, where in the *small aggressor* condition, participants read the text in parenthesis and in the *large aggressor* condition participants read the text in brackets:

> Imagine you are in the mood for a cup of coffee. You can either go to Starbucks or an independent coffee shop called Joe's Java. (Joe's Java) [Starbucks] just moved in directly across the street from (Starbucks) [Joe's Java] and is now in direct competition with them.

Participants were then asked to indicate their purchase likelihood on a seven-point scale for both of the coffee shops, "How likely would you be to go to Joe's Java (Starbucks)?" (1 = not likely; 7 = very likely).

Results

We analyzed the results using a mixed model ANOVA with competitive framing (*small aggressor* versus *large aggressor*) as the independent variable, and purchase likelihood for Starbucks and Joe's Java as the repeated measure. We found a main effect for brand indicating a higher likelihood to go to Joe's Java over Starbucks ($F(1, 64) = 12.17, p = 0.001$), no main effect for competitive framing ($F(1, 64) = 0.73, NS$), and a significant interaction between competitive framing (*small aggressor* versus *large aggressor*) and brand on purchase likelihood ($F(1, 64) = 5.31, p < 0.03$). Participants were significantly less likely to go to Starbucks in the *large aggressor* condition than in the *small aggressor* condition (2.54 vs. 3.85; $t(64) = 2.42, p < 0.02$). Joe's Java's purchase likelihood was higher in the *large aggressor* condition than in the *small aggressor* condition; though, the difference was not significant (5.23 vs. 4.40; $t(64) = 1.53, NS$).

These results show that consistent with H3, large brands are punished for competing intensively. Although the small brand benefitted under this condition, the change was not significant. Furthermore, small brands are neither rewarded nor punished for intense competition. Thus, whether being "competitive" in the marketplace is bad for brands depends upon whether the brand is big or small.

General discussion

Talking about your competition is often viewed as taboo in the world of marketing. Forrester Research analyst Josh Bernoff proclaims, "It's a truism in the marketing world that you don't, in general, talk about your competitors." (Bernoff 2008) Altimeter analyst Jeremiah Owyang states that, "There's some unwritten law that companies shouldn't talk about their competition (unless you're criticizing them). It's welded deeply into nearly every corporate culture." (Owyang 2008) Many brands take pains to avoid mentioning their competition.

However, some brands explicitly highlight their competition, drawing consumers' attention to it in an attempt to frame the larger game being played out in the marketplace – a game in which consumers play a critical role. A sign in a local coffee shop reads, "When you say tall, do you mean small, medium, or large?" poking fun at the pretentious sizing (tall, grande, and venti) used by its competitor Starbucks to evoke Italian coffee culture. The owner of an independent bookstore hangs a sign over its cash register that reads, "Find it here. Buy it here. Keep *us* here," that discourages customers from showrooming books in the store and then purchasing them online from its competitor Amazon.

These small brands may be onto something. In this chapter, we demonstrate the effect of positioning brands in competition with one another and show that highlighting competition can help a brand when it is situated within a salient popular battle – in this case protecting small, local brands from large, national players. We find that support for small, local brands goes up when faced with a competitive threat from a large, national brand, versus when it is alone or in competition with a similar brand. This support translates into increased purchase intention and purchase frequency. We outline the conditions under which brands should highlight or avoid competitive narratives to their advantage.

Brands, both big and small, can use the "framing the game effect" to motivate or mute politicized consumption. For example, Jim Koch, the founder of Boston Beer Company, makers of Samuel Adams, vociferously compares his small, independent brewery to the behemoth, Anheuser Busch whenever he can, claiming "Anheuser Busch spills more beer than we make every year" and "Sam Adams' current sales volume of 6,000 cases a month represents less than a minute of production for Anheuser-Busch," framing the game to his advantage. Over the years, as Samuel Adams has become the dominant player in the craft beer segment, Koch continues to position his company as small versus Anheuser-Busch, rather than as large versus the other small, independent craft brewers, "Being the largest craft brewer is like being the tallest pygmy. You're still not ready to play for the Nuggets. To give you some perspective, Anheuser-Busch is almost 200 times our size." Following the takeover of Anheuser-Busch by Belgian's InBev, Boston Beer Company became the United States' largest independent brewery, with a market capitalization of $740 million, a mantle that Koch is not comfortable wearing out in public. In 2010, Boston Beer Company's advertising campaign entitled "Growing Up Small" attempted to dispel the growing perception among consumers that Samuel Adams was a large brand. In the ad, consumers are asked how big Samuel Adams was; responses vary from "huge" to "25 percent of the market." The commercial then reveals that Samuel Adams still has less than 1 percent market share of the beer category, reminding consumers of its diminutive competitive position. Despite the objective reality that he is running a big brand, Koch deftly reframes the competitive game to benefit the Samuel Adams brand and to garner support from consumers who want to express their political views through their purchasing.

Many grass roots and governmental programs have sprouted up to help small businesses compete. "Small Business Saturday" is an effort sponsored by American Express that encourages shoppers in the US to shop small on the day following Black Friday, the Friday following the Thanksgiving holiday, which is often the busiest shopping day of the year given its proximity to Christmas. This research can help umbrella programs and organizations better position their marketing messages to frame the game to more effectively tap into consumers' inherent desire to support weaker competitors.

Brands, both big and small, can differentially narrate their brand positions to frame a competitive context that works to their advantage to strengthen consumers' preference. Future research could explore whether this enhanced preference leads to the formation of differential types of consumer-brand relationships. Given the emotional profile associated with feelings of political activism, we hypothesize that consumers who purchase products after being influenced by competitive framing may find themselves in relationships with brands that fall further along the socio-emotional side of the spectrum than the functional. These relationships may be marked by stronger emotional connections, connections with the self, and a sense of shared responsibility and purpose that characterizes interdependence, three of the markers of Brand Relationship Quality (Fournier 1994). Framing the game might not only influence preference, liking, and choice, but also frame the evolutionary path that the consumer's relationship with the brand will take.

References

Adorno, T.W. and M. Horkheimer (1944) "The Culture Industry: Enlightenment as Mass Deception", *The Consumer Society Reader*, eds J.B. Schor and D.B. Holt. New York: The New Press: 3–19.

Aggarwal, P. (2004) "The Effects of Brand Relationship Norms on Consumer Attitudes and Behavior", *Journal of Consumer Research*, 31 (1): 87–101.

Avery, J., N. Paharia, A. Keinan, and J.B. Schor (2010) "The Strategic Use of Brand Biographies", *Research in Consumer Behavior*, ed. R.W. Belk, Vol. 10. Bingley, UK: Emerald Group Publishing Limited: 213–229.

Bernoff, Josh (2008) "Should You Talk About Your Competitors?" *Empowered*, April 3, 2008, http://forrester.typepad.com/groundswell/2008/04/should-you-talk.html.

Devinney, T., P. Auger, and G. Eckhardt (2010) *The Myth of the Ethical Consumer*. Cambridge: Cambridge University Press.

Firat, F. and A. Venkatesh (1995) "Liberatory Postmodernism and the Re-enchantment of Consumption", *Journal of Consumer Research*, 22 (3): 239–267.

Fournier, S. (1994) *A Consumer-Brand Relationship Framework for Strategic Brand Management*. Doctoral Dissertation, University of Florida.

Fournier, S. (1998) "Consumers and Their Brands: Developing Relationship Theory in Consumer Research", *Journal of Consumer Research*, 24 (4): 343–373.

Harrison, R., T. Newholm, and D. Shaw (2005) *The Ethical Consumer*. London: Sage Publications.

Heath, J. and A. Potter (2004) *Nation of Rebels: Why Counterculture Became Consumer Culture*. New York: Harper Business.

Holt, D.B. (2002) "Why Do Brands Cause Trouble? A Dialectical Theory of Consumer Culture and Branding", *Journal of Consumer Research*, 29 (1): 70–90.

Hosein, H. and H. Hughes (2006) *Independent America: The Two-Lane Search for Mom and Pop: CreateSpace*. Independent America Media Inc.

Inglehart, R. and W. Baker (2000) "Modernization, Cultural Change, and the Persistence of Traditional Values", *American Sociological Review*, 65 (1): 19–51.

Klein, N. (2000) *No Logo*. New York: Picador Press.

McAlexander, J.H., J.W. Schouten, and H.F. Koening (2002) "Building Brand Community", *Journal of Marketing*, 66 (1): 38–54.

Micheletti, M. (2003) *Political Virtue and Shopping: Individuals, Consumerism and Collective Action*. New York: Palgrave Macmillan.

Micheletti, M., A. Follesdal, and D. Stolle (2006) *Politics, Products, and Markets: Exploring Political Consumerism Past and Present*. New Brunswick, NJ: Transaction Publishers.

Muniz, A. and T.C. O'Guinn (2001) "Brand Community", *Journal of Consumer Research*, 27 (4): 412–432.

O'Guinn, T.C. and A.M. Muniz, Jr. (2004) "The Polit-Brand and Blows Against the Empire: The Collectively Approved Brands of the New-New Left", *Advances in Consumer Research*, 31, Provo, UT: Association for Consumer Research, 100.

O'Guinn, T.C. and A.M. Muniz, Jr. (2005) "Communal Consumption and the Brand", *Inside Consumption: Frontiers of Research on Consumer Motives, Goals, and Desires*. New York: Routledge: 252–272.

Owyang, J. (2008) "The 3 'Impossible' Conversations for Corporations," *Web Strategist*, February 24, 2008, www.web-strategist.com/blog/2008/02/24/what-corporations-should-but-fail-to-talk-about/.

Paharia, N., J. Avery, and A. Keinan (2014) "Positioning Brands versus Large Competitors to Increase Sales", *Journal of Marketing Research*, 51 (6): 647–656.

Paharia, N., A. Keinan, J. Avery, and J.B. Schor (2011) "The Underdog Effect: The Marketing of Disadvantage and Determination through Brand Biography", *Journal of Consumer Research*, 17 (5): 775–790.

Schor, J.B. (1998) *The Overspent American*. New York: Basic.

Spector, R. (2005) *Category Killers: The Retail Revolution and its Impact on Consumer Culture*. Boston, MA: Harvard Business School Press.

Tan, E. (2007) "Survey 'Good is the New Black' Consumers in Cone Study Say They Won't Buy Your Products if They Don't Like Your Practices", *Advertising Age*, July 12, 2007, http://adage.com/article/news/survey-good-black/119214/.

Thompson, C.J. and Z. Arsel (2004) "The Starbucks Brandscape and Consumers'

Anticorporate Experiences of Glocalization", *Journal of Consumer Research*, 31 (3): 631–642.

Thompson, C.J. and G. Coskuner-Balli (2007) "Enchanting Ethical Consumerism: The Case of Community Supported Agriculture", *Journal of Consumer Culture*, 7 (3): 275–303.

Thompson, C.J., A. Rindfleisch, and Z. Arsel (2006) "Emotional Branding and the Strategic Value of the Doppelganger Brand Image", *Journal of Marketing*, 70 (1): 50–64.

Zhao, Z., J.G. Lynch Jr., and O. Chen (2010) "Reconsidering Baron and Kenny: Myths and Truths about Mediation Analysis", *Journal of Consumer Research*, 37 (August): 197–206.

3

THE ROLE OF CULTURAL CAPITAL IN CREATING "GLOCAL" BRAND RELATIONSHIPS

Dannie Kjeldgaard, Søren Askegaard, and Giana M. Eckhardt

Introduction

It is well established in the marketing literature that consumers have a variety of relationships with brands (Fournier 1998). There is now an annual conference dedicated to exploring the nature of these relationships (Brands and Brand Relationships), and the current volume is the second major book to explore this topic in depth. One aspect of consumers' relationships with brands that remains relatively unexplored, however, is how brand relationships may evolve and change in a global context. That is, when a consumer experiences Carlsberg beer in the USA, Africa, Hong Kong, and Brazil, does the nature of the relationship stay the same across these contexts, especially seeing as how the brand positioning may be vastly different in each of these locales given competitive differences, the level of market development, and consumer culture differences? This is precisely the issue we wish to explore in this chapter.

We argue that brands are not global or local to a consumer because of their country of origin, but rather, because of the nature of the cultural myths that a brand chooses to invoke in a particular context. Thus, country of origin is much less straightforward in today's creolized, hybridized global marketplace and should be considered as contextualized product–place imagery. Consequently, brands have much more freedom and flexibility to position themselves in a way that is strategically savvy, and their positioning does not have to be consistent around the world. We demonstrate how cultural capital can be used in varying ways to create these myths and illustrate how one global brand – Carlsberg Beer – has varied its use of local and global cultural capital around the world. Essentially, our model recognizes that consumers have "glocal" relationships with brands. That is, the relationship can be global or local depending on the type of cultural capital evoked and consumers' interpretation of it. Furthermore, "glocal" indicates that global relations always are locally instantiated and local relations must be understood in relation to the global. We offer recommendations for when to invoke global or local cultural capital in brand positioning to account for these glocal relationships.

Global and local culture in brand symbolism

Global branding can be said to involve two dimensions: market presence and brand image. In the discussion of what constitutes a global brand, the two dimensions are often intermingled so that a global brand is construed as one that 1) is present globally, i.e., sold in so many different markets that it is perceived as being present everywhere, and 2) its brand image as perceived by consumers is partly the perception of this globality: it is used as a global symbol (Holt *et al.* 2004; Steenkamp *et al.* 2003).

Leveraging the cultural mythologies of the global and the local for brand competition can be understood as forms of cultural capital (Bourdieu 1984; Ger 1999). Cultural capital alongside economic and social capitals are particular resources that determine power within particular socio-cultural fields. The concept of cultural capital views cultural sets of skills and knowledge as assets that can be brought into play in different fields. While traditionally used to analyze consumption and taste patterns, Bourdieu in his later work applied his apparatus to marketplace phenomena such as real estate (2005), which he defined as a particular social field of economic transactions. Transferring the concept of cultural capital to branding allows us to analyze how brands must take into account which forms of cultural capital are deemed legitimate within particular market contexts. Just as global companies may attempt to obtain local cultural capital (through brand acquisition, for example), local brands can use global cultural capital for both home and export markets.

It is important to understand how to use global and local cultural capital strategically because the interpretation of brand meaning is highly contextual. A brand may be imbued with global or local meanings, or both. For example, Alden *et al.* (1999) point out that many global brands originating in the US may become dissociated with the US at a global level since they have become part of "the global consumption set," but, at a local level within the US, they may be perceived as quintessentially American and hence be considered as culturally local or national. While a brand may be interpreted as global, this globality is further subject to consumer interpretation. For example, the global brand McDonald's, while a powerful symbol of the West in China, can also be used to support local cultural values such as in-group harmony in the Chinese market (Eckhardt and Houston 2002). The brand's meaning as global can hence serve as a symbolic resource for local cultural issues.

In some cases, brands that have a global market presence can benefit from establishing brand symbolism that expresses the exotic or foreign (what Alden *et al.* 1999 term "foreign consumer culture positioning"). These types of brands leverage local cultural capital to a global market level. This type of branding strategy often relies on a product-place image where the origin of the product testifies to specific values or qualities (e.g., watches from Switzerland). When foreign consumer culture positioning is used, the brand may nevertheless be perceived of as being part of the "global consumption set" by being acknowledged as a brand that has a global presence and consumer following. Riefler (2012) suggests that consumers categorize brands in terms of perceived brand origin and perceived globality. We go beyond this in suggesting that how consumers do this will differ in varying regions of the world. In sum, global brands can invoke global, local, or foreign cultural capital in their brand positioning (Kipnis *et al.* 2014), depending on where they are from and what the fit is between their country of origin and their position in the global marketplace in varying competitive spaces.

Cultural capital and global branding

Figure 3.1 offers a framework that organizes the diverse findings and the often disparate empirical evidence of the global-local cultural dynamic of global branding. Our model is a visualization of the complex dynamic between the types of cultural capital (global-local) and how these work at different levels of brand/market competition (local-global). In other words, the figure represents a visualization of the competitive fields of global brand competition. Each of the quadrants represents different competitive fields determined by market level and the type of cultural capital that can be transformed into brand assets.

Cultural Capital

	Global	*Local*
Global	Global branding	Country of origin appeals Exotic aura
Local	Global brands in local markets Local globals Global aura	Local branding Local aura Nostalgia

Market Level

FIGURE 3.1 Deployment of local and global cultural capital

Global cultural capital/global market level

In the upper left quadrant, the field is constituted from competition using global cultural capital at the global market level. In the literature, this encompasses what has been referred to as global branding. Global branding refers to the kind of brand competition frequently referenced in international marketing literature: the traditional dualistic and antagonistic battles between dominant global iconic brands such as Pepsi-Cola and Coca-Cola, or Windows versus Linux (see Steenkamp *et al.* 2003). Brands utilize their global cultural capital on a worldwide field of competition for power. For example, see HSBC's globally uniform positioning in terms of global market presence in the banking domain, as exemplified by its current branding campaign, "In the future …".[1] Brands are not trying to localize in this field, but tend to seek a consistent image across cultural boundaries, and that image is global and not from a particular country (Holt *et al.* 2004).

Global cultural capital/local market level

Next, in the lower left quadrant of global cultural capital at the local market level, we see brands leveraging global cultural capital to capture local markets. Here the allusion to globalness is used in brand positioning strategies, typically by global or foreign brands, and seeks to capture local markets and fight off local competition – the strategic perspective outlined by Levitt (1983). Typically, we see global iconic brands enter local markets and transform competition and the cultural meaning of existing marketplace structures such as product categories. For example, Askegaard and Csaba (2000) demonstrate how Coca Cola entered the Danish market and forced local competitor Jolly Cola to alter the type of cultural capital it used to try to remain successful in its local market. In other words, the logics of competition for power in the field were altered.

Global cultural capital can also be used by local brands in their domestic marketplace. Local brands that are in a situation where the legitimate form of brand symbolism for a product is global can be forced to establish global cultural capital. For example, this strategy has been used by Chinese brands Haier and Lenovo; Haier focused on penetrating the US market to accumulate global cultural capital in order to compete in the Chinese market, and Lenovo purchased IBM's laptop division to do the same (Wang 2008).

In this quadrant, we also see a positioning strategy in which brands seek to cloak themselves in a global aura through Anglo-sounding names (cf. Eckhardt 2005). That is, some brands have not acquired global cultural capital per se (for example, through acknowledgement of global market presence), but use brand symbolism to create a global aura that allows them to compete in their local marketplace. One study showed how local coffee shop owners took pride in the authenticity of their mimicking of the standards set out by the global chain Starbucks and, hence, sought to leverage global cultural capital against local competitors (Kjeldgaard and Östberg 2007). This mimicry can also be in the form of exoticism such as when the Asian brand Tiger Beer explicitly draws upon its Asian cultural heritage in its global branding efforts (Cayla and Eckhardt 2008) in Western markets, while not emphasizing traditional stereotypes of Asian culture in the Asian region. There, the brand emphasizes the urban global lifestyles of Asian metropolises; hence leveraging global cultural capital at 'local' market levels.

Local cultural capital/global market level

In this quadrant, local cultural capital is a source of competitive advantage leveraged in global competitive fields. This encompasses much of the strategy discussed in literature pertaining to country-of-origin (Magnusson *et al.* 2011). These country-of-origin appeals can take the form of umbrella brands such as 'Danish Design' or IKEA's blatant references to their Swedish heritage to leverage local cultural capital that is recognized as valuable in global markets. Other examples are ham from Parma and wines from France or many of its wine-producing regions (e.g., the umbrella brand of Grand Vin de Bourdeaux). The literature stream that theorizes how and why country-of-origin appeals are successful is applicable to understanding the cultural dynamics in this quadrant (for an overview, see Roth and Diamantopolous 2009). While being global in terms of market scope, these brands rely on specific country-of-origin imagery and, hence, draw on local cultural capital. This category thus more systematically differentiates global brands into those that rely on global cultural capital from those that rely on local cultural capital, a distinction missing in much of the literature on global branding.

Similar to the global aura, another strategy in this field is to construct symbolism that connotes "foreignness." That is, brands that do not necessarily possess local cultural capital seek to be perceived as if they do. For example, the US ice cream brand Haagen-Dazs seeks to establish a "Euro/Swiss" brand image through its non-US sounding brand name for the global market. That way they can capitalize on country-of-origin beliefs surrounding Swiss ice cream without actually accruing the local capital they would gain if they were really from Switzerland. This is similar to Steenkamp's (2014) idea of cultural arbitrage, where a company such as Apple, for example, will emphasize "Designed in California," to try and overcome the negative country of origin implications of being made in China.

One strategy for making sure that local cultural capital may not be copied is to use systems of authentication (Ger 1999), which are exemplified by the French AOC system for wine that ensures that only wines produced in specific regions with particular technologies can carry that label. The flows of the globalizing ethnoscapes may also form the ground for a type of global branding based on appealing to ethnic cultural identity dispersed transnationally. Such "diaspora branding" is seen, for example, in the international marketing of the Turkish cola brand Cola Turka which is distributed in Western European markets with a large Turkish migrant population (Özkan and Foster 2005).

Local cultural capital/local market level

In the field constituted by local cultural capital at the local market level, brands leverage their local cultural capital to compete in the local marketplace, as described in Ger (1999). Often discussed in the literature as the opposite of global branding, local branding implies a branding strategy in each marketplace that is localized and inconsistent across markets. Particularly if the brand is local rather than global, there will often be an affinity with or allusion to nationalism, seeking to establish a brand that emphasizes its natural belonging to a given market on the basis of historical legitimacy. Hence, local branding uses local cultural capital to be able to make these claims to legitimacy: often the amount of years the firm has operated in the marketplace, the use of local workers to make the products, and the use of local ingredients. Essentially, utilizing local cultural capital implies that the brand knows the marketplace more intimately than a global brand, and can appeal to the unique identity of local consumers in a way that global brands cannot (Ger 1999).

Similar to the global aura and exotic aura already discussed, local aura strategy is often used by foreign brands that wish to compete in a market field where local cultural capital is deemed legitimate. Creating a local aura allows a global brand to appropriate local cultural capital and hence to appear local, which involves adaptation to local cultural contexts and systems of meaning. This is often done through acquisition strategies, since local brands possess innate local cultural capital, and also because there might be an inherent problem of legitimacy among consumers if the brand which has established well-known global cultural capital (e.g., a global presence) at the same time attempts to appear local.

For example, Nestlé's ownership of Perrier and San Pellegrino, the quintessentially French and Italian brands of bottled water, is well concealed (Douglas *et al.* 2001). Nestlé as a conspicuous carrier of global cultural capital would not be able to claim itself a legitimate local brand in the French and Italian bottled water markets, nor at the global level. These brands are carriers of a local cultural capital which can be leveraged locally as well as globally. The concealed nature of the ownership may help in maintaining local cultural capital, but not necessarily. One might argue that this is an example of a brand with global cultural capital that seeks to compete in fields where local cultural capital has higher value at both local and global levels.

Finally, some brands, in establishing themselves as legitimate bearers of local cultural capital, will rely on local pride. This can be done either by conjuring up imagery of local sociocultural history, such as a venerated Soviet-era cheese brand in contemporary Russia (Kravets and Örge 2010), or by demonstrating the brand's historical presence in the particular market setting and playing on national sentiments, such as emphasizing how much local employment is provided by the brand (Strizhakova *et al.* 2008).

In sum, our framework provides managers with a template for analyzing the competitive situation for brands in multiple market contexts. For example, Amis and Silk (2010) provide a compelling in-depth analysis of the multiple meanings pertaining to the beer brand Guinness across different cultural contexts as one way of illustrating how brand management needs to think beyond the classic dualisms of global-local, cultural-non-cultural, and national-international in order to capture the multi-layered polysemy of global brands. The Guinness brand, they underline, "has a currency that varies upon the ontological constitution of particular consumer groups" (Amis and Silk 2010: 175). Guinness is simultaneously just another beer brand in a global selection of beers, yet, in Africa, it is deeply linked to a certain pan-Africanness through its linkage with the movies featuring Michael Power, the "black James Bond", and is also a nostalgic reference to their Ireland home for the Irish diaspora. We might want to add a fourth signification pertaining to the role of Guinness as a symbol of quintessential Irishness, consumed by non-Irish in countless hyper-real Irish pubs across the global marketplace. Consequently, the framework suggested here seems to be able to capture and systematize quite neatly the various symbolic productions of Guinness that for Amis and Silk (2010) constitute the complexity of the brand's meanings. A simple mapping of the cultural capital at stake, as done by our framework, may make the seemingly endless complexities of a cultural approach to branding much easier to relate to and bring about active usage by brand managers.

Case study: Carlsberg

In the following, we use our model in an analysis of the competitive brand positioning situation for another global beer brand, Carlsberg. This analysis is developed from secondary resources such as popular and trade media, as well as informal interviews and insights from company marketing communications, in line with case study recommendations from Kates (2007). Carlsberg is a brand with a strong position in its home market of Denmark where it is an iconic national brand (Holt 2004), and it possesses a brand image of globalness (Holt et al. 2004) as well as a global market presence, hence offering an exemplary case to illustrate the model. Carlsberg is the world's fourth largest brewery corporation with net revenues exceeding 66 billion DKK in 2013, and a portfolio of over 500 brands.

This case illustrates how the competitive situation is more complex than much of the global brand literature would suggest, in that global brands face new competitive fronts due to cultural movements that arise from globalization. Importantly, our analysis suggests that one consistent response to these varying competitive fronts is not necessarily the most desirable response, and thus that brand positioning should not always be consistent globally.

Global cultural capital/global market level

In much of its brand positioning, Carlsberg draws on global cultural capital: most notably exemplified by its tagline, "That calls for a Carlsberg." Introduced in 2011, this tagline positions the beer as a reward for the drinker's hard work. The campaign focuses on humankind's greatest achievements (landing on the moon, climbing Mt Everest), and positions Carlsberg as the appropriate reward for such endeavors (Silverstein 2011), rather than focusing on Carlsberg's Danish origins. Carlsberg uses this global brand positioning to compete with other major beer brands that constitute the global set; that is, other brands that also rely on global cultural capital, such as Heineken and Budweiser (Gammelgaard and Dörrenbächer 2013). The competition between Carlsberg and Heineken is an ongoing drama in the international beer market. Heineken's global campaign "Open your world," also introduced in 2011, focuses on Heineken being a strong and reliable brand in new situations, with the brand being defined as worldly, open minded, and confident, using the tagline, "Born in Amsterdam, raised by the world" (O'Neill 2013). Carlsberg is in competition with Heineken regarding which brand can be more global, and calls on its global cultural capital to continue competing in an increasingly globalized competitive field (Swinnen 2011). The global presence of Carlsberg historically enables the company to position itself as part of the global consumption set.

Global cultural capital/local market level

In contrast to the above, Carlsberg competes in its national market of origin, Denmark, as a "global national" player. Here, Carlsberg faces competition from national breweries that draws upon global cultural capital, in particular around Odense where its market share is considerably lower than the national level.[2] Since this is seemingly a case of out-localing the globals (Ger 1999), the response from Carlsberg has been to mobilize the most global of capitals, namely money, by offering the local leading football team a lucrative sponsorship contract with which the large local brewery cannot compete, a thinly veiled attempt to simply buy some local sympathy. The national dominance of the Carlsberg Corporation in the Danish beer market has furthermore provoked resistance from a number of micro-breweries. According to the manager of micro-brewery Refsvindinge, the motivation for launching the successful craft beer brand Ale no. 16 was to "provide something better than Carlsberg." The brewery explicitly draws on global micro-brew culture in branding its product an "ale" (personal interview). So, while global cultural capital was, in one sense, a competitive advantage for Carlsberg, other forms of global cultural capital were mobilized by local competitors.

Local cultural capital/global market level

Here, Carlsberg faces competition at the global level from brand name competitors that leverage local cultural capital on a global scale. This can be in the form of exoticism such as that used by the Asian brand Tiger Beer, which explicitly draws on its Asian cultural heritage in its global branding efforts in the West (Cayla and Eckhardt 2008), or those that reference specific artisanal traditions, such as many of the Belgian Trappist beers that market their products on the basis of centuries of accumulated artisanal knowledge in monasteries (Beverland *et al.* 2008). The response from Carlsberg has been to launch two lines of craft beers under the sub-brands "Jacobsen" (the name of its nineteenth-century founder) and "Semper Ardens," realizing that the Carlsberg name is too associated with global competition within the standard pilsner beer market. This enabled Carlsberg to become a legitimate player in the craft beer market.

Local cultural capital/local market level

Here, the global and national-dominant brand image of Carlsberg acts as fuel for references to specific product-place imagery and local cultural traditions aimed at local markets. One such example is the local brand "Springtime in Funen" (*Fynsk Forår*) that refers to a specific locality in Denmark (as well as a piece of classical music) from a brewery that does not distribute outside of Denmark. Yet the micro-brew industry, whether drawing on local or global cultural capital, has, in less than five years, attained a significant position in the Danish beer market. The number of micro-breweries has expanded from nine breweries in 2000, to 24 in 2003, and to more than 120 in 2012.[3] We see this as a result of the demand for cultural differences expressed through brands, rather than the dominant idea in global branding literature that consumers always prefer the global brand to the local (e.g. Holt *et al.* 2004; Steenkamp *et al.* 2003). In much of its branding strategy towards the home market, Carlsberg leverages its historically accumulated local cultural capital. For example the 'That calls for a Carlsberg' slogan is hardly ever used in the home market, where Carlsberg instead runs campaigns featuring prominent Danish actors in everyday situations to illustrate how much the brand is part of everyday life. A famous campaign that played explicitly on being *the* national beer was a series of commercials in the 1990s ironically playing with well-known Scandinavian self-perceptions of collectivity and solidarity using the slogan 'Our beer'.[4] This strategy enabled Carlsberg to sustain its role as a national iconic brand (Holt 2004).

Interestingly, Carlsberg has been able to successfully establish brand symbolism from both local and global cultural capital, defying much normative brand strategy literature recommending brand image consistency across markets. Furthermore, in the standardization/adaptation debate, the question is often whether adaptation should be made to the cultural contexts of exports. Carlsberg has inversely executed this by adapting to the home market cultural context and using a relatively standardized strategy globally. Carlsberg still has a way to go in terms of managing how its cultural capital is utilized, though. For example, the French brand Kronenbourg 1664, acquired jointly by Carlsberg and Heineken in 2008, recently had its ads removed from television in the UK by the government because it was thought that the ads implied the beer was French, when it is actually brewed in Manchester, England (Poulter 2014).

Discussion

Having a global standardized brand image is not necessarily desirable or possible. This has implications for the assessment and discussion of the power of global brands, and the nature of the relationship between consumers and brands on a global scale. On the consumer side, brands are part of the spread of globally-shared values that consumers identify with and also part of the construction of imagined social spaces through brand practices (Cayla and Eckhardt 2008; Steenkamp and de Jong 2010). On the producer side, branding has become a common managerial approach to think about and manage cultural meanings – whether local or global – in the construction of brand image and brand positions (Askegaard 2006). Consequently, branding can be said to be a phenomenon that is both exemplary of globalization, as well as a driver for it. The literature on global and local appeals, to some extent, deals with the local and global as essential sets of symbolism which, in some cases, emerge in creolized form (e.g., Zhou and Belk 2004; Hung *et al.* 2007). However, we argue that the symbolism of the global and the local emerge as the result of brand positioning in varying competitive fields. Our argument hence situates and provides an explanatory framework for previous findings on the variety of consumer preferences for global or local appeals (e.g., Steenkamp and de Jong 2010).

From a managerial perspective, for a brand such as Carlsberg, the framework we develop helps systematize and explicate the types of brand competition that they are facing and offers a template for considering which types of cultural capital should be utilized in these competitive situations. For example, in the competitive fields that rely on local cultural capital, a brand development or brand acquisition strategy might prove most successful, since local culture is the legitimate cultural logic for competition. Future research can investigate how a brand can combine global and local cultural capital, if they are operating in a market where more than one positioning simultaneously exists.

Importantly, our framework and analysis suggests that a consistent brand image is not always desirable for global brands, given the varying discourses in particular markets around the world. The global brand literature emphasizes consistency as a key to success (e.g., Johansson 2009); we contend that global brands should emphasize local, global or creolized cultural capital dependent upon the competitive situation in varying local or regional markets. Even if demand for global brands is increasing around the world, à la Levitt (1983), how those brands compete will not necessarily be homogenized or consistent. This analysis is in line with Strizhakova, Coulter and Price's (2012) findings that show consumers' cultural identities are not static, but evolving, and that these transformations are more noticeable in markets undergoing larger shifts. Thus, brands need to shift in line with global consumers' shifts. This analysis is also in line with recent findings by Brown, McDonough and Shultz (2013), who suggest that ambiguous brands (which do not have clarity of meaning, but rather, identities that are imprecise) have increased longevity in terms of consumer appeal, as consumers can attach varying salient meanings to the brand over time.

Brands draw on mythologies of the global, the foreign, the national, and the local in constituting brand symbolism, and we help systematize when and why particular mythologies will be appropriate for brand competition, in order to assist managers in navigating the complex world of global cultural branding. Consumers' relationships with brands will change based on varying contexts in varying regions of the world, and brands need to be able to draw from a pool of global and local cultural capital to respond. In sum, our framework helps to decouple brand positioning from country of origin, and provides managers with a map of how to harness global and local cultural capital as strategic resources.

Notes

1   www.hsbc.com/about-hsbc/advertising/in-the-future.
2   www.fyens.dk/article/207603:Business-Fyn—Carlsberg-stormer-Fyn-for-at-faa-markedsandele.
3   www.business.dk/foedevarer/frygt-for-konkursboelge-blandt-mikrobryggerier.
4   www.business.dk/ledelse/fra-vores-oel-til-verdens-oel.

References

Alden, D.L., J.B. Steenkamp, and R. Batra (1999) "Brand Positioning Through Advertising in Asia, North America, and Europe: The Role of Global Consumer Culture", *Journal of Marketing*, 63 (January): 75–87.

Amis, J. and M.L. Silk (2010) "Transnational Organization and Symbolic Production: Creation and Managing a Global Brand", *Consumption, Markets & Culture*, 13 (2): 159–179.

Askegaard, S. (2006) "Branding as a Global Ideoscape", *Brand Culture*, eds J. Schroeder and M. Salzer-Mörling. London, Routledge: 91–102.

Askegaard, S. and F. Csaba (2000) "The Good, the Bad, and the Jolly: Taste, Image, and Symbolic Resistance to the Coca-Colonization of Denmark", *Imagining Marketing*, eds S. Brown and A. Patterson. London: Routledge: 124–140.

Bourdieu, P. (1984) *Distinction: A Social Critique of the Judgement of Taste*. London: Routledge.

Bourdieu, P. (2005) *The Social Structures of the Economy*. Cambridge: Polity Press.

Beverland, M.B., A. Lindgreen, and M.W. Vink (2008) "Projecting Authenticity through Advertising: Consumer Judgments of Advertisers' Claims", *Journal of Advertising*: 37 (1): 5–15.

Brown, S., P. McDonough, and C. Shultz (2013) "*Titanic:* Consuming the Myths and Meanings of an Ambiguous Brand", *Journal of Consumer Research*, 40 (4): 595–614.

Cayla, J. and G.M. Eckhardt (2008) "Asian Brands and the Shaping of a Transnational Imagined Community", *Journal of Consumer Research*, 35 (2): 216–230.

Douglas, S.P., C. Samuel Craig, and E.J. Nijssen (2001) "Integrating Branding Strategy Across Markets: Building International Brand Architecture", *Journal of International Marketing*, 9 (2): 97–114.

Eckhardt, G.M. (2005) "Local Branding in a Foreign Product Category in an Emerging Market", *Journal of International Marketing*, 13 (4): 57–79.

Eckhardt, G.M. and M.J. Houston (2002) "Cultural Paradoxes Reflected in Brands: McDonalds in Shanghai, China", *Journal of International Marketing*, 10 (2): 68–82.

Fournier, S. (1998) "Consumers and Their Brands: Developing Relationship Theory in

Consumer Research", *Journal of Consumer Research*, 24 (1): 343–373.

Gammelgaard, J. and C. Dörrenbächer (2013) *The Global Brewery Industry – Markets, Strategies, and Rivalries*, London: Edward Elgar Publishing, Inc.

Ger, G. (1999) "Localizing in the Global Village: Local Firms Competing in Global Markets", *California Management Review*, 41 (4): 64–83.

Holt, D. (2004) *How Brands Become Icons*, Cambridge, MA: Harvard University Press.

Holt, D., J.A. Quelch, and E.L. Taylor (2004) "How Global Brands Compete", *Harvard Business Review*, 82 (9): 68–75.

Hung, K., S. Li, and R. Belk (2007) "Glocal Understandings: Female Readers' Perceptions of the New Woman in Chinese Advertising", *Journal of International Business Studies*, 38 (6): 1034–1051.

Johansson, J. (2009) *Global Marketing*, 5th ed. Boston, MA: McGraw Hill.

Kates, S. (2007) "The Extended Case Method in Consumer Research", *Handbook of Qualitative Research Methods in Marketing*, ed. R. Belk. London: Edward Elgar: 175–185.

Kipnis, E., A. Broderick, and C. Demangeot (2014) "Consumer Multiculturation: Consequences of Multi-Cultural Identification for Brand Knowledge", *Consumption, Markets and Culture*, 17 (3): 231–253.

Kjeldgaard, D. and J. Östberg (2007) "Coffee Grounds and the Global Cup: Glocal Consumer Culture in Scandinavia", *Consumption, Markets and Culture*, 10 (2): 175–187.

Kravets, O. and Ö. Örge (2010). Iconic Brands. A Socio-material Story. *Journal of Material Culture*, 15 (2): 205–232.

Levitt, T. (1983) "The Globalization of Markets", *Harvard Business Review*, 61 (3): 92–102.

Magnusson, P., S.A. Westjohn, and S. Zdravkovic (2011) "'What? I thought Samsung was Japanese': Accurate or Not, Perceived Country of Origin Matters", *International Marketing Review*, 28 (5): 454–472.

O'Neill, T. (2013) "Raised by the World: Heineken Brand Profile", *The Drum*, September 2, 2013.

Özkan, D. and R.J. Foster (2005) "Consumer Citizenship, Nationalism, and Neoliberal Globalization in Turkey: The Advertising Launch of Cola Turka", *Advertising & Society Review*, 6 (3), www.volkskunde.uni-muenchen.de/vkee_download/derya/oezkan_colaturka.pdf.

Poulter, S. (2014) "Cantona's French Beer Advert is Barred: Commercials that Boasted of Gallic Superiority of Kronenbourg 1664 Banned because it's Actually Brewed in Manchester", *Daily Mail*, February 12.

Riefler, P. (2012) "Why Consumers Do (Not) Like Global Brands: The Role of Globalization Attitude, GCO and Global Brand Origin", *International Journal of Research in Marketing*, 29 (1): 25–34.

Roth, K.P., and A. Diamantopoulos (2009) "Advancing the Country Image Construct", *Journal of Business Research*, 62 (7): 726–740.

Silverstein, B. (2011) "Carlsberg Calls for New Brand Positioning", *BrandChannel*, April 5.

Steenkamp, J.B. (2014) "How Global Brands Create Firm Value: The 4V Model", *International Marketing Review*, 31 (1): 5–29.

Steenkamp, J.B. and M.G. de Jong (2010) "A Global Investigation into the Constellation of Consumer Attitudes toward Global and Local Products", *Journal of Marketing*, 74 (November): 18–40.

Steenkamp, J.B., R. Batra, and D.L. Alden (2003) "How Perceived Brand Globalness Creates Brand Value", *Journal of International Business Studies*, 34 (1): 53–65.

Strizhakova, Y., R. Coulter, and L.L. Price (2008) "Branded Products as a Passport to Global Citizenship: Perspectives from Developed and Developing Countries", *Journal of International Marketing*, 16 (4): 57–85.

Strizhakova, Y., R. Coulter, and L. Price (2012) "The Young Adult Cohort in Emerging Markets: Assessing their Glocal Cultural Identity in a Global Marketplace", *International Journal of Research in Marketing*, 29 (1): 43–54.

Swinnen, J. (2011) *The Economics of Beer*, Oxford: Oxford University Press.

Wang, J. (2008) *Brand New China: Advertising, Media and Commercial Culture*. Cambridge, MA: Harvard University Press.

Zhou, N. and R. Belk (2004) "Chinese Consumer Readings of Global and Local Advertising Appeals," *Journal of Advertising*, 33 (3): 63–76.

PART II

Brands, identities, and self-expression

4

BOYS WILL BE BRANDS

Exploring male consumer-brand relationships

Aliette Lambert and John Desmond

Introduction

> The shelf below his bathroom mirror is a battlefield. Occasionally he tries to blame his girlfriend, but the truth is that half the items fighting for territory on the strip of zinc are his. The ranks of grey, white, and black vessels resemble advancing chess pieces. Their provenance is mysterious: he wouldn't be able to tell you exactly when Kiehl's Blue Herbal Astringent Lotion and Clarins Active Face Wash insinuated themselves into his morning routine. Not to mention Clinique M Lotion and American Crew Classic Wax. He certainly didn't rush out and buy them all at once. It was a slow accretion; a steady assault on his subconscious until each of these products seemed essential. It hardly seems possible that there was a time when a razor, foam, water and soap would have sufficed, followed by a quick blast of deodorant.
>
> *(Tungate 2008: 11)*

The above vignette conveys the evolving nature of men's consumption habits and offers a glimpse of the potential for men to engage in consumer-brand relationships ("each of the products seemed essential"), as well as the latent intonations of femininity still associated with consumption ("he tries to blame his girlfriend"). The quote positions a man as a less-than-eager consumer whose products inevitably inveigle their way into his routine, his life, and even his identity ("It was a slow accretion; a steady assault on his subconscious"). This accords somewhat with a conception that the realm of consumption and shopping is women's work (Veblen 1899; Edwards 1997; De Grazia and Furlough 1996), and, given traditional associations of women with nurturing, relationships, and consumption, it made sense for Fournier (1998) to disregard men and focus on relations between women and brands. This conception, however, obscures important aspects of the historical relation between masculinity, appearance, and consumption that must be acknowledged in developing an understanding of contemporary consumer-brand relations, as men have been targeted by mass-mediated idealized images of masculinity at least since the late eighteenth century (Mosse 1996; Desmond 2002).

This chapter emphasizes the purposive nature of men's brand relationships within their identity projects (Fournier 1998; Arnould and Thompson 2005). We first provide a historical context to argue that a specific male archetype, the narcissistic dandy historically located on the fringes of masculinity given 'feminine' concerns with appearance and shopping, is today mainstream, both located in advertising and accepted as a form of (commercial) masculinity. Dandyism, we contend, is pivotal to the formation of a 'New Man' for whom engagement in consumer culture is acceptable (Beynon 2002), thus underpinning men's propensity to participate in consumer-brand relationships, and not only with product categories congruent with normative masculinity such as fast cars, beer and sports. We then demonstrate through findings from our study on consumer-brand relationships (Lambert and Desmond 2013) the individual nature of men's brand relationships, the significance of these relationships to identity, and the nuanced forms of masculinity, from conventional to dandy-like, evident within male consumer identity projects.

Historical context

Activities such as shopping, meticulously styling hair and picking out the perfect cologne are not necessarily considered 'masculine' or thought to occupy men on a regular basis. However, market research suggests a surge of male engagement in the marketplace, with a recent Key Note report (Hughes 2014) noting "the taboo of male grooming (changing) into something of a necessity" and a Mintel report (Mintel 2013) observing that the launches of beauty and personal care products targeted at men have increased by 70 percent globally from 2007 to 2012. Gendered assumptions of consumption-related practices as "women's work" are deeply embedded in the social subconscious and, along with Fournier's (1998) female-only participant pool, prompt questions about men's brand relationships. Moreover, consumer research lacks systematic inquiry on gender (Bettany *et al.* 2010) and research on the male consumer is underdeveloped at best (Tuncay and Otnes 2007), despite consumption trends. Existing research tends to focus on tensions of masculinity given blurred gender roles in postmodernity (Gentry and Harrison 2010; Hein and O'Donohoe 2014); fantasies of recapturing traditional masculinity (Belk and Costa 1998, Holt and Thompson 2004); and male solidarity through brand communities (Schouten and McAlexander 1995; Kozinets 2001). Whilst Zayer and Neier's (2011) study is valuable in extending Fournier's (1998) brand relationship typology to men, it does not dwell on the role of brand relationships in consumer identity projects, a focus of Fournier's work and this chapter. In order to build a foundation for this line of inquiry, we first briefly outline the historical relationship between men and consumption.

Although men *have* historically shied away from shopping and consumption associated culturally with female territory, this has never been so for a particular archetype embodied by the eighteenth-century dandy. The dandy character is exemplified in Beau Brummell, a rather effeminate man whose unrivalled sense of taste won favor amongst elite men anxious over sartorial display at a time when fashions were quickly changing (Kelly 2006). The relation of dandyism to mainstream masculinity has changed over the intervening centuries, but has been present throughout. At times, as with Brummell and prior to the First World War with 'mashers' and 'swells' who were also preoccupied by appearance and shopping, expression of an aberrant masculinity received a cautious welcome from the mainstream (Shannon 2006). However, as with Oscar Wilde, or as occurred in parts of Europe between the two World Wars, this character was cast out from "good" society, labeled as a countertype to ideals of masculinity, and a source of contamination to the racial stock (Mosse 1996). Ultimately, dandified figures enduring through history purposively sought identity through consumption, and thus underpin male consumer-brand relationships.

Male propensity toward brand relationships is further evident in the 1960s British Rocker, embodying a hyper-masculine image similar to the American Harley-Davidson brand subculture described by Schouten and McAlexander (1995), including interest in heavy motorcycles, rock music, leathers and beer. Interestingly, this "branded" subculture emerged as a reaction against dandified Mod subculture, deliberately fashioned through commodity selection to be antithetical in every way to the rockers (Hebdige 1988). Scooters (Vespas or Lambrettas) were combined with musical style (*The Who* or *The Kinks*) and clothing (sharp Italian suits, button-down shirts, olive green anoraks) to express the Mods' sophistication compared to their peers (Hebdige 1988). Here, Hebdige (1988) usefully extends consideration of identity beyond the idea of the extended self (Belk 1988; 2013) and the role played by goods in the reflexive identity project of late modernity (Giddens 1991), expressive of a particular form of femininity or masculinity (Fournier 1998; Holt and Thompson 2004; Tuncay and Otnes 2007), by focusing on how groups of teenagers in the 1960s used brands as marker goods to protect their chosen identity from symbolic contamination. Accounts of subcultures of consumption and brand communities (Schouton and McAlexander 1995; Kates 2002; Kozinets 2001; Muniz and Schau 2005) further underpin male consumer-brand relationships in this way, by demonstrating brand selection as contributing to group and individual identity.

By the 1980s, the objectification of men was spurred by mass media programs, advertisements, and perhaps most notably, male lifestyle magazines such as *Men's Health* and *GQ* (Edwards 1997; Patterson and Elliot 2002). In these publications, advertising was no longer separate from editorial; the entire magazine took advertising for its form. Thus, the crafting of identity through consumption of brands filtered to the mainstream. Benyon (2002) contends that this sea change in men's relations to brands occurred as a consequence of the decline of the "old industrial man" and the rise of the 1980s "yuppie," whose character was fashioned along more self-expressive, materialistic lines. Embodied by dubious characters such as Gordon Gekko in the movie *Wall Street*, the yuppie used conspicuously recruited weapons of style, from power-look suits to his Filofax and Porsche, as means to help make his way to the top (Edwards 1997: vii). The yuppie blended the dandy's attention to appearance and love of shopping with the image of a successful businessman who signaled status through powerful brands, setting a stage for widespread commercial masculinity in the form of the narcissistic, sophisticated, and urbane metrosexual (Simpson 2002; Shugart 2008). The mainstream metrosexual is often considered threatening to "conventional and normative" masculinity (Shugart 2008: 281) given his 'feminine' love of brands and consumption, along with an ambiguous sexuality. This ambiguity is unsurprising given extensive use of gay window advertising in the 1980s and 1990s, whereby gay men were targeted through mainstream ads given a preconception that they enjoyed higher disposable income and a tendency to use consumption to "reinforce sexual orientation" (Edwards 1997: 74; Kates 2002). By the dawn of the new millennium, luxury brand advertising appeals brazenly challenged dominant heterosexual representations of gender, most notably in a 2007 advertisement for Armani briefs featuring David Beckham – a clearly heterosexual role model – in a provocative pose. These mass-market appeals shift dandyism into the mainstream and foster a propensity for men to cultivate a self-image through brand relationships. Threats to hegemonic masculinity are well documented in consumer research studies highlighting men's fantasies of recapturing "dying" forms of masculinity (Holt and Thompson 2004; Belk and Costa 1998). Gentry and Harrison (2010: 75) note: "Males are facing tensions in the marketplace between conforming to social expectations about what it means to be a man and the desire to break away from the constraints of hegemonic masculinity through consumption." In all, this "New Man" embraces blurred gender lines in a postmodern setting where the once marginal figure of the dandy is now mainstream. How this plays a role in the "everyday" man's identity project and relationship with brands remains underexplored.

Empirical research

The above account shows both that men can engage in brand relationships and how the historic figure of the effeminate consuming man – the dandy – has infused modern masculinity, encouraging commercial masculinity and thus fostering brand relationships. Consumer research remains fragmented; its study of men and understanding of the male consumer is underdeveloped (Tuncay and Otnes 2007). Although Zayer and Neier (2011) explore consumer-brand relationships, applying Fournier's (1998) typology to men, identity and the nature of these relationships requires further consideration. Thus, we conducted a study (Lambert and Desmond 2013) focusing on male consumer-brand relationships and narcissism, the former of which will be explored in this chapter. We used narcissism as a lens through which to examine brand relationships in that study, given that men's foray into consumption is often labeled as a narcissistic pursuit, reflected in accounts of the dandy and metrosexual (Edwards 1997; Beynon 2002). Initially, we conducted a pilot to ascertain whether men actively engage in brand relationships to the same extent as women, finding that participants instantly distanced themselves from brand culture (Holt 2002), beginning with what seemed to be a practiced denial, "I don't really care about brands," but, later commenting upon recalling favorite brands: "I guess I engage with brands more than I thought." This, along with the dearth of research in the area, piqued our curiosity as we set forth into the main data collection phase.

Study design

In all, we interviewed seven (self-defined heterosexual) men about their relationships with brands. The four men selected for interviews, described in Table 4.1, comprised the main study and were drawn from a group of 25 postgraduate students at a UK university, ages 20 to 30, based on Narcissistic Personality Inventory scores (Raskin and Terry 1988). As noted in Table 4.1, two scored in the top 10 percent and two scored in the bottom 10 percent. Semi-structured depth interviews, allowing for deeper understanding of the participants' experiences (Guba and Lincoln 1994), were then conducted, addressing life histories, personality traits, and relationships with brands. Given the small size of the postgraduate community at this university, all participants were socially acquainted with the first author (interviewer) to similar degrees (and also acquainted with one another), which provided for richness of data (Mick and Buhl 1992). Whereas Fournier (1998) selected three women from different generations, showing the divergent nature of identity and brand use in each life stage, these participants were in the same transitional emerging adult life stage (Arnett 2004). We recognize the status of our participants as Western European and privileged, being relatively wealthy and attending an elite university at the time of the study. Interview sessions lasted up to three hours, with two hours recorded on average, and were subsequently transcribed. Conversation before and after the interview is accounted for through field notes; follow-up questions were asked as needed. Three of the four interviews were conducted in the participant's home for access to his possessions, and the first author was able to later visit the fourth participant's home.

Data analysis

Data analysis was conducted much like it was in Fournier's 1998 study, through an idiographic method that allowed for constant comparison and a parts-to-whole analysis (Thompson *et al.* 1989) in which individual cases are constructed through thick description analyzed individually and then compared to other cases. For the purposes of this chapter, we have analyzed the data particularly pertaining to brand relationships in order to 1) discover themes related to men's brand relationships and 2) to compare these relationships to the female consumer–brand relationships in Fournier's 1998 study.

Findings

There was no question as to whether men *could* have brand relationships: this was immediately obvious with all participants, and evident in the literature. Like women, these men use brand relationships as "symbolic resources for the construction and maintenance of identity" (Elliott and Wattanasuwan 1998: 132). Most prominently, we found four distinctive identity projects bound up in purposive selection of brands, much like in Fournier's (1998) study. Although each participant is navigating the emerging adult life stage through consumption, we found that brands are purposively engaged to express *individual* identity. Furthermore, in line with research on tensions of masculinity (Gentry and Harrison 2010; Hein and O'Donohoe 2014), we observed nuanced forms of masculinity, including adherence to conventional masculinity and expressions of dandyism, throughout the cases. First, we present a discussion of common themes including: 1) the influence of females, 2) "fear of the feminine", and 3) the individual nature of male consumer identity projects. Then, we present individual participant cases (see Table 4.1).

Three common themes

The first commonality amongst the participants is the influence of females (particularly mothers) in brand selection and shopping processes. This is reminiscent of traditional gender norms (i.e., mothers shopping *for* their sons) in which the realm of consumption is relegated to women (Edwards 1997); participants only mention fathers when speaking of traditional male-oriented purchases, such as buying a suit (Ben) or choosing a brand of shaving razor (Stephen). This is also indicative of the emerging adult life stage (Arnett 2004) in which young adults rely on parents while in the process of gaining independence. James notes: "My mom is highly involved in the process of buying clothes, but lately, you know, as I've gotten older, I have more and more developed independence, but I'm still wearing lots of stuff that she has, you know, bought for me." This is similar to Vicki (Fournier's youngest participant) "inheriting" some of her mother's brand loyalties.

A second theme amongst the participants is a "fear of the feminine," or "an aversion to buying products that have feminine connotations" (Otnes and McGrath 2001: 117; Hein and O'Donohoe 2014). This emerged particularly from the two participants most aligned with metrosexual and dandy-like consumption behavior (Chris and James, high NPI scorers), but was also demonstrated by other participants through adherence to male gender norms and shared reluctance to admit brand loyalty or, as Ben states, "an emotional attachment to an abstract thing." These men are not as forthright as the women in Fournier's (1998) study, and are even private about brand relationships, perhaps less keen to admit to their "backstage" habits (Goffman 1959) in order to present the constructed front as a fait accompli. We further extend "fear of the feminine" to include fear of ambiguous sexual orientation; the equivocal nature of sexuality both of the

TABLE 4.1 Participant information and summary of themes

CHRIS: 23 YEARS OLD, HIGH NPI SCORE (29); 30 BRANDS MENTIONED

IDENTITY THEMES: Metrosexual. Need for recognition. Attention to perfecting appearance as fashion-forward. Conscientious of avoiding the feminine.

BRAND RELATIONSHIPS/TYPOLOGY: Wide selection of mass-marketed luxury brands; Few deep attachments.
Neutrogena (marriage of convenience), Oral B (arranged marriage), Calvin Klein (compartmentalized friendship), Armani (underwear, fling; perfume, compartmentalized friendship), Dolce Gabbana (fling), D-Squared (courtship)

JAMES, 25 YEARS OLD, HIGH NPI SCORE (29); 36 BRANDS MENTIONED

IDENTITY THEMES: Future-oriented identity project; dandy-like appearance that is not fashion forward, but carefully cultivated through high status brands.

BRAND RELATIONSHIPS/TYPOLOGY: Very brand aware and conscious of brand status. Deep but disposable attachments (if something better comes along).
The White Company (marriage of convenience); Bionsen (best friendship); Zegna (committed partnership); van Laack (best friendship); Sevens (best friendship); Rimowa (courtship); Wella (courtship)

BEN, 25 YEARS OLD, LOW NPI SCORE (9); 15 BRANDS MENTIONED

IDENTITY THEMES: Crafting an identity that foregoes a youthful self who experiments with brands, in favor of a mature, classic self-image reflective of his hardworking, ambitious nature. Attentive to his clean-cut, conservative appearance through deep brand relationships, many from childhood.

BRAND RELATIONSHIPS/TYPOLOGY: Not very brand oriented but has some specific, long-lasting brand relationships
Nivea (kinship/dependency); Adidas (best friendship); Hugo Boss (committed partnership); Armani (enmity)

STEPHEN, 25 YEARS OLD, LOW NPI SCORE (12); 20 BRANDS MENTIONED

IDENTITY THEMES: Individual style centered on a passion for vintage products and a desire for uniqueness

BRAND RELATIONSHIPS/TYPOLOGY: Not very brand oriented, but very loyal to specific brands that adhere to his style or serve him well
Abercrombie & Fitch (best friendship); Rimowa (best friendship); Apple (committed partnership); Omega (best friendship); Porsche (best friendship)

---

metrosexual and dandy seems to prompt a need from Chris and James to reinforce their heterosexuality. For example, Chris mentions on the topic of shampoo: "Fruity, fruity. It has to be fruity. It sounds stupid but I like most the one that smells like a woman. But I can't use them because they are too womanized … it's just gay if I would smell like that." Similarly, James reinforces his heterosexual orientation by distinguishing his preferred shop assistant as homosexual, and expresses discomfort in recalling the shop assistant, admiring him in a pair of Sevens jeans, commenting, "Your ass just looks great in this!"

The third common theme is that relationships with brands remain an individual pursuit. There is no mention of shopping as a communal activity engaged in with male friends – Chris asserts: "I never go with my friends." Rather each participant either shops alone or with parents (typically mothers). There is no talk of comparing brands with friends, as demonstrated by Vicki who often discusses friends when discussing brands (Fournier 1998). The few occasions in which friends are mentioned occur either to reinforce status or to establish an undesired self. When discussing his favorite store, James recounts that his friend assumed it to be the store in the 'posh' area, to which James replied, "Yeah, that's the one!" Ben refers to Chris as the 'fashion kid' in order to reinforce his own classic and mature brand selection.

Individual thematic analysis

This section explores individual themes of each participant. See Table 4.1 for a summary.

Chris (high NPI): the metrosexual

One of the most prominent themes in Chris's narrative is his painstaking attention to appearance and the image he portrays to others. Many of his habits are reminiscent of the metrosexual. He mentions early in the interview that he is a person who "very much likes to be liked" and frequently sees himself "worse than I am." Thus, for Chris, recognition is important, reflected in his extensive engagement with brands, and a particular penchant for the signaling power of conspicuous prestige brands (Vigneron and Johnson 1999). Chris is very particular about the (designer) brands that he selects. He wants to be fashionable and sees himself as a bit of a trendsetter:

> I want to be a person where the people say, "Oh he's really fashionable," but I wouldn't say I am a person who tries things out. But to be honest sometimes I just check like if you see … on the TV just Beckham walks there and wears this, and ah looks good, then I might wear it. But I am not the person who wears it first. But usually since, it sounds stupid, but since [my home country] is so back in trends and I am very internationalized, I usually set, very often, trends or I wear something before other people.

Here, we see influences of celebrity culture and media, as well as the inversion of the male gaze (Patterson and Elliott 2002) as Chris admires David Beckham, who is appropriately named by Simpson (2002) as the archetypal metrosexual. It also draws in the theme of invidious consumption (Kates 2002) – or, in this case, employing brands in order to both receive attention and invoke the envy of others.

Chris is branded down to his underpants, using many brands that may be considered luxury, such as his preferred Calvin Klein underwear, of which he has amassed over 30 pairs: "I ordered Armani, Dolce Gabbana and Calvin Klein, and they [Calvin Klein] were simply the ones who made the most comfortable ones, they're famous and they were the cheapest, actually." Chris seems to attentively select brands that communicate his identity project of a young, fashion-forward guy. He likes to wear stylish, slim-fit clothes from recognizable brands that are young, hip, and liberal (e.g., he finds Ralph Lauren "too conservative" because they "cut [clothes] like you're fat"). His favorite brand is DSquared, which he describes as "the craziest most expensive brand I've ever seen." On its website, the brand uses the adjectives 'young, attractive, metropolitan' to describe itself as "dandy swag," words suggestive of a metrosexual (Shugart 2008). DSquared describes its collection as "created for a cosmopolitan dandy, a young handsome guy who wears fitted suits with a cooler twist as he wants to stand out wherever he is." (DSquared Classic 2014) This seems directly relevant to Chris's identity project, as it squares with Chris's desire to be fashionable and aligns with dandy-like and metrosexual tendencies.

Also characteristic of a metrosexual, Chris is a perfectionist when it comes to his appearance. He describes his obsession with the fit of a button-down shirt: "I care a lot about shirts. I try them on, if they don't fit, I bring them to a guy who fits them. They have to be perfect." Chris's diligent care for his appearance is further reflected in his many consumption rituals from going to the hairdresser every few weeks to using multiple toothpastes to brush his teeth. Tuncay and Otnes (2007) note that men are increasingly using personal products previously deemed "feminine," and Chris certainly fits this description, with highly ritualized use of products from Neutrogena moisturizer, to £30 hair wax (allowing him to remold his hair up to 12 hours after initial use), to colognes. Moreover, Chris doesn't just grab "whatever" brand. Rather, he tests many different options before selecting the perfect product. For example, Chris tested (owned) over 15 colognes before deciding that Armani Diamonds was the perfect scent for him, and also purchased the deodorant and aftershave. But, perhaps indicative of a stigma against brands as a feminine pursuit or against "consumer-as-dupe," Chris asserts that he does not feel loyal to the brand: "I wouldn't say I am loyal to Armani, I just love this perfume … I mean I have two Armani perfumes but it is just because I think Armani makes really good perfumes." However, Chris later admits to trusting (and relying on) big brands versus brands from "smaller companies," as he expects their products to be "tested, quality good, uh and you always get the same product." This evokes Elliot and Wattanasuwan's (1998) observation that brands are important pillars of trust and providers of comfort in an uncertain "postmodern" environment. Chris's reliance on big brands may also be indicative of mainstream status and thus powerful signals in the gaining of recognition from others.

James (high NPI): the traditional, future-oriented dandy

While Chris is concerned with fashion, crafting a future self preoccupies James; he continually distinguishes between his current "student" self and his future "professional" self. Moreover, it was evident throughout the interview that James is modeling his career after his father's position as a high-level executive for a major fast-moving consumer goods brand; at the time of this interview, James had recently accepted a graduate job at a rival company.

Most of the brands James mentions are luxury brands; he asserts: "The more expensive, the more I like it!" Indicative of future-orientation, James frequently qualifies discussions of the brands (most of which he already owns) with "I'll definitely buy this brand all the time when I am working." For example, although he doesn't care much about appearance in a student setting, he fondly recalls a hair styling product he once tried: "Oh yeah there's actually one product I used once and I want to buy that again because I was very happy with it, it's called Wella High Hair or something, and it's a pomade, you know the stuff they use in Elvis Presley age. But I'll use the hair gel at a later point in time." James seems particularly concerned with the quality and status of the brands he owns: "I would always try to get, well higher class, upper class kind of brand," brands he perhaps deems "worthy" of an executive. For example, he displays a van Laack dress shirt that he will "totally buy all the time" when he has a salary, noting the superior quality and signature button stitch that only those of a certain status would recognize, asserting: "This shirt is just so me, as you can tell." This signifies an inclination to affiliate his current self with a future "executive" self. James does mention that he would switch brands if something better comes along, if he finds something "like really posh that would fit me well"; this theme is further discussed in Lambert and Desmond (2013).

James tends to revere certain brands he finds unfit for "student life" situations, like his van Laack shirt. Another key example is James's most prized possession, his Zegna coat. The brand story below elicits feelings of happiness, love (Ahuvia 2005), and nostalgia stimulated by long-term engagement with the brand, not least through inheriting a Zegna tuxedo from his father that he has worn on special occasions for the past six years. James describes the coat, which he keeps at his parent's home:

> J: 'I've got a coat that's worth over £1000 … the thing is I have worn it once, which is ridiculous but that coat is absolutely, utterly beautiful. It's great.
> I: What's the brand?
> J: Zegna, it's my favorite brand … It's one of those brands you hear if you've got more money … it's absolutely terrific … I really love that brand. I had a perfume from them, and I will use the perfume again. I will always only use this perfume. It was a gift for my 18th birthday from an Italian friend of mine who knew I love Zegna, and it is an Italian brand so he gave it to me. But yeah that coat, that Zegna coat. It's a Zegna coat. It's just great because we

were at [an upscale men's store where his father also shops] … my mom just looked at the coat, was like, well my mom always likes to buy stuff for me … And then you know I got the coat and I'm really happy and I'll always use it, and it's beautiful. But, you know, you have to have the right situation to wear it. I can't just wear it to the university! It would be ridiculous! …When you're in a certain, how do you say? In a certain peer group, certain level, you know, students, we would always go to pub where you just take the coat and put it in the corner. If I'm with my parents and we go to the opera or a fine restaurant, where they actually take the coat, so once I reach a certain level, it makes more sense for me to use that coat for, you know, really taking care of, cause I like to take care of my things. I expect people to take care of my things.

Evident in the passage is James's committed, long-lasting brand relationship with Zegna, as well as the nature of his ideal self-identity project. Unlike Chris, James does not proclaim to be stylish or attentive to his appearance, remarking, after being questioned about any other habits in his morning routine, "yeah well [I use] deodorant, and that's it" (although it is a specific type of deodorant, Bionsen, which he justifies in terms of it being natural and aluminum free). But he is precise in crafting a professional identity, an identity to which he aspires. In many ways, that identity is reminiscent of Beau Brummell, the original dandy. On the one hand, Brummell was conservative, popularizing a sober bourgeois dress code amongst the aristocracy. On the other hand, he demanded quality of materials and superior cut and style of his clothing, and relentlessly pursued an extravagant lifestyle of conspicuous consumption (Auslander 1996: 92). Perhaps, in James we see a dandy consumer: he is not obsessive when it comes to appearance, in contrast to the fashionable metrosexual, but methodical in selecting high quality, status brands, thereby cultivating a polished appearance. He relentlessly pursues a (future) identity based on conspicuous consumption of expensive brands and status symbols, dreaming of his SieMatic kitchen, caressing his plush White Company towels, displaying the versatility of his glimmering Rimowa suitcase.

Ben (low NPI): the (new) conventional man?

Rather than test identity through fashion and brands like Chris and James, Ben is committed to forming an identity that matches his hardworking and ambitious work ethic instilled by his parents. He *is* similar in this way to James, but does seem to not engage in conspicuous consumption. As such, most of Ben's brand relationships are homegrown, either inherited from his family (Nivea) or part of the milieu in which he was raised (Adidas), and reflective of his desire for a classic, understated self-image (Hugo Boss). Ben finds it difficult to understand any emotional attachment he might have to a brand, despite his committed brand relationships. Perhaps Ben's most dedicated brand relationship is with Nivea, a product he has used since childhood. In fact, this is his only personal care brand;

he has an array of its men's line products, from shower gel to deodorant to aftershave.

> If I go back like, being whatever, being bathed as a young kid, as a baby, then definitely Nivea was around because my mom bought this kind of stuff ... I will also always have it, so. That's probably a reason; you grew up into this and your mom says well it is good to use this, your dad says well this is the best aftershave I use. Then you try it, you're convinced and you stick with it.

At first, he was reluctant to admit attachment, but then, chuckling to himself, he remembered once leaving all of his Nivea products at his parent's home; running to the store to buy some products, he was bitterly disappointed when he could not find any: "I was like oh God, no Nivea there. They only had the spray version of deodorant. That's just annoying, but that does prevent me from buying anything else." For Ben, these life-long product attachments stem from trust: he remains loyal "because you have a certain trust and comfort in getting the quality you expect, or they promise to deliver." In his words: "why change a winning team?"

Ben is also loyal to brands that assist him in forging an identity project predominately organized around a maturing, hardworking, and ambitious persona, foregoing his wild teenage self. This is reflected in his penchant for traditional, classic brands. Referring to the participant Chris, he states:

> If you look at Chris, for example, he is just the fashion kid. I mean he's still got the [All-star] Chucks and all of that stuff. I mean, I had them myself, but there's a certain point – especially baggy jeans, hip hop clothing, this kind of stuff – gone. I would never wear this again, you know? But I figured out for myself as well just yeah, just wear some classy things. You can never go wrong with white polos; you can never go wrong with nicely cut jeans.

His favorite brand of clothes, which he states with fervor, is Hugo Boss, asserting: "German Brand. Simple cut." He is most attracted by their "understatement in fashion" that is not "poseur-like" and instead is "very classic, traditional." He derides luxury brands that charge extra for "gimmicks," noting of Hugo Boss: "It's nothing you know that will pop out like any Armani suit, any other fancy stuff that you pay a hundred quid on top just for the brand name." This elicits a theme of concern with keeping a classic, almost professional, appearance now that he has reached a certain age: "I do criticize some of my friends for not being that caring about fashion ... One of my friends just recently bought [Puma Formula 1] shoes that we all wore when we were 18 and I was like, 'no God you didn't!'" And wise to the market, he notes: "I like to dress properly and I'm not really sloppy ... I said a few years ago I definitely want to go to work in a suit every day, a Barney Stinson [from the television show *How I Met Your Mother*] sort of thing, just suits, man!" Ben's evolving identity project from young to grown up, from a boy to a man, from fun to serious, is mirrored in his brand relationships, many of which are life-long.

His practical nature and few brand relationships, most of which are masculine and traditional, are perhaps most indicative amongst the cases of conventional masculinity, but his attention to appearance (i.e., using branded personal care products, attending to the cut of his clothing) demonstrates changing male consumption patterns and nuances in masculinity.

Stephen (low NPI): the individual

Stephen exhibits an identity project focused on a desire to be unique and a reverence for vintage products. This is reflected in brands to which he is very loyal; he thoughtfully describes his relationship with specific brands, but eschews any allegations of loyalty to brands in general. He also describes vintage products that he owns ("There's no school like old school!"), from a 1968 Omega automatic watch, to his 1973 yellow Porsche 911, both of which he carefully maintains. He notes:

> I like old products. I think if you look at an old car which is 30 years old and we can see how it works actually and when you sometimes even can fix it yourself, that just inspires me and I really just love it. Or when I had tough times nearly two years ago, I needed to have like a hobby which is totally different from my other work and my other life, so I renovated an old chair. And it was just, like, amazing and very cool to, yeah, rebuild this chair on your own and see the finished product in the end, which you did.

Stephen's love for "old" products translates to his brand relationships as he seeks brands that specifically either *are* original in their design, such as his beloved "old-school" and "unchanged for 50 years" Rimowa suitcase, or modern but resembling a 1960s James Bond or "lord-of-the-manor" style. For this reason, he is very loyal to Abercrombie and Fitch, describing:

> I like Abercrombie and Fitch. Sometimes I buy Abercrombie and Fitch from the United States via the Internet. I don't like the brand and I don't like the shops – they are awful! … But sometimes they have really decent clothes like in these old, uh you don't know it, but it's like a TV series which is in Germany but is based in England, in Cornwall, and you see the people wearing the lovely trench coats and lovely land lord clothes, and I like such kind of things, which sometimes Abercrombie and Fitch offers.

For Stephen, it isn't necessarily the brand image, or what others think; rather, it is the style that fits with his identity project, one that seeks uniqueness in channeling his passion for 1960s style. For example, one of Stephen's favorite items is a pair of red trousers: "Of course I'm dressing sometimes like you know with the red trousers um which is not so like normal or standard" – and he is bothered when someone else wears them.

A brand story that highlights Stephen's loyalty to specific brands and fondness for special things concerns his relationship with his Apple MacBook Pro; Stephen notes: "I bought it [my MacBook] in the first place because it was something special, and I like things that are unique and special ... My Mac is an awesome product – never experienced a single problem. I went with it through the whole world and it never collapsed." Stephen speaks about his products such as his Rimowa suitcase or his MacBook, as "best friends" (Fournier 1998) who have been "through the whole world" with him. He also accessories these products appropriately; for example, he has a vintage-style leather satchel to carry his MacBook and a set of antique-style earbud headphones. Stephen's engagement with brands serves the purposive project of the self, to complement his antique products, such as his car and watch, with modern products that fit this image rather than impress others. Stephen's story is somewhat reminiscent of Fournier's oldest participant, Jean (1998: 350), and also Ben. Like Jean and Ben, Stephen's attachments to brands have an "enduring nature" and he has many "deeply held commitments." He is consistent in his purchase choices, staunchly loyal to a few brands that directly contribute to an identity project reflecting a desire for individuality and passion for vintage products.

Discussion

The above four cases show that men *do* engage in brand relationships in ways that purposively serve their individual identity projects. In analyzing the data on brand relationships, four distinct identity projects emerge, indicating the consumption-oriented nature of these young men's identity projects (Belk 1988, 2013; Arnould and Thompson 2005). Interestingly, as observed in Lambert and Desmond (2013), consumer-brand relationship themes tend to align with participants' narcissistic tendencies. Both high NPI scorers, Chris and James, seek to impress others (actual or hypothetical audiences) through use of luxury brands and attentiveness to style. Chris does so in ways suggestive of the metrosexual, concerned with fashion and engaging with mass-marketed luxury brands, whilst James aligns with a dandy character concerned with a classy, though muted, appearance composed of extremely high-status brands. This squares with conceptions of the metrosexual and dandy as narcissistic. While explored further in Lambert and Desmond (2013), we note the finding that narcissistic participants tend to engage with brands agentically, compared to non-narcissistic participants who exhibit a communal nature and long-term brand loyalties. For example, Ben partakes in long-term brand relationships rooted in childhood, typically in the form of committed partnerships and best friendships. With similar types of brand relationships, Stephen expresses an unwavering passion for vintage products and a desire to be unique, carefully crafting his identity and conscientious of the symbolic purpose of each brand with which he engages, at least in the case of visible brands (e.g., he is not concerned with personal care brands). Chris and James conversely tend to engage in shallow brand relationships, such as casual friends/buddies and flings, with occasional dependencies and extended courtships.

Another notable theme (also mentioned in the Findings section) is a shared reluctance to disclose brand loyalties. This likely indicates that, despite nuanced forms of masculinity evident in the cases, hegemonic masculinity remains a powerful force. Along these lines, Gentry and Harrison (2010) show the reinforcement of hegemonic masculinity in media, despite the fact that gender roles in "real life" are "changing rapidly." It is evident that all participants are attentive toward appearance and self-image, a dandy-like tendency, but in different ways. This demonstrates the pervasiveness of commercial masculinity and the fluidity of male gender norms (Shugart 2008), thus rendering dandyism or metrosexuality as a characteristic of certain masculinities, rather than as a lifestyle or character. But despite these shifting masculinities, shared reluctance remains as perhaps an inevitable inclination to conform to normative conceptions of masculinity. The common themes discussed in the findings (including the backstage nature of male brand relationships, fear of the feminine, and the influence of females), all intimate a perceived stigma against male engagement in consumer culture. There is an "everybody's-doing-it-but-nobody's-talking-about-it" ethos to male brand relationships, a reticence to admit brand loyalty, which unwittingly reinforces gender stereotypes of consumption as feminine. Yet this reluctance also denotes divergent meanings and social implications in brand engagement for men and women – perhaps brands are more obviously meaningful, more tangible in women's lives, and perceived as less important, or less socially acceptable, in men's lives. From our observations, brands seem to play *as much* of a role in the identity projects of these men as with Fournier's (1998) female participants. Both sets of participants express individual identities through brand relationships, which are purposive in their lives. Interestingly, the male participants are in the same life stage as Vicki, and similar themes emerge: a transitional life phase, a testing of products (especially with Chris) and somewhat of a fragmentation of self (such as with James who lives in the future with only one foot in the present). Still, the divergent ways that identity is expressed within the same life stage is intriguing: four individual identities and four very different manners of relating to brands emerge. This is suggestive of an expression of unique identity through brand use, as well as the inescapability of consumption-oriented identity projects (Arnould and Thompson 2005; Holt 2002; Kozinets 2002). Moreover, the stigma of engaging with brands surrounding male brand relationships leaves lingering questions for future research, questions that have important implications for researchers and practitioners alike.

Implications and conclusion

The exploratory research presented in this chapter contributes to a foundation for exploring men and brand relationships (along with Zayer and Neier 2011) and serves to further dispel the myth of consumption as women's work. Moreover, this chapter has important implications for both managers and academics: namely, it shows that men *can* and *do* engage in consumer-brand relationships purposive to their lives. Managers in particular must consider that men engage in brand relationships in similar ways to women, and that the nature of masculinity is nuanced, evolving away from the traditional gender norms often propagated through media (Gentry and Harrison 2010). For academics, this chapter introduces important themes for further exploration, such as: the relationship of narcissism with gender and consumption; the role of gender in consumer identity work and brand relationships; and tensions between normative and "alternative" forms of masculinity. We also acknowledge many other areas for research, ranging from quantitative studies aimed at identifying trends to questions of differences in both sexuality and culture, given more traditional gender norms in varying cultural contexts. On this note, we recognize the limitations of this study, including the privileged status of the limited number of participants, as well as the focus on the emerging adult life stage. These limitations provide scope for further exploration of men in different life stages, of different nationalities, and at different income levels, as well as scope for a much larger study. In all, this chapter provides a fruitful foundation for further investigations of the male consumer and men's relationships with brands.

References

Ahuvia, A.C. (2005) "Beyond the Extended Self: Loved Objects and Consumers' Identity Narratives", *Journal of Consumer Research*, 32 (1): 171–184.

Arnett, J.J. (2004) *Emerging Adulthood: The Winding Road from the Late Teens through the Twenties*. New York: Oxford University Press.

Arnould, E.J. and C.J. Thompson (2005) "Consumer Culture Theory (CCT): Twenty Years of Research", *Journal of Consumer Research*, 31 (4): 868–882.

Auslander, L. (1996) "The Gendering of Consumer Practices in Nineteenth-Century France", *The Sex of Things: Gender and Consumption in Historical Perspective,* eds V. de Grazia and E. Furlough. Berkeley, CA: University of California Press: 79–112.

Belk, R.W. (1988) "Possessions and the Extended Self", *Journal of Consumer Research*, 15 (2): 139–168.

Belk, R.W. (2013) "Extended Self in a Digital World", *Journal of Consumer Research*, 40 (3): 477–500.

Belk, R.W. and J.A. Costa (1998) "The Mountain Man Myth: A Contemporary Consuming Fantasy", *Journal of Consumer Research*, 25 (3): 218–240.

Beynon, J. (2002) *Masculinities and Culture*. Buckingham: Open University Press.

Bettany, S., S. Dobscha, L. O'Malley, and A. Prothero (2010) "Moving Beyond Binary Opposition: Exploring the Tapestry of Gender in Consumer Research and Marketing", *Marketing Theory*, 10 (1): 3–28.

De Grazia, V. and E. Furlough (1996) *The Sex of Things: Gender and Consumption in Historical Perspective*. Berkeley, CA: University of California Press.

Desmond, J. (2002) "The Stereotype of Manliness", *Proceedings of the Sixth Conference on Gender, Marketing and Consumer Behaviour, June*, eds P. McLaran and E. Tissier-Desbordes, Association for Consumer Research: 227–239.

DSquared Classic (2014) corporate website, www.dsquared2.com/special/classic_men, accessed April 30, 2014.

Edwards, T. (1997) *Men in the Mirror: Men's Fashion, Masculinity and Consumer Society*. London: Cassell.

Elliott, R. and K. Wattanasuwan (1998) "Brands as Symbolic Resources for the Construction of Identity", *International Journal of Advertising*, 3: 17–20.

Fournier, S. (1998) "Consumers and Their Brands: Developing Relationship Theory in Consumer Research", *Journal of Consumer Research*, 24 (4): 343–353.

Gentry, J. and R. Harrison (2010) "Is Advertising a Barrier to Male Movement toward Gender Change?", *Marketing Theory*, 10 (1): 74–96.

Giddens, A. (1991) *Modernity and Self-Identity: Self and Identity in the Late Modern Age.* Cambridge: Polity.

Goffman, E. (1959) *The Presentation of Self in Everyday Life.* New York: Doubleday.

Guba, E. and Y. Lincoln (1994) "Competing Paradigms in Qualitative Research", *Handbook of Qualitative Research,* eds N.K. Denzin and Y.S. Lincoln. London: Sage: 105–117.

Hebdige, D. (1988) *Hiding in the Light: On Images and Things.* London: Routledge.

Hein, W. and S. O'Donohoe (2014) "Practicing Gender: The Role of Banter in Young Men's Improvisations of Masculine Consumer Identities", *Journal of Marketing Management*, 30 (13–14): 1293–1319.

Holt, D.B. (2002) "Why Do Brands Cause Trouble? A Dialectical Theory of Consumer Culture and Branding", Journal of Consumer Research, 29 (1): 70–90.

Holt, D.B. and C.J. Thompson (2004) "Man Of Action Heroes: The Pursuit of Heroic Masculinity in Everyday Consumption", Journal of Consumer Research, 31 (2): 425–440.

Hughes, K. (2014) "Key Note Market Report", *Youth Fashionwear.* Richmond-Upon-Thames: Harlequin House.

Kates, S.M. (2002) "The Protean Quality of Subcultural Consumption: An Ethnographic Account of Gay Consumers", Journal of Consumer Research, 29 (3): 383–399.

Kelly, I. (2006) Beau Brummell: The Ultimate Man of Style. New York: The Free Press.

Kozinets, R.V. (2001) "Utopian Enterprise: Articulating the Meanings of Star Trek's Culture of Consumption", *Journal of Consumer Research*, 28 (1): 67–88.

Kozinets, R.V. (2002) "Can Consumers Escape the Market? Emancipatory Illuminations from Burning Man", *Journal of Consumer Research*, 29 (1): 20–38.

Lambert, A. and J. Desmond (2013) "Loyal Now, but not Forever! A Study of Narcissism and Male Consumer–Brand Relationships", *Psychology and Marketing*, 30 (8): 690–706.

Mick, D.G. and C. Buhl (1992) "A Meaning-Based Model of Advertising Experiences", *Journal of Consumer Research*, 19 (3): 317–338.

Mintel.com (2013) "Beauty and Personal Care Product Launches Targeted to Men Increase by 70% over the Past Six Years", Mintel.com, www.mintel.com/category/press-centre/beauty-and-personal-care, accessed October 22, 2014.

Mosse, G.L. (1996) *The Image of Man: The Creation of Modern Masculinity.* Oxford: Oxford University Press.

Muniz Jr., A.M. and H.J. Schau (2005) "Religiosity in the Abandoned Apple Newton Brand Community", *Journal of Consumer Research*, 31 (4): 737–747.

Otnes, C. and M.A. McGrath (2001) "Perceptions and Realities of Male Shopping Behaviour", *Journal of Retailing*, 77 (1): 111–137.

Patterson, M. and R. Elliott (2002) "Negotiating Masculinities: Advertising and the Inversion of the Male Gaze", *Consumption, Markets and Culture*, 5 (3): 231–249.

Raskin, R. and H. Terry (1988) "A Principal-Components Analysis of the Narcissistic Personality Inventory and Further Evidence of its Construct Validity", *Journal of Personality and Social Psychology*, 54 (5): 890–902.

Schouten, J.W. and J.H. McAlexander (1995) "Subcultures of Consumption: An Ethnography of the New Bikers", *Journal of Consumer Research*, 22 (1): 43–61.

Shannon, B.A. (2006) *The Cut of His Coat: Men, Dress and Consumer Culture in Britain, 1860–1914.* Athens, OH: Ohio University Press.

Shugart, H. (2008) "Managing Masculinities: The Metrosexual Moment", *Communication and Critical/Cultural Studies*, 5 (3): 280–300.

Simpson, M. (2002) "Meet the Metrosexual", *Salon.com*. www.salon.com/2002/07/22/metrosexual/, accessed October 22, 2014.

Thompson, C.J., W.B. Locander, and H.R. Pollio (1989) "Putting Consumer Experience Back into Consumer Research: The Philosophy and Method of Existential-Phenomenology", *Journal of Consumer Research*, 16 (2): 133–146.

Tuncay, L. and C. Otnes (2007) "Exploring the Link between Masculinity and Consumption", *Brick And Mortar Shopping in the 21st Century*, ed. T. Lowrey. New York: Lawrence Erlbaum Associates: 153–168.

Tungate, M. (2008) *Branded Male: Marketing to Men*. London: Kogan Page Publishers.

Veblen, T. (1899) *The Theory of the Leisure Class*. Oxford: Oxford University Press.

Vigneron, F. and L.W. Johnson (1999) "A Review and a Conceptual Framework of Prestige-Seeking Consumer Behavior", *Academy of Marketing Science Review*, 1 (1): 1–15.

Zayer, L.T. and S. Neier (2011) "An Exploration of Men's Brand Relationships", *Qualitative Market Research: An International Journal*, 14 (1): 83–104.

5

BRAND RELATIONSHIPS AND SELF-IDENTITY

Consumer use of celebrity meaning to repair a compromised identity

Jennifer Edson Escalas and James R. Bettman

Many consumer behavior researchers have made the assertion that people engage in consumption behavior to construct their self-concepts and to create their personal identities (e.g., Richins 1994; McCracken 1989; Belk 1988). In particular, brand meanings are used to create and define a consumer's self-concept (Levy 1959). McCracken (1989) asserts that such brand meaning originates in the culturally constituted world, moving into goods via the fashion system, word of mouth, reference groups, subcultural groups, the media, and, importantly for our purposes, celebrities. In this chapter, we build on research that shows that a celebrity endorser may provide a bundle of meanings that become associated with the brands he or she endorses (Miller and Allen 2012). We theorize, and demonstrate in a study, that brand meaning based on celebrity endorsement is appropriated by consumers as they construct their self-identities through brand choices, using the congruency between such celebrity-generated brand meaning and the consumers' desired self-image. Furthermore, we show that this process is more likely to occur for consumers with compromised self-identities, specifically, those who are low in social complexity.

Theoretical development

In general, consumers purchase products and brands for various reasons. On the one hand, consumers value products' instrumental features and attributes, which provide tangible benefits such as salt adding flavor or pens enabling people to write. On the other hand, sometimes consumers form a special relationship with products or brands, ascribing meaning to these brands that makes them worth more than the value of the sum of their features or instrumental benefits. As an example of special meaning, a consumer may become particularly attached to a certain brand of pens. This brand may symbolize prestige and achievement to the consumer, and using this brand may communicate the consumer's intelligence and status to others. Thus, the pen brand has become incorporated into the consumer's sense of self. It represents a part of who he or she is and can be used to communicate who he or she is to others.

Brand relationships based on self-identity construction

How does meaning become associated with brands? In order to understand this process, we must recognize that brands have symbolic properties extending beyond their functional benefits. As symbols, brands take on meaning when they join with, add to, and reinforce the way consumers think about themselves (Levy 1959). To achieve their identity goals, people use brands to create and represent self-images and to present these images to others or to themselves (Huffman *et al.* 2000). For example, our research has shown that consumers use brands to construct their self-identity and present themselves to others based on the congruency between brand-user associations and self-image associations (Escalas and Bettman 2003, 2005).

The set of brand associations can be more meaningful the more closely it is linked to the self. We study this self-brand linkage by conceptualizing consumers' interactions with brands as a constructive, active process. To extend the "life is a stage" metaphor of Goffman (1959), brands may be considered to be props used by actors for character development. In our research, we focus on self-brand connections, rather than specific brand associations or brand attitudes, because we believe that self-brand connections measure the extent to which symbolic brand meanings are incorporated into a consumer's self-concept (Escalas 2004).

Self-brand connection may be considered one facet of the relationship paradigm proposed by Fournier and others (e.g., Fournier 1998). Fournier identifies six dimensions of brand relationship quality (BRQ). The self-brand connection concept is most similar to the BRQ dimension entitled "self-concept connections" and could thus be considered a subset of BRQ. The self-concept connections dimension of BRQ focuses on brands as vessels of symbolic meaning, with this meaning appropriated by consumers as they use brands' symbolic properties to meet self-related needs.

Compromised identity repair for low social complexity

Consumer researchers have recognized for a long time that people consume in ways that are consistent with their sense of self (Sirgy 1982). Although early research tended to focus on broad conceptual issues surrounding consumers and their sense of self, recent research takes a more granular approach, breaking down the relationship between identity concerns and consumption to look at the effects of specific self-related goals on consumer behavior. For example, consumers with strong self-enhancement goals tend to form self-brand connections to brands used by aspiration groups, that is, groups for which the consumer wishes to become a member (Escalas and Bettman 2003). Similarly, consumers with strong self-verification goals tend to form self-brand connections to brands used by groups to which the consumer actually belongs, in order to confirm his/her self-identity (Escalas and Bettman 2003).

In this chapter, we focus on a specific self-motivation: the extent to which consumers engage in self-identity construction via brands to repair their compromised self-identities. Brands provide useful meanings and connections that help consumers meet self-identity construction needs. These needs may often be salient when consumers' identities are compromised, which creates a liminal state where one's identity needs to be reconstructed. Schouten (1991) proposed that the consumption of aesthetic plastic surgery can be viewed as an active, symbolic reconstruction of self-identity. He found that consumers in a transitional or compromised state (in that they had lost a particular role or aspect of self, or gained a new one) engaged in consumption to develop an integrated new self-concept. Mehta and Belk (1991) studied how Indians who immigrated to America used possessions with cultural and symbolic symbolism to construct their sense of self and identity during the transitional period of assimilating into a new culture. Finally, Chaplin and John (2005) find a similar self-construction process utilizing brands that evolves with the development of children into adolescence, a time where one's self-concept is clearly compromised, growing and developing with age.

This chapter examines one instantiation of compromised identity to see if it augments the self-construction process resulting in self-brand connections: low social complexity. Social complexity is defined as joining and maintaining membership in diverse groups. The social support inherent in social complexity provides a buffering effect against stress and loneliness, as well as being positively related to personal and collective self-esteem (Wann and Hamlet 1994). We expect consumers low in social complexity to engage in ongoing attempts to repair their self-identity, because they feel isolated, have low self-esteem, and may be undergoing stress. We theorize that these consumers may appropriate brands' symbolic meanings as part of that reconstruction, or identity repair, process.

Thus, we assert that when consumers have compromised identities, they may appropriate brand symbolism to navigate their ever-changing sense of self, using brands to construct a desired self-image and to communicate their evolving self-identity to others. We now turn our focus to look at one source of symbolic brand meaning that is particularly relevant given the recent growth in social media: celebrity endorsement.

Celebrity endorsement

With the rise of social media and reality television, some refer to our times as the social era of celebrity (Solis 2011). Kim Kardashian receives $10,000 to tweet about products; Abercrombie & Fitch paid Jersey Shore stars *not* to wear their products on the reality television show; and stars like Katy Perry, Justin Bieber, and Lady

Gaga have more Twitter followers than the populations of many countries (e.g., Katy Perry has over 49 million followers as of September 2013 according to TwitterCounter.com). About 20 percent of US ads in traditional media feature celebrities (Solomon 2009), and the percentage of ads using celebrities in other countries, such as Japan, is thought to be even higher. Adly.com offers over two thousand celebrities for endorsement deals through Twitter, with projected revenues of over five million dollars in 2013 (Cassidy 2013).

Traditional explanations of celebrity endorsement persuasion effects are based on the source effects literature and find that 1) celebrity endorsement increases the attention paid to an ad (Buttle *et al.* 2000); 2) celebrities are generally attractive, which helps persuasion when consumers are worried about social acceptance and others' opinions (DeBono and Harnish 1988) or when the product is attrac-tiveness-related (Kahle and Homer 1985; Kamins 1990); 3) celebrities may be credible sources if they have expertise in a particular area, such as an athlete endorsing shoes (Ratneshwar and Chaiken 1991) or a beautiful model endorsing make-up (Baker and Churchill 1977); and 4) celebrities are often well-liked, possibly leading to identification and consumer persuasion in an attempt to seek some type of relationship with the celebrity (Belch and Belch 2007).

In dual process attitude models (e.g., Elaboration Likelihood Model [ELM]; Petty *et al.* 1983), celebrities are often considered a peripheral cue: they are important in persuasion only when consumers are not involved in the product category or in processing the ad. However, celebrities may provide central information when an aspect of the celebrity matches the product (as with beauty products and attractiveness; Kahle and Homer 1985). Also, as affective peripheral cues, celebrity endorsements may have an impact on sales in mature categories (MacInnis *et al.* 2002). Additionally, research has shown that source congruence, that is, the match between the celebrity's image and the brand's image, is an important influence on brand beliefs and attitudes under conditions of high involvement/elaboration (Kirmani and Shiv 1998), especially in situations with multiple endorsers and multiple endorsements (Rice *et al.* 2012).

Celebrity as source of meaning

Our approach differs from these more traditional explanations of celebrity endorsement effects on persuasion, focusing instead on the cultural meanings associated with celebrities. We examine celebrity endorsement based upon McCracken's (1989) perspective: as consumers construct their self-concept by using brands, they appropriate the symbolic meanings of brands; these meanings may be derived, in part, from celebrity endorsement (see also Miller and Allen, 2012). Celebrities come to personify various characteristics that may be useful to consumers for building the self, and these symbolic properties become associated with brands via celebrity endorsers.

In our consumer society, people often look to celebrities for meaning. Thomson (2006) asserts that attachment to celebrities comes from celebrities' perceived abilities to meet consumers' autonomy and relatedness needs (and not harm competence needs). O'Guinn (1991) finds that consumers are motivated to worship celebrities in order to fulfill social and even spiritual needs. Celebrities play the role of modern heroes who help individuals make sense of their lives in a society that no longer reveres historical and/or mythological heroes (Campbell 2008). Despite the commercial nature of modern celebrity in our society, celebrities may provide life lessons valued by our culture, such as illustrating the wages of sin, punishment for hubris, or the benefits of self-mastery (Gabler 2000). Celebrities create a source of common experience around which society can build a nationwide or even global community.

Celebrities encapsulate meaning on a number of levels, including both broad cultural ideas, such as values and norms, and more idiosyncratic individual meanings, such as what it means to be cool, smart, or successful. Being a fan of celebrities also allows consumers to connect with popular culture, while maintaining individuality in their choice of which celebrities to "worship" (Klapp 1969). Celebrities use mass media to create their identity, which the consumer culture interprets; then, in a circular fashion, the celebrities' own meaning is also created by the products they endorse (Ferris 2007). Consumers in turn use the meanings they themselves fashion for celebrities to construct their own personal identities (Marshall 1997).

Celebrity endorsement and self-identity goals

In this chapter, we assert that consumers appropriate desired celebrity-based meanings by using brands associated with celebrities to construct and communicate the consumers' self-concepts. Celebrity endorsement provides useful meanings and connections that help consumers meet self-related needs, such as self-construction and self-presentation. These needs may often be salient when a consumer's sense of self is compromised, which creates a liminal state where one's identity needs to be reconstructed (Schouten 1991). Thus, we argue that when consumers have compromised self-identities, they will be motivated to engage in self-construction and will be more likely to look to celebrities for meaning. In this chapter, we focus on social complexity as one type of compromised self-identity, which is particularly relevant in the case of celebrity endorsement because lack of social complexity leads individuals to look to celebrities for meaning and is also associated with celebrity worship (Maltby *et al.* 2004). Thus, we expect consumers low in social complexity to look to celebrities for meaning in an ongoing attempt to repair their self-identity, and, as part of this process, to form self-brand connections with the celebrity–endorsed brands.

Hypotheses

Based on the theory above, we believe that brand associations may be captured from celebrity endorsement and used by individuals to construct their self-concepts. We also propose that as a result of this active self-construction process, consumers incorporate brands into their notions of self, forming self-brand connections.

> *H1:* Consumers will use the meanings created by celebrity endorsement in self-identity construction, resulting in self-brand connections.

The addition of specific self-motives can provide insight into the self-construction processes used by consumers. In our framework, celebrity-based brand associations can help consumers achieve self-goals in a manner consistent with their predominant or currently activated self-motivations (Escalas and Bettman 2003). Thus, our theory implies that our hypothesized endorsement effects will be stronger when self-needs relevant to constructing one's self-identity are high. Specifically, this chapter examines how consumers look to celebrities to repair identities that have been compromised due to low social complexity.

> *H2:* The effect of celebrity endorsement on self-brand connections will be moderated by the extent to which consumers have active self-identity construction goals; in particular, we expect a more pronounced effect of celebrity endorsement for low social complexity consumers compared to high social complexity consumers.

The role of congruence

Consumers do not look to all celebrities for meaning indiscriminately. Based on previous research (e.g., Kirmani and Shiv 1998; Rice *et al.* 2012), in order for celebrity endorsement to have an effect on self-brand connections, there must be source congruence: that is, a match between the celebrity image and the brand image. Source congruence occurs when one or more of the aspects of a celebrity's image are congruent with one or more of these aspects of a brand's image, such as associations regarding the celebrity's personality traits, social roles, past experiences, category membership, behavior, abilities, and social relationships. McCracken's (1989) view also suggests that a symbolic "match" should exist between the celebrity image and the brand image in order for the celebrity endorsement to be effective. A generic, well-liked celebrity endorsement will not have the same "punch" as a celebrity endorsement where the image of the celebrity matches the image of the brand.

Going beyond celebrity-brand congruence, we propose that a three-way match is actually necessary for an effective endorsement. If one thinks about celebrity endorsement in terms of balance theory (Heider 1946), a triangle of congruence is necessary between the brand, celebrity, and consumer. The effect of celebrity endorsement on self-brand connections thus depends upon three variables: the extent to which the consumer aspires to be like the celebrity, the extent to which the celebrity image matches the brand image, and the extent to which the consumer's desired self-image matches the brand image. We expect participants who do not possess a self-image (or do not desire a self-image) similar to the positioning of a brand's image will reject a celebrity endorsement, even if the celebrity image is congruent with the brand image.

> *H3:* The effect of celebrity endorsement on self-brand connections will be moderated by the extent to which there exists congruence between and among the celebrity, the brand, and the consumer.

Taking these three hypotheses altogether, our expectation is that consumers who are low in social complexity will be most receptive to celebrity endorsements when there is a three way match between the celebrity's image, the consumer's self-image, and the brand's image, building self-brand connections as they appropriate the celebrity's symbolism through the brand to reconstruct their identity, which has been compromised by low social complexity.

Study

This study examines whether low social complexity augments the influence of celebrity endorsement on self-brand connections (Hypotheses 1 and 2) by measuring social complexity, defined as joining and maintaining membership in diverse groups. In this study, we also explore the notion of three-way source-brand-participant congruence (Hypothesis 3) by manipulating the extent to which the celebrity's image matches the product category being advertised (here, an athletic version of a fictitious Montrex brand watch) and measuring the extent to which participants consider themselves to be athletes (to match the positioning of the athletic watch stimulus).

Method

Participants

The experiment was administered via a web-based facility affiliated with a major research university. A total of 131 US residents from an online panel responded to a randomized invitation to participate, ultimately yielding a usable sample of 118 participants after the removal of approximately the top and bottom 5 percent of participants based on the time taken to complete the study (N = 13, completion time range: five minutes to nearly four hours; mean: 16 minutes, top 5 percent: over 70 minutes, bottom 5 percent: under 8 minutes). Up to three email notifications over a one week period were used to secure cooperation, and the chance to win one of three drawings for a $100 prize served as an incentive.

Procedure

Participants were asked to complete a battery of individual difference scales, including social complexity and their personal degree of athleticism (counterbalanced: half saw the individual difference scales first, half at the end; there were no significant order effects, so the two conditions were collapsed). Next, participants were asked to read a biography of either actor Will Smith (male participants) or actress Angelina Jolie (female participants) that emphasized either their dramatic abilities (low source congruence) or their athletic abilities (the high source congruence condition for the stimulus sports watch). After reading the short bio, participants were shown an ad for the fictitious watch brand, Montrex, using a sports watch as the stimulus and listing sports watch related features. Participants then rated the degree to which they had self-brand connections with the Montrex athletic watch, followed by manipulation checks and demographic variables.

Independent and dependent variables

Participants were randomly assigned to source congruence conditions. We measured social complexity, using a seven item scale developed by Wann and Hamlet (1994) that includes items such as "I tend to be a member of many different groups," "I actively seek out new group memberships," and "I am identified with a variety of different groups," (0 to 100, $\alpha = 0.83$). Our primary dependent variable, self-brand connections (SBC), was measured using the seven item scale developed by Escalas (2004), which includes such items as "This brand reflects who I am," "I feel a personal connection to this brand," and "I consider this brand to be me," (0 to 100, $\alpha = 0.97$). Given our athletic watch stimulus brand, we also measured the extent to which the participants perceived of themselves as being athletic, with three items: "I am an athletic person," "I work out regularly," "I consider myself to be a good athlete;" (0 to 100, $\alpha = 0.92$). This measure represents participant congruence.

Manipulation checks and covariates

In order to test our manipulation of source congruence, we asked about the perceived athleticism of the actor with three items ("this celebrity is in good physical shape," "this celebrity is very athletic," and "this celebrity is an excellent athlete," (0 to 100, $\alpha = 0.83$). Gender was also included as a covariate in the models, because female participants saw Angelina Jolie, while male participants saw Will Smith as the celebrity endorser.

Results

The model used to analyze self-brand connections was a between-subjects GLM model, with gender as a covariate and three factors, with all their interactions: source congruence (manipulated), social complexity (measured, continuous), and participant congruence (measured, continuous).

Manipulation checks

The source congruence manipulation was successful, with a significant effect on the celebrity athleticism manipulation check (high congruence = 70.90, low congruence = 65.17; $F(1, 117) = 4.13, p < 0.05$).

Hypotheses tests

We find only one significant effect in our model: the three-way interaction of social complexity, source congruence, and participant congruence ($F(1, 117) = 4.18, p < 0.05$; Figure 5.1 graphically presents these results, using dichotomous variables for source congruence and participant congruence for graphical purposes). In support of our three hypotheses, we find that the results for low social complexity drive the interaction: high participant congruence (48.15) is significantly different from low participant congruence (18.71) in the high source congruent condition (top panel in the figure; $F(1, 117) = 9.00, p < 0.01$) for consumers low in social complexity, but none of the contrasts in the high social complexity model reach significance (bottom panel in the figure, $Fs(1, 117) < 1.06$, ns).[1] The interpretation of this interaction is that for those consumers with compromised identities due to low social complexity, the effect of celebrity endorsement on self-brand connections depends upon the extent to which the celebrity image matches the brand image (that is, source congruence), and the extent to which the consumer's self-image matches the brand image (that is, participant congruence). We find that low social complexity participants who do not perceive themselves to be athletic reject brands designed for athletes and endorsed by an athletic celebrity. In addition, participants who are not motivated to repair a compromised self-identity (high social complexity) also are not affected by the celebrity endorsement.

Discussion of results

Our study demonstrates that consumers who are not socially complex look to celebrities for meaning more than consumers who have highly complex social networks (Hypotheses 1 and 2). By providing social support, social complexity provides a buffering effect against stress and loneliness and enhances personal and collective self-esteem (Wann and Hamlet 1994). Thus, in this study, those high in social complexity do not look to celebrities for meaning as much as those more vulnerable consumers who are low in social complexity and look to celebrities for fulfillment and meaning (Maltby *et al.* 2004). We also successfully manipulate source congruence by highlighting a celebrity trait, in this case athleticism; we only find a positive effect on self-brand connections for low social complexity participants when there is a celebrity–brand image match and a participant–brand image match (Hypothesis 3).

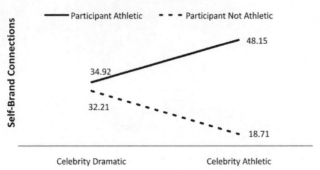

Low Social Complexity

Self-Brand Connections

——— Participant Athletic   - - - Participant Not Athletic

34.92

48.15

32.21

18.71

Celebrity Dramatic   Celebrity Athletic

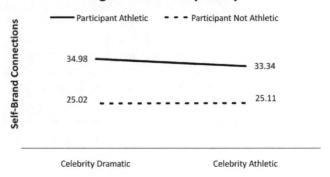

High Social Complexity

Self-Brand Connections

——— Participant Athletic   - - - Participant Not Athletic

34.98   33.34

25.02   25.11

Celebrity Dramatic   Celebrity Athletic

FIGURE 5.1 Effect of social complexity, source of congruence, and participant congruence on self-brand connections

Conclusion

Our key contribution stems from our proposition that symbolic celebrity meaning can be used by consumers motivated to construct their self-identity, with consumers with a compromised self-identity being more likely to look to celebrities for meaning. Our study shows that consumers who have low social complexity report higher self-brand connections for brands with images that are congruent with the image of a celebrity and their own self-image. The self-identity construction function of celebrity meaning is an important extension of the celebrity endorsement literature; our findings demonstrate that consumers are motivated by their self-construction needs to utilize brand associations derived from celebrity endorsement in a contingent fashion to create and present their self-identities. In our study, self-construction needs stem from low social complexity, which compromises the consumers' self-identity.

Our research raises some interesting questions for future research. First, while we propose that as modern heroes, celebrities are uniquely suited to be used for self-identity construction by consumers, one might ask whether consumers with compromised self-identities are generally more likely to use external cues to meaning. Second, perhaps compromised consumers are more likely to be persuaded by ads that make reference to the self. For example, future research could explore whether consumers with compromised self-identities are more persuaded by ads using self-referencing appeals, self-conscious emotion, or nostalgia involving a link to a past self. Third, in this chapter, we focused our attention on only one of the six dimensions of consumer-brand relationships identified in Fournier's (1998) BRQ paradigm. Future research could explore whether the process of using brands to help consumers construct their self-concepts also affects the other five BRQ dimensions, namely partner quality, love/passion, intimacy, interdependence, and commitment.

Our research may also shed light on the adoption of social media to follow celebrities in our modern culture. For example, a Pew Research Center study (Smith 2011) reports that the majority of Twitter users are under the age 34, with half of those users under the age of 24. While one might argue that young people are early adopters of technology in general, the most followed individuals on Twitter are celebrities, such as Lady Gaga, Justin Bieber, and Katy Perry (TwitterCounter.com 2013). Perhaps young people, whose identities are still under construction, are more likely to look to celebrities for meaning and thus adopt social media as part of that endeavor.

Our studies are not without limitations. Given our quest for internal validity, we used a fictitious brand in our research. Therefore, the level of self-brand connections to this brand is consistently below the scale midpoint. While challenging, future research might explore the use of real brands, with pre-existing connections to consumers and idiosyncratic brand associations, to extend our findings to more positive self-brand connections. Measuring social complexity is also not without limitations: there could be unmeasured constructs correlated with social complexity, such as loneliness, social exclusion, or isolation, which are driving our results.

Our findings should be useful to marketers attempting to manage brand meaning in a number of ways. First, when should marketers use a celebrity endorser in an advertising campaign? Our finding that consumers with self-identity construction goals respond more strongly to a celebrity appeal might imply that products with symbolic benefits might be well-served by celebrity endorsements. Second, we find that celebrity endorsements have the most impact for consumers constructing self-identity when the brand image and the celebrity image match. This means marketers need to understand both what their brand already means to their target consumers and what their target consumers believe about the meaning of a potential celebrity endorser. Marketers often make celebrity endorsement decisions based on an overall likeability score; our congruency results reveal that the symbolic image or meaning of the celebrity is every bit as important as the likeability index. Marketers may also be tempted to use celebrities to build new images for their brands, but such endeavors may prove challenging if they try to change a brand image to be too far afield from its current symbolic meaning by using a celebrity endorser with a radically different image. The result may not be an image change, but a failed advertising campaign.

In sum, we believe the self-brand connection scale captures the transfer of meaning from celebrity to brand to consumer (McCracken 1989). We have focused on the effect of celebrity endorsement on self-brand connections as an important part of consumers' construction of self. The set of associations consumers have about a brand is an important component of brand equity (Keller 1993). Therefore, the notion that consumers form a relationship with a brand as they use the brand's symbolic associations for self-construction is important to marketing managers. When consumers' self-concepts are linked to a brand, then the company behind the brand may be able to gain an enduring competitive advantage, because this type of identity-based relationship is difficult for competitors to imitate. Our studies show that using celebrity endorsers to enhance such connections appears to be more successful when consumers' identities have been compromised or are in flux.

Note

1   Further, a spotlight analysis revealed a significant interaction between source congruence and participant congruence one standard deviation below the mean of social complexity ($F(1, 117) = 7.53, p < 0.01$) but not one standard deviation above the mean ($F(1, 117) < 1, ns$).

References

Baker, M.J. and G.A. Churchill Jr. (1977) "The Impact of Physically Attractive Models on Advertising Evaluations", *Journal of Marketing Research*, 14 (November): 538–555.

Belch, G.E. and M.A. Belch (2007) *Advertising and Promotion: An Integrated Marketing Communications Perspective.* New York: The McGraw Hill Companies, Inc.

Belk, R.W. (1988) "Possessions and the Extended Self", *Journal of Consumer Research*, 15 (September): 139–168.

Buttle, H., J.E. Raymond, and S. Danzinger (2000) "Do Famous Faces Capture Attention?", *Advances in Consumer Research*, 27: 245–249.

Campbell, J. (2008 [1949]) *The Hero with a Thousand Faces.* Novato, CA: New World Library.

Cassidy, M. (2013) "What Does Celebrity Shilling Look Like In A Post-Snooki Age? Adly Speaks Up", *Forbes*, April 24, 2013.

Chapin, L.N. and D. Roedder John (2005) "The Development of Self-Brand Connections in Children and Adolescents", *Journal of Consumer Research*, 32 (June): 119–129.

DeBono, K.G. and R.J. Harnish (1988) "Source Expertise, Source Attractiveness, and the Processing of Persuasive Information: A Functional Approach", *Journal of Personality and Social Psychology*, 55 (4): 541–546.

Escalas, J.E. (2004) "Narrative Processing: Building Consumer Connections to Brands", *Journal of Consumer Psychology*, 14 (1 & 2): 168–179.

Escalas, J.E. and J.R. Bettman (2003) "You Are What They Eat: The Influence of Reference Groups on Consumer Connections to Brands", *Journal of Consumer Psychology*, 13 (3): 339–348.

Escalas, J.E. and J.R. Bettman (2005) "Self-Construal, Reference Groups, and Brand Meaning", *Journal of Consumer Research*, 32 (December): 378–389.

Ferris, K.O. (2007) "The Sociology of Celebrity", *Sociology Compass*, 1 (1): 371–384.

Fournier, S. (1998) "Consumers and Their Brands: Developing Relationship Theory in Consumer Research", *Journal of Consumer Research*, 24 (March): 343–373.

Gabler, N. (2000) *Life: The Movie: How Entertainment Conquered Reality*. New York: Random House, Inc.

Goffman, E. (1959) *The Presentation of Self in Everyday Life*. Garden City. NY: Doubleday & Company, Inc.

Heider, F. (1946) "Attitudes and Cognitive Organization", *Journal of Psychology: Interdisciplinary and Applied*, 21 (1): 107–112.

Huffman, C., S. Ratneshwar, and D.J. Mick (2000) "Consumer Goal Structures and Goal-Determination Processes: An Integrative Framework", *The Why of Consumption: Perspectives on Consumer Motives, Goals, and Desires*, eds R. Ratneshwar, D.G. Mick, and C. Huffman. New York: Routledge Press: 9–35.

Kahle, L. and P.M. Homer (1985) "Physical Attractiveness of the Celebrity Endorser: A Social Adaptation Perspective", *Journal of Consumer Research*, 11 (March): 954–961.

Kamins, M.A. (1990) "An Investigation of the 'Match-Up' Hypothesis in Celebrity Advertising: When Beauty May Be Only Skin Deep", *Journal of Advertising*, 19 (1): 4–13.

Keller, K.L. (1993) "Conceptualizing, Measuring, and Managing Customer-Based Brand Equity", *Journal of Marketing*, 57 (January): 1–22.

Kirmani, A. and B. Shiv (1998) "Effects of Source Congruity on Brand Attitudes and Beliefs: The Moderating Role of Issue-Relevant Elaboration", *Journal of Consumer Psychology*, 7 (1): 25–47.

Klapp, O.E. (1969) *The Collective Search for Identity*. New York: Holt, Rinehart, and Winston.

Levy, S.J. (1959) "Symbols for Sale", *Harvard Business Review*, 37 (July–August): 117–24.

MacInnis, D.J., A.G. Rao, and A.M. Weiss (2002) "Assessing When Increased Media Weight of Real-World Advertisements Helps Sales", *Journal of Marketing Research*, 39 (November): 391–407.

Maltby, J., L. Day, L.E. McCutcheon, M.M. Martin, and J.L. Cayanus (2004) "Celebrity Worship, Cognitive Flexibility, and Social Complexity," *Personality and Individual Differences*, 37: 1475–1482.

Marshall, P.D. (1997) *Celebrity and Power: Fame in Contemporary Culture*. Minneapolis, MN: University of Minnesota Press.

McCracken, G. (1989) "Who Is the Celebrity Endorser? Cultural Foundations of the Endorsement Process", *Journal of Consumer Research*, 16 (December): 310–321.

Mehta, R. and R. Belk (1991) "Artifacts, Identity, and Transition: Favorite Possessions of Indians and Indian Immigrants to the United States", *Journal of Consumer Research*, 17 (March): 398–411.

Miller, F.M. and C.T. Allen (2012) "How Does Celebrity Meaning Transfer? Investigating the Process of Meaning Transfer with Celebrity Affiliates and Mature Brands", *Journal of Consumer Psychology*, 22 (4): 443–452.

O'Guinn, T.C. (1991) "Touching Greatness: The Central Midwest Barry Manilow Fan Club", *Highways and Buyways: Naturalistic Research from the Consumer Behavior Odyssey*, ed. R.L. Belk. Provo, UT: Association for Consumer Research: 102–111.

Petty, R. E., J.T. Cacioppo, and D. Schumann (1983) "Central and Peripheral Routes to Advertising Effectiveness: The Moderating Role of Involvement", *Journal of Consumer Research*, 10 (September): 135–146.

Ratneshwar, S. and S. Chaiken (1991) "Comprehension's Role in Persuasion: The Case of Its Moderating Effect on the Persuasive Impact of Source Cues", *Journal of Consumer Research*, 18 (1): 52–62.

Rice, D.H., K. Kelting, and R.J. Lutz (2012) "Multiple Endorsers and Multiple Endorsements: The Influence of Message Repetition, Source Congruence, and Involvement on Brand Attitudes", *Journal of Consumer Psychology*, 22 (2): 249–259.

Richins, M.L. (1994) "Valuing Things: The Public and Private Meanings of Possessions", *Journal of Consumer Research*, 21 (December): 504–521.

Schouten, J.W. (1991) "Selves in Transition: Symbolic Consumption in Personality Rites of Passage and Identity Reconstruction", *Journal of Consumer Research*, 17 (March): 412–430.

Sirgy, J.M. (1982) "Self-Concept in Consumer Behavior: A Critical Review", *Journal of Consumer Research*, 9 (3): 287–300.

Smith, Aaron (2011) "Twitter Update", *Pew Research Center*, June 1, 2011, www.pewinternet.org/2011/06/01/twitter-update-2011/.

Solis, Brian (2011) "Ad.ly CEO Arnie Gullov-Singh on the Social Era of Celebrity Endorsements", *Revolution with Brian Solis*, www.podcasts.com/revolution/episode/ad.ly-ceo-arnie-gullov-singh-on-the-social-era-of-celebrity-endorsements.

Solomon, M.R. (2009) *Consumer Behavior: Buying, Having, and Being.* Upper Saddle River, NJ: Pearson Education, Inc,/Prentice Hall.

Thomson, M. (2006) "Human Brands: Investigating Antecedents to Consumers' Strong Attachments to Celebrities", *Journal of Marketing*, 70 (July): 104–119.

TwitterCounter.com (2013) The Top 100 Most Followed on Twitter, http://twittercounter.com/pages/100.

Wann, D.L. and M.A. Hamlet (1994) "The Joiner's Scale: Validation of a Measure of Social Complexity", *Psychological Reports*, 74: 1027–1034.

6

HOW LONELY CONSUMERS RELATE TO BRANDS

Insights from psychological and marketing research

Christopher R. Long, Sukki Yoon, and Mike Friedman

Why bother thinking about loneliness? For many consumers, a day without smartphones, Facebook, Twitter, and Skype – not to mention an array of email accounts – would seem incomplete. Immediate connections to friends and family are almost always at our fingertips, in our pockets, or on a desk in front of us. In this highly-connected context, opportunities for communication with others appear to be growing daily. For that reason, it may be surprising that many of us inhabit demographic categories in which loneliness is a problem whose prevalence may be expected to increase.

Specifically, recent surveys indicate that loneliness is a regular feature of the lives of people of all ages, with estimated prevalence rates ranging from 5 percent to 32 percent (e.g., Masi *et al.* 2011). On top of this, researchers anticipate increases in loneliness in the US and other cultures who share certain population-level characteristics, including increased numbers of older adults, increased numbers of dual-career couples and single-person households, and reduced rates of fertility (Masi *et al.* 2011). Furthermore, there is even evidence that loneliness may spread through networks of friends and acquaintances, as if it were contagious (Cacioppo *et al.* 2009).

Taking seriously the idea that loneliness may be a complication faced by an increasing number of consumers, this chapter begins with a review of what psychologists and other researchers have learned about the experience of loneliness and its consequences. As this book focuses on consumer-brand relationships, we then explore how loneliness influences our consumption habits. We will consider in detail what consumer behavior researchers – including the authors of this chapter – have discovered about loneliness's effects, and we will end the chapter by using findings from psychology and marketing research to develop actionable insights for readers interested in better understanding how to reach lonely consumers. In sum, this chapter reviews the existing literature on loneliness and consumer behavior and describes a series of exploratory studies designed to better understand some of the links between loneliness and consumer-brand relationships.

The psychology of loneliness

Loneliness is an aversive feeling, typically resulting from the conclusion that we are not experiencing adequate levels of social connection or support. Its function can be conceptualized as a call to action – a signal for us to try to reach out to others – and some of us may be genetically predisposed to experience this signal more intensely than do others (Cacioppo *et al.* 2014). However, to understand the effects of the loneliness signal on consumer behavior, it is important to consider the consequences of the effects of loneliness on people's thinking.

A central aspect of the psychology of loneliness is its often intense influence on cognition, which, in turn, can have a powerful effect on moods. In particular, the feeling of loneliness may often lead to rumination – repetitive, generally unproductive thinking – about one's deficits in social support, social contact, or social competence. This kind of thinking appears to be an important link between loneliness and negative health outcomes, such as sad moods and sleep disruptions (Zawadzki *et al.* 2013). Underscoring this point, a recent analysis of 50 research studies showed that the most effective interventions for loneliness are those that focus on improving maladaptive ways of thinking (Masi *et al.* 2011). From this perspective, it makes sense to conceptualize loneliness as encompassing both the judgment that one's needs for social connection are not being met, as well as the many harmful effects that result from the conclusion that one's life no longer seems satisfying (Mellor *et al.* 2008).

Of course, the effects of loneliness are not limited to dissatisfaction with life: researchers have connected loneliness to smoking, problems with food and alcohol consumption, and decreased exercise (DeWall and Pond 2011; Miller 2011). Loneliness seems to predict disruptions with managing distress as well as with sleeping, both of which could lead to emotional and physical health difficulties (Cacioppo *et al.* 2002; Jaremka *et al.* 2013). In fact, among older adults, the effects of loneliness are such that it has been identified as a mortality risk (Newall *et al.* 2013; Steptoe *et al.* 2013).

Before considering the effects of loneliness on consumer behavior, it is important to note that the psychology of loneliness may be different at different stages of the human lifespan. For example, psychologists have emphasized different aspects of adolescents' experiences of loneliness compared to those of older adults; a meta-analysis of 149 studies involving older adults found that loneliness in that population was predicted by low social network quality, lack of contact with friends and neighbors, low socioeconomic status, living in a nursing home, and being a woman (Pinquart and Sörensen 2001).

In contrast, adolescent loneliness has been shown to be composed of both family-related loneliness and peer-related loneliness, with different predictors and outcomes associated with each type (Goossens *et al.* 2009; Teppers *et al.* 2014). Similarly, shyness may play an important role in adolescent loneliness (Woodhouse *et al.* 2012), in a way that is not reflected in the loneliness of older adults. For reasons like these, as we shift our focus to the influence of loneliness on consumer behavior, we should remember that loneliness may have different consequences for adolescent consumers than it does for older adult consumers.

Loneliness and consumer behavior

Marketing researchers have identified several specific types of effects of loneliness on consumer behavior. For example, one area of research has examined differences between lonely and non-lonely consumers' ways of shopping for and consuming goods and services. There is evidence that lonely consumers use the shopping experience in a compensatory way; for them, shopping may be an attempt to fulfill interpersonal needs that are unmet in other aspects of their lives (Lastovicka and Sirianni 2011). Specifically, certain lonely consumers may rely on shopping experiences to generate social interaction. Automated experiences (e.g., self-service checkouts) in a retail environment appear to have a particularly negative impact on lonely consumers' shopping satisfaction (Forman and Sriram 1991), presumably because it deprives them of desired social contact. Similarly, a survey of older consumers found that feelings of loneliness predicted patterns of shopping behavior: compared to non-lonely older consumers, lonely older consumers were more likely to use a mall shopping environment for diversion and aesthetic purposes, as well as to fulfill basic consumer needs, such as eating or the consumption of services (e.g., by using mall-based hair salons and banks [Kim *et al.* 2005]).

Other research has shown that consumption of or perceived connection to consumer objects may help individuals combat the negative psychological effects of loneliness. For example, loneliness has been found to prompt a sense of social connection with non-human entities, including consumer objects (e.g., alarm clocks, pillows [Epley *et al.* 2008]). Furthermore, among individuals with a positive relationship history (i.e., who generally experience relationship security), consumption of comfort food can buffer against feelings of loneliness in response to threats of social rejection (Troisi and Gabriel 2011). Both of these findings suggest that consumer goods may offer a protective function against the negative feelings of disconnection that often accompany loneliness.

A third research stream has investigated the different types of products that lonely vs. non-lonely consumers seek out. For example, when lonely consumers are allowed to express their preferences without social scrutiny, they distance themselves from products endorsed by the majority of consumers and gravitate toward products endorsed by a minority of consumers (Wang *et al.* 2012). It appears that lonely consumers are relatively uninterested in the majority-endorsed products because these seemingly popular products do not fit with their feelings of loneliness. Thus, lonely consumers seem unable or unwilling to connect with products embraced by a social environment from which they feel distant. A related recent study examined how researcher-induced feelings of loneliness influence consumers' product preference and choice (Wan *et al.* 2014). The results show that, when socially excluded consumers perceive the cause of their exclusion as unchanging (vs. temporary), they are more likely to perceive themselves as unique, which then leads them to choose distinct or unique products. Both of these sets of studies converge upon the conclusion that lonely consumers are drawn to products that are different than those used or proposed by the majority; the outcomes in both cases are choices that deviate from the norm.

Taken together, these three areas of research suggest that lonely consumers could use the consumption process, perceived connection with objects of consumption, or particular types of product choice to try to cope with some of the negative psychological consequences of loneliness. As documented by the research findings presented above, it is not inconceivable that shopping and other more general aspects of the consumption process can temporarily relieve feelings associated with loneliness. However, as a continued strategy across time, consumption behavior in itself is perhaps a sub-optimal solution. A recently-published six-year longitudinal study tracked the evolution of consumers' loneliness and materialism across time (Pieters 2013). This research found evidence that loneliness and materialism reinforce one another over time, placing consumers in a "material trap" in which materialism leads to loneliness, which, in turn, often leads to greater materialism. Furthermore, loneliness appeared to have a greater influence on subsequent materialism than the other way around. Based on these findings, one would be hesitant to recommend a prescription of "retail therapy" (e.g., Atalay and Meloy 2011) to cure consumers of their feelings of loneliness in a lasting way!

Our research on loneliness and consumer-brand relationships

Shopping and consumption may not be long-term cures for loneliness, but it is clear that shopping for, consumption of, and connection with goods and services are strategies that consumers may use to try to manage the effects of loneliness. This idea – paired with the fact that loneliness seems to be increasing in prevalence across several demographic categories – suggests that marketers could benefit from increased understanding of the specific effects of loneliness on consumer choice. As noted earlier, researchers have shown that lonely consumers appear particularly disinterested in making choices that fit in with or conform to the majority of people's preferences. However, those studies seemed to focus on the effects of loneliness on one-time consumption choices and not on repeat-purchase opportunities with customers' previously preferred brands. To learn more about how loneliness might influence consumers' perceptions of favored brands, we designed a series of exploratory studies in which we induced feelings of loneliness and social isolation in consumers; then, we assessed their attitudes toward brands that they had nominated as having been helpful to them.

Before conducting our first study, we were unsure of what results to expect. On the one hand, we were familiar with the research reviewed above that suggests that lonely people seek connection even with non-human entities and physical objects. To us, that research indicated that lonely consumers could perhaps demonstrate particular loyalty to brands that had forged an enduring positive presence in their lives.

On the other hand, we were aware of the possibility that negative feelings associated with loneliness might spill over into lonely consumers' evaluations of even familiar brands. However, we knew that Wang and colleagues (2012) had explained lonely consumers' relative disinterest in majority-endorsed products by arguing that popular-seeming products may seem incongruous with feelings of loneliness. At least in their case, these effects were not accounted for by consumers' level of depression or desire for uniqueness. Instead, it appears that the lonely consumers felt unable or unwilling to connect with products embraced by a social environment from which they felt distant.

Rather than identifying a connection with brands as compensation for loneliness, Wang and colleagues' results suggest that lonely consumers' evaluations are influenced by feelings of disconnection: How well does this product or brand fit with current feelings of relative isolation? In this way – as we explain below – we found that lonely consumers in our studies evaluated their regularly used brands more negatively than did non-lonely consumers. In four separate exploratory studies, we found evidence that loneliness-primed consumers felt less connected to familiar and helpful brands or products.

Study 1

Across our studies, we activated consumers' feelings of loneliness using three different methods: a computer game (Study 1), subliminal primes (Study 2), and the manipulated results of a personality measure (Studies 3 and 4). For each study, university student participants completed all tasks individually in a laboratory on computers set in private cubicles. In Study 1, participants were told that they would complete two unrelated tasks: a "Cyberball" task and a brand rating task.

The Cyberball task was a virtual ball-tossing game featuring four characters, one of which was controlled by the participant. The task, which is widely used in research on social exclusion, allows participants to use computer keys to designate to which of the three computer-controlled characters their character would toss the ball (Williams and Jarvis 2006). Their character then waits until it receives the ball again before the participant is once more asked to choose to whom to toss the ball. In the social exclusion version of the task, the participant receives the ball only three times before the computer-controlled characters target the remaining approximately 25 throws exclusively at one another. In the non-exclusion version, the participants' character receives the ball regularly. Across many studies (e.g., Williams 2007), the social exclusion condition has been shown to generate negative emotional responses consistent with effects of interpersonal social exclusion.

Following the Cyberball task, participants were presented with the brand rating task. First, on-screen instructions directed them to type the name of a brand that was important to them. Specifically, they were instructed that the brand should be meaningful to them, used every day, and have an impact on their daily life.

After choosing a brand, participants rated their closeness to the brand using a measure of brand engagement in self-concept (BESC; Sprott *et al.* 2009). This scale assesses the degree to which consumers incorporate brands into their self-concept. Items include "I have a special bond with the brands I like" and "I consider my favorite brands to be a part of myself." We modified the items to target the participants' selected brands (e.g., "I have a special bond with the brand I selected").

When we calculated the scale scores, we found that participants in the social exclusion condition subsequently indicated significantly less BESC than did participants in the non-exclusion condition.

Study 2

Study 2 was in most respects identical to Study 1; however, we wanted to find out if the results of Study 1 would generalize to new methods and measures, so Study 2 used a subliminal priming task in place of the Cyberball task, and a general evaluation of brand attitude as part of the brand rating task.

Here, participants were told that their participation would entail completion of two unrelated tasks: a "cognitive" task and a brand rating task. The first task was a subliminal loneliness priming procedure adapted from a similar task developed by Arndt and colleagues (1997) and was presented to participants as a computer-based "Word-Relation Task." The task presented participants with two emotionally-neutral words, like "LETTUCE" and "CALCULATOR," and instructed participants to respond by pressing a certain key if they felt the words seemed related, or a different key if they felt the words seemed unrelated. Participants did not know that for the 27 milliseconds between the two words of each pair, they were exposed subliminally to a third word. For 15 trials, half the participants were exposed to the word "ALONE," intended to activate concepts relevant to loneliness, and the other half saw the word "TABLE," intended to activate concepts unrelated to social concerns. When masked by the words that preceded and followed the primes, 27 milliseconds is sufficient time to allow for non-conscious perception of the primes but is insufficient for conscious recognition.

Following the priming task, participants were presented with the brand selection instructions from Study 1. After selecting a brand, participants rated their attitude toward to this brand (Crites *et al.* 1994). Participants indicated their evaluations along four dimensions: positive/negative, like/dislike, good/bad, and desirable/undesirable.

Mirroring the results of Study 1, participants subliminally primed with "ALONE" subsequently indicated significantly less positivity toward their selected brands than did participants who were primed with "TABLE."

Study 3

To further extend the findings of Studies 1 and 2, Study 3 incorporated a new method to manipulate feelings of loneliness – false feedback on a personality measure – and it incorporated a measure of brand loyalty.

Participants were told that their participation would entail completion of two unrelated tasks: a personality measure and a brand rating task. The first task was an adaptation of a loneliness activation procedure developed by Wildschut *et al.* (2006), presenting participants with either of two versions of a 10-item "Southampton Loneliness Scale" to complete. In the heightened-loneliness condition, the items were worded to promote participant agreement (e.g., "I sometimes feel alone"), and no matter the participants' responses, each participant received the following feedback: "Your responses place you at the 67th percentile of the loneliness distribution at [your university] (i.e., you scored higher than 67 percent of your peers). This indicates that you are well above average on loneliness compared with other undergraduates [here]." Participants in this condition were then asked to list three reasons why they scored well above average in loneliness.

In the low-loneliness condition, the items were worded to reduce participant agreement (e.g., "I always feel alone"), and no matter the participants' responses, each participant received the following feedback: "Your responses place you at the 12th percentile of the loneliness distribution at [your university] (i.e., you scored lower than 88 percent of your peers). This indicates that you are very low on loneliness compared with other undergraduates [here]." Participants in this condition were then asked to list three reasons why they scored very low in loneliness.

Following the personality feedback, participants were presented with the brand selection instructions used in Studies 1 and 2. After selecting a brand, participants rated their attitude toward to this brand according to the measure used in Study 2. Then, they completed a brief measure of brand loyalty (Chaudhuri and Holbrook 2001). Items included: "I intend to keep purchasing this brand as long as it is available" and "I feel committed to this brand."

Similar to Study 2, participants in the heightened-loneliness condition indicated significantly less positivity toward their selected brands than did participants in the low-loneliness condition. In addition, participants in the heightened-loneliness condition indicated significantly less loyalty toward their selected brands than did participants in the low-loneliness condition.

Study 4

For Study 4, we wanted to get a sense of whether the findings from the first three studies would generalize to any brand or if they were limited to brands that participants found personally useful. As in Study 3, participants were told that their participation would entail completion of two unrelated tasks: a personality measure and a brand rating task. The first task was the loneliness priming procedure modified from Wildschut *et al.* (2006), presenting participants with either the heightened-loneliness or low-loneliness version of the 10-item personality scale.

However, following the personality task, participants were presented with a new set of brand selection instructions. This time participants were instructed to list two brands about which they had a positive opinion. Specifically, they were asked to list the name of a brand of shoes that helps them achieve the goal of being physically fit. Then, they were asked to list the name of a brand that helps other people – but not them – achieve the goal of being physically fit.

Next, approximately half of the participants from each loneliness condition were randomly assigned to use the BESC measure from Study 2 to rate their closeness to the brand that helped them (i.e., their instrumental brand). The remaining participants from each loneliness condition were randomly assigned to complete the BESC measure with respect to the brand that helped others (i.e., their non-instrumental brand).

As would be expected, we found that participants showed a higher BESC for brands that had helped them rather than for non-instrumental brands. More importantly, though, we also found that for the instrumental brands, the loneliness feedback led to significantly lower BESC, but it had no effect on BESC for non-instrumental brands. This result suggests that at least some effects of loneliness are negative, but that these effects may not apply to consumers' evaluation of every brand.

Synthesis and managerial implications

Research summary and synthesis

Loneliness is an aversive feeling which typically results from the assessment that one is not experiencing sufficient levels of social connection or support. A large body of psychological research has documented relationships between loneliness and reduced psychological and physical health. While psychologists have focused largely on the clinical, cognitive, and social implications of loneliness, marketing researchers have revealed some basic associations among loneliness and different aspects of consumer behavior. First, consumer behavior research on loneliness suggests that lonely consumers use the shopping experience to fulfill interpersonal needs that are otherwise unmet in their lives. Indeed, interpersonal contact made through the shopping experience appears to be an important benefit of shopping behavior for lonely consumers. Second, consumption behavior can potentially help combat the negative psychological feelings produced by loneliness. Specifically, research suggests that lonely consumers can seek connection with and gain some comfort from consumer objects in order to combat feelings of disconnection that are provoked by loneliness. Finally, some consumer behavior research suggests that lonely consumers are more likely to prefer and choose products that deviate from the norm.

The focus of this book is consumer-brand relationships, and, in contrast to previous research reviewed above, the original research we present in this chapter speaks to the links between loneliness and consumer-brand relationships. Although we view our current findings as somewhat exploratory, the results of the studies we have conducted all seem to point in the same direction. In Studies 1, 2, and 3, activating feelings of loneliness led consumers to evidence lower brand engagement in the self-concept, brand attitude, and brand loyalty. In Study 4, we found evidence that the effect of loneliness is particularly negative for brands that a consumer has used successfully, and that it may not impact brands with which the consumer does not have an established relationship. It is noteworthy that the primary finding of these studies – that loneliness leads consumers to give more negative evaluations of preferred brands – was robust across different manipulations of loneliness and different measures of brand evaluation. Furthermore, the results of Study 4 give some indication of a potential boundary condition of the loneliness-brand evaluation link. Specifically, lonely consumers evidenced reduced self-brand connections only with brands that were useful to them (i.e., that allowed them to achieve a desired goal). In a similar manner to that evidenced for personal relationships, loneliness seems to cause disruption or distance between consumers and brands (or people) with whom they have a satisfying, pre-existing relationship.

In this way, our research is generally consistent with existing psychological research on the interpersonal implications of loneliness. While the psychological literature suggests that, for some people, loneliness can result from individuals' tendency to withdraw from interpersonal contact (cf., Watson and Nesdale 2012), our research on loneliness and consumer-brand relationships suggests that loneliness can lead consumers to take greater distance from brands with which they have an existing relationship.

Managerial implications

A first implication of the existing research on loneliness and consumer behavior suggests that marketers understand the social motivations that are inherent in the shopping experience. Indeed, particularly for lonely consumers, the social interaction that the shopping experience entails can be an important driver of shopping behavior. This suggests that marketers and managers should be especially attentive to specific interpersonal aspects of service employees' interactions with customers. Given that certain demographic groups (e.g., older adults, shut-ins, or single-person households) may be more likely to be lonely, extra care and interpersonal attention can be paid to enhance the shopping experience and increase customer satisfaction for businesses that serve these consumers.

In addition, the research we conducted has implications for marketing and communication strategies for target groups who are likely to be lonely. Our research on loneliness and consumer-brand relationships suggests that such populations are likely to take psychological and attitudinal distance from familiar or favored brands. Marketers can perhaps engage in specific communication strategies with these populations – for example, relational marketing strategies that emphasize connection with and support for consumers –in order to guard against consumer withdrawal. It may be that, if particular brands provide lonely consumers a feeling of potential connectedness, such consumers may respond to those brands' efforts with a willingness to maintain and even enhance existing brand relationships.

In sum, a great deal of research from across the field of marketing has shown that the relationships people have with brands can have many of the same qualities as human interpersonal relationships, and our research on loneliness and consumer-brand relationships is no exception. Echoing research on the psychological implications of loneliness, our work shows how, under circumstances of loneliness, consumer-brand relationships can suffer. An important take-home message of the current research, and indeed much of the research discussed in this book, is that consumers' relationships with brands share a strong similarity with consumers' relationships with other people.

References

Arndt, J., J. Greenberg, T. Pyszczynski, and S. Solomon (1997) "Subliminal Exposure to Death-Related Stimuli Increases Defense of the Cultural Worldview", *Psychological Science*, 8 (5): 379–385.

Atalay, A.S. and M.G. Meloy (2011) "Retail Therapy: A Strategic Effort to Improve Mood", *Psychology and Marketing*, 28 (6): 638–660.

Cacioppo, J.T., S. Cacioppo, and D.I. Boomsma (2014) "Evolutionary Mechanisms for Loneliness", *Cognition and Emotion*, 28 (1): 3–21.

Cacioppo, J.T., J.H. Fowler, and N.A. Christakis (2009) "Alone in the Crowd: The Structure and Spread of Loneliness in a Large Social Network", *Journal of Personality and Social Psychology*, 97 (6): 977–991.

Cacioppo, J.T., L.C. Hawkley, L.E. Crawford, J.M. Ernst, M.H. Burleson, R.B. Kowalewski, W.B. Malarkey, E. Van Cauter, and G.G. Bernston (2002) "Loneliness and Health: Potential Mechanisms", *Psychosomatic Medicine*, 64 (3): 407–417.

Chaudhuri, A. and M.B. Holbrook (2001) "The Chain of Effects from Brand Trust and Brand Affect to Brand Performance: The Role of Brand Loyalty", *Journal of Marketing*, 65 (2): 81–93.

Crites, S.L., L.R. Fabrigar, and R.E. Petty (1994) "Measuring the Affective and Cognitive Properties of Attitudes: Conceptual and Methodological Issues", *Personality and Social Psychology Bulletin*, 20 (6): 619–634.

DeWall, C.N. and R.S. Pond (2011) "Loneliness and Smoking: The Costs of the Desire to Reconnect", *Self and Identity*, 10 (3): 375–385.

Epley, N., S. Akalis, A. Waytz, and J.T. Cacioppo (2008) "Creating Social Connection through Inferential Reproduction", *Psychological Science*, 19 (2): 114–120.

Forman, A.M. and V. Sriram (1991) "The Depersonalization of Retailing: Its Impact on the 'Lonely' Consumer", *Journal of Retailing*, 67 (2): 226–243.

Goossens, L., M. Lasgaard, K. Luyckx, J. Vanhalst, S. Mathias, and E. Masy (2009) "Loneliness and Solitude in Adolescence: A Confirmatory Factor Analysis of Alternative Models", *Personality and Individual Differences*, 47 (8): 890–894.

Jaremka, L.M., C.P. Fagundes, R. Glaser, J.M. Bennett, W.B. Malarkey, and J.K. Kiecolt-Glaser (2013) "Loneliness Predicts Pain, Depression, and Fatigue: Understanding the Role of Immune Dysregulation", *Psychoneuroendocrinology*, 38 (8): 1310–1317.

Kim, Y., J. Kang, and M. Kim (2005) "The Relationships among Family and Social Interaction, Loneliness, Mall Shopping Motivation, and Mall Spending of Older Consumers", *Psychology and Marketing*, 22 (12): 995–1015.

Lastovicka, J.L. and N.J. Sirianni (2011) "Truly, Madly, Deeply: Consumers in the Throes of Material Possession Love", *Journal of Consumer Research*, 38 (2): 323–342.

Masi, C.M., H. Chen, L.C. Hawkley, and J.T. Cacioppo (2011) "A Meta-Analysis of Interventions to Reduce Loneliness", *Personality and Social Psychology Review*, 15 (3): 219–266.

Mellor, D., M. Stokes, L. Firth, Y. Hayashi, and R. Cummins (2008) "Need for Belonging, Relationship Satisfaction, Loneliness, and Life Satisfaction", *Personality and Individual Differences*, 45 (3): 213–218.

Miller, G. (2011) "Why Loneliness is Hazardous to your Health", *Science*, 331 (1): 138–140.

Newall, N.E., J.G. Chipperfield, D.S. Bailis, and T.L. Stewart (2013) "Consequences of Loneliness on Physical Activity and Mortality in Older Adults and the Power of Positive Emotions", *Health Psychology*, 32 (8): 921–924.

Pieters, S. (2013) "Bidirectional Dynamics of Materialism and Loneliness: Not Just a Vicious Cycle", *Journal of Consumer Research*, 40 (4): 615–631.

Pinquart, M. and S. Sörensen (2001) "Influences on Loneliness in Older Adults: A Meta-Analysis", *Basic and Applied Social Psychology*, 23 (4): 245–266.

Sprott, D., S. Czellar, and E. Spangenberg (2009) "The Importance of a General Measure of Brand Engagement on Market Behavior: Development and Validation of a Scale", *Journal of Marketing Research*, 46 (1): 92–104.

Steptoe, A., A. Shankar, P. Demakakos, and J. Wardle (2013) "Social Isolation, Loneliness, and All-Cause Mortality in Older Men and Women", *Proceedings of the National Academy of Sciences of the United States of America*, 110 (15): 5797–5801.

Teppers, E., K. Luyckx, T.A. Klimstra, and L. Goossens (2014) "Loneliness and Facebook Motives in Adolescence: A Longitudinal Inquiry into Directionality of Effect", *Journal of Adolescence*, 37 (5): 691–699, www.sciencedirect.com/science/article/pii/S014019711300167X, accessed April 28, 2014.

Troisi, J.D. and S. Gabriel (2011) "Chicken Soup Really is Good for the Soul. 'Comfort Food' Fulfills the Need to Belong", *Psychological Science*, 22 (6): 747–753.

Wan, E.W., J. Xu, and Y. Ding (2014) "To Be or Not To Be Unique? The Effect of Social Exclusion on Consumer Choice", *Journal of Consumer Research*, 40 (6): 1109–1122.

Wang, J., R. Zhu, and B. Shiv (2012) "The Lonely Consumer: Loner or Conformer?", *Journal of Consumer Research*, 22 (6): 1116–1128.

Watson, J. and D. Nesdale (2012) "Rejection Sensitivity, Social Withdrawal, and Loneliness in Young Adults", *Journal of Applied Social Psychology*, 42 (8): 1984–2005.

Wildschut, T., C. Sedikides, J. Arndt, and C. Routledge (2006) "Nostalgia: Content, Triggers, Functions", *Journal of Personality and Social Psychology*, 91 (5): 975–993.

Williams, K.D. (2007) "Ostracism: The Kiss of Social Death", *Social and Personality Psychology Compass*, 1 (1): 236–247.

Williams, K.D. and B. Jarvis (2006) "Cyberball: A Program for Use in Research on Interpersonal Ostracism and Acceptance", *Behavior Research Methods*, 38 (1): 174–180.

Woodhouse, S.S., M.J. Dykas, and J. Cassidy (2012) "Loneliness and Peer Relations in Adolescence", *Social Development*, 21 (2): 273–293.

Zawadzki, M.J., J.E. Graham, and W. Gerin (2013) "Rumination and Anxiety Mediate the Effect of Loneliness on Depressed Mood and Sleep Quality in College Students", *Health Psychology*, 32 (2): 212–222.

7

IDENTITY DEGRADING BRANDS

Zeynep Arsel and Scott Stewart

Brands are complex symbolic sources that serve multiple constituencies (Diamond *et al.* 2009; Levy 1959). For consumers, they serve as resources for individual identity management and expression strategies (Holt 2004; Holt 2002). This resource capacity of a brand lies in its power to harbor narratives that help one to build and express a coherent sense of self (Arnould and Thompson 2005). Additionally, brands serve as publicly visible cues to signal identity (Berger and Ward 2010) when people actively engage in impression management (Goffman 1959). As a result, people develop bonds with their brands similarly to the ways they form relationships with other humans (Fournier 1998). For example, one could have a bond akin to a childhood friendship, as in the case of someone who uses Estée Lauder, because the brand evokes nostalgic memories of their mother (Fournier 1998). These relationship types vary from love (Batra *et al.* 2011), to symbiotic partnerships, to dysfunctional secret affairs.

Whereas the use of brands as symbols to build, express, and signal identities in constructive and co-constitutive contexts has been discussed thoroughly within academic literature, little has been written on cases of dysfunctional relationships. Specifically, except for Kozinets' (2001) depiction of the stigmatization of the Star Trek fan community, and members' subsequent legitimization efforts, situations of people discovering themselves in relationships where the brand's meaning system is perceived as identity degrading are understudied. When brand meanings are identity enhancing, the brand serves its identity purpose: people benefit from using them as favorable resources for their identity projects and desirable social signals. However, if they are identity degrading or stigmatized, these meanings could actually hurt the identity goals of the owners. In this chapter, we investigate the latter, and inquire about the ways individuals relate to brands that they have a strong relationship with, despite subjectively perceiving them as identity degrading.

Unpacking brand-identity connections

Consumption is a vehicle for self-presentation, especially for high self monitors (Graeff 1996; Kim *et al.* 2009). Three decades ago, Solomon (1983) argued that consumers reflexively evaluate product symbolism to socially perform their identities. While doing this, they frequently rely on what Cooley (1902) calls the *looking glass self*, the process by which individuals reflexively appraise themselves from the perspective of another. Frequently, they role-play from another's position to discern how others see them (Mead 1934). This reflective appraisal also facilitates the formation of one's self-concept (Felson 1985) and is used in performing social roles through consumption (Solomon 1983) and signaling social boundaries. This performance-based view is further theorized by Han *et al.* (2010) who suggest a differential status signaling model. For example, well-off individuals with low status needs prefer subtle signals, such as esoteric designs and invisible logos. This finding is also supported by Berger and Ward (2010), who demonstrate how people show off to others in their own strata and dissociate themselves from lower classes. However, people with high need for status and low economic resources prefer to use loud signals to associate themselves with higher classes while dissociating themselves from other unwealthy consumers (Han *et al.* 2010). Other researchers demonstrate that consumers forge connections with brands to serve their identity projects and align their selves with ingroups (Escalas and Bettman 2005). Similarly, Thompson, Rindfleisch, and Arsel (2006) show how brands provide authenticating narratives for consumers' identity projects through marking symbolic distinctions. But beyond signaling and boundarymaking, brands also infiltrate deeper into our identities by serving as identity-building narratives.

According to Holt (2004), identity value is a component of a brand that helps people to use it for self-expression. He describes the value as a symbolic salve that provides solutions to significant and collectivized anxieties in a society (Holt 2004; Holt 2006). The mass-mediated meaning systems or brand mythologies that circulate in the marketplace (Cayla and Eckhardt 2008; Diamond *et al.* 2009; Giesler 2012; Thompson and Arsel 2004) frequently intersect with broader sociocultural forces and emerge as complex and compelling sociocultural resources. In return, these resources filter into consumer interpretive strategies, such as using brand meanings to assert national identities (Dong and Tian 2009) or manage moral conflicts (Luedicke *et al.* 2010). For example, in the latter case, people use the Hummer brand and its mythology to support their moralistic narratives of American exceptionalism and individualism. Similarly, brands provide symbolic blankets to assuage existential insecurities (Rindfleisch *et al.* 2009) or resolve identity contradictions (Holt and Thompson 2004). Lastly, extending from dyadic constitutions, these connections can be further embedded into social networks that bolster consumer-brand connections, as well as human sociality (Muniz and O'Guinn 2001; Rindfleisch *et al.* 2009; Schau *et al.* 2009; Schouten and McAlexander 1995). Cova (1997) suggests that brands possess a *linking* function that serves to foster connections between members of the society. In existing literature, this link is depicted in a range from weak ties, such as corporate imposed communities (McAlexander *et al.* 2002), to the quasi-religious experience of brand cults like that of Apple (Belk and Tumbat 2005; Muñiz and Schau 2005).

One tenet that is taken from this body of research is that these strong communal, affective and identity-enhancing bonds are integrated into one's self in an enduring fashion (Batra *et al.* 2011; Belk 1988). Thus, they are fairly inalienable and contingent on the culturally constituted meanings associated with a brand that relationally transfer to the consumer, regardless of the valence of these meanings (Arsel and Thompson 2011). For example, when their favorite brands do not perform well, or are publicly criticized, consumers' self-concepts are impaired (Cheng *et al.* 2011). Given the fact that brand meanings are created by a range of social actors, most of whom are outside managerial control (Thompson *et al.* 2006), and layered in a complex and intertextual gestalt (Diamond *et al.* 2009), how do people relate to brands that they perceive as identity degrading, and how do they further manage these brand-mediated meanings to pursue their identity goals?

Apple: a case study

To illustrate our point, we take the Apple brand and its consumers as a case. Apple has become increasingly popular within the past decade, climbing to the top of the world's most valuable brands list (Millward Brown 2012). It often garners unparalleled media attention, leading to a strong presence in the popular culture. Furthermore, Apple is what Han *et al.* (2010: 15) label as a *prominent* brand, one that "has visible markings that help ensure observers recognize [it]." Finally, Apple has a history of strong identity-based relationships (Muñiz and Schau 2005; Park *et al.* 2010) that are frequently compared to cultish devotion (Belk and Tumbat 2005), perhaps best exemplified by mass mourning and grieving after the co-founder Steve Jobs' passing (Penenberg 2011). At the same time, Apple has also attracted a lot of criticism and parody, and generated its own doppelganger image (Giesler 2012; Thompson *et al.* 2006). We suggest that these characteristics provide us with an excellent opportunity to pursue our inquiry.

Our data predominantly consists of in-depth interviews with consumers of Apple products. We recruited 13 Apple users through online calls for participation. The salience of the brand to our participants' identities was further confirmed during the interview process. The interviews either took place in person, or through videoconference in cases where the participants were not local. Interviews were semi-structured, which allowed the researcher to enter the interview with a premeditated schedule of discussion, but also granted the freedom to discuss topics conversationally. The dialogue started with basic background questions and then evolved into ones that focused on experiences related to Apple, as well as meanings and anecdotes about the brand's use in public. The recordings amounted to 146,936 words of transcribed data.

Interviews were interpreted through a hermeneutical process (Thompson 1997). Through the data collection and analysis processes, we also conducted passive netnography (Kozinets 2010) in Apple online communities and familiarized ourselves with the fan discourses. This familiarization was integral to our analysis, and it enabled us to enter interview situations with insider knowledge, build easier rapport, and understand the references made by the study participants. We analyzed the interviews in multiple iterations. First, we performed idiographic analysis of each interview transcript focusing on brand-identity connections (Fournier 1998). This was followed by a cross-participant analysis, repeatedly revisiting individual interviews. The back-and-forth iterative analysis was continued until we reached theoretical clarity.

Apple's identity degrading meanings

Apple, which started as an underdog brand (Paharia *et al.* 2011) of modest origins, is now the most valuable brand in the world (Elliott 2013). The brand's meta-narrative also changed from a revolutionary (as expressed in its classic *1984* Super Bowl ad) to a global Goliath with an escalating dark side (McLaughlin and Bridgman 2013). This dramatic evolution of the brand's popular image (Giesler 2012) has also filtered into how its consumers perceive the value it brings to their identities.

In our case, while some of our participants found Apple's identity value-enhancing, others' appraisals were not always positive. For these people, doppelganger images (Thompson *et al.* 2006) of Apple, as a product that is often associated with pretentious people, have infiltrated into their brand-mediated self-appraisals. As a result, they develop confusion and ambivalence about what exactly they portray to others as a consumer of the company's products. This is the case of Brandon. Throughout his interview, Brandon continuously shows ambivalence about his brand-mediated identity:

> The way I saw Apple users, before I was an Apple user, was: really obsessed with the product. They are really stuck on themselves for using it. So even though I think I'd like people to think of me as Justin Long, I also worry that they think of me as a pompous asshole: "Look at me I have these Apple products for everyone to see, and think I am better than everyone because I have them."

Brandon's desire to be thought of as Justin Long is in reference to Apple's commercials in which a young and hip brand personification, played by actor Justin Long, mocks the middle-aged and square PC personification. Brandon is concerned that he would be mistaken for a pompous, arrogant, and smug person, the antithesis of the cool, easygoing, and creative Apple user that the company seeks to portray. Brandon worries that social observers view him negatively, not because he has received actual negative feedback, but because he himself viewed Apple users negatively prior to purchasing their products. When asked if he has ever heard about these assumptions from others, he responds: "Nobody ever says it to me; but because I thought that about other people, I assume people think that about me."

Roger thinks even more negatively of the Apple brand's identity reflections. When asked about his thoughts on other Apple users, he immediately starts to disengage himself from the stereotype:

> *Roger:* Well I don't think I'm a typical Apple user actually. It is a little disappointing in a way, how people kind of follow Apple blindly. Whenever Apple comes out with the latest thing, people are lined up around the corner all over the world to buy it. And I think that doesn't show a lot of critical judgment.
>
> *Interviewer:* Have you ever had people make that assumption about you?
>
> *Roger:* Yeah, for sure. If they see me using a Mac, people will make a quick judgment. So if they don't know me, then people will make that assumption. Doesn't happen that often, but if anyone makes a judgment, then that's pretty much what they assume; that's the demographic that everyone knows from the news and things like that. So I think that's just what they figure everyone is.
>
> *Interviewer:* How do you feel about it when you're lumped in like that?
>
> *Roger:* Well, I kind of feel that I would like to set the record straight.

Relationship with an identity degrading brand

So how do people manage their identities when they acknowledge that being associated with the brand has degrading effects on their identities? How do they set the record straight? Perhaps one assumption is that they will stop using this brand. However, if they already have strong existing relationships with the brand, even after considering the possibility that it does not signal an ideal image, they might not simply abandon it (Arsel and Thompson 2011). Rather, they strategically convert these negative appraisals into a sophisticated moral identity play; or they enter into a dysfunctional and dependent relationship with it.

Brand as a public moral pivot

Luedicke *et al.* (2010) have shown that brands can serve as central figures in moralistic identity work. Through confronting other consumer groups on the basis of morality, people not only derive identity value, but also reinforce symbolic distinctions. Whereas Luedicke *et al.* (2010) have shown how Hummer consumers use the brand as an embellishment for their moralistic identity play, our participants choose Apple as an oppositional target for their moral identity work, despite still consuming it. In other words, although consuming its products, they confront Apple's meaning system. This moralized dissociation is frequently framed as being immune to Apple's marketing communications, declaring personal sovereignty and distilling pure functional utility from products (Holt 2002). For example, Jason, who throughout the interview asserted that he uses Apple products for purely functional reasons, differentiates himself from the stereotypical gullible Apple consumer:

Interviewer: Is there a stereotypical Apple user from what you've seen, if you were to picture a person in your head?

Jason: Oh, yeah, totally. I believe a stereotypical Apple user would probably be a hipster. You're familiar with that term I'm guessing?

Interviewer: Yeah.

Jason: So out here in San Francisco, our hipsters, like hipsters everywhere, are unique in many ways. Our hipsters totally, have a $100 Bianchi bike, then change [it] into a fixed gear bike. They wear skinny jeans, they don't wear helmets, and they all have a chrome bag or a Timbuktu bag with, with a Mac in it. And like that's just them goin' around. Then they go to coffee shops, and go on IM and, you know, whatever. So, that would be the stereotypical Apple user.

When asked later if he feels misrepresented by these people, Jason refuses to play the identity game and declares, "If every single hipster bought that machine, I still probably would have bought the Mac product, because of what it was." While he ostensibly refuses to identify with the meaning system that the brand offers, he still subtly constructs identity value through the brand, albeit through an oppositional narrative. Whereas existing research has discussed how oppositional narratives are utilized by brand community members to reinforce consciousness of kind against the non-members (Muniz and O'Guinn 2001), in our case, our participants refuse to claim connections to other Apple users, and instead derive status from the lack of these connections. Roger, whom we quoted earlier regarding his assumptions of being mistaken as a shallow trend seeker, elaborates:

Interviewer: When you see these people on the news, or out there in [city of residence], does that affect you in any way? You were saying you're disappointed. Does that actually make you feel a connection to them at all?

Roger: When I say disappointed, I shouldn't. I guess that is making a judgment. But it's actually a different demographic than myself, or it feels like. I guess [I'm] disappointed in that I think just in general I think people should be a little more critical. Just sort of make informed decisions. I think that the people who are lined up around the corner: that's the face of Apple, and that's the demographic that Apple is, is definitely going for. I'm not the demographic they're going for. I'm not good business for that.

Convinced that the brand does not bring any desirable identity value to them, these participants choose to forge a symbolic distinction to the stereotypical user of the brand and its mass-mediated meaning system. Unlike Luedicke *et al.*'s (2010) Hummer consumers who use moral narratives around the brand as enhancing mythical embellishments in their moral identity play, our participants use Apple for a more counterintuitive expressive strategy. In this case, they disentangle the Apple mythology from the actual product, and dissociate themselves from its community. In the end, they constitute their identity through declaring who they are not – the typical superficial Apple user – thus drawing symbolic boundaries and deriving relational status through the process. In this process, Apple's meaning system serves as the pivotal hinge on which they rely.

Denying a failed relationship partner

The second strategy we identify is employed when a brand transgresses a relationship. Prior research has shown that not all brand transgressions result in dissolution of consumer-brand connections, and, in some cases, a transgression could serve to revive a fading relationship (Aaker *et al.* 2004). In our case, however, we show an even more striking pattern: denial of such transgressions. In these instances, consumers are trying to keep their relationship with the brand unscathed. For example, Stacy recounts how her MacBook failed irrecoverably, only a month after her warranty expired. However, rather than being frustrated with the malfunction, she considers herself lucky for having the funds available to purchase another one:

> I got a Mac in my first year, and it was the white plastic one. And then, literally like a month after my warranty ran out, it just exploded. Actually, [the] motherboard or something happened with it, and I went to Mac, and they were as nice as they could have been but there was nothing they could do. And I still don't know what the problem was, but I needed a new computer. It was lucky that I had like some money set aside, um … 'Cause I need to get a Mac again. I definitely had the decision to get, the same one that I had, or to get the new one.

Our participants disregard product failures in order to continue their connections with the Apple brand and maintain the identity value they derive from being a member of this community. Their willingness to disregard transgressions causes them to enter into a dysfunctional dependency relationship with the brand (Fournier 1998) reflected in their contradictory brand-related narratives. For example, throughout the interview, William insists that Apple is a high quality brand, only to negate this later in the interview:

> So an Apple user, an Apple fan, they understand that they're paying more, but they know they're paying more not just for nothing, not just because it has an Apple logo on it. They're paying more for the quality.
> [Later]
> My [Apple] Time Capsule literally just stopped working. I figured the hard drive crashed or some electronic failure. And this was probably about a year and a half after I had it. And it wasn't surprising because I knew they had some liability issues. Again, no company's perfect. Apple has made products periodically that have liability issues.

Brand as a secret relationship partner

The above examples demonstrate cases when the brand fails its users through some functional transgression. Our data also shows that symbolic transgressions occur when social observers make disparaging remarks about the brand's users. In these cases, Apple is not failing as a technology product, but rather failing as a provider for desirable identity meanings. Instead of fighting these criticisms and risking their social connections (or morally pivoting through them, while losing their brand identity-connections), our participants choose to treat the criticism as an invalid appraisal. Patrick elaborates:

> People will joke and say that you've drunk the Kool-Aid. You've joined the cult. You've got your Apple phone, you won't go back. They've got you, they've got you where they want you! But it's generally more in a joking sense, it's not anything where they're trying to be mean or discriminate that I'm an Apple person.
> [Later]
> I don't really buy into what other people think about, about my purchases. I bought it because I wanna use it. You're free to think whatever you want. And you can make up some elaborate story about how I have 700 iPhones at home, or 700 iPods 'cause I buy every revision that comes out. That's your opinion and you're entitled to it.

Here, despite outsiders' criticism of his unconditional loyalty, and despite transgressions from the brand, Patrick continues to bond with Apple. To manage their brand-mediated identities against disparaging comments, or to avoid being confronted by outsiders regarding their failed products, these participants isolate their brand use from the social observers. Brandon, whom we quoted earlier, admits that he tries "not to use [his] phone as much if those kinds of comments come out." For these participants, even though Apple is a strong relationship partner, it is a dysfunctional relationship they would rather keep secret from the observing others in an attempt to manage the cognitive dissonance arising from this transgression.

Discussion and considerations

In this chapter, we expand consumer-brand relationships to cases where the brand is perceived to be identity-degrading either due to its functional failure, or undesirable associations. We argue that extant literature does not adequately discuss such attachment types where consumer-brand bonds are dysfunctional. Furthermore, we extend the existing research that suggests that the brand gestalt incorporates a myriad of meanings (Diamond et al. 2009), including those that are disparaging (Thompson et al. 2006). We demonstrate that a brand's identity value to its consumer is not monolithic or universally enhancing, but rather, is interpreted through social context. These contextualized interpretations are further reformulated in complex consumer-brand relationships. Our findings also highlight how identity value – even when undesirable – is managed socially as a resource on which to capitalize.

The strategies we discuss also demonstrate how behaviors that are depicted in earlier studies serve distinct identity goals. First, we show how anti-brand moralism (Luedicke *et al.* 2010), in fact, serves to derive identity value from a brand, albeit through dissociation. Second, we show how disregard of brand transgressions (Aaker *et al.* 2004) or insistence of staying in dysfunctional dependent brand relationships (Fournier 1998), serve consumer identity goals: by denying the transgressions, such as product failures, individuals dissociate themselves from the undesirable associations that the brand carries.

Like all work, this piece comes with limitations. We start with a small sample and a unique case, but beyond methodological consideration, our space restrictions limit the scope of our discussion. Our aim in this chapter is to point to an underexplored aspect of consumer-brand relationships: that we do not always have functional and productive partnerships with brands, and that loyalty does not necessarily root itself via identity enhancing brand meanings. Opening a door for inquiry, we suggest a few considerations for researchers interested in future studies.

Our modest sample did not account for variations in interpersonal differences. For example, while differing levels of self-monitoring have been shown to affect how individuals behave in the presence of others, the construct is not measured in our study. We posit that self-monitoring tendencies can mediate these relationship styles. Another question that requires a more longitudinal approach concerns the turning point in a consumer-brand relationship trajectory when one becomes aware of these identity-disparaging meanings. We suggest that when people recognize these identity-disparaging meanings late in a relationship, they might feel locked in, or act in denial regarding these narratives. Whether they would ever gravitate towards identity degrading brands in earlier stages of relationships, despite negative meanings, is also an important question.

References

Aaker, J., S. Fournier, and S.A. Brasel (2004) "When Good Brands Do Bad", *Journal of Consumer Research*, 31 (1): 1–16.

Arnould, E.J. and C.J. Thompson (2005) "Consumer Culture Theory (CCT): Twenty Years of Research", *Journal of Consumer Research*, 31 (4): 868–882.

Arsel, Z. and C.J. Thompson (2011) "Demythologizing Consumption Practices: How Consumers Protect Their Field-Dependent Identity Investments from Devaluing Marketplace Myths", *Journal of Consumer Research*, 37 (5): 791–806.

Batra, R., A. Ahuvia, and R.P. Bagozzi (2011) "Brand Love", *Journal of Marketing*, 76 (2): 1–16.

Belk, R.W. (1988) "Possessions and the Extended Self", *Journal of Consumer Research*, 15 (2): 139–168.

Belk, R.W. and G. Tumbat (2005) "The Cult of Macintosh", *Consumption Markets and Culture*, 8 (3): 205–217.

Berger, J. and M. Ward (2010) "Subtle Signals of Inconspicuous Consumption", *Journal of Consumer Research*, 37 (4): 555–569

Cayla, J. and G.M. Eckhardt (2008) "Asian Brands and the Shaping of a Transnational Imagined Community", *Journal of Consumer Research*, 35 (2): 216–230.

Cheng, S.Y.Y., T. Barnett White, and L.N. Chaplin (2011) "The Effects of Self-Brand Connections on Responses to Brand Failure: A New Look at the Consumer-Brand Relationship", *Journal of Consumer Psychology*, 22 (2): 280–288.

Cooley, C.H. (1902) *Human Nature and the Social Order*. New York: C. Scribner's Sons.

Cova, B. (1997) "Community and Consumption: Towards a Definition of the 'Linking Value' of Product or Services", *European Journal of Marketing*, 31 (3): 297–316.

Diamond, N., J.F. Sherry, A.M. Muñiz, M.A. McGrath, R.V. Kozinets, and S. Borghini (2009) "American Girl and the Brand Gestalt: Closing the Loop on Sociocultural Branding Research", *Journal of Marketing*, 73 (3): 118–134.

Dong, L. and K. Tian (2009) "The Use of Western Brands in Asserting Chinese National Identity", *The Journal of Consumer Research*, 36 (3): 504–523.

Elliott, S. (2013) "Apple Passes Coca-Cola as Most Valuable Brand", *The New York Times*, September 29, 2013.

Escalas, J.E. and J.R. Bettman (2005) "Self Construal, Reference Groups, and Brand Meaning", *Journal of Consumer Research*, 32 (3): 378–389.

Felson, R.B. (1985) "Reflected Appraisal and the Development of Self", *Social Psychology Quarterly*, 48 (1): 71–78.

Fournier, S. (1998) "Consumers and Their Brands: Developing Relationship Theory in Consumer Research", *Journal of Consumer Research*, 24 (4): 343–373.

Giesler, M. (2012) "How Doppelgänger Brand Images Influence the Market Creation Process: Longitudinal Insights from the Rise of Botox Cosmetic", *Journal of Marketing*, 76 (6): 55–68.

Goffman, E. (1959) *The Presentation of Self in Everyday Life*. Garden City, NY: Doubleday Anchor.

Graeff, T.R. (1996) "Image Congruence Effects on Product Evaluations: The Role of Self-Monitoring and Public/Private Consumption", *Psychology and Marketing*, 13 (5): 481–499.

Han, Y.J., J.C. Nunes, and X. Dreze (2010) "Signaling Status with Luxury Goods: The Role of Brand Prominence", *Journal of Marketing*, 74 (4): 15–30.

Holt, D.B. (2002) "Why Do Brands Cause Trouble? A Dialectical Theory of Consumer Culture and Branding", *Journal of Consumer Research*, 29 (1): 70–91.

Holt, D.B. (2004), *How Brands Become Icons: The Principles of Cultural Branding*. Boston, MA: Harvard Business School Press.

Holt, D.B. (2006) "Jack Daniel's America", *Journal of Consumer Culture*, 6 (3): 355–377.

Holt, D.B. and C.J. Thompson (2004), "Man-of-Action Heroes: The Pursuit of Heroic Masculinity in Everyday Consumption", *Journal of Consumer Research*, 31 (2): 425–440.

Kim, H.M., S. Sen, and K. Wilcox (2009) "Why Do Consumers Buy Counterfeit Luxury Brands?", *Journal of Marketing Research*, 46 (2): 247–259.

Kozinets, R.V. (2001) "Utopian Enterprise: Articulating the Meanings of Star Trek's Culture of Consumption", *The Journal of Consumer Research*, 28 (1): 67–88.

Kozinets, R.V. (2010) *Netnography : Doing Ethnographic Research Online* (1st ed.). Los Angeles, CA: Sage Publications Ltd.

Levy, S.J. (1959) "Symbols for Sale", *Harvard Business Review*, 37 (March–April): 117–124.

Luedicke, M.K., C.J. Thompson, and M. Giesler (2010) "Consumer Identity Work as Moral Protagonism: How Myth and Ideology Animate a Brand Mediated Moral Conflict", *Journal of Consumer Research*, 36 (6): 1016–32.

McAlexander, J.H., J.W. Schouten, and H. Koenig (2002) "Building Brand Community", *Journal of Marketing*, 66 (1): 38–54.

McLaughlin, C. and T. Bridgman (2013) "Dark Side Competition: Apple and the Human Costs of Production", *Academy of Management Proceedings*, Academy of Management Meeting, January 2013 (Meeting Abstract Supplement) 18032.

Mead, G.H. (1934) *Mind, Self & Society from the Standpoint of a Social Behaviorist*. Chicago, IL: The University of Chicago Press.

Millward Brown (2012) "2012 BrandZ Top 100", www.millwardbrown.com/BrandZ/Top_100_Global_Brands.aspx, accessed June 28, 2012.

Muniz, A.M. and T.C. O'Guinn (2001) "Brand Community", *Journal of Consumer Research*, 27 (March): 412–432.

Muñiz, A.M. and H.J. Schau (2005) "Religiosity in the Abandoned Apple Newton Brand Community", *Journal of Consumer Research*, 31 (4): 737–747.

Paharia, N., A. Keinan, J. Avery, and J.B. Schor (2011) "The Underdog Effect: The Marketing of Disadvantage and Determination through Brand Biography", *Journal of Consumer Research*, 37 (5): 775–790.

Park, C.W., D.J. MacInnis, J. Priester, A.B. Eisingerich, and D. Iacobucci (2010) "Brand Attachment and Brand Attitude Strength: Conceptual and Empirical Differentiation of Two Critical Brand Equity Drivers", *Journal of Marketing*, 74 (6): 1–17.

Penenberg, A.L. (2011) "The Meaning Of Steve Jobs ", www.fastcompany.com/1786436/the-meaning-of-steve-jobs, accessed October 26, 2011.

Rindfleisch, A., J.E. Burroughs, and N. Wong (2009) "The Safety of Objects: Materialism, Existential Insecurity, and Brand Connection", *Journal of Consumer Research*, 36 (1): 1–16.

Schau, H.J., A.M. Muñiz, and E.J. Arnould (2009) "How Brand Community Practices Create Value", *Journal of Marketing*, 73 (5): 30–51.

Schouten, J.W. and J.H. McAlexander (1995) "Subcultures of Consumption: An Ethnography of the New Bikers", *Journal of Consumer Research*, 22 (1): 43–61.

Solomon, M.R. (1983) "The Role of Products as Social Stimuli: A Symbolic Interactionism Perspective", *Journal of Consumer Research*, 10 (3): 319–329.

Thompson, C.J. (1997) "Interpreting Consumers: A Hermeneutical Framework for Deriving Marketing Insights from the Texts of Consumers' Consumption Stories", *Journal of Marketing Research*, 34 (4): 438–455.

Thompson, C.J. and Z. Arsel (2004) "The Starbucks Brandscape and Consumers' (Anti-Corporate) Experiences of Glocalization", *Journal of Consumer Research*, 31 (3): 631–642

Thompson, C.J., A. Rindfleisch, and Z. Arsel (2006) "Emotional Branding and the Strategic Value of the Doppelganger Brand Image", *Journal of Marketing*, 70 (1): 50–64.

PART III

Humanizing and anthropomorphizing brands

8

BEFRIENDING MR. CLEAN

The role of anthropomorphism in consumer-brand relationships

Jing Wan and Pankaj Aggarwal

Introduction

Mr. Clean is a line of cleaning products owned by Procter and Gamble since 1958. Over the years, Mr. Clean has strengthened its human persona by appearing as the police officer "Grimefighter," as a "changed man" when a new formula was introduced, and most recently, in the 2013 "Origin" commercial, as someone who has been working hard from his childhood days to serve the cause of fighting grime to help others. This is just one example of a brand that has been given human form and characteristics with the implicit belief that endowing brands with such humanlike traits makes for a more successful brand performance in the marketplace (Aggarwal and McGill 2007; Shaffer 2014). Presumably, this is because consumers would be more likely to relate to the brand in a personalized manner and form relationships with it as if it was a human being. Understanding how and why consumers anthropomorphize products and brands sheds light on the efficacy of anthropomorphism as a marketing strategy and as a building block for the formation of brand relationships.

In this chapter, we review recent work in psychology and marketing to explore how and why anthropomorphizing brands affects the relationships that consumers form with brands. We then propose a theoretical model that a) links anthropomorphism and brand relationships, and b) offers directions for future investigation in this area.

Although marketers have long employed a number of differentiation tools, such as brand equity (Keller 1993), brand image (Park *et al.* 1986), and brand personality (Aaker 1997; Plummer 1985) to create and sustain strong brands, research in the past two decades has focused on a relatively novel yet potent phenomenon of brand differentiation: brand relationships (Fournier 1998). This line of research suggests that people sometimes form relationships with brands in much the same way they form relationships with other people in social contexts (Aggarwal 2004; Fournier 1998; Muniz and O'Guinn 2001). Seminal work by Fournier (1998) suggests that consumer-brand relationships traverse a wide spectrum of relationship types – from casual acquaintances, to close friendships, arranged marriages, committed partnerships, flings, one-night stands, and secret affairs. Other researchers have noted that the norms that underpin different types of relationships are unique, and depending on the relational type, consumers' evaluation of the brand will depend on whether the brand's actions are consistent with the norms of that particular type of relationship (Aggarwal 2004).

The relationship metaphor, borrowed from social psychology to gain insights into consumer behavior, has fascinated both researchers, as well as practitioners, resulting in a recent flurry of research activity in the area. It is interesting to note that most of the work in the area has focused on understanding the consequences of forming different relationship types, and often uses relationship types as a moderating factor to explain differences in consumer behavior. Surprisingly, however, research on consumer-brand relationships is relatively silent on the antecedents of different types of relationships, and how they are formed. Arguably, brand anthropomorphism is an important anteceding factor for the formation of consumer-brand relationships. Understanding why people tend to so easily view non-human entities as humanlike, and how this tendency affects the way brands are evaluated, can be very insightful, and help us to better understand the very interesting phenomenon of consumer-brand relationships.

What is anthropomorphism?

Although research on anthropomorphism in marketing only emerged within the last two decades, the concept of anthropomorphism extends back centuries. Some of the earliest evidence of anthropomorphism is an ancient sculpture from over 30,000 years ago, showing a human body with the head of a lion (Dalton 2003), suggesting that humans have long been imbuing non-human entities (e.g., a lion) with human attributes. The word anthropomorphism originates from the Greek words "anthropos" (human) and "morphe" (shape or form); that is, anthropomorphism is the phenomenon by which non-human entities are given human shape or form. Epley, Waytz and Cacioppo (2007: 864) note that anthropomorphism is the "tendency to imbue the real or imagined behavior of non-human agents with human-like characteristics, motivations, intentions, or emotions". Anthropomorphism pervades human judgment and is prevalent in almost all cultures and aspects of human life, particularly in religion, art, and storytelling.

Most religions (with the notable exceptions of Judaism and Islam) tend to reflect human form in the images of gods, goddesses, and other divine entities. The Greek philosopher Xenophanes famously said that if horses and cattle could depict their gods, their gods too would look like horses and cattle, respectively. It is not surprising, then, that anthropologists like Guthrie (1993) suggest that anthropomorphism is a phenomenon that comes very naturally and easily to humans, and that the human brain has an innate tendency to see the "human" in natural phenomenon and events. Anthropomorphism also pervades literature across diverse cultures such as the Indian *Panchatantra* and the Greek *Aesop's Fables* – both of which are collection of stories about anthropomorphized animals that highlight useful everyday principles of life. More recent classics, such as *Alice in Wonderland* and *The Jungle Book*, and the popularity of movies like *The Lion King*, as well as the variety of Disney characters, such as Mickey Mouse and Donald Duck, also highlight the pervasiveness of anthropomorphism in literature and art.

Anthropomorphism is pervasive in our modern day life in part due to the numerous ways in which marketers often encourage consumers to see their products and brands as humans by imbuing brands with human-like personalities and imagery (Aaker 1997; Biel 2000). There are countless examples of anthropomorphized representations of brands, such as Mr. Peanut, Tony the Tiger, the Michelin Man, the Pillsbury Doughboy, or the Geico Gecko. Brands are even given names that strongly signal specific roles and familial relationships, such as Aunt Jemima, Uncle Ben's or Dr. Pepper. All this is done presumably to make the brands more endearing and desirable to consumers and ultimately to entice consumers to choose these brands over others. It is not surprising then that consumers are able to form a variety of different relationships with brands – relationships that range from casual acquaintances, to close friendships, committed partnerships, flings, and one-night stands (Fournier 1998). These types of relationships that consumers form with brands necessitate that the consumers first perceive the brand as human-like or possessing human-like qualities. After all, what would it mean to form a close friendship with a brand if the consumer does not perceive the brand to possess qualities similar to that of human friends? Indeed, it is likely that imbuing a brand with human traits activates a human schema, which then increases the likelihood of anthropomorphizing the brand (i.e., a consumer is then more likely to perceive the brand as a complete human). Subsequently, if the brand is seen as a person, it is more likely that a consumer will form a relationship with the brand. Further, the humanlike attributes of a brand (e.g., its personality traits) can influence the types of relationships that consumers form with the brand.

In the following sections, we examine why people anthropomorphize inanimate entities, and how this tendency can affect the way consumers evaluate and engage with products and brands. We outline future lines of research and offer predictions about how anthropomorphism can influence the types of relationships that consumers form with brands. The goal of this chapter is to use the interesting phenomenon of brand anthropomorphism to better understand the process by which consumer-brand relationships are first formed and then nurtured over time.

Why anthropomorphize?

Why do people have this tendency to ascribe human-like characteristics to non-human entities? Three explanations have been offered for the tendency to anthropomorphize (see Guthrie [1993] for a review). One explanation is that doing so comforts people by providing relationships or companionship. This view sees anthropomorphism as stemming from wishful thinking; people who wish to have more relationships in their everyday lives use products to fill the void left by a scarcity of human relationships. A second explanation is that people anthropomorphize to make better sense of the world around them. People use what they are familiar with – their knowledge of themselves – and ascribe human-like characteristics to events or entities to better account for outcomes and things that they know less about. Finally, Guthrie (1993) suggests that anthropomorphizing may be seen as a cognitive and perceptual strategy akin to making a bet that the world is human-like: a bet that has more upside potential than downside risk. From an evolutionary perspective, making this bet may have allowed humans to develop a mechanism to help people identify potential predators (Guthrie 1993). While this mechanism may yield false positive results, such as identifying a tree with human-like limbs as an enemy, the upside is that it would also lead to correctly identifying predators if and when they were around in the environment – something crucial for survival. In addition, the tendency to anthropomorphize may be a developmental trait, where young children learn about human interactions and relationships, and then overgeneralize them to interactions with non-humans (Guthrie 1993).

Building upon the propositions by Guthrie (1993), Epley *et al.* (2007) later proposed a three-factor model to explain why people anthropomorphize so readily. The first factor is the accessibility and applicability of anthropocentric knowledge. From a cognitive perspective, when people view objects that share traits with humans (e.g., physical shape, movement, voice, etc.), the human schema becomes more readily accessible, which increases the likelihood of the object being anthropomorphized by the observer. Thus, people tend to engage with the environment around them by using self-knowledge and human category knowledge. For example, the similarity of a non-human object's movement to human movement leads observers to perceive the object as being alive (Tremoulet and Feldman 2000); in addition, if the speed of the object is more in line with natural human speed, then the object is more likely to be perceived as being human-like (Morewedge *et al.* 2007).

Consistent with this explanation, marketers often take advantage of human schema activation by employing brand characters and mascots. Brown (2010) finds that marketers are most likely to use stylized human beings as brand characters or mascots, followed by domesticated animals. Further, the popularity of the brand animal is directly correlated with the species' physiological (shape) and psychological (presence of mind) distance from humankind. Even when the object is completely inanimate – that is, the object is without a conscious mind and without movement – observers are still able to detect human-like features. When faced with a row of soft drink bottles of varying sizes, consumers prefer to see them as a "family" of products rather than a "line" of products (Aggarwal and McGill 2007). Humans also have a strong tendency to detect faces in inanimate objects (Guthrie 1993), likely because recognition of faces and facial expressions is crucial for successful social interactions. Consumers are able to identify facial expressions on cars (with headlights as eyes and the grille as a mouth), and the emotion that they perceive from the expression affects how they evaluate the car (Aggarwal and McGill 2007; Landwehr *et al.* 2011; Maeng and Aggarwal 2014; Windhager *et al.* 2008).

While the first factor noted by Epley *et al.* (2007) is cognitive and based on people's knowledge structures, the second and third factors provide a motivational perspective. The likelihood of an individual anthropomorphizing an object depends on two motivational states of the individual: sociality motivation and effectance motivation. Humans have a need for affiliation and belongingness (Baumeister and Leary 1995), and when this need is activated (i.e., when people feel lonely or isolated, and hence are eager to seek out and form social connections), there is an increased likelihood of anthropomorphizing non-human objects. Consistent with this, Puzakova, Kwak, and Rocereto (2009) suggest that certain personality traits may increase the likelihood of anthropomorphizing: consumers who have a high need for belonging and those who rate highly for chronic loneliness may have a stronger tendency to anthropomorphize brands and use anthropomorphism as a way to fulfill their needs for social connections. Epley *et al.* (2008) demonstrate in a series of experiments that people who are lonely compensate for their lack of social connections through anthropomorphizing animals, and even gadgets, thereby creating a sense of connection with these nonhumans.

The sociality motivation also affects the way consumers perceive anthropomorphized objects. The innate desire for social connection suggests that, when individuals perceive the object to be human-like, they employ social norms typically used in social interactions. For example, when consumers consider their old products as being imbued with human-like characteristics, they are less willing to replace them with newer models (Chandler and Schwarz 2010) because it is socially inappropriate to get rid of "friends" or "family members" when they get old. When people perceive a non-human entity to have a presence of mind, they are more likely to treat the entity with care and concern (Waytz *et al.* 2010), and because of this, when an anthropomorphized object delivers an emotional appeal (e.g., a humanized light bulb saying, "I am burning. Please turn me off!"), individuals are more likely to comply (Ahn *et al.* 2014).

The third factor – effectance motivation – arises from individuals' need to understand and predict their environment and reduce uncertainty. Similar to making inferences about other people's behavior by using the self as a reference point, individuals anthropomorphize non-humans in order to comprehend and predict the behavior of objects (Dawes and Mulford 1996). By using a familiar reference point (i.e., human behavior), individuals feel that they have more control over their environment, and are better able to explain ambiguous elements in their surroundings (Burger and Copper 1979). Epley *et al.* (2008) identify the need for control as a personality variable that determines the likelihood of anthropomorphizing. Individuals who have a high need for control are more likely to anthropomorphize animals whose behaviors are unpredictable – which suggests that anthropomorphizing these animals enables their behavior to become more understandable. Puzakova *et al.* (2009) posit that having a high need for control induces consumers to explain brands' behaviors through anthropomorphic representations (e.g., intentions, desires) of the brand. Kim and McGill (2011) provide some evidence in support of this proposition: products that are seen as being risky (e.g., a slot machine) are preferred only when the product is anthropomorphized, because humans, especially those who feel empowered, can exert control over other (more predictable) humans, but not over (more unpredictable) objects. Furthermore, Guthrie (1993) notes that anthropomorphic propensity increases during times of uncertainty and rapid technological change, which likely explains why complex products like computers are ascribed with human-like traits and are treated as similar to humans (Nass and Moon 2000; Nass *et al.* 1996).

In sum, the human tendency to anthropomorphize non-human entities, driven by a need to make sense of the world around them, begins in early childhood and is likely rooted in evolution. Observers are more likely to anthropomorphize objects when features of the object activate the human schema (e.g., through human-like movement or facial expressions, etc.). Factors internal to the observer can also affect the likelihood of anthropomorphism. That is, when individuals are motivated to form social relationships, or when they are motivated to understand the behavior of non-human objects, they are more likely to view objects as more human-like. Consumers may also *prefer* personified products and brands for similar reasons: 1) the product/brand would fit with their activated human schema, 2) the product/brand can satisfy the need to form social connections, or 3) the product/brand would be more predictable and controllable.

Consumer evaluation of anthropomorphized products and brands

Much of the literature on anthropomorphism focuses on the reasons why individuals anthropomorphize and the circumstances under which anthropomorphism is more likely to occur, as outlined above. The authors of the paper that first brought anthropomorphism to the attention of consumer behavior research argue that "products that can be 'humanized' are often seen as stronger candidates for long-term business success" (Aggarwal and McGill 2007). Delbaere, McQuarrie, and Phillips (2011) posit that advertising that uses anthropomorphism (in the form of inanimate spokescharacters, mascots, and brand animals) is more likely to elicit positive emotional responses from consumers. They go on to demonstrate that consumers like brands that induce anthropomorphic feelings, and that consumers form positive attributions of these brands' personalities.

However, simply anthropomorphizing products – that is, imbuing products with human-like traits – does not always increase positive evaluations. The relationship between consumers and brands/products is more nuanced. The types of roles that brands play and the features and functions of products also need to be taken into consideration. For instance, consumers prefer cars that have "aggressive eyes" and a "smiling mouth" to cars that are simply smiling (Landwehr *et al.* 2011). In a recent series of experiments, we find that desire for social connection does not always increase liking for anthropomorphized products (Wan and Aggarwal 2014). In fact, when the product is seen as being primarily functional and serving a specific purpose, desire for social connection decreased preference for these products, presumably because "using" a "person" to complete a task is socially inappropriate. These results are consistent with recent work that distinguishes between two different roles assigned to brands of being a servant or a partner to the consumer (Aggarwal and McGill 2012). Servants are brands that are bought or used to serve a particular goal: the onus of accomplishing the job of satisfying the consumer's need is on the brand – the brand is outsourced to do the task, as it were. Partners, on the other hand, are brands that are seen as co-producers of fulfilling the consumers' needs along with the consumers themselves. We suggest that consumers with a need for social connection may find some roles to be more desirable than other roles (Wan and Aggarwal 2014). That is, when a product is seen in instrumental terms and is meant to serve a specific purpose, it is more likely to be perceived as a servant when anthropomorphized. And since servants do not fit in the "friend" schema, such an anthropomorphized product would not receive strong positive evaluations. On the other hand, if a product is meant to be consumed for its own sake, it would more likely be perceived as a partner when anthropomorphized, and hence seem more desirable.

Recent research has further noted the negative downstream consequences of brand humanization (Puzakova *et al.* 2013). This research suggests that an anthropomorphized brand can lead to lower consumer evaluations when the brand faces negative publicity due to wrongdoings. Consumers who believe in personality stability (i.e., entity theorists) view anthropomorphized brands that undergo negative publicity less favorably than non-anthropomorphized brands. In contrast, consumers who advocate personality malleability (i.e., incremental theorists) are less likely to devalue an anthropomorphized brand from a single instance of negative publicity. Kim and McGill (2011) find that consumers who perceive themselves as having little power prefer non-anthropomorphized risky products such as slot machines compared to consumers who are high in power, who prefer anthropomorphized risky products.

The findings outlined here suggest that merely anthropomorphizing products and brands is not always the best strategy to improve evaluations; the attributes and purpose of the brand and product need to be considered. Consumers are not always more likely to form positive relationships with products and brands simply because they are human-like. For example, weak relationships between the consumer and brand may result if the consumer's consumption goals do not match the type of "person" the brand is. Furthermore, the relationships between the brand and consumer may even turn sour after a brand's wrongdoing if consumers believe in the stability of personality traits. The attributes of the consumer and the attributes of the products and brands need to be taken into account during the formation of positive relationships, and when determining whether or not anthropomorphism would be effective in improving brand evaluations.

Implications of anthropomorphism for brand relationships

While anthropomorphizing brands will not always lead to the formation of relationships with brands, anthropomorphism is a necessary antecedent of brand relationships. That is, brands must be viewed as humans – humans who have intentions, emotions, and agency – in order for consumers to form relationships with them. It is still not fully understood what determines the particular types of relationships consumers form with brands, but understanding why consumers anthropomorphize and the contexts in which anthropomorphic products and brands will be favored provides interesting avenues for future research. In the following sections, we propose some possible factors and contexts in which brand anthropomorphism can inform and guide consumer-brand relationships. We examine the potential role of three anteceding variables of anthropomorphism – knowledge accessibility, sociality motivation, and effectance motivation – and other individual and contextual factors in affecting the formation of consumer-brand relationships (see Figures 8.1, 8.2, and 8.3 for a conceptual model).

Knowledge accessibility

As noted before, one cognitive factor that leads to a greater likelihood to anthropomorphize is when people are confronted with stimuli that make the knowledge about human schema more accessible, such as when products are endowed with features that resemble human traits. When that happens, people interact with brands much as they might interact with people, since that seems the natural and right way to behave. Of course, depending upon the particular stimuli that are incorporated in the products, the type of human schema that is made salient might differ, resulting in a different type of interaction and relationship being forged with that brand. For example, work by Aggarwal and McGill (2007) shows that a smile is associated with the schema of a spokesperson, but a frown is not, and it is this schema congruity that leads to a preference for a car that is smiling and presented as a spokesperson over the one that is frowning and presented as a spokesperson.

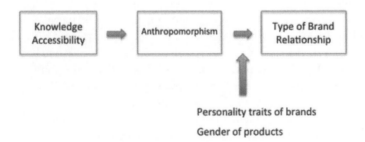

FIGURE 8.1 Antecedents of anthropomorphism: the role of knowledge accessibility on the formation of consumer-brand relationships

Personality traits (of products)

Brands are perceived to have distinct personality traits, just as people do (Aaker 1997), and these brand personality traits are likely to result in different relationships being forged with the brand. While there is little empirical work in consumer behavior that links anthropomorphism with brand personalities, it is worth recognizing that imbuing a brand with human personality traits would activate the human schema and increase the chance of anthropomorphizing a given brand. Further, the types of personality traits a brand possesses can influence the types of relationships that consumers form with the brand. Prior research on brand personality shows that sincere personality leads to a durable long-term committed partnership, while an exciting brand personality leads to a fling-like relationship (Aaker *et al.* 2004). Nobre, Becker, and Brito (2010) report that brand personality is a strong positive predictor of consumer-brand relationships on the dimensions of passion and intimacy-loyalty – that is, when consumers perceive a brand to possess human traits such as intensity and confidence, they are more likely to form passionate and intimate relationships with the brand. More recent research finds that the ratio of width to height of car-faces follows the same pattern of preference as the ratio of width to height of human-faces: the higher the ratio, the greater the attribution of dominance to the anthropomorphized cars (Maeng and Aggarwal 2014). However, unlike dominant human-faces that are less preferred, dominant car-faces are favored since possessions are more likely to be seen as reflective of the self, thereby helping people feel more empowered and strong. Thus, through activating consumers' human schema, brand personalities can guide the formation of unique and distinct consumer-brand relationships.

Gender (of products)

As noted earlier, prior research has noted that computers are sometimes seen in gender stereotypical ways, especially if they are associated with male or female voices (Nass *et al.* 1997). More recent work suggests that use of different languages might lead to different levels of anthropomorphism, as well as different attribution of male versus female traits to non-human objects. Thus, work by Kim *et al.* (2014) suggests that gendered languages, such as French that assigns male or female gender to objects like tables, chairs, etc. (by using he or she to refer to them), are more likely to lead to anthropomorphism compared to more neutral languages like English (that use "it"). Furthermore, depending upon whether a product is referred to as a "he" or a "she", it is assigned more male or female stereotypical traits. Consumers might then form different types of relationships with products and brands depending upon the language used in the particular country, as well as whether the product is referred to as a "he" or a "she". Clearly, the use of brand characters, and assigning them male or female form such as a the Michelin Man or the Land O'Lakes woman is likely to lead to different types of relationships being forged with these brands.

Sociality motivation

As noted earlier, one underlying motivation as to why people tend to anthropomorphize non-human entities is in order to fulfill the need for social connections. There are social and individual contexts where the sociality motivation might be particularly strong, which would then result in greater likelihood of forming strong relationships with brands.

Culture

There is a plethora of research in psychology and marketing highlighting the relevance and value of examining cross-cultural differences, and how those differences influence consumer behavior (see Markus and Kitayama 1991 for a review). One factor that has been identified as a key dimension that separates different cultures is the concept of self-construal, or the extent to which people perceive themselves to be independent versus interdependent. The main distinction between these two types of self-construal is that independent people focus relatively more on themselves while interdependent people focus relatively more on others around them. The interaction of culture and the need for social connection provides an interesting context to examine the formation of consumer-brand relationships. One may argue that because people in interdependent cultures value social relations more (Markus and Kitayama 1991), they would be more likely to anthropomorphize brands and form intimate/close relationships with such anthropomorphized brands. Conversely, interdependent people might perceive themselves to already have sufficient functional relationships in social domains, and thus they may not need to rely on brands to fulfill their sociality needs. As such, independent rather than interdependent consumers might anthropomorphize more and form more close relationships with brands as substitutes for human relationships.

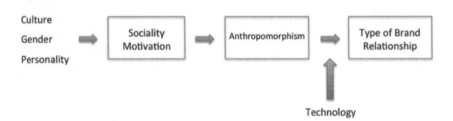

FIGURE 8.2 Antecedents of anthropomorphism: the role of sociality motivation on the formation of consumer-brand relationships

Gender (of consumers)

Gender research suggests that women respond better to appeals of togetherness and interdependence, compared to men (Wang *et al.* 2000), while men respond better to appeals of separateness and independence, compared to women. Furthermore, women are more likely to consider brands as active relationship partners, compared to men (Monga 2002). While both men and women consider how they act toward brands, women (and not men) also consider how brands act toward them. These findings suggest that women might, in fact, be more likely, relative to men, to anthropomorphize brands and then form close relationships with these anthropomorphized entities. Other related work sheds further light on the issue by noting that, within the interdependence context, women focus more on the relational aspects of interdependence, whereas men focus more on the collective aspects of interdependence (Gabriel and Gardner 1999). This research then suggests a more nuanced hypothesis, outlining that women might be more likely to form more dyadic consumer-brand relationships, while men might be more likely to form relationships at a group level akin to the idea of brand communities, noted by Muniz and O'Guinn (2001).

Personality traits (of consumers)

It has been noted in past research that certain personality traits, such as chronic loneliness, increases the propensity to anthropomorphize as a way to compensate for lack of human connections (Epley *et al.* 2008; Puzakova *et al.* 2009). If this is the case, then one would expect that people who show these personality traits might also be more likely to seek out and form close and durable relationships with brands on an ongoing basis.

Technology

One crucial aspect of our fast changing world is the role of technology and the extent to which technology is integral to our everyday living, as manifested in our usage of many different 'avatars' to represent our digital selves. Prior research suggests that machines are also gender stereotyped (Nass, Moon and Green 1997), given personalities like human personalities (Nass *et al.* 1995), and treated with politeness (Nass *et al.* 1999) and with norms of social interaction such as reciprocity (Moon 2000). President Obama's recent visit to Japan where he infamously bowed to a robot, saying later that "they were too lifelike," further demonstrates how normal and easy it might be to form social connections with machines, especially those that take on a physical form that resembles human form. Other examples like voice recognition technology, fingerprint sensors, and the iPhone's Siri function all show the great strides that technology has made in our everyday lives. As technology advances to simulate humans in shape, speech, action, and performance, people will be more likely to anthropomorphize these gadgets and relate to them just as they would to other people.

Effectance motivation

The effectance motivation suggests that people have a great need to make sense of the world around them and reduce uncertainty so they have better control over their environment. Consequently, situations that naturally offer greater risks or uncertainties are likely to lead to a greater likelihood of anthropomorphism, which, in turn, might lead to a greater likelihood to form relationships with these products or brands. However, because the motivation is not driven by a need for social connection, it is likely that the types of relationships formed as a result of effectance motivation are qualitatively different.

Uncertain or risky contexts

Prior research has found that risky contexts lead to a preference for products that are anthropomorphized. Thus, Kim and McGill (2011) show that in a high-risk context, such as gambling, people prefer a slot machine that is anthropomorphized, compared to the one that is not anthropomorphized. Further, they observe this effect only for those consumers who perceive themselves to be high in power, suggesting that the preference for the anthropomorphized slot machine is driven by a desire to exercise "control" over the unpredictable machine. Conversely, those low in power like the anthropomorphized slot machine much less, suggesting that they fear being controlled by a humanized entity that is more powerful than them, particularly in a context that is seen as high risk. This suggests that if we were to identify naturally occurring or otherwise high-risk contexts and situations, consumers may be more likely to relate to anthropomorphized products there, especially if they feel empowered. Thus, doctors and other health practitioners who are in high risk situations and often feel empowered might prefer anthropomorphized products to help them meet their goals. Others who might be in similar situations include frontline workers in various domains, such as the military, firefighting, education, etc. Presenting the products and brands that these people work with as anthropomorphized entities might forge stronger relationships and more effective performances.

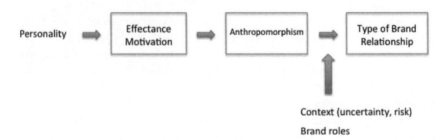

FIGURE 8.3 Antecedents of anthropomorphism: the role of effectance motivation on the formation of consumer-brand relationships

Personality traits (of consumers)

Recent work has identified two personality traits as being associated with greater propensity to anthropomorphize as a way to understand and to control the environment: the need for closure and the need for control (Epley *et al.* 2008; Puzakova *et al.* 2009). Given this, one can argue that people who are high on these two personality traits are not just likely to anthropomorphize brands, but also likely to form a certain type of relationships with the brands around them. Arguably, the need to control would lead these people to try and "use" the brands to manage their environment better around them. The question that future researchers might find worthwhile to examine is whether such consumers are more likely to form asymmetrical and unequal relationships with brands, akin to treating the brands as slaves or servants.

Brand roles

Sometimes consumers think of brands in the role of a partner, and at other times think of brands in the role of a servant (Aggarwal and McGill 2012). As explained previously, servant brands are used to serve a particular goal, and partner brands are perceived as collaborators and co-producers of fulfilling consumers' needs. While a social connectedness motivation might be more likely to lead to perceiving the anthropomorphized brand as a "partner" to the consumer, the effectance motivation is likely to make salient the need to control the environment, resulting in a greater likelihood of forging a servant-like relationship with the anthropo-morphized brand. Wan and Aggarwal (2014) find evidence supporting this proposition by showing that when consumers expect the brand to serve a specific function, they consider its usefulness and instrumentality, and tend to prefer anthropomorphized brands "to get the job done." Arguably, when consumers feel less empowered, but think of the brand in terms of instrumentality, they may prefer a "boss" brand, especially if it is seen as a benevolent master, much like a luxury brand that is desirable.

Conclusion

Although anthropomorphism as a concept is as ancient as religion, research in the consumer domain on anthropomorphism did not emerge until recent years. The use of anthropomorphism in advertising is still increasing in popularity because companies believe they will have an edge over their competitors if they personify their products and brands (Shaffer 2014). However, Shaffer (2014) warns practitioners that modern consumers may be oversaturated with conventional anthropomorphic advertisements, which use the typical talking animal or other anthropomorphic spokescharacter (e.g., GEICO's talking gecko). Consumers may view these types of advertisements as too blatant or "cheesy." This does not at all suggest that eliciting anthropomorphic feelings in consumers is ineffective in influencing consumers' preference and engagement with such brands and products; in fact, Shaffer (2014) encourages marketing managers to explore methods by which one may induce anthropomorphism in more innovative ways. He cites a series of ads for IBM as innovative, as they use more subtle ways to elicit anthropomorphism (e.g., an ad with captions reading, "Trains now queue for passengers"). The large restaurant chain, Subway, used a particularly novel form of anthropomorphism in a product placement on a television show. Subway has engaged in many blatant product placements on various network television shows (e.g., NBC's *Chuck*, CBS's *Hawaii Five-0*). In 2013, Subway went so far as to literally humanize its brand and inserted the human character "Subway" into the storyline on NBC's comedy *Community*. The "Subway" character even formed a fling-type relationship with one of the main characters of *Community*, which was later reflected by that character's mixed positive and negative attitude toward actual Subway sandwiches.

Understanding the efficacy of anthropomorphism in a marketing context and how it influences the formation of brand relationships is more important than ever, especially with the continual growth of social media. Brands now have an actual voice through social media platforms, and can engage one-on-one with consumers in real time. Direct interactions with brands through Facebook, Twitter, or Instagram, and the indirect observation of brands' interactions with other consumers would easily allow consumers to ascribe personality traits to brands and to view brands as possessing intentions and emotions. Even Mr. Clean has "his" own Facebook and Twitter accounts, where "he" writes in the first-person and makes cleaning related puns. Social media makes it simple for consumers to engage with brands, and through repeated interactions, consumer-brand relationships are more likely to be formed. The propensity to anthropomorphize will rise as consumers try to make sense of the modern world that is characterized by rapid technological changes and other uncertainties. The question is whether, in this fast-paced and technology-focused world, the types of relationships that we develop with others, including brands, will prove to be more long-term and fulfilling or merely a means to achieve some other goals that we cherish more.

References

Aaker, J. (1997) "Dimensions of Brand Personality", *Journal of Marketing Research*, 34 (3): 347–356.

Aaker, J., S. Fournier, and S. Brasel (2004) "When Good Brands Do Bad", *Journal of Consumer Research*, 31 (1): 1–16.

Aggarwal, P. (2004) "The Effects of Brand Relationship Norms on Consumer Attitudes and Behavior", *Journal of Consumer Research*, 31 (1): 87–101.

Aggarwal, P. and A. McGill (2007) "Is That Car Smiling at Me? Schema Congruity as a Basis for Evaluating Anthropomorphized Products", *Journal of Consumer Research*, 34 (4): 468–479.

Aggarwal, P. and A. McGill (2012) "When Brands Seem Human, Do Humans Act like Brands? Automatic Behavioral Priming Effects of Brand Anthropomorphism", *Journal of Consumer Research*, 39 (2): 307–323.

Ahn, H., H. Kim, and P. Aggarwal (2014) "Helping Fellow Beings Anthropomorphized Social Causes and the Role of Anticipatory Guilt", *Psychological Science*, 25 (1): 224–229.

Baumeister, R. and M. Leary (1995) "The Need to Belong: Desire for Interpersonal Attachments as a Fundamental Human Motivation", *Psychological Bulletin*, 117 (3): 497–529.

Biel, A. (2000) "Converting Image into Equity", *Advertising's Role in Building Strong Brands*. eds D. Aaker and A. Biel. Hillsdale, NJ: Erlbaum: 67–82.

Brown, S. (2010) "Where the Wild Brands Are: Some Thoughts on Anthropomorphic Marketing", *The Marketing Review*, 10 (3): 209–224.

Burger, J. and H. Copper (1979) "The Desirability of Control", *Motivation and Emotion*, 3 (4): 381–393.

Chandler, J. and N. Schwarz (2010) "Use Does Not Wear Ragged the Fabric of Friendship: Thinking of Objects as Alive Makes People Less Willing to Replace Them", *Journal of Consumer Psychology*, 20 (2): 138–145.

Dalton, R. (2003) "Lion Man Takes Pride of Place as Oldest Statue", *Nature News*, www.nature.com/news/2003/030904/full/news030901-6.html, accessed May 5, 2014.

Dawes, R. and M. Mulford (1996) "The False Consensus Effect and Overconfidence: Flaws in Judgment or Flaws in How We Study Judgment?", *Organizational Behavior and Human Decision Processes*, 65 (3): 201–211.

Delbaere, M., E. McQuarrie, and B. Phillips (2011) "Personification in Advertising", *Journal of Advertising*, 40 (1): 121–130.

Epley, N., A. Waytz, and J. Cacioppo (2007) "On Seeing Human: A Three-Factor Theory of Anthropomorphism", *Psychological Review*, 114 (4): 864–886.

Epley, N., S. Akalis, A. Waytz, and J. Cacioppo (2008) "Creating Social Connection through Inferential Reproduction Loneliness and Perceived Agency in Gadgets, Gods, and Greyhounds", *Psychological Science*, 19 (2): 114–120.

Epley, N., A. Waytz, S. Akalis, and J. Cacioppo (2008) "When We Need a Human: Motivational Determinants of Anthropomorphism", *Social Cognition*, 26 (2): 143–155.

Fournier, S. (1998) "Consumers and Their Brands: Developing Relationship Theory in Consumer Research", *Journal of Consumer Research*, 24 (4): 343–353.

Gabriel, S. and W. Gardner (1999) "Are there 'His' and 'Hers' Types of Interdependence? The Implications of Gender Differences in Collective versus Relational Interdependence for Affect, Behavior, and Cognition", *Journal of Personality and Social Psychology*, 77 (3): 642–655.

Guthrie, S. (1993) *Faces in the Clouds*. 1st edn. New York: Oxford University Press.

Keller, K. (1993) *Strategic Brand Management: Building, Measuring, and Managing Brand Equity*. 2nd edn. Upper Saddle River, NJ: Prentice Hall.

Kim, S. and A. McGill (2011) "Gaming with Mr. Slot or Gaming the Slot Machine? Power, Anthropomorphism, and Risk Perception", *Journal of Consumer Research*, 38 (1): 94–107.

Kim, H., A. Weibrauch, B. Shiv, and P. Aggarwal (2014) "Do the French Take Better Care of Things than the English? Gendered Language and Anthropomorphism", Unpublished Working Paper.

Landwehr, J., A. McGill, and A. Herrmann (2011) "It's Got the Look: The Effect of Friendly and Aggressive 'Facial' Expressions on Product Liking and Sales", *Journal of Marketing*, 75 (3): 132–146.

Maeng, A. and P. Aggarwal (2014) "Striving for Superiority: Face Ratio, Anthropomorphism, and Design Preferences", *Advances in Consumer Research*, 42 (January): 594.

Markus, H. and S. Kitayama (1991) "Culture and the Self: Implications for Cognition, Emotion, and Motivation", *Psychological Review*, 98 (2): 224–253.

Monga, A. (2002) "Brand as a Relationship Partner: Gender Differences in Perspectives", *North American Advances in Consumer Research Volume 29*, eds S. Broniarczyk and K. Nakamoto. Valdosta, GA: Association for Consumer Research: 36–41.

Moon, Y. (2000) "Intimate Exchanges: Using Computers to Elicit Self-disclosure from Consumers", *Journal of Consumer Research*, 26 (4): 324–340.

Morewedge, C., J. Preston, and D. Wegner (2007) "Timescale Bias in the Attribution of Mind", *Journal of Personality and Social Psychology*, 93 (1): 1–11.

Muniz Jr, A. and T. O'Guinn (2001) "Brand Community", *Journal of Consumer Research*, 27 (4): 412–432.

Nass, C. and Y. Moon (2000) "Machines and Mindlessness: Social Responses to Computers", *Journal of Social Issues*, 56 (1): 81–103.

Nass, C., B. Fogg, and Y. Moon (1996) "Can Computers be Teammates?", *International Journal of Human-Computer Studies*, 45 (6): 669–678.

Nass, C., Y. Moon, and P. Carney (1999) "Are People Polite to Computers? Responses to Computer-Based Interviewing Systems", *Journal of Applied Social Psychology*, 29 (5): 1093–1109.

Nass, C., Y. Moon, and N. Green (1997) "Are Machines Gender Neutral? Gender-Stereotypic Responses to Computers with Voices", *Journal of Applied Social Psychology*, 27 (10): 864–876.

Nass, C., Y. Moon, B. Fogg, B. Reeves, and D. Dryer (1995) "Can Computer Personalities be Human Personalities?", *International Journal of Human-Computer Studies*, 43 (2): 223–239.

Nobre, H., K. Becker, and C. Brito (2010) "Brand Relationships: A Personality-Based Approach", *Journal of Service Science and Management*, 3 (2): 206–217.

Park, C., B. Jaworski, and D. MacInnis (1986) "Strategic Brand Concept-Image Management", *Journal of Marketing*, 50 (4): 135–145.

Plummer, J. (1985) "How Personality Makes a Difference", *Journal of Advertising Research*, 24 (6): 27–31.

Puzakova, M., H. Kwak, and J. Rocereto (2009) "Pushing the Envelope of Brand and Personality: Antecedents and Moderators of Anthropomorphized Brands", *Advances in Consumer Research*, 36: 413–420.

Puzakova, M., H. Kwak, and J. Rocereto (2013) "When Humanizing Brands Goes Wrong: The Detrimental Effect of Brand Anthropomorphization amid Product Wrongdoings", *Journal of Marketing*, 77 (3): 81–100.

Shaffer, J. (2014) "Innovating Advertising: Conventional vs. Innovative Anthropomorphic Advertising Approaches in the Twenty-First Century", *Advertising and Society Review*, 15 (1).

Tremoulet, P. and J. Feldman (2000) "Perception of Animacy from the Motion of a Single Object", *Perception*, 29 (8): 943–952.

Wan, J. and P. Aggarwal (2014) "Spending Time with Mr. Lexus and Paying Money to Doughboy: The Effect of Time and Money on Preference for Anthropomorphized Products", *Advances in Consumer Research*, 42 (January): 738.

Wang, C., T. Bristol, J. Mowen, and G. Chakraborty (2000) "Alternative Modes of Self-Construal: Dimensions of Connectedness-Separateness and Advertising Appeals to the Cultural and Gender-Specific Self", *Journal of Consumer Psychology*, 9 (2): 107–115.

Waytz, A., J. Cacioppo, and N. Epley (2010) "Who Sees Human? The Stability and Importance of Individual Differences in Anthropomorphism", *Perspectives on Psychological Science*, 5 (3): 219–232.

Windhager, S., D. Slice, K. Schaefer, E. Oberzaucher, T. Thorstensen, and K. Grammer (2008) "Face to Face: The Perception of Automotive Designs", *Human Nature*, 19 (4): 331–346.

9

ANTHROPOMORPHISM AND CONSUMER-BRAND RELATIONSHIPS

A cross-cultural analysis

Mandeep Kaur Ghuman, Li Huang, Thomas J. Madden, and Martin S. Roth

An anthropomorphizing tendency refers to an inherent preference for regarding nonhuman objects as human-like. Consequently, entities ranging from God to nature, and animals to robots are eligible to be humanized (Epley *et al.* 2007). As suggested by Fournier (1998), the abstract entity, such as a brand, could serve as a relationship partner, based on a premise that the brand may be humanized by the consumer. While a great deal of research has paid much attention to the antecedents of anthropomorphism in general (Epley *et al.* 2007; Cohen and Johnson 2009; Waytz *et al.* 2010), little research focuses on when and why consumers anthropomorphize the brand and how this brand anthropomorphism affects consumer-brand relationships. Although some consumer researchers have recently studied brand anthropomorphism and its marketing consequences (e.g., Aggarwal and McGill 2007; Labroo *et al.* 2008; Eyssel *et al.* 2010; Landwehr *et al.* 2011), they have not yet looked into the antecedents from a cultural perspective and its consequences on consumer-brand relationship quality. We propose that brand anthropomorphism, which is driven by general anthropomorphizing tendencies, differs across cultures because of variances in cognitive human knowledge and market industrialization. Furthermore, the degree of brand humanization affects the strength of consumer-brand relationship quality. The current study thus fills an important research gap by empirically testing this prediction and providing an interesting exploration across diverse cultural and industrial contexts.

Literature review and hypotheses development

Culture, the anthropomorphizing tendency, and anthropomorphism

Every individual has a certain stable level of inherent tendency to anthropo-morphize nonhuman entities depending on his or her culture, education, need for cognition, and interaction with human and nonhuman agents (Epley *et al.* 2007). Waytz, Cacioppo and Epley (2010) term this inherent individual tendency as 'Anthropomorphizing Tendency', and posited that the anthropomorphizing tendency of an individual predicts their anthropomorphism of any particular agent. They also developed the individual differences in anthropomorphism questionnaire (IDAQ) to measure the anthropomorphizing tendency of a particular individual and capture differences in anthropomorphizing tendencies across individuals. IDAQ is a manifestation of a more general human tendency to anthropomorphize nonhuman agents, and is based on the measurement of the anthropomorphism of three types of stimuli – animals (fish, cow, cheetah, insect, and reptile), nature (mountain, ocean, environment, tree, and wind), and technology (television, robot, car, computer, devices, and machines). Thus, the IDAQ scale measures anthropomorphic judgments across targets, but, in totality, it indicates general anthropomorphizing tendency.

Culture is known to influence how well people relate to and depend upon each other. In individualist cultures, child-rearing patterns emphasize self-reliance, independence, and self-actualization, while child-rearing patterns in collectivist cultures emphasize conformity, obedience, and reliability (Triandis 1989). As a result, people in individualist societies are independent, have fewer social relationships, act as individuals rather than as members of a group, and make their decisions independently of others. In contrast, individuals in collectivist societies are interdependent and are deeply embedded in many social relationships. They constantly think of themselves in the context of other people and as a part of social groups (Roth 1995).

Due to relationship orientation, human knowledge is highly accessible in collectivist cultures. Epley, Waytz and Cacioppo (2007) assert that the accessibility of human knowledge is a cognitive determinant of anthropomorphism. The higher the accessibility of human knowledge, the greater is the tendency to anthropomorphize the nonhuman. Therefore, individuals in collectivist cultures apply easily accessible human knowledge with little correction when describing nonhuman entities. So, even when they see nonhumans, they are likely to connect to them at a human level because collectivists in general are trained to connect to other humans on a regular basis. This suggests that people in collectivist cultures are more likely to perceive the human in nonhuman entities. In contrast, in individualist cultures, human knowledge is relatively less accessible, and people are less likely to anthropomorphize nonhuman agents.

Based on the above discussion, we posit that people in collectivist cultures have a higher tendency to anthropomorphize nonhuman entities. This is in line with Asquith (1986) who discusses that while studying primates, Japanese primatologists attributed a theory of mind to animals, but Westerners did not. Japanese primatologists studied several groups of single species together and focused on their social structures, while Westerners conducted single group studies and focused on the individual characteristics. He argues that the social approach of Japanese primatologists might be a phenomenon rooted in their cultural orientation towards inter-individual relationships. Our proposition is also in line with previous research that proves culture to be an important determinant of human behavior in general, and consumer behavior in particular (e.g., Bian and Forsythe 2012; Zhang *et al.* 2014). As a corollary, we also expect that people in collectivist cultures will be more likely to anthropomorphize brands available in the marketplace. Therefore, we test the following hypotheses:

> *H1a*: People in collectivist cultures are more likely to have a tendency to anthropomorphize than people in individualist cultures.
> *H1b*: People in collectivist cultures are more likely to have greater brand anthropomorphism than people in individualist cultures.

Market development, the anthropomorphizing tendency, and anthropomorphism

As the acquisition and accessibility of human knowledge encourages anthropomorphism, analogously, acquisition and accessibility of nonhuman knowledge reduces anthropomorphism (Epley *et al.* 2007). When knowledge about nonhuman agents is higher, people are more likely to use this knowledge when reasoning about them, and hence are less likely to anthropomorphize. People in economically developed and industrialized Western countries are exposed to a wider array of mechanical and technological objects (e.g., cars, computers, mobile phones, etc.). Therefore, they have a relatively more elaborate knowledge of nonhuman entities and, hence, relatively less tendency to anthropomorphize. In their cross-cultural study on robots, Li, Patrick Rau and Li (2010) found that German people had less positive attitudes toward a sociable robot than Chinese and Korean people. They argue that due to higher exposure to industrial robots, German people prefer to have more sense of control and to use robots as tools or machines, rather than using them as companions or personal service providers. Thus, we propose that individuals in developed nations are more likely to view nonhuman objects in non-anthropomorphic terms, and therefore are less likely to anthropomorphize. We hypothesize:

> *H2a*: People in less economically developed countries are more likely to have a tendency to anthropomorphize than people in more developed countries.
> *H2b*: People in less economically developed countries are more likely to have greater brand anthropomorphism than people in more developed countries.

Anthropomorphism and brand relationship quality

Fournier (1998) has posited that brands can also serve as viable relationship partners, such as friends and marriage partners. Consumers are not only concerned about a brand's features and benefits, but also how it contributes as a relationship partner (Kervyn *et al.* 2012; Fournier and Alvarez 2012). Consumers' emotional attachment to a brand leads to various desired marketing outcomes such as consumer retention, satisfaction, recommendations, a reluctance to brand switch, a willingness to share more information with the company, a favorable attitude towards brand extensions, and a willingness to pay price premiums (Thomson *et al.* 2005; Fedorikhin *et al.* 2006; Smit *et al.* 2007).

Existing research suggests that for a brand to serve as a legitimate relationship partner it must be perceived by consumers as possessing human-like characteristics (Fournier 1998; Puzakova *et al.* 2009; Aggarwal and McGill 2012). This suggests that brand anthropomorphism influences relationship-building between consumers and brands. However, anthropomorphism of a brand would be more likely for individuals who have a higher tendency to anthropomorphize than for individuals who have a lower tendency to anthropomorphize. Therefore, we propose that anthropomorphizing tendency is an antecedent of brand anthropomorphism, and that brand anthropomorphism predicts the quality of relationship between the consumer and the brand (see Figure 9.1). Thus, we test the following hypotheses:

> *H3a*: Anthropomorphizing tendency is positively associated with brand anthropomorphism.
> *H3b*: Brand anthropomorphism is positively associated with the quality of consumer-brand relationship.

Research methodology

As posited by Hypotheses 1 and 2, collectivism and market development influence anthropomorphism. Therefore, data were collected from three countries varying in collectivism and market development: China, India, and the United States. The United States represents a culture low on collectivism, while China represents a culture high on collectivism. India is in the middle (Hofstede 2001; House *et al.* 2004). With respect to market development, as measured by GDP per capita, the United States is the highest. India and China are significantly lower than the United States, with China being slightly higher than India.

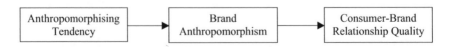

FIGURE 9.1 Conceptual model

Data were gathered from student populations in a university in Beijing in China, a northern university in India, and a southeastern university in the United States. The paper and pencil questionnaire was administered in English in India and the United States. The questionnaire was translated into Mandarin for use in China and then translated back into English. Results reported here are based on 257 responses from the Chinese sample, 140 responses from the Indian sample, and 212 responses from the United States sample. The mean age of respondents was 18.27 (China), 22.58 (India), and 20.81 (United States). In the samples, 41.5 percent (China), 53.6 percent (India), and 57.5 percent (United States) were males.

Measures

Anthropomorphizing tendency (AT)

Anthropomorphizing tendency was measured using the 15-item IDAQ scale developed by Waytz, Cacioppo, and Epley (2010). IDAQ asks to what extent nonhuman agents such as animals, technology, and nature have intentions, free will, emotions, consciousness, and minds of their own (see Appendix).

Brand anthropomorphism

For measuring brand anthropomorphism, responses were elicited for two products – mobile phones and athletic shoes. These products were chosen as they were popular among university students in all of the three countries. If respondents owned more than one brand, they were asked to identify their favorite among these. Their responses pertained to the identified brand. Brand anthropomorphism was measured using five items (11-point scales) derived from the IDAQ scale. Respondents were asked to what extent your mobile phone (or athletic shoe) has intentions, free will, emotions, consciousness, and a mind of its own (see Appendix).

Quality of the consumer-brand relationship

Fournier (1998) proposed Brand Relationship Quality (BRQ) as a seven-faceted indicator of the quality, strength and depth of a consumer-brand relationship. The seven facets include love, passion, self-connection, nostalgic connection, personal commitment, intimacy, and brand partner quality. The scale for BRQ utilized in this research consists of 16 items (measured on seven-point scales) adapted from Ekinci, Yoon and Oppewal (2005). Fourteen of the BRQ scale items measure the seven relationship facets proposed by Fournier (1998) and the remaining two measure the trustworthiness of the brand (see Appendix). Consumer responses for BRQ were also elicited for both mobile phones and athletic shoes.

Reliability of measures

The reliability (Cronbach's Alpha) coefficients for the multi-item measures for the constructs are provided in Table 9.1. The measures of internal consistency exceed the common threshold of 0.70 for the measures of anthropomorphism and brand relationship quality for all three countries. The measures of anthropomorphizing tendency pass the threshold as well except for the measures of technology for the Indian sample, which was 0.69.

Analysis and results

Cross-cultural and market development comparisons of anthropomorphizing tendency (AT)

A one-way ANOVA was conducted to test for differences in AT of people in China, India, and the United States. The mean AT values for China, India, and the United States are 4.39, 4.36 and 3.18 respectively. Overall ANOVA results indicate that the national differences in AT are significant ($p < 0.001$). For country level comparisons, since sample sizes are unequal, we use post-hoc Scheffe tests. As shown in Table 9.2, there is no significant difference in AT between China and India, while both China and India are significantly higher than the United States in AT. The differences support the market development Hypothesis 2a that Chinese and Indian consumers have higher AT than those in the United States. The cross-cultural hypothesis H1a is partially supported, in that AT is higher in China and India than in the United States, but not supported in that no AT difference was found between China and India.

TABLE 9.1 Cronbach's alpha for multi-item measures

| | Anthropomorphising Tendency | | |
	Animal	Nature	Technology
China	0.87	0.89	0.89
India	0.71	0.76	0.69
USA	0.81	0.81	0.89

| | Brand Anthropomorphism | | Brand Relationship Quality | |
	Mobile Phone	Athletic Shoes	Mobile Phone	Athletic Shoes
China	0.86	0.85	0.88	0.92
India	0.76	0.87	0.84	0.89
USA	0.91	0.93	0.92	0.92

TABLE 9.2 Post-hoc comparison of AT across three countries

(I) Country	(J) Country	Mean Difference (I-J)	Std. Error	Sig.
China	USA	1.21073*	0.16512	0.000
	India	0.02788	0.18709	0.989
India	USA	1.18285*	0.19449	0.000
	China	-0.02788	0.18709	0.989
USA	India	-1.18285*	0.19449	0.000
	China	-1.21073*	0.16512	0.000

Note: $\star$Significant at the 0.01 level.

Cross-cultural and market development comparisons of brand anthropomorphism

Now we test Hypotheses 1b and 2b for brand anthropomorphism of mobile phones (AM) and athletic shoes (AA). One way ANOVA was conducted with AM and AA as dependent variables. Overall ANOVA results for both AM and AA reveal significant differences across three countries ($p < 0.001$). Post-hoc Scheffe test results show that AM and AA do not differ between Chinese and Indian consumers, but are significantly higher compared to the United States consumers (see Table 9.3). Therefore, we find support for Hypothesis 1b and partial support for Hypothesis 2b.

TABLE 9.3 Post-hoc comparison of AM and AA across three countries

Dependent Variable	(I) Country	(J) Country	Mean Difference (I-J)	Std. Error	Sig.
AM	China	USA	0.88636*	0.19768	0.000
		India	-0.22245	0.22402	0.611
	India	USA	1.10881*	0.23304	0.000
		China	0.22245	0.22402	0.611
	USA	India	-1.10881*	0.23304	0.000
		China	-0.88636*	0.19768	0.000
AA	China	USA	1.24138*	0.19052	0.000
		India	-0.42835	0.21582	0.140
	India	USA	1.66973*	0.22421	0.000
		China	0.42835	0.21582	0.140
	USA	India	-1.66973*	0.22421	0.000
		China	-1.24138*	0.19052	0.000

Note: $\star$Significant at the 0.01 level.

Anthropomorphism and brand relationship quality – model testing

We conducted structural model analysis (using AMOS 18) to test our predictions on the antecedents and consequences of brand anthropomorphism. There are five model constructs in the structural model as shown in Figure 9.2. The model proposes that brand anthropomorphism is an endogenous construct resulting from the exogenous construct anthropomorphizing tendency.

As given in the methodology, the measures of brand anthropomorphism used here were adapted from the anthropomorphizing tendency scale, and, therefore, we first assessed the discriminant validity between anthropomorphizing tendency and brand anthropomorphism using the method suggested by Fornell and Larcker (1981). All the constructs were found to possess discriminant validity in each of the three countries.

Further, the model shown in Figure 9.2 was fit for each product (mobile phones and athletic shoes) in each of the three countries. The models fit the data quite well as shown by the chi-square statistics and fit indices shown in Table 9.4. For all models, the p-value for the chi-square is >0.05 indicating good fit. Additionally,

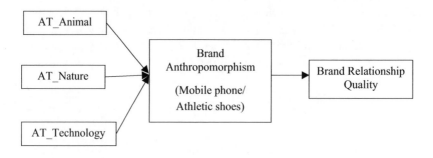

FIGURE 9.2 The structure model

TABLE 9.4 Model fit indices

Country	Chi²	df	p-value	RMSEA	CFI	CMIN/df
Mobile Phone						
China	7.10	3	0.07	0.07	0.99	20.37
India	7.26	3	0.06	0.10	0.96	2.42
USA	3.82	3	0.28	0.04	0.99	1.27
Athletic Shoes						
China	2.49	3	0.48	0.00	1.0	0.83
India	0.94	3	0.82	0.00	1.0	0.31
USA	1.92	3	0.59	0.00	1.0	0.64

common fit indices such as the RMSEA, CFI and CMIN/df also indicate very good fit.

The parameter estimates of the proposed structural links are presented in Table 9.5. The links from AT[N] and AT[T] are significant for all three countries for mobile phones. There is a difference between the Chinese sample and the Indian and US samples with respect to the link from AT[T] to anthropomorphism. The coefficients for the Indian and US samples are the same (0.39) and significantly lower than the Chinese sample (0.62). Only for the Chinese sample is there a significant path from anthropomorphism to BRQ. The results for mobile phones show, for the Chinese sample, an effect of AT[T] on brand anthropomorphism, which enhances BRQ. For the Indian and US samples, there is an effect from AT[N] and AT[T] on brand anthropomorphism, but this does not enhance brand relationship quality. Further, the link from AT[A] to anthropomorphism is significant for the US sample for athletic shoes; however, the path is negative. The effects of the other two AT agents [Nature and Technology] are significant and positive for all three cultures. The relationship between anthropomorphism and brand relationship quality is significant in all three countries for athletic shoes.

Discussion and conclusions

Anthropomorphism has recently attracted the attention of both psychologists and marketers. The present cross-national study adds to theory both by distinguishing between the constructs of anthropomorphizing tendency and brand anthropomorphism and examining country characteristics as antecedents of anthropomorphizing tendency.

TABLE 9.5 Parameter estimates for the model shown in Figure 9.2

Country	AT[A]->AM	AT[N]->AM	AT[T]->AM	AM->BRQ
Mobile Phone				
China	—	0.19	0.62	0.25
India	—	0.27	0.39	—
USA	—	0.20	0.39	—
Athletic Shoes				
	AT[A]->AA	AT[N]->AA	AT[T]->AA	AA->BRQ
China	—	0.38	0.33	0.43
India	—	0.33	0.40	0.30
USA	–0.14	0.36	0.26	0.26

Note: Only significant (p < 0.05) estimates are shown.

Our findings suggest that in China and India, people have higher anthropomorphizing tendencies than people in the United States. Differences in market development and culture appear to explain these differences. In collectivist cultures (China and India), people are interdependent and live closer to each other and, therefore, have higher accessibility of human knowledge than people in individualist cultures (the United States). Further, due to greater economic development, people in the West may have higher exposure to mechanical and technological objects and, therefore, have higher accessibility of nonhuman knowledge than people in the East. In line with Asquith (1986) and Li, Patrick Rau, and Li (2010), our results provide compelling evidence that anthropomorphism varies cross-nationally; it is higher in the Eastern cultures due to their collectivism and lower industrialization, and lower in the Western cultures due to their individualism and higher industrialization.

Model testing reveals that anthropomorphizing tendency predicts brand anthropomorphism, but it is true for the tendency to anthropomorphize non-animate (nature and technology) stimuli only. The tendency to anthropomorphize animals is not related to brand anthropomorphism in China and India, and is negatively related to brand anthropomorphism in the United States. This suggests that general tendency to anthropomorphize non-animate things only predicts anthropomorphism of non-animate things, and the anthropomorphism of animals may not be generalized to anthropomorphism of non-animate things like brands.

Next, our study provides cross-national support that anthropomorphism predicts brand relationship quality, specifically that the greater the level of brand anthropomorphism, the greater the tendency to have quality relationships with brands. Our results held across two unique product categories – mobile phones and athletic shoes. For athletic shoes, the association between anthropomorphism and brand relationship quality holds in all three countries. But for mobile phones, the relationship is found to be significant in China only. This is possibly due to the fact that Chinese people may anthropomorphize technology more than people in India and in the United States, and their tendency to anthropomorphize technology drives their relationships with technological brands (mobile phone brands). Additional research on product category differences and anthropomorphism, particularly in terms of technological disparities, is needed.

Past research finds that brand anthropomorphism motivates consumers to achieve successful social interaction with the brand (Aggarwal and McGill 2012). In this study, we extend the study of brand anthropomorphizing by finding that anthropomorphism increases the likelihood of formation of human-like emotional bonds with brands. This finding is significant as consumers' emotional relationships to brands lead to various marketing outcomes such as consumer retention, satisfaction, recommendations, a reluctance to switch brands, a willingness to share more information with the company, a favorable attitude towards brand extensions, and a willingness to pay price premiums (Thomson *et al.* 2005; Fedorikhin *et al.* 2006; Smit *et al.* 2007).

Theoretical and managerial implications

Our findings have implications for both theory and practice. Our results suggest that the general human tendency to anthropomorphize non-animate things, but not animals, predicts anthropomorphism of brands. Further, accessibility of human knowledge is one of the primary factors that accounts for variation in anthropomorphism. Markets lower in economic development and cultures higher on collectivism have high accessibility of human knowledge, and, therefore, exhibit a higher tendency to anthropomorphize. Finally, it is extensively acknowledged that consumers may form human-like relationships with brands (Fournier 1998). Our study adds to existing knowledge by empirically finding that individuals with higher tendencies to anthropomorphize have higher tendencies to bond with brands and to build quality relationships with them.

Our findings have significant implications in the marketing arena. The anthropomorphizing tendency is inherent in every human being and is prevalent in all cultures. Therefore, whether or not marketers provide anthropomorphic cues to consumers, the anthropomorphism of products and brands is likely. Therefore, while designing products and brands, and while assessing consumer evaluations of products and brands, we recommend that marketers should think in anthropomorphic terms to better predict consumer evaluations.

Next, we find that anthropomorphism enhances brand relationship quality. Although all human beings have an inherent tendency to anthropomorphize, marketers can facilitate brand anthropomorphism by using marketing strategies that suggest the anthropomorphism of products and brands. Strategies, such as the use of metaphors, may facilitate brand anthropomorphism; e.g., a stain cleaner as a tough man and complex software as friendly, would encourage brand anthropomorphism and, hence, would lead consumers to establish stronger and higher quality brand relationships.

Further, based on data from three countries, our study finds that consumers in Eastern cultures are more likely to anthropomorphize brands than their counterparts in Western nations are. This suggests that marketing strategies promoting brand anthropomorphism may yield better marketing outcomes in cultures high in collectivism and in less industrialized countries.

Limitations and future research

This research has certain limitations that imply future research directions. First, our results may be specific to the student population used in the study. Therefore, the same study may be replicated with consumers sharing other demographic profiles to establish generalizability of the findings. Second, our study focuses on two product categories. Studies with other product categories as target stimuli would also be useful, in particular ones that differ technologically and in social situation usage. Third, in the mobile phone category, we find that brand anthropomorphism predicts brand relationship quality in China, but not in the other two countries.

This may be explained by a higher level of anthropomorphism of technology in China; however, future research on additional environmental characteristics may help to explore the issue in depth. Fourth, previous research suggests that a brand could also be an enemy for a consumer (Fournier 1998). As anthropomorphism increases the strength of positive relationships with a brand that is liked, likewise it may also increase the strength of negative relationships with a brand that is disliked, which is an interesting avenue for future research. Finally, based on our finding that anthropomorphism strengthens consumer-brand relationships, we posit that anthropomorphism–based marketing strategies should result in increased marketing effectiveness. Assessment of financial outcome relationships is yet to be established empirically and offer another important avenue for future research.

Appendix

Items used to measure anthropomorphizing tendency (11-point scale: 0-not at all, 10-very much)

1 To what extent does the average fish have free will?
2 To what extent does the average mountain have free will?
3 To what extent does a television set experience emotions?
4 To what extent does the average robot have consciousness?
5 To what extent do cows have intentions?
6 To what extent does a car have free will?
7 To what extent does the ocean have consciousness?
8 To what extent does the average computer have a mind of its own?
9 To what extent does a cheetah experience emotions?
10 To what extent does the environment experience emotions?
11 To what extent does the average insect have a mind of its own?
12 To what extent does a tree have a mind of its own?
13 To what extent does the wind have intentions?
14 To what extent does the average reptile have consciousness?
15 To what extent does technology – devices and machines for manufacturing, entertainment, and productive processes (e.g., cars, computers, television sets) – have intentions?

Items used to measure brand anthropomorphism for mobile phone and athletic shoes (11-point scale: 0-not at all, 10-very much)

1 Have you ever considered that your mobile phone (athletic shoes) has intentions?
2 Have you ever considered that your mobile phone (athletic shoes) has free will?
3 Have you ever considered that your mobile phone (athletic shoes) experiences emotions?
4 Have you ever considered that your mobile phone (athletic shoes) has consciousness?

5   Have you ever considered that your mobile phone (athletic shoes) has mind of its own?

Items used to measure BRQ (7-point scale: 1-not at all, 7-very much):

Passion:

1   It is a feeling of loss when I have not used this brand for a while.
2   Something would definitely be missing in my life should this brand not exist anymore.

Intimacy:

3   I have the feeling that I really understand this brand.
4   It feels like I have known this brand for a long time.

Self-Connection:

5   This brand and I have lots in common.
6   This brand reminds me of who I am.

Nostalgic Connection:

7   This brand reminds of things I have done or places I have been.
8   This brand will always remind me of a certain period in my life.

Love:

9   I have feelings for this brand that I do not have for a lot of other brands.
10   If it is about mobile phones, this brand is my favorite brand.

Partner Quality:

11   This brand has always been good to me.
12   This brand treats me as an important and valuable customer.

Personal Commitment:

13   This brand can always count on me.
14   I will continue using this brand in the near future.

Trust:

15   I trust this brand.
16   This brand is an honest brand.

References

Aggarwal, P. and A.L. McGill (2007) "Is that Car Smiling at Me? Schema Congruity as a Basis for Evaluating Anthropomorphized Products", *Journal of Consumer Research*, 34 (4): 468–479.

Aggarwal, P. and A.L. McGill (2012) "When Brands Seem Human, Do Humans Act Like Brands? Automatic Behavioural Priming Effects of Brand Anthropomorphism", *Journal of Consumer Research,* 39 (2): 307–323.

Asquith, P.J. (1986) "Anthropomorphism and the Japanese and Western Traditions in Primatology", *Primate Ontogeny, Cognition, and Social Behaviour*, eds J.G. Else and P.C. Lee. Cambridge: Cambridge University Press: 61–71.

Bian, Q. and S. Forsythe (2012) "Purchase Intention for Luxury Brands: A Cross Cultural Comparison", *Journal of Business Research*, 65 (10): 1443–1451.

Cohen, A. and K. Johnson (2009) "Religion, Culture, and the Personification of Non Human Entities", paper presented at *Metanexus Conference,* July 18–21, Phoenix, Arizona.

Ekinci, Y., T.H. Yoon, and H. Oppewal (2005) "An Examination of the Brand Relationship Quality Scale in the Evaluation of Restaurant Brands", *Advances in Hospitality and Leisure*, edition 1, Emerald Group Publishing Limited, 1: 189–197.

Epley, N., A. Waytz, and J.T. Cacioppo (2007) "On Seeing Human: A Three-Factor Theory of Anthropomorphism", *Psychological Review*, 114 (4): 864–886.

Eyssel, F., F. Hegel, G. Horstmann, and C. Wagner (2010) "Anthropomorphic Inferences from Emotional Nonverbal Cues: A Case Study", conference proceedings *RO-MAN 2010 IEEE*, September 13–15: 646–651.

Fedorikhin, A., C.W. Park, and M. Thomson (2006) "How Far Do Feelings Go? How Attachments Influence Brand Extensions", *Advances in Consumer Research*, 33: 631.

Fornell, C. and D. Larcker (1981) "Evaluating Structural Equation Models and Unobservable Variables and Measurement Error", *Journal of Marketing Research*, 18 (1): 39–50.

Fournier, S. (1998) "Consumers and Their Brands: Developing Relationship Theory in Consumer Research", *Journal of Consumer Research*, 24 (3): 343–372.

Fournier, S. and C. Alvarez (2012) "Brands as Relationship Partners: Warmth, Competence and In–Between", *Journal of Consumer Psychology*, 22 (2): 177–185.

Hofstede, G. (2001) *Culture's Consequences: Comparing Values, Behaviors, Institutions, and Organizations Across Nations*. London: Sage.

House, R.J., P.J. Hanges, M. Javidan, P.W. Dorfman, and V. Gupta (2004) *Culture, Leadership, and Organizations, The Globe Study of 62 Societies*. Thousand Oaks, CA: Sage.

Kervyn, N., S.T. Fiske, and C. Malone (2012) "Brands as Intentional Agents Framework: How Perceived Intentions and Ability Can Map Brand Perception", *Journal of Consumer Psychology*, 22 (2): 166–176.

Labroo, A., R. Dhar, and N. Schwarz (2008) "Of Frog Wines and Frowning Watches: Semantic Priming, Perceptual Fluency, and Brand Evaluation", *Journal of Consumer Research*, 34 (6): 819–831.

Landwehr, J.R., A.L. McGill, and A. Herrmann (2011) "It's Got The Look: The Effect of Friendly and Aggressive 'Facial' Expressions on Product Liking and Sales", *Journal of Marketing*, 75 (3): 132–146.

Li, D., P.L. Patrick Rau, and Y. Li (2010) "A Cross Cultural Study: Effect of Robot Appearance and Task", *International Journal of Social Robotics*, 2 (2): 175–186.

Puzakova, M., H. Kwak, and J.F. Rocereto (2009) "Pushing the Envelope of Brand and Personality: Antecedents and Moderators of Anthropomorphized Brands", *Advances in Consumer Research*, 36: 413–420.

Roth, M.S. (1995) "The Effects of Culture and Socioeconomics on the Performance of Global Brand Image Strategies", *Journal of Marketing Research*, 32 (2): 163–175.

Smit, E., F. Bronner, and M. Tolboom (2007) "Brand Relationship Quality and Its Value for Personal Contact", *Journal of Business Research*, 60 (6): 627–633.

Thomson, M., D.J. MacInnis, and C.W. Park (2005) "The Ties That Bind: Measuring the Strength of Consumers' Emotional Attachments to Brands", *Journal of Consumer Psychology*, 15 (1): 77–91.

Triandis, H.C. (1989) "The Self and Social Behavior in Differing Cultural Contexts", *Psychological Review*, 96 (3): 506–520.

Waytz, A., J. Cacioppo, and N. Epley (2010) "Who Sees Human?: The Stability and Importance of Individual Differences in Anthropomorphism", *Perspectives on Psychological Science*, 5 (3): 219–232.

Zhang, S., J. van Doorn, and P.S.H. Leeflang (2014) "Does the Importance of Value, Brand and Relationship Equity for Customer Loyalty Differ Between Eastern and Western Cultures?", *International Business Review*, 23 (1): 284–292.

10

THE POST-HUMAN FUTURE OF BRANDS

Robert V. Kozinets

Predicting the future

> There are bits of the literal future right here, right now, if you know how to look for them. Although I can't tell you how; it's a non-rational process.
>
> *William Gibson, in Johnston (1999)*

How would we predict the future of brands? How would brand management change if we could predict the future? What is the future of brand management?

In this chapter, I use a cultural history perspective to create projective understandings, and I also assume two things: first, that the brand experience is becoming increasing tied into the entertainment experience; and second, that the entertainment experience is becoming more immersive, more powerful, more responsive, more omni-channeled, and more digital. Across both of these elements, we see notions of brands as archetypal personalities with stories co-existing with notions of brands as identity tools and resources for people's collective and individual identity creation, maintenance, and transformation projects.

If we accept this, then we accept that brands have become: popular culture, immersively digital, essential to consumer identity, and archetypal identities in themselves.

The question then becomes, 'Where should we look to project these changes in brands toward the future?' The use of professional futurists by corporate interests has, as Andrew Ross tracks in *Strange Weather* (1991), a long history. Many of these professional futurists have understandably been science fiction authors.

This chapter looks towards science fiction visions as sources of projective ideas regarding the future of brands. The three books that comprise William Gibson's *Bridge* trilogy are used as an idea source and as raw data, which led me to other sources and theories. Throughout this process, which constitutes one part of a much larger research project, I seek to perform future-oriented pattern recognition that can inform our understanding of the trajectory of brands at a macro-social and cultural level, one that tells us about concepts in historical trajectory, a form of both research and development prognostication and theory generation.

William Gibson's work

William Gibson is best known, and highly quoted, for his genre-defining novel, *Neuromancer* (1999), which coined the term and concept of the information universe called "cyberspace." This notion was further developed through the highly conceptual and philosophical Wachowski Brothers film *The Matrix* (1999), later expanded into a trilogy. In Gibson's *Neuromancer* trilogy future, information astronauts were blasted into cyberspace using various drugs and implements. The link to classic science fiction is fascinating, in that launching people into interplanetary outer space evolves into launching people's conscious awareness into notional digital computer space. In *Neuromancer*, we also witness the next major evolution in our planetary species: the complex artificial intelligence (AI) computer program "Wintermute" slides its expansionary subprograms into the Internet to become a fully conscious self-aware being.

This chapter centrally considers another book: William Gibson's 1996 novel *Idoru* (1997). *Idoru* takes place in "what can now loosely be called the *Bridge* sequence [trilogy] of *Virtual Light*, *Idoru*, and *All Tomorrow's Parties*" (Murphy 2003: 72). This trilogy takes place in a time between our own and the more technologically and socially sophisticated, almost magical, future era of *Neuromancer*. *Idoru* is the second and, thus, "bridge" novel of this sequence of books written to link the time between present and future, and it offers the reader "a subtly complex engagement with the post/human tapestry of presence, pattern, simulation, virtuality, and digital/corporeal embodiment" (Murphy 2003: 72).

The book deeply engages with the idea of celebrity as brand, and brand as celebrity. It takes a hard-hitting stance towards the interaction between popular culture, digital devices, and individual shallowness. Global culture is incredibly complex, people are extremely good at producing technologies, and individuals are more stereotypical corporate puppets than actual human beings. The key mantra for this future is "popular culture is the test bed of our futurity". Everyone lives to be a brand, and every brand is the key to social being.

Digital embodiment

In Gibson's future, the digital is becoming embodied. We see a perfect example of this with Rei Toei. Rei is a virtual creation, an *idoru*, a synthetic media star. Toei is described as "a personality-construct, a congeries of software agents, the creation of information-designers, she is akin to what I believe they call a 'synthespian,' in Hollywood" (Gibson 1997: 21). Gibson does not invent the word or concept here, but borrows this word from others. In fact, synthespians already exist.

dk-96, the creation of Japanese entertainment software conglomerate HoriPro Inc., was released in 1996 as "Kyoko Date." dk-96, or Kyoko Date, recorded her own music single, released on CD as *Love Communication*. The content also included a videostream of her walking along major urban streets in Japan and the US. Kyoko Date even has a biography that bespeaks her heritage as both American and Japanese, born at a US Army Base located close to Tokyo (Gaouette 1998). Kyoko Date is really not a digital creation, but a digital hybrid: her entire look, face, and body came from paid, but now rendered anonymous, human female models whose faces and body language were digitized in a recording process known as Full Motion Capture. Very much like Rei Toei, Kyoko Date inspired a broad male fan following, those who knew a deep and abiding desire for a perfect woman that they were just as likely to have as any of the perfect human celebrities. This desire was, in a Lacanian sense, perfect. This was a desire that went on and on, for it could never be fulfilled by any physical woman. They had a longing for a woman who only existed digitally. According to Lacan (1964), unfulfillable desire is the perfect, most pure, desire. It may well be that these gentlemen were so in love with dk-96 precisely because they knew they could never physically experience her. Perhaps, her image play is the strongest play, after all, for them, or the only play necessary for becoming a fan.

Gibson plays with desire throughout *Idoru*, hanging tantalizing hints that all we want is pure want: that celebrity, and especially that of Rei Toei's variety, exists as "aggregates of subjective desire." What does this say about brands, and to brand theorists and managers?

To Gibson, there are no doubts about what brand management is at its core, and where brand managers should be focusing their attention. To him, brand work is about building in consumer society "an architecture of articulated longing" (Gibson 1997: 178). If we need an example closer to North America, we only have to look at Lara Croft (Murphy 2003), or indeed at so many of the now iconic superheroines on display at ComicCons. If you are lustily, deeply, and madly in love with Wonder Woman, Supergirl, or even She-Hulk, then you are set up for the same kind of fantastic desire disappointment.

What would it mean to have a brand become such a thing? Is a brand already, in some ways, such a thing? Might we think of the Old Spice Guy, Isaiah Mustafa, as a similarly unattainable, but also perfect performance of manhood, something whose interactive response campaign made it close to an avatar, more like a long interactive advertisement? Celebrity, in the case of the Old Spice Guy, was directly attached to the brand, yet interactive, and openly available as files on YouTube, to be watched on demand and shared. What would it mean to think of the Old Spice Guy evolving digitally into a virtual creation like Rei Toei? This could be the future of brands: as AI entities that enact brand personalities and stories in interactive ways, with particular audiences, perhaps even in an on-demand manner with particular individuals.

Post-human branding

We have heard much talk of human branding, from scholars such as Thomson (2006), Parmentier (2011), and Fournier and Eckhardt (2013). Increasingly, people are brands (e.g., a celebrity or microcelebrity brand) (Marwick and Boyd 2011).

We can see the process of personal and human branding manifesting itself through another type of digital transformation. In this case, we learn a branding lesson from a rock and roll figure, much larger than life, who has attained mega-stardom in the rock and roll arena with his band Lo/Rez, of which he is the lead singer. Named Rez, he is like a bigger and longer lasting Mick Jagger, and almost comparable to a modern Elvis. He is an incredibly popular figure with the entertainment and news media and throughout social media.

However, as we learn in *Idoru*, Rez is a complete personal brand empire unto himself. He commands a huge media, entertainment, and fashion licensing empire, and generates significant motion pictures, videos, and music sales. And, yet, he is an empty shell of a person, somehow completely hollowed out. He is like a shadow, an alien, a digital cloud of static: he is not traceable or even recognizable as an actual human being. He has no private life at all. He is a licensed image, and in his somewhat inconvenient simultaneous incarnation as an aging human male he must continually alter and surgically change his body to try to match the popular and expected image of himself – a trait of insecure self-treatment that seems the most human thing anyone can do.

In these sections, Gibson is already drawing our attention to the implications of personal and human branding, of taking our personalities and goals and life projects and making brands of them. The inevitability of the project infuses his future vision. Its widespread nature is apparent. To personally brand is commonplace. Everyone will soon be managing themselves as their own brand, in an increasingly careful and deliberate way.

The marriage of the humanized brand and the branded human

In *Idoru*, the marriage of humanized brand and branded human is physical, not metaphorical, and therein lies the struggle.

The digital construct Rei Toei appears on Rez's system and asks him to marry her. Rez is a flesh and blood human who is so famous, he has become entirely digital, his every move captured, sold, and shared online. Rei Toei is a digital construct, made to seem human, interacting with people as if she were Turing-test real, and then seeking, Pinocchio-like, to become a real girl.

The resolution in this tension between the natural and the digital is epitomized in the marriage of Rei Toei, the media industry-constructed software celebrity, and Rez, the media industry-constructed human celebrity. Can the two truly unite in holy matrimony: the computer construct and the aging rock star? A man and a program of a woman?

In one place in the novel, science fiction guru Gibson speaks through rock god

Rez's voice of "new modes of being" and "the alchemical marriage" (Gibson 1997: 229). This allusion to alchemy invokes his higher referents for the union, what mystical psychologist Carl Jung (1963) called the *Mysterium Coniunctionis*, the sacred marriage or union of opposites. This mystical union of digital humans and human digitality is a perfect metaphor for our current evolution: we meet in the nether grounds of the numinously technological attention market and marry our images, our self-creating brand images that are co-created by and co-creating us.

What is the link between the digital world, and the world of physical human beings? The key is held in what we currently call 3D printing, but which is really a set of technologies still to be more fully defined and named. Nanotechnology is involved, a future nano-assembler that is a military grade, highly top secret, and in limited supply version of a 3D printer, which can create matter from digital instructions. In the resolution, Rei does indeed become human and physical, manifesting through nanotechnology into a real, live body. However, she does it in a way that displays that, although she is now materialized, she is clearly not human. For, she arrives in many places at once, exact and perfect digital duplicates. From being zero, suddenly there is not just one being, as with humans, but many Rei Toeis.

Now, as many, is she both more attainable and less desirable? Or, because her humanity still eludes her, is she even more desirable? Desire for the unattainable is at the very heart of contemporary consumer culture, and thus it is at the very heart of brands – their unspoken, almost never realized and, ultimately, paradoxical secret (Shakar 2001; Brown *et al.* 2003).

When a brand assumes human form, it enables a paradox of desire: it can become both more desirable and more attainable. Its attainability, if limited to the digital world of screens, still places it as out of reach as a Hollywood star. However, the brand becomes much more intimate, much more complex, if it is also a product or a service, a place, an idea, or a human brand.

We crave our supergods

Archetypes are everywhere. Can we see the Jolly Green Giant as an archetypal and folkloric figure, as Sullenberger (1974) does? Wrapped in leaves, giant and green, he is clearly a fertility figure of the kind mythologically identified by James Frazer in *The Golden Bough* (1922). The giant is an ancient European harvest figure, long established and associated with the color green, the garland, the wrapping in leaves, the way he paternalistically presides over the bountiful crop. As Sullenberger (1974: 55) clearly explains, the campaign works. It worked in 1974. It was already an established, if formulaic, economic success, a standout of early brand building in the competitive world of food marketing, and it is still working today. The brand remains a viable brand. The Giant is still quite limited in his repertoire, still not very active or interactive. He 'ho ho hoes' on cue at the end of the commercial. His mere presence is almost his story, but he does have mythological potential.

In service, think of figures like Ronald McDonald and his retinue, and Chuck E. Cheese. The United States, along with Japan, truly pioneered and continues to pioneer such branding experiments. Experiments in which brands become simultaneously human, mythological, and commercial; they become ways to enact great human themes on the level of marketplace decisions and purchases.

As Grant Morrison explains in *Supergods*, "we live in the stories we tell ourselves. In a secular, scientific rational culture lacking in any convincing spiritual leadership, superhero stories speak loudly and boldly to our greatest fears, deepest longings, and highest aspirations. They're not afraid to be hopeful, not embarrassed to be optimistic, and utterly fearless in the dark." (Morrison 2011: xvii).

Hopeful and powerful, yet enacted at the level of the marketplace rather than explicitly at a mystical level of religious or spiritual elevation, brands offer us opportunities for certain kinds of super-heroic transformation at a cost. Plastic surgery, adventure travel, a new car: all offer certain kinds of identity transformation, available for a price.

What happens when we marry such potential to interactive AI agents, who take over as the voice of brands, similar to the emerging voice of brands that is required when social media accounts are managed, such as for personified food service brands like Taco Bell or Wendy's? Such is the modern marketplace. Such are the promises of brands.

Five convergences

The following is some speculative historical theorization, drawn from *Idoru* and Gibson's *Bridge* trilogy. There is currently emerging a meta-convergence of five already major social and media convergences:

1 communicative media
2 the internet of things
3 the maker movement
4 collective intelligence
5 artificial intelligence

As a result of these convergences, we can no longer think of brands as linked to products, to consumer markets, or to even to exchanges of matter. The net effect of these technological convergences has been to unlink brands from matter entirely. Brands are no longer products; of course, this has been the case for a long time, ever since the first brand extension was discovered.

As a consequence, brands have become unbound from material substrates in exactly the same way that thought unbinds minds from brains.

What are the two brand trends that Gibson is relating to us through *Idoru*? First, brands are changing into and inhabiting human beings through evolving information software and AI. Second, human beings are digitally extending and reinventing themselves into higher order constructs of strategically managed personal brands, social brands, which have semi-autonomous 'agentic' elements of individual power and influence.

In the future, brands may be governed by AIs. They may become sophisticated, responsive, intelligent personalities, tied to products, services, places, notions, and people. Not only might brands become personalities, but they may also become sites, nodes of data processing and intelligence gathering. A brand would not only be a transmitting, processing, and thinking-deciding personality-imbued intelligence itself, but it would also serve, in archival fashion, as a vast space of play, information, and decision-making for popular society itself, the next evolution of popular culture.

This particular reading of William Gibson's *Bridge* trilogy reveals five interstitial areas or key convergences in the worlds of mass-mediated communications and information technologies. Because these alterations change matter into mind, and mind into spectacle, they elevate brand personalities to AI celebrities. To enfold human imagination, these AI forms will be assistants in the hero stories and mythic tales that we write for ourselves, that we use to structure our tales, the tales we tell others of ourselves, that we wish others to share, and that we love to use to sacralize our consumption and everything else we do in our everyday life.

Interdependence

Are people also brands, and brands also people? To what extent are they or were they ever independent? Many people already are, and many more will be brands; many brands will also be people. We talk about anthropomorphized brands, such as Mr. Clean, the Blendtec guy, or the Old Spice Guy, but will brands one day have the potential and power to court us? To manifest in our information systems? To alter to our likes and dislikes, learning how to make us love them more and more, simultaneously fulfilling and stoking our desires? To begin dreaming, generating new images, taking actions such as manifesting to someone and proposing marriage?

What Gibson suggests to us is that brands are transforming into unique, higher-dimensional constructs – a medial middle ground and digital interstices in which human beings can evolve into code, and code beings can evolve into something more human: a convergence built upon other convergences.

Using personal branding concepts and personal technological devices, such as smartphones, apps, laptops, movie screens, computer screens, video channels such as YouTube, microcelebrity fan payment plans, and digital television, people will increasingly become empowered to transcend their limitations and become part of the technocapitalistic money-and-status-machine sold by media industries. Even Google will promote your personal brand for micropayments.

Our story: my story and yours

Using the most sophisticated intelligence and technological reality creation tools ever available, we are creating all sorts of social informational experiments. The central novel form these narratives increasingly take is that of the collective dream, visible clearly through science fiction, comic books, and in self-help psychology. Beneath it all, hero myths abound. This is the collective dream, a narrative heart. This is our story, a story of good and evil that clearly beats beneath stories like *The Lord of the Rings* and *Game of Thrones* as well as *Virtual Light, Idoru,* and *All Tomorrow's Parties* – the three books of the *Bridge* trilogy. Casting the *Bridge* trilogy as one would a set of casting stones, I see a human future where brands are at least as real as the people who use them, and human-brand "relationships" that draw us to a new digital reality where we meet in between, in the realm of the human brand where brands become human and humans become brands. In this burgeoning reality, each of us will also be a brand manager who manages the value, capital resources, narrative flow, and public image of our own personal brand, or even a stable of other brands, owned by people and corporations of various sorts and stripes.

Ordinary people may be less so, but extraordinary ones will be candidates for courtship and proposals by large corporations. When we blog and have impressive Klout scores and social media influence, we really are somebody. We are other people's heroes. In some sense, this digital future might be good, and also a bit wrong. Yet, it may turn out that having our biological and social fantasies professionally managed, edited, and played back to us endlessly in story form will turn out to be all that we will ever need.

The search for natural culture

To be a person today is to be part of a collective human effort to understand ourselves: who you really are, what really matters to yourself only, and what matters to all of us. I call this the search for natural culture. We all want to know what we really believe. What we really care about. What we really need. What we really love. The "really" part is the important part. This is the widely recognized search for truth, in the form of the genuine and authentic self.

This search effort is, by definition, relational. It involves our relationship to one another as well as our relationship to what we find to be the world around us. Each of us is on a collective quest to find an understanding of our own individual relationship to nature, and also to culture.

Human relationship consumption is, at its core, the source of all other consumption, and motivating all of this is our collective modern quest for a sense of who we are in this moment: our natural culture. That distinct element, culture, is that one thing which we do not ever forget not to take for granted. Culture is the difference that differentiates and the difference that is entirely and eternally the same across all of us. In this age, natural culture is found by embracing technology. Technology is our most natural manifestation. We are fully artificial beings, and thus concurrently fully genuine in our artifice.

Consider that our times are times in which digital technology is necessary to be cool and social. Digital technology is required to be a productive worker, a good consumer, and a member of society. Technology itself has become not only indispensable, but natural. Speaking of this in relation to national culture, speaking for the robophilic techno-embracers of Japanese culture, Idoru's creator Kuwayama explains: "We [the Japanese people] have never developed a sinister view of technology, Mr. Laney. It is an aspect of the natural, of oneness. Through our efforts, oneness perfects itself" (Gibson 1997: 314).

Certainly since industrialization began in the UK, we have not seen the rise of technology-based capitalism spread as quickly or as successfully as it has today, accommodating the development of today's age of "high" technology, which combines entertainment, information, communications, and social systems. This is the natural form and language of our global civilization, a still-developing, contested, conflicted, complex network of competing and coordinating interests and influences. Conveyed within them all is an age of amazing images, amazing selves, and amazing personal brand self-images. It is from within this deeply cultural sphere that Gibson chooses to immerse us in brand images that have become human, and human images that are becoming brands.

In conclusion, this chapter contemplates the future of brands in technocapitalism and technoculture. It also seeks to do more than this. It prognosticates brands as future actualizations of entertainment and media descriptions of the future. The "methodology" or method of prediction comes not from some statistical flavor of argument, not from some mathematical, but instead a cultural extrapolation.

Science fiction is assumed to be type of Einsteinean thought experiment. Moreover, it is one in which the stock market of popular culture population ecology has had the effect of elevating the best work and the most evocative predictions. We can look at these as successful professional fictional extrapolations of possible technological and social futures. Science fiction is the test bed of brand futurity. This chapter and its method have assumed that science fiction books can help us adapt to and shape our understanding of brands.

In that future, human beings increasingly extend their personal brands into digital spaces, and corporate brands simultaneously seek to manifest their influence in human social worlds. The two meet in the realm of digital branding and human brands, converging in five separate technology developments and accelerating the interweaving of corporate and organizational influence with ordinary human social life. It is a world we already see in development, and a reality that could be greatly changed by the emergence of AI brand entities, brands that think, relate, and speak back.

Brands that we genuinely know, and that genuinely know us: could this truly be the post-human future of brands?

References

Brown, S., R. V. Kozinets, and J. F. Sherry, Jr. (2003) "Teaching Old Brands New Tricks: Retro Branding and the Revival of Brand Meaning", *Journal of Marketing*, 67 (July): 19–33.

Fournier, S. and Eckhardt, G. (2013) "Managing a Corporeal Brand", Compro Biz Blog Network, September 24, 2013.

Gaouette, N. "Sirens of Cyberspace." *The Christian Science Monitor*, July 2, 1998.

Gibson, W. (1994) *Virtual Light*. New York: Bantam.

Gibson, W. (1997) *Idoru*. New York: Berkley, 1997.

Gibson, W. (1999) *All Tomorrow's Parties*. New York: Putnam.

Gibson, W. (1999) *Neuromancer*. New York: Ace.

Johnston, A. (1999) "William Gibson: *All Tomorrow's Parties*: Waiting for the Man", *Spike Magazine*, August 1, 1999, www.spikemagazine.com/0899williamgibson.php.

Jung, C.J. (1963) *Mysterium Coniunctionis: An Inquiry into the Separation and Synthesis of Psychic Opposites in Alchemy*, Volume 14 in *The Collected Works of C. G. Jung*, eds M. Fordham and H. Read. Princeton, NJ: Princeton University Press.

Lacan, J. (1964) *The Seminar, Book XI, The Four Fundamental Concepts of Psychoanalysis*, ed. J.A. Miller, trans. 1977 A. Sheridan,. New York: W.W. Norton & Co.

Marwick, A. and D. Boyd (2011) "To See and Be Seen: Celebrity Practice on Twitter", *Convergence* 17 (2): 139–158.

Morrison, G. (2011) *Supergods*. New York: Spiegel & Grau.

Murphy, G. (2003) "Post/Humanity and the Interstitial: A Glorification of Possibility in Gibson's Bridge Sequence," *Science Fiction Studies*, 30 (1): 72–90.

Parmentier, M.A. (2011) "When David Met Victoria: Forging a Strong Family Brand", *Family Business Review*, 24 (3): 217 –232.

Ross, A. (1991) *Strange Weather: Culture, Science, and Technology in the Age of Limits*. New York: Verso.

Shakar, A. (2001) *The Savage Girl*. New York: HarperCollins.

Sullenberger, T.E. (1974) "Ajax Meets the Jolly Green Giant: Some Observations on the Use of Folklore and Myth in American Mass Marketing", *The Journal of American Folklore*, 87 (January–March): 53–65.

Thomson, M. (2006) "Human Brands: Investigating Antecedents to Consumers' Strong Attachments to Celebrities", *Journal of Marketing*, 70 (3): 104–119.

PART IV
#BrandsOnline

11

FROM STRANGER TO FRIEND

Shaping consumer-brand relationships with social media

Renée Richardson Gosline

The average consumer appears to have an increasingly intimate connection with technology products. She looks at her smartphone first thing in the morning and directly before she sleeps at night; she spends 82 percent of her mobile minutes on 41 applications (apps). She uses these apps for everything from shopping and entertainment, to social networking, to creating and sharing content (Gupta 2013; Nielsen 2012). Does the increasingly intimate access to, and use of, these social media applications translate into more intimate relationships with sponsor brands? That is, beyond mere purchase consideration, can using an app deepen the relationship between consumer and brand, moving it from an exchange-based connection to a more interpersonal and communal one (Aggarwal 2004; Fournier 1998)?

Although app-based media has allowed consumers to connect with brands in unprecedented ways, little empirical evidence exists to show that it actually strengthens the relationships between brands and their consumers. On the contrary, what little evidence exists about the impact of apps emphasizes the importance of their utility: apps need to serve a function in order to provide value (Dohnert 2013; Goodson 2011). These studies suggest a transactional, "what have you done for me lately," exchange-based view of the role of apps. Recent research has suggested that apps can increase brand purchase if they work in some manner to provide something of utility such as information, entertainment, or a service (Bellman *et al.* 2011). Other research points to the importance of consumers' ability to customize and exercise control over the app to driving increasing app usage (Kim *et al.* 2013).

Though these studies examine new media, their theoretical perspectives appear to be consistent with an old media exchange-based view of consumers. They do not address the impact of new media (such as apps) on brands in two key ways: first, the exchange-based view of app efficacy overlooks the increasingly interpersonal dimensions of the ways in which consumers create meaning for their brands (McCracken 1986). This is crucial, not only because of the increasing intimacy that consumers have with digital media, but because marketers seek to create intense, active loyalty relationships that can affect brand equity in the long term (Keller 2009). I argue that apps are important beyond their mere exchange-based utility because they enable consumers to construct their digital extended selves (Belk 2013) and engage in identity work that creates new meaning for their brands (Arnould and Thompson 2005; Schau and Gilly 2003). Thus, a consumer-brand relationship perspective is essential to gaining a more nuanced understanding of the impact of apps on the ways in which consumers view their corresponding brands.

Second, the little existing research on the impact of apps on brands is not based on experimental tests in a real field setting. Rather, the current evidence is primarily based on anecdotal cases, content analyses of existing apps, or lab-based tests of existing apps. To understand the impact of apps, theory must be developed that is based on a methodological approach that is both rigorous and experimental in nature to minimize confounding variables and to allow causal conclusions, as well as based in a real field setting similar to the one managers face for the purpose of external validity.

In the meantime, firms both large and small seem to be jumping on the app bandwagon, with some viewing it as a key strategic asset, and others perhaps out of fear of getting left behind by competitors (Forrester 2011). Contemporary apps are not predominantly commerce or transaction-based; rather, today's offerings are dominated by apps that allow brands to connect with consumers in other ways: via providing entertainment or information, and via social networking. These added-value (non-exchange) offerings beg the question: is this money well spent? We need to better understand the relative impact of these aspects of app-based media on consumer-brand relationships. Do added-value features, such as the opportunity to connect with friends, the ability to customize, and/or the capacity to discover new information, actually strengthen a consumer's relationship with a brand? In this chapter, I explore this question, in an effort to better understand how apps build value and meaning for consumers, and generate loyalty to their brand sponsors beyond what one would expect from mere transactional interactions between the consumer and the brand.

I suggest that apps are most effective in strengthening consumer-brand relationships when consumers are able to enhance their digital extended selves by engaging in identity work that conveys a desired social identity (Belk 2013; Arnould and Thompson 2005). I argue that perceived brand trustworthiness is essential to the development of higher-order consumer-brand relationships. My results suggest that brand managers should recognize and facilitate image-enhancing social identity work if they want to build more positive brand relationships and trust with consumers. Taken together, these findings shed light on the strategic impact of apps on brands and contribute to the development of consumer-brand relationship theory. I choose to define the scope by focusing on entertainment apps in order to better understand their implications for the development of communal relationships and their impact on brand resonance (Keller 2012, 2001; Aggarwal 2004). This choice stands in contrast to an emphasis on apps that enable commerce between a consumer and the brand. In some respects, the utilized example presents a more conservative test of what creates a truly engaging app, as users have no real utility-based need to compel usage (i.e., as they do with mobile banking or shopping apps).

Viewing impact through the consumer-brand relationship lens

Brands can be more than mere products; people may connect to their brands in ways similar to the manner in which they connect with other people. There may be loyal connections, dysfunctional relationships, arms-length business acquaintanceships, and perhaps everything in between. Consider the recent fallout when the popular app Instagram (with 150 million monthly active users) changed its policy in 2012 and claimed it had the right to sell users' photographs without obtaining their permissions. The reactions amongst consumers included emotions most often associated with soap opera storylines: betrayal, anger, and passion. Loyal app user and famous actor Jonah Hill (with 3 million Twitter followers) tweeted: "Instagram, you were my favorite app and you stabbed me in the back. I feel like I just married you and you slept with my best friend" (posted on Twitter 12/18/2012 3:57 p.m.)

Despite his anguish, Mr Hill continues to use Instagram. Though his usage of the product is stable, should he be deemed brand loyal? A more nuanced description could adjudicate between the self-described best friend relationship Mr Hill had with the app prior to its policy change and the new relationship state characterized by dislike. Managers need to be able to understand and measure these differences in relational type if they are to truly create brand equity and minimize their vulnerability to losing their customers to competitors. Viewing the impact of marketing strategy through the lens of consumer-brand relationships (CBR) can revolutionize the way we understand traditional notions of brand loyalty and brand consideration.

Consumer-brand relationship theory leverages metaphors from interpersonal relationships as guides for brand relationships (Fournier 1998). Though early characterizations of consumer behavior viewed consumers' interactions with products as a series of exchanges, a more sociological view is called for, given the way that digital media has structured consumers' interactions with both their brands and one another (Prahalad and Ramaswamy 2004a; Smelser and Swedberg 2010). In CBR, a continuum ranging from more formal interactions (e.g., business transactions) to more personal relationships draws inspiration from research on human-to-human interpersonal relationships (Wish et al. 1976; McCall 1970). This work suggests that we may develop a deeper understanding of consumer attitudes by employing language that describes human relationships (e.g., "friend", "fling", "enemy"), to describe consumer-brand relationships.

Yet, there is a paucity of work that links this theoretical perspective with the burgeoning social media phenomenon of apps (cf., Leigh and Thompson 2011;

Hennig-Thurau *et al.* 2010). I argue that this bridge must be built to help us understand the relative importance of the features that uniquely characterize social media, such as customization, network effects, and the discovery of new information via formal and informal sources.

How then might we measure the impact of app-based social media through the consumer-brand relationship lens? Instead of binary measures of purchase (yes or no), or superficial "likes" on Facebook corporate pages, we can employ nuanced relationship constructs. For instance, an ostensibly loyal repeat-purchaser could characterize her relationship to a brand in any of a number of ways: dislike, stranger, business acquaintance, fling, or friend. Consider the aforementioned case of Jonah Hill: he might describe his relationship with the Instagram app as having gone from "friend" to "dislike."Yet, Mr Hill's repeated usage of the product would likely mask this change in the nature of his relationship to the brand. A manager who measures brand loyalty as a behavioral measure with sales figures alone would miss this important relational change, and perhaps be surprised when a competitor is able to convert users who have been harboring dislike toward the brand. Similarly, a manager who fails to understand the nature of the "friend" relationship may be undervaluing the relationship's potential. I seek to address this issue by using CBR constructs to measure the impact of app-based social media on the way consumers relate to brand sponsors.

Identity work

I argue that apps can impact consumer-brand relationships, but the practical problem remains: how? App-based social media offers consumers the opportunity to do everything from connecting to social networks, to customizing experiences, to discovering new information content. How do these features impact a consumer-brand relationship? I argue that one key aspect of this phenomenon is the sociological construct of identity work, and suggest that this is a mechanism for the strengthening of consumer-brand relationships.

Consumers are identity seekers and makers who engage in digital self-presentation to enhance the status of the digital extended self (Arnould and Thompson 2005; Schau and Gilly 2003). What we decide to "post" or share in social media shapes the way others view us, our social identities, and how we view others (Rentfrow and Gosling 2003, 2006; Tajfel and Turner 1979). Identity work includes the range of activities in which individuals engage to create, present, and maintain a sense of the self in a social setting that is congruent with and supportive of their self-concept (Sveningsson and Alvesson 2003; Snow and Anderson 1987). This is consistent with our understanding of self-presentation (Goffman 1959), but takes on a whole new meaning in the digital domain. Apps are a part of the digital media revolution that has ushered in an era of consumer empowerment, wherein consumers interact with firms to co-create value and meaning (Deighton and Kornfeld 2009; Prahalad and Ramaswamy 2004a). Identity work affects these meanings that consumers ascribe to products (Thompson and Haytko 1997).

I theorize that social media that enables identity work can enhance the image of the digital self and serve to strengthen consumer-brand relationships (Belk 2013). Enabling consumers to tend to their digital selves can make them look and feel important, and can create interpersonal consumer-brand connections that are much more characteristic of true brand loyalty than mere repeat transactional exchanges. What might this identity work look like within the confines of a consumer-app relationship? The "likes" that we earn, the "friends" that we accrue, and the comments that we make and receive are all part of this identity work. Using apps that allow us to interact with social network members, express ourselves through customization, and discover information that increases our expertise leads to this identity work, which I argue can positively impact how we relate to the brands that sponsor these apps.

Identity work enabled by embeddedness, customization, discovery

Social media apps can enable identity work, yet little is understood about what specific aspects of these media facilitate this process and what the implications are for consumers' relationships with brands. I address this by focusing on three aspects of app usage: social embeddedness, customizability, and discovery. These features have been identified as key aspects of consumer behavior in the digital space (Belk 2013; Deighton and Kornfeld 2009; Schau and Gilly 2003; Miller 1995). I will explain each of these concepts below and discuss how they may be operationalized in experimental research, including a field experiment that I have conducted at MIT.

Social embeddedness refers to the fact that social actors exist within relational, institutional, and cultural contexts and cannot be seen as atomized decision-makers maximizing their own utilities (Granovetter 1985). This is an important aspect of economic behavior, as it presents neither the traditional economic undersocialized view of consumers (as it takes into account the social connections that affect behavior), nor an oversocialized view (as it continues to allow consumers to have their own agency).

With regard to digital media, social media apps that allow social embeddedness have the critical feature of direct interactions with consumers and consumer communities (Prahalad and Ramaswamy 2004b). The question remains whether facilitating these consumer-to-consumer (C2C) interactions in a social media app is beneficial to the sponsor brand. I have conducted experimental research to explore the role of social embeddedness by examining the impact of making and interacting with friends while using a brand-sponsored app. If these interactions facilitate identity work, I expect that consumers will have opportunities to enhance the digital self, thereby strengthening the consumer-brand relationship.

A second aspect of social media that has received great attention is the opportunity for customization. Customization refers to the ability of an individual to modify or build an app experience according to individual or personal specifications or preferences, for instance, customizing a virtual automobile. Previously, the firm and the consumer had distinct roles of production and consumption, respectively (Porter 1980). However, the meaning of value and the process of value creation are now rapidly shifting from a product- and firm-centric view to person-alized consumer experiences (Prahalad and Ramaswamy 2004a). This view of co-creation is consistent with the work of von Hippel and the lead user co-creation of innovations (Urban and von Hippel 1988; von Hippel 1986). Examples of brands that benefit from the joint development of new products and services are Linux and Apache. This is indicative of the rise in consumer empowerment, where creation of the brand does not rest solely in the hands of the firm.

It may be, then, that consumers have greater trust in that which they have helped to create, which could strengthen their relationship to a brand. Given consumer empowerment in the digital space, we must explore the role of customization. There is certainly enough interest in customization that it would appear to be a key aspect of app-based social media: a Google search of the terms "customize" and "app" returns 125,000,000 hits that attempt to guide consumers and firms through the processes of customizing apps. If customization in an app allows the user to fashion the experience according to his or her preferences, it may serve to enable social identity work. Like the bumper stickers on a car or the photo collection on a desk, customization in an app may allow us to create and maintain the identity we wish to convey to others. This can positively impact the strength of the consumer-brand relationship.

Finally, the third aspect of social media that I will examine is the role of information discovery in shaping consumers' relationships with branded apps. Allowing for access to informal sources of information (e.g., blogs) demonstrates that the brand is not trying to have complete control over the information, instead providing consumers with an uncensored source of information that may be trusted more so than official corporate sources are. Perceived trustworthiness is a key element of relationship-building and has been conceptualized as a determinant of relationship quality and firm credibility (Urban 2005; Moorman *et al.* 1992). A branded app that permits the discovery of uncensored (and, perhaps even unflat-tering) information may lead to greater trust in the brand sponsor (Liberali, Urban and Hauser 2012). Moreover, the discovery of information may enhance the consumers' social identity, allowing them to appear as experts who possess novel, early information (Wojnicki and Godes 2008). As a result, I expect that apps that feature opportunities for discovery enable social identity work, to the benefit of consumer-brand relationships. I suggest that information is currency in the digital world, and enabling discovery will create value for the consumer.

An exploratory experiment

I conducted an exploratory experiment in order to begin to address the issues discussed above, testing the three independent variables (embeddedness, customization, and discovery) by having participants use a design game app. Embeddedness was operationalized as a binary measure of the presence or absence of a social networking feature in the app. Participants were randomly assigned to a *high embeddedness* condition and introduced to one another via a scavenger hunt activity. Consistent with popular social media offerings, these consumers could "friend" one another, make posts, give feedback on one another's car designs, and have off-topic (non-vehicle related) discussions in message board threads. The activities in the *high embeddedness* condition were not only provided to ensure verisimilitude with real apps, but also to enable identity work in the social network. I captured behavioral measures as well as self-reported measures of the degree to which participants felt a sense of community and felt comfortable participating in the community. I created a variable for social identity work based on these behavioral and attitudinal measures (Cronbach's $\alpha = 0.73$), and labeled it identity work.

The second independent variable, customization, was operationalized as a large or small suite of customization options. For instance, participants in the *high customization* condition had dozens of choices of graphics and accoutrement (e.g., pets) to add to their designs in the app.

Finally, the third variable, discovery, was operationalized as the presence or absence of links to informal sources of information outside of the app (e.g., blogs). Therefore, some of the participants experienced apps that contained uncensored posts and comments that were at times critical of the sponsor brand. This allowed participants to explore links to discover novel information from informal sources (as opposed to from official corporate websites). This was important to test the impact of the discovery of informal information. People in the *low discovery* condition were not presented with these links.

I employed a 2x2x2 factorial design, and participants were randomly assigned to experimental conditions, each based on a combinational permutation of the independent variables. In addition to the measures above, I captured self-reported liking of the app ("overall app rating"), and consumers' ratings of the trustworthiness of the sponsor brand ("trustworthiness"). I use these additional measures for covariate analyses.

The possible incarnations of consumer-brand relationships are perhaps as diverse as the individual participants and the various brands they use, potentially varying in terms of affect, strength, and tenor. As a result, past research has examined various sub-groups of the universe of relationships in the CBR typology. Here, I focus on six relationship types that may be viewed hierarchically: dislike, stranger, business acquaintance, fun fling, someone I hope to know someday, and friend. This approach is consistent with past CBR research and relies on the consumer to think about the brand using interpersonal metaphors (Fournier 1998). In my study, I also provided descriptive language to ensure clarity of each relationship type.

Based on three waves of data collection over a two-month period, I measured the changes in consumer-brand relationships based on the six-tiered relationship hierarchy, ranging from "dislike" to "friend." The measure of self-reported perceived brand trustworthiness serves as a check of whether the relationship hierarchy was internally valid. Indeed, a correlation analysis indicates that the trustworthiness of the brand increases in a linear fashion along each rung of the relationship ladder.

Embeddedness enabled identity work behavior ($\beta = 3.38$, $p = 0.000$). To the extent that consumers receive image-enhancing feedback and are able to develop their digital extended selves in a social network, social media applications can serve to strengthen the brand relationship, even when controlling for the ingoing relational type. Of the three independent variables tested, embeddedness appears to have the strongest impact (relative to low embeddedness) on social identity work, and, consequently, on consumer-brand relationships.

Opportunities for customization of a social media app do enable identity work behaviors, but only when interacting with the embeddedness variable. This interaction between embeddedness and customization is significant, supporting the importance of both of these variables for the development of an effective social media app strategy ($\beta = 0.938$, $p = 0.001$). This underscores the "social" part of social media – identity work needs an audience, and self-expression via customization does not have the same impact without social embeddedness in a network.

Moreover, I found that opportunities for the discovery of uncensored information in a social media app enable identity work behaviors ($\beta = 0.27$, $p = 0.008$). This positively impacts the strength of the consumer-brand relationship, controlling for embeddedness, customization, and the ingoing relational form. Finally, I find that discovery also provides enjoyment. Consumers like jumping over to independent blogs to discover new information; this exploration increases their overall ratings of the app ($\beta = 0.356$, $p = 0.01$), which also positively impacts the consumer-brand relationship.

Discussion

The rise of social media and explosion in popularity of apps has been noted by marketing practitioners and scholars alike. As consumers increasingly amass apps and spend more of their waking hours using digital media, we need rigorous research on the potential of social media for building brand equity. There is a relative paucity of evidence, however, that demonstrates the efficacy of these apps. I believe that this chapter begins to address this matter.

The evidence discussed here suggests that embeddedness, customization, and discovery work uniquely, but in tandem, to allow consumers to develop a relationship with the brand on their own terms. Social media is most effective in strengthening consumer-brand relationships when consumers are able to enhance the digital extended self by engaging in identity work that reflects a desired social identity. Identity work enables this process and mediates the relationship between the app-based independent variables (embeddedness, customization, and discovery), and the resulting consumer-brand relationship strength. My results suggest that brand managers should recognize and facilitate image-enhancing social identity work if they want to build more positive brand relationships with consumers. I also identify perceived brand trustworthiness as correlated with increasing relationship strength.

My study additionally indicates that understanding the ingoing consumer-brand relationship is important. Though I was able to strengthen these brand relationships with an experimental manipulation, the pre-experiment relationship state still plays a significant role in the outgoing state (β = 0.667, $p < 0.000$). This suggests that social media strategies may be adapted according to the existing relationship that a consumer has with a brand. Future research could further investigate this. It is reasonable to consider that consumers have different expectations of a brand friend than they do of a brand business acquaintance, and that this could have implications for the type of marketing communication that is desired. Moreover, identifying consumers who dislike the brand may have funding implications, as this is likely the most difficult relationship to change.

I do not suggest here that the goal for each brand is to ascend the relationship hierarchy and cultivate friend relationships with its consumers. On the contrary, consumer-brand relationship theory is based on an understanding of consumer needs, and consumers may not see the need for higher-order relationship dynamics with every brand. Nevertheless, understanding these needs and how they shape brand relationships will be essential for developing true brand loyalty, both in the new digital arena and the conventional one.

References

Aggarwal, P. (2004) "The Effects of Brand Relationship Norms on Consumer Attitudes and Behavior", *Journal of Consumer Research*, 31 (1): 87–101.

Arnould, E.J. and C.J. Thompson (2005) "Consumer Culture Theory (CCT): Twenty Years of Research", *Journal of Consumer Research*, 31 (4): 868–882.

Belk, R.W. (2013) "Extended Self in a Digital World", *Journal of Consumer Research*, 40 (3): 477–500.

Bellman, S., R.F. Potter, S. Treleaven-Hassard, J.A. Robinson, and D. Varan (2011) "The Effectiveness of Branded Mobile Phone Apps", *Journal of Interactive Marketing*, 25 (4): 191–200.

Deighton, J. and L. Kornfeld (2009) "Interactivity's Unanticipated Consequences for Marketers and Marketing", *Journal of Interactive Marketing*, 23 (1): 4–10.

Dohnert, J. (2013) "The Key to Branded Apps Is to Uncover Their Consumer Utility", January 25, 2013, www.clickz.com/clickz/news/2238592/the-key-to-branded-apps-is-to-uncover-their-consumer-utility, accessed January 16, 2014.

Forrester, Inc. (2011) "Why, How, and When to Jump on the Mobile App Bandwagon", July 11, 2011, http://forrester.typepad.com/groundswell/2011/07/why-how-and-when-to-jump-on-the-mobile-app-bandwagon.html, accessed January 16, 2014.

Fournier, S. (1998) "Consumers and their Brands: Developing Relationship Theory in Consumer Research", *Journal of Consumer Research*, 24 (4): 343–353.

Goffman, E. (1959) *The Presentation of Self in Everyday Life*. Garden City, NY: Anchor.

Goodson, S. (2011) "How To Make Amazing Branded Apps", November 4, 2011, www.forbes.com/sites/marketshare/2011/11/04/how-to-make-amazing-branded-apps/

Granovetter, M. (1985) "Economic Action and Social Structure: The Problem of Embeddedness", *American Journal of Sociology*, 91 (3): 481–510.

Gupta, S. (2013) "For Mobile Devices, Think Apps, Not Ads", *Harvard Business Review*, 91 (3): 70–75.

Hennig-Thurau, T., E.C. Malthouse, C. Friege, S. Gensler, L. Lobschat, A. Rangaswamy, and B. Skiera (2010) "The Impact of New Media on Customer Relationships", *Journal of Service Research*, 13 (3): 311–330.

Keller, K.L. (2001) *Building Customer-Based Brand Equity: A Blueprint for Creating Strong Brands*, Boston, MA: Marketing Science Institute.

Keller, K.L. (2009) "Building Strong Brands in a Modern Marketing Communications Environment", *Journal of Marketing Communications*, 15 (2–3): 139–155.

Keller, K.L. (2012) "Understanding the Richness of Brand Relationships: Research Dialogue on Brands as Intentional Agents", *Journal of Consumer Psychology*, 22 (2): 186–190.

Kim, E., J.S. Lin, and Y. Sung (2013) "To App or Not to App: Engaging Consumers via Branded Mobile Apps", *Journal of Interactive Advertising*, 13 (1): 53–65.

Leigh, T.W. and S.A. Thompson (2012) "On The Complexity of Managing Brand Relationships in a Social Media World", *Consumer-Brand Relationships: Theory and Practice*, eds S. Fournier, M. Breazeale and M. Fetscherin. London: Routledge: 317–350.

Liberali, G., G.L. Urban and J.R. Hauser (2012) "Competitive Information, Trust, Brand Consideration and Sales: Two Field Experiments", *International Journal of Research in Marketing*, 30 (2): 101–113.

McCall, G.J. (1970) "The Social Organization of Relationships", *Social Relationships*, ed. G.J. McCall *et al.* Chicago, IL: Aldine Publishing Company: 3–34.

McCracken, G. (1986) "Culture and Consumption: A Theoretical Account of the Structure and Movement of the Cultural Meaning of Consumer Goods", *Journal of Consumer Research*, 13(1): 71–84.

Miller, H. (1995) "The Presentation of Self in Electronic Life: Goffman on the Internet", Paper presented at the Embodied Knowledge and Virtual Space Conference, Goldsmiths' College, University of London, June 1995, 9.

Moorman, C., G. Zaltman, and R. Deshpandé (1992) "Relationships between Providers and Users of Market Research: The Dynamics of Trust", *Journal of Marketing Research*, 29: 314–28.

Nielsen (2012) "State of the App Nation – A Year of Change and Growth in U.S. Smartphones", www.nielsen.com/us/en/insights/news/2012/state-of-the-appnation-a-year-of-change-and-growth-in-u-s-smartphones.html, accessed January 14, 2014.

Porter, M.E. (1980) *Competitive Strategy: Techniques for Analyzing Industries and Competitors*. New York: The Free Press.

Prahalad, C.K. and V. Ramaswamy (2004a) "Co-creation Experiences: The Next Practice in Value Creation", *Journal of Interactive Marketing*, 18 (3): 5–14.

Prahalad, C.K. and V. Ramaswamy (2004b) *The Future of Competition: Co-Creating Value with Customers*. Boston, MA: Harvard Business School Press.

Rentfrow, P.J. and S.D. Gosling (2003) "The Do Re Mi's of Everyday Life: The Structure and Personality Correlates of Music Preferences", *Journal of Personality and Social Psychology*, 84 (6): 1236–1256.

Rentfrow, P.J. and S.D. Gosling (2006) "Message in a Ballad: The Role of Music Preferences in Interpersonal Perception", *Psychological Science*, 17 (3): 236–242.

Schau, H.J. and M.C. Gilly (2003) "We are What We Post? Self-presentation in Personal Web Space", *Journal of Consumer Research*, 30 (3): 385–404.

Smelser, N.J. and R. Swedberg (2010) *The Handbook of Economic Sociology*, Princeton, NJ: Princeton University Press.

Snow, D.A. and L. Anderson (1987) "Identity Work among the Homeless: The Verbal Construction and Avowal of Personal Identities", *American Journal of Sociology*, 92 (6): 1336–1371.

Sveningsson, S. and M. Alvesson (2003) "Managing Managerial Identities: Organizational Fragmentation, Discourse and Identity Struggle", *Human Relations*, 56 (10): 1163–1193.

Tajfel, H. and J.C. Turner (1979) "An Integrative Theory of Intergroup Conflict", *Intergroup Relations: Essential Readings. Key Readings in Social Psychology*, eds Michael A. Hogg and Dominic Abrams. New York: Psychology Press. 94–109.

Thompson, C.J. and D.L. Haytko (1997) "Speaking of Fashion: Consumers' Uses of Fashion Discourses and the Appropriation of Countervailing Cultural Meanings", *Journal of Consumer Research*, 24 (1): 15–42.

Urban, G. (2005) *Don't Just Relate – Advocate!: A Blueprint for Profit in the Era of Customer Power*. Englewood, NJ: Pearson Education.

Urban, G.L. and E. von Hippel (1988) "Lead User Analyses for the Development of New Industrial Products", *Management Science*, 34 (5): 569–582.

von Hippel, E. (1986) "Lead Users: A Source of Novel Product Concepts", *Management Science*, 32 (7): 791–805.

Wish, M., M. Deutsch, and S.J. Kaplan (1976) "Perceived Dimensions of Interpersonal Relations", *Journal of Personality and Social Psychology*, 33 (4): 409–420.

Wojnicki, A.C. and D. Godes (2008) "Word-of-Mouth as Self-Enhancement", Harvard Business School Marketing Research Paper, No. 06–01.

12

HOW SOCIAL MEDIA INFLUENCERS BUILD A BRAND FOLLOWING BY SHARING SECRETS

Barbara Bickart, Soyean Kim, Seema Pai, and Frédéric Brunel

In a post on his blog "Live Your Legend" (http://liveyourlegend.net), entrepreneur and blogger Scott Dinsmore shared 35 "honest, personal stories, fears and facts you don't know about me" (Dinsmore 2013). Some of these stories included incidents that may have been embarrassing or painful to reveal to his audience, including an arrest in high school and his love of Taylor Swift music. Given the intimate and distressing nature of some of these revelations, one has to wonder what motive could have compelled Scott to share very publicly these 35 secrets with his large audience of readers. Although we all have a certain part of the self that we hesitate to share with others for fear of embarrassment, shame, or potentially even greater negative consequences, revealing secret information can also lead to at least two types of positive outcomes. First, keeping a secret is stressful and burdensome (Pennebaker 1989, 1990), and therefore revealing it to others can be cathartic and therapeutic. Second, because revealing secrets to others makes one more vulnerable, it can serve as a signal of trust in the relationship partners (e.g., Altman and Taylor 1973) and, thus, it can be a foundational mechanism through which relationships are built and deepened. Although all participants in social media conversations might from time to time reveal secrets, one group that may especially benefit from disclosing secrets online are opinion leaders and influencers, such as bloggers and microbloggers (Kim *et al.* 2013). In this paper, we focus on this last group and seek to inform how and why bloggers, and other influencers, might share secrets online.

Even though there are potential positive consequences to sharing secrets, there are also significant risks. First, as people try to become influencers and opinion-leaders and build themselves as brands, they give up privacy in exchange for celebrity (Belk 2013) and, thus, revealing intimate details or secrets can cost obvious further loss of personal privacy. Second, it can be argued that many secrets should remain undisclosed because disclosure may lead to personal embarrassment and the disapproval of others (e.g., Bok 1983; Larson and Chastain 1990; Stiles 1987; Wegner and Erber 1992), thereby nullifying the positive effects of sharing intimate details. In the offline world, this concern over disapproval (or rejection) functions as a barrier, which prevents individuals from being fully open about their secrets (Kelly 1998; Kelly and McKillop 1996). Yet, because of increased anonymity as well as the physical and interpersonal distancing that the online medium provides, these downsides may not seem so extreme. Although, in our context, the opinion leader is usually known, the audience members typically are not known by the blogger; there is no direct face-to-face interaction, and the relationship between an audience member and the blogger is more "imagined" rather than one based on actual interactions. Therefore, using the relative cloak of anonymity and distancing provided by online communication, influencers may share deep and sometimes dark secrets with total strangers in a bid to increase their persuasiveness and better connect with their audience. Anecdotally at least, this seems to be true. For example, it has been suggested that individuals frequently share their emotions, fears, and wishes, and disclose every intimate detail of their lives on their blogs, Facebook posts, and Twitter mentions (Feiler 2014; Fowler 2012).

In this chapter, we examine when and why these influencers share secrets online. Based on an exploratory survey with 48 bloggers and the literature on secret sharing, we examine the use of secret sharing as a strategy for audience building. We then describe the types of secrets that influencers disclose, as well as their motives for sharing these secrets and the emotions associated with this behavior. Past research on secret sharing suggests that people share secrets primarily to unburden themselves and gain validation and support from others, as well as to build stronger relationships (Derlega and Grezelak 1979). Our findings support that online influencers share secrets primarily to build their brand following (increase their influence, gain the loyalty of their audience and build the size of their audience), and we find little evidence, if any, that secret sharing is consciously used to unburden and cleanse the soul. Therefore, based on what bloggers are willing or able to admit, it seems that online influencers share secrets for strategic reasons rather than for improving their own psychological well-being.

The chapter is organized as follows. First, we define what a secret is. We then discuss our survey methodology. We look at the results of our survey in the light of what is already known about secret sharing in the social psychology literature. Finally, we discuss secret sharing as a personal brand building tool and directions for future research.

What is a secret?

According to the *Oxford Dictionary*, a secret is defined as something that is "not meant to be known by others." Similarly, psychologists define a secret as information that is deliberately kept hidden from other people (Margolis 1974). Anything that exists, either in the real physical world or in the imagination, can become a secret, whether they are facts, feelings, observations, or objects, as long as they are consciously hidden from others (Wismeijer 2011). Context can also affect what is perceived to be a secret. For example, a person may be comfortable disclosing identifying information (such as an address or phone number) to a friend or colleague, while, in an online context, they may want to keep this information secret. Likewise, art critics are free to discuss the ending of a show among themselves, but are professionally bound to keep it a secret when they write about it in a public forum.

Some researchers conceive of a secret as "active inhibition of disclosure" (e.g., Pennebaker 1989). A secret, however, is not merely the opposite of self-disclosure (i.e., the act of revealing personal information to others) (Collins and Miller 1994) because the secret-keeping process feels burdensome and stressful (Pennebaker 1989; 1990). It is, therefore, an effortful process that requires cognitive and emotional resources (Frijns 2005; Lane and Wegner 1995; Wegner 1989; 1992; 1994; Wegner *et al.* 1994), while not disclosing personal information does not require such efforts. In other words, different from "self-disclosure inhibition," the secret keeping process requires individuals to exert energy and resources to ensure that the secret can be kept hidden from others.

To summarize, a secret is generally defined as "a conscious and effortful process of social selective information exchange that requires cognitive resources and that can be experienced as an emotional burden" (Wismeijer 2011: 308). A secret indicates not only a secret keeping process, but also that information is kept hidden.

Having defined what a secret is, we go on to investigate secret sharing by influencers in online settings. The goal of our study is to find out how bloggers think about secret sharing, whether they do it, what constitutes a secret in their mind, why they do it, and how they feel about it.

Study

To examine these issues, we conducted an exploratory survey of a convenience sample of bloggers. Bloggers represent one type of online influencer. A complete and accurate sampling frame of bloggers does not exist, so we created a list using "top blog" lists in different domains. The blog categories included lifestyle/fashion, parenting, health and fitness, sports and recreation, theater, pets, cooking, photography, and self-help. We limited our sample frame to blogs that were primarily managed by an individual (versus a collaborative blog like *The Daily Beast*) and the categories selected tend to fit this criterion. A research assistant visited blogs on the lists and, whenever possible, identified the name of the primary blogger and an email address. Through this process we were able to compile a list of 208 bloggers with names and email addresses. Of these, 12 email addresses did not work.

A Qualtrics survey was sent by email to the bloggers. In addition, two reminder emails were sent to those who had not yet completed the survey. Participants were offered a chance to win a $100 Amazon gift card for their participation. We obtained 48 complete responses, with a final response rate of 24 percent. To assess selection bias, we compared the distribution of blog topics among final respondents and the original list. There was some selection bias. Specifically, we had a higher response rate from theater and pet bloggers, and a relatively lower response rate from fashion/lifestyle bloggers.

Survey description

Bloggers were asked to participate in a survey about how they connect with their audiences. The survey included questions about their strategies to communicate with their audience, whether or not they share secrets, and examples of secrets shared, motives for sharing secrets and emotions experienced when sharing secrets. The survey took approximately ten minutes to complete.

Sample description

In terms of audience size, the blogs in the sample reported having between 100 and 8 million visitors per month, with a median audience of 12,000. About 47 percent of blogs had between 5,000 and 50,000 visitors per month. In terms of the types of blogs, the most common categories were performing arts/theatre (30 percent), lifestyle/fashion (17 percent), followed by personal development and health and fitness (both 13 percent) and pet (11 percent). Other categories included food and cooking, sports and recreation, and parenting.

About 49 percent described their audience as primarily female, and 49 percent as both male and female. Fifty-seven percent of the participants acknowledged that they made money from their blog, with 22 percent of those claiming the blog as their primary source of income. Seventy-eight percent of the participants were between the ages of 21 and 50, and about two thirds (64 percent) were female.

Findings

Do online influencers share secrets?

There are challenges to measuring the prevalence of secret sharing by online influencers. First, what may seem like a secret to some is not a secret to others. Second, what constitutes a secret in an online context where influencers are often communicating with strangers may be different from what constitutes a secret in an offline context. Finally, influencers may not want to admit to sharing secrets because this behavior may potentially break a social rule (e.g., polite conversation norms might dictate that secret sharing be avoided so as not to embarrass oneself or the audience), or is a transgression of a professional code of conduct. We attempted to address this issue in our survey by first asking participants an open-ended question about how they connected with their blog audience, followed by a question asking whether they used a specific set of communication strategies, including various forms of personal disclosures/secret-sharing.

For the open-ended question, we asked influencers how they built a connection with their audience and had them list up to three different strategies. Approximately 27 percent of the participants listed some form of personal disclosure as one of their connection strategies. Some illustrative comments included "telling stories about personal experiences," "showing vulnerability," "sharing frustrating and difficult moments," and "sharing a mix of personal details." While not all of these responses strictly constitute secret sharing, they do indicate a desire to reveal personal information to connect with the audience. Other common strategies included interacting with the audience members via the comment system and asking and answering questions to stimulate conversation (54 percent), the use of multiple social media platforms to engage with their audience members (44 percent), developing an interest in whatever topics their readers are interested in and tailoring their content accordingly (29 percent), and being honest and authentic (17 percent). Interestingly, a desire for honesty and authenticity can probably also lead to secret sharing, as it would imply reduced inhibition and lesser impression management.

Additional evidence that secret sharing occurs comes from our close-ended responses. We asked people to rate the frequency with which they used a list of strategies to communicate with their audience on a scale of 1 to 7 with 1 being Never and 7 being Very Frequently. Table 12.1 shows the mean values for all of the strategies on the list.

We conducted a factor analysis of these items and the five starred items in Table 12.1 loaded on a single factor that explained 26 percent of the overall variance. We interpret this factor as disclosure of private information and details. A high score on this factor is not evidence of secret sharing in a strict sense. However, it is

TABLE 12.1 Mean ratings on use of communication strategies

	Mean	Std Dev.
★ I provide my own personal viewpoint on topics of interest	6.19	1.10
I respond personally to posts and questions	5.83	1.48
I try to be as responsive as possible to my audience's needs	5.75	1.42
I disclose any incentives I may receive	5.73	1.77
I look for new information to share	5.67	1.52
I try to be objective	5.50	1.73
★ I disclose private and intimate details about my life	5.08	1.87
★ I reveal information about my personal life	4.37	1.77
I share my emotions and feelings	4.31	1.70
★ I reveal information about my identity (such as where I live and work)	4.12	2.02
I post and comment on other bloggers' sites	3.77	2.13
I accept commercial incentives	3.73	2.09
★ I post pictures of myself and/or family	3.04	1.75

Note: Measured on a 7-point scale from 1 = Never to 7 = Very Frequently. (n = 48)

evidence that these respondents rely on disclosure of personal details as a communication strategy. From the means, it is clear that these were among the most common strategies used, particularly sharing one's own personal point of view and disclosing private and intimate details about one's life.

Finally, when asked explicitly if they had ever shared a secret with their social media audience, 19 percent of the respondents said yes. This question differentiates secret sharing from mere information disclosure by allowing the respondents to determine what does or does not constitute a secret. In addition, while we are limited by the small sample size, we do see a (non-significant) tendency for bloggers who make money from their blogs to admit to secret sharing more (22 percent) than those who do not (15 percent). This finding suggests that, as the potential risks and financial consequences of "turning-off" an audience increase, bloggers do not "play it safe," and secret sharing is at least as, if not more, prevalent in money-making blogs, suggesting that secret sharing is not viewed as having a major downside. We also constructed a scale using the five starred items in Table 12.1. We find that the respondents who said that they shared secrets scored significantly higher on this disclosure of private information scale ($M = 5.56$) versus those who said they did not ($M = 4.47$, $F\ 1.46 = 6.55$, $p < 0.01$). Our results suggest that as bloggers and online influencers seek to build their personal brand and following, they use disclosures of intimate personal information, and that, for a subset of these people, this means sharing information they consider to be a secret. In addition, we have some evidence that these are deliberate strategies rather than accidental disclosures.

What are the different types of secrets?

We find that although many respondents reported engaging in the disclosure of intimate and personal information, when asked specifically whether or not they had shared a secret, only nine participants said yes. Therefore, there may be a semantic distinction between what constitutes a secret in the eyes of these online influencers versus the more general conceptualizations of secrets that one may encounter in the perception of the broader population. These influencers are people with a very public personal brand and persona, and thus that fact alone has likely shifted the barrier between the private and the public domain, making them less likely to consider something disclosed to be a secret. When one lives in the public eye, one trades off privacy for fame (Belk 2013) and thus has fewer secrets. Further, with every instance of personal disclosure, bloggers might raise the bar for what they consider to be a secret. Thus, over time, it becomes more difficult for them to even think about past instances when they shared a secret since that category gets smaller over time.

To better understand the types of secrets shared by our online influencers, we asked them to list an example of a secret they had shared. Among the participants who said that they shared a secret with their social media audience, we found three general types of secrets. The largest category (5 out of 9) was secrets regarding physical or mental health; most of these were conditions where there was the possibility of social stigma, such as eating disorders and/or mental health issues. The second category constituted secrets about relationships. Here again, there were some extreme examples including personal abuse. The final category was revealing spoilers to an audience about shows prior to airing. Revealing this information could be perceived as a violation of professional norms, in particular, depending on how that information was obtained. For instance, one blogger was able to get spoilers about a television show by covertly photographing the set. Our findings are consistent with work suggesting that secrets are likely to indicate negative or stigmatizing personal information about the secret keepers (Norton *et al.* 1974) since people have a tendency to hide their most traumatic, embarrassing, or disturbing personal experiences and to report them as their secrets.

In addition, we included a close-ended list of different types of secrets that people might share on social media. The nine people who indicated that they had shared a secret with their audience indicated whether or not they had shared a secret of each type. The three biggest categories (six people each) were secrets about their family, secrets about a relationship, and a personal confession. This finding is somewhat surprising given that across various ranges of topics, researchers find that sexual secrets and the desire for a romantic relationship are considered as the most secretive personal information (e.g., Hill *et al.* 1993; Kelly 1998; Kelly *et al.* 2001). Other research on online sharing shows that while anonymity may not be the main driver (or motive) of online secret sharing, it certainly stimulates individuals to share their private details more freely online (Barak and Gluck-Ofri 2007; Suler 2004). It is possible that this relative anonymity and physical distancing are enabling our respondents to reveal these types of secrets to their audience. We also find that people are less likely to share secrets regarding their work life or gossip about other people. Overall, our findings indicate that the secrets shared by these influencers tend to be very self-focused, suggesting that they may be wary of implicating others, and that whatever social benefit might be derived from sharing secrets is mainly obtained by providing new information about the self. For the blog categories in our sample, violating other peoples' privacy would detract from building one's own personal brand. Therefore, if secrets are to be shared, they are likely to be about the self or an abstract target object.

Why do people share secrets?

As previously discussed, the notion of secret implies an overt effort to conceal. At some point, however, individuals may decide to share a secret, and thus the information is no longer "secret" for the recipient. Therefore, it is interesting to understand why people might abandon their previous concealment strategy and opt for disclosure. Psychologists have found that the sharing of secrets is driven mainly by five motives: self-clarification, social validation, social control, expression, and relationship development (Derlega and Grezelak 1979). The self-clarification motive stems from a communicator's need to recognize his or her position. By telling one's private story to others, people can clarify their thinking and views. People can also tell secrets for social validation, that is, to confirm their sense of being and self-esteem through how they are viewed by others. Further, secret sharing can be a form of social currency, and, thus, acts as a type of social control that can be used to reward and control the behaviors of others. In addition, the motive for expression suggests that disclosing personal emotional events to others is a compelling human need or impulse (Rimé 1995; Tait and Silver 1989). People frequently share their secrets simply because they cannot resist the urge to share, responding to their need for expression and unburdening. Finally, given the human need to belong or connect to a group or community (Baumeister and Leary 1995), a basic motive for sharing secrets is to develop relationships (e.g., Wismeijer 2011). By making themselves vulnerable to others, people may seek to build trust and, thus, stronger relationships. This relationship building often implicates norms of reciprocity, where parties to a relationship reciprocate the counterparty's secret sharing to develop an equitable, intimate bond. A secondary motive associated with relationship building is a motive to draw on one of the main benefits of a strong relationship: the ability to gain help or support from others.

In order to discern the online influencers' motives for secret sharing we asked our informants to list, in an open-ended question, the reasons for sharing the secret that they had previously described. In addition, we also had them rate a list of 16 possible motives on a 7-point Not at all Important/Important scale (see Table 12.2).

We did not see any evidence of either self-clarification or social validation as a motive for secret-sharing within our sample, nor did our influencers talk about sharing secrets simply out of a compelling need to express themselves. Of the five

TABLE 12.2 Mean ratings on use of secret sharing motives

	Mean
To be authentic	6.44
To build a relationship with my audience	6.00
To be more closely connected to my audience	5.67
To express my feelings	5.56
To help my audience understand me better	4.78
To persuade or influence people	4.67
To gain new insights	4.56
To gain catharsis	4.11
To feel positive about myself	4.00
To feel better	3.78
To relieve stress	3.63
To reciprocate secret sharing by members of my audience	3.33
To get help or support	2.89
To cleanse my soul	2.67

Note: Rated on a 7-point scale, with 1 = Not at all Important and 7 = Important. (n = 9)

motives suggested in the literature, the only motive that directly fits our data is the relationship development motive. Relationship development is achieved by two main strategies – helping others and building trust with the audience. For example, one blogger stated sharing secrets online, "helped my readers understand that they are not alone and to gain their trust," while another said, "I felt I had an honest relationship with the audience I had built and I thought disclosing my story would be a help to others." Another respondent replied, "Everything I share is to help others learn from the situation. I don't expose for shock value. I won't write about a difficult or private situation unless I can share what I've learned that can bring more happiness into people's lives."

In addition to the motives discussed in the secret sharing literature, our data highlights another motive for secret-sharing that seems unique to online influencers, namely a desire to create unique or novel content. Per our data, respondents tended to share secrets that were about under-shared or under-discussed topics, which, in turn, enabled them to create unique content that differentiates their blog from other websites and helps to build their personal brand. For instance, one respondent mentioned that, "There's a lot of clinical information regarding pregnancy available, but less sharing about emotional struggles." Another blogger had this to say regarding their motivation behind sharing a secret: "I felt it would provide an interesting perspective on a topic that is rarely discussed openly." A related, but slightly different, example of secret sharing that enables the creation of unique content is providing impersonal information that the audience would not be privy to otherwise. For example, multiple theater bloggers mentioned providing plot endings or spoilers to shows prior to actual public performance or airing. While these types of spoilers might be perceived as a breach as of professional conduct in some instances, they are also another avenue through which bloggers can add value for their audience.

The responses to the closed-ended list (shown in Table 12.2) are consistent with the above. Two out of the three highest rated reasons are about relationship building (e.g., to build a relationship with my audience, to be more closely connected to my audience). In addition, the highest rated reason was to be authentic. In social media, authenticity can be considered the Holy Grail of brand relationship building and persuasion. Additionally, in contrast to the existing literature on secret sharing, the need for support and the cleansing of one's soul are the lowest rated reasons on the list and do not appear to be very important at all. These findings provide further evidence that for these online influencers, secret sharing is a strategic decision rather than a form of self-therapy or unburdening.

Overall, our findings show that in contrast with the motives identified in the psychology literature on secret sharing, most of the motives identified by these online influencers are "other-focused" as opposed to being focused on the person sharing the secret. These other-focused motives reveal a focus on the audience, and when we also consider that most of the secret sharing content was about the self, we found that the strategies and tactics used by our informants are consistent with a customer-centric approach to personal brand building.

Emotional outcomes of secret sharing

As mentioned previously, one of the key characteristics of a secret is that there are strong emotions associated both with keeping the secret, as well as the potential outcomes from disclosing it. Given that, we were interested in looking at the impact that secret-sharing has on the online influencers themselves. As mentioned earlier, secret-sharing by online influencers involves a tradeoff. Traditionally, there are barriers to secret sharing that mostly revolve around a fear of disapproval or rejection (Kelly 1998; Kelly and McKillop 1996). In particular, we were interested in whether these influencers were worried about potential disapproval from their readers upon sharing a secret.

However, what we find instead is that secret sharing by online influencers leads to a mix of positive and negative emotions with positive emotions appearing to dominate. Across 14 emotions, we had the participants rate how they felt when they shared the secret (5-point Strongly Disagree/Strongly Agree scale). The top emotions were pride (M=3.89), anxiety (M=3.78), and content (M=3.67), followed by relieved (M=3.56), excited (M=3.44), and pleased (M=3.44) respectively. Participants felt relatively no shame (M=1.44), sadness (M=1.44), or embarrassment (M=2.11), emotions which are sometimes associated with secret sharing (Manen and Levering 1996; Newth and Rachman 2001). These results indicate that the influencers felt relatively good upon sharing secrets with their audience, and there are very limited indications that secret sharing among these influencers was emotionally taxing.

Taking these findings with the bloggers' stated motives for secret sharing suggests that these influencers feel as though they have helped their audience members and/or increased trust with their audience through the process of secret sharing, both of which further enhanced their personal brand.

Conclusion

Our exploratory study of secret sharing among online influencers reveals several key findings. First, we are able to establish the prevalence of disclosure of intimate personal information among online influencers. However, at the same time, there is relatively limited self-reporting of what this group of informants considered "secret sharing." We believe that because online influencers have a public persona, they have a higher bar for what is considered to be a secret, and that the bar is constantly being raised as they engage in intimate personal disclosures. However, longitudinal and more controlled studies would be needed to provide more direct support for these conjectures.

Second, we find that secret sharing among these influencers is a strategic and purposeful, rather than accidental, brand building act. This conclusion is supported by our findings that the secrets shared by these bloggers tend to be about the self and abstract objects and not about others, perhaps because talking about others could be damaging to the bloggers' personal brands. In addition, their motives for secret sharing are focused on relationship development, authenticity, and providing novel information, rather than receiving support or cleansing one's soul. Finally, there appears to be low social or emotional costs to secret sharing and the emotional outcomes are mostly positive.

We see some important differences between secret sharing among these online bloggers versus what has been described in the secret sharing literature. First, the very understanding of what kind of information might be considered a secret seems to differ in this domain; the types of secrets that are shared are potentially more extreme, even though the audience is much larger. In addition, the secrets are confined to certain topics that help enhance the personal brand. Finally, the motives for sharing secrets appear to be quite different in that there is much more of a focus on how the secret will help build a relationship and less focus on self-related outcomes. In fact, it appears that bloggers use secret sharing as one way of providing differentiated content and value to their customers.

Our conclusions are limited by the methodology that we used in the study. First, we have a small convenience sample of bloggers, who are just one type of online influencer. Without the ability to probe, we were not able to get the depth of understanding on what a secret means to these people and the risks associated with sharing secrets. We asked people about why they share secrets, but did not ask questions about why they did *not* share secrets. It is also possible that we are underestimating the prevalence of secret sharing because these people live in the public eye and have a higher threshold for what constitutes a secret. We hope that future research can illuminate these issues.

Finally, our methodology does not allow us to assess the outcomes associated with secret sharing, limiting our ability to develop specific implications for bloggers. Anecdotally, from our own observation of various blogs, posts that involve what can be construed as secret sharing appear to get significant engagement including comments, questions, and reciprocal secret sharing from audience members. In addition, the effectiveness of secret sharing is likely to vary with the characteristics of the blog and, consequently, the audience and our sample size does not allow for us to examine this issue. For example, secret sharing is likely to be more effective in communally oriented blogs versus those that are exchange oriented. Clearly, additional research is needed to better understand the exact process through which secret sharing as a strategy helps with personal brand building, relationship development, and gaining a loyal following.

To summarize, a key to building one's online brand and following is to develop strong relationships and provide unique content and value to the audience. Selective secret sharing appears to be one approach that online influencers can use towards this goal. Our hope is that this initial investigation into secret sharing spurs additional research on this strategy, as well as on the broader phenomenon of online personal brand building.

References

Altman, I. and D.A. Taylor (1973) *Social Penetration: The Development of Interpersonal Relationships*. Oxford: Holt, Rinehart, and Winston.

Barak, A. and O. Gluck-Ofri (2007) "Degree and Reciprocity of Self-Disclosure in Online Forums", *Cyber Psychology and Behavior*, 10 (3): 407–417.

Baumeister, R.F. and M.R. Leary (1995) "The Need to Belong: Desire for Interpersonal Attachments as a Fundamental Human Motivation", *Psychological Bulletin*, 117 (3): 497–529.

Belk, R.W. (2013) "Extended Self in a Digital World", *Journal of Consumer Research*, 40 (3): 477–500.

Bok, S. (1983) "The Limits of Confidentiality", *Hastings Center Report*, 13 (1): 24–31.

Collins, N.L. and L.C. Miller (1994) "Self-Disclosure and Liking: A Meta-Analytic Review", *Psychological Bulletin*, 116 (3): 457–475.

Derlega, V.J. and J. Grezelak (1979) "Appropriateness of Self-disclosure", *Self-Disclosure: Origins, Patterns, and Implications of Openness in Interpersonal Relationships*, ed. G.J. Chelune. San Francisco, CA: Jossey-Bass: 151–176.

Dinsmore, S. (2013) "Honest, Personal Stories, Fears and Facts You Don't Know About Me". http://liveyourlegend.net/authenticity-101-what-i-wish-you-didnt-know-about-me/.

Feiler, B. (2014) "Secret Histories: In an Age of Lessening Privacy, Some Family Secrets Persist", *The New York Times*, January 17, 2014, www.nytimes.com/ 2014/01/19/fashion/Family-Secrets.html

Fowler, G.A. (2012) "When the Most Personal Secrets get Outed on Facebook", *Wall Street Journal*, October 13, 2012, http://online.wsj.com/news/articles/SB10000872396390444165804578008740578200224

Frijns, T. (2005) "Keeping Secrets: Quantity, Quality and Consequences" (Doctoral Dissertation). http://hdl.handle.net/1871/9001

Hill, C.E., B.J. Thompson, M.C. Cogar, and D.W. Denman (1993) "Beneath the Surface of Long-Term Therapy: Therapist and Client Reports of their Own and each other's Covert Processes", *Journal of Counseling Psychology*, 40 (3): 278–287.

Kelly, A.E. (1998) "Clients' Secret Keeping in Outpatient Therapy", *Journal of Counseling Psychology*, 45 (1): 50–57.

Kelly, A.E. and K.J. McKillop (1996) "Consequences of Revealing Personal Secrets", *Psychological Bulletin*, 120 (3): 450–465.

Kelly, A.E., J.A. Klusas, R.T. von Weiss, and C. Kenny (2001) "What is it about Revealing Secrets that is Beneficial?", *Personality and Social Psychology Bulletin*, 27 (6): 651–665.

Kim, S., B. Bickart, F. Brunel, and S. Pai (2013) "Can Your Business Have 1 Million Friends? Understanding and Using Blogs as One-to-One Mass Media", *Organizations and Social Networking: Utilizing Social CRM to Engage Consumers*, eds E.Y. Li, S. Loh, C. Evans, and F. Lorenzi. Hershey, PA: IGI Press: 125–152.

Lane, J.D. and D.M. Wegner (1995) "The Cognitive Consequences of Secrecy", *Journal of Personality and Social Psychology*, 69 (2): 237–253.

Larson, D.G. and R.L. Chastain (1990) "Self-Concealment: Conceptualization, Measurement, and Health Implications", *Journal of Social and Clinical Psychology*, 9 (4): 439–455.

Manen, M.V. and B. Levering (1996) *Childhood's Secrets: Intimacy, Privacy and the Self Reconsidered*. New York. Teachers College Press.

Margolis, G.J. (1974) "The Psychology of Keeping Secrets", *The International Journal of Psycho-Analysis*, 1 (3): 291–296.

Newth, S. and S. Rachman (2001) "The Concealment of Obsessions", *Behaviour Research and Therapy*, 39 (4): 457–464.

Norton, R., C. Feldman, and D. Tafoya (1974) "Risk Parameters across Types of Secrets", *Journal of Counseling Psychology*, 21 (5): 450–454.

Pennebaker, J.W. (1989) "Confession, Inhibition, and Disease", *Advances in Experimental Social Psychology*, ed. R. Berkowitz. New York: Springer: 22: 211–244.

Pennebaker, J.W. (1990) *Opening Up: The Healing Power of Confiding in Others*. New York: Morrow & Co.

Rimé, B. (1995) "Mental Rumination, Social Sharing, and the Recovery from Emotional Exposure", *Emotion, Disclosure and Health*, ed. J.W. Pennebaker. Washington, DC: American Psychological Association: 271–291.

Stiles, W.B. (1987) "I have to Talk to Somebody: A Fever Model of Self-disclosure", *Self-disclosure: Theory, Research, and Therapy*, eds V.J. Derlega and J.H. Berg. New York: Plenum Press: 257–282.

Suler, J. (2004) "The Online Disinhibition Effect", *Cyber Psychology and Behavior*, 7 (3): 321–326.

Tait, R. and R.C. Silver (1989) "Coming to Terms with Major Negative Life Events", *Unintended Thought*, eds J.S. Uleman and J.A. Bargh. New York: Guilford Press: 351–382.

Wegner, D.M. (1989) *White Bears and Other Unwanted Thoughts: Suppression, Obsession, and the Psychology of Mental Control*. New York: Penguin Press.

Wegner, D.M. (1992) "You Can't Always Think What You Want: Problems in the Suppression of Unwanted Thoughts", *Advances in Experimental Social Psychology*, ed. M.P. Zanna. San Diego, CA: Academic Press: 25: 193–225.

Wegner, D.M. (1994) "Ironic Processes of Mental Control", *Psychological Review*, 101 (1): 34–52.

Wegner, D.M. and R. Erber (1992) "The Hyperaccessibility of Suppressed Thoughts", *Journal of Personality and Social Psychology*, 63 (6): 903–912.

Wegner, D.M., J.D. Lane, and S. Dimitri (1994) "The Allure of Secret Relationships", *Journal of Personality and Social Psychology*, 66 (2): 287–300.

Wismeijer, A. (2011) "Secrets and Subjective Well-Being: A Clinical Oxymoron Emotion Regulation and Well-Being", *Emotion Regulation and Well-Being*, eds I. Nyklicek, A. Vingerhoets, and M. Zeelenberg. New York: Springer: 307–323.

13

CUSTOMER-TO-CUSTOMER RELATIONSHIP MANAGEMENT (CCRM)

How marketers can successfully engage consumers online

Molan Kim and Scott A. Thompson

Traditionally, marketers have acted as brand curators, controlling all of the messaging surrounding a brand and its products. With the rise of social media, marketers' roles are being transformed. Consumers are increasingly participating in brand consumer collective environments, such as brand communities and consumption communities (Muñiz and O'Guinn 2001; McAlexander *et al.* 2002). Consumer-to-consumer (C2C) interactions in these brand consumer collectives generate benefits for both firms and customers (Bendapudi *et al.* 1996). The value of a brand's products is enhanced through unpaid product support in the form of frequent C2C helping behavior (Muñiz and O'Guinn 2001). Additionally, the firm benefits from positive word of mouth (WOM), enhanced brand loyalty, and increased sales (Thompson and Sinha 2008).

While the C2C interactions in these environments generate value for firms, marketers often find themselves on the outside of these interactions looking in. Because they do not own or control these environments, marketers are unable to directly control the content of discussions (Fournier and Lee 2009). Consumers are free to complain about features or their experiences with products and services, share companies' proprietary information, or offer advice on how to use products in unintended ways. Faced with this reality, marketers are struggling with the questions of whether, and, if so, how and when they should attempt to interact in brand consumer collectives. Attempts at engagement risk negative reactions (Muñiz and O'Guinn 2001), and it is unclear what beneficial outcomes marketers can realistically achieve by participating, and which roles facilitate positive outcomes. Traditional customer relationship management (CRM) strategies, which seek to engage consumers directly in one-to-one relationships, are impractical in these environments (Boulding *et al.* 2005), due to the complicated relationships between each customer and the brand, between each customer and the community, among each customer and his or her peer customers, and between each customer and the company. Instead, marketers must employ Customer-to-Customer Relationship Management (CCRM) strategies, which require marketers to select the appropriate role they wish to assume within a consumer community.

The purpose of this study is threefold: first, we examine the range of roles marketers currently assume within large, online C2C environments; second, we examine consumer responses to marketers who assume these different roles; third, we examine the consequences consumers' reactions have for the associated firm and its products. In doing so, we provide new insights into the range of options available to marketers seeking to adopt a CCRM strategy, as well as insights into the relative impact of these approaches on consumer responses.

The benefits of consumer-to-consumer interactions for firms

Gartner's 2012 CRM Report predicts that companies that engage in customer support through consumer brand communities will achieve relational benefits, including C2C helping, increased customer loyalty, and self-motivated customer maintenance, as well as reap the financial benefits of cost reduction from easy, almost free, response and assistance to customer needs (Gartner Inc. 2012). Furthermore, C2C interactions can address issues that firms cannot readily address themselves. For example, a common source of customer service calls is the failure of a customer to read the product manual or documentation (BBC News 2009). However, firms cannot tell customers to go back and read the manual without risking a negative customer reaction. Thus, firms are trapped in a situation where they know the root cause of the customer's problems with a product (failure to read the manual), but they fear pointing to the obvious solution.

This problem is also a common source of consumers' requests for help from fellow consumers. However, consumers are not restrained by the same expectations placed upon firms. Consumers in C2C environments often defend the brand in question, noting that the failure is the user's fault and respond with the rude, often-used acronym RTFM (Read the F*ing Manual). A quick search of a large computer related community, Hardforum.com, reveals that RTFM appears in over 500 discussion threads and even has a dedicated "RTFM" Wikipedia page. More importantly, when consumers address another consumer's problem with this response, a curious thing frequently happens: they go back and read the manual. And even more remarkably, the consumer with the problem frequently returns to report that the problem was solved, acknowledge their error, and thank fellow consumers. As one consumer openly admitted on Hardforum.com, "Well, I think I fixed my instability problem with my 780's. Moral of the story is RTFM."

Thus, today's C2C networked environments are critical places where consumers not only berate firms and products, but also defend and assist them – when they feel so inclined. The task facing marketers is identifying and effectively implementing relational strategies that promote such beneficial C2C interactions. Though some practitioners have realized the significance of these benefits, many still hesitate to participate in consumer brand communities, possibly fearing unfavorable responses or outright rejection from community members. Therefore, the first challenge for marketers is identifying which initial roles they can assume when trying to join these communities that will generate favorable responses and build positive relationships.

Theoretical background

Prior research on consumer communities has primarily focused on the role of identity and identification in consumption. In the case of brand communities, research has focused on consumers' identification with a particular brand of product (e.g., Muñiz and O'Guinn 2001). In other types of consumer communities, the focus has been on consumers' identifications with an organization or product category (e.g., Bhattacharya and Sen 2003). But, across the various types of consumption communities, the emphasis has been on the relationships among consumers and with the brand or product. In comparison, there is a lack of work on the part played by relationships between consumers and members of the firms that represent brands and products.

The literature on interorganizational relationships suggests that the roles played by company representatives impact how individuals within and outside the firm respond (e.g., Grayson 2007). In the same vein, research on human relationships between members of groups suggests that perceptions of others' warmth and competence influence responses (Fiske *et al.* 1999, 2002). Within marketing, research has built on Fiske's work to show that perceptions of brands' warmth and competence influence consumers' responses to brands (Fournier and Alvarez 2012). These perceptions are also relevant to individual employees representing the brand. Yet, there is currently little research on how the roles played by company representatives affect consumer responses within consumption communities. In the subsequent sections, we build on prior research by drawing on Fiske's framework to develop an understanding of how the roles assumed by representatives influence how members of communities respond.

Marketer CCRM participation roles – warmth and competence

Social psychology researchers have suggested that a focal group member's judgment of outsiders is determined by two dimensions: warmth and competence (Cuddy *et al.* 2007; Fiske *et al.* 1999, 2002; Glick and Fiske 2001; Judd *et al.* 2005). This stream of research has suggested that affective responses towards other people depend upon the relative level of perceived warmth and competence. Specifically, when people evaluate a focal person's level of warmth as high, they are more prone to have positive social reactions towards that person and are less likely to reject him or her (Fiske *et al.* 2002; Jackman 1994). More importantly, this warmth-based response tends to be sustained regardless of the perceived level of competence (Jackman 1994). Applying this theory to the C2C community context, it could be expected that, if a marketer who assumes a certain role in a C2C community is evaluated as warm by the community's members, the marketer is likely to be welcomed and responded to positively by those members.

On the other hand, consumer members' responses to a marketer assuming a role associated with a high competence level seems to be more complex. Social psychology researchers have shown that if someone is perceived to have high competence but low warmth, people are likely to treat the person as an out-group member, resulting in negative affective responses to the person (Fiske *et al.* 2002). However, researchers later note that competence is critical when trying to influence the intentions of others (Cuddy *et al.* 2008). In line with this, the consumer literature suggests that WOM and purchase intentions are more likely to be influenced by the seller's level of competence than their warmth (Aaker *et al.* 2010; Berger *et al.* 2007). Therefore, in an attempt to implement CCRM strategies within a C2C interactive community, this study suggests that if a marketer assumes a role associated with high competence, other consumer members' responses are likely to be determined by the helpfulness of the marketer's actions within their community. However, when a marketer fails to prove helpful, consumer members are likely to show a negative emotional response to a marketer's participation in their community.

Path dependencies in roles

In the real world, it is common that a marketer who assumes an initial role that is linked to high warmth (e.g., social engagement) may later wish to expand their role to include competence related interactions (e.g., technical assistance), once they feel secure in their acceptance within a consumer community. Yet, the existing literature has not examined how this type of role transition and multiple role possession may influence consumers' responses toward marketers. Furthermore, little work has been done on whether starting with a role perceived as high in one dimension, either warmth or competence, limits or facilitates the ability to add roles viewed as high in the other.

As noted, regardless of the level of competence, if someone is perceived to have a high level of warmth within a group, other members' favorable biases towards them will increase, which leads to a positive response toward that person's activities in that group. This finding suggests that once socially engaged and accepted as an in-group member, marketers are likely to be welcomed by other members, even when they assume an additional role that is linked to high competence. However, it is less clear whether the opposite path is available – marketers transitioning from a role based on high competence to a social role based on high warmth.

Study

To examine the roles marketers assume in these environments and their consequences, we employed a three-stage research process. First, we identified four large online consumer communities generated by third parties or by consumers spanning three product areas: computers, audio/video equipment, and men's clothing and fashion. The specific web-based consumer communities selected were: 1) HardOCP, 2) TechPowerUp, 3) CNET, and 4) Styleforum. Each of these online communities ranks among the largest within their product category and has existed for five to ten years. Due to their size and prominence, numerous firms have attempted to engage in CCRM by joining and participating in these communities.

In the second stage, we identified user accounts associated with the marketers participating in these environments. Individual data was gathered and analyzed through hermeneutic analyses of a wide range of discussions among a total of 245,487 consumers spanning a time period from 2003 to 2012. A total of 67 company representatives were identified as a result of these analyses. All messages posted by these representatives were then downloaded and examined by two expert judges. The roles employed by the representatives were identified through an iterative process, with disagreements resolved through discussions between the judges (Spiggle 1994; Thompson 1997). Finally, each representative was coded based on the initial role they assumed upon joining the community as well as on subsequent roles they attempted to assume. In the third and final stage, all C2C messages posted prior to, during, and after a participation event by one of the 67 representatives were collected and examined. These messages provide insights into how C2C behavior was influenced by participation from company representatives acting in different roles.

Results

Using an iterative agreement and re-defining process, four distinct participation roles assumed by marketers across the communities were identified: 1) social, 2) usage support, 3) sales support, and 4) product co-development. In a *social* role, a representative primarily focuses on interacting with fellow members, rather than acting on behalf of the firm or brand. This includes sharing their love of using products in general, expressing their sense of connection with fellow consumers, engaging in discussions about the product category as a whole, and participating in rituals and traditions common to the community (Muñiz and O'Guinn 2001). These types of activities are associated with high warmth in Fiske's warmth/competence framework (Fiske *et al.* 1999, 2002). In a *usage support* role, the focus is on assisting existing customers within community settings in the use of the firm's products. This supports another primary function of consumption communities: assisting fellow consumers in the use of a brand or product (Muñiz and O'Guinn 2001). This role includes answering questions, assisting in the troubleshooting of problems, and escalating difficult problems to other companies' usage support staffs. Thus, the representative acts as a traveling usage support agent who attempts to intercept and address problems that consumers take to a C2C community.

A *sales support* role involves providing assistance with the purchase of products. However, it differs from social and usage support roles in that sales support is not an activity that community members normally engage in with fellow members. Sales support roles involve two sub-roles – pre-sales promotions and post-sales support – with representatives engaging in one or both. In a pre-sales promotion role, representatives provide consumers with information intended to encourage or stimulate purchase, including supplying information on discounts and providing special deals or coupons to community members. In a post-sales support role, representatives serve to facilitate the completion of a purchase through providing assistance with order processing, product customization, delivery tracking, and product returns.

Finally, in a *product co-development* role, company representatives interact with community members for the purpose of soliciting assistance with product design and development. This role also deviates from activity normally associated with consumption communities (Muñiz and O'Guinn 2001). In this role, company representatives facilitate customer discussions about current and upcoming products, invite members to "beta test" unreleased products, and seek feedback on desired features or changes.

Table 13.1 lists each identified representative and the role he or she assumed upon entry into the community. Furthermore, once established in a community, Table 13.1 reveals that some representatives attempted to expand their interactions to encompass other roles. Table 13.1 catalogs each representative under every role they attempted to subsequently assume. To illustrate these roles in practice, five cases were selected from the overall dataset as representative of each role. These cases encompass six of the 67 representatives in the data and illustrate not only the roles they assume, but how these roles influence consumer behaviors.

Case 1: Social roles (JonGerow for BFG Technologies)

The HardOCP forum is one of the highest traffic computer enthusiast communities on the Internet, providing members with an environment to exchange information on the purchase and use of computers and computer components. *JonGerow* joined HardOCP forum in April 2008. *JonGerow* worked for BFG Technologies, a well-known computer components company, providing products ranging from power supplies, to video cards, to external hard drives targeted at enthusiasts. He shared his employment status with other members by using "BFG PSU Product Manager" at the beginning of the join date. However, he primarily engaged in social interactions with community members that were not directly related to BFG or its products, posting a wide range of messages across sub-forums based on his passion for computer hardware in general. For example, in a thread dedicated to the lavish spending of a retail executive in Las Vegas, he joined in light-hearted ridicule of the executive for buying expensive bottled water:

JonGerow
FWIW: Fiji is the only bottled water you can get at the hotels in Vegas. And at a whopping $7 for a small bottle, I'll drink tap … thanks

TABLE 13.1 Roles of company representatives

Initial Roles:

Social	Usage Support	Sales Support		Product Co-Development
		Pre-Sales	*Post-Sales*	
sherkelman, JonGerow, Redbeard, Icejon, Velocity_Micro, edborden, Zebbo, neliz, JF-AMD, yfyf, Mauro, Jay-D, Shirtmaven, drewtronius, blake, MalfordOfLondon, OakStreetBootmakers, Uotis, Equus Leather, Nick A, chorse123, Mr.Samsung	Juan_Jose, Gary Key, Jacob FreemanPeter_Moeller, Mike Clements, Rkoth814, andyOCZ, Tony Ou, Heather Taylor, Josh Covington, XFXSupport, Tt Enthusiasts,Retell, Xnine, MushkinSean, Antec_Jessie, Mad Catz Rich, CoolIT.Susan, Guy_4HM, Epaulet, Saddleback Leather, blkblk,chrisRVA, Gordon Yao Tailors, Samsung_HD_Tech	ClubIT DealMaster, Shane Vance, Monarch Deals, Newegg Webmaster, RodenGray, Fahim, TATE and YOKO, Wrong Weather, Michel Porteneuve	Michael Grey, John Malley, Blondie133, jdarwin, EVGA_JakeC, Tt Tech, PowerColor	tt-enthusiasts

TABLE 13.1 continued

All Roles:

Socialization	Usage Support	Sales Support		Product Co-Development
		Pre-Sales	Post-Sales	
sherkelman, JonGerow, Redbeard, Icejon, Velocity_Micro, edborden, Zebbo, neliz, JF-AMD, yfyf, Mauro, Jay-D, Shirtmaven, drewtronius, blake, MalfordOfLondon, OakStreetBootmakers, Uotis, Equus Leather, Nick A, chorse123, Mr.Samsung	Juan_Jose, Gary Key, Jacob Freeman, Icejon, sherkelman, JonGerow, Peter_Moeller, Mike Clements, Rkoth814, andyOCZ, Velocity_Micro, Tony Ou, Heather Taylor, Josh Covington, XFXSupport, edborden, Tt Enthusiasts,Retell, Xnine, MushkinSean, Zebbo, Antec_Jessie, neliz, Mad Catz Rich, CoolIT.Susan, JF-AMD, Guy_4HM, Epaulet, Jay-D, Saddleback Leather, Shirtmaven, blklblk,chrisRVA, Gordon Yao Tailors, Nick A, Mr. Samsung, Samsung_HD_Tech	ClubIT DealMaster, Shane Vance, Monarch Deals, Newegg Webmaster, Velocity_Micro, neliz, yfyf, Mauro, Guy_4HM, RodenGray, Fahim., Epaulet, Jay-D, Saddleback Leather, Shirtmaven, drewtronius, blake, blklblk, MalfordOfLondon, chrisRVA, TATE and YOKO, OakStreetBootmakers, Uotis, Gordon Yao Tailors, Equus Leather, Nick A, Wrong Weather, chorse123, Michel Porteneuve	sherkelman, JonGerow, Michael Grey, John Malley, Blondie133, jdarwin, EVGA_JakeC, Shane Vance, Rkoth814, andyOCZ, Velocity_Micro, Tt Tech, Heather Taylor, Josh Covington, neliz, PowerColor, Mauro, Guy_4HM, RodenGray, Fahim., Epaulet, Jay-D, Saddleback Leather, Shirtmaven, blklblk, TATE and YOKO, Gordon Yao Tailors, Wrong Weather	tt-enthusiasts, Redbeard, yfyf, Mauro, Jay-D, Shirtmaven, drewtronius, blake, MalfordOfLondon, OakStreetBootmakers, Uotis, Equus Leather, Nick A, chorse123

Notably, members responded to this and other comments posted by *JonGerow* as they would other members, without derogating them as originating from an outside marketer.

This does not mean that BFG did not benefit from *JonGerow*'s involvement in the community. Indeed, as his social role became established, members in the community became more inclined to defend BFG products and were more vocal in their support. Furthermore, when the brand was criticized by a member, fellow members frequently joined these discussions to defend *JonGerow* and the BFG brand. The following exchange, in which *Murky44* criticizes BFG products, illustrates this:

> **Murky44**
> i am very un-fond of BFG units. They cost a premium, yet their rail regulations are inferior to those that cost 100 dollars less. That is pretty much unacceptable to me.

At this point, one would normally expect community members to be somewhat incredulous of the marketer's defense of his firm's products and pricing, tending to side with fellow member *Murky44*. However, the exact opposite happens as *HOOfan_1* and *Zero82z* join the conversation and defend BFG and *JonGerow*:

> **HOOfan_1**
> *To murky44:* $100 for a very good 1000W unit is a Premium? In fact … I haven't seen any BFG units that I would say are overpriced. I'd say they have a pretty superior rail designation. 216W for molex, floppy and SATA, 336W for each of 3 6pin & 8 pin PCI-E sets, over 216W for the CPU connector, up to 216W for the ATX connector. Please tell me what is inferior about that?
>
> **Zero82z**
> *To murky44:* Do you have any evidence to back up those statements? Also, considering the LS-1000 is $100, I doubt you'd find any 1kW PSUs for $0 that perform any better.
>
> Of course, if you have any examples that can help me understand where you're coming from, I'm all ears.

These two customer members showed cynical attitudes towards a fellow customer, while citing examples of superior BFG products and advocating the BFG's position. Significantly, after the postings from *HOOfan_1* and *Zero82z*, *Murky44* did not complain again.

Case 2: Transitioning between social and sales support roles (Mauro for Farinelli's)

Mauro joined Styleforum in March 2006. His initial interactions were social in nature, participating as a "Member" in several sub-communities dedicated to a variety of discussions about men's fashion. In this social role, *Mauro* exchanged fashion tips and was greeted and welcomed by other fellow members who shared his interests. In August 2008, he started to work for Farinelli's, a boutique carrying high-end men's jeans and sportswear. Although Styleforum policy recommended company representatives use "Vendor" as their user title, *Mauro* declined to change his title, preferring to emphasize the social role he had built within the community. Nonetheless, he acted as a representative on behalf of Farinelli's, posting information on the company's sales and customer service until he stopped working for Farinelli's in April 2011.

Mauro's case is an example of a representative who assumed a social role and then transitioned to a sales support role. Curiously, consumers continued to treat Mauro consistent with his initial social role, even after his affiliation with Farinelli's was announced. Furthermore, his refusal to change his user title to "Vendor" was accepted, with no complaints or criticisms being offered by fellow consumers over almost three years.

Case 3: Usage support roles (Mr. Samsung and Samsung_HD_Tech for Samsung Electronics

Samsung_HD_Tech joined CNET forum in an explicit usage support role in October 2008 without first establishing himself in a social role. At the time of joining, he stated that the purpose of his participation was to provide assistance to Samsung customers regarding technical issues when using Samsung products. As part of this role, he was officially assigned to CNET forum by Samsung Electronics since a sub-forum dedicated to Samsung was created within the community. Interestingly, when *Samsung_HD_Tech* joined, another Samsung representative, *Mr. Samsung*, had already been a member since March 2007. However, *Mr. Samsung* had originally joined in an unofficial capacity, assuming a social role as a fellow audio/video enthusiast, while attempting to help fellow members where he could. Only later did he expand his participation to include an official usage support role, once his employer became aware of his membership in this particular community. When this occurred, *Mr. Samsung* made the following post announcing his new official usage support role (emphasis in bold made by the authors):

> **Title: Let the Samsung Forums begin ... by Mr__Samsung**
> Hello CNET members. I'm Mr. Samsung. **As you would expect, I work for Samsung**. About a year ago I started posting on the CNET forums when I saw people had questions about Samsung products. I often found myself on CNET looking for answers to my own questions so I figured I would throw my hat into the ring and give back a little. At the time, this wasn't an official Samsung program. I just started answering questions and soon I found myself on the forums all the time. When my upper management found out what I was doing, I thought they would tell me to

stop or even worse – hire a PR person to take my place and start posting scripted answers that were run by our legal department three times before it was approved. Instead they stepped up and told me I should work with CNET to make this official so our current and future customers know that I'm really a Samsung employee … I'm better suited to answer questions from people who are looking to buy or set up an HD product but I'll try to answer any question you have. Ok … So let the Samsung Forums begin! Let's see where this takes us.

Mr. Samsung.

As was the case with *Mauro* of Farinelli's, members welcomed *Mr. Samsung's* additional role, while still treating him as a fellow in-group member. And like *Mauro*, even after taking on his new role, *Mr. Samsung* did not use any official title or attachment reflecting his status as "Samsung Rep." In contrast, *Samsung-HD-Tech* attached the Samsung official logo to the end of each of his postings.

Despite both serving in usage support roles, consumers' response to *Samsung_HD_Tech* and *Mr. Samsung* differed remarkably. When seeking help, customers preferred asking for help from *Mr. Samsung*. On the other hand, they tended to direct complaints about disappointing experiences with Samsung products to *Samsung-HD-Tech*. However, the most notable difference came when the representatives were unable to provide assistance in the technical support role. This sometimes occurred when products were purchased outside of the US. When *Mr. Samsung* noted that he was unable to assist, the lack of service was nonetheless greeted with gratitude for his efforts. In contrast, when faced with the same situation and providing the same response, *Samsung_HD_Tech* received critical responses that also included criticisms of Samsung as a brand. This disparity suggests that a social role not only leads to more favorable responses to the representative and the brand, but it can also buffer against failures in other roles, including the failure to resolve consumer problems and complaints.

Conclusively, *Mr. Samsung's* case illustrates the reactions engendered by marketers providing usage support after establishing a warm social role. While still cheering *Mr. Samsung's* effort to explain irresolvable problems with Samsung products, customer members complained loudly when *Samsung_HD_Tech* gave the same response as *Mr. Samsung*. Similar discrepancies in the treatment of social versus non-social role marketers were witnessed in observed communities. Indeed, once a social role was established with high warmth, marketers could expect more positive customer responses than when they initially assume a usage support role.

Case 4: Sales support roles, pre-sales activities (ClubIT DealMaster for ClubIT.com)

ClubIT DealMaster joined HardOCP forum in September 2005 as an "Official ClubIT Rep" for the online computer components store, ClubIT.com. *ClubIT DealMaster* continued to participate in the community until August 2007, with the store closing a year later. From the beginning, *ClubIT DealMaster* stated that his purpose for participating in the community was to post information about deals and coupons of ClubIT products, commonly posting messages with titles such "Good deals for Hmembers," "Here is your deal," "Coupon for a 10 percent discount," and so on. Members did not make an effort to treat *ClubIT DealMaster* as a fellow community member, and *ClubIT DealMaster* never assumed a social role. Although customer members sometimes asked *ClubIT DealMaster* for assistance with the use of ClubIT products, *ClubIT DealMaster* did not respond to those questions, limiting his role to sales promotions. Consequently, replies or responses to his postings usually numbered only one or two, from those members who were interested in the deal. Absent was the kind of praise for the brand seen with representatives such as *JonGerow* of BFG Technologies.

Case 5: Product co-development roles (tt-enthusiasts for Thermaltake)

tt-enthusiasts joined HardOCP in July 2011 as an "Official Thermaltake Representative", actively seeking consumer feedback as part of Thermaltake's product development efforts. Below is one of the solicitations *tt-enthusiasts* made to the community, seeking assistance:

> **tt-enthusiasts, Official Thermaltake Representative**
> What Can thermaltake Do For You?
> Hello,
> Thermaltake is actively working on getting community feedback on existing and future Thermaltake products. We would like you as the enthusiast community to provide feedback on your experience with present Thermaltake product, and also any product, idea or changes you would like to see from Thermaltake in the future. Thermaltake is here to support the enthusiast community and we would like to address any issues or concerns you have so that your experience with Thermaltake is excellent and our products will improve to better suit your needs. Please feel free to discuss, comment or provide suggestions as we are here for you and we are willing to work directly with you to assist with any issues that may arise. We have opened a Thermaltake support section in the Thermaltake forums so that you have a place to seek assistance or make suggestions on existing Thermaltake products or what you would like to see from Thermaltake.
> Thank you Thermaltake Enthusiasts support

Remarkably, this call for assistance received 114 replies and 6,655 views. A subsequent request for product development feedback received a further 20 replies and 1,212 views. Given the importance of consumer feedback to successful new product development (Payne *et al.* 2008; Woodruff and Flint 2006), this represents a valuable contribution by community members to the firm. Notably, *tt-enthusiasts* had not established any other roles, including a social role, prior to making this call for assistance. This suggests that firms can request, and receive, assistance with product development in C2C environments, even in the absence of prior social ties. However, *tt-enthusiasts* was consistently treated as an outside representative, rather than a member of the community.

Discussion

As shown in Table 13.1, company representatives can take on various roles to effectively engage with customers in consumption communities as part of CCRM strategies. Some roles are assumed in response to direct requests from customers, while other roles are assumed because of companies' desires to take advantage of C2C interactions to achieve the firm's goals. Table 13.1 also demonstrates that some company representatives subsequently expand into other roles. The challenge facing marketers is determining which role to assume when entering a C2C community and how to manage the subsequent engagement process.

The results of this research suggest both opportunities and hazards for marketers. First, marketers who enter communities need not fear automatic rejection simply by virtue of their affiliation with a firm. Marketers who initiated their memberships in usage support roles, product development roles, and sales support roles were welcomed when they provided information or assistance that is of value to members. Representatives may choose to employ more direct CCRM strategies, emphasizing the traditional role of a marketer. Sales promotion and customer services are well-known and oft-used marketing activities that have been employed to build and maintain relationships with customers. ClubIT assigned a number of representatives in both the HardOCP and TechPowerUp forums to provide support to customers. Furthermore, members were willing to provide feedback on existing and future products, even in the absence of prior social relationships with marketers.

However, members can be highly critical of marketers and the firm if the members feel that marketers' actions were not beneficial to the community's members. This risk of negative word of mouth was particularly high when marketers engaged in usage support roles. If a firm failed to resolve a problem to the satisfaction of one member, other members frequently joined in advocating and complaining on that member's behalf. This resulted in series of C2C interactions that generated damaging word of mouth about the firm and its products.

Second, the findings show that marketers are able to successfully seek and be welcomed into social roles within communities, even when their affiliation with the firm is publicized from the outset. They are treated as members of the in-group, leading to more favorable responses to the marketer personally, as well as to their communications (Brown 2000; Hogg and Abrams 2003). More importantly, this favorability bias extends to the brand and its related products. Indeed, as seen with *JonGerow*, this in-group bias can lead to favorable changes in C2C communications, even in discussions in which the marketer did not participate. As a result, consumers engaged in C2C interactions are more willing to defend the firm and its products and attribute failures to fellow consumers' actions (e.g., "RTFM"). As such, we find that marketers who assume a social role are viewed as a peer member by other customer members, consistent with Fiske's warmth–competence framework.

Third, once established in a social role, marketers are able to expand into other roles without forfeiting their social standing. This was witnessed in each community, with marketers expanding from a social role into other roles such as usage support and sales support. Fiske's framework has traditionally treated roles as static and mutually exclusive. This finding extends Fiske's work by revealing that roles can change and expand over time. Furthermore, marketers with an established social role were consistently treated more favorably in other roles, suggesting that these changes are interdependent. This positive bias, stemming from the existing social role, was particularly evident in usage support roles when the marketer was unable to provide assistance. When initially assuming a usage support role, marketers do not receive the "benefit of the doubt," and instead are treated as "cold, competent" actors, judged solely on the benefit members received from them. As a result, in the absence of a prior role, consumers responded negatively to failure to provide support, even when the marketer had a long history of helping community members. Worse, this cold, competent reaction extended to members' WOM about the products themselves. On the other hand, marketers with a prior social role received sympathetic treatment when failing to provide usage support, often receiving appreciation for their efforts. Just as important, this failure did not engender the same negative C2C discussions seen with usage support representatives who did not have a social role. This suggests that assuming a social role not only enhances the effectiveness of other roles, but may also mitigate risks associated with them.

Finally, the results suggest that there may be a troubling path dependency phenomenon when it comes to assuming additional roles. Marketers frequently expand their involvement from a social role into a variety of other roles. As noted, this approach leads to an in-group bias that enhances the subsequent roles. However, it is less clear whether the opposite path is available, with marketers transitioning from other roles into a social role. Notably, of the 67 representatives studied in this paper, none managed to transition to a social role if a prior role had been established. This is consistent with prior research which has found that, once discomfort or hostility is generated, negative attitudes may not be easily overcome (Tax and Brown 1998). This raises the prospect of a path dependency in CCRM strategies, such that if a marketer enters a community in a role which marks them as cold and competent, they may find it difficult to later achieve in-group status. Marketers should therefore seek to establish a social role first, prior to engaging in non-social roles, in order to ensure the associated benefits. Otherwise, marketers may encounter path dependencies that can make establishing a social role difficult or even impossible later.

CCRM **199**

References

Aaker, J., K.D. Vohs, and C. Mogilner (2010) "Nonprofits are Seen as Warm and For-Profits as Competent: Firm Stereotypes Matter", *Journal of Consumer Research*, 37 (2): 224–237.
BBC News (2009) "Gadget Problems Divide the Sexes", http://news.bbc.co.uk/2/hi/technology/8346810.stm.
Bendapudi, N., S.N. Singh, and V. Bendapudi (1996) "Enhancing Helping Behavior: An Integrative Framework for Promotion Planning", *Journal of Marketing*, 60 (July): 33–49.
Berger, J., M. Draganska, and I. Simonson (2007) "The Influence of Product Variety on Brand Perception and Choice", *Marketing Science*, 26 (8): 460–472.
Bhattacharya, C.B. and S. Sen (2003) "Consumer-Company Identification: A Framework for Understanding Consumers' Relationships with Companies", *Journal of Marketing*, 67 (2): 76–88.
Boulding, W., R. Staelin, M. Ehret, and W.J. Johnston (2005) "A CRM Roadmap: What We Know, Potential Pitfalls, and Where to Go", *Journal of Marketing*, 69 (October): 155–167.
Brown, R. (2000) "Social Identity Theory: Past Achievements, Current Problems and Future Challenges", *European Journal of Social Psychology*, 30 (6): 745–778.
Cuddy, A. J.C., S.T. Fiske, and P. Glick (2007) "The Bias Map: Behaviors from Intergroup Affect and Stereotypes", *Journal of Personality and Social Psychology*, 92 (4): 631–648.
Cuddy, A. J.C., S.T. Fiske, and P. Glick (2008) "Warmth and Competence as Universal Dimensions of Social Perception: The Stereotype Content Model and the BIAS Map", *Advances in Experimental Social Psychology*, 40 (March): 61–149.
Fiske, S.T., J. Xu, A.C. Cuddy, and P. Glick (1999) "(Dis)respecting versus (Dis)liking: Status and Interdependence Predict Ambivalent Stereotypes of Competence and Warmth", *Journal of Social Issues*, 55 (3): 473–489.
Fiske, S.T., A.J.C. Cuddy, P. Glick, and J. Xu (2002) "A Model of (Often Mixed) Stereotype Content: Competence and Warmth Respectively Follow From Perceived Status and Competition", *Journal of Personality and Social Psychology*, 82 (6): 878–902.
Fournier, S. and C. Alvarez (2012) "Brands as Relationship Partners: Warmth, Competence and In-Between", *Journal of Consumer Psychology*, 22 (2): 177–185.
Fournier, S. and L. Lee (2009) "Getting Brand Communities Right", *Harvard Business Review*, April: 105–111.
Gartner Inc. (2012) "Predicts 2012: CRM Customer Service and Support Staggers into the Posthuman Age", www.gartner.com/resId=1846919.
Glick, P. and S.T. Fiske (2001) "Ambivalent Stereotypes as Legitimizing Ideologies: Differentiating Paternalistic and Envious Prejudice", *The Psychology of Legitimacy*, eds J.T. Jost and B. Major. Cambridge: Cambridge University Press: 278–306.
Grayson, K. (2007) "Friendship versus Business in Marketing Relationships", *Journal of Marketing*, 71 (October): 121–139.
Hogg, M.A. and D. Abrams (2003) "Intergroup Behavior and Social Identity", *The Sage Handbook of Social Psychology*, eds M.A. Hogg and J. Cooper. London: SAGE: 407–422.
Jackman, M.R. (1994) *The Velvet Glove: Paternalism and Conflict in Gender, Class, and Race Relations*. Berkeley, CA: University of California Press.
Judd, C.M., L. James-Hawkins, V. Yzerbyt, and Y. Kashima (2005) "Fundamental Dimensions of Social Judgment: Understanding the Relations between Judgments of Competence and Warmth", *Journal of Personality and Social Psychology*, 89 (6): 899–913.
McAlexander, J.H., J.W. Schouten, and H.F. Koenig (2002) "Building Brand Community", *Journal of Marketing*, 66 (January): 38–54.
Muñiz, A.M. Jr. and T.C. O'Guinn (2001) "Brand Community", *Journal of Consumer Research*, 27 (4): 412–432.

Payne, A.A., K. Storbacka, and P. Frow (2008) "Managing the Co-creation of Value", *Journal of the Academy of Marketing Science*, 36 (1): 83–96.

Spiggle, S. (1994) "Analysis and Interpretation of Qualitative Data in Consumer Research", *Journal of Consumer Research*, 21 (December): 491–503.

Tax, S.S. and S.W. Brown (1998) "Recovering and Learning from Service Failure", *Sloan Management Review*, 40 (1): 75–88.

Thompson, C.J. (1997) "Interpreting Consumers: A Hermeneutical Framework for Deriving Marketing Insights from the Texts of Consumers' Consumption Stories", *Journal of Marketing Research*, 34 (November): 438–455.

Thompson, S.A. and R.K. Sinha (2008) "Brand Communities and New Product Adoption: The Influence and Limits of Oppositional Loyalty", *Journal of Marketing*, 72 (November): 65–80.

Woodruff, R.B. and D.J. Flint (2006) "Marketing's Service-Dominant Logic and Customer Value", *The Service-Dominant Logic of Marketing: Dialog, Debate, and Directions*, eds R.F. Lusch and S.L. Vargo. Armonk, NY: M.E. Sharpe: 183–95.

PART V

Relationship threats and endings

14

THE UNFAITHFUL BRAND

When flirting with new customer segments, make sure you are not already married

Marius K. Luedicke and Elisabeth A. Pichler-Luedicke

Today I heard about your new strategy to target Turkish advertisements and assortments on the TV, which led to me losing a piece of the patriotic attachment to MySave. After watching the report on ORF [Austrian national TV], I am profoundly disappointed with your course of action, and will from now on do my shopping at your competitors, even against my own will.

(Hubert, email to MySave)

When the marketing manager of MySave (a pseudonym) opened his email inbox on a sunny morning in Fall 2008, he was quite surprised to find it filled with emails from dozens of angry customers like Hubert. What had happened? What had made these customers so angry? He started reading the emails and quickly realized that the Turkish magazine that his company had displayed in one of their stores had become a stone of contention. A national report had been televised the day before on his company's efforts to better serve Turkish customers. The magazine was one part of this project. But why, he wondered, would his company's attempt to target a growing Turkish customer segment become such a problem? Let us take a step back to gain a better understanding of this issue.

MySave and its customers are part of a globalizing system in which national borders have become more permeable, and even rural societies are more culturally diverse than at any other time in human history (Barber 1995; Bauman 2004). Marketers operating under such conditions, therefore, encounter a whole new range of possibilities to engage with culture (Peñaloza and Gilly 1999). For example, a butcher who has never thought about religious butchering practices before may now choose to produce halal and kosher foods to attract Muslim or Jewish customers; a restaurant owner may attract new customers by offering dishes from around the world; and the marketer of a telecommunications company may offer special communication plans for immigrants to call their families back home.

Companies that master such ethnic or multicultural marketing practices may reap significant benefits from creating culture-specific market offerings or establishing new markets that cater to immigrant consumers (Costa and Bamossy 1995). Customers who value their nurtured and long-lasting relationships with these companies may, in turn, perceive these companies' efforts to build new customer relationships with immigrant consumers either with admiration or, as we will show below, with contempt that results from a feeling that the relationship is akin to a committed marriage. For marketers, it seems important to understand the sources of backlash against their multicultural marketing practices in order to avoid such backlash in the future. This includes finding ways to respond to hostile reactions without jeopardizing existing consumer-brand relationships or devaluing their brand's equity (Costa and Bamossy 1995; Peñaloza and Gilly 1999).

In this chapter, we focus on four emails, representative of several dozen that a MySave supermarket brand manager received after the televised report on the company's plans for targeting Turkish customers. Our goal is to reveal four intersecting sources of backlash that serve to explain why MySave's first deliberate, and well-intentioned, move into multicultural marketing failed. To this end, we begin by describing the social context in which the incident occurred. Then, we introduce the relationship partners that were involved in the conflict. Next, we take a closer look at four emails sent from one relationship partner to the other that illustrate the relational dynamics at hand. Lastly, we summarize our findings and the managerial contributions of this study.

The context

In the last 50 years, Europe has become a haven for about 63 million immigrants from around the world. European politicians have made it one of their top priorities to build structures that support the integration of these immigrants into the cultures and societies of their respective countries. However, notable shifts to the political right in recent European elections provide only one piece of evidence that significant problems persist on this political front (Higgins 2014). For most native Europeans, enduring encounters with people from foreign cultural backgrounds were relatively rare over the last few decades. However, these enduring encounters have slowly become the norm, rather than the exception, for citizens of today's functionally differentiated societies (Harman 1988; Hellmann 1998). Due to its emotional and relational significance for the individuals and groups involved, immigration ranks among the most influential drivers of socio-cultural change, but also of social conflict (Barber 1995; Bauman 2004; Huntington 1993).

Our story takes place in Tyrol, a picturesque county in Western Austria. Tyrol is home to the iconic ski resorts of St Anton, Sölden, and Kitzbühel with about 715,800 people – 11.8 percent non-Austrian citizens and 1.6 percent Turkish nationals (Statistik Austria 2013a). The group of Turkish immigrants, around which our conflict unfolds, made first contact with Austrians in the 1960s. At the time, Tyrolean companies began to recruit workers from the Turkish countryside to fill the vacant jobs in their thriving textile factories. Around 16,000 men accepted the Austrian companies' invitation and supplied their hard work in return for an income that allowed them to accumulate modest wealth for themselves and their families back home.

Without these migrant workers, the Tyrolean industry would not have been able to meet the rapidly growing international demand for its products and, therefore, would not have grown into one of the country's wealthiest regions. In the wake of the 1970s economic crisis, however, Austrian companies encouraged many of their Turkish guest workers to continue working for them and settle down in Austria for good, rather than going back home to their families in Turkey. The Turks' conversion from guest workers to immigrants changed the relationship of indigenous and immigrant Austrians and caused a range of social tensions. Today, more than 110,000 Turkish citizens live in Austria, working in a broad range of occupations and contributing their share to the gross domestic product.

The relationship partners

To better understand what aggravated and prompted the email writing by MySave customers in Tyrol, let us take a closer look at the three relationships partners involved in this incident.

The MySave brand

MySave, the commercial partner in this conflict, is a chain of Austrian grocery stores that has been serving customers in the province of Tyrol since 1920. MySave, first named after its founder, started out as a small local food store in Innsbruck, the capital of Tyrol. Later, the founder acquired a bakery and began to expand the business regionally. In the 1970s, the company changed its name to MySave and gradually turned the business into a full-fledged modern supermarket chain.

Deeply rooted in Tyrolean culture, retail, and production, the MySave brand has become a favorite shopping destination for many Tyroleans. The company is also respected and liked for its ecological and social responsibility, as well as for its innovativeness in retail design, regional products, and corporate responsibility. In its home market, MySave has become one of the largest food retailers and stocks about 20 percent of its assortment with regionally-sourced products. Today, the founder's sons and grandsons manage the company and are widely regarded as diligent, regionally rooted entrepreneurs who have modestly built the company in the interest of the local community.

Several years ago, owing to a shortage of qualified native Austrian sales personnel, MySave began to recruit more and more staff members from the ranks of second and third generation Turkish immigrants. Today, the company's employees with Turkish backgrounds are typically born in Tyrol, speak the local dialect fluently, and are widely recognized by local customers as friendly and competent staff.

The indigenous customers

Tyrol is a province in Western Austria, proud of a tradition of about 6,000 years occupying the region. Over the last 2,000 years, Tyrol was consecutively part of the Roman Empire, the duchy of Bavaria, the Habsburg Empire, and the German Nazi Reich. Since 1955, Tyrol has been a province of the Republic of Austria and is a Christian-dominated province. Some of its first cathedrals, such as St Jacob in Innsbruck, were built as early as 1100 AD. Tyroleans predominantly vote conservative (about 39 percent of the vote in 2013 elections), but a significant part of the population votes for the ecological party (12 percent) and the populist anti-immigrant party (9.3 percent) (Tirol 2013). Many Tyrolean families have lived in the province for several generations and feel strongly connected to their natural surroundings, culture, and people.

As we will show, the Tyroleans who wrote the emails describe themselves as loyal MySave customers and feel passionately about this local brand. They feel equally passionately about the Turkish immigrant group, harboring mostly feelings of resentment towards the immigrants. Other research we conducted in this context indicates that indigenes struggle with accepting Turkish "guest" workers and consumers as full-fledged "citizens" with equal rights and opportunities. For many Tyroleans, even second and third generation Turks still are viewed as aliens that threaten the homogeneous social fabric of their rural towns.

The immigrant customers

Over the last five decades, since the arrival of the first Turkish guest workers, the Turkish-origin population in Tyrol has made remarkable progress. The proportion of Turkish men that are employed almost matches that of the indigenous population (78 percent of Turks vs. 79.3 percent of Austrians), whereas the percentage of employed Turkish women is about 40 percent lower than their Austrian counterparts. Many Turkish families have worked their way up to middle-class economic standards, owning houses in indigenous neighborhoods and sending their children to institutions of higher education (Statistik Austria 2009). These findings suggest that many Turks have successfully acculturated to the foreign culture. Nevertheless, 67 percent of Turkish immigrants in Austria express frustration with the discrimination they face. Furthermore, 77 percent of Austrians claim that they do not support the policy of "no expulsion [of immigrants] when jobs are rare," nor do these Austrians believe that immigrants should have "full political participation" (Statistik Austria 2013b: 97).

MySave, as an employer of many young Turkish women, seems to have a good reputation among Austrian Turks. Due in part to its role as a Turkish employer and also to the growth potential offered by Turkish customers, MySave was interested in finding new ways to reach out to their Turkish workers and customers.

The emails

The above sections provide insight into the broader social circumstances surrounding the MySave incident. The following excerpt from our conversation with a MySave manager explains what happened the day before the angry customer emails began flooding his mailbox:

> In Fall 2008, our company ran a one-page advertisement in a Turkish magazine, which we displayed in our supermarkets in Talberg [pseudonym]. In return for the advertising placement, we agreed to display the magazine in our stores. The magazine sat on a stand-up display, hidden somewhere in the back of the store, where few people took notice. However, when the national evening news aired a short report about the Turkish magazine on television, people became enraged. We received many emails from customers, some with very vehement criticism. Many of these people threatened to never buy from our stores again unless the Turkish magazines were removed. Many expressed harsh feelings towards MySave and disappointment with our choices.
>
> *(Manager at MySave headquarters, Interview 2010)*

From conversations with other witnesses, we learned that some indigenes gathered together to demonstrate in front of one of the stores where the magazine had first been displayed. These indigenes demanded the magazine be removed from their store immediately or they would never return to the company again.

We have selected four emails from all the responses received that best illustrate the four key aspects (e.g., marriage, incomprehension, betrayal, and anxiety) of this triangular relationship and the conflict that arose from them. The names of the email authors are presented as pseudonyms.

Hubert and his MySave marriage

The email that Hubert sent to MySave begins as follows:

> For decades we have been the most loyal customers of [the company's founder] and subsequently MySave. In the sixties and seventies I was already biased towards [the company's founder] and then to MySave. I was taught by my parents that we should play our role and support the local economy by shopping there [and at other local companies]. Since nowadays only MySave remains [of all the local suppliers] and because the assortment [of MySave] encompasses many Tyrolean products, we have remained faithful customers. In the past, we have bought around 80 percent of our monthly goods from your stores.

Hubert's email vividly documents the kind of relationship that he experiences with the MySave brand. In Fournier's (1998) terms, it is a voluntary relationship, as well as a positive and enduring one. Hubert explains that he has shopped at MySave since his childhood in the 1960s and, therefore, can be legitimately considered one of the company's "most loyal customers." His many years of shopping at MySave also endow him with a sense of communal purpose: for him, to support MySave and its Tyrolean producers also translates into support for Tyrol. In this sense, Hubert sees both the region Tyrol and the company MySave as part of his extended self (Belk 1988), and thus sees himself and the company as part of a community that shares the same fate (Aggarwal 2004; Fiske 1992). He implies that he expects a similar faithfulness from the company towards him. Even though Hubert reports being just 80 percent faithful to his retail partner, he expects fidelity and monogamy from MySave.

The text that follows next in his email is the section that we have cited above as an opener to this chapter. Therein, Hubert tells MySave that the company's approach to Turkish customers has made him lose a piece of his patriotic loyalty to the brand and that he finds this very disappointing. He also proclaims that he will terminate the 50-year-old relationship – against his "own will" – and begin buying from other supermarkets. From this choice of words, we learn that Hubert perceives MySave's attempt to attract Turkish customers to their brand as an act of unfaithfulness to him. It shows that Hubert understands his relationship with MySave as something akin to marriage between MySave and the indigenous Austrians, a group to which he belongs. To convey this sense of marriage, Hubert formulates his email in a language that partners would normally use to break up ("I heard that;" "I am disappointed;" "I will no longer," etc.). He also dramatizes his proverbial divorce from MySave by first emphasizing the strength of his own faith brought to the relationship, before he bemoans the company's failure to reciprocate.

Hubert's email continues as follows:

> It is sad that a traditional Tyrolean company with local roots does not set great value on us Tyroleans any more, with the help of whom you have become this big, but instead follows a path now, that no Tyrolean could ever expect to find for himself in Turkey.

Hubert considers the company's new policy to be an all-encompassing and fatal development for Tyroleans. He expresses his feelings as an underappreciated customer and frustration with the perceived lack of gratitude he receives from MySave for the purchases he has made to support their company over the decades. But what exactly is taken away from Hubert as a result of MySave's actions? Let us take a look at another email to find out.

Anton and the misunderstanding about integration

> Ladies and Gentlemen, With regards to the TV broadcast yesterday, I would like to inform you – even though you are probably not interested in that (because you care more about our Turkish fellow citizens now) – that I and my entire family (even though it won't have much of an impact) will avoid MySave stores in the future. It must be a joke that rather than expecting from immigrants to integrate you even help them with your Turkish magazine to not adapt. Nothing against foreigners, that is not my intention, but everywhere on the planet one has to conform, why not here? I don't think that I will ever find a German magazine in a Turkish supermarket. Best and last greetings, Anton.

Anton uses a similar marital infidelity storyline and dramatic voice in his message. He proclaims that MySave is obviously no longer on the same page as him and that he and his entire family will, therefore, terminate the relationship ("will avoid … in the future"). In contrast to Hubert, who has argued the marital betrayal with more patriotic sentiments, Anton bolsters his case for relational betrayal with immigration policy. Anton, on the other hand, feels betrayed by MySave because the company fails to expect "immigrants to integrate" and instead directly accommodates these customers' needs. In strict acculturation theoretical terms, Anton himself expects Turkish citizens to assimilate (rather than integrate), which essentially means that the group should abandon its Turkish culture and language in favor of the Austrian culture and language. He perceives that MySave is attempting to integrate Turkish citizens by allowing Turkish language to enter the Tyrolean supermarkets. For Anton, this choice is wrong, and he believes it should not be taking place at MySave, because "one has to conform" everywhere else. The reason for his disappointment is that his identity, like Hubert's, is inextricably linked to the region and the supermarket brand that plays a significant role therein. In Anton's view, however, MySave does not join forces with him and other compatriots in protecting the Austrian community and the marital consumer-brand relationship that supports it. Instead, the brand proactively opens the Tyrolean ranks to the other group. Particularly noteworthy is the dramatic scripting of this email. Like Hubert, Anton first formally announces that he will end the relationship ("I would like to inform you … will avoid …"). Then, he explains that he does so because he no longer feels sufficiently appreciated by MySave, and because he feels like he is being passed over in favor of a new partner ("because you care more about our fellow Turkish citizens now"). His formal address ("Ladies and Gentlemen") and formal tone ("would like to inform you") are offset by an anger-laden valediction, which underlines the sincerity of his chagrin and the finality of his split-up ("Best and last greetings"). Anton's short tragic play thus conveys a strong sense of relational trouble induced by an unfaithful partner.

The first two drivers of this indigenous backlash, a sense of unfairness that results from Turks getting the same customer rights as native Tyroleans and a sense of mismatch when it comes to the ways in which Tyroleans deal with immigrants, expose the broad sense of betrayal that certain Austrian consumers experience when their beloved regional brand appears to prefer another customer segment to them. The next email that we will take a glance at provides a more nuanced understanding of Hubert's and Anton's conviction about the nation's imminent decline, stemming from Turkish immigration.

Friederike and the decline of the nation

> To start with I must remark that I have shopped at MySave regularly and with pleasure, that I value the offering very much. Today I have heard about the new activity of handing out free magazines in Turkish language on Tirol heute [Tyrol today; local TV news]. The Head of Marketing said that "it hasn't been purposely planned, it has just come about." More hypocrisy really just isn't possible... For just how stupid is one regarded as a Tyrolean customer??? To encourage favor with Turkish migrants, to reel in even more foreign customers, that is simply the worst. Everyone who lives in Austria has a responsibility to learn the culture and the language. This multicultural glorification has gone all wrong in many parts of Europe and it's destroying Austria. And now the managers at MySave go down on their knees before people who are unwilling to integrate. Now Turkish magazines, then Turkish posters, until a few years from now I will be stared at for speaking German...? MySave is losing me as a customer, I hope many other Tyroleans as well. Without best regards, Friederike.

Like Hubert and Anton, Friederike used to be a loyal customer of MySave and found great pleasure in nurturing this relationship. Similar to the other two customers, she also perceives MySave's activities as a violation of a marital-type of consumer–brand relationship and declares the abrupt ending of this partnership ("MySave is losing me as a customer"). Akin to Anton's writing, the nature of the relationship break-up as one-sided and non-consensual, driven by anger and disappointment, is expressed clearly throughout Friederike's goodbye letter, again with quite an unfriendly ending ("Without best regards").

In Friederike's letter we can note an additional relational facet to those Hubert has already expressed. She perceives the marketing manager's response to the backlash as dishonest ("More hypocrisy really just isn't possible...") and as an affront to herself and other Austrian customers ("For just how stupid is one regarded as a Tyrolean customer???"). This interpretation moves beyond Anton's assumption of a misunderstanding and ascribes intentionality to MySave's cheating and deceiving. For Friederike, such behavior is, in marriage relational terms, unacceptable and inevitably leads to the end of the relationship.

The metaphors that she uses for bolstering her point are revealing. For Friederike, the MySave marketers "go down on their knees before people who are not willing to integrate." This image implies an inverted power relationship, in which the Turkish minority dictates the Austrian majority company's course of action. It is because of this image that Friederike believes that integration of immigrants is "destroying Austria" and will eventually make her a foreigner in her own town ("be stared at for speaking German"). In relationship theoretical terms, Friederike's narrative documents a case in which MySave violates the terms of a community relationship in favor of a market relationship. This particular type of taboo trade-off is infamous for causing backlash against brands that commit it (McGraw *et al.* 2012).

Let us next consider Anna's email, which adopts a different tone and provides further insight into the type of relationship she has with the company and the reasons for her backlash.

Anna and the imperiled austrian culture

> Hello dear MySave team, I have been living abroad for some time and to my horror recently discovered, from a forwarded email, what has happened not too long ago in my home country. I am not at all predisposed to racism, neither do I have any prejudices against anyone… Still I ask myself: "Is this really necessary?" Have our ancestors not fought hard to keep in possession what we have today, what we may live/experience? Our craftsmanship is known across the world and I myself all too often rave about the outstanding bread that can be bought e.g. at Baguette [the bakery shop within many MySave supermarkets]. I do not want to claim that other countries bake "worse," but in Tyrol it's just different, you just taste the difference. The variety and freshness of the products and the modern appealing architecture, that's what makes me visit a MySave store rather than one of your competitors (when I am at home from time to time). You just feel "comfortable" there. Merely I am terrified at the idea of what might come next. (Maybe products labeled in two languages? Maybe soon bilingual leaflets in the mail box?) Please don't get me wrong, but I think we must preserve our culture as effectively as possible and MySave simply belongs to it, too. However, I doubt that such a campaign is a positive contribution to this. With kind regards, Anna.

Anna uses less of the marital unfaithfulness and breakup language than the other three authors. Instead, she adopts the perspective of a previously committed relationship partner who has left the country and sends a piece of advice to a friend back home. Her letter is remarkable in various ways. First, she expresses her (quite drastic) feeling of "horror" upon learning from friends about the situation involving the Turkish magazine. This case was apparently discussed in her social circles leading to quite an uproar. Then, in order to make sure that she is not associated with the right-wing political spectrum, she insulates herself against accusations of being racially prejudiced. Next, she praises the particular character of Austrian culture and craftsmanship and how they manifest in MySave's bakery products. Apparently, she is "terrified" (again quite a drastic term) by recent changes in this cultural setup and by her own imagination of what will come next ("bilingual leaflets"). The goal of her email is to convince MySave to "preserve" Tyrolean culture, of which she, in line with Hubert, considers herself and MySave a part. On this relational background, Anna seems to expect that MySave, by allowing Turkish language to enter their supermarkets, is only at the beginning of a process of cultural decline that should be conquered early on. Such an outcome is, in her mind, unrelated to racist discrimination, but to cultural protectionism instead.

Of the four authors, Anna is the relationship partner with the most casual relationship to MySave, whereas Anton, Hubert, and Friederike clearly write more from the position of a marriage partner with an unfaithful spouse. Perhaps, Anna does not threaten MySave with the prospect of terminating her relationship with the brand because she does not see herself as married to MySave, but rather views herself as a friend who hopes her advice can lead to the betterment of the company.

The resolution

The managers at MySave were caught unprepared by these customers' dramatic backlash against their targeting of Turkish customers. Within a day of receiving the outraged emails, the managers decided to remove the Turkish magazines from their displays. The public relations manager announced in public that the company did not intend to pursue a strategic marketing plan specifically catering to Turkish customers, but simply wanted to connect better with their valued Turkish employees and their families. They did not expect or intend to offend anyone.

Conclusions and marketing implications

Why, we have asked in this chapter, would it be upsetting for indigenous consumers to discover that their favorite local supermarket brand wanted to reach out to an immigrant customer group? There are many possible and overlapping explanations for this outrage: from radical conservatism, to racist ideology, to territorial protectionism among indigenes. Each of these reasons is important because of the perceived impact it has on the relationship between the consumer and the brand. With that understanding, we have focused our attention on the relational factors that drive the situation. Our text analysis of dozens of emails sent to MySave in anger and frustration sheds light on these drivers.

1   Three of the four consumers cited in this chapter use specific wording that reveals that they perceive themselves as partners in a marriage-type of relationship with the MySave brand. This relationship diagnosis is founded in the notion that both partners have supported each other over decades. These authors' agitated responses to MySave's flirtation with Turkish customers

suggest that these indigenous customers see their relationship with the company as a long-standing exclusive relationship between MySave and only the indigenous community. This type of relationship entails expectations of privileged treatment and, importantly, the expectation that any move towards including other members in the marriage requires approval by both partners. This finding confirms and provides some contextual nuance to experimental consumer research on taboo trade-offs between community and exchange relational logics (Aggarwal 2004; McGraw *et al.* 2012).

2   The study further shows that indigenous customers see MySave as part of an Austrian social and cultural system that is threatened by the growth of Turkish immigrants. Consumers like Anton, Hubert, and Friederike expect Turkish immigrants to assimilate to Austrian culture by adopting it as their own, and see great danger in Austrians accommodating (even the slightest bit) the needs of Turkish consumers. MySave, by allowing the Turkish language into their stores, appears to breach this (one-sided, intangible) social contract, an act that these indigenous customers perceive as high treason.

3   Indigenous customers interpret MySave's decision to serve Turkish customers as an act of weakness in the face of changing market forces, and thus as an erosion of Tyrolean community boundaries. This interpretation of the situation renders MySave a spouse that can no longer be trusted. Consumers such as Friederike and Anna take this weakness as an opportunity to speculate how much more the company will be willing to give in to Turkish customers' needs, and, thus, feel alienated as MySave's existing relationship partners.

Many of the offended partners' interpretations and socio-cultural projections are either factually wrong or, at least, misguided. The authors tend to speak from an emotionally aroused position and resort to exaggerated, unrealistic inferences. For example, how would the quality of MySave bakery bread become compromised when MySave chooses to advertise to Turks? How exactly would Austrian customers suffer from Turkish customers being served as well? And who could, given the historical data (Sassen 1999), reasonably expect Austria to turn into a Turkish-dominated country when Turkish citizens are treated as equal consumer citizens? Regardless of the validity and ethical legitimacy of these angry customers' claims, their perceptions of a Turkish intrusion into their marriage with MySave matters enough to these consumers to encourage them to write angry emails and make resolutions to boycott the brand, creating a legitimate marketing problem.

From the above backlash against MySave's move to multiculturalism, three practical insights emerge for marketers considering targeting minority customer groups. First, in cultural contexts, such as the one described above, indigenous consumers sometimes see themselves as symbolically married to their longstanding commercial partners and expect these brands to be faithful to them in return. For them, "faithful" means, for example, that the brand does not connect with customers that these existing partners try to keep at a distance, i.e., outgroups. Marketers that consider "flirting" with new customer segments may, therefore, find it useful to explore a) how their existing relationship partners relate to a potential new partner, and b) to what extent the existing partners perceive the marriage as open or monogamous.

Second, when marketers decide to 'flirt' with new customer segments that might enflame the passion of existing customers, it becomes important for brands to address the existing partners' sense of privilege. The hierarchy between the old and the new relationship partners may be influenced by racial or sociocultural ideologies, but could also depend on the length of a relationship. Consider, for instance, how one feels when the telecommunications company to which one has been loyal for years makes generous offers to attract new customers, while withholding such offers from existing customers. In the above case, MySave may be better advised to introduce products that signal an interest in the existing relationship partner, while targeting the Turkish community more indirectly. For example, offering Turkish products in original Turkish language packaging might be less of a problem when these products carry a MySave-branded label in German, promoting these products to Tyroleans as a new line of ethnic products. A product with large-print Turkish language and small- (or no) German language print that appears to be exclusively designed for Turkish customers is, in turn, more likely to produce undesirable responses, such as feelings of betrayal. The first option conveys a sense of indigenous (including MySave's) ownership and control over the innovation process, whereas the second case conveys just the opposite sense to the critical existing customer base. Introducing such products to an outgroup is more likely to be seen by the ingroup as an introduction to the other culture, a move that seems more focused on the existing partner than on the new one.

Third, and in light of the above insights surrounding relational power dynamics, displaying a Turkish-language magazine that indigenes cannot decipher in an indigenous store might be too bold of a first step for targeting a new customer segment. A product offering that inherently precludes the existing partner – in this case through a language barrier – suggests that the marketer is trying to build parallel relationships and is flaunting them in front of the marriage partner. For indigenous customers, such as the customers cited herein, this feels like catching an unfaithful spouse in flagrante. A more inclusive approach might include a gradual introduction of products and communications that respect (or even directly acknowledge) the interest of the original partner, while still allowing the marketer to court the new intended target.

This study highlights some of the important dynamics that marketers should consider when flirting with new customer segments. Based on our findings, marketers are well advised to first explore the nature of their relationship with existing customers to determine its parameters and then study how this existing customer group relates to the potential new target group. If the marketer determines that the brand is already considered to be in an exclusive marriage with its existing customers, then they have to proceed with caution when they target new types of customers, particularly if the relationship between existing customers and the new customers is strained. Marketers should consider creating new products or promotions that acknowledge and respect the existing relationship while still courting the new target. In so doing, marketers may gradually introduce the existing partner to the idea of an open marriage.

References

Aggarwal, P. (2004) "The Effects of Brand Relationship Norms on Consumer Attitudes and Behavior", *Journal of Consumer Research*, 31 (1): 87–101.

Barber, B.R. (1995) *Jihad vs. McWorld*. New York: Times Books.

Bauman, Z. (2004) *Wasted Lives. Modernity and its Outcasts*. Cambridge: Polity Press.

Belk, R.W. (1988) "Possessions and the Extended Self", *Journal of Consumer Research*, 15 (2): 139–168.

Costa, J.A. and G. Bamossy (1995) *Marketing in a Multicultural World: Ethnicity, Nationalism, and Cultural Identity*. Thousand Oaks, CA: Sage.

Fiske, A.P. (1992) "The Four Elementary Forms of Sociality: Framework for a Unified Theory of Social Relations", *Psychological Review*, 99 (4): 689–723.

Fournier, S. (1998) "Consumers and Their Brands: Developing Relationship Theory in Consumer Research", *Journal of Consumer Research*, 24 (4): 343–373.

Harman, L.D. (1988) *The Modern Stranger. On Language and Membership*. Berlin, New York and Amsterdam: Mouton de Gruyter.

Hellmann, K. (1998) "Fremdheit als soziale Konstruktion: eine Studie zur Systemtheorie des Fremden" [Strangeness as a Social Construction: A Study on the Systems Theory of Foreigners], *Die Herausforderung durch das Fremde*, ed. H. Münkler. Berlin: Akademie Verlag: 401–459.

Higgins, A. (2014) "Populists' Rise in Europe Vote Shakes Leaders", *The New York Times*, www.nytimes.com/2014/05/27/world/europe/established-parties-rocked-by-anti-europe-vote.html?, accessed February 11, 2104.

Huntington, S.P. (1993) "The Clash of Civilizations", *Foreign Affairs*, 72 (3): 22–49.

McGraw, A.P., J.A. Schwartz, and P.E. Tetlock (2012) "From the Commercial to the Communal: Reframing Taboo Trade-offs in Religious and Pharmaceutical Marketing", *Journal of Consumer Research*, 39 (1): 157–173.

Peñaloza, L. and M.C. Gilly (1999) "Marketer Acculturation: The Changer and the Changed", *Journal of Marketing*, 63 (3): 84–104.

Sassen, S. (1999) *Guests and Aliens*. New York: The New Press.

Statistik Austria (2009) *Arbeits- und Lebenssituation von Migrantinnen und Migranten in Österreich. Modul der Arbeitskräfteerhebung 2008* [Labor and Living Situation of Migrants in Austria]. Wien: Bundesamt für Statistik.

Statistik Austria (2013a) "Bevölkerung nach Staatsangehörigkeit und Geburtsland" [Population by Nationality and Birth Country], www.statistik.at/web_de/statistiken/bevoelkerung/bevoelkerungsstruktur/bevoelkerung_nach_staatsangehoerigkeit_geburtsland/index.html - reiter_table [2.5.2013].

Statistik Austria (2013b) Bundesamt für Statistik. Kommission fur Migrations- und integrationsforschung der Osterreichischen Akademie der Wissenschaften [Federal Office of Statistics: The Austrian Academy of Science Commission for Migrations and Integrations], Vienna.

Tirol, L. (2013) "Wahlergebnisse Landtagswahl 2013" [Election Results, Landtagswahl, 2013], http://wahlen.tirol.gv.at/landtagswahl_2013/index.html, accessed February 5, 2014.

15

DYADS, TRIADS AND CONSUMER TREACHERY

When interpersonal connections guard against brand cheating

Miranda Goode, Mansur Khamitov, and Matthew Thomson

Consumers develop committed and meaningful relationships with brands (Fournier 1998), yet still sometimes buy or use options that compete directly with these "relationship partners." Consistent with a relationship metaphorical view of consumer-brand relationships, this activity might be understood as a form of cheating or infidelity, a topic that has been reviewed at length in the interpersonal literature, but is emergent in marketing.

From psychological research, we know that cheating in a relationship where there exists an expectation of exclusivity can be a dramatic event that is typically regarded as a major transgression of norms (Baumeister *et al.* 1994; Whitty 2003). Indeed, interpersonal relationships that are highly committed, satisfying, and important are generally reasonably well protected from cheating behavior (Drigotas *et al.* 1999; Glass and Wright 1985; Buss and Shackelford 1997; Liu 2000).

Turning to brand relationships, what remains to be seen is if and how cheating operates. Do consumer-brand relationship partners adhere to rules of exclusivity? From a behavioral point of view, what does commitment to a particular cherished brand look like? In what ways might cheating manifest itself? Informed by social and consumer psychological research, we report the results of three studies that together examine this nascent area of brand cheating, which we define as the act of buying and/or using a different brand within the same category in which a consumer has a strongly committed relationship with another brand. Notably, this definition does not reflect switching to a new brand on a permanent basis. With brand cheating, the consumer has no intention of undermining or harming the focal brand relationship, but does occasionally "step out" on the favored brand.

Literature

Interpersonal infidelity

Research on human relationships defines infidelity as a "sexual and/or emotional act engaged in by one person within a committed relationship where such an act occurs outside of the primary relationship and constitutes a breach of trust and/or violation of agreed upon norms" (Blow and Hartnett 2005: 191–192). Reflected in this view, infidelity encompasses two components: behavioral (e.g., sexual infidelity) and emotional (e.g., flirting, temptation) (Allen *et al.* 2005; Glass and Wright 1992; Blow and Hartnett 2005; Whitty 2003). This research reflects a distinction between thoughts and actions, though it is fairly common for both to co-exist in the same extra-dyadic pursuit (Thompson 1983; DeSteno and Salovey 1996). The consequences of both types of cheating can be dire, and may include reduced relationship satisfaction and investment, increased divorce proneness, and actual divorce (Drigotas *et al.* 1999; Previti and Amato 2004). The major predictors of infidelity can be categorized into three groups: relational, individual, and situational/contextual.

Relationship factors

Relationship factors increase the risk of infidelity. For example, if relationship partners are dissatisfied, if there is stress and conflict, and if the dyad lacks love and affection, cheating is more likely (Atkins *et al.* 2001; Buss and Shackelford 1997; Previti and Amato 2004; Treas and Giesen 2000; Drigotas *et al.* 1999). However, relationships do not need to be highly unhappy or conflict-ridden for cheating to occur. For example, Atkins *et al.* (2001) shows that married adults who were "not too happy" were almost four times more likely to have extramarital sex than those ones who were "very happy," but those whose marriages were "pretty happy" were still twice as likely to report extramarital sex as "very happy" people. This finding suggests that even people in relatively happy relationships cheat.

Individual factors

Trait characteristics are also linked with infidelity. For example, individuals with low conscientiousness and agreeableness, high narcissism and psychoticism, depleted self-control, or insecure attachment styles are more likely to cheat (Buss and Shackelford 1997; Schmitt 2004; Gailliot and Baumeister 2007; Allen and Baucom 2004), as are previously divorced people and those who married young (Atkins *et al.* 2001; Wiederman 1997). At the other end of the spectrum, people holding non-permissive attitudes toward extramarital sex, those who attend religious services, and those who possess biblical beliefs are less likely to report infidelity and more likely to be sexually exclusive (Burdette *et al.* 2007; Treas and Giesen 2000; Wiederman 1997). There is mixed evidence as to whether and how gender and age predict infidelity (Allen and Baucom 2004; Atkins *et al.* 2001; Treas and Giesen 2000; Wiederman 1997).

Situational factors

Finally, cheating on a relationship partner is predicted by various situational or contextual factors, such as employment status, workplace opportunities, income, and work-related travel (Atkins *et al.* 2001; Treas and Giesen 2000; Træen and Stigum 1998). Further, availability of alternatives (Saunders and Edwards 1984) and perceived reference group norms (Buunk and Bakker 1995) are also important influences.

Brand cheating

Prior research on services has marshaled evidence of a link between commitment and exclusivity as an indicator of "true" consumer loyalty (Aurier and N'Goala 2010; Walz *et al.* 2012). Specifically, these studies imply that commitment to a given service relationship is associated with enhanced odds of exclusive patronage behaviors and usage, and that such "monogamy" is possible in a service context.

With respect to consumer-brand relationships, it has been suggested that "monogamy" is possible in "committed partnerships" that are governed by rules of exclusivity (Fournier 1998). Similarly, exclusive brand purchasing may be associated with stronger brand attachments (Grisaffe and Nguyen 2011). However, even well-established and popular brands have a hard time protecting themselves against cheating. Consumers frequently exhibit only a weak sense of exclusivity with brands and often have transient or multi-brand loyalties (Fournier 1998; Sung and Choi 2010).

Various types of brand relationships have been proposed, one of which is a brand fling (Alvarez and Fournier 2012), an emotionally intense and identity-pertinent brand relationship of a relatively short-lived nature. Brand flings take on many forms and develop over a distinct cycle, starting with a strong attraction, peaking with substantial resource investment, and then ending. Several other relationship types might seem to be linked to brand cheating, such as secret affairs and one-night stands (Fournier 1998; Ji 2002), but they are nonetheless distinct from what we examine. We start from the position that a consumer has a strong and committed relationship with a focal brand within a certain category and his or her infidelity is not intended to harm that focal brand. Thus, a brand fling or secret affair represents the type of relationship that a cheating consumer might pursue in addition to the committed relationship that is our starting point.

Given the paucity of research on brand cheating, we examined what consumers thought of the issue. We started by exploring various online consumer forums and found mixed results. Importantly, there were starkly contrasting positions on whether brand cheating exists or "counts" as cheating. For example, some customers believed cheating is possible:

"I am in the early stages of cheating on one of the longest-standing relationships of my (consumer) life. I have betrayed Apple."

(Male, www.news.yahoo.com)

"I have a confession to make: I've been cheating on my toothpaste brand."

(Male, www.corebrand.com)

"I have cheated on my silicone free routine since going natural … My partner in crime is Organix Renewing Moroccan Oil Weightless Healing Dry Oil Spray."

(Female, www.naturallycurly.com)

While the notion of brand cheating certainly resonated among these consumers, others were highly skeptical:

"I don't get the idea of 'cheating.' The primary goal is a product that meets our needs and is not priced over products of the same result and quality."

(Female, www.beautytech.com)

"One really can't 'cheat' on a dive shop."

(Male, www.scubaboard.com)

"The idea that you could even say 'cheating on Apple' is pathetic."

(Male, www.news.yahoo.com)

This suggests that for some customers, brand cheating exists but for others, it is a stretch. Next, we report the results of a study that examines the issue more systematically.

Study 1

Because there is little work on brand cheating, we carried out a study that would allow greater immersion into consumers' thoughts and feelings about the phenomenon. We expected to find mixed perspectives on brand cheating (similar to what we saw in online consumer discussions), as well as other themes.

Method

We carried out a series of phenomenological interviews (Thompson *et al.* 1989) with 20 non-student consumers recruited at a large university (55 percent female; M_{age} = 34.2 years). We recruited consumers who self-identified as having at least one brand to which they were strongly committed. Interviews averaged about 30 minutes each. Respondents received $10 for their participation. Respondents were asked at the start of each interview to list at least one or more brands to which they felt deeply committed. These brands became the focus of our interview. Respondents were asked a series of questions that started broadly (e.g., "tell me the story of one or two very important experiences you had with this brand") and then narrowed (e.g., "would you say that you always try to buy only this brand?") to more closely align with the topic of infidelity.

Results

We started with an idiographic analysis of transcripts (Mick and Buhl 1992; Thompson *et al*. 1990; Thompson *et al*. 1994). Recurrent themes were identified based on transcript interpretation, and information from individual brand stories was subsequently considered individually and collectively in light of these themes. Based on these efforts, we uncovered themes that parallel those in the interpersonal literature.

Respondents distinguished between the idea of cheating (e.g., feeling tempted or fantasizing) versus the act of cheating (e.g., actually buying a different brand), a result similar to the emotional and behavioral (physical) infidelity captured by interpersonal research. Another interesting pattern emerged such that even strong and committed brand relationships do not always protect consumers from pursuing alternative brands in the same category. For instance, one respondent who was committed to Blackberry said: "If HTC came out with another phone that was totally cool and innovative and different, then I would look at it … The loyalty goes so far." This observation seems to parallel findings from the interpersonal literature that even people in happy relationships are susceptible to physical (behavioral) infidelity. Importantly, opportunity factors (e.g., the presence of attractive alternatives) in the branding context seemed to trigger cheating much like it does in interpersonal relationships. As an example, one respondent indicated "I think I'd be more likely to waive the Gap, where there's a market, I think, with more variety … With the Gap, there are a lot of different alternatives. I can find much the same, probably, product at a lot of low retailers."

Four additional themes emerged:

Brand cheating does not exist

A number of respondents were of the opinion that it is not possible to cheat on a brand. For example, when asked to imagine buying a different brand from her cherished one (Zara), one respondent said "No, I don't think I would feel bad. I would feel OK with it. I don't feel like I would be cheating on Zara." Similarly, another respondent speaking about having bought a brand (Avanti) other than the one she claims to be committed to said "I don't feel like I'm being disloyal to Vichy…" Another respondent said: "I don't think it really counts as cheating, but I wouldn't feel bad if another brand like Adidas or Reebok, for example, if they had a shoe that was on sale or that was of equal good quality that was cheaper. I wouldn't feel bad."

For some, then, the concept of cheating on a brand was a stretch: "I don't feel unfaithful. No. I don't think an item deserves faithfulness."

Monogamous brand relationships

Conversely, many respondents did behave "exclusively" with a focal brand. A number of respondents said that they generally operated within a framework something akin to monogamy. For example, one respondent said "I am loyal and exclusive just to Michael Kors … For purses and wallets and watches, I stayed just true to Michael Kors. I don't even look at other brands to be honest." Another talked about her general refusal to shop at different retailers: "If I'm looking for something specific and I don't find it there, I usually wait and come back and look again when a new collection comes in. I've steered away from going to other stores, I feel like because I know I'll usually find what I need there, I'll just wait and go back."

Similarly, one respondent explained her exclusive repurchase behavior with Lululemon, "With the yoga wear, there's a sense of exclusivity, because I know what they have, I know that I like it, I know what size I am, I know that I'm not going to be disappointed."

First chance to say no

A third theme we identified is somewhat contrasted to this exclusive view, namely that remaining committed to the brand could be achieved not by *being* exclusive, but by going through certain motions. That is, respondents also talked about their commitment to a particular brand being fulfilled not by buying *only* from that brand, but by essentially giving that brand the first chance to satisfy their needs.

For example, "Yes, definitely that would be my first choice that I would go in there and check for availability of things that I'm looking for. If it's not there, then I would try other places." Similarly, another said of her brand, Zara: "Yeah, that's what usually happens. Zara is the first place and everything else is the second option." Still another indicated that "if I had a choice, I would always choose [Starbucks]. I mean, if I were somewhere where they didn't have a Starbucks, then yeah, I would go someplace else." Finally, one expended "quite a bit of effort to start there [Sandro] if I am specifically looking for something," while another said, "I always look to Nike first before something else." Two other respondents said, "I'll always give them that courtesy. Go in and see what they [Honda] have to offer," and that "I would probably look at North Face first and exhaust those options before I would consider something else." This idea seems to capture some aspect of "a right of first refusal," whereby the committed consumer will go first to the focal brand and, then, will move on only after that attempt fails.

Interpersonal connections

We also detected a pattern that emerged from looking across the findings on cheating, exclusivity, and a right of first refusal: more of the respondents who seemed to believe both that cheating was possible and that rules of exclusivity might apply to consumer-brand relationships also talked about the brand relationship facilitating an interpersonal relationship. For example, one brand seemed to be a relationship "enabler" for a particular respondent and her sister:

> "For Michael Kors, it's actually a little thing I have with my sister. It started a few years ago. We just went to the States, and we went into one of his stores and just fell in love with their product and have been loyal ever since … It's something I share with my sister. We usually go shopping at the same time. It's a special time that we always share together like a sister time. We enjoy it. We go through their websites together. We go on special trips to the States together. Our purpose is specifically for Michael Kors. It's just something that I enjoy to do with my sister. It's a special bonding time we have … I am loyal and exclusive just to Michael Kors. Something in my head is set to that level with Michael Kors. It's just like exclusive to me."

Our interpretation is that the brand helps to strengthen the respondent's relationship with her sister and thus that the relationship with the brand is a means to that interpersonal end. Another example involved a mother talking about her exclusive relationship with a particular food brand because of her child:

> "The Jif peanut butter started out because my son likes peanut butter and he only likes this one brand … He would only eat that peanut butter, and then we started eating it because we were buying it and we actually got to like it better … It's attached to my son … We're only eating Jif. Now, if I'm at a restaurant, if they didn't have Jif, which they don't tend to, I would just not eat peanut butter … If Jif peanut butter wasn't available, I wouldn't eat peanut butter. I just would eat something else."

In this case, the respondent's commitment to the brand has a lot to do with her son. The fact that the brand is associated with an important person means a lot to her. This theme of exclusivity is further reflected in the narrative of another respondent talking about a sports brand: "Growing up I was an athlete. I played competitive basketball and that sort of thing … My family was all Nike wearers … I always felt like I was betraying Nike when I was younger wearing an Adidas shirt or something like that." The respondent juxtaposes Nike as the "family" brand and feelings of betrayal that would arise from using a competing brand.

Conversely, respondents spoke about brands where there was no third party involvement and reflected an attitude that it would be fine to buy competing brands. They would not feel "remorse or anything at all" or "like I was betraying anyone." One such example was "If your family is working in Ford, you stay with Ford. I'm not like that. I have no relations to Honda. The only thing they've done good to me is give me a good product, a reliable product over the years, which I wanted and they owned up to it."

These results suggest that some consumers feel like cheating on a brand is possible and that rules of consumer-brand exclusivity may exist and be linked to involvement of a third party. We take this as preliminary evidence that "triadic" brand relationships might buffer against brand infidelity due to the social capital associated with that interpersonal relationship, while "dyadic" brand relationships are less constrained and preclude exclusivity expectations. A triadic brand relationship is one that implicates an interpersonal third party (i.e., some form of interpersonal bond) whereas a dyadic brand relationship implicates only the consumer and the brand.

Dyadic vs. triadic brand relationships

Relationship theorists have pointed out that brands may be either ends unto themselves, or a means to maintaining interpersonal bonds (e.g., Fournier 2009). That is, consumers form relationships both directly and solely with brands, and also with other people who are fans of the brand (Schouten and McAlexander 1995; Thomson *et al.* 2005). The distinction seems to parallel our qualitative result concerning triadic versus dyadic consumer-brand relationships.

We theorize that in the branding context, the interpersonal relationship facilitated by the brand relationship may help to protect against cheating. In buying or using a competing brand in the same category, a person involved in a "triadic" brand relationship may feel as if she is betraying a person who is important to them. Conversely, when a brand relationship is dyadic, consumers may not think interaction with the brand is governed by norms of exclusivity, making emotional or behavioral "cheating" more likely.

Study 2

We conducted a survey of consumers to investigate the possibility that the involvement of a third party – an interpersonal link associated with the consumer and the brand – might help protect that committed brand relationship from infidelity.

Method

We conducted an online survey with 175 adult respondents using a private research panel (55 percent female; M_{age} = 52.2 years). After collecting covariates (age, gender, materialism), we next asked respondents to name a brand "that is very important to you and that you are committed to buying and using in the future." After listing the self-selected brand, respondents completed three measures of relationship strength: one measure of commitment (Fletcher *et al.* 2000), and two measures of attachment (Thomson *et al.* 2005; Park *et al.* 2010).

Respondents then answered six questions intended to assess interpersonal connection, the degree to which a third party was involved with their brand relationship (e.g., "Using this brand provides me a sense of contact with people who care for me and whom I care for"; see Appendix 15.1), followed by measures of brand substitutability (e.g., "It would be relatively easy for me to replace this brand with a new one"), monogamy (e.g., "Using a brand within the same product or service category as [brand] would be wrong"), a right of first refusal (e.g., "I always start with looking at [brand] first before I look at any other brand in the same product or service category"), emotional cheating (e.g., "How often do you fantasize about using or buying other brands...") and behavioral cheating (e.g., "Other than [brand], how many different brands in the same product or service category have you *actually used or bought* in the past 12 months?"). Based on respondent feedback, we also coded for whether the brand represented a product or service. The analysis included three other covariates (age, gender, and materialism). Using Structural Equation Modeling, we constructed a model using latent measures in AMOS (all associated Cronbach alphas > 0.84) with missing values imputed and ML bootstrapping (1,000 iterations). We started with a saturated model, with a right of first refusal, emotional cheating, and behavioral cheating as the outcomes, and retained paths if $p < 0.10$. The results below reflect the final model (*Chi-sq.* = 1147.94; *DF*= 486; *CMIN/DF*= 2.36; *CFI*= 0.86; *RMSEA*= 0.09).

Results and discussion

Respondents reported having generally strong relationships with their selected brands. For example, the average commitment score was 5.47 (on a 7-point scale) and the average attachment score ranged from 4.59 to 5.09 (depending on which metric is used). These results suggest that consumers were cheating on a strong and committed relationship as opposed to contemplating exiting permanently to a different brand.

Relationships that had higher scores on interpersonal connection were stronger ($\gamma = 0.65$, $p < 0.05$) and more closely linked with monogamous expectations ($\gamma = 0.45$, $p < 0.05$), which in turn influenced perceptions of the brand as lacking substitutes ($\gamma = -0.33$, $p = 0.05$). Thus, it seems that triadic relationships simultaneously bolster brand relationships and provide a protective perception of rarity or irreplaceability. This perception that the focal brand is less substitutable itself impacts a right of first refusal ($\gamma = -0.20$, $p < 0.01$). Those who gave a particular brand this right of first refusal were much less likely to engage in emotional cheating ($\gamma = -0.44$, $p < 0.01$), while more materialistic people were more likely to engage in emotional cheating ($\gamma = 0.17$, $p < 0.01$). Behavioral cheating was predicted only by emotional cheating ($\gamma = 0.63$, $p < 0.01$) and whether the brand was product- (=0) or service- (=1) oriented ($\gamma = 0.24$, $p < 0.01$).

TABLE 15.1 Study 2 summary statistics and correlations

Construct	Summary Statistics			Correlation Matrix									
	M	SD	alpha	(1)	(2)	(3)	(4)	(5)	(6)	(7)	(8)	(9)	(10)
(1) Commitment	5.47	1.19	0.96										
(2) Attachment (Thomson et al.)	5.09	1.24	0.93	**0.76**									
(3) Attachment (Park et al.)	4.59	1.39	0.90	**0.62**	**0.75**								
(4) Monogamy	3.76	1.39	0.94	**0.26**	**0.32**	**0.40**							
(5) Materialism	3.53	1.21	0.90	0.11	**0.20**	**0.24**	0.06						
(6) Interpersonal	3.51	1.63	0.92	**0.41**	**0.58**	**0.66**	**0.47**	**0.16**					
(7) Difficulty Replacing	4.25	1.42	0.86	**0.26**	**0.34**	**0.41**	**0.44**	0.13	**0.45**				
(8) Emotional Cheating	2.83	1.53	0.91	-0.04	0.12	0.10	0.03	**0.19**	**0.25**	-0.10			
(9) Behavioral Cheating	2.84	1.91	0.95	0.02	0.04	0.00	-0.11	0.14	0.11	**-0.17**	**0.63**		
(10) Right of First Refusal	4.87	1.26	0.80	**0.20**	**0.19**	0.12	0.03	**-0.22**	0.05	**0.20**	-0.13	-0.02	

Note: **Bold** = p< 0.05

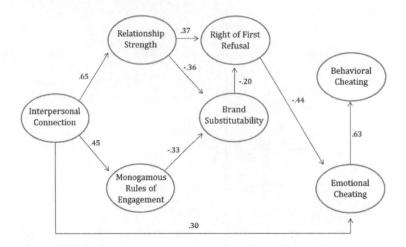

Results of ML Bootstrapping (iterations = 1,000) analysis; *Chi-sq.*= 1147.94; *DF*= 486; *CMIN/DF*= 2.36; *CFI*= .86; *RMSEA*= .09; all paths *p* < .05; Materialism (covariate) impacts Emotional Cheating (γ = .17, p< .02); Brand Type dummy (0 = product; 1 = service) impacts Behavioral Cheating (γ = .24, p< .01); all other covariates (age, gender) are not significant.

FIGURE 15.1 Study 2 SEM results

While all of these results broadly confirm that triadic consumer-brand relationships help to prevent cheating and reinforce a right of first refusal by virtue of monogamous expectations, we also found an unexpected positive effect. Namely, increasing scores on interpersonal connection were linked directly to increased emotional cheating (γ = 0.30, p< 0.01). This result was unexpected and seems to suggest that there is something about a consumer-brand relationship involving a third-party that encourages flirting with other brands. It is fairly clear that there is some form of unmeasured moderator that would help to explain why this interpersonal connection variable sometimes protects against cheating and, at other times, seems to facilitate emotional cheating.

Study 3

We undertook Study 3 to probe the unexpected main effect from Study 2 that increasing interpersonal connection predicted increased emotional cheating. We carried out an experiment on MTurk (n = 292) in which we manipulated whether the focal brand that respondents self-selected was connected to other people:

> Now, we want you to think about a specific brand that you are committed to buying and using in the future and that you generally use alone [with other people in mind]. That is, when you think about or use this brand, it does not link you in any way to other people (e.g., family, friends) – it's just

yours [it links you in some way to other people (e.g., family, friends) – it's something you share].

In addition to measuring all the same constructs as we did in Study 2 (in much the same manner), we made two changes: first, based on an examination of Study 2 results, we noted that the people associated the chosen brands also varied on another dimension: time. Specifically, we noted that the interpersonal relationships varied in their time orientation (i.e., with some occurring in a person's past while others were contemporary and ongoing). So, we speculated that the time-orientation of the associated relationship might matter. We assessed this idea using multi-item measures of the past (e.g., "Reminds me of an important friend from my past"; $\alpha = 0.81$), present (e.g., "Reminds me of a person who is important to me now; $\alpha = 0.82$) and future (e.g., "Will help me carry on a tradition"; $\alpha = 0.75$) relationship orientation. Second, we included a measure of need for belonging (e.g., "I do not like being alone"; $\alpha = 0.89$) to see if this might add explanatory power. In most other respects, Study 3 paralleled Study 2. See Appendix 15.1 for details about the measures.

Results and discussion

All measures showed reasonable reliability ($\alpha > 0.75$). We analyzed the results using Process macro (Hayes 2012; model 8, moderated-mediation). Since our focus is on understanding the direct effect of interpersonal connection on emotional cheating, we included all the other variables contemplated in Study 2 (e.g., relationship strength, monogamy) as covariates in order to account for their variance. Figure 15.2 shows the specific approach.

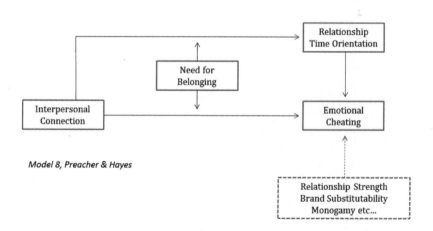

FIGURE 15.2 Study 3 model

Our initial analysis revealed that the past and present orientation of the associated relationships had no impact on emotional cheating. Future orientation, however, did have an effect, but in a manner that insinuated a need for belonging (NFB). The results are as follows:

(a) Among respondents with low levels of need for belonging, increased interpersonal connection significantly reduced emotional cheating (i.e., the conditional direct effect was only significantly negative when NFB was low).
(b) Among those with high NFB, the indirect path from interpersonal connection to emotional cheating through future orientation was significantly positive (i.e., the conditional indirect effect was positive and the confidence interval did not contain zero only when NFB was high).

These results confirm that the relationship between interpersonal connections and emotional brand cheating may operate differently as a function of differences in levels of need for belonging. The fact that increased interpersonal connection significantly reduced emotional cheating only among respondents with low levels of need for belonging seems to suggest that, for this group of consumers, brands that are able to become facilitators of important interpersonal relationships may qualify for a kind of "special status." If people who generally do not experience high levels of need for belonging experience strong bonds with other people – with brands playing the role of facilitators of such bonds – the brands that they use may be somewhat insulated from emotional cheating. Conversely, the fact that increased interpersonal connection increases emotional cheating among respondents with high levels of need for belonging (through future orientation) suggests that brands used by this group of consumers do not enjoy similar levels of protection from emotional cheating. Indeed, it suggests that a consumer may use other people as a conduit for experimenting with new brands, perhaps based on their potential meanings or other related aspirations.

Conclusions

Our findings suggest that triadic brand relationships are different from dyadic ones. The involvement of a third party can, to some extent, protect against emotional and behavioral cheating, and reinforce a focal brand's special status as having a "right of first refusal". For certain consumers, brands are a means to an end and help to facilitate important interpersonal relationships. Such triadic consumer-brand relationships are guided by expectations of monogamy, while dyadic relationships are ends to themselves. Consumers involved in dyadic relationships do not feel it is "wrong" to fantasize about or buy competing brands.

There is, to date, little work on brand cheating. Through our investigation, we have introduced a framework and empirical results that will hopefully inspire additional research. Our findings offer insight to marketers who wish to position their brands within an existing interpersonal relationship.

Appendix

APPENDIX 15.1 Key Measures

Monogamy	Using a brand within the same product or service category as XYZ would be wrong.
	When I think about other brands in the same product or service category that XYZ is in, it is important to me that I only use or buy XYZ.
	If I bought a brand apart from XYZ in the same product or service category, I would feel guilty.
	If I bought a brand apart from XYZ in the same product or service category, I would feel uncomfortable.
	If I bought a brand apart from XYZ in the same product or service category, I would feel embarrassed.
	If I bought a brand apart from XYZ in the same product or service category, it would be a betrayal.
Interpersonal Connection	XYZ helps me feel closer to my friends and family.
	Using XYZ provides me a sense of contact with people who care for me and whom I care for.
	XYZ will always remind me of a particular important person in my life.
	When I use or think about XYZ, it really reminds me of the people I care about.
	XYZ helps me get love and affection from people I care for.
	Using XYZ is a good way to reinforce the relationships I have with certain people.
Difficulty Replacing	It would be relatively easy for me to replace XYZ with a new one.
	The kinds of qualities XYZ has are ones that I can easily find in another brand.
	XYZ does things for me that would be hard to replace.
	I doubt I could ever find another similar brand to XYZ.
	XYZ is truly unlike any other.
	XYZ has no substitute.
Emotional Cheating	In the past year, how often have you imagined using or buying other brands in the same product or service category as XYZ?
	In the past year, how often have you fantasized about using or buying other brands in the same product or service category as XYZ?
	In the past year, how often have you become excited about using or buying other brands in the same product or service category as XYZ?
	In the past year, how often have you been tempted to use or buy other brands in the same product or service category as XYZ?
Behavioral Cheating	Other than XYZ, how many different brands in the same product or service category have you actually used or bought in the past 12 months?
	Other than XYZ, how many different brands in the same

	product or service category do your foresee using or buying during the next 12 months?
	Other than XYZ, how many different brands in the same product or service category do you foresee using or buying on one and only one occasion during the next 12 months?
Right of First Refusal	I would try another brand in the same product or service category only when I made sure that XYZ is not able to offer me what I need.
	I always start looking at XYZ first before I look at any other brand in the same product or service category.
	I always consider XYZ first, and only after that I may consider other brands in the same product or service category.

References

Allen, E.S. and D.H. Baucom (2004) "Adult Attachment and Patterns of Extra-dyadic Involvement", *Family Process*, 43 (4): 467–488.

Allen, E.S., D.C. Atkins, D.H. Baucom, D.K. Snyder, K.C. Gordon, and S.P. Glass (2005) "Intrapersonal, Interpersonal, and Contextual Factors in Engaging in and Responding to Extramarital Involvement", *Clinical Psychology: Science and Practice*, 12 (2): 101–130.

Alvarez, C. and S. Fournier (2012) "Brand Flings: When Great Brand Relationships are not Made to Last", *Consumer-Brand Relationships: Theory and Practice*, eds S. Fournier, M. Breazeale, and M. Fetscherin. London and New York: Routledge: 74–96.

Atkins, D.C., D.H. Baucom, and N.S. Jacobson (2001) "Understanding Infidelity: Correlates in a National Random Sample", *Journal of Family Psychology*, 15 (4): 735–749.

Aurier, P. and G. N'Goala (2010) "The Differing and Mediating Roles of Trust and Relationship Commitment in Service Relationship Maintenance and Development", *Journal of the Academy of Marketing Science*, 38 (3): 303–325.

Baumeister, R.F., A.M. Stillwell, and T.F. Heatherton (1994) "Guilt: An Interpersonal Approach", *Psychological Bulletin*, 115 (2): 243–267.

Blow, A.J. and K. Hartnett (2005) "Infidelity in Committed Relationships I: A Methodological Overview", *Journal of Marital and Family Therapy*, 31 (2): 183–216.

Burdette, A.M., C.G. Ellison, D.E. Sherkat, and K.A. Gore (2007) "Are There Religious Variations in Marital Infidelity?" *Journal of Family Issues*, 28 (12): 1553–1581.

Buss, D.M. and T.K. Shackelford (1997) "Susceptibility to Infidelity in the First Year of Marriage", *Journal of Research in Personality*, 31 (2): 193–221.

Buunk, B.P. and A.B. Bakker (1995) "Extradyadic Sex: The Role of Descriptive and Injunctive Norms", *The Journal of Sex Research*, 32 (4): 313–318.

DeSteno, D.A. and P. Salovey (1996) "Evolutionary Origins of Sex Differences in Jealousy? Questioning the 'Fitness' of the Model", *Psychological Science*, 7 (6): 367–372.

Drigotas, S.M., C.A. Safstrom, and T. Gentilia (1999) "An Investment Model Prediction of Dating Infidelity", *Journal of Personality and Social Psychology*, 77 (3): 509–524.

Fletcher, G.J.O., J.A. Simpson, and G. Thomas (2000) "The Measurement of Perceived Relationship Quality Components: A Confirmatory Factor Analytic Approach", *Personality and Social Psychology Bulletin*, 26 (3): 340–354.

Fournier, S. (1998) "Consumers and Their Brands: Developing Relationship Theory in Consumer Research", *Journal of Consumer Research*, 24 (4): 343–373.

Fournier, S. (2009) "Lessons Learned about Consumers' Relationships with Their Brands", *Handbook of Brand Relationships*, eds D. MacInnis, C.W. Park, and J.R. Priester. New York: Society for Consumer Psychology: 5–23.

Gailliot, M.T. and R.F. Baumeister (2007) "Self-Regulation and Sexual Restraint: Dispositionally and Temporally Poor Self-Regulatory Abilities Contribute to Failures at Restraining Sexual Behavior", *Personality and Social Psychology Bulletin*, 33 (2): 173–186.

Glass, S.P. and T.L. Wright (1985) "Sex Differences in Type of Extramarital Involvement and Marital Dissatisfaction", *Sex Roles*, 12 (9–10): 1101–1120.

Glass, S.P. and T.L. Wright (1992) "Justifications for Extramarital Relationships: The Association between Attitudes, Behaviors, and Gender", *The Journal of Sex Research*, 29 (3): 361–387.

Grisaffe, D.B. and H.P. Nguyen (2011) "Antecedents of Emotional Attachment to Brands", *Journal of Business Research*, 64 (10): 1052–1059.

Hayes, A.F. (2012). "PROCESS: A Versatile Computational Tool for Observed Variable Mediation, Moderation, and Conditional Process Modeling [White Paper]", www.afhayes.com/public/process2012.pdf.

Ji, M.F. (2002) "Children's Relationships with Brands: True Love or One-Night Stand?" *Psychology & Marketing*, 19 (4): 369–387.

Liu, C. (2000) "A Theory of Marital Sexual Life", *Journal of Marriage and the Family*, 62 (2): 363–374.

Mick, D. and C. Buhl (1992) "A Meaning-Based Model of Advertising Experiences", *Journal of Consumer Research*, 19 (3): 317–338.

Park, C. W., D.J. MacInnis, J.R. Priester, A.B. Eisingerich, and D. Iacobucci (2010) "Brand Attachment and Brand Attitude Strength: Conceptual and Empirical Differentiation of Two Critical Brand Equity Drivers", *Journal of Marketing*, 74 (6): 1–17.

Previti, D. and P.R. Amato (2004) "Is Infidelity a Cause or a Consequence of Poor Marital Quality?" *Journal of Social & Personal Relationships*, 21 (2): 217–230.

Saunders, J.M. and J.N. Edwards (1984) "Extramarital Sexuality: A Predictive Model of Permissive Attitudes", *Journal of Marriage and the Family*, 46 (4): 825–835.

Schmitt, D.P. (2004) "The Big Five Related to Risky Sexual Behaviour across 10 World Regions: Differential Personality Associations of Sexual Promiscuity and Relationship Infidelity", *European Journal of Personality*, 18 (4): 301–319.

Schouten, J.W. and J.H. McAlexander (1995) "Subcultures of Consumption: An Ethnography of the New Bikers", *Journal of Consumer Research*, 22 (1): 43–61.

Sung, Y. and S.M. Choi (2010) "I Won't Leave You Although You Disappoint Me: The Interplay Between Satisfaction, Investment, and Alternatives in Determining Consumer–Brand Relationship Commitment", *Psychology & Marketing*, 27 (11): 1050–1074.

Thompson, A.P. (1983) "Extramarital Sex: A Review of the Research Literature", *The Journal of Sex Research*, 19 (1): 1–22.

Thompson, C., W.B. Locander, and H.R. Pollio (1989) "Putting Consumer Experience Back into Consumer Research: The Philosophy and Method of Existential Phenomenology", *Journal of Consumer Research*, 16 (2): 133–146.

Thompson, C., W.B. Locander, and H.R. Pollio (1990) "The Lived Meaning of Free Choice: An Existential-Phenomenological Description of Everyday Consumer Experiences of Contemporary Married Women", *Journal of Consumer Research*, 17 (3): 346–361.

Thompson, C., H.R. Pollio, and W.B. Locander (1994) "The Spoken and the Unspoken: A Hermeneutic Approach to Understanding the Cultural Viewpoints That Underlie Consumers' Expressed Meanings", *Journal of Consumer Research*, 21 (3): 432–452.

Thomson, M., D.J. MacInnis, and C.W. Park (2005) "The Ties that Bind: Measuring the Strength of Consumers' Emotional Attachments to Brands", *Journal of Consumer Psychology*, 15 (1): 77–91.

Træen, B. and H. Stigum (1998) "Parallel Sexual Relationships in the Norwegian Context", *Journal of Community and Applied Social Psychology*, 8 (1): 41–56.

Treas, J. and D. Giesen (2000) "Sexual Infidelity among Married and Cohabiting Americans", *Journal of the Marriage and the Family*, 62 (1): 48–60.

Walz, A.M., K. Celuch, and N.G. Robinson (2012) "'I Will Have No Other!' – The Role of Communication and Trust in Driving Exclusive Behavior", *Journal of Consumer Satisfaction, Dissatisfaction and Complaining Behavior*, 25: 80–95.

Whitty, M.T. (2003) "Pushing the Wrong Buttons: Men's and Women's Attitudes Toward Online and Offline Infidelity", *Cyber Psychology and Behavior*, 6 (6): 569–579.

Wiederman, M.W. (1997) "Extramarital Sex: Prevalence and Correlates in a National Survey", *The Journal of Sex Research*, 34 (2): 167–74.

16

THIS BRAND IS JUST NOT THAT INTO YOU

Exploring the role of firm integrity in how consumers react to customer firing

Martin Mende, Maura L. Scott, Katherine N. Lemon, and Scott A. Thompson

Building consumer-brand relationships has been a central marketing paradigm for decades (Fournier 1998; Palmatier *et al.* 2006). The sophistication of customer relationship management (CRM) provides numerous organizational benefits, but its increasing analytical power also prompts novel ethical challenges. Firms analyze customer profitability more than ever and might *actively dissolve* relationships with consumers who fall short of profit metrics or require disproportionate resources (Mittal *et al.* 2008). For instance, in 2007, Sprint-Nextel terminated more than 1,000 customers who called its customer service too frequently. Internet-bank ING Direct closes 3 to 4 percent of accounts a month, finding it cost-prohibitive to maintain customers requiring high levels of attention (Pasha 2005). Even in medical services, provider-initiated relationship dissolution is increasing, as some doctors stop treating unprofitable Medicaid patients (Bishop *et al.* 2011).

In parallel, business publications also suggest that firms terminate relationships with undesirable customers; for instance, *Harvard Business Review* featured "It's Time to Fire Some of Your Customers" (Tjan 2011), and *Businessweek-Bloomberg* featured "Save Your Company by Firing Your Customers" (Schmitt 2011). Although initial work supports abandoning unprofitable customers (Hänlein *et al.* 2006), little research has examined *Firm-Initiated Relationship Ending* (FIRE) – the steps taken by a firm to dissolve a relationship – and its impact on consumers (except Johnson *et al.* 2011, Study 3). Whether FIRE should become managerial practice depends, partly, on how consumers react to it. Most firms profess to be customer-oriented, because customer-orientation is usually profitable. However, firms that fire customers may violate ethical principles of CRM, which "is inherently an ethical activity," because relationships cannot be "sustained without a solid moral foundation" (Murphy *et al.* 2007: 38). Indeed, Mittal *et al.* (2008: 99) emphasize that "ethical and legal issues can arise when companies decide to divest customers" because FIRE "may directly contradict the principles of corporate social responsi-bility." This notion is crucial for marketers, because consumer-perceived violations of ethical norms can result in considerable damage to a firm's/brand's reputation and market value (Hänlein and Kaplan 2009; Mittal *et al.* 2008).

Against this background, we present a conceptual framework and exploratory empirical insights into how customer-perceived firm integrity influences consumers' response to FIRE. We focus on firm integrity and related downstream effects, because popular opinion suggests "that the cause of the problems of American corporations is one of poor, greedy and/or unethical leadership" (Kochan 2004: 224). Thus, if consumers consider FIRE to be unethical, this may trigger negative responses toward the firm that might compound the initial problem of unprofitable customers. For instance, consumers who perceive a company to violate ethical norms may have a lower evaluation of the brand (e.g., reduced willingness-to-pay) and lower brand loyalty (e.g., repurchase intentions and behaviors) (Mohr *et al.* 2001; Stanaland *et al.* 2011), which can harm a brand's reputation and its market value (Luo and Bhattacharya 2006).

FIRE and blame attributions

Despite some pioneering contributions (Hänlein and Kaplan 2009; Mittal *et al.* 2008), marketing research provides little insight into how consumers respond to FIRE. We build on attribution theory and social exclusion theory, and begin our conceptualization with the attribution of causal responsibility. Attribution research underlines the human need to account for the causality of events, especially for unexpected and unfavorable outcomes (Bradbury and Fincham 1990; Shaver and Drown 1986). People's causal attributions for negative events predominately capture whether something internal or external brought about the outcome (Hall *et al.* 2003). Thus, the interplay of self-blame and other-blame helps explain how people respond to negative events (Tennen and Affleck 1990). Especially in the context of relationship dissolution, not only explaining why it occurs, but also attributing causal responsibility between the self and the partner is of great psycho-logical importance (Weiss 1975). In parallel, social exclusion theory suggests that people respond to ostracism by appraising the meaning, cause, and reasons for being excluded; this appraisal is an important determinant for their cognitive, affective, and behavioral response (Williams 2007). Against this background, we explore how the allocation of causal responsibility – or blame[1] – between firm and customer influences customer responses to FIRE. Specifically, we focus on the interplay of two factors (blame and cause) from the consumers' perspective.

Firm-assigned blame: customer or firm

On the one hand, as it initiates the dissolution, the firm attributes blame in its communicated judgment to the customer about which party has caused the need to end the relationship (customer or firm).[2] For example, a firm stating that a relationship is ending due to the customer violating business norms (e.g., abusing the firm's return policy or loyalty program), blames the customer (e.g., Williams 2013). A firm stating that management issues prevent it from profitably serving its customers (e.g., firm's cost structure), blames itself. A key factor in our model is the message the customer receives from the firm about where the blame for FIRE lies.

Customer-perceived cause: customer or firm

On the other hand, because people are particularly likely to engage in sense-making in response to unexpected and unfavorable outcomes (Bradbury and Fincham 1990; Shaver and Drown 1986), upon learning about the firm's intent to end the relationship, customers assess the firm's blame attribution in light of their own perception of where the cause rests. Customers may perceive the cause to be inconsistent with the firm's assigned blame. Specifically, insights about self- and other-blame (Hall *et al.* 2003) suggest that customers can perceive either themselves or the firm as having caused the dissolution, and this perception may be consistent or inconsistent with the firm's assigned blame. We focus on the interaction of these two conceptual components: the firm's assigned blame, and the customer's perception as to which party has caused the termination. Thus, we conceptualize four FIRE configurations (Figure 16.1).

Discrepancies between cause and assigned responsibility are not uncommon during relationship ending. For instance, incongruent attributions can occur in the context of employee termination, because firms might deliberately assign blame to

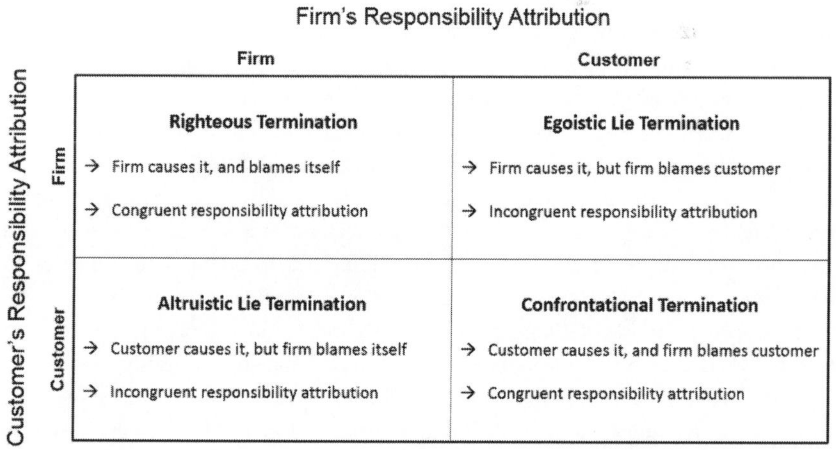

Firm's Responsibility Attribution

	Firm	Customer
Firm	**Righteous Termination** → Firm causes it, and blames itself → Congruent responsibility attribution	**Egoistic Lie Termination** → Firm causes it, but firm blames customer → Incongruent responsibility attribution
Customer	**Altruistic Lie Termination** → Customer causes it, but firm blames itself → Incongruent responsibility attribution	**Confrontational Termination** → Customer causes it, and firm blames customer → Congruent responsibility attribution

Customer's Responsibility Attribution (vertical axis label)

FIGURE 16.1 Firm-initiated relationship ending configurations as a function of responsibility attributions

the wrong party during a termination to protect their own or a worker's reputation (e.g., stated lay-off due to profitability shortfalls when the cause is lack of employee skill) (Moore *et al.* 2007), which may be inconsistent with what the employee perceives to be the cause (e.g., awareness of their own lack of skill). Similar discrepancies might occur related to FIRE. Figure 16.1 displays two forms of customer-perceived deception due a discrepancy (incongruence) between customer-perceived cause and firm-assigned blame. In the *altruistic lie termination* (lower left, Figure 16.1) the firm 'packages' its decision by mis-assigning blame deliberately to itself although the cause for the dissolution is customer-based (e.g., misbehavior).Vice versa, under the *egoistic lie termination* (upper right) the firm mis-assigns blame to the customer although the cause lies with the firm. While this may appear far-fetched, this – at least partly – seems to have been Sprint-Nextel's approach when firing customers because they frequently called customer care, given their dissatisfaction with the firm. The two remaining configurations represent congruence between perceived cause and blame, yet they vary in the extent to which the termination is centered on consumers. Under *righteous termination* (upper left), the firm causes the need to dissolve the relationship and it declares itself responsible. Here, the firm is perceived as being truthful and accepting responsibility for negative outcomes. In contrast, we refer to *confrontational termination* (lower right) if a customer has caused the termination and the firm blames him/her.

FIRE and some of its consequences

Given the interplay between firm-assigned blame and customer-perceived cause, we hypothesize consequences of FIRE in terms of customer-perceived firm integrity, customers' willingness to adapt their behavior, and negative word-of-mouth (WOM) intentions. WOM is a familiar variable in marketing, but firm integrity and willingness to adapt require elaboration. Despite the strong focus on corporate ethics related to the financial crisis, the impact of firm integrity on CRM is under-researched. There is no universally accepted definition of firm integrity (Brown 2006), but, drawing on literature on business ethics (Bendixen and Abratt 2007; Brenkert 2004; Maak 2008), we synthesize the facets of ethics, benevolence, and absence of greed into our concept of customer-perceived firm integrity. Second, we examine customers' willingness to adapt their behavior to avoid termination. Being socially excluded triggers a reflective stage that can lead to prosocial responses (Williams 2007). That is, people aim to regain their threatened connections through cognitive and behavioral modifications. For instance, workers were willing to work harder on a group-project with coworkers who had just excluded them (Williams and Sommer 1997). This insight is relevant for firms considering FIRE. For example, customers who abused a firm's refund policy might be willing to respond prosocially by stopping such behavior to forego FIRE. If customers adapt their behavior, relationships may be altered from unprofitable into profitable ones, and negative outcomes such as consumers' anti-brand actions (Johnson *et al.* 2011; Mittal *et al.* 2008), and resulting damage to firm reputation and value are likely reduced if not avoided. Thus, our interest in this variable "willingness to adapt" points to the idea of customer relationship turnaround management rather than customer firing.

The interaction of firm-assigned blame with customer-perceived cause

Two insights about interpersonal relationship termination and attributions predict a main effect of firm-assigned blame: First, people's reactions to relationship dissolution are typically negative (Weiss 1975). Second, people accept less responsibility for negative than for positive relationship events; indeed, they tend to minimize self-attributions for difficulties and tend to assign blame to their partner (Sillars and Scott 1983). Therefore, firms blaming customers (vs. themselves) should trigger more negative responses to FIRE. This main effect notwithstanding, our focus is on the interaction between the firm's blame attribution (firm vs. customer) and the customer-perceived cause (firm vs. customer). Four considerations explain this interplay and its effects: first, honesty is one of the most positive personality traits (Argyle and Henderson 1984), and people who learn that they have been lied to typically react negatively (Pontari and Schlenker 2006). Hence, congruence between firm-assigned blame and customer-perceived cause (confrontational termination, righteous termination) may be beneficial in terms of customer response to FIRE. Second, there is, however, a dilemma between honesty and the norm of being kind to partners. Honesty itself can be hurtful and trigger harmful outcomes (e.g., criticizing a partner) (Zhang and Stafford 2008). Hence, customers should respond to confrontational termination (customer-caused, customer-blamed) more negatively than to righteous termination (firm-caused, firm-blamed). Third, people sometimes tell partners minor lies rather than the truth in order to avoid hurt feelings (Kaplar and Gordon 2004). Although lies are often regarded as morally wrong, the acceptability of lying is related to its motivation (Backbier *et al.* 1997). Egoistic, self-serving lies (told for one's gain or at another person's expense) are perceived more negatively than altruistic lies (e.g., to be polite) (Pontari and Schlenker 2006). Taken together, although both incongruent terminations conflict with people's preference for honesty, we expect that an egoistic lie termination triggers particularly unfavorable customer responses. Fourth, corporate scandals and the economic crisis have reduced public trust in commercial entities (Herbst 2010; Love 2009). Consumers might not expect firms to accept responsibility after causing negative outcomes (George 2009). Hence, if a firm accurately blames itself, customers might be positively surprised and respond less unfavorably in terms of perceived firm integrity, willingness to adapt, and WOM. Thus, righteous termination might help mitigate negative consequences. In synthesis, we expect the main effect of the firm's blame attribution to be moderated by the customer-perceived cause for FIRE:

H1: When the firm assigns blame to itself, customers will respond more favorably if they perceive the cause to rest with the firm (vs. customer); when the firm assigns blame to the customer, customers will respond less favorably if they perceive the cause to rest with the firm (vs. customer).

The mediating role of firm integrity

We expect customer-perceived firm integrity to mediate the link between FIRE and behavioral intentions (customers' willingness to adapt, WOM), building on two theoretical arguments: first, ostracized people direct their attention to the social exclusion episode to interpret and appraise its meaning (Williams 2007). The idea that ostracized individuals interpret their exclusion experience links to our second argument, the concept of reciprocity (Gouldner 1960). In relational contexts, individuals reciprocate benevolence and consideration (or lack thereof) that they receive from a partner (Dirks and Ferrin 2002). Hence, customers' perception that the firm's decision to end the relationship is driven by a low (high) level of integrity should trigger more (less) negative behavioral intentions.

H2: The effect of the customer-perceived cause-by-firm-assigned blame interaction on behavioral intentions is mediated by customer-perceived firm integrity.

Study 1: exploratory experiment

Consistent with our framework, we manipulated four termination scenarios to test H1 and H2. Simulating a firm firing customers from its loyalty program (e.g., Williams 2013), we asked participants to imagine being a member in the loyalty discount program of a bookstore (called 'Arena Books'), which mirrored the program of a large US bookstore as follows: for a $25 annual membership fee, members receive 40 percent off hard cover books and 20 percent off CDs, DVDs, paperback books, and sale items. Participants were told they intended to renew their membership. Because (un-)profitability is a major reason for FIRE (Mittal *et al.* 2008), this was the firm's rationale for FIRE in all conditions. Accordingly, participants received a letter from Arena Books, communicating its decision to end the membership upon its expiration (in one month). This letter manipulated the firm-assigned blame factor as follows:

Firm-Assigned Blame [Customer/Firm]: After careful analysis, we have determined that [your shopping patterns/our business practices] make it costly to adequately serve you as a customer.

Recall that customers interpret a firm's termination message in light of their own attributions as to which party caused the need for FIRE. Therefore, we manipulated customer-perceived cause as follows:

> *Customer-Perceived Cause* [Customer/Firm]: Although the service was good and you are satisfied with the program, you realize that over the last year in the program, [you used/the firm implemented] the program in a way that was probably not very profitable for Arena Books over the long term.

Pretest of manipulations

Participants (N = 45) read the scenario for one of the four conditions. They next indicated the customer-perceived cause " this situation was primarily caused by:" (1 = You, the Customer, 7 = Itself, the Company), ($M_{CPC\ Customer}$ = 3.15 vs. $M_{CPC\ Firm}$ = 6.35, $F(1, 41)$ = 47.16, $p < 0.001$). They also rated firm-assigned blame "the bookstore primarily blames:" (1 = You, the Customer, 7 = Itself, the Company); ($M_{FAB\ Customer}$ = 1.47 vs. $M_{FAB\ Firm}$ = 5.08, $F(1, 41)$ = 40.20, $p < 0.001$). Other effects were non-significant.

Main study

We ran a 2 (customer-perceived cause: customer, firm) × 2 (firm-assigned blame: customer, firm) between-subjects experiment with undergraduate participants (N = 303). We manipulated customer-perceived cause and firm-assigned blame as described above, and measured firm integrity, willingness to adapt, and negative WOM with items from prior research (Table 16.1).

Analyses revealed the following results (detailed in Table 16.2).

ANOVA of *willingness to adapt* (a = 0.82) revealed a firm-assigned blame main effect ($F(1, 299)$ = 6.00, $p < 0.05$), and a customer-perceived cause×firm-assigned blame interaction ($F(1, 299)$ = 11.89, $p < 0.001$), supporting H1. The customer-perceived cause main effect was non-significant ($p > 0.25$). ANOVA of WOM (a = 0.79) revealed similar results, including the predicted two-way interaction ($F(1, 299)$ = 6.21, $p < 0.05$), supporting H1. ANOVA of the integrity index (a = 0.91) revealed a firm-assigned blame main effect ($F(1, 299)$ = 11.93, $p < 0.001$), and a customer-perceived cause×firm-assigned blame interaction ($F(1, 299)$ = 10.96, $p < 0.001$). The firm-assigned cause main effect was non-significant ($p = 0.27$).

Mediation analysis

First, we examined mediation of firm integrity on *willingness to adapt*. Our model was comprised of the customer-perceived cause×firm-assigned blame interaction as the independent variable, the customer-perceived cause and firm-assigned blame factors as covariates, and firm integrity as the mediator (Preacher and Hayes 2008; Zhao *et al.* 2010). The mean indirect effect from the bootstrap analysis excluded zero for firm integrity ($a \times b$ = 0.52; 95% confidence interval 0.22 to 0.88). The

TABLE 16.1 Summary of measurement items

Construct	Measurement Items
Firm Integrity	
Adapted from Bies and Tripp (1996), Johnson *et al.* (1996), Mayer and Davis (1999)	• Arena Books always looks out for its customers' interests. • Arena Books goes out of its way to make sure its customers are not harmed. • Arena Books cares for its customers' welfare. • Arena Books is willing to make sacrifices for its customers. • Arena Books is ethical when making business decisions. • Arena Books considers the welfare of consumers when making business decisions. • Arena Books is greedy. [R] • This bookstore wants to earn as much as possible. [R] • This bookstore wants to earn more than a reasonable outcome. [R] • This bookstore prefers to get as much as possible. [R] • The bookstore is motivated by selfish rather than unselfish concerns. [R]
Behavioral Intentions	
Willingness to Adapt (derived from Young and Klingle 1996)	• I would be willing to adjust my purchasing behavior with Arena • Books given the letter the firm has sent me. • I would be willing to increase my purchases at Arena Books if it would help to maintain my membership in the Value Client Program. • I would be willing to change my purchasing behavior in the interest of my membership in the Value Client Program.
Negative WOM (Bougie *et al.* 2003)	• I would warn other consumers about this bookstore. • I would not recommend this bookstore to other people. • I would discourage friends and relatives to do business with this bookstore.

Note: Items were recorded on 7-point disagree/agree scales

direct effect c (1.22) was significant, indicating complementary mediation. Next, we tested the mediating role of firm integrity on *negative WOM*, with an analogous model. The mean indirect effect from the bootstrap analysis was negative and significant with 95 percent confidence interval excluding zero for firm integrity ($a \times b = -0.43$; 95% confidence interval -0.77 to -0.14). In summary, firm integrity mediates the relationship between the customer-perceived cause × firm-assigned blame interaction and both willingness to adapt and negative WOM intentions, supporting H2. Another important component of perceived firm integrity is its relationship to customers' emotional responses, which we examine in exploratory Study 2, a field study related to an actual FIRE event.

TABLE 16.2 Study 1 – Firm integrity and behavioral intentions as a function of customer-perceived cause and firm-assigned blame in relationship dissolution

	Customer-Perceived Cause	Firm-Assigned Blame	N	Firm Integrity M (SD)	Willingness to Adapt Behavior M (SD)	Negative WOM M (SD)
Confrontational	Customer	Customer	70	3.13[a] (1.11)	3.19[a] (1.52)	4.31[a] (1.50)
Altruistic Lie	Customer	Firm	68	3.15[a] (0.99)	3.02[a] (1.59)	4.40[a] (1.67)
Egoistic Lie	Firm	Customer	79	2.56[b] (1.22)	2.38[b] (1.52)	5.33[b] (1.36)
Righteous	Firm	Firm	86	3.44[c] (1.17)	3.42[a] (1.48)	4.56[a] (1.50)

Notes: In each column, different superscripts (a, b, and c) indicate that the means are significantly different at $p < 0.05$. For example, for firm integrity, the altruistic lie termination (M = 3.15) is significantly different than the egoistic lie termination (M = 2.56); but the altruistic lie termination (M = 3.15) is not significantly different than the confrontational termination (M = 3.13).

Study 2: Consumer response to Sprint's FIRE

Study 1 focused on first-person accounts of consumers who experience FIRE. In 2007, much of the negative response to Sprint's FIRE initiative came from consumers who were not targeted, but reacted upon learning about Sprint's actions. Since the above mechanisms underlying blame attribution are also operative when judging the treatment of others, our framework may account for how observing consumers react to the *termination of others*. Accordingly, Study 2 examines the reactions of consumers who learn about FIRE, but are not targeted themselves; as such, Study 2 sheds light on the broader issue of the extent to which FIRE might damage a firm's reputation beyond the customers it targets. Study 2 captures both the mediating role of firm integrity and emotional responses to this actual FIRE event. To do so, we content-analyzed consumer posts from a website in response to Sprint's 2007 FIRE initiative. In its termination letter, Sprint blamed the targeted customers for causing the dissolution by making excessive service inquiries. Consistent with our above theorizing, Study 2 captures which party (firm or terminated customer) *the observing consumers* believe to have caused the relationship termination. Although Sprint blamed its customers, observing consumers may draw their own conclusions regarding which party caused the relationship to fail (Sprint by providing bad service, or customers by calling Sprint frequently). The fact that observing consumers' causal attributions may (not) be consistent with Sprint's blame target results in two configurations. First, if the observing consumer's cause attribution is congruent with the firm's blame target, the configuration reflects *confrontational termination* (customer causes it, Sprint blames the customer). Second, despite Sprint blaming the customer, observers may attribute responsibility to Sprint. This incongruence between the observer's attribution and the firm's attribution reflects *egoistic lie termination* (Sprint caused it, but blames customers). Study 2 explores how consumers respond to Sprint in light of these two FIRE configurations.

Design

The website consumerist.com covered Sprint's 2007 actions and policies around firing 1,000 customers, including Sprint's termination letter (which blamed customers for excessive complaining). Commenting on this coverage, consumers posted a total of 173 comments (posted by 131 users).[3] We content-analyzed these posts in a two-stage process. First, two coders (unaware of the study purpose) coded each message based on whether it suggested that either the terminated customer or Sprint had caused the relationship dissolution.[4] Disagreements were resolved through discussion (Kolbe and Burnett 1991). Next, coders rated each message from –3 to +3 on two variables: the poster's portrayal of Sprint's integrity, and the poster's emotional response.[5] Both variables exceeded the 0.667 minimum reliability threshold for drawing initial conclusions ($\alpha_{Integrity} = 0.737$; $\alpha_{Emotion} = 0.744$) (Krippendorff 2004).

Results

Out of 173 messages, 103 (59.5 percent) messages indicated that FIRE was caused by Sprint, and 70 (40.5 percent) messages indicated that FIRE was caused by customers. Overall, the posts displayed a negative emotional response ($M = -0.62$; $MD = -0.50$), and conveyed negative portrayals of Sprint's integrity ($M = -0.55$; $MD = -0.50$). This is consistent with media accounts which reported negative public reactions to Sprint's actions. To evaluate the impact of causal attributions on firm integrity and emotional responses, we conducted one-way ANOVAs with the message as the unit of analysis.[6] The ANOVA on firm integrity revealed a significant main effect of cause attribution, $F(1, 172) = 168.80$, $p < 0.01$. When Sprint was the cause, perceived firm integrity was negative ($M = -1.46$). One consumer referred to terminations as "the Sprint way:" "Apparently, that's the Sprint way: Don't solve the problems, just find some sheep that won't bleat when you screw 'em. We [firm where consumer works] have a volume deal with Sprint. I'm going to forward this to a few of the higher-ups and see if I can't make it clear that Sprint isn't a company we should be associating with." However, when the fired customers were the cause, firm integrity was portrayed positively ($M = 0.78$). Some even applauded Sprint's fairness: "He was probably a low value, low profit, high maintenance customer ... They even paid his last bill and waived the ETF [early termination fee], which they don't have to do." Another posted: "I think many people would disagree with me, but I think this is an honorable way for them [Sprint] to end this." The ANOVA on emotional responses also revealed a significant cause main effect, $F(1, 172) = 86.97$, $p < 0.01$. When Sprint was the cause, messages contained negative emotional responses ($M = -1.20$). For example, regarding Sprint's claim that consumers were terminated for excessive service calls, one observer wrote: "I think it is a poor business practice to drop a paying customer because you think he calls you too much. ... if they don't want your business and they don't want to fix your problem ... so be it!" Another noted:

"Sprint sucks and I hope this idiotic decision hurts their bottom line." In contrast, when fired customers were perceived to be the cause, messages reflected a slightly positive emotional response ($M = 0.23$). One consumer stated: "Kudos to Sprint for doing this. PR wise it didn't look bad at all to me. I assumed it was for excessive [profanity] whiners."

Exploring mediation

Portrayals of firm integrity tended to coincide with emotional response; those expressing a negative view of Sprint's integrity often also displayed negative emotions. Thus, the impact of causal attributions on emotional response may be mediated by firm integrity. We explored this mediation by conducting a bootstrapping analysis (Preacher and Hayes 2008; Zhao et al. 2010). The model included causal attributions as the independent variable, firm integrity as the mediator, and emotional response as the dependent variable. Confidence intervals with 5,000 bootstrap samples at the 95 percent level excluded zero ($a \times b = -1.24$; 95% CI = -1.60 to -0.91), suggesting that perceived firm integrity indeed functions as a mediator.

Summary and discussion

In times in which firms frequently identify up to 30 percent of their customers as unprofitable (Hänlein and Kaplan 2009), and in which dysfunctional customer behavior is on the rise (Berry and Seiders 2008), firms increasingly consider FIRE. However, the marketing literature provides managers with little insight into the mechanisms that influence how customers respond to FIRE. To shed light on some of these mechanisms, we examine the role of firm integrity in the context of four FIRE configurations. Our studies suggest that the interaction between the customer's and the firm's account for which party (customer vs. firm) causes the dissolution influences perceived firm integrity, which, in turn, drives customers' behavioral intentions (e.g., willingness to adapt, negative WOM) (Study 1) and their affective responses (Study 2).

The fact that perceived firm integrity mediates the association between FIRE and customers' behavioral response underscores the notion that corporate scandals have hurt public trust in American corporations (Brenkert 2004; Kochan 2004), and that consumers now particularly scrutinize firms and expect them to behave in a manner that exhibits integrity. If a company decides to engage in FIRE, our findings guide managers toward the righteous termination as the preferred way to live up to this expectation: if firms cause the need to dissolve relationships, they ought to take responsibility for it. Customers – to some extent – recognize such organizational righteousness. Accordingly, righteous termination triggers the least detrimental impact on firm integrity (Study 1). Interestingly, perceived firm integrity was significantly *lower* for altruistic lie termination than for righteous termination. This is somewhat surprising, because an altruistic lie termination is aligned with a customer-serving philosophy such that the firm takes blame on behalf of customers. Firms – even when working to dissolve a relationship – might deliberately choose an altruistic lie termination to protect the customer's and the company's reputation. Although this approach could be considered taking the "high road," the results from Study 1 suggest that the deceptive discrepancy between firm-assigned blame and customer-perceived cause may still undermine the firm's altruistic intent. While our data cannot speak to the underlying mechanism driving this result, customers might reject this approach, because they attribute a lack of professionalism to the firm, or because they feel patronized, similar to people seeing through a breakup themed around a pseudo-empathetic rationale of "it's not you, it's me." Notably, companies likely trigger the most detrimental effects with an egoistic lie termination, which resulted in the lowest firm integrity, the lowest willingness to adapt, and the highest intentions to spread negative WOM. In conclusion, our exploratory results seem to suggest that managers are ill-advised to use deceptive approaches that resemble 'packaged' forms of FIRE: neither altruistic lie nor egoistic lie terminations minimize the detrimental impact of dissolution. Indeed, customers seem to dislike deceit even if it is meant to soften FIRE (i.e., altruistic lie termination).

Expanding insights from Study 1, and consistent with our framework, Study 2 further suggests that consumers' judgments of cause and blame influence perceived firm integrity and emotional responses toward FIRE, even when they themselves are not targeted. Therefore, Study 2 sheds light on the public perception of FIRE *beyond* the customers as firm targets, which is crucial for marketers to understand the risk of FIRE damaging the firm's brand reputation. The corresponding results for confrontational termination ("deserved firings") are especially interesting. While one might expect firms not to be portrayed negatively for terminating customers who are responsible for causing FIRE, we find that the firm's integrity is actually portrayed *positively* for terminating such customers. This insight seems consistent with deservingness theory that argues that observers can respond with pleasure (schadenfreude) when others *deservingly* receive negative outcomes (Feather et al. 2011). A related rationale for this result might indicate the observers' economic self-interest, such that they assume that firing costly customers may reduce the firm's service prices and fees for surviving customers.[7]

While we recognize why managers consider abandoning customers (Hänlein et al. 2006), FIRE triggers the risk of harming consumer and firm well-being.[8] Therefore – in contrast to what some business press suggests[9] – FIRE might not always be the best option. Notably, Keller and Lehmann (2006: 742) urged scholars to explore whether "there [are] systematic ways to migrate unprofitable customers into profitable relationships." Accordingly, we explore customers' willingness to adapt their behavior to salvage the relationship. We find that customers – provided the firm displays righteous behavior– signal a certain willingness to adapt behaviors that are suboptimal for firms. This insight is consistent with the idea that one consequence of ostracism is a person's attempt to fortify relational needs (e.g., belonging) via prosocial behavior (Williams 2007). Inspired by this idea of customer turnaround management, companies could legitimately point to problems if they exist, but might be better off working with customers to make the relationship less dysfunctional (more profitable) rather than ending it. We provide some first exploratory insights, but more research on customers' prosocial response is needed to develop customer turnaround management as a potentially superior alternative to FIRE.

This notion also relates to limitations of our work. Although scenarios in laboratory experiments are an established approach to studying social exclusion and rejection in marketing and psychology (Ward and Dahl 2014; Williams 2007), more work is needed on FIRE in non-laboratory settings. A challenge is gaining access to consumers and companies in the context of FIRE. Firms often do not readily admit to dissolving relationships (Mittal *et al.* 2008), which makes it difficult to find consumers who have been fired. Despite these challenges, FIRE is a fertile area for further research in various ways: first, attribution theory shows that people can allocate responsibility not only to a partner, but can also blame environmental conditions (Tennen and Affleck 1990). Hence, marketers could study whether the firm blaming third parties or other externalities (e.g., economic downturn) changes consumer responses to FIRE. Second, because justice theory is a fruitful lens for the study of employee termination (Bennett *et al.* 1995), marketers could examine how perceived distributive, procedural, and interactional justice influence customer response to FIRE. For example, in 2009, American Express offered to pay some of its cardholders $300 each to pay off their account balances and close their accounts. It would be interesting to study what effects such monetary incentives have on terminated customers' perceived distributive justice, and on customers who are not targeted by dissolution. Similarly, the idea of turnaround management includes giving targeted customers a warning. This raises the question at which point in time and in which form such warnings are most effective (e.g., letter vs. face-to-face) for successful customer turnarounds, and to what extent this approach might influence customer-perceived procedural justice. Three additional research avenues emerge related to the role of the brand in the context of FIRE: first, Aaker's (1997) influential research suggests that a brand's particular personality might be an important moderating factor in explaining consumer responses to FIRE. For instance, could consumers respond to FIRE more negatively if the firm's brand personality emphasizes facets of "sincerity" (e.g., cheerfulness, honesty, down-to-earth) relative to a brand personality that emphasizes facets of ruggedness (e.g., toughness)? Second, Fournier's (1998) seminal work on consumer-brand relationships suggests that responses to FIRE might also be influenced by the type of relationship the consumer has developed with the brand. For instance, consumer responses to FIRE are likely to be more intense and negative in the context of a "committed partnership" or "best friendship" than a "casual friendship." A third platform could focus on the consumers' personalities and examine consumer-brand relationships in light of attachment theory (e.g., Swaminathan *et al.* 2008; Mende and Bolton 2011), which suggests that certain consumers (those who are high in attachment anxiety toward a brand) are likely to respond particularly sensitively to FIRE, whereas other consumers (those high in attachment avoidance toward a brand) may not display a strong response. Finally, besides these conceptual avenues, additional research opportunities arise under methodological considerations. Our exploratory work drew on attribution theory and social exclusion theory and was guided by a hypothesis-testing framework, which is an established approach in scholarly marketing research (Armstrong *et al.* 2001). However, we note that alternative approaches seem equally fruitful. For instance, expanding our Study 2, an alternative avenue would be to conduct a netnographic exploration of consumers' responses to FIRE. Such a netnography (Kozinets 2002) might provide particularly rich insights into how consumers experience being fired by a company, and how observing (i.e., non-targeted) consumers interpret and respond to such FIRE actions.

Notes

1   While some scholars outline nuanced distinctions between responsibility and blame (e.g., Shaver and Drown 1986), others use (causal) responsibility and blame interchangeably (e.g., Morrison and Robinson 1997). Because it is not the goal of this chapter to assess this subtle distinction, we use the terms interchangeably.

2   Our distinction between customer and firm is a categorical approach. Researchers predominantly adopt either such a categorical or a dimensional approach to attributions (Hall *et al.* 2003). Weiner's theory (1974) is dimensional as it conceptualizes attributions via locus, stability, and controllability. However, the majority of studies on attributions for negative events assess attributions as categories (e.g., allocating the blame to self or others) (Hall *et al.* 2003). Proponents of this approach argue that it is "a more promising method of assessing attributions because these may more accurately reflect the way people think when they make attributions [and] there is also evidence that people do not generally agree on where specific causes should be located on Weiner's dimensions" (Hall *et al.* 2003: 516).

3   This website was not dedicated to Sprint customers or cell phone products, and a careful examination of the messages found that none of the posters indicated directly or indirectly that they were terminated themselves.

4   During the process, poster identity was hidden from the coders. Doing so avoided two confounds. First, clever or rude usernames could influence the coders. Second, knowing which messages belonged to a given poster risked earlier messages by that poster influencing the coding of later messages.

5   Scores at the extremes on integrity (-3, +3) indicate the message portrayed firm integrity negatively (-3; e.g., dishonest, unethical, selfish) or positively (+3; honest, ethical, unselfish). A score of -3 on emotional response indicates that the message contained strong negative emotions toward Sprint (e.g., anger, hurt); a score of +3 indicates strong positive emotions in response to the firm's actions (e.g., admiration, happiness).

6   Since some consumers posted more than one message, the analysis was also performed with the poster rather than the message as the unit of analysis, based on the first message posted by each consumer. The results closely matched, suggesting that repeat posting did not influence the results. Specifically, cause attribution showed a significant main effect on firm integrity, $F(1, 130) = 149.06, p < 0.01$, and emotional response, $F(1, 130) = 83.70, p < 0.01$. Furthermore, for both variables, mean responses were more negative when cause was attributed to Sprint rather than the customer (-1.58 versus 0.90 for firm integrity and -1.32 versus 0.33 for emotional response).

7   We thank one of the anonymous reviewers for this insight. While this logic might help

explain the focal response among observing customers, it overlooks that the number of customers who pay the firm's fixed costs becomes smaller as a function of FIRE; consequently, the firm's prices may actually rise (Mittal *et al.* 2008). Clearly, more research is needed to better understand these mechanisms.

8 Despite the *relative* differences between the corresponding scores, the *absolute* values of the dependent variables (DVs) send a cautionary message; the majority of absolute values of the DVs are below the midpoints (< 4) of scales indicating positive responses (willingness to adapt) and above the midpoints (> 4) of scales indicating negative responses (negative WOM). This insight might caution companies that consider or practice FIRE.

9 Frequently, business press (and related blogs) recommend to fire the "unprofitable, the time wasters, and the crazy-makers" (*Businessweek* 10/2007; www.marketingmo.com/how-to-articles/customer-service/when-to-fire-your-customer).

References

Aaker, L.J. (1997) "Dimensions of Brand Personality", *Journal of Marketing Research*, 34 (3): 347–356.

Argyle, M. and M. Henderson (1984) "The Rules of Friendship", *Journal of Social and Personal Relationships*, 1 (2): 211–237.

Armstrong, S.J., R.J Brodie, and A.G. Parsons (2001) "Hypotheses in Marketing Science: Literature Review and Publication Audit", *Marketing Letters*, 12 (2): 171–187.

Backbier, E., J. Hoogstraten, and K.M. Terwogt-Kouwenhoven (1997) "Situational Determinants of the Acceptability of Telling Lies", *Journal of Applied Social Psychology*, 27 (12): 1048–1062.

Bendixen, M. and R. Abratt (2007) "Corporate Identity, Ethics and Reputation in Supplier–Buyer Relationships", *Journal of Business Ethics*, 76 (1): 69–82.

Bennett, N., C.L. Martin, R.J. Bies, and J. Brockner (1995) "Coping with a Layoff: A Longitudinal Study of Victims", *Journal of Management*, 21 (6): 1025–1040.

Berry, L.L. and K. Seiders (2008) "Serving Unfair Customers", *Business Horizons,* 51 (1): 29–37.

Bies, R.J. and T.M. Tripp (1996) "Beyond Distrust: Getting Even and the Need for Revenge", *Trust and Organizations*. Thousand Oaks, CA: Sage: 246–260.

Bishop, T.F., A.D. Federman, and S. Keyhani (2011) "Declines in Physician Acceptance of Medicare and Private Coverage", *Archives of Internal Medicine*, 171 (12): 1117–1119.

Bougie, R., R. Pieters, and M. Zeelenberg (2003) "Angry Customers Don't Come Back, They Get Back: The Experience and Behavioral Implications of Anger and Dissatisfaction in Services", *Journal of the Academy of Marketing Science*, 31 (4): 377–393.

Bradbury, T.N. and F.D. Fincham (1990) "Attributions in Marriage: Review and Critique", *Psychological Bulletin*, 107 (1): 3–33.

Brenkert, G.G. (2004) *Corporate Integrity and Accountability*. Sage.

Brown, M.T. (2006) "Corporate Integrity and Public Interest: A Relational Approach to Business Ethics and Leadership", *Journal of Business Ethics*, 66 (1): 11–18.

Dirks, K.T. and D.L. Ferrin (2002) "Trust in Leadership: Meta-Analytic Findings and Implications for Research and Practice", *Journal of Applied Psychology*, 87 (4): 611–628.

Feather, N.T., I.R. McKee, and N. Bekker (2011) "Deservingness and Emotions", *Motivation and Emotion*, 35: 1–13.

Fournier, S. (1998) "Consumers and Their Brands: Developing Relationship Theory in Consumer Research", *Journal of Consumer Research*, 24 (3): 343–373.

George, B. (2009) "After the Crisis: Restoring Trust in U.S. Leaders", *BusinessWeek*, November 24, 2009.

Gouldner, A.W. (1960) "The Norm of Reciprocity: A Preliminary Statement", *American Sociological Review*, 25 (2): 165–170.

Hall, S., D.P. French, and T.M. Marteau (2003) "Causal Attributions Following Serious Unexpected Negative Events: A Systematic Review", *Journal of Social and Clinical Psychology*, 22 (5): 515–536.

Hänlein, M. and A.M. Kaplan (2009) "Unprofitable Customers and Their Management", *Business Horizons*, 52 (1): 89–97.

Hänlein, M., A.M. Kaplan and Schoder, D. (2006) "Valuing the Real Option of Abandoning Unprofitable Customers When Calculating Customer Lifetime Value", *Journal of Marketing*, 70 (3): 5–20.

Herbst, M. (2010) "Berkshire Tops in Reputation Poll, Banks Near Bottom", *BusinessWeek*, April 5, 2010.

Johnson, A.R., M. Matear, and M. Thomson (2011) "A Coal in the Heart: Self-relevance as a Postexit Predictor of Consumer Anti-Brand Actions", *Journal of Consumer Research*, 38: 108–125.

Johnson, J.L., J.B. Cullen, T. Sakano, and H. Takenouchi (1996) "Setting the Stage for Trust and Strategic Integration in Japanese–U.S. Cooperative Alliances", *Journal of International Business Studies*, Special Issue: 981–1004.

Kaplar, M.E. and A.K. Gordon (2004) "The Enigma of Altruistic Lying: Perspective Differences in What Motivates and Justifies Lie Telling Within Romantic Relationships", *Personal Relationships*, 11 (4): 489–507.

Keller, K.L. and D.R. Lehmann (2006) "Brands and Branding: Research Findings and Future Priorities", *Marketing Science*, 25 (6): 740–759.

Kochan, T.A. (2003) "Restoring Trust in American Corporations: Addressing the Root Cause", *Journal of Management and Governance*, 7 (3): 223–231.

Kolbe, R.H. and M.S. Burnett (1991) "Content-Analysis Research", *Journal of Consumer Research*, 18 (2): 243–250.

Kozinets, R.V. (2002) "The Field Behind the Screen: Using Netnography for Marketing Research in Online Communities", *Journal of Marketing Research*, 39 (1): 61–72.

Krippendorff, K. (2004) *Content Analysis: An Introduction to its Methodology* (2nd edn). Thousand Oaks, CA: Sage.

Love, A. (2009) "Dousing the Passion for Greed", *Bloomberg BusinessWeek*, October 23, 2009.

Luo, X. and C.B. Bhattacharya (2006) "Corporate Social Responsibility, Customer Satisfaction, and Market Value", *Journal of Marketing*, 70 (4): 1–18.

Maak, T. (2008) "Undivided Corporate Responsibility: Towards a Theory of Corporate Integrity", *Journal of Business Ethics*, 82 (2): 353–368.

Mayer, R.C. and J.H. Davis (1999) "The Effect of the Performance Appraisal System on Trust for Management", *Journal of Applied Psychology*, 84 (1): 123–136.

Mende, M. and R.N. Bolton (2011) "Why Attachment Security Matters: How Customers' Attachment Styles Influence their Relationships with Service Firms and Service Employees", *Journal of Service Research*, 14 (3): 285–301.

Mittal, V., M.E. Sarkees, and F. Murshed (2008) "Managing Unprofitable Customers", *Harvard Business Review*, 86 (4): 94–103.

Mohr, L.A., D.J. Webb, and K.E. Harris (2001) "Do Consumers Expect Companies to be Socially Responsible? The Impact of Corporate Social Responsibility on Buying Behavior", *Journal of Consumer Affairs*, 35 (1): 45–72.

Moore, S., L. Grunberg, E. Greenberg, and P. Sikora (2007) "Type of Job Loss and its Impact on Decision Control, Mastery, and Depression", *Current Psychology*, 26 (2): 71–85.

Morrison, E.W. and S.L. Robinson (1997) "When Employees Feel Betrayed: A Model of

How Psychological Contract Violation Develops", *Academy of Management Review*, 22 (1): 226–256.

Murphy, P.E., G.R. Laczniak, and G. Wood (2007) "An Ethical Basis for Relationship Marketing: A Virtue Ethics Perspective", *European Journal of Marketing*, 41 (1/2): 37–57.

Palmatier, R.W., R.P Dant, G. Grewal, and K.R. Evans (2006) "Factors Influencing the Effectiveness Relationship Marketing: A Meta-Analysis", *Journal of Marketing*, 70 (4): 136–153.

Pasha, S. (2005) "4% interest … Why not Bank Online?", *CNN.com*, http://money.cnn.com/2005/10/02/pf/debt/internet_banking/, accessed August 14, 2014.

Pontari, B.A. and B.R. Schlenker (2006) "Helping Friends Manage Impressions: We Like Helpful Liars But Respect Nonhelpful Truth Tellers", *Basic and Applied Social Psychology*, 28 (2): 177–183.

Preacher, K.J. and A.F. Hayes (2008) "Asymptotic and Resampling Strategies for Assessing and Comparing Indirect Effects in Multiple Mediator Models", *Behavior Research Methods*, 40 (3): 879–891.

Schmitt, J. (2011) "Save Your Company by Firing Your Customers", *Businessweek*, April 5, 2011, www.businessweek.com/managing/content/apr2011/ca2011045_952921.htm, accessed August 14, 2014.

Shaver, K.G. and D. Drown (1986) "On Causality, Responsibility, and Self-blame: A Theoretical Note", *Journal of Personality and Social Psychology*, 50 (4): 697–702.

Sillars, A.L. and M.D. Scott (1983) "Interpersonal Perception between Intimates: An Integrative Review", *Human Communication Research*, 10 (1): 153–176.

Stanaland, A.J.S., M.O. Lwin, and P.E. Murphy (2011) "Consumer Perceptions of the Antecedents and Consequences of Corporate Social Responsibility", *Journal of Business Ethics*, 102 (1): 47–55.

Swaminathan, V., K.M. Stilley, and R. Ahluwalia (2009) "When Brand Personality Matters: The Moderating Role of Attachment Styles", *Journal of Consumer Research*, 35 (6): 985–1002.

Tennen, H. and G. Affleck (1990) "Blaming Others for Threatening Events", *Psychological Bulletin*, 108 (2): 209–232.

Tjan, A.K. (2011) "It's Time to Fire Some of Your Customers", *Harvard Business Review Blog*, http://blogs.hbr.org/tjan/2011/08/its-time-to-fire-some-of-your.html, accessed August 14, 2014.

Ward, M.K. and D.W. Dahl (2014) "Should the Devil Sell Prada? Retail Rejection Increases Aspiring Consumers' Desire for the Brand", *Journal of Consumer Research*, 41 (October).

Weiner, B. (1974) *An Attributional Theory of Motivation and Emotion*, New York: Springer.

Weiss, R.S. (1975) *Marital Separation*. New York: Basic Books.

Williams, K.D. (2007) "Ostracism", *Annual Review of Psychology*, 58: 425–452.

Williams, K.D. and K.L. Sommer (1997) "Social Ostracism by Coworkers: Does Rejection Lead to Loafing or Compensation?", *Personality and Social Psychology Bulletin*, 23 (7): 693–706.

Williams, P. (2013) "Supreme Court Reluctant to Expand Frequent Flier Lawsuits", *NBC News*, December 3, 2013, www.nbcnews.com/business/travel/supreme-court-reluctant-expand-frequent-flier-lawsuits-f2D11687495, accessed August 14, 2014.

Young, M. and R.S. Klingle (1996) "Silent Partners in Medical Care: A Cross-Cultural Study of Patient Participation", *Health Communication*, 8 (1): 29–53.

Zhang, S. and L. Stafford (2008) "Perceived Face Threat of Honest but Hurtful Evaluative Messages in Romantic Relationships", *Western Journal of Communication*, 72 (1): 19–39.

Zhao, X., J.G. Lynch Jr, and Q. Chen (2010) "Reconsidering Baron and Kenny: Myths and Truths of Mediation Analysis", *Journal of Consumer Research*, 37: 197–206.

17

COMMUNITAS INTERRUPTUS

Consumer experiences of leaving community

James H. McAlexander and Beth Leavenworth DuFault

Introduction

Leaving is a fundamental part of living. We leave the womb, we leave home, we leave school, we leave loves, we leave careers, and, ultimately, we leave life itself. Leaving seems like it should be easy. A simple statement, "I quit," seems adequate. But, leaving can be hard. It can be messy. It can be complicated and it can hurt. Leaving can also be liberating and exhilarating. The heartbreak and joy of leaving home, hearth, and love has been the heart of epic blockbusters, the soul of the poet's craft, and the lifeblood of masterpiece novels. Even the comparatively more mundane experiences of leaving jobs and lifestyles have created the story arcs of Oscar-winning movies and *New York Times* bestsellers. Leaving resonates at the core of our human existence. Yet, the lived experience of leaving has remained relatively unexamined in consumer behavior literature.

The literature provides compelling insights into many of the vital human relationship concerns and issues that impact and are impacted by consumer behaviors (Fournier 1988). However, in cases of relationship endings and community exit, there is much less work. The scholarly locus of concern has been largely on forward movement into a new life space, rather than on the experience of leaving itself. Consumer behavior scholars who have begun to capture aspects of the lived experience of exit (cf. McAlexander 1991; Schouten and McAlexander 1993; Penaloza 1994, Arsel and Thompson 2011, Russell and Schau 2014; Ustuner and Holt 2007; McAlexander 2011) reveal the importance of understanding better what appears, when examined closely, to be a protracted process that does not match the dominant theoretic work associated with linear passage and transition models (Van Gennep 1960; Erikson 1959; Sheehy 1976).

This chapter integrates longitudinal research across our work that has examined the experiences of consumers who leave diverse relationships that have been central to their lives and identities (McAlexander 1991; McAlexander *et al.* 1993; DuFault 2011; DuFault 2013; Price and DuFault 2014). Our research with respect to leaving deeply invested relationships have included people that navigate departure from the Harley-Davidson brand, marriages, employment, faith communities, and neighborhoods. An important note of terminology: we will refer to those informants who are leaving these important relationships as "Travelers." We do so because the leaving process, across all of our studies of those who have had relationships that were deeply held with brands and communities, share a similar trajectory. Contrary to being a linear path leading to a fixed ending point of "closure," the path is instead, as the Beatles penned years ago, "a long and winding road."

We see that the journey of leaving becomes complicated as ties that have been important and valued become burdensome. Leaving is also complicated by ties that informants wish to maintain, but fear losing. There are roadblocks and exit barriers, and many have experiences that preclude leaving, at least for a time. Thus, informants who seek to leave different communities and relationships experience switchbacks, forks, obstacles, crashes, unexpected turns, and even races back to the beginning. We choose to use the term "Traveler," rather than "leaver" or "one who has left" to emphasize our scholarship's main finding, the Leaving Loop (see Figure 17.1).

The Leaving Loop describes a relationship departure that is messy, lengthy, circuitous, iterative, and may never be fully accomplished. The following Traveler, who is working to leave her faith community, describes her road:

> While being supportive, my husband feels as if I have given up, that I am refusing to see the good in the Church. In tears yesterday, I told him I just don't know if I can go back to church. He told me he thinks I'm not trying anymore … It's been fourteen years of my hanging on by a thread, and I am tired.
>
> *(Burton 2009: 51)*

The lived experience of leaving

The exit from a tightly knit collectivity is experienced as a tangle of relationship ties that are continually stretched, pulled, and severed as the Traveler seeks the exit. The communities being left have been entwined with consumers' identities, construction of lifestyle, and consumption constellations. For many, these connections have been central to their sense of purpose and life meaning. The stretching of ties too strong to break often pulls the Traveler back. Accepted scholarship has described the process of transition as one that begins with processes of separation and a liminal period where one feels disconnected, or between statuses, and a transition is deemed complete when one is integrated into a new status (Turner 1969; Rosow 1976; Van Gennep 1960). However, we find that this integration does not always occur. We have seen Travelers mired in a liminal state

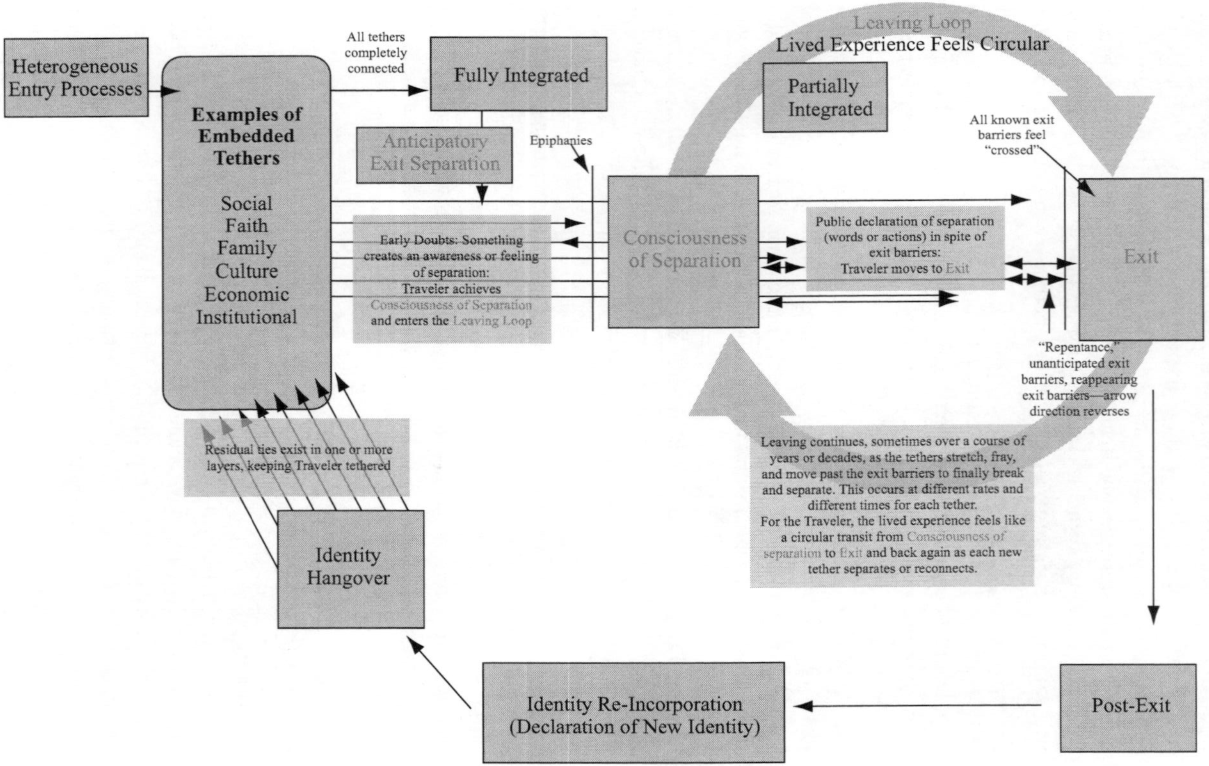

Heterogeneous Entry Processes
Examples of Embedded Tethers
Social
Faith
Family
Culture
Economic
Institutional
All tethers completely connected
Fully Integrated
Anticipatory Exit Separation
Epiphanies
Early Doubts: Something creates an awareness or feeling of separation: Traveler achieves Consciousness of Separation and enters the Leaving Loop
Consciousness of Separation
Leaving Loop
Lived Experience Feels Circular
Partially Integrated
Public declaration of separation (words or actions) in spite of exit barriers: Traveler moves to Exit
All known exit barriers feel "crossed"
Exit
"Repentance," unanticipated exit barriers, reappearing exit barriers—arrow direction reverses
Leaving continues, sometimes over a course of years or decades, as the tethers stretch, fray, and move past the exit barriers to finally break and separate. This occurs at different rates and different times for each tether.
For the Traveler, the lived experience feels like a circular transit from Consciousness of separation to Exit and back again as each new tether separates or reconnects.
Residual ties exist in one or more layers, keeping Traveler tethered
Identity Hangover
Identity Re-Incorporation (Declaration of New Identity)
Post-Exit

FIGURE 17.1 Leaving process model (for formerly highly integrated community members)

of leaving and staying that, like Doctor Doolittle's "pushmi-pullyu" trying to decide upon a direction, can last indefinitely. This sentiment is expressed by an anonymous Traveler (as reported in a forum that caters to people navigating the Leaving Loop within the Mormon faith): "Now, I feel like my soul is tied between two poles – one that continues to pretend, and the other that longs to express my true feelings. I am tearing in half."

In our research, we see the messiness of the leaving process expressed poignantly by informants leaving communities that require separation from people, places, brands, and products that have been important pillars of identity. This exit from community does not happen "all at once" in any of our research. As reported by McAlexander (2011), an informant who had been in a deeply committed relationship with a Harley-Davidson branded motorcycle and its associated community, shared with great sadness, a partner-imposed sale of his motorcycle: "It was either keep the bike or keep the marriage." The sale of the motorcycle, however, did not result in a complete personal abandonment of his identity as a Harley brand community member. When probed about his feelings regarding the brand and community, he continues to be uncertain as to whether he has left Harley-Davidson or not. These kinds of feelings are typical of others we have interviewed, as echoed by another informant:

> I loved my Harley. I rode with the guys from work almost every week. It was great. When the baby came, we really wanted to get into a house of our own. I sold the Harley for the down payment. I figure in a couple of years, when my wife is working again, I'll get another bike, definitely another Harley-Davidson.

On its face, this may seem a less meaningful experience than for those that we have studied exiting a religious community or a marriage. However, these deeply committed Harley-Davidson owners who reach a point of self or other-imposed exit from the Harley subculture, describe the experience of the Leaving Loop as a difficult, long, and complicated process.

Our findings reveal that the protracted experience of the Leaving Loop is more common than one might expect. Indeed, most of the informants across these studies experience an iterative process wherein they realize they want to leave, they decide to leave, they initiate exit from parts of the community, they then discover the personal costs of exit, and they end up backtracking to restore ties that they discover that they don't want broken. This iterative process is variable, dependent upon the depth of ties within the relevant group, and with the status and capital amassed (Bourdieu 1984) within the collectivity they were attempting to leave (Ebaugh 1984; Schouten and McAlexander 1995; Arsel and Thompson 2011; McAlexander *et al.* 2014). While variable, the Leaving Loop appears to be ubiquitous.

The experiences of the leaving loop

We find that the trajectories of leaving for the Travelers in all of the contexts we have studied, surprisingly, mirror each other. Our discussion will focus on the shared thematic experiences of separation from community and the impediments that forestall departure.

Entry: an epiphany

In our studies, a consciousness of separation – an epiphany (cf. Press and Arnould 2011) – was consistently the driving motivator that initiated the leaving process. This epiphany often began with the questioning of basic beliefs, for example: whether the Traveler "truly believed" in church doctrines; whether they were "in love;" or whether they really fit in as a "Harley person." Informants experienced a realization that resulted in questioning the hold that the consumption community, institution, or other relevant relationships had upon them. For Sandy, the epiphany moment that moves her to separation from her faith has to do with the church's reaction to her gay brother: "He was destroyed (by the church) for not doing anything wrong. He only had one partner. They loved each other. That partner just happened to be a male not a female. I don't see that there was anything wrong with this." Sandy could not reconcile the church's treatment of her brother with her notion of Christian love, and consequently entered the Leaving Loop. We see that epiphanies like these can become cascading fissures of the belief system upon which the committed collectivity membership rests.

While epiphany was the first step, it was just an entry point into the Leaving Loop for the Travelers. In our study of a faith community, leaving did not occur immediately upon the realization that the Traveler no longer believed the tenets of the religion. The abandonment of a long-term marriage did not occur in an instant when it dawned on a spouse that they were not in love with their partner. Leaving did not occur when an employment situation became untenable. As one teacher leaving employment in a school district said: "They moved our location. It was nicer, but we were the step children on the site. When we didn't even get a copier code, I thought, 'That's it.' But I stayed and taught and acted like the move was a good thing." A church member when asked, "Why did you keep going?" after he no longer believed, replied:

> Because it would affect my social standing and my interactions … the minute I started saying, you know I'm really not interested in being part of the church anymore, then I would be the guy they had to save as the lost sheep. Or, they would just stop having interest in being with me.

We observed varying responses to this epiphany of separation while Travelers stay within the community. Travelers, like the informant above, may appear to others to be deeply integrated while they are fully engaged in navigating the Leaving Loop.

Other Travelers exercise voice (Hirschman 1970) while in the Leaving Loop. Voice provides opportunities to maintain what Travelers see as productive and meaningful engagement with the community and its members. Our interviews of Travelers reveal that in exercising voice, many see themselves as adopting the role of the "loyal opposition." Some Harley owners, for example, increasingly uncomfortable with the company's relationship with "yuppies" continued to participate in their own Harley community while wearing their Harley insignia upside down to signal their distress (McAlexander 2011). The teacher, above, motivated her students to write letters of complaint to administration about the lack of printed copy lesson materials.

After the legitimacy of the relevant brand community, relationship, product, or institution has been brought into question in a way that releases its hold on the consumer and motivates them to consider leaving, many Travelers proceed on the road to exit. This seems, at first, to the Travelers to be a clear case of "in" or "out," as in the teacher's observation, above. However, it often turns out to be, as it did for her, a long and difficult journey. This experience reflects that character of what we call the "Leaving Loop."

The leaving loop

We find that "leaving," even after strong epiphanies of desired separation from community, is an ongoing experience of untangling different tethers of embeddedness. There are a multitude of "gossamer threads" (or embedded ties) of varying strength that connect us to communities (Baldwin 1950; Boorstin 1973; Friedman *et al.* 1993; McAlexander *et al.* 2003). Leaving a community can be a process of disconnecting significant and powerful bonds. These ties individually might seem like fragile microfibers, but entwined together they strongly bind members to the community. Our data reveal that for highly integrated members of disparate collectivities, these microfibers can extend the experience of leaving to an entire lifetime in such a way that a complete departure never takes place. This interconnected embeddedness is reinforced as the collectivity being left overlaps with other significant groups that the Traveler does not wish to leave behind. These groups may include employers and work peers, family, and social circles (Phillips 1998). Significantly, our findings show that these points of connection and resistance are diverse in nature, and exist in distinctive aspects of both social and personal identity. To leave is to untangle and untie these varied tethers. This experience is protracted as these connections stretch, fray, and break at differing rates and times. The process of leaving can feel like being at the beginning of a race, but bound to the starting line by multiple bungee cords of varying lengths, strengths, widths and materials. As the race starts, the various ties are unraveled, broken, or held at different times and in different ways, ever-exerting differentiated pulls back to the starting gate.

Important to our research is the revelation that these different layers of embeddedness are navigated and resolved at uneven rates, often at completely different times and experienced in unpredictable ways. The ties stretch, fray, break or hold sometimes independently, and are sometimes influenced by the break in another tie. Further, the tethers can reattach as moments of repentance and unanticipated exit barriers are encountered. The iterative experience emically feels recursive to the Traveler, as they make a break in one tie only to find they are "held" by others, including ones they thought they had already broken.

Communication to others: public performance

The markers that most strongly signal the breaking of each tether of embeddedness can best be described as the public performance of an act or ritual that separates oneself from the community on that particular level (cf. Kates 2002). This public performance can be achieved with either words or action. The same separation rituals may have occurred privately prior to the public leap, but the public acts and presentations that are declarations of separation and markers of exit seem to those watching the Traveler to be a rejection of the collectivity. As the Traveler becomes more comfortable performing identity at odds with the collective he or she is leaving, more ties are broken. At the same time, new ties are made outside the collective and former ties are reknit together in different types of socially constructed relationships that now exist outside of the Traveler's membership in the collective.

We term this entire iterative and circular process the "Leaving Loop" because the connections, weak and strong, on the various tethers, as they continually hold, sever, and reattach, create the distinctive pendulum-like experience of "living leaving." Common to our informants in the Leaving Loop was their describing of yet another epiphany of another tie that held them after they thought they had left. Marcus, an informant who moved from a stigmatized neighborhood and spent two decades on the other side of the country, moved back to buy his mother's house. He spoke repeatedly about the negative aspects of the neighborhood, refuted the positives, and expanded upon why he did not live there. When asked why he moved back, he paused a long time, and finally said, softly: "I associate that house with my mother, and it took me a lot of time to get over that. But I couldn't."

The Leaving Loop can last for months, years, or a lifetime, and thus is worthy of focus. In the Leaving Loop, the Traveler is liminal, as he or she works toward, but has not yet accomplished, a full post-community autonomous identity. We consider The Leaving Loop, and the lived experience of circularity while being a Traveler trying to exit community, to be a key finding of this research. Due to the nature of the embeddedness of the various ties, the varying rates of separation, and varying length and strength of the embeddedness, leaving feels at times as if one has split identities, or like living in two worlds. To some Travelers who have long, elastic, weak bungee cord ties, eventually the tethers rest easily and are not felt strongly. These are Travelers who are able to reconcile "staying" in one layer of embeddedness while "leaving" in another. To others, however, the split identity causes great pain as the separation process is navigated. A forum poster reflects on this uncomfortable situation: "For years I struggled to live in both worlds. It became obvious to me, however, that they were worlds in collision."

At the time of this writing, some Travelers in each of our contexts have continued to live in the two worlds: in the collective, and, in their life, in separation from that collective. They make constant micro- and macro-corrections to avoid collisions. Below, we share data to reveal the Travelers' emic experiences of the phenomenon of feeling the embedded tethers holding them in the Leaving Loop. These tethers have been deemed field dependent capital in the work on leaving a faith consumption community (McAlexander *et al.* 2014), but, to the Traveler, they are experienced simply as ties that are, in turn, easy, difficult, or impossible, to break.

Experiences of the leaving loop

Personal choices of individual family members have consequence for family identity (Price and DuFault 2014). To act in ways misaligned with a family's shared sense of engagement in such things as faith, social activities, or recreation can be upsetting to other family members. The Traveler often would prefer to not distress the family, or at least to avoid a full scale eruption of conflict. Many times, the Traveler specifically does not want to lose the family tie and fears this consequence most of all. The consequences of leaving a collectivity that affects the identity of other family members creates stress and anxiety for both those who leave and for those who are left behind, as informants Peter and Sara communicate about the effect leaving their faith community had upon their son: "That – that really hurt him. His junior year he started getting in with a group of friends he really liked – they were a lot of fun, he loved hanging out with him. Then the moment they found out he wasn't LDS they didn't hang out with him anymore."

As a result, exit from a faith, a marriage, a neighborhood, or even a brand that gives personal or reflected identity to others in the family can create distress and even uproar. This may seem obvious in the case of faith, but we observe that family contention may appear at the very first signs of fissures that signal an intent to leave – and thus the family tie may be the first tether felt pulling back against exit from any community. For example, as informant Cindy said about leaving employment in the school community that was changing:

> My family was upset when I drove out to interview [in another school district]. My husband said, "Think about what you're doing. This school district is important to us." I said, "But the kids don't go there anymore." He said, "That doesn't matter. It's your identity." I was like, "Yeah, right." But he was right. It was like we did all lose that connection – to the schools, to the town, to the people.

Family is also the tether that most often persistently pulls the Traveler back into alignment over a protracted exit. Failure to attend church or its activities, absence from family events, consumption of proscribed products (e.g., caffeinated beverages, alcohol, Japanese motorcycles), taking off a wedding band, stopping by model homes in a new neighborhood – these and more are powerful signals of exit to family members from the various collectives in our contexts, even though they might go completely unnoticed by others. Prior informants have used what is called "anticipatory socialization" to traverse the oftentimes lengthy leave-taking of exit: for instance, a law student planning to divorce his spouse studied divorce law, and another husband considering leaving insisted that his wife return to school (McAlexander *et al.* 1993). To those who become aware, these consumer behaviors are perceived correctly as markers of leaving.

Members of a Traveler's family who do not want to leave the collective, and the Traveler him or herself, may be complicit in delaying the public show of exit. A faithful Mormon wife dutifully hid all of the alcohol and put the coffee maker in the cupboard before her husband's family came to visit to hide the fact that her husband was leaving the Mormon faith. One informant's spouse was fully aware that his partner desired divorce and was taking steps toward leaving, but both kept up consumer behaviors that provided a shield and facade of union in order to avoid losing the social and economic capital that was entrenched within the partnership. Members of a collective may also work consciously to install exit barriers by flaunting and strengthening ties linking the Traveler to the collective in question, to oppose exit. An informant's husband began planning weekly family get-togethers with both sets of in-laws and all adult children, and made scrap books of happy times, after his wife initiated a conversation about a trial separation.

Membership in the brand and consumer collectives that we study contributes broadly to the structure of the informants' lives. We observe that these collectives enrich, frame, and impact their sociocultural status. Often, we find that Travelers are held in community by the pain of losing sociocultural status, friendships, and career opportunities if they exit. Sociocultural status change due to leaving can be difficult whether moving "up" or "down." Informant Janice moved to a more upscale community and has stayed there. She has, however, continued to work in the economically distressed community from which she left and maintains her sociocultural ties there. She talks passionately about leaving:

> From that point on, whenever you said you were from [our town], you were like someone to be watched, someone that was not to be trusted, someone who was poor, someone – so wherever you went, people had this infamous – not famous, but infamous – mentality about [our town].

Even though she has left the neighborhood, like the informant who has sold his Harley, she still considers herself part of the former community. She became a community development activist. She is there every week and has her offices there. Although it has been decades since she moved, and she readily indicates the stigma she was escaping, Janice talks about herself as a resident.

Travelers still in community often develop impression management strategies to avoid severing sociocultural tethers that would be threatened by public signs of exit before they are ready to leave. Informant Sam spoke of what he said Mormons call the "100 mile" rule:

> Actually, in my opinion, that's a very standard path guys follow. I remember growing up and hearing about my granddad going on the deer hunt and not finding out until I was fourteen or fifteen that that meant going hunting and drinking with his buddies. That's what the deer hunt was for, maybe kill a deer, maybe not!

Participation in relationship collectives and subcultures can have a great effect on a person's ability to maintain their lifestyle. For instance, a faith community can impact career choice and career performance. For one informant, a degree from a church-owned university on his resume, and his visible faith participation, provided entrée to high status clients of the same faith. When it was publicly apparent that he had left the church, he lost important clients who were a large portion of his practice. To lose clients is to risk livelihood and lifestyle. Further, the reputation and friendships that one has in a job often come from the persona one has played while in it. Feeling the pull of this tether – where staying in community would prevent economic loss – has caused Travelers in our contexts to delay leaving.

Identity consequences

Identity is socially constructed, and deeply embedded relationships in collectivities and relationships construct parts of that sense of self (cf. Belk 1986). In religion, for example, one is surrounded by people who share a common belief system, and thus beliefs and aspirations are mirrored, enacted, rewarded, and deviations punished by a surrounding and relatively homogeneous audience. In a marriage, identity is as part of a dyad, the dyad itself is embedded within larger family networks, and resources are combined to work toward shared family and extended family identity goals. In a brand or consumption community, such as that of Harley owners, identity is also performed and the performance is reflected back by a Harley owner's riding peers. In all contexts, when interacting with people who are "outsiders," one can also see personal identity reflected back, as the "audience" reacts to the consumer's performance. In a sense, one can receive affirmation or approbation of identity by all with whom one interacts (Goffman 1959).

When identity performance is adjusted during leaving and doesn't align well with the community membership, there can be repercussions. A Traveler reveals this identity performance misalignment as she chooses to wear a sleeveless shirt as she is beginning to leave the Mormon faith:

> Just sleeveless. That right away targets me as not-Mormon. Because I'm not wearing garments. I mean, it's not a big deal anywhere else because I'm not wearing anything super low-cut or anything, but sleeveless – especially around here, you immediately go – oh, they're not Mormon.

Goffman (1959) talks at length about the small, informal, generally unnoticed ceremonies that permeate everyday interaction – the ones that only feel unnatural to self and other when they don't happen. In the social community, discordant micro-signals are noted and reacted upon in the everyday life experience as the Traveler finds above.

You can never leave: the identity hangover

Interviews with informants after symbolic ceremonies of leaving (asking to be taken off the rolls of the church, receiving a divorce decree, selling a Harley, handing in a letter of resignation from a job, or moving from their lifelong neighborhood) reveal an important aspect of the Leaving Loop. Even after formal exit, some of the tethers are still embedded. Although the Traveler enters the equivalent of a new frontier, with the possibility of being free from the affiliation to the former collectivity, exit often comes with residual hangover (cf. Ebaugh 1988). Informants can be reluctant to inform current community members that they have left. Informant Sandy reveals: "I haven't shared it with the Mormon portion of my Facebook community. It isn't because of getting back to my father, I just don't know where the discussion would be beneficial to all of us." Informant Cindy says: "I change the subject before work comes up with my friends from [that city]. It's like I don't have any legitimate ties to them anymore. What if a large part of our friendships rested on me having a position with the school district?"

Even after formal resignation, ties with family, friends, and work colleagues who are still members of the community that was left are maintained. Further, there is a lifelong decision of whether or not to identify yourself as an "ex," whether to reveal your history or keep it hidden, and with whom to share what. As Janice says about her old neighborhood:

> Trying to make someone understand … "Look, there's some really nice people that live there, you know? They've got a bad reputation, but nice people." Unless you've been there – like you've been, now you've been to my mom's – now you see that all of us just don't live in that kind of ghetto mentality that we're – that that's what we're known for. And that there's some really nice people in [our town], and it's hard to explain that.

Janice is uncomfortable not being a member of her neighborhood in one circumstance, and uncomfortable being a member of her neighborhood in another. This stems, in part, from the portion of the identity hangover that is the lingering and persistent feelings the ex-member has toward the collective. The attachment of some of the tethers may persist past formal exit. Further, if one defines oneself as an "ex," then one is de facto defined by being in opposition to that particular something.

We end this overview of our studies on leaving by reflecting that if trying to exit a deeply embedded collectivity or relationship is often a long and winding road with no real finish line, there must be many disparate definitions of the phrase "I've left." When is one done leaving a relationship? As one informant, Michael, said when discussing his 12 years of exit from the Mormon faith and its community: "The song, 'Hotel California'… 'You can check out any time you like but you can never leave.' You can never leave! You *cannot* ever leave. You can't."

This research adds to our understanding of consumer behavior while consumers are in life transitions that involve leaving community, and specifically opens new areas of potential research into our understanding of the experience for consumers that leave brands and brand community. The long and winding process of exit that consumers experience while embedded in the Leaving Loop offers intriguing opportunities for additional study.

References

Arsel, Z. and C.J. Thompson (2011) "Demythologizing Consumption Practices: How Consumers Protect their Field-Dependent Identity Investments from Devaluing Marketplace Myths", *Journal of Consumer Research*, 37 (February): 791–806.

Baldwin, M. (1950) *I Leap Over the Wall: Contrasts and Impressions After Twenty-Eight Years in a Convent*. New York: Rhinehart.

Belk, R.W. (1986) "Possessions and the Extended Self", *Journal of Consumer Research*, 15 (2): 139–168.

Boorstin, D. (1973) *The Americans: The Democratic Experience*. New York: Random House.

Bourdieu, P. (1984) *Distinction: A Social Critique of the Judgement of Taste*. Cambridge, MA: Harvard University Press.

Burton, D.J. (2009) "Braving the Borderlands … Reconnecting with a Former Faith?", *Sunstone*, July: 51.

DuFault, B. (2011) "Mom's the Boss: Social Capital and Motherhood in the Workplace", Paper Presented at University of California, Berkeley International Sociological Research Symposium, Berkeley, CA, May 2011.

DuFault, B. (2013) "Black Flight and the Changing Marketplace in a Shifting Urban Landscape", Paper Presented at Anthropology of Markets and Consumption Conference, University of California Irvine, March 2013.

Ebaugh, H.R.F. (1984) "Leaving the Convent: The Experience of Role Exit and Self-Transformation", *The Existential Self in Society*, eds J.A. Kotarba and A. Fontana. Chicago, IL: The University of Chicago Press: 156–176.

Ebaugh, H.R.F. (1988) *Becoming an Ex: The Process of Role Exit*. Chicago, IL: The University of Chicago Press.

Erikson, E.H. (1959) *Identity and the Life Cycle*. New York: International Universities Press.

Fournier, S. (1988) "Consumers and Their Brands: Developing Relationship Theory in Consumer Research", *Journal of Consumer Research*, 24 (4): 343–353.

Friedman, M., P.V. Abeele, and K. De Vos (1993) "Boorstin's Consumption Community Concept: A Tale of Two Countries", *Journal of Consumer Policy*, 16 (1): 35–60.

Goffman, E. (1959) *The Presentation of Self in Everyday Life*. New York: Anchor Books.

Hirschman, A.O. (1970) *Exit, Voice, and Loyalty: Responses to Decline in Firms, Organizations, and States*, Vol. 25. Cambridge, MA: Harvard University Press.

Kates, S.M. (2002) "The Protean Quality of Subculture Consumption: An Ethnographic Account of Gay Consumers", *Journal of Consumer Research*, 29 (3): 383–399.

McAlexander, J.H. (1991) "Divorce, the Disposition of the Relationship and Everything",

Advances in Consumer Research, 18 (1): 43–48.

McAlexander, J.H. (2011) "Communitas Interruptus", *Proceedings of the European Association for Consumer Research Conference*, 19: 401–405.

McAlexander, J.H., J.W. Schouten, and S.D. Roberts (1993) "Consumer Behavior and Divorce", *Research in Consumer Behavior*, 6: 153–184.

McAlexander, J.H., J.W. Schouten, and H.F. Koenig (2003) "Building Brand Community", *Journal of Marketing*, 66 (1): 38–54.

McAlexander, J.H., B.L. DuFault, D.M. Martin, and J.W. Schouten (2014) "The Marketization of Religion: Field, Capital, and Consumer Identity", *Journal of Consumer Research*, 41 (3): 858–875.

Penaloza, L. (1994) "Atravesando Fronteras/Border Crossings: A Critical Ethnographic Exploration of the Consumer Acculturation of Mexican Immigrants", *Journal of Consumer Research*, 21 (June): 32–54.

Phillips, R. (1998) "Religious Market Share and Mormon Church Activity", *Sociology of Religion*, 59 (2): 117–130.

Press, M. and E. Arnould (2011) "How does Organizational Identification Form?: A Consumer Behavior Perspective", *Journal of Consumer Research*, 38 (4): 650–666.

Price, L. and B. DuFault (2014) "Consumption as a Catalyst in the Heterogeneous and Open-Ended Project of Becoming a Family", Presented at International Consumer Culture Theory Conference, Helsinki, Finland.

Rosow, I. (1976) "Status and Role Change Through the Life Span", *Handbook of Aging and the Social Sciences*, eds R.H. Binstock and E. Shanes. New York: Van Nostrand Reinhold Co.: 457–482.

Russell, C. and H.J. Schau (2014) "When Narrative Brands End: The Impact of Narrative Closure and Consumption Sociality on Loss Accommodation", *Journal of Consumer Research*, 60 (6): 1039–1062.

Schouten, J.W. and J.H. McAlexander (1993) "Market Impact of a Consumption Subculture: the Harley-Davidson Mystique", *European Advances in Consumer Research Volume 1*, eds W. Fred Van Raaij and Gary J. Bamossy. Provo, UT: Association for Consumer Research: 389–393.

Schouten, J.W. and J.H. McAlexander (1995) "Subcultures of Consumption: An Ethnography of the New Bikers", *Journal of Consumer Research*, 22, (1): 43–61.

Sheehy, G. (1976) *Passages: Predictable Crises of Adult Life*. New York: E. P. Dutton.

Turner, V. (1969) *The Ritual Process: Structure and Anti-Structure*. New York: Aldine de Gruyter.

Ustuner, T. and D.B. Holt (2007) "Dominated Consumer Acculturation: The Social Construction of Poor Migrant Women's Consumer Identity Projects in a Turkish Squatter", *Journal of Consumer Research*, 34 (1): 41–56.

van Gennep, A. (1960) *The Rites of Passage*. London: Routledge.

18

CONSUMERS' EXPERIENCE OF BRAND WITHDRAWAL

Unfolding consumption bereavement theory

Cristel Antonia Russell and Hope Jensen Schau

Brands come and brands go. Sometimes called brand pruning, brands are discontinued for a myriad of reasons including failure to capture market share, failure to meet financial targets, inconsistency with firm objectives, a realization that brands offered by the same firm are cannibalizing each other's sales, obsolescence, poor product quality, regulatory mandates, or recessions causing firms to decrease the breadth of their offerings (Clifford 2009; Hemlock 2009; Kumar 2003; Ng 2014). While these are compelling rationales for a firm to withdraw a branded product or service, consumers may not wish to end their relationships with favored brands.

Drawing on interpersonal relationship theory, Fournier (1998) asserts that consumers form relationships with brands, and that brands have the capacity to be active relationship partners. Brands often entice consumers to begin a relationship, but they can also end a relationship, such as when the firm withdraws a brand from the marketplace. Despite the prevalence of brand discontinuation, research on how brand withdrawals impact consumers and their relationships with brands is scant (cf. Fajer and Schouten 1995). Prior research (Muñiz and Schau 2005; Russell and Schau 2014) suggests that, like interpersonal relationships, consumer-brand relationships do not end abruptly due to marketplace withdrawals, and often linger through consumer-initiated action.

Research in the interpersonal relationship discipline has long documented the ways in which people adjust to losses. This literature can thus shed light on how consumers may respond to the loss of a brand relationship partner. Drawing theoretically from loss and grief research and empirically from consumers' narratives, we unfold a theory of *consumption bereavement* that captures consumers' experiences following the market withdrawal of a favored product and service.

Theoretical framework

Consumer-brand relationships (CBRs)

The parallel between human relationships and how consumers relate to brands has a rich tradition in consumer research, from Fournier's (1998) work on inanimate brands, to public figures and human brands (Levy 1962; Thomson 2006), television characters (Russell *et al.* 2004), and service providers (Price and Arnould 1999). Longevity of interaction beyond a single or even a few encounters is key to the definition of a relationship and even to its status (Berscheid and Peplau 1983); therefore, Fournier (1998) views time (enduring versus short-term) as a prominent dimension of a consumer-brand relationship. Her research presupposes temporality as indicative of consumer commitment such that long-term relationships with brands are assumed stronger than shorter term, or "casual" relationships.

Consumers do not develop relationships with all brands, but may with favored brands. Brands may even be beloved (Ahuvia 2005; Day 1983; Lastovicka and Sirianni 2011). Some scholars advocate the construct "share of heart" to capture a "consumer's product commitment" and "the nature and strength of the emotional bonds to the brands" (Day 1983: 6).

Here, we examine the dissolution of committed consumer-brand relationships in the face of "managerially imposed stressors" (Fournier 1998: 363), namely when firms exit the relationship through marketplace withdrawal. We parallel the withdrawal of the brand from the market to consumer abandonment and even to the brand's "death." A vivid example of this parallel in the market is consumers' collective enactment of a funeral complete with procession and eulogy to commemorate the discontinuation of the first mass-produced electric car, General Motors' EV1. Devoted EV1 consumers drew on funeral rituals to cope with the loss of their beloved electric car (Pool 2003). More recently, the cancellation of 72-year-running soap opera *The Guiding Light* triggered outcry from fans and motivated the launch of grief-counseling sites (Jacobs 2009).

Marketplace withdrawals

Literature on marketplace withdrawals has been relatively meager. While Fajer and Schouten's (1995) theoretical framework of the dissolution of consumer-brand relationships focuses on voluntary consumer rejection, due to dissatisfaction or disloyalty, Fournier (1998) accounts for the "managerial decision to terminate" the consumer-brand relationship when Karen discusses Mary Kay ceasing production of Moisture Lipstick (363). Mao, Luo and Jain (2010) later examined the impact of product discontinuation on individual consumers' perception and evaluation of the firm, but not the experience of loss, per se. The first research addressing consumers' experience of market withdrawals (Russell and Schau 2014) offered insights into how fans cope with the end of their favored television series and revealed the positive impact of sociality on consumer loss accommodation.

Our project examines how individual consumers react to the end of brand production. We study the final phases of the brand production and the impact on consumers who are, at the height of the brand production, not necessarily involved in strong brand communities and not necessarily actively protesting the withdrawal.

Involuntary loss

Within consumer research, there is a growing body of knowledge on the voluntary disposition of goods, such as meaningful possessions (Lastovicka and Fernandez 2005) or heirloom and wealth (Bradford 2009; Price *et al.* 2000). In comparison, literature on involuntary dispossession is scant. Hill's seminal article (1992: 284) found that children whose cherished possessions were left behind due to homelessness expressed deep anxiety about their loss but also fantasized and dreamt that they might someday retrieve them in an attempt to cope and "restore the self to wholeness." Unanticipated losses, because they are sudden and unpredictable, trigger an adjustment process different from that documented in the voluntary disposition process. Research conducted with consumers facing the loss of animal companions (Stephens and Hill 1996) or material loss due to a natural disaster (Baker *et al.* 2007; Delorme *et al.* 2005) has shown that the involuntary loss of possessions to which people are strongly attached can be extremely painful, involving sadness, crying, or searching. Researchers suggest that the process parallels human grieving, involving initial "deep sorrow at the dissolution of the emotional bonds" they had (Stephens and Hill 1996: 201) but eventually leading to a rebuilding and adjustment phase (Delorme *et al.* 2005).

Responses to loss

Responses to loss have been studied extensively in anthropology, sociology, and human loss, specifically in the field of death studies (Raphael 1983). A common affective response across these loss scenarios is grief (Parkes and Weiss 1983), sometimes referred to as an emotional syndrome (Shear and Shair 2005). Acute grief might involve painful yearning and longing for the lost one, including strong feelings of separation, deprivation, and anguish, and, most prevalently, sadness (Rando 1988; Stroebe and Schut 1999).

"Grief work" is a forced perceptual shift to cope with the imposed loss (Parkes 2006). The term was coined by psychiatrist Erich Lindemann (1944) to describe the tasks (Fitzgerald 1994) and processes that must be actively completed in order to resolve the grief in a healthy fashion. Grief is generally viewed as running a phasic course, although individuals facing loss often oscillate back and forth between them (Raphael 1983). Models developed to outline this process, notably Bowlby's stage theory of grief (1979) and Worden's grieving process (1991), begin with numbness and disbelief/denial, which may be interrupted at times by outbursts of anger or deep despair. This phase gives way to a period of strong emotions as awareness of the loss develops, leading to yearning and protest. At this stage, there is often an overriding urge to search for the lost person/object and a desire to recover it. Eventually, searching is abandoned and the irrevocability and permanence of the loss is recognized, leading to a phase of despair, which can include withdrawal from people and activities and an overall loss of interest. Finally, coming to terms with the loss and resuming a new normal life bring about a recovery phase, allowing closure and recalibration of one's life without the lost object/person. This last phase may include the reinvestment of the emotional energy into new tasks (Leick and Davidson-Nielsen 1991) and the development of relationships that can fulfill the roles previously fulfilled by the lost person or object (Worden 1991). Successful recovery following a loss requires that individuals accept the reality of the loss and work through the pain of the grief. These stages of grief have applied across a range of domains from the loss of a relationship partner to divorce or break-up (cf. Herman 1974) to the adaptation processes caused by relocation (Fried 1966) or job change (Deits 1988). The same stages may thus emerge when losing a brand to which one is strongly attached.

Many researchers have recognized the importance of the social process surrounding loss and grief (Fowlkes 1990; Rosenblatt *et al.* 1976). In the initial period following the loss, when most people feel stunned and unable to accept the loss, individual reactions can vary from calm withdrawal to seeking the company of others. Social support for the expression of grief is often viewed as providing a way to share the pain (Parkes 1993). Interpersonal relationships exert an obvious influence on making sense of a loss and social sharing allows the cultivation of a collective memory (O'Donohoe and Turley 2005). Because consumption is frequently a social process, connecting people around shared brands (Muñiz and O'Guinn 2001), the withdrawal of a brand may also trigger the loss of the social links that the brand enabled (Russell and Schau 2014).

Post-loss adaptation

Continuing bonds

A large body of research has investigated continuing bonds following a loss. Although the urge to search for the lost object or person is considered a normal reaction (Parkes 1996), there is a debate over whether the purpose of grief work should be to sever the bonds in order to make new attachments and construct a new identity (Silverman and Klass 1996). Retaining bonds may be maladaptive and pathological (Bonanno and Field 2001), leading to high dependency and chronic grief (Parkes and Weiss 1983). Yet, some theorists propose that continuing bonds can be a healthy part of the survivor's ongoing life. Still, continued attention to the loss at the expense of other emotional involvements is normative for a limited time only. Often, one is able to become involved intellectually or emotionally with others, through a process called transference.

Transference

Freud (1917) referred to the incremental divestment of libido from memories of the lost object as decathexis, and he viewed recovery as recathexis, the redirection of libido from the memory of the lost person to available survivors which allows removing the cause of the pain and renewing opportunities for pleasure in life. Indeed, according to adult attachment theory, previous relationship patterns can reemerge when people form new relationships (Andersen and Cole 1990). The process of transference refers to what happens when a perceiver in a new relationship infers information about it based on representations from previous significant relationships, including memories and affective responses. Transference is most likely triggered when previous relationships are salient which is why it is especially applicable to chronically accessible significant-other representations such as those emerging in the case of losing a person or an object to whom one is strongly attached (Andersen *et al.* 1995). Because transference applies to a greater degree when there is more resemblance between the old and the new relationship objects (Brumbaugh and Fraley 2006), as in the brand extension context, transference in the case of a brand withdrawal may thus be affected by the similarities between the lost brand and potential new brands.

Method

Using consumer narratives, we capture consumers' experience of firm-imposed market exits. The study focuses on consumers' retrospective accounts of a market withdrawal, allowing us to capture the experience of the withdrawal and uncover consumers' strategies for coping with them.

Data

The data consist of consumer narratives written about their experience with a withdrawn brand. Sixty-six fourth-year university students (in the US and New Zealand) partook in the study for extra course credit (38 females, $M_{age} = 21.6$). Following Schau *et al.*'s (2009) finding that it is common for consumers to document personal brand histories, respondents were asked to select a product or service brand that they consumed but that had been discontinued and to write a detailed narrative of their experience of the brand and its withdrawal. The instructions were general and simply advised the participants to first describe their history with the brand, the ways in which they used/consumed the brand, what the brand meant to them, and then to describe how they felt when the brand was discontinued, how they coped without it and, if they knew in advance that it was going to be discontinued, how they prepared for it. They were encouraged to be introspective and rich with details. They were given one week to produce this narrative and complete a questionnaire where they reported how long they had used the brand, the year when it was discontinued, and some demographic data.

Data analysis

Narratives were analyzed using an iterative coding procedure focusing on relationships between the codes (Glaser and Strauss 1967; Miles and Huberman 1994). Patterns of experiences were sought and identified within individual narratives (idiographic analysis), across informants' narratives (nomothetic analysis) (Mick and Buhl 1992; Thompson et al. 1990). Consensus was reached regarding themes and patterns of themes.

Findings

Narratives focused on a range of products that on average had been withdrawn over six years prior, even longer than their average time of consumption (4.56 years). Consumers wrote about discontinued technology products and services (33.3 percent), television programs that had been cancelled (25.0 percent), foods and drinks (29.6 percent) or health and beauty products (9.3 percent) that were no longer available, retail stores that had closed (5.6 percent), or entertainment products that had been withdrawn (5.6 percent).

Phases of loss

The analysis reveals a distinct phasic pattern across narratives: 1) a stage of numbness and disbelief/denial at the withdrawal, 2) a period of strong negative emotions as the withdrawal is contemplated, 3) a phase of yearning and protest where consumers search for the withdrawn brand, 4) a stage where searching is abandoned and the irrevocability of the withdrawal is recognized, leading to an emotional state akin to despair, which can include an overall loss of interest in the product category as a whole, and 5) a recovery phase consisting of two options: 5A) transference where consumers resume a new life without the brand that may include investment in a new relationship that can fulfill the void left by the withdrawal, or 5B) continuation of the consumer-brand relationship apart from the corporation. Narrative analysis also reveals evidence of the social embeddedness of consumer-brand bonds. Specifically, when consumers describe using and appreciating the brand with others during the active CBR, consumers also report experiencing heightened emotion and behavioral manifestations across all phases of dissolution above. The more social the consumption was, the more consumers continue the CBR apart from the corporation.

Denial

During the denial phase, consumers describe feeling "numb" or "shocked" and deny the marketplace withdrawal, offering alternative explanations to explain their inability to purchase the brand. One narrative about AGA, a restaurant, vividly demonstrates this stage: "My initial reaction was shock and surprise as it never crossed my mind that the restaurant would close, as their business seems to be really good whenever I was there. My second reaction was to ask around to see if they had actually relocated instead of discontinuing their service." For other examples please see Table 18.1.

Negative emotions

Consumers realize the brand has been withdrawn and express negatively valenced emotions like anger, disappointment, and sadness. Narratives conveyed these emotional experiences in a variety of ways. One consumer wrote simply, "When Big Fresh [grocery store] closed its doors it was a sad day." Similarly a consumer notes, "I was very upset when, at some point, I didn't see Tab Energy drinks gracing the shelves of the convenience, drug, and grocery stores as before." Others elaborated on their negative emotions, tying them to unrealized value, "I also remember how sad I was when I was told that the facility (Discovery Zone activity park) in my town had closed. Not only was I sad that I would never be able to play in that amazing jungle gym anymore, but I would never be able to cash in my tickets that I had been saving up." For more examples, please see Table 18.1.

Search

Consumers search for remnants of the brand or bastions of brand availability in the marketplace. Narratives commonly relayed the experience of searching in a straightforward manner, "When we couldn't find it [Uncle Toby popping corn] at the supermarket, it made us search for it even more so. We would go to the snack-food aisle of different supermarkets just to check whether it had come back." Consumers were persistent in their searching efforts, sometimes traveling great distances to find their brand,

> I went to the dairy [convenience store] the day after I had heard the news on the radio but unfortunately for me they [Snifters candy] had already sold out. The thing was, the product had actually been discontinued some time before news actually broke in the mainstream media, so what was out on the shelves of shops was basically the last boxes of Snifters actually produced … On the radio I had heard that the best chance in finding Snifters was to go to old dairies in small suburbs.

Consumers were also known to pay exorbitant prices when the brand was located, "It is still possible to purchase the Microsoft Trackball Explorer, but for extremely high prices. Slightly used Trackballs can be found on eBay or related web-sites for several hundred dollars. This is almost four times as much as the price that my father paid for his many years ago." Find more data in Table 18.1.

TABLE 18.1 Consumer-brand relationship dissolution phases data table

Phase	Description Data Excerpts
1	**Denial** – Consumers deny the withdrawal, offering alternative explanations to explain their inability to purchase the brand.
	Lakme (sun screen): "Lakme had stopped manufacturing the product. This was an absolute shock to me. Why would Lakme take such a step?"
	Clark Foam (surfboard component): "I just started working for the surf industry when Clark Foam decided to close its doors. I was shocked that such a successful business could just close down within a matter of a day."
	Georgie Pie (restaurant chain): "I remember I would have been around the age of seven when I heard the rumour that McDonalds was buying out Georgie Pie. Of course, being that age, I didn't really pay attention or believe that it was going to happen."
2	**Negative Emotions** – Consumers realize the brand has been withdrawn and express negatively valenced emotions such as anger, disappointment, and sadness.
	Friends (TV program): "My mom and I were on the couch watching and dreading every time the commercials would come on. I remember the very last episode like it was yesterday. It ended with all six friends putting their keys to the apartment that they shared so many memories in on the counter top. When the credits rolled on the page I started crying to my mom."
	M&M Crispy (candy): "When crispy M&Ms disappeared from the shelves, the ads were also lost, so I miss seeing the ads on TV... [I was] sad that they had discontinued."
	Biore (face wash): "I felt really dissatisfied and regretful when this happened. I have been using Biore for over 8 years and now the products have disappeared."
	Hot Line (retailer): "It was quite sad to see a retailer who offered genuine service, and good quality and relatively well priced garments go out of business."
3	**Search** – Consumers search for remnants of the brand or bastions of brand availability in the marketplace.
	Johnson and Johnson Bebe (face wash): "The 'old' range began to slowly disappear in the stores. Going shopping for beauty products, I had to really search for this 'old' and perfect facial cleanser. Sometimes I even had to go to a couple of different stores to finally find it."
	Pop Tarts (breakfast/snack food): "It wasn't until continued attempts to source the product fell short that I realized it was no longer available."
	Lorac Lip Polish (cosmetic): "After four and a half years of using the lip polish, I noticed that I was running out and desperately need to pick up another bottle at Sephora. Upon my arrival to the Lorac stand, I was extremely confused. I could not find the lip polishes. They were nowhere in sight."

TABLE 18.1 continued

Phase	*Description*
	Data Excerpts

4	**Despair/Hopelessness** – Consumers realize the finality of the brand's withdrawal and experience a sense of hopelessness and impotence at the firm-imposed alienation.

Nintendo 64 (video game system): "I felt helpless as I watched this devoted machine move rapidly into the realms of uselessness; as if it were a beloved family pet becoming old and decrepit."

Friends (TV program): "It felt as though the characters would still be living, but we would just not get to see what was happening to them … The last episode was very emotional, and it really did feel as though we were leaving people we knew, and that we would never get to see them again."

Spice Girls (musical act): "When the Spice Girls broke up it was very upsetting to me and to my friends. The Spice Girls were our icons and as young girls we imagined their "break up" as an issue among their friendship, not a "growing up" opportunity for them. We took the break up personal and wondered if they ever considered how we, their fans, felt. As a fan I felt like they abandoned me."

5A	**Recovery/Transference** – Consumers accept the brand withdrawal, learn a new consumption experience without the brand and begin to invest energy into alternative brands to fill the void of the withdrawal.

Biore (face wash): "Biore launched back their face wash products into the Indonesian market. The face wash has totally different packaging and have different contents. The product has moisturizer to prevent skin from further drying after washing. I was excited when I heard about this. When I asked a friend of mine to bring one for me when she came to Auckland, unfortunately and surprisingly, the product didn't suit me anymore. I am not sure as to why this had happened. Is it because of the moisturizer substance added to the face wash? Or has my skin adapt to the Dove face wash already? However I do feel that for now, I am still going to stick with my Dove face wash."

AGA (restaurant): "Most importantly, I and my friends tried finding restaurants with similar ambience and the laid back atmosphere that we were most comfortable in. In the end, we found another place to get together but we would always compare the place to AGA restaurant."

SBTB (TV program): "Now that *Saved By the Bell* has been discontinued for many years I have adopted new teen dramas to follow in place of the old gang. No other show will ever have the same characters, or make the same impact on me growing up as *Saved By the Bell* did."

5B	**Recovery/Continuation** – Consumers continue their consumer-brand relationship beyond firm-imposed dissolution.

Friends: "To cope with the loss, many people – myself included, have turned to previous seasons and episodes to 'visit' the characters we know and love. Often my friends and I will YouTube *Friends* episodes and scenes that we enjoy, or montages of our favorite characters."

Clark Foam (surfboard component): "The majority of them I still keep and store in my priceless collection in California."

Despair/hopelessness

Consumers realize the finality of the brand's withdrawal and experience a sense of hopelessness and impotence at the firm-imposed alienation. One narrative describes the betrayal and hopelessness a consumer experienced when she realized her favorite sun screen left the market, "After I gave up the idea of buying the gel [Lakme Sun Expert] from the retail stores, I decided to look for them online. The only message I came across was this – 'No Stock'." She later opts to keep the packaging her last Lakme Sun Expert came in and use it to house the substitute sunscreen she deems inferior in order to experience the Lakme scent. Another narrative about a consumer's relationship to her Ford Bronco describes despair, "The Bronco was a great vehicle that will be dearly missed by me and everyone who knew me as owning 'Bronco Splash'." Based on this experience, she opted to never commit herself emotionally to another vehicle because the experience of the Bronco's market withdrawal had left her feeling too vulnerable. For more data examples please see Table 18.1.

Transference

Consumers accept the brand withdrawal, learn a new consumption experience without the brand and begin to invest energy into alternative brands to fill the void of the withdrawal. One consumer accepts the withdrawal and life without the branded snack Planter's Cheez Balls "because there was no substitute for the distinct taste." Another narrative explains that finding a substitute for the original CBR required a lot of time and effort, "I wouldn't go so far as to say a piece of my identity was lost with the discontinuation of my favorite energy drink [Tab Energy], I would say that it took me quite a while to find a substitute that lived up to the legend I had built in my own mind." Other examples are in Table 18.1. Overall, one third of participants did not replace the brand.

Continuation

Consumers accept the withdrawal but opt to continue their consumer-brand relationship beyond firm-imposed dissolution. As we see with the Lakme example above where the consumer put her new sunscreen into the old Lakme box to experience the withdrawn brand's scent, some consumers will go to great lengths to retain some of a favored brand's attributes. Continuation is a difficult phase to enact and works best for products where consumers can capture almost perfectly some elements of their active brand experience (e.g., television programs, movies, films, food recipes). One narrative reveals, "To continue the *Friends* odyssey in our household, we bought the DVD collection of the 10 best *Friends* episodes as voted by viewers." Similarly, another described continuing a CBR with a defunct television program *Freaks and Geeks* by renting and buying DVDs since the show does not air anywhere on broadcast or cable channels. Another reveals how consumers continue their relationship with a Kentucky Fried Chicken seasonal menu item through purchasing it, taking it home, and freezing it, where the menu item has been completely discontinued, "I know for a fact that some island visitors to New Zealand do purchase large amount of KFC and freeze it and transport it to their home countries to eat at a later date." For more data, refer to Table 18.1.

Social embeddedness of consumer-brand bonds

Consumer-brand bonds exist within a complex social network that includes consumers collectively consuming and appreciating brands. Narratives demonstrate that consumers co-consume during the active stage of the CBR, most prevalently within the family, "My parents and younger brother and sister were also big fans of the show and because we were all very busy with work, school, and other activities, watching *Friends* as a family while eating dinner became a Wednesday night ritual that we all looked forward to." Co-consumption extends beyond families to close others, "My childhood memories of *Georgie Pie* [restaurant] are associated with my birthdays and my friends' birthdays." *Georgie Pie* was consumed collectively as part of themed birthday celebrations that many children fondly remember. Another narrative demonstrates co-consumption within friend networks, "My friends and I used to have '*OC* viewing parties' every Thursday night where we all screamed at the television during the drama packed episodes and complained how we could never find a boyfriend as great as Seth Cohen or Ryan Atwood." Here, the brand experience was a form of bonding inextricably linked to the friend network.

When a market withdrawal threatened the consumer-brand bond and collective consumption was a critical part of consumer-brand relationship, narratives emphasized continuation of the consumer-brand bond in the absence of the corporation. A narrative regarding *Friends* shows co-consumption and maintaining the bond in the post withdrawal period, "Not only did I watch *Friends* on TV, I also watched reruns online, and DVD sets of the show's previous seasons. *Friends* was watched at my house, at friends' houses, and after the show finished, at university halls and flats in the form of re-runs." Here, the narrative demonstrates the continuation of the CBR beyond withdrawal which was fueled by collective brand consumption. Another narrative describes adamantly recommending Bebe facial wash to her younger sister who began to co-consume the product as part of a nightly ritual. When Bebe was withdrawn from the market, the consumer had some advance warning and purchased a year's supply of Bebe to use until either the brand was brought back to market or an adequate substitute emerged. At the time of the narrative, almost a year out, the consumer and her sister were continuing the bond through the stockpile.

Discussion

Popular press examples suggest that, particularly in cases of complete brand withdrawal, the death analogy may be quite apt to describe the dissolution of the consumer-brand relationship (Blackburn 2009; Clifford 2009; Gaulin 2007; Gomstyn 2009). Many journalists reporting on consumer reactions to marketplace withdrawals have used the language of grief and the analogy of mourning (Clifford 2009; Stephenson 2008; Wooler 2009; Yew 2009). Previous academic research had hinted that grieving-like processes emerge when people face the involuntary loss of possessions (Delorme *et al.* 2005; Stephens and Hill 1996) or consumption experiences special to them (Otnes *et al.* 2008; Russell and Schau 2014). Yet, to date, very little research had addressed the stage of consumer-brand relationships when production of the brand ceases (Fournier 1998). Here, we provide initial evidence of a phasic process that ensues when consumers face brand withdrawal.

Toward a model of consumption bereavement

Consumption bereavement refers to the situation of facing the loss, through withdrawal, of a significant brand and the adaptation process that ensues. Consumption bereavement is associated with emotional reactions, such as sadness or distress, which are akin to grief, and behavioral manifestations, such as social sharing or rituals that characterize mourning. Most consumers work through their grief, gradually adjust, and eventually come to terms with this loss over the course of time. They might relocate the loss emotionally by investing into other brands, and they might continue their relationship with the brand and other consumers of the brand even after the brand is withdrawn. We summarize the consumption bereavement process in Figure 18.1, recognizing that relational trajectories may

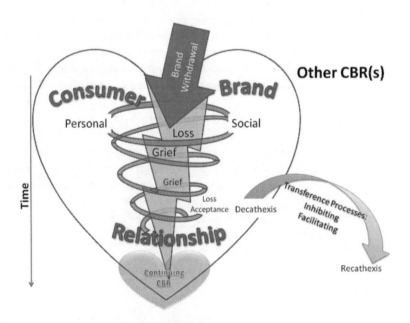

FIGURE 18.1 Model of consumption bereavement

differ based on the consumer's relationship history, the circumstances of the withdrawal, the availability of surrogate brands, etc.

The heart

Depicted by a heart-shape connoting the share of heart concept, consumer-brand relationships (CBRs) are important and sometimes enduring. They are comprised of personal and social elements that fuel consumers' relationships with favored brands. The size of the heart captures the intensity and strength of the consumer-brand relationship.

The arrow

When a firm withdraws a brand, consumers may suffer an imposed, painful loss creating a fissure in the CBR, affecting the personal and social dimensions.

The fissure

The cracked space within the CBR necessitates an elaborate consumer coping and adjustment process, that evolves in a manner similar to grieving. The intensity of the grief is affected by the length and depth of the consumers' relational history with the brand.

The downward spiral

The downward spiral reflects the evolution of the CBR after the withdrawal. Over time, consumers adjust to the new reality without their active brand relationship partner and, as consumers work through their grief and acceptance of the loss increases, both their personal attachment and social engagement reduce in intensity. Trajectories down this spiral may differ from consumer to consumer, with some transferring their allegiances to other brands (transference), others continuing their relationships (small heart), and some getting 'stuck' in the spiral, unable to resolve their grief.

Transference ribbon arrow

With grief decreasing and acceptance of the loss increasing, consumers may extricate themselves from the relationship, divesting emotional resources (decathexis). Consumers prepare for a new emotional outlay onto a new relationship partner (recathexis). The process of divesting from the previous relationship partner and reinvesting emotional resources in a new relationship partner is called the transference process. This process can be either inhibited or facilitated by the attributes of the new relationship partner.

Small heart

The continued CBR is shown in the figure as a smaller heart that takes on its own albeit lesser CBR. It is lesser because the relationship partner is no longer active and the relationship is sustained through the consumer's memory, imagination, continued consumption, as well as social sharing with other consumers of the brand.

Adaptive coping with consumption bereavement

Our data reveal that the length and severity of consumption bereavement differs depending on the degree to which consumers are personally attached to the brand and the degree to which they socialize with other brand consumers. They reveal the social dynamics associated with the managerially imposed stressor. When the brand is co-consumed, or when the consumer is part of a community of brand consumers, consumption bereavement is more severe, indicating that the loss not only of the brand itself but also of the social links it enabled. At the same time, social sharing following a withdrawal eases bereavement, showing that freely expressing yearning for the loss can be therapeutic (Raphaël 1983).

Market withdrawals appear to be relatively manageable stressors. In most cases, consumers facing the loss of a favored brand eventually come to terms with the loss of their active relationship partners. They move from a loss-orientation to a restoration-orientation, reorganizing their consumption and, transferring their allegiance to a new brand (Stroebe and Schut 1999). Nonetheless, for a significant portion of our participants, recalibration of their consuming life without the brand does not include reinvesting into new brands and developing replacement relationships (Leick and Davidson-Nielsen 1991; Worden 1991). Few consumers are unable to come to terms with their loss and complete the bereavement process, although, for brands with deep emotional and social connections, complicated grief is possible (Russell and Schau 2014).

Consumers may go to great lengths to continue their bond with a brand after withdrawal by stockpiling or re-experiencing the product as it was when it was in production. This finding is in line with bereavement research that proposes that the resolution of bereavement does not necessarily entail severing previous bonds (Silverman and Klass 1996). In our study, consumers watched re-runs or bought boxed sets of media brands that had been discontinued in order to maintain their relationship under new conditions (no brand evolution). Strong interpersonal connections around the brand and social sharing fuel the continuing relationship.

Managerial implications

Given the growing need for companies to streamline their brand portfolios, such as when Procter & Gamble's decided to cut its brand portfolio in half (Ng 2014), understanding that consumer-brand relationships may extend beyond the life of the brand implies that brand withdrawal strategies and consumer-brand relationship management 'post mortem' should be integral to a brand manager's responsibilities. Understanding consumption bereavement of favorite brands can assist brand managers in the planning and handling of brand deletions, before, during, and after the actual withdrawal. The bereavement model suggests that preparing consumers for the demise of their favorite brand can help them prepare themselves emotionally, as well as socially. Brand managers may be able to ease the emotional impact of the withdrawal by announcing it ahead of time and by engaging with consumer brand communities to help them prepare. Offering rationales for the withdrawal and assisting consumers with finding resources to cope, in particular through social media, are useful tactics to ease their pain. During the withdrawal period, companies may offer consumers the option to stockpile and organize celebratory events that feature memorabilia and review happy times of the brand's life. Companies could also actuate transference and direct consumers toward other brands in their portfolio by offering free trials or communicating the potential for surrogate brands to fill the void left by the defunct brand.

Future research

Although our findings in this chapter inform our understanding of the emotional symptomatology and the behavioral manifestations of consumption bereavement, there are several limitations that highlight opportunities for future research. First, our findings are based upon consumers' narratives of recalled market withdrawals rather than consumer perceptions collected at the time of market exit. Did the passing of time romanticize the market withdrawal? Second, we focus exclusively on the post-withdrawal phase. We demonstrate manifest behaviors and consumer perceptions associated with firm-imposed market withdrawals, but do not illuminate the anticipatory stage. How do consumers react to anticipation of a brand withdrawal? Is it the same or different than in cases where there is a rapid and unanticipated brand withdrawal? Research suggests that such cases may trigger even greater suffering and, instead of sadness, anger (Bonnano and Field 2001) and protest such as those witnessed by Muñiz and Schau (2005) and Otnes *et al.* (2008) in consumer communities that refused to accept brand withdrawals. Third, there may be aspects of transference that could not be observed in this research because they are more applicable to tangible consumption goods, such as the notion of linking objects, which provides a connection with the deceased that will transmute over time, but be long lasting (Volkan 1981). Lastovicka and Fernandez (2005) identified the process of iconic transfer, whereby consumers transfer the private meaning from a disposed object to an icon, hence retaining the private meanings beyond physical separation. Iconic transfer allows physical detachment without psychological detachment and may be a mechanism for consumers to cope with the loss of a withdrawn brand. Finally, given that grief and bereavement processes in the context of brand relationships are likely to be different from those of human relationships, further research is needed to investigate the specificities of consumption bereavement. For instance, future research should evaluate whether institutional factors that normalize or give structure to mourning behaviors in the context of human bereavement are also at play when consumers deal with the loss of a favorite brand. Do consumers who acknowledge the consumption bereavement process have or long for structure in their mourning rituals?

Conclusion

This research shows that the withdrawal of a brand from the market is perceived as a loss and triggers a process of adaptation to the loss awash with emotions and behaviors similar to those witnessed in classical bereavement. We introduce the term *consumption bereavement* to capture the process followed when consumers experience the cessation of a favored brand's production, one to which they relate as an active relationship partner.

References

Ahuvia, A.C., (2005) "Beyond the Extended Self: Loved Objects and Consumers' Identity Narratives", *Journal of Consumer Research*, 32 (1): 171–184.
Andersen, S.M. and S.W. Cole (1990) "Do I Know You? The Role of Significant Others in General Social Perception", *Journal of Personality and Social Psychology*, 59 (3): 384–399.
Andersen, S.M., N.S. Glassman, S. Chen, and S.W. Cole (1995) "Transference in Social Perception: The Role of Chronic Accessibility in Significant-Other Representation", *Journal of Personality and Social Psychology*, 69 (1): 41–57.
Baker, S.M., D.M. Hunt, and T.L. Rittenberg (2007) "Consumer Vulnerability as a Shared Experience: Tornado Recovery Process in Wright, Wyoming", *Journal of Public Policy and Marketing*, 26 (1): 6–19.
Berscheid, E. and L.A. Peplau (1983) "The Emerging Science of Relationships", *Close Relationships*, ed. H.H. Kelley. New York: W.H. Freeman: 1–19.
Blackburn, R. (2009) "Aussie Pontiac Lovers Mourn Demise of Brand", www.drive.com.au, accessed June 10, 2009.
Bonanno, G.A. and N.P. Field (2001) "Examining the Delayed Grief Hypothesis across 5 Years of Bereavement", *American Behavioral Scientist*, 44 (5): 798–816.
Bowlby, J. (1979) *The Making and Breaking of Affectional Bonds.* London: Tavistock.
Bradford, T.W. (2009) "Intergenerationally Gifted Asset Disposition", *Journal of Consumer Research*, 36 (June): 93–111.
Brumbaugh, C.C. and R.C. Fraley (2006) "Transference and Attachment: How Do Attachment Patterns Get Carried Forward from One Relationship to the Next?", *Personality and Social Psychology Bulletin*, 32 (4): 552–560.
Clifford, S. (2009) "Condé Nast Closes Gourmet and 3 Other Magazines", *The New York Times*, www.nytimes.com/2009/10/06/business/media/06gourmet.html, accessed April 30, 2014.
Day, E. (1983) "Share of Heart: What Is It and How Can It Be Measured?", *Journal of Consumer Marketing*, 6 (1): 5–12.
Deits, B. (1988) *Life After Loss: A Personal Guide to Dealing with Death, Divorce, Job Change and Relocation.* Tucson, AZ: Fisher Books.
Delorme, D.E., G.M. Zinkhan, and S.C. Hagen (2005) "The Process of Consumer Reactions to Possession Threats and Losses in Natural Disaster", *Marketing Letters*, 15 (4): 185–199.

Fajer, M.T. and J.W. Schouten (1995) "Breakdown and Dissolution of Person-Brand Relationships", *Advances in Consumer Research*, 22: 663–667.

Fitzgerald, H. (1994) *The Mourning Handbook*. New York: Simon and Schuster.

Fournier, S. (1998) "Consumers and Their Brands: Developing Relationship Theory in Consumer Research", *Journal of Consumer Research*, 24 (March): 343–373.

Fowlkes, M.R. (1990) "The Social Regulation of Grief", *Sociological Forum*, 5 (4): 635–652.

Freud, S. (1917) "Mourning and Melancholia", *Standard Edition of the Complete Psychological Works of Sigmund Freud*. London: Hogarth.

Fried, M. (1966) "Grieving for a Lost Home, Psychological Costs of Relocation", *Urban Renewal: The Record and the Controversy*, ed. J.Q. Wilson. Cambridge, MA: MIT Press: 359–379.

Gaulin, P. (2007) "The Most Irritating Consumer Trend: Discontinued Products", *AC: Associated Content* (February 22), http://associatedcontent.blogspot.com/.

Glaser, B.G. and A. Strauss (1967) *The Discovery of Grounded Theory: Strategies for Qualitative Research*. Hawthorne, NY: Aldine Transaction.

Gomstyn, A. (2009) "Goodbye Buys: 8 Stores, Brands You Miss. Garden Retailer Smith & Hawken is the Latest Brand Consumers are Mourning", *ABC News Business Unit*, July 15, 2009, http://abcnews.go.com/Business/Story?id=8087908&page=1, accessed April 30, 2014.

Hemlock, D. (2009) "Recession a Cold Bucket of Water for Swimwear Designers", *Sacramento Bee* (July 22).

Herman, S.J. (1974) "Divorce a Grief Process", *Perspectives and Psychiatric Care*, 12 (3): 108–112.

Hill, R.P. (1992) "Homeless Children: Coping with Material Losses", *Journal of Consumer Affairs*, 26 (2): 274–287.

Jacobs, D.L. (2009) "Grief Counseling from the Soap Shrink: How to Cope When the Light Goes Out", http://marlenadelacroix.com/?p=253, accessed April 30, 2104.

Kumar, N. (2003) "Kill a Brand, Keep a Customer", *Harvard Business Review*, December: 86–95.

Lastovicka, J.L. and K.V. Fernandez (2005) "Three Paths to Disposition: The Movement of Meaningful Possessions to Strangers", *Journal of Consumer Research*, 31 (4): 813–824.

Lastovicka, J.L. and N.J. Sirianni (2011) "Truly, Madly, Deeply: Consumers in the Throes of Material Possession Love", *Journal of Consumer Research*, 38 (2): 323–342.

Leick, N. and M. Davidson-Nielsen (1991) *Healing Pain: Attachment, Loss and Grief Therapy*. New York: Routledge.

Levy, S.J. (1962) "Phases in Changing Interpersonal Relations", *Merrill-Palmer Quarterly*, 8 (2): 121–128.

Lindemann, E. (1944) "Symptomatology and Management of Acute Grief", *American Journal of Psychiatry*, 101 (6): 141–148.

Mao, H., X. Luo, and S.P. Jain (2009) "Consumer Responses to Brand Elimination: An Attributional Perspective", *Journal of Consumer Psychology*, 19 (3): 280–289.

Mick, D.G. and C. Buhl (1992) "A Meaning-Based Model of Advertising Experience", *Journal of Consumer Research*, 19 (December): 317–338.

Miles, M.B. and A.M. Huberman (1994) *Qualitative Data Analysis*. Thousand Oaks, CA: Sage Publications.

Muñiz, A.M. Jr and T.C. O'Guinn (2001) "Brand Community", *Journal of Consumer Research*, 27 (March): 412–432.

Muñiz, A.M. Jr and Schau, H.J. (2005) "Religiosity in the Abandoned Apple Newton Brand Community", *Journal of Consumer Research*, 31 (March): 737–747.

Ng, S. (2014) "P&G to Shed More Than Half Its Brands", *Wall Street Journal*, http://online.wsj.com/ articles/procter-gamble-posts-higher-profit-on-cost-cutting-1406892304, accessed August 3, 2104.

O'Donohoe, S. and D. Turley (2005) "Till Death Do Us Part? Consumption and the Negotiation of Relationships Following a Bereavement", *Advances in Consumer Research*, 32: 625–626.

Otnes, C., J. Yang, B.E. Ilhan, and N. Tami (2008) "Consumer Mourning and Coping with the Loss of Strategic Rituals: The Case of Marshall Field & Co", *Advances in Consumer Research*, 36: 688.

Parkes, C.M. (1993) "Bereavement as a Psychosocial Transition: Processes of Adaptation to Change", *Handbook of Bereavement: Theory, Research, and Intervention*, eds M.S. Stroebe, W. Stroebe, and R.O. Hansson. Cambridge: Cambridge University Press: 91–101.

Parkes, C.M. (1996) *Bereavement: Studies of Grief in Adult Life*. London: Penguin.

Parkes, C.M. (2006) *Love and Loss: The Roots of Grief and Its Complications*. New York: Routledge.

Parkes, C.M., and R. Weiss (1983) *Recovery from Bereavement*. New York: Basic Books.

Pool, B. (2003) "Eulogy for GM EV1: Drivers Find Outlet for Grief over EV1s GM is Reclaiming its Electric Cars, so Fans Conduct a Mock Funeral", *Los Angeles Times* (July 25).

Price, L.L. and E.J. Arnould (1999) "Commercial Friendships: Service Provider–Client Relationships in Social Context", *Journal of Marketing*, 63 (October): 38–56.

Price, L.L., E.J. Arnould, and C.F. Curasi (2000) "Older Consumers' Disposition of Special Possessions", *Journal of Consumer Research*, 27 (September): 179–201.

Rando, T.A. (1988) *Grieving: How to Go On Living When Someone You Love Dies*. Lexington, MA: Lexington Books.

Raphaël, B. (1983) *The Anatomy of Bereavement*. New York: Basic Books, Inc.

Rosenblatt, P.C., R.P. Walsh, and D.A. Jackson (1976) *Grief and Mourning in Cross-Cultural Perspective*. New Haven, CT: Human Relations Area File Press.

Russell, C.A. and H.J. Schau (2014) "Coping with the End of Narrative Brands: The Impact of Narrative Closure and Consumption Sociality on Loss Accommodation", *Journal of Consumer Research*, 40 (April): 1039–1062.

Russell, C.A., A.T. Norman, and S.E. Heckler (2004) "The Consumption of Television Programming: Development and Validation of the Connectedness Scale", *Journal of Consumer Research*, 31 (1): 150–161.

Schau, H.J., A.M. Muniz Jr., and E.J. Arnould (2009) "How Brand Community Practices Create Value", *Journal of Marketing*, 73 (5): 30–51.

Shear, K. and H. Shair (2005) "Attachment, Loss, and Complicated Grief", *Developmental Psychobiology*, 47 (3): 253–267.

Silverman, P.R. and D. Klass (1996) "What is the Problem?", *Continuing Bonds: New Understandings of Grief*. Philadelphia, PA: Routledge: 3–30.

Stephens, D.L. and R.P. Hill (1996) "The Loss of Animal Companions: A Humanistic and Consumption Perspective", *Society and Animals*, 4 (2): 189–210.

Stephenson, K. (2008) "Mormons Mourn Postum's Passing", *The Salt Lake City Tribune* (January 1).

Stroebe, M.S. and H. Schut (1999) "The Dual Process Model of Coping with Bereavement: Rationale and Description", *Death Studies*, 23 (3): 197–224.

Thompson, C.J., W.B. Locander, and H.R. Pollio (1990) "The Lived Meaning of Free Choice: An Existential-Phenomenological Description of Everyday Consumer Experiences of Contemporary Married Women", *Journal of Consumer Research*, 17 (3): 346–361.

Thomson, M. (2006) "Human Brands: Investigating Antecedents to Consumers' Stronger Attachments to Celebrities", *Journal of Marketing*, 70 (3): 104–119.

Volkan, V.D. (1981) *Linking Objects and Linking Phenomena: A Study of the Forms, Symptoms, Metapsychology, and Therapy of Complicated Mourning*. New York: International Universities Press.

Wooler, R. (2009) "Mourning Max Factor in the US", *JC Report* (June 22).

Worden, J.W. (1991) *Grief Counseling and Grief Therapy: A Handbook for the Mental Health Practitioner*. New York: Springer.

Yew, M.A. (2009) "Car Enthusiasts Mourn the End of Pontiac", *The Toronto Star* (April 28).

PART VI

Building the brand-driven organization

19

BUILDING BRANDS FROM THE INSIDE OUT

Three practitioner stories

Chris Allen and Matt Carcieri

In the not-too-distant past, most brands executed against a standard template. They promised functional and emotional benefits and used paid communications to persuade people to buy into their promise. Through consistent delivery of the benefit, the brand engendered trust. This was the essential formula for brands like Kodak, Maxwell House, Quiznos, and Oldsmobile.

Today, the marketing landscape looks very different. In their assessment of brands, savvy consumers look beyond communications (which they increasingly avoid). Instead, they interrogate a brand's behavior across all aspects of its enterprise. They discern the brand's meaning by how the brand acts, not just by what it says.

At the same time, consumers are now looking for higher significance in their brands (Allen *et al.* 2008). Beyond the promise of trusted performance, consumers use brands to satisfy their needs for belonging and self-esteem. They use them to affect their self-image and identity (Fournier 1998; Springfield and Sharma 2012). As Ken Roman, former chairman and CEO of Ogilvy & Mather put it: "Brands began as guarantors of reliability and quality in consumer products, and have evolved into representations of a way of life" (Roman and Maas 2003: 12).

In their discernment of a brand's meaning, consumers have an ever-widening view into the brand's inner workings and its governing precepts. The rise of the Internet has yielded greater transparency, breaking down the walls between manufacturers and consumers, between internal operations and external experience.

In this new paradigm, the most important currency is *shared values*. It is the platform upon which the strongest consumer-brand relationships are built. Consider brands like Whole Foods, Chipotle, Natura, and Patagonia. With their emphasis on sustainability and community, these brands garner deep commitment from consumers. In fact, the more visible the values – and the more authentically they are acted upon and reaffirmed – the more magnetic the bond with values-based customer cohorts.

TABLE 19.1 Comparing two modes of brand-building

	Conventional	Culture Based
General Orientation	External	Internal → external (inside out)
Governing Concept	Functional or emotional benefit promise	Organizational purpose and values
Primary Form of Engagement	Persuasion through brand communications	Actualizing values through brand behaviors
Key Currency of the Consumer-Brand Relationship	Trust	Shared values

The companies that are forging the strongest values-based connections have a different operating style. Whereas the focus of conventional brand organizations is almost exclusively external, the orientation of values-focused firms is "inside-out." That is, they view marketplace outcomes as a manifestation of their internal identity and intentionality. Instead of being "communications-led" (the work of marketers), these brands are "culture-based" (actualizing enterprise values across the organization).

To better understand this alternative operating style, we took a look inside some of its leading practitioners. Here, we describe qualitative research conducted with three firms that emphasize brand building from the inside out. Their stories illuminate the scenarios where the approach is most applicable and identify practices that foster success.

Interview approach

Featured companies

The three companies profiled here were selected from a larger project examining organizations that cultivate internal culture to affect brand meaning. There are important similarities and differences among the companies. Two – Innocent and Method – are small consumer products companies that are often called out as exemplars of a new brand building style (cf. Gamechangers 2014; Garfield and Levy 2013; Stengel 2011). Both have fewer than 500 employees. The third – Motorola Solutions – is a global business-to-business firm with 22,000 employees. However, all three demonstrate an active stance regarding an ideal or purpose (Mackey 2011) and a commitment to acting on their values. This, in turn, yields a sustainable point of difference and a deep bond with their customers.

- *Innocent Drinks.* From its headquarters in the Ladbroke Grove neighborhood of London, Innocent Drinks markets nutritious beverages and quick meals, with 100 percent pure fruit smoothies as the anchor product. Their products do not reach North America, but are distributed in 18 European countries plus Russia. In 2009, Innocent's three founders sold a minority stake to Coca-Cola Company. In 2013, Coca-Cola increased its stake to over 90 percent, providing the platform for Innocent's global expansion. Innocent's stated purpose is to *make natural, delicious food and drink that helps people live well and die old*.

- *Method*. From its headquarters in San Francisco, Method designs and markets naturally-derived personal and household cleaning products. In 2012, Method merged with Belgium-based Ecover in a combined effort to scale up for global expansion; however, the Method and Ecover brands have maintained distinct identities. As *people against dirty*, Method champions happy, healthy cleaning in the home, while at the same time working to fundamentally alter what they refer to as "dirty" business practices.

- *Motorola Solutions*. Motorola Solutions provides data communication solutions and telecommunication gear for public and private sector customers around the world. For example, first responders in 100+ countries rely on Motorola radios to stay connected in crisis situations. Motorola Solutions' stated purpose is *to help people be their best in the moments that matter*.

The interview process

The general objective for all interviews was to explore how companies act on their stated purpose and values inside the organization in ways that could affect external stakeholders' views about the brand. The descriptions and conclusions offered here are based on 20 in-depth interviews with senior executives in the three companies. These executives had diverse roles, including senior marketers and product/brand managers, but also human resources, operations, and the three chief executive officers. The interviews were conducted onsite at corporate headquarters and included tours of the facilities and workspaces. All interviews were audio-recorded and transcribed for subsequent analysis.

A standardized guide was used for all interviews across companies, but it allowed for exploration of unique themes volunteered by each participant. The interviews began with a general question about current and previous roles. Participants were then asked to explain, in their own words, the essential, shared purpose of the organization and how purpose and values influence operations in their sphere of responsibility. Often, this involved elaborating on the pithy phrases that serve as insider jargon typical in robust corporate cultures. Specific probes also explored internal events and rituals that involve reinforcement of values. Additionally, there was a general line of questioning regarding consumers/end users and their appreciation (or lack thereof) of purpose and values.

Principal discoveries from the interviews are discussed next, beginning with Innocent. Synthesis and conclusions are offered at the end.

Innocent drinks

We were struck by the distinctiveness of Innocent's culture as soon as we entered the playfully decorated headquarters, dubbed the Fruit Towers (a nod to the John Cleese television series *Fawlty Towers*). Here is how one interviewee described her first impression: "I got goose bumps. I just walked in and thought, 'Wow! What a place!' It made me laugh. I wasn't laughing at them; it just made me feel incredibly energized and positive."

The central lounge area contains picnic tables, a ping-pong table, and foosball. The floor is covered in Astroturf. Lighthearted images and sayings fill the walls.

The first tenet on Innocent's list of organizational values is "be natural." This describes both their product philosophy and their maxim for living, and is a key part of the value system that Innocent's consumers "buy into." Inside the walls of Fruit Towers, that "be natural spirit" can be seen in the employees' style of dress (many wear shorts and flip-flops) and in the backyard-barbeque manner in which employees interact (there is, in fact, a barbeque on the premises, and employees often gather round for a taste of sausage).

To be clear, the folks at Innocent are serious about business. There is plenty of rigor and process and a hard-charging results orientation; however, their business discipline is complemented by an idiosyncratic worldview, which is fueled by a distinctive set of practices. One example is the "Lord and Lady of the Sash" ceremony. As part of a company-wide meeting every Monday morning, the leaders crown an employee to recognize his or her actions in support of company values. This Monday morning "values jam" – a spirited and quirky celebration of values – is part of what makes Innocent, Innocent.

Perhaps the biggest lever in sustaining Innocent's culture is new-hire selection. The company invests a great deal of time in recruiting, and it places a premium on cultural fit. According to Group Operations Director Steven Spall, "A lot of effort goes into hiring against the values." The company conducts multiple rounds of interviews. "The last two rounds of that are: do we really believe this person is going to deliver against the values?", says CEO Douglas Lamont.

By building and maintaining a team of values cohorts, the culture at Innocent becomes self-perpetuating and self-reinforcing. Employees innately understand the guard rails for brand-related behavior, and they practically demand certain parameters of decision-making from the leadership team. CEO Lamont says, "[The employees] are the ones knocking our doors down if they sense we're moving away from the ideal."

With such a strong internal culture, Innocent's values naturally "leak out" into the marketplace. For example, the "be natural" spirit comes out in the brand's voice and its stance toward consumers. One manifestation is Innocent's playful bottle label, which invites people to "pop round for a visit" to the company headquarters.

The day's final interview was with Dan Germain, Innocent's Group Head of Brand and Creative. Speaking about Coca-Cola's buy-out of the brand, he had this to say about his new colleagues:

> There's a bunch of stuff that we do that they [Coke] look at – our traditions, our Innocent moments – they've been over here and experienced it, and they've said, "We don't really understand why you do that or why you started doing that, but please don't stop doing that, because it seems to work."

Since assuming ownership of the UK-based drink brand, the Atlanta bosses have left the brand's unique culture untouched. While they may not understand the inside-out approach to brand building, they understand that it is a key source of the brand's success.

Method

Method is a Certified B Corporation, committed to designing safe and environmentally-conscious products (Ryan and Lowry 2011). They have a concise values directory – including calls to action like "innovate, don't imitate," "care like crazy," and "keep Method weird." Method's devotion to culture is similar to Innocent's, to include the company-wide, Monday morning values jam; California-casual dress code; and plenty of Astroturf. Method also invests considerable time and energy in new-hire selection, prioritizing values fit.

The first interview at Method was with Eric Ryan, co-founder and chief Brand Architect. He made the point that being values-driven does not imply a lack of traditional business savvy or a philanthropy-first mindset.

> We need to make money to follow our mission. If we truly believe in the social impact of our business, every dollar we invest back in the business that gets somebody to choose a non-toxic alternative is ultimately the way we go to work every day and create the most good in the world.

Subsequent interviews with the chief marketing officer and chief financial officer, and with product managers holding MBAs from the likes of Harvard and Michigan, reaffirmed Ryan's premise that Method has all the conventional business skills in place. But, it was an interview with the vice president of operations that highlighted the profound influence of values on decision making within Method.

Method's dramatic growth in recent years now justifies its own manufacturing and distribution center (previously, all Method products were produced by contract manufacturers). This is a very big deal for everyone at Method, and especially for the vice president of operations. Here's how the building process took shape within the guard rails of Method's brand values.

Like any business searching for a building site, Method started with criteria involving things like proximity to suppliers and intermodal transportation. Method identified 150 sites in the Midwest that covered the basics, but then eliminated most of these with the mantra of "no cornfields." In the end, they chose a site in the Pullman neighborhood on Chicago's south side. In the late1800s, George Pullman developed this area into the first planned industrial community in the US, but decades of neglect had left his factories and the neighborhood in a state of decay.

Method's leaders bought into Mayor Emanuel's vision to help revive Chicago's south side. Drew Frasier, Method's CEO, explained the decision this way: "What it came down to was: how best does this facility and its location reinforce our mission, our values, and our brand?" Method's values lead them to place a high priority on community re-development. "We felt we could have a profound impact beyond soap," he said. Five of the 22 acres in the Method tract will be occupied by buildings; the rest will be gardens and green space. Sidewalks, not fences, will mark the property's boundaries. Method's point of view is that it is hard to become part of a community by building fences.

Given Method's values, it is no surprise that they are also working closely with the US Green Building Council in pursuit of LEED certification. Method has positioned the project to be on track for LEED Platinum certification. A 225-foot tall, refurbished wind turbine will supply a significant share of the plant's energy and enhances the LEED rating. According to the vice president of operations, Garry Embelton: "We're on track to capture the most LEED points of any facility ever, for our industry." "Care like crazy" is a value fulfilled at Method.

While Method's investment in its new Pullman plant is a dramatic demonstration of how purpose and values affect strategic choices, this is by no means a standalone event. Another example from the Method portfolio is its ocean plastic packaging initiative. It turns out that there are massive fields of plastic trash afloat in the Pacific Ocean. Frequently, large swaths of this debris wash ashore on beaches across the Pacific region.

Method sends its employees to trashed Pacific beaches to sort plastic waste that will ultimately be harvested for use in the manufacture of new bottles containing hand-wash products. Given the costs involved, anything packaged in ocean plastic will never contribute to Method's profitability, and Method does not pretend to be solving the problem of ocean plastic. They are simply trying to make more people aware that this problem exists. They are *people against dirty*, and this is a very big dirty. As expressed by Katie Molinari, Method's chief Architect of Buzz: "I've been with Method for six years. When we launched packaging made out of ocean plastic – just to be part of a small company that can do that is a very cool thing!"

In building its first manufacturing facility, Method has made many unique choices, dictated by both business considerations and values. Inevitably, these choices will "leak out" into the public's consciousness. 160,000 motorists each day will see the factory's wind turbine along the Dan Ryan Expressway. Journalists will embrace stories about the company's relations with its neighbors. Method will earn new brand advocates and deepen its relationship with existing ones, powered by shared values.

Motorola solutions

The prominent feature of Motorola Solutions' headquarters in Schaumburg, Illinois is not Astroturf. It is larger-than-life images of customers on the job with a

Motorola product, in their moments that matter. Much like Innocent and Method, Motorola's leaders actively affect internal culture through devotion to purpose and values. However, rituals like weekly, company-wide, face-to-face values jams are not an option in a global company with thousands of employees. The strategy to build the Motorola Solutions brand is inside out, as it is at Innocent and Method, but the execution is adapted to its size and scale.

Motorola's stated purpose is to *help people be their best in the moments that matter*, and it is reaffirmed through a commitment to values like being innovative, passionate, and accountable in supporting the needs of their unique customer segments. As is typical in any values-driven culture, the language is abstract and aspirational, and with this comes an authenticity challenge. Can one embrace the purpose day-in, day-out, year-in, year-out? How do we remind employees of the purpose in ways that make it more than a slogan or wall poster? Leaders at Motorola were remarkably self-aware of the authenticity challenge. Eduardo Conrado, Senior Vice President, Marketing and IT framed it this way: "I think the initial heavy lifting is finding [your] purpose. Then, making it authentic over time, if you're going to work on it for multiple years, that's where you're going to put a lot of your efforts."

At Motorola, they are perfecting the practice of story capture and story sharing to establish authenticity with internal and external stakeholders. The focal construct in the stories is always customers in specific moments that matter. A dispatcher alerting police of fleeing suspects in Toliara, Madagascar; an engineer inspecting a dam in Skien, Norway; a police officer viewing real-time video of a terrorism suspect in Boa Vista, Brazil – these and hundreds of other examples of "moments that matter" are being systematically captured and shared inside Motorola Solutions. There is a template for story capture that emphasizes elements like the exact time and place, the hero of the story, and the problem/conflict that the hero overcame. Stories are shared internally through a worldwide closed-circuit TV system, in weekly communications to employees, and via the oversized images of "customer heroes" in all the lobbies of Motorola's 27 locations around the world. Conrado explained all this activity very simply: "Employees at the end of the day are very representative of the brand, so if you start from within, it will show itself on the outside."

Story capture and sharing have become contagious at Motorola Solutions, in a way that reaffirms the purpose and values of the company. CEO Greg Brown referred to the practice as "additive to the foundation of the firm." He also relayed a story – stemming from his participation at a Major City Chiefs' Recognition Dinner – that illustrates an important byproduct of inside-out brand building. The Major City Chiefs' Dinner is an event where first responders from around the world are recognized for remarkable acts of valor. Award recipients are asked to say a few words, and one of them had this to say about Motorola:

> I want to thank the Major City Chiefs, and I want to thank my boss, but I also want to thank Greg Brown. The reason I thank you, Mr Brown, is not

out of being polite. It's because all of the officers in here are in scary moments or dark moments, and the only partner I have on my watch is my Motorola radio. I thank you for providing me this, for my moments that matter, that are too frequent to arise. I know what a moment that matters means. It's what I do. It's what we all do.

Relationship building is fundamental for the B2B firm (Dwyer *et al.* 1987). At Motorola Solutions those relationships are self-evident, but the basis for that relationship is no different than it would be for Innocent or Method. Motorola's customers have an emotional connection with the brand; the two parties share a deep appreciation for the need to be one's best in *the moments that matter*.

Synthesis and conclusions

Each of the companies represented here exhibits intentional execution of the inside-out approach to brand building. In comparison to conventional brands – whose focus is largely external (using paid communications to persuade consumers to buy into their promise) – these "culture-based" brands start from within, manifesting internal values in all aspects of their behavior. By authentically affirming a definitive set of values, they garner deep commitment from values cohorts.

In all three firms, we observed a comprehensive agenda for orchestrating the internal culture. All three made programmatic interventions, the efforts were ongoing, and they touched all parts of the enterprise. Inside-out brand building is not just a "marketing thing," it is an interdisciplinary agenda.

Although there are many potential ways to orchestrate a brand culture, our research revealed four practices that may be effective for other firms seeking to embrace this new style. Naturally, this approach must begin with a formal declaration of purpose and values. Once defined, these practices serve to systematically embed the purpose and values.

1 *Physical space design* – All three companies use physical workspace to affirm values. At Motorola Solutions, oversized images of customer heroes in "moments that matter" are everywhere on the walls. At Method and Innocent, the central lounge areas with couches and green Astroturf communicate a sense of place where we can and will gather regularly to be our natural selves. In our interview with Innocent's CEO, he emphasized the importance of "making sure those small things are in place in the office, with some silly things on the walls as well" – like photos of all the Lords and Ladies of the Sash. "The small things are a daily reminder of what makes us unique."

2 *Rituals* – At both Innocent and Method, the employees' workweek begins with a "values jam." While sometimes informal, the agenda for the Monday morning meetings serves to perpetually reaffirm brand values, keeping them salient in everyday work. Dan Germain told us that eliminating the Monday morning company-wide meeting "would be cataclysmic" for Innocent.

3   *Hiring for values fit* – For both Innocent and Method, new-hire selection is a
     critical lever for sustaining the culture. Both companies invest a great deal of
     time in recruiting, placing a premium on values fit. As expressed by another
     of Innocent's senior leaders:

> A job candidate asked me recently, "How do you make people be the
> values?" Needless to say, that candidate didn't get very far. Because I
> must say that those who are successful, you can see they have the values
> that we aspire to, and you can see by their CV and experiences and the
> way they conduct themselves that they "get it." They want to be here
> because they understand what it is that we do and where and how we
> do it.

4   *Story capture and story sharing* – Motorola systematically uses stories to instill the
     organization's purpose and values. This includes both a template for capturing
     stories and a system for internal sharing. Even though they appear on the
     surface as less deliberate, Innocent and Method are equally savvy about
     storytelling. The fundamental agenda of their Monday morning values jams is
     storytelling in service of celebrating values. This provides largely the same
     benefit at Innocent and Method as it does at Motorola.

Once inculcated, purpose and values becomes a filter for decisions and behaviors.
This was evident in all three companies, but we can see it most pointedly in
Method's choices in building its first manufacturing facility. When a manufacturing
plant signals the values of its builder, consumers will see that plant as a reflection
of the brand. If consumers share the builder's values, the basis for a relationship has
been established. When manufacturing sites become a totem for brand meaning,
one has to acknowledge that the paradigm for brand building has shifted. This is a
paradigm that emphasizes building the brand from the inside out.

References

Allen, C., S. Fournier, and F. Miller (2008) "Brands and Their Meaning Makers", *Handbook
    of Consumer Psychology*, eds C.P. Haugtvedt, P. Herr, and F.R. Kardes. New York: Lawrence
    Erlbaum Associates: 781–822.
Dwyer, F.R., P. Schurr, and S. Oh (1987) "Developing Buyer-Seller Relationships", *Journal
    of Marketing*, 51 (2): 11–27.
Fournier, S. (1998) "Consumers and their Brands: Developing Relationship Theory in
    Consumer Research", *Journal of Consumer Research*, 24 (4): 343–73.
Gamechangers (2014) http://gamechangers500.com/, accessed April 2, 2014.
Garfield, B. and D. Levy (2013) *Can't Buy Me Like: How Authentic Customer Connections Drive
    Superior Results.* New York: Penguin Group.
Mackey, J. (2011) "What Conscious Capitalism Really Is", *California Management Review*, 53
    (3): 83–90.
Roman, K. and J. Maas (2003) *How to Advertise.* New York: Thomas Dunne Books.

Ryan, E. and A. Lowry (2011) *the method Method*. New York: Penguin Group.

Springfield, S. and P. Sharma (2012) "Brand Humanity: Transforming the Business of Building Brands", *Consumer-Brand Relationships*, eds S. Fournier, M. Breazeale, and M. Fetscherin. London: Routledge: 382–94.

Stengel, J. (2011) *Grow: How Ideals Power Growth and Profit at the World's Greatest Companies*. New York: Crown Business.

20

BRANDING TERROR

Building notoriety in violent extremist organizations

Michael Breazeale, Erin G. Pleggenkuhle-Miles, Gina Scott Ligon, and Mackenzie Harms

> What links these [terrorist] groups, experts say, is no longer a centralized organization but a loose ideology that any group can appropriate and apply as it sees fit while gaining the mystique of a recognized brand name.
>
> *(Hubbard 2014)*

As the world reeled from the unprecedented September 11, 2001 attacks on the United States by al-Qaeda, another event grabbed headlines and the attention of an American public that, while no stranger to domestic terrorism, had been introduced to foreign attacks on home soil only four months earlier. Daniel Pearl, the *Wall Street Journal's* South Asia bureau chief, was kidnapped by an al Qaeda affiliated organization, and, one month later, a video of his decapitation was aired all over the world. Both the kidnapping and the beheading were viewed as a propaganda opportunity by the Violent Extremist Organization (VEO) (Krause-Jackson and Capaccio 2011). Most accounts suggested that the long-term effect of the release of the video was successful in drawing the attention of people around the globe (Lentini and Bakashmar 2007). Viewed objectively, such tactics to promote the brand of global jihad are not that different from more traditional branding efforts employed by much-loved consumer brands. An organization had used its knowledge of its target market to stage a promotion that would resonate with them, filmed the event, released the video, and then allowed its own customers to spread the message virally. As is often the case with the best viral marketing, the promotion engaged an audience far larger than originally planned due to the surprising nature of the content. Consider WestJet Airlines surprising its passengers with Christmas gifts in December 2013. WestJet recorded the Christmas wishes of 250 passengers via a virtual Santa as they boarded a four-hour cross-country flight. Then, with the help of 150 staff members, they surprised those passengers upon their arrival with their requested gifts on the baggage carousel in place of their suitcases (Moran 2013), leading many of the nearly 36 million viewers who watched the video on WestJet's YouTube channel (http://bit.ly/westjetpromo) to ask whether this was a Christmas miracle or a sickly sweet public relations stunt.

With only one fatality, the beheading of Daniel Pearl was less lethal than the attacks of September 11, but equally impactful due to the malevolent creativity of the action. Examined from a purely analytical standpoint, this was a parsimonious and elegant branding event. With far fewer financial and human resources than WestJet's Christmas campaign, al-Qaeda achieved even more viral success and notoriety than the airline and solidified their reputation as the world's premier provider of terror. Indeed, the Islamic State of Iraq and Syria (ISIS), formerly an ally of al-Qaeda (Sly 2014), has recently attempted to recreate the success of that event by releasing a video of the beheading of another American journalist, James Foley.

Both scenarios employed branding strategy to garner attention and endear the focal brand to its intended target audience, but no research to date has examined the implementation of traditional branding strategies to both create and strengthen the relationships that violent extremist organizations (VEOs) have with their followers and the public. Additionally, no research has studied the other outcomes of these branding tactics on the organizations that implement them, such as fundraising and co-branding opportunities. In this chapter, the authors will present a conceptual justification for the application of brand theory to the notoriety of VEOs and lay out a research agenda that will model specific branding strategies that VEOs employ to gain prominence, and the outcomes that result. Up until this point, the dangerous potential of VEOs has traditionally been evaluated based upon lethality (i.e., body count) (Asal and Rethemeyer 2008). If this research is successful, governments may possess a new tool that allows them to predict which organizations possess the tools to become dangerous *before* their body count rises. This chapter proposes that factors that contribute to the prominence and brand reputation (and notoriety) of business organizations will contribute in comparable ways to VEOs. Using case-based evidence, we suggest the conditions under which marketing theories apply to and potentially even predict outcomes for VEOs.

Background

Theoretical models continue to advance our understanding of the impact that even subtle marketing strategies have on traditional organizations' performance. Both marketing and management scholars have also shown that the prominence and reputation of an organization can play a critical role in an organization's economic performance and other measures of success (Fombrun and Shanley 1990; Roberts and Dowling 2002). Uncertainty remains, however, about the generalizability of these theoretical models in their application to non-traditional organizations. Despite obvious differences in organizational goals, VEOs share many structural similarities with business organizations (e.g., formalization, centralization, and hierarchy) that contribute to their overall performance (Ligon *et al.* 2013). Many of the performance measures of a business organization are also valid for VEOs (e.g., revenues, talent recruitment, and strong brand community).

The term "violent extremist organization" (VEO) is used to describe collections of individuals who prescribe to an ideological or belief-based mission and engage in violence in order to execute that mission (Ligon *et al.* 2013). Beyond their similarities in structure, operations, and performance outcomes, VEOs are similar to other types of organizations in that their complexity, unique characteristics, and continual evolution make them difficult to study in an empirical, controlled laboratory setting. Yet VEOs' "products" – terror, violence, and destruction – typically have a markedly different type of societal impact from those of more traditional organizations. Therefore, the importance of this research lies in the fact that the ability to predict VEO outcomes, based on an analysis of their marketing activity, could provide insight for defense and security communities, conserve economic resources, contribute to political stability, and save lives.

Our research question is direct – Can brand and reputation theories predict the notoriety of VEOs and contribute to their successful growth? Case evidence gathered from a Department of Homeland Security-funded effort (Ligon 2012) will allow us to demonstrate the overlap of branding and organizational theories on prominence and reputation in the VEO domain.

Conceptualization

Although brand identity and reputation represent disparate research streams in the fields of marketing and management respectively, both constructs relate to the way that an organization is perceived by the public and both contribute to desired organizational outcomes. To explore the applicability of these theories to VEOs, we briefly summarize known theory and discuss their relevance to non-traditional organizations.

The importance of brand

There are many definitions used to describe what a brand is, but perhaps the simplest is that a brand is a product offering from a known source (Kotler and Keller 2011). This definition suggests that brands come with a set of expectations – a reputation. Contributing to that reputation are the brand elements that the marketer designs to convey the brand's story, as well as associations with the brand, such as co-branding opportunities and active brand communities. For marketers lucky enough to create and manage a strong brand that resonates with consumers, benefits accrue that include the ability to imbue products with unique associations, a source of competitive advantage, symbolic representation of the brand promise, and a means of easily identifying the brand's products (Keller 2013). Well-loved brands like Coca-Cola and Apple also see significant brand benefits that include strong financial performance and the ability to recruit and retain top employee talent.

Readers of this book will also recognize that strong brands benefit from the relationships that consumers form with them (Fournier 1998). These relationships can result in emotional attachment (Fedorikhin *et al.* 2008; Thomson *et al.* 2005), attitudinal and behavioral loyalty (Chaudhuri and Holbrook 2001; Fader and Schmittlein 1993), and even love (Batra *et al.* 2012; Carroll and Ahuvia 2006). The quality of those relationships depends on a sense of interdependence, intimacy, commitment, passion, self-brand connection, and brand partner quality. The results of a strong relationship include accommodation by the consumer, willingness to forgive the brand for perceived transgressions, biased partner perceptions, devaluation of alternatives, and attribution biases (Fournier 1998).

All of the previously cited research describes traditional brands, but the authors of this chapter suggest that the findings are equally relevant for non-traditional brands such as VEOs. The very basis of followers' relationships with VEO brands are the same feelings that constitute brand relationship quality for fans of Coke and Apple, and the zeal of the fans of brands that include Jeep and Apple has often been described as extreme or "cult-like" (Belk and Tumbat 2005; Muñiz and O'Guinn 2001). Let us consider the Jemaah Islamiyah brand.

The terrorist organization Jemaah Islamiyah was founded in 1993 as a group of jihadists committed to engaging in violence to establish an Islamic state in Indonesia, Malaysia, the Philippines, southern Thailand, and Singapore. Jemaah Islamiyah initially received little public and governmental attention, but the organization would later go on to be considered one of the most violent and effective terrorist organizations worldwide, despite engaging in fewer attacks than many organizations with comparable infamy (e.g., al Qaeda, the Irish Republican Army). What factors about Jemaah Islamiyah contributed to its rise in global notoriety, and how did that notoriety influence its performance?

Jemaah Islamiyah operated throughout the 1990s without conducting any successful attacks. However, by the year 2000, Jemaah Islamiyah had attracted the attention of al Qaeda, which offered covert financial support for the planning of a series of Christmas Eve bombings. On Christmas Eve in 2000, Jemaah Islamiyah simultaneously bombed 39 Christian churches across Indonesia, resulting in nearly 150 fatalities and injuries (START 2012). Following this attack, Jemaah Islamiyah was officially endorsed by al Qaeda as an ally (co-branding). Over the next two years, Jemaah Islamiyah members were trained in al Qaeda camps; al Qaeda substantially increased funding to the organization, as well as provided new members, and the ranks of both active members and passive supporters (McCauley and Moskalenko 2008) grew (a growing brand community). In 2002, Jemaah Islamiyah committed another infamous attack, the Bali bombings, which resulted in over 500 fatalities and injuries. Rather than aiming for hard targets such as opposing military or religious groups, the Bali bombings aimed for soft targets: two nightclubs that were frequented by western tourists. This particular attack resulted in a great deal of media attention, in that nightclub party-goers were photographed with injuries and carnage. These images – and the subsequent attention they obtained for the brand – propelled the US to add Jemaah Islamiyah to the Foreign Terrorist Organization watch-list.

During this time period, Jemaah Islamiyah grew from a lesser-known brand to one with a stronger identity. It did so by 1) co-branding with al Qaeda, 2) producing a more high profile product, and 3) delivering on its brand promise in highly visible ways that were consistent with the brand's identity. The result for the Jemaah Islamiyah brand was a larger and more loyal brand community. Specifically, prior to the media attention, estimates indicated the group had approximately 100 members. However, as a result of the increased attention from these attacks, the group had up to 1,000 active members in 2012 (Crenshaw 2014). Just as traditional organizations with strong brands attract more investors and higher stock prices, so too do VEOs attract the attention of sympathizers willing to donate time and money to further the organization's cause (McCauley and Moskalenko 2008).

The role of reputation

Reputational research crosses disciplines. As a construct, reputation has been defined a number of ways, operationalized in a variety of contexts, studied in varying degrees at every level of analysis, and is, by its very nature, interdisciplinary (see Table 1 in Rindova *et al.* 2005: 1036). Strong reputations are rent-producing assets with substantial economic value because they are difficult to imitate. As such, organizational reputation as a source of competitive advantage is well established in both the marketing (e.g., Shamsie 2003) and management (e.g., Fombrun and Shanley 1990) literature. Prior research has examined how firms construct reputation; such as through market signals (e.g., Fombrun and Shanley 1990), market actions (e.g., Clark and Montgomery 1998), patterns of resource flows (Dierickx and Cool 1989), and the combination of resource flows and strategic communications (Rindova and Fombrun 1999). While organizations create and manage their reputations through various means, the reputation of an organization is simultaneously impacted by the industries to which they belong (spillover effects) and the non-market (political, economic, social, and cultural) environments in which they operate. Taken together, we know that a strong reputation can protect traditionally studied organizations during times of crises; can the same be said when the organizations' business *is* crisis?

Research has demonstrated that favorable organizational reputation has economic benefits (Fombrun and Shanley 1990; Roberts and Dowling 2002), and there exists a plethora of anecdotal evidence. Consider Mattel's ability to ride out massive toy recalls in 2007, or Apple's ability to thrive despite the lack of significant product breakthroughs in recent years. Other research might attribute this successful maneuvering to their celebrity status. The nature of celebrity is well grounded in research and most often refers to social actors that "attract large-scale public attention and elicit *positive* emotional responses from the public" (Ranft *et al.* 2006: 283, italics added). It should be noted that while celebrity can be purposively created and managed, it is not something that can merely be granted. Rather, it is a byproduct of interactions between an actor and a public. Celebrity often increases access to resources, such as raw materials, capital markets, or human capital (Rindova *et al.* 2006). While celebrity may be the positive byproduct for traditional organizations, notoriety, for VEOs, can elicit similar benefits. Let us revisit the example of Jemaah Islamiyah.

Following the Bali bombings, the global media attention Jemaah Islamiyah received from major international news sources increased by 1,800 percent (Ligon *et al.* 2014b). Over the next year, Jemaah Islamiyah became officially designated as a terrorist organization by several international governments (third-party certification), including the United Kingdom and the United States. For VEOs, just as for other organizations, celebrity status and prominence are often granted through 1) third-party certifications (e.g., media rankings, certification of achievement), 2) co-branding with high-status actors (e.g., al Qaeda), as well as 3) significant media attention (Rindova *et al.* 2005). Jemaah Islamiyah also gained a notable reputation as a major threat within their culture and relative to other terrorist organizations. As a result, their ability to fundraise via legal and illegal avenues increased substantially (enhanced economic benefits), as did support in terms of membership, training, and the ability to recruit members with highly desirable traits (e.g., specialized expertise, high socioeconomic status) (Ligon *et al.* 2014a). As this example suggests, Jemaah Islamiyah engaged in efforts to promote its ideology – or brand – which led to increased media attention and global prominence, resulting in higher notoriety and more opportunities for fundraising and recruitment.

Performance outcomes

Brand reputation matters because of its impact on organizational performance. Traditional performance measures include sales, shareholder value, and innovation, among other key performance indicators. While the most common metric of VEO performance is that of lethality, or total attributed deaths per year (Asal and Rethemeyer 2008), other elements of performance are also central to the sustainability of a given VEO. Specifically, there are at least three indices of VEO performance that have gained traction in the security studies literature: 1) fundraising, 2) achievement of objectives, and 3) organizational size or growth.

First, fundraising is critical to plan and execute attacks. The 9/11 attacks cost al Qaeda between $400,000 and $500,000 (National Commission on Terrorist Attacks upon the United States 2004). Funds were required to select and train participants, obtain visas, travel to the United States, and facilitate communications between the plot leader and participants outside the United States. Pre-9/11, it was estimated that al Qaeda had an operating budget of approximately $30 million a year, which allowed the organization to finance this complex set of activities by members. Put simply, without funds, terrorist organizations are less able to reign terror.

Another performance outcome is the obtainment of political goals associated with the VEO's ideology. For example, in present day Iraq and Syria, there are three main VEOs with the ideological objective of establishing an Islamic State. Al-Nusra Front, the Islamic State in Iraq and Syria (ISIS), and al Qaeda Central all have political goals of imposing strict Sharia law and taking over the states of Iraq and Syria. However, as of now, these groups are not cooperating with each other. Thus, another performance outcome evident by the present conflict is the achievement of political objectives – which of these VEOs, if any, will be in charge of the region? Establishing a loyal brand community and a prominent reputation versus those of rival VEOs will likely play a significant part in the outcome of the current and future conflicts (Al-Monitor 2014).

Finally, and related to lethality, fundraising, and goal accomplishment, a central and perhaps most important performance outcome of VEOs is the capacity to share their ideologies with others. Experts in terrorism research agree that radicalizing others to identify with and join the ideological cause is the primary focus of leaders and active members (Horgan 2013). Thus, converting non-radicals to "believers" is executed through online mechanisms (Wiktorowicz 2013), promotional events such as concerts (Simi and Futrell 2010), and friendship (Sageman 2008). Increasing members – or even sympathizers – serves at least two pragmatic and one ideological goal. First, having a larger number of individuals sympathetic to the cause provides access to more diverse talent and expertise. This was evidenced in a recent call from Boko Haram to partner with al Shabaab members to cross-train on social media strategies (Ligon *et al.* 2014a). Second, increasing membership also helps gain greater access to diverse types of funding sources. The Tamil Tigers of Sri Lanka greatly increased their operations when they were able to radicalize members of the Tamil diaspora living in Canada (Ligon *et al.* 2010). Finally, most ideologies associated with VEOs have the imperative of converting more individuals to believers. For example, in present day Iraq, non-believers (i.e., Christians) have a stamp painted on their houses as a marker from the group ISIS that these individuals have yet to convert to radical Islam (Jensen 2014). This serves as a warning to the inhabitants, but also demonstrates the ideological imperative members feel to increase their brand communities. While lethality is certainly part of the outcomes of malevolent creativity and objective accomplishment of goals, body count may not always be the best measure of VEO performance.

Attacks, which can function as promotional efforts that gain media attention, are a central mechanism that leads to the eventual performance of lethality, fundraising, achieving objectives, and radicalization of more members. Consider the 2013 Boston Marathon bombing. This bombing resulted in three fatalities, a relatively low number of casualties when compared to other high-impact terrorist attacks. However, the symbolic nature of the target rendered this event deeply psychologically destructive to the American people (Drake 1998), further evidence that lethality alone is not the only index of VEO performance that indicates the effectiveness or success of terrorists. Also noteworthy is the fact that much of the initial speculation regarding the initiators of the attack focused on al-Qaeda, later proven not to be the perpetrators, a testament to the strong brand reputation of that organization.

VEOs may engage in behaviors that are inhumane above and beyond the lethality of their mission in order to gain media attention or prominence in the minds of stakeholders (Gil *et al.* 2013). For instance, while the videotaped beheading of journalist Daniel Pearl resulted in only one death, it created substantial psychological damage for the millions who viewed or read about the event. As with any organization, additional efforts made by VEOs to differentiate themselves are expected to be related the strength of the organization's ideology or brand image. Based on the research supporting the link between brand image and efforts to differentiate in the branding and market literature, the following conceptual model is proposed relating to VEOs:

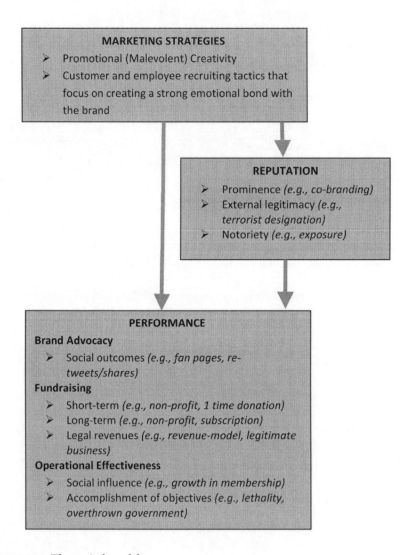

FIGURE 20.1 Theoretical model

The model

The proposed model is parsimonious. VEOs that implement effective marketing strategies should see their reputation enhanced. Those same strategies and the prominent reputation to which they contribute will positively impact their performance. The difficulty lies in developing effective measures that can demonstrate the model's ability to predict important outcomes. Before discussing empirical methods of testing this model, let us apply the model in full to a historically notable VEO with known performance outcomes: The Japanese Red Army (1971–2001).

Application: the branding story of the Japanese Red Army

The Japanese Red Army (JRA) leveraged high profile attacks to gain notoriety for its leftist cause throughout Israel, Singapore, and Palestine. The attack at Lod Airport in Tel Aviv on May 30, 1972 demonstrated malevolent (promotional) creativity as this group met religious travelers at baggage claim and aimed deliberately at them. The attack, sophisticated and well-planned, allowed JRA members to coordinate grenade explosions with ammunition reloads, thus creating a steady stream of attacks even when one member needed to tend to his weapon. The attack, which lasted 30 minutes, left 26 people dead and 80 seriously injured (Burns 2000). Two of the assailants committed suicide immediately to avoid arrest, while the third was arrested and later imprisoned in Israel (Farrell 1990).

As a result of this attack, air transportation was changed forever. Given the great deal of media attention the attack garnered (notoriety), Israel instated extensive security measures at all airports, and the West followed suit within months (Farrell 1990). In addition, other VEOs formed formal alliances, or co-branded, with JRA. For example, the Palestinian Liberation Front Party (PLFP) later released videos of JRA members at its training camps and other recruitment films (Box and McCormack 2004). Finally, the US designated JRA as a Foreign Terrorist Organization in 1997 given escalation of activities (Foreign Terrorist Organizations n.d.).

While social media were not as prevalent during the JRA reign, brand advocacy could be measured by the distribution of the recruiting films the group produced (Box and McCormack 2004). In addition, the group engaged in a series of fundraising strategies that were both short-term (e.g., bank robberies) and long-term (e.g., hijacking planes to negotiate with the Japanese government for a ransom of $6 million). In terms of operational effectiveness, JRA did see a rise in membership, particularly in the 1980s and 1990s when they were seen as the most powerful terrorist group on airplanes. They also accomplished additional objectives, such as prisoner release. Just 13 years after one of the Lod Airport attackers was imprisoned, JRA successfully negotiated with Israel for his early release from a life sentence (Smith 2007). It seems the imprisonment and deradicalization of the group's leader Shigenobu Fusako, a living symbol of the JRA brand, was the catalyst to the group's disbanding in 2001. The group was officially taken off of the FTO (foreign terrorist organization) list in 2001.

Next steps: empirically testing the model

Similar to more conventional research, there exist government terrorism databases (e.g., the Global Terrorism Database, LaFree and Dugan 2007) that provide a starting point in testing empirical models based on the theoretical constructs framed here. These, in conjunction with scholarly publications in the terrorism domain (e.g., *Terrorism and Political Violence Journal*) and publicly available records (e.g., news reports, government records), provide sound avenues for developing measures in an open-source method. In developing ideas for empirically testing the model developed here, we worked from an interdisciplinary understanding, whereby we took traditional measures and identified measurable markers of them for a VEO context. Below are examples of various strategies we suggest for empirically examining the proposed relationships.

First, let us consider how to measure marketing strategies. Promotional creativity, taken in the VEO context, becomes the malevolent creativity of a VEO's terrorist attacks. A Likert-type assessment could be developed that would take into consideration the overall cost of the activity weighed against its impact. Effective customer recruiting tactics designed to gain new followers or subscriptions following an ad campaign could be similarly applied to VEO's by measuring the number of new followers or growth in membership following a terrorist attack.

Moving on to consider ways in which to measure reputation, just as we take stock of co-branding arrangements between traditional organizations (e.g., McDonalds and Disney), one could quantitatively assess a VEO's relationships with other groups such as al Qaeda's training of Jemaah Islamiyah soldiers. External legitimacy is granted through third parties. For instance, in determining the legitimacy of a traditional organization, we might use a ranking measure (e.g., Fortune 500, US News and World Report MBA rankings) or a government certifi-cation (e.g., a member of the Better Business Bureau). This is easily transferrable to the VEO context, wherein one could assess a VEO's external legitimacy by counting the number of foreign terrorist designations (FTOs) it holds. FTO designation means that anyone who is found contributing funds to the organi-zation can have *all* of their assets frozen, thus indicating that foreign governments consider the VEO to be a prominent threat. Notoriety, or celebrity status, is traditionally linked to an organization's figurehead and the amount of media exposure he or she garners. Such exposure in the VEO context can be evaluated by assessing the number of media hits a given VEO receives and evaluating the valence of those hits (e.g., moderately positive, extremely negative).

Finally, we turn to performance. Just as brand advocacy might be measured in terms of known supporters of a traditional organization, we could also measure brand advocacy by the membership of the VEO, as it is assumed that any member of a VEO is an advocate for its cause – or brand. While sales or financial performance is often what we measure in terms of performance of more traditional organizations, in the VEO space, we turn to fundraising as an important performance outcome with multiple indicators (Freeman 2011). Some VEO revenue comes in the form of one-time donations to the cause. Longer reaching are the funds that come into the organization via pledged ongoing support from sympathizers, the equivalent of a subscription business model. Most of these individuals may believe they are actually donating to a humanitarian cause rather than supporting the violent actions of a VEO (e.g., the Tamil Tigers of Sri Lanka launched a long-term donor campaign for repressed Tamil minorities and then funneled profits to weapons acquisition; Flanigan 2008). Even more important for sustaining a VEO over time is the legitimate business model of funding in which the VEO owns and operates a legal business and funnels its profits into VEO activities. For example, the US Department of Treasury lists hundreds of organizations on its Specially Designated Nationals List (SDN) that are owned or controlled by VEOs or their members. While Executive Order 13224 prohibits US citizens from donating to groups on the FTO list, more successful VEOs develop business models and financial acumen to rival conventional organizations. For example, the Provisional Irish Republican Army (PIRA) owns a portfolio of small businesses, such as supermarkets, cafes, pubs, and slot machines, in Belfast, Derry, and other counties. It also has extensive property investments (Moloney 2003).

We could also consider performance in terms of operational effectiveness. Management research would look at this through measures of slack or fiscal efficiency, whereas branding research might consider growth of followers or increase in sales following the launch of a new advertising campaign. Within the VEO context, we could consider performance in terms of its growth in social influence, such as growth in membership or span of reach. Alternatively, we could also measure a VEO's performance in a more traditional sense, in terms of its lethality. As demonstrated here, there exist concrete methods for examining these non-traditional organizations utilizing measures that are not that dissimilar to measures commonly applied in branding research.

Conclusion

Preliminary evidence suggests that the model does indeed predict the performance outcomes of VEOs included in the START database (Ligon *et al.* 2014c). This suggests that the model could be applied to startup VEOs, allowing governments to intercede before branding tactics allow them to produce the performance outcomes included in the model. This study exemplifies the notion that branding relationship strategies are not limited to traditional commercialized firms and contributes to the fledgling research on nontraditional branding. It further suggests that other branding concepts may also be effective in studying these non-traditional organizations. For example, customer relationship management (CRM), supply chain management, and social media marketing tactics are all employed by

VEOs, yet we know very little about the differences that are indicative of these strategies when carried out by these organizations.

We know that people turn to strong brands for support when they are lonely (Holt 2002, 2004; Puzakova *et al.* 2009) or frightened (Dunn and Hoegg 2013). When the chosen brand is a VEO, however, that support may actually serve to enhance that fear or loneliness, thus creating a vicious cycle that reinforces the relationship with the brand. VEOs, when viewed as brands, represent strong symbols, beacons calling out to the disenfranchised and zealous, and the actions of those who are drawn to these extreme brands take on added significance due to the deadly ramifications of their advocacy. Therefore, the ability of researchers to predict which VEO will be the "next big thing" in terror takes business research to a higher level of relevance to society at large.

References

Al-Monitor Website (2014), "Rift Grows between Jabhat al-Nusra and ISIS", www.al-monitor.com/pulse/ar/security/2013/11/isis-jabhat-nusra-rift-syria-jordan-1.html#, accessed July 25, 2014.

Asal, V. and R.K. Rethemeyer (2008) "The Nature of the Beast: Organizational Structures and the Lethality of Terrorist Attacks", *The Journal of Politics*, 70 (April): 437–449.

Batra, R., A. Ahuvia, and R.P. Bagozzi (2012) "Brand Love", *Journal of Marketing*, 76 (2): 1–16.

Belk, R.W. and G. Tumbat (2005) "The Cult of Macintosh", *Consumption Markets and Culture*, 8 (3): 205–217.

Box, M. and G. McCormack (2004) "Terror in Japan: The Red Army (1969–2001) and Aum Supreme Truth (1987–2000)", *Critical Asian Studies*, 36 (1): 91–112.

Burns, J. (2000) "Lebanon Grants Political Asylum to 1 of 5 Japan Terrorists", *The New York Times*, March 18, www.nytimes.com/2000/03/18/world/lebanon-grants-political-asylum-to-1-of-5-japan-terrorists.html, accessed January 21, 2014.

Carroll, B.A. and A.C. Ahuvia (2006) "Some Antecedents and Outcomes of Brand Love", *Marketing Letters*, 17 (2): 79–89.

Clark, B.H. and D.B. Montgomery (1998) "Deterrence, Reputations, and Competitive Cognition", *Management Science*, 44 (1): 62–82.

Chaudhuri, A. and M.B. Holbrook (2001) "The Chain of Effects from Brand Trust and Brand Affect to Brand Performance: The Role of Brand Loyalty", *Journal of Marketing*, 65 (2): 81–93.

Crenshaw, M. (2014) "Mapping Militant Organizations", http://web.stanford.edu/group/mappingmilitants/cgi-bin/groups, accessed July 25, 2014

Dierickx, I. and K. Cool (1989) "Asset Stock Accumulation and Sustainability of Competitive Advantage", *Management Science*, 35 (12): 1504–1511.

Drake, C.J. (1998) "The Role of Ideology in Terrorists' Target Selection", *Terrorism and Political Violence Journal*, 10 (2): 53–85.

Dunn, L. and J.A. Hoegg (2013) "The Impact of Fear on Emotional Brand Attachment", conference paper presented at *Consumer-Brand Relationships Conference*, May 20, Boston, MA.

Fader, P.S. and D.C. Schmittlein (1993) "Excess Behavioral Loyalty for High-Share Brands: Deviations from the Dirichlet Model for Repeat Purchasing", *Journal of Marketing Research*, 30 (4): 478–493.

Farrell, W.R. (1990) *Blood and Rage – The Story of the Japanese Red Army*. Lexington, MA: Lexington Books.

Fedorikhin, A., C.W. Park, and M. Thomson (2008) "Beyond Attitude and Fit: The Effect of Emotional Attachment on Consumer Responses to Brand Extensions", *Journal of Consumer Psychology*, 18 (4): 281–291.

Flanigan, S.T. (2008) "Nonprofit Service Provision by Insurgent Organizations: The Cases of Hizballah and the Tamil Tigers", *Studies of Conflict and Terrorism*, 31 (6): 499–518.

Fombrun, C. and M. Shanley (1990) "What's in a Name? Reputation Building and Corporate Strategy", *Academy of Management Journal*, 33 (2): 233–258.

Foreign Terrorist Organizations, Bureau of Counterterrorism, US Department of State, www.state.gov/j/ct/rls/other/des/123085.htm, accessed February 20, 2015.

Fournier, S. (1998) "Consumers and Their Brands: Developing Relationship Theory in Consumer Research", *Journal of Consumer Research*, 24 (March): 343–353.

Freeman, M. (2011) *Financing Terrorism Case Studies*. Farnham: Ashgate.

Gill, P., J. Horgan, S.T. Hunter, and L.D. Cushenberry (2013) "Malevolent Creativity in Terrorist Organizations", *The Journal of Creative Behavior*, 47 (2): 125–151.

Holt, D.B. (2002) "Why Do Brands Cause Trouble? A Dialectical Theory of Consumer Culture and Branding", *Journal of Consumer Research*, 29 (1): 70–90.

Holt, D.B. (2004) *How Brands Become Icons: The Principles of Cultural Branding*. Boston, MA: Harvard Business School Press.

Horgan, J. (2013) *Psychology of Terrorism*. London: Routledge.

Hubbard, B. (2014) "The Franchising of Al Qaeda", *New York Times*, January 25, www.nytimes.com/2014/01/26/sunday-review/the-franchising-of-al-qaeda.html?_r=0, accessed July 25, 2014.

Jensen, J. (2014) "ISIS Making Good on Promise to Kill Christians", www.10news.com/news/isis-making-good-on-promise-to-kill-christians-07212014), accessed July 21, 2014.

Keller, K.L. (2013) *Strategic Brand Management: Building, Measuring, and Managing Brand Equity* (4th Edn). New York: Prentice-Hall.

Kotler, P. and K.L. Keller (2011) *A Framework for Marketing Management* (5th Edn). New York: Prentice-Hall.

Krause-Jackson, F. and T. Capaccio (2011) "Al-Qaeda Saw 'Opportunity' in Killing Journalist Daniel Pearl in Pakistan", *Bloomberg*, January 20, www.bloomberg.com/ news/2011-01-20/al-qaeda-saw-daniel-pearl-kidnapping-a-target-of-opportunity-study-says.html, accessed July 25, 2014.

LaFree, G. and L. Dugan (2007) "Introducing the Global Terrorism Database", *Terrorism and Political Violence*, 19: 181–204.

Lentini, P. and M. Bakashmar (2007) "Jihadist Beheading: A Convergence of Technology, Theology, and Teleology?", *Studies of Conflict and Terrorism*, 30 (4): 302–325.

Ligon, G.S. (2012) *Organizational Determinants of Violence and Performance*. Grant Proposal to National Consortium on Studies of Terrorism and Responses to Terrorism (START), Department of Homeland Security Center of Excellence.

Ligon, G.S., D. Derrick, and M. Harms (2014a) "Convergence of Cyber and CWMD in Non State Actors", Final Technical Report for United States Strategic Command, Task Order 30.

Ligon, G.S., M. Harms, and D.J. Harris (2014b) "Organizational Determinants of Violence and Performance: START L.E.A.D.I.R. Study and Dataset", Final Technical Report Brief for the Department of Homeland Security and the National Consortium for the Studies of Terrorism and Responses to Terrorism.

Ligon, G.S., Z. Leahy, M. Versella, C. Troyan, and C. Gibson (2010) "Structure Differences between Violent and Non-Violent Ideological Organizations", Paper presented at the 2010 *Society of Industrial and Organizational Psychology Annual Conference*, Atlanta, GA.

Ligon, G.S., P. Simi, M. Harms, and D.J. Harris (2013) "Putting the 'O' in VEOs: What Makes an Organization?" *Dynamics of Asymmetric Conflict*, 6 (1–3): 1–25.

Ligon, G., M. Breazeale, E. Pleggenkuhle-Miles, M. Harms, and S. Woracek (2014c) "Branding Destruction: Applying a Marketing Framework to the Notoriety of Violent Extremist Organizations", working paper, University of Nebraska, Omaha.

McCauley, C.R. and S. Moskalenko (2008) "Mechanisms of Political Radicalization: Pathways toward Terrorism", *Terrorism and Political Violence*, 20 (3): 415–433.

Moloney, E. (2003) *A Secret History of the IRA*. New York: W.W. Norton and Co.

Moran, L. (2013) "WestJet Airlines Surprises Passengers with Gifts after They Touch Down from Flights", *New York Daily News,* December 11, www.nydailynews.com/news/world/airline-surprises-passengers-christmas-gifts-article-1.1544292, accessed July 25, 2014.

Muniz Jr., A.M. and T.C. O'Guinn (2001) "Brand Community", *Journal of Consumer Research*, 27 (4): 412–432.

National Commission on Terrorist Attacks (2004), *The 9/11 Commission Report: Final Report of the National Commission on Terrorist Attacks Upon the United States.* New York: Norton.

National Consortium for the Study of Terrorism and Responses to Terrorism (START) (2012) "Global Terrorism Database", www.start.umd.edu/gtd, accessed July 25, 2014.

Puzakova, M., H. Kwak, and J.F. Rocereto (2009) "Pushing the Envelope of Brand and Personality: Antecedents and Moderators of Anthropomorphized Brands", *Advances in Consumer Research*, 36: 413–420.

Ranft, A.L., G.R. Ferris, R. Zinko, and M.R. Buckley (2006) "Marketing the Image of Management: The Costs and Benefits of CEO Reputation", *Organizational Dynamics*, 35 (3): 279–290.

Rindova, V.P. and C. Fombrun (1999) "Constructing Competitive Advantage: The Role of Firm-Constituent Interactions", *Strategic Management Journal*, 20: 691–710.

Rindova, V.P., T.G. Pollock, and M.L.A. Hayward (2006) "Celebrity Firms: The Social Construction of Market Popularity", *Academy of Management Review*, 31 (January): 50–71.

Rindova, V.P., I.O. Williamson, A.P. Petkova, and J.M. Sever (2005) "Being Good or Being Known: An Empirical Examination of the Dimensions, Antecedents, and Consequences of Organizational Reputation", *Academy of Management Journal*, 48 (December): 1033–1049.

Roberts, P.W. and G.R. Dowling (2002) "Corporate Reputation and Sustained Superior Financial Performance", *Strategic Management Journal*, 23 (12): 1077–1093.

Sageman, M. (2008) *Leaderless Jihad*. Philadelphia, PA: University of Pennsylvania Press.

Shamsie, J. (2003) "The Context of Dominance: An Industry-Driven Framework for Exploiting Reputation", *Strategic Management Journal*, 24 (3): 199–215.

Simi, P. and R. Futrell (2010) *American Swastika: Inside the White Power Movement's Hidden Spaces of Hate*. New York: Rowman and Littlefield.

Sly, L. (2014) "Al-Qaeda Disavows any Ties with Radical Islamist ISIS Group in Syria, Iraq", *The Washington Post*, February 3, www.washingtonpost.com/ world/middle_east/al-qaeda-disavows-any-ties-with-radical-islamist-isis-group-in-syria-iraq/2014/02/03/2c9afc3a-8cef-11e3-98ab-fe5228217bd1_story.html, accessed November 6, 2015.

Smith, P.J. (2007) *The Terrorism Ahead: Confronting Transnational Violence in the Twenty-First Century*. Armonk, NY: M.E. Sharpe.

Thomson, M., D.J. MacInnis, and C. Whan Park (2005) "The Ties That Bind: Measuring the Strength of Consumers' Emotional Attachments to Brands", *Journal of Consumer Psychology*, 15 (1): 77–91.

Wiktorowicz, Q. (2013) Working to Counter Online Radicalization to Violence in the United States, February 5, www.whitehouse.gov/blog/2013/02/05/working-counter-online-radicalization-violence-united-states, accessed July 25, 2014.

21
IDENTITY TENSIONS IN BUSINESS-BASED BRAND RELATIONSHIPS

Benjamin Lawrence and Patrick J. Kaufmann

Chick-fil-A is a privately held family owned business that was started in 1946 by Truett Cathy. Since then, the company has steadily grown and is currently the largest quick-service chicken restaurant chain in the United States with over 4.6 billion in sales and 1,700 restaurants (www.chick-fil-a.com). Low franchisee turnover, 5 percent a year, is attributed to highly committed franchisees that identify strongly with the company, its brand, and its values (Schmall 2007). Chick-fil-A carefully selects individual franchisees that believe in its faith-based corporate purpose "to glorify God by being a faithful steward of all that is entrusted to us," and asks questions about family and faith during the interview process (Ventura 2006). In line with its values, it is closed on Sundays so that all "franchised Chick-fil-A operators and restaurant employees should have an opportunity to rest, spend time with family and friends, and worship if they choose to do so" (www.chick-fil-a.com). Franchisees feel like part of this franchise family and care deeply for Cathy and the organization. In return, they work tirelessly towards success (Ventura 2006; Schmall 2007; Dobrzynski 1996). This model of selecting and socializing franchisees to identify strongly with the organization and its values is not unique to Chick-fil-A. Other distribution systems including direct selling organizations such as Amway, Shaklee, and Mary Kay, also engender strong identification between contractors and the organization (Pratt and Foreman 2000; Biggart 1989). These companies encourage and successfully develop emotional attachments between their independent contractors and the identities of their organizations, founders, and brands. They reinforce the roles that their operators value and seek.

In this chapter, we explore the relationships that channel members have with the brands and companies they represent. We draw on ethnographic research to explore two primary identity tensions observed in one prominent form of distribution – franchising. We also provide some preliminary quantitative work in support of our qualitative findings. We posit that channel members seek relationship partners that reinforce one of four unique identity types and their associated values. Tensions arise between franchisees and their corporate partners when conflicting roles surrounding these two key dimensions of identity are imposed by the organization.

Identity and identification

Identification and identity are interrelated constructs. An individual or organization constructs its identity through the process of identification, a process of coming to know who we are in relation to environmental objects. Identification has been described as the process in which an individual comes to see an object (e.g., an individual, group, organization, symbol, product) as being definitive of oneself or, as Pratt (1998) terms, the object as "self referential." Identification is a cognitive perception of psychological interconnectiveness with a target object when an individual forms a psychological connection with that object. Thus, identification is the degree to which a person defines himself with the same attributes as the target object. This psychological connectedness does not necessarily imply behavioral or affective antecedents or outcomes of such identity overlap including loyalty or prosocial behavior (Ashforth and Mael 1989). Identification simply describes the "oneness" of self and object and not the potential outcomes including attachment and commitment.

Within the field of organizational behavior, various theoretical approaches have been applied to the study of identification including social identity theory (Tajfel and Turner 1979) and identity/role theory (Stryker 1968). Role theory takes a sociological approach and examines identity construction through the enactment of salient roles. It is through the enactment of these roles with others that individuals come to view their own identity.

Identification in marketing has focused primarily on consumers and four main foci of identity construction: the product or object (Richins 1994; Belk 1988; Ball and Tasaki 1992; Wallendorf and Arnould 1988), brand (Fournier 1998; Escalas and Bettman 2003) or brand community (McAlexander *et al.* 2002; Schouten and McAlexander 1995; Muñiz and O'Guinn 2001) and more recently the company (Bhattacharya and Sen 2003; Ahearne, Bhattacharya, and Gruen 2005). Branding scholars have talked about identification processes as central to understanding a consumer's relationship with those objects (Fournier 1998). A large stream of research points to the importance of object and symbols, including brands in the construction of one's self concept, in expressing one's identity and in developing consumers' relations with brands or objects. Researchers have embraced the constructs of attachment *et al.* 2005, 89), extended-self (Ball and Tasaki 1992; Wallendorf and Arnould 1988; Tian and Belk 2005; Kleine *et al.* 1995), and self-brand connections (Escalas 1997; Escalas 2004; Escalas and Bettman 2000; Escalas and Bettman 2003) in defining a consumer's identity overlap with brands or objects. Strong attachment to an object (brand) is predicated on overlap of the characteristics between the focal object and the self, while self-brand connection is defined as the extent to which individuals have incorporated brands into their self-concept (Escalas and Bettman 2000). Similarly, extensions of the self are predicated on identification processes linking the self with the object.

As the importance of such identifications with brands and the communities they engender have taken a prominent role in marketing theory and practice, corporate management of brand identity, including a set of associations about the brand, has been heralded as the "cornerstone" of successful brand strategy (Aaker 1991; Aaker 1996; Keller 1993). Such brand strategy involves managing multiple facets of brand identity with both internal and external stakeholders. This view of branding assumes that the firm has control of the brand identity and, through management of the brand associations, can engender various stakeholders to identify with them. Unlike a postmodern view of branding in which stakeholders are meaning-makers in the brand identity process, creating and enhancing identification with the brand, Aaker's view of branding mirrors that of corporate identity scholars (Olins 1992; Margulies 1977; Van Riel and Balmer 1997; Balmer 1998) in that the distinctive identity of the corporation is controlled and communicated to various stakeholders.

The study of identity and identification has also taken on increased importance within the domain of organizational behavior as traditional company structures have given way to greater mobility and disaggregation between the workforce and the integration of more non-traditional work relations (Pfeffer and Baron 1988). Within marketing, many channel relations take on such disaggregated structures as agents of the firm work to distribute products, acting as intermediaries between the company and the consumer. Though these agents work outside the traditional boundaries of the firm, they are often considered, by themselves and the firm, as members of the overall organization. Two exemplars of such relational forms include direct selling and franchising, where individuals work as independent agents, but take on the identity of the firm in their interactions with the consumer. In such contexts, identification between the individual and firm has been explored by sociologists and organizational theorists (e.g., Biggart 1989; Pratt 2000). However, in the field of marketing channels, researchers have failed, for the most part, to explore the impact of identity alignment or misalignment between such agents and principals (for exceptions see Grayson 2007; Heide and Wathne 2006, Hughes and Ahearne 2010). Though norms have been posited as a way to reduce opportunism (and the commensurate monitoring costs) by aligning the self-interests of channel members (Brown et al. 2000; Heide and John 1992), the specific role of identification of channel members with the brand or corporate partner has not been thoroughly investigated.

Franchising, one prominent form of channel relationship, provides an excellent context to examine identity-based relationships. Charismatic franchise pioneers such as Ray Kroc (McDonald's), Colonel Saunders (KFC), and Truett Cathy built franchise systems with highly committed franchisees that identified strongly with the franchisor (Dobrzynski 1996; Darden 2002; Love 1986). Franchising agreements create a unique relationship between franchisor and franchisee. A franchisee, although an independent legal entity, often resembles a quasi-employee of the firm. Unlike traditional employees, franchisees exist outside the boundaries of the firm, yet they can potentially have long term, multi-generational relationships with the systems and brands within which they operate. Unlike employees who have a hierarchical relationship with the firm, franchisees often view themselves as independent contractors who are in a partnership with the franchisor. Like contract workers (George and Chattopadhyay 2005) or union members (Fullagar and Barling 1991), franchisees have multiple, sometimes competing, work groups with which to identify.

Methodology and data

This chapter is informed by qualitative fieldwork and quantitative surveys reported in other work (Lawrence and Kaufmann 2011, Lawrence and Kaufmann 2014). Three sources of data were used in the ethnographic stage of data collections: secondary data available via mass media channels, participant observations at franchisee events, including association conferences, and unstructured interviews with those with experience with franchising. Formal interviewees were purposively sampled (Patton 2001). In addition to the 36 recorded interviews, informal discussions with over 100 individual franchisees helped to inform this chapter. Our quantitative data included survey data collected from three companies in two distinct industries resulting in 207 completed surveys, a total response rate of 14 percent. In order to capture the cognitive connection between franchisees and the companies and brands they represent, we utilized scales in the literature used to measure identification. These measures provided a simple and well accepted measure of the cognitive connection between franchisee and franchisor. Please see an adapted version of Bergami and Bagozzi's pictoral scale (2000) of identification (Appendix 21.1). Organizational identity type was measured using a scale adapted from Deshpandé *et al.* (1993) that was constructed from the work of Quinn (1988) (see Appendix 21.2).

Identity value dimensions

As mentioned previously, organizational identity scholars have highlighted competing identity claims in organizations as potential sources of conflict (e.g., Golden-Biddle and Rao 1997; Glynn 2000; Foreman and Whetten 2002). Organizations can also have hybrid identities (Golden-Biddle and Rao 1997; Glynn 2000) with both normative (e.g., we are a family) and utilitarian (e.g., we are a profit center) dimensions. Such hybrid identities cause tension for the organization as members work to resolve the contradiction when seemingly opposing identities co-exist. The literature on brand identity points to the importance of brand personality, defined as the set of human characteristics associated with a given brand, as central to consumers' identification processes (Aaker 1997). Like brands, an organization's identity has been proposed as an analog to an individual's personality (Whetten 2006). Our qualitative data initially revealed several salient tensions between the individual franchisee and franchisor. These tensions revolved around six identity dimensions (communal–individualistic, secure–venturesome, aggressive–satisfied, autonomous–dependent, stable–dynamic and nostalgic–progressive). In accessing the literature in franchising and more broadly in channels of distribution, these tensions were further condensed to encompass two primary tensions around the roles of an entrepreneur and employee and the roles of a family member and investor. Tensions arise between the franchisee, who represents the brand, and the franchisor when conflicting roles surrounding these two key dimensions of identity are imposed.

The franchise family

> This brand is all about family – my own family, your family, and the KFC franchisee family … What really makes KFC so special is the number of second- and third-generation franchisees in the business who are building on what their parents or grandparents started. This brand is all about family – families in the business and the KFC franchisee family – franchisees helping one another as family.
>
> *(KFC Franchisee)*

During our fieldwork, we were often struck by the common use of the family metaphor to describe franchisee system membership. Though some have referred to the franchise relationship as a marriage (Bradach 1998), a metaphor used to describe interorganizational commitment (Morgan and Hunt 1994), few researchers have examined the familial type of relationships embedded in channels of distribution (see Biggart 1989 for an exception). While observing franchisee behavior, we witnessed close bonds and affection between longtime franchisees and the brands they inhabit. Iconic founders are often described as father figures.

> And so [the founder] was "the dad." And he had this dream and this belief, and he built the company. He really believed that if his franchisees were successful, then he would be successful … It was a family.
>
> *(Tom)*

> Now [the Founder] didn't have any money … in those days people were very friendly and everything. They'd ask [the Founder] if he'd wanna stay with 'em, and he'd love it, 'cause otherwise he was sleeping in his car; he couldn't afford a motel. And, so, he then became friends and family with all these various people he was bringing into his family [The Franchise]. He always thought about it as his family [The Franchise]…
>
> *(Susan)*

Susan feels a moral responsibility to help other community members. She describes a time when she was ready to purchase a new store but found a franchisee who was closer who wanted the territory.

> Well, I found out another man, Jeff Smithton, was closer, and he wanted the territory. So I said, oh great Jeff, go for it. You know, I mean, gave him my information and everything. Well, I thought I was closer, and the company told me I could have it – never any conflict. It was just, you know, my brother wanted it, and so go for it Jeff.
>
> *(Susan)*

She describes her community as unique and special.

> You know, it's just … we have a different feeling among ourselves than any other group that I've ever seen, including [franchise system] or [franchise system]. [Franchise system] franchisees are, what's best for me, you know. And, we don't feel that way. It's what's best for our fellow franchisee and the family.
>
> *(Susan)*

Given the influx of new franchisees and changes in ownership over time, considerable tension revolves around norms of a family relationship versus those of a business. The coexistence of norms of business and friendship has been highlighted as one tension that exists among organizations (Albert and Whetten 1985; Golden-Biddle and Rao 1997) and between exchange partners (Price and Arnould 1999; Heide and Wathne 2006; Grayson 2007). In describing these social relations as embodied in organizations, early work on organizational identity adopted two basic identity types – normative and utilitarian (Albert and Whetten 1985). Quinn's (1988) competing values model highlights the "human relations model" and the "rational goal model" as embodying these two competing values. The human relations model embodies values of a family where loyalty, cohesion, teamwork, and personal relations define the organization. In contrast, the rational goal model embodies values of the marketplace, where achievement, competition, production, and aggressiveness define its culture. This framework of competing values has been adopted by marketing researchers (Deshpandé *et al.* 1993) in examining the influence of culture on customer orientation of the firm. In their framework, Deshpande *et al.* use the terms "clan" and "market" to describe these two competing organizational types.

Heide and Wathne (2006) propose that gaps between governance structures that reflect such values and the identity roles assumed by exchange partners (friend or businessperson roles) can lead to mismatches. They propose that such mismatches can lead to higher governance costs and retaliatory actions by exchange partners. Different franchisees within a singular franchise system may adopt different role identities, one embodying communal qualities (I am a family member that takes care of other members) and the other embodying individualistic qualities (I am an investor and have no loyalty to my fellow franchisees that don't produce). The salient contrast or assimilation between these identities is fundamental to understanding an individual franchisee's identification in such systems. Long time franchisees who have been socialized to internalize family values with their brand adopt a communal orientation. When the organization fails to live up to these communal brand values and acts in accordance with market values of self interest, tensions between the values of the organization and franchisee emerge. Newer franchisees that have not been acculturated to this communal orientation fail to experience this tension, as their role aligns with that of an investor whose purpose is self-interest driven profit seeking. In fact, new franchisees may fail to identify with the system that continues to treat its members in a communal fashion (i.e., forgiving franchisees that fail to perform).

The rugged entrepreneur

Overall, franchisees view themselves as fundamentally different from company employees and, more generally, from the population as a whole. Franchisees often speak about franchising in terms of an entrepreneurial spirit or protestant ethic (Weber 2002), embodying values of industriousness, self-reliance, independence, and moral fortitude, and also look to their relationship with the brand to reinforce these values. These values of hard work and resilience are exemplified by the quotes of famous franchise founders: Colonel Sanders in his mantra *The Hard Way*, Dave Thomas of Wendy's,[1] Ray Kroc of McDonalds,[2] and Tom Monaghan of Domino's.[3] The franchisee gatherings we attended frequently echoed this belief in hard work and moral fortitude. These values were instilled in the brand and in its associated meanings, often including the symbolic markers of the founders and their entrepreneurial ethic. Tensions between franchisee and franchisor often revolved around limiting franchisee autonomy. James has been a franchisee since 1974, when he "saw an ad in the *LA Times* that said, 'be your own boss, own a [franchise name] franchise'". For James, being a franchisee is all about fulfilling his role as an independent operator and being a rugged individualist. Identity tensions arise when the franchise system challenges his autonomy by working to centralize decision making and increase uniformity in the system.

> Everyone sees themselves as an independent contractor, and everyone wants their rights as independent contractors preserved. We didn't buy a job. We bought businesses because we're entrepreneurs, and sometimes that entrepreneurial spirit gets in the way. And [the franchisor] feels that there should be a more centralized view, or a more cohesive view, and, the way we see it is, we're all entrepreneurs, no one knows my neighborhood better than I do.
>
> *(James)*

James values his independence above all else. In fact, he views the image of a benevolent franchisor as antithetical to his views of franchising.

I was in a breakout session at an IFA, where a gentleman who was president and CEO of a franchise chain of dry cleaners, stood up and said that his philosophy was to treat his franchisees as a benevolent dictator. And I danced all over his head. I took over the room. I got a standing ovation. (Laugh) I mean because, I think the worse thing in the world any franchisor can do is be a benevolent dictator. It stifles growth. We didn't buy a job. If you wanna be a benevolent dictator, then run company stores and have employees and not franchisees. The minute you franchise, you're giving an entrepreneur a right to make a living and make decisions.

(James)

James's juxtaposition of an employee characterized as subordinate versus a self-governing franchisee was reiterated by others in his system and by the franchisee body at large. At their national franchisee conference, the loss of autonomy on the part of franchisees was a central theme in franchisee discussions.

During the question and answer session, a franchisee gets up and states that "if you take the entrepreneurial spirit out of this business this business will die." This feeling is particularly prevalent for longtime franchisees that have witnessed an erosion in their autonomy over time. Newer franchisees (many of which are former corporate employees) are thought to "toe the line" and don't know any better.

(Field notes)

Such tensions often surface when the franchise system tries to enforce policies to standardize operations or directly challenge the autonomy of individual franchisees by demanding uniformity. As a long time franchisee, James considers himself an expert on the local market, expertise that he has been able to apply and profit from because of his autonomy.

Sometimes they [the company] make suggestions and we say "what are they thinking?" And I don't wanna say I know it all, but I was 23 years old when I bought my store. And, there's been times when they've rolled out a program, and I've said, won't be here three months from now, and sure enough. And so I wish they would … take our local knowledge.

(James)

James is very proud of his store. During a personal tour, he highlighted how his store was different from other stores in his franchise system. His autonomy as an independent contractor afforded him the ability to profit from his extensive knowledge of his unique customers. Contrasting the value of his knowledge gained through autonomy with that of a hierarchical system based on subordination, James highlights the tension between the franchise system's identity and his own.

I believe that a teacher believes that he knows more than every one of his students. And I believe that a manager or supervisor believes that he's smarter than all the folks that work under him. That's why he's a manager or supervisor. The plant manager's smarter than the supervisor who's smarter than the foreman, who's smarter than all the workers. And ... it's really strange when I'm in Fresno sometimes, having a conversation with a category manager, who's ... hasn't been alive as long as I've been doing this. So I'm talkin' to some 30 year old, and I don't have anything against 30 year olds, but I'm talkin' to some 30 year old, who's telling me about his strategy to sell more product X. Yeah, and I'm like, utilize the knowledge from the street. But I think it's just human nature, that Fresno, the folks sitting in the ivory tower in Fresno, and I just say that as a term, the folks sitting in the ivory tower in Fresno, think they know more about convenience retailing than we do, when the, the reverse is obviously true.

I don't want some guy at headquarters in Fresno sitting down with Nabisco negotiating a deal that is quote unquote in my best interest. I want to sit down with Nabisco and negotiate the deal that is in my best interest. No one knows better than me what is best for me.

(James)

For James, the most salient identity tension revolves around values of autonomy and dependence. This was shared by others in the system who feel threatened when their roles of successful entrepreneurs are challenged by a franchisor who treats them as managers.

They are dictating things that are, in my opinion, completely out of the realm of their responsibilities. For example, telling you how many people, how many of your employees that you have, have to be certified order writers, and it's none of their business. I don't have any certified order writers, yet I've got the highest volume stores in Las Vegas; three years ago it was the highest volume store in the United States, and I don't have any certified order writers.

(Troy)

They wanna control everything ... they've narrowed it down to the point of where we have to buy everything from them, 85 percent has to come from their recommended sources, which leaves us a 15 percent leeway to buy from whom whomever we wish. So ... we're, we're, we're losing, we're losing our independent contractor status. They're not mentioning that, and they're not saying that, but basically we really are. We're just becoming glorified store managers as far as I can see. So there's a lot of unhappiness amongst the franchise community because of this. There's been a lot of people who have left the system because of this.

(Robert)

This infringement of autonomy includes steps to limit franchisee product selection, move to a uniform menu and service standards, and enforcement of capital investment requirements. These tensions are particularly acute in older systems, where the autonomy of longtime franchisees is often challenged with newer contracts that further limit franchisee autonomy. These feelings of autonomy may evolve over time as longtime franchisees view their knowledge as superior to the corporation and feel they can succeed independently of franchisor assistance. Moves by the corporation to usurp this autonomy by treating franchisees as employees who must follow rules are met with significant resistance in light of the perceived personal investment franchisees have made in the brands. In comparing their own situation with that of corporate employees, franchisees often state that they have "considerable skin in the game" and "If I can't pay the bills, no one is going to save me" while the corporate officers will just move on.

The franchise-relational form, unlike other entrepreneurial ventures results in "controlled self employment with an entrepreneurial partnership" (Weaven and Frazer 2006: 227). As self-employed, franchisees may see themselves as distinct from employees who are under the direct control of the firm. Yet, being contractually tied to the franchisor, they are also part of a larger organization that provides support on which they are dependent. The franchisor must balance perceptions of dependence and autonomy while working with a diverse set of franchisees (new vs. multi-generational franchisees, family owned versus multi-unit operators). Though franchisees are often sold on the fact that they are going to run their own business as independent contractors, they are in fact dependent, to a great extent, on the actions of the firm. Franchisees, therefore, can see the organization as either hierarchically authoritative or as a source of autonomy. Quinn (1988) identifies such contrasting organizations as either an "Open Systems Model" that embodies values of an "Adhocracy," where dynamism, innovation, and creativity define its culture, or as an "Internal Process Model" that embodies values of a "Hierarchy", where stability, control, and procedures define its culture. Deshpandé et al. (1993) also use the terms "Autocracy" and "Hierarchy" to describe these two competing organizational types.

Franchise researchers have highlighted autonomy as a key attribute in a franchisee's decision to enter into franchise relationships (Dant and Gundlach 1999; Kaufmann and Stanworth 1995). Franchisees with no prior experience with franchising may seek the independence promised under the mantra of "being your own boss." However, franchisees with prior self-employment experience may seek various dependence-based support features of franchising, including training and operational support. These initial perceptions of independence or dependence may also change over time. Older franchisees, feeling that they have developed an understanding of the system, are more likely to feel like they can succeed independent of the franchisor (Peterson and Dant 1990). A gap between a franchisee's perceived independence and the current organization's identity as it relates to facilitating such autonomy creates tension in such a system.

Other franchisees may seek a relationship with the organization that is highly structured and dependent. Individuals who have been self-employed may seek the comfort and support offered by a dependent franchise relationship. Take, for example, the following quote from a story about a Subway franchisee featured in a *New York Times* article on franchising.

> For Mr. Gurwitz, joining Subway was a welcome respite from the myriad decisions he has to make in running the convenience store, which he co-owns with his father. "They give you the operations manual, which is as thick as the New York City telephone book, and it tells you within a millimeter how thick to slice the onions," said Mr. Gurwitz, who spent two weeks at the Subway training center in Milford, Conn. "If you have a question about anything, you'll find it in the operations manual." Indeed, Mr. Gurwitz discovered that many issues were no longer his sole responsibility. "Someone stubs his toe in the store, you call the Subway legal department," he said. "How many convenience stores have a legal department?" Research and development, pricing and menus – all are handled for him. By contrast, he said, "With the convenience store, I'm everything."
>
> *(Flaherty 2001)*

Our fieldwork confirmed that some new smaller franchisees may seek franchising for the structured conformity and comfort that such a relationship brings. Deborah, a franchisee for seven years, describes such a relationship.

> I don't think you really have to have a business degree I think you have to be teachable and that's the key thing … at [orientation] they give you the basics, as I would assume most franchisors do. They give you everything you need to actually run the business.
>
> *(Deborah)*

When franchise systems mature, longtime franchisees increasingly view themselves as self-reliant, and tensions arise when an organization continues to treat them as subordinates when they view themselves as equal partners in the relationship. This may be particularly salient for franchisees when the legitimacy of franchisor management is brought into question. When founders transfer ownership to a new management team, they do not transfer the legitimacy and social capital that they often enjoy. Neither do founders transfer the entrepreneurial sprit with which they imbue the brand. How franchisees view the organization, as reaffirming such roles of entrepreneur or employee in such circumstances, is critical to understanding franchisee-franchisor relationships.

Identity dimension framework

The model shown in Figure 21.1 shows four types of organizational identity types: hierarchy, autocracy, clan and market. Tensions between hierarchy and autocracy

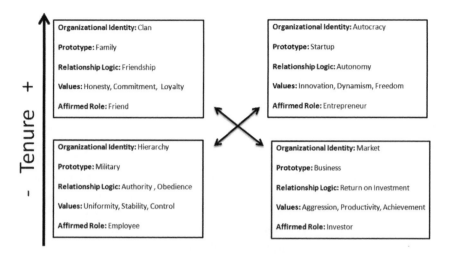

FIGURE 21.1 Identity dimension framework
Source: Adapted from: Quinn 1998, Deshpandé 1993

identities revolve around values related to autonomy and authority, while tensions between identities of a clan and market identities revolve around business norms of self interest and communal norms of loyalty and commitment. Each identity is detailed below.

We define a Hierarchy organizational identity, the prototype of which is a military organization, as based on obedience to authority. Members are controlled by procedures and rules that govern behavior and order relationships. Such organizations rely exclusively on norms of authority where values of uniformity, stability, and control dominate. Members follow policies and procedures in return for security and stability. The salient role that is reaffirmed is that of an employee who has no authority to question superiors, but follows scripts that define his or her appropriate behavior.

An Adhocracy identity, the prototype of which is a startup, is based on values of innovation, dynamism, and freedom. In such organizations, individuals are guided by the logic of autonomy where freedom to express new ideas and creativity is encouraged. These organizations rely on visionary leaders to guide their members' actions. The salient role that is reaffirmed is that of an entrepreneur who has complete authority to chart his or her own course.

We define a Market identity, the prototype of which is a business firm, as based on self-interest seeking economic rational behavior, where employees are controlled through monetary incentive. In such organizations, employees are paid for their work and, in exchange, are expected to produce goods equal to that value. Such organizations rely exclusively on norms of business (Heide and Wathne 2006) where individuals are calculative and are motivated by maximizing self-interest. An organization's actions, such as eliminating employees who fail to produce to their marginal cost, are accepted under such a business norm. In such a relationship, the role that is most strongly reaffirmed is that of an investor, whose interest in the relationship is driven solely by the expectation of profit and whose commitment to the organization is based on return, and not on an emotional attachment to the firm or its members.

In contrast to a Market identity, a Clan identity, the prototype of which is a family and exemplified by religious, political, or socially based organizations, is based on empathy, interdependence, caring, shared responsibility, and shared sacrifice. These organizations rely on normative control rather than economic incentive to guide their members' actions. Such organizations rely exclusively on norms of friendship (Heide and Wathne 2006), where individuals are cooperative and self-sacrificing. In such a relationship, the role that is most strongly reaffirmed is that of a family member whose interest in the relationship is driven by an emotional attachment to the organization and for caring for the good of the group.

Various models of organizational identification have proposed tenure with an organization as an antecedent of identification (Dutton *et al.* 1994; Bhattacharya *et al.* 1995; Mael and Ashforth 1992). Results investigating the relationship between tenure and higher levels of organizational identification have been mixed. Some researchers have found a positive relationship between tenure and identification (Barker and Tompkins 1994; Mael and Ashforth 1992), while others have found null effects (George and Chattopadhyay 2005; Ilyer *et al.* 1997). George and Chattopadhyay (2005) propose that mixed results may be because tenure acts as a step function, only becoming significant at certain junctures in the relationship. However, such mixed results could also point to more complex interaction between the multiple dimensions of the organizational identity over time.

As franchisees develop and maintain friendships with other franchisees and organizational members over time, tenure should enhance franchisees' communal identity orientation. Longtime franchisees are also more likely to have trans-generational and complex familial relationships with the brand. Family members may work together in multi-unit franchise companies or own independent franchise units within the same system. As business and family gatherings coexist and memories of such brand events are stored and retrieved from memory, the brand becomes a central focus of the family. Longtime franchisees, feeling that they have a thorough understanding of the system, are also more likely to feel as though they can succeed independent of the franchisor (Peterson and Dant 1990). Therefore, as franchisees' tenure in the system increases, role identities should align more with organizational identities that reflect the values of a clan and an autocracy.

Quantitative results

Even though we had hoped to compare across perceived identity types (i.e., by comparing those who perceive their organization as a Clan versus Market and

Hierarchy versus Autocracy), very few respondents rated their franchisor high on values reflected by a Clan or Autocracy (the top quartile of both consisted of ratings above only 20 points). Therefore, our analysis focuses on perceptions of one identity type (e.g., comparing those respondents rating their franchisor high on values of Market versus those rating their franchisor low on values of Market). Ratings for Market and Hierarchy identity types provided adequate distribution to allow for a comparison between those scoring in the upper quartile (Hierarchy ≥ 50, Market ≥ 40) versus lower quartile (Hierarchy ≤ 15, Market ≤ 10). Thus, we focus the following analysis on perceptions of franchisors on these two identity types.

In order to test the interaction of tenure on perceived identity, we conducted a mean split of tenure, creating two groups that comprised a similar number of respondents, one high in tenure (>10 years) and those low in tenure (≤10). As described above, we split organizational identity ratings into two groups: those who scored in the top quartile and those who scored in the bottom quartile. This created cell sizes that were large enough to satisfactorily test the hypothesis (Low Tenure/Low Hierarchy n=25, High Tenure/Low Hierarchy n=22, Low Tenure/High Hierarchy n=24, High Tenure/High Hierarchy n=27) (Low Tenure/Low Market n=33, High Tenure/Low Market n=24, Low Tenure/High Market n=18, High Tenure/High Market n=31).

We ran a 2(Tenure: Hi/Low) × 2(Identity Type: Hi/Low) ANCOVA controlling for company, number of outlets, brand identification, and brand-franchisor overlap. Results showed a significant interaction between the degree to which franchisees viewed the organization as having values of a market (Hi/Lo) and tenure in the organization (Hi/Lo) (F(2,97) = 11.93, p < 0.01) (see Figure

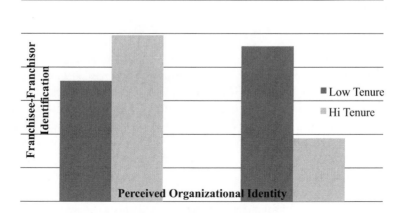

FIGURE 21.2 Perceived market identity × tenure

21.2). Planned contrasts show a significant difference in long term franchisees' identification across levels of perceived market identities ($M_{HiMarket}$ = 1.94, $M_{LowMarket}$ = 3.47; F (1,97) = 11.57, p < 0.01). Furthermore, when compared with older franchisees, newer franchisees have higher identification with a franchisor they view as high on market values ($M_{LowTenure}$ = 1.94, $M_{HiTenure}$ =3.31; F (1,151) = 8.44 p < 0.01). In regards to our predictions regarding identification with perceived hierarchical identities, results did not support our claim that longtime franchisees are more likely to identify with autocratic organizations. These null results may be the resultant of measurement error or sample bias due to our small sample size.

Conclusion

We argue that relationships between channel members are contingent on reaffirming certain role identities and the values associated with these identities. Perceptions that the franchisor is oriented towards values of a market are found to negatively impact longtime franchisees' identification with the franchisor. Though the data did not allow for a direct comparison between perceptions of a franchisor high in clan and business values, based on the competing values framework, the results suggest that when compared with short term franchisees, longtime franchisees will identify more strongly with a franchisor that is viewed as embodying the values of a clan.

The relationship between various foci of identity including the brand, corporate owners, founders, and collectives is an important avenue for future research. Competing identity claims are inevitable given that large conglomerates often own a portfolio of brands. Companies even hide the fact that competing identity claims may exist, for example, when a parent company owns a subsidiary and the brand identity of the subsidiary and that of the parent have opposing meanings (e.g., Dagoba and Cadbury, Odwalla and Pepsi, Tom's of Maine and Colgate-Palmolive, Burt's Bees and Clorox). Most consumers fail to gain such knowledge or have limited incentive to look for such information. However, there are instances when identity misalignment between the actions of the firm and the meanings of the brand are uncovered. Take, for example, Dove's "Real Beauty Campaign" that generated publicity when consumers revealed that Unilever, Dove's parent company, also owned Axe. If a corporation is seen to abandon its brand identity or fails to stay true to its brand promise, brand evangelists and passionate consumers can actively fight back by disidentifying with a company and its brand. In most consumer contexts, inconsistencies in brand identity lead the consumer to abandon the brand and seek an alternative brand that they feel aligns with their self-concept. However, in cases where the brand is so central to an individual's self-concept, as in the case of a longtime loyal user of the brand, an individual may create an alternative identity distinct from that which the corporation portrays. An individual may therefore continue to identify strongly with a brand by detaching the meanings of the brand from the corporation itself, thus maintaining a sense of cognitive consistency. The company may continue to reinforce one brand identity while the consumer or brand community constructs an alternative brand identity.

In a channel setting, such identity separation may be even more salient, given the nature of the relationship.

Future research needs to examine more closely the two related routes to identification, role reinforcement, and value congruency. Though identity theory and social identity theory have emerged from two separate theoretical camps (see Hogg *et al.* 1995; Stets and Burke 2000 for comparisons of the two theories), there seems to be considerable opportunity to examine the relationship between roles and values and their impact on brand relationships. Research in the consumer realm has focused exclusively on values as the driving force of identification (Bhattacharya *et al.* 1995; Bhattacharya and Sen 2003), while in the channel literature, roles have dominated (Heide and Wathne 2006; Grayson 2007). An interesting avenue for future research could examine potential conflicts that arise when a relationship partner in a channel setting reflects your values but treats you in a way that is incongruent with a salient role identity. For example, brands that espouse the values of friendship, but in interactions treat you as a business partner.

Lastly, future work should examine how business-based brand relationships differ from those in the consumer space. Given the commitment some channel members have with the brand and the potential for instability on the part of its corporate owners, future work should examine the unique relationship between a brand's identity and its corporate owners. Understanding these tensions has important implications for channel management.

Appendix

APPENDIX 21.1 Measure of perceived franchisor identity

1: What is (Franchisor) like? (Please distribute 100 points)

_____ points for A

(A) (Franchisor) is a very close knit group. They treat each other like an **extended family** and seem to share a lot of themselves with each other. **Loyalty and tradition** guide their actions and they emphasize **human resources.**

_____ points for B

(B) (Franchisor) is very **dynamic and entrepreneurial.** They are willing to stick their neck out and take risks. Commitment to **innovation** and **development** guide their actions and they emphasize **growth** and **acquiring new resources.**

_____ points for C

(C) (Franchisor) is very **formal and structured.** Established procedures generally govern what they do. **Formal rules and policies** guide their actions and they emphasize **permanence and stability.**

_____ points for D

(D) (Franchisor) is very **outcome and achievement oriented.** They are primarily concerned with getting the job done and being competitive. **Tasks and goal accomplishment** guide their actions and they emphasize **competitive actions and achievement.**

APPENDIX 21.2 Franchisor identification measure

> 4: Imagine that one of the circles on the left represents **your own self definition or identity** (who you are) and the other circle at the right represents (**Franchisor's) Identity** (who they are). Please check which letter best represents the level of overlap between your own and CI's identities.

ME   (Franchisor)

☐A: Far Apart

☐B: Close Together But Separate

☐C: Very Small Overlap

☐D: Small Overlap

☐E. Moderate Overlap

☐F: Large Overlap

☐G: Very Large Overlap

☐H: Complete Overlap

Notes

1   "If there are things you don't like in the world you grew up in, make your own life different."
2   "Luck is a dividend of sweat. The more you sweat, the luckier you get."
3   "No matter what an individual decides to become, hard work and determination is very important in today's competitive world. You may also encounter hardships along the way, but you must not get discouraged and you push on in order to fulfill your goals."

References

Aaker, D.A. (1991) *Managing Brand Equity: Capitalizing on the Value of a Brand Name*. New York: Free Press.

Aaker, D.A. (1996) *Building Strong Brands*. New York: Free Press.

Aaker, J.E. (1997) "Dimensions of Brand Personality", *Journal of Marketing Research*, 34 (3): 347–356.

Ahearne, M., C.B. Bhattacharya, and T. Gruen (2005) "Antecedents and Consequences of Customer-Company Identification: Expanding the Role of Relationship Marketing", *Journal of Applied Psychology*, 90 (3): 574–85.

Albert, S. and D.A. Whetten (1985) "Organizational Identity", *Organizational Identity; A Reader*, ed. L.L. Cummings and B.M. Straw, Vol. 7. Greenwich CT: JAI Press: 263–295.

Ashforth, B.E. and F. Mael (1989) "Social Identity Theory and the Organization", *Academy of Management Review*, 14 (1): 20–39.

Ball, A.D. and L.H. Tasaki (1992) "The Role and Measurement of Attachment in Consumer Behavior", *Journal of Consumer Psychology*, 1 (2): 155–172.

Balmer, J.M.T. (1998) "Corporate Identity and the Advent of Corporate Marketing", *Journal of Marketing Management*, 14 (8): 963–996.

Barker, J.R. and P.K. Tompkins (1994) "Identification in the Self-Managing Organization Characteristics of Target and Tenure", *Human Communication Research*, 21 (2): 223–240.

Belk, R.W. (1988) "Possessions and the Extended Self", *Journal of Consumer Research*, 15 (2): 139–68.

Bergami, M. and R.P. Bagozzi (2000) "Self-Categorization, Affective Commitment and Group Self-Esteem as Distinct Aspects of Social Identity in the Organization", *British Journal of Social Psychology*, 39 (4): 555–577.

Bhattacharya, C.B. and S. Sen (2003) "Consumer–Company Identification: A Framework for Understanding Consumers' Relationships with Companies", *Journal of Marketing*, 67 (2): 76–88.

Bhattacharya, C.B., H. Rao, and M.A. Glynn (1995) "Understanding the Bond of Identification: An Investigation of its Correlates among Art Museum Members", *Journal of Marketing*, 59 (4): 46–57.

Biggart, N.W. (1989) *Charismatic Capitalism: Direct Selling Organizations in America*. Chicago IL: University of Chicago Press.

Bradach, J.L. (1998) *Franchise Organizations*. Boston, MA: Harvard Business Press.

Brown, J.R., C.S. Dev, and D.J. Lee (2000) "Managing Marketing Channel Opportunism: The Efficacy of Alternative Governance Mechanisms", *Journal of Marketing*, 64 (2) (April): 51–65.

Dant, R.P. and G.T. Gundlach (1999) "The Challenge of Autonomy and Dependence in Franchised Channels of Distribution", *Journal of Business Venturing*, 14 (1): 35–67.

Darden, R. (2002) *Secret Recipe: Why KFC is Still Cookin' After 50 Years*. Irving, TX: Tapestry Press.

Deshpandé, R., J.U. Farley, and F.E. Webster Jr (1993) "Corporate Culture, Customer Orientation, and Innovativeness in Japanese Firms: A Quadrad Analysis", *Journal of Marketing*, 57 (1): 23–37.

Dobrzynski, J.H. (1996) "Chicken Done to a Golden Rule", *New York Times*, April 3.

Dutton, J.E., J.M. Dukerich, and C.V. Harquail (1994) "Organizational Images and Member Identification", *Administrative Science Quarterly*, 39 (2): 239–263.

Escalas, J.E. (1997) "Meaningful Self-Brand Connections and Consumer Product Experience Stories", *Advances in Consumer Research*, 24: 309.

Escalas, J.E. (2004) "Narrative Processing: Building Consumer Connections to Brands", *Journal of Consumer Psychology*, 14 (1): 168–180.

Escalas, J.E. and J.R. Bettman (2000) "Using Narratives to Discern Self-identity Related Consumer Goals and Motivations", *The Why of Consumption, Contemporary Perspectives on Consumer Motives, Goals, and Desires*, eds C. Huffman, D.G. Mick, and S. Ratneshwar. London: Routledge: 237–258.

Escalas, J.E. and J.R. Bettman (2003) "You are What They Eat: The Influence of Reference Groups on Consumers' Connections to Brands", *Journal of Consumer Psychology*, 13 (3): 339–348.

Flaherty, J. (2001) "By the Book: Individuality Vs. Franchising; Trading Spark of Creativity For the Safety of Numbers", *New York Times*, February 17, Business.

Foreman, P. and D.A. Whetten (2002) "Members' Identification with Multiple-Identity Organizations", *Organization Science*, 13 (6): 618–635.

Fournier, S. (1998) "Consumers and Their Brands: Developing Relationship Theory in Consumer Research", *Journal of Consumer Research*, 24 (4): 343–353.

Fullagar, C. and J. Barling (1991) "Predictors and Outcomes of Different Patterns of Organizational and Union Loyalty", *Journal of Occupational Psychology*, 64 (2): 129–143.

George, E. and P. Chattopadhyay (2005) "One Foot in Each Camp: the Dual Identification of Contract Workers", *Administrative Science Quarterly*, 50 (1): 68–99.

Glynn, M.A. (2000) "When Cymbals Become Symbols: Conflict Over Organizational Identity Within a Symphony Orchestra", *Organization Science*, 11 (3): 285–298.

Golden-Biddle, K. and H. Rao (1997) "Breaches in the Boardroom: Organizational Identity and Conflicts of Commitment in a Nonprofit Organization", *Organization Science*, 8 (6): 593–611.

Grayson, K. (2007) "Friendship Versus Business in Marketing Relationships", *Journal of Marketing*, 71 (4): 121–139.

Heide, J.B. and G. John (1992) "Do Norms Matter in Marketing Relationships?", *The Journal of Marketing*, 56 (2): 32–44.

Heide, J.B. and K.H. Wathne (2006) "Friends, Businesspeople, and Relationship Roles: A Conceptual Framework and a Research Agenda", *Journal of Marketing*, 70 (3): 90–103.

Hogg, M.A., D.J. Terry, and K.M. White (1995) "A Tale of Two Theories: A Critical Comparison of Identity Theory with Social Identity Theory", *Social Psychology Quarterly*, 58 (4): 255–269.

Hughes, D. and M. Ahearne (2010) "Energizing the Reseller's Sales Force: The Power of Brand Identification", *Journal of Marketing*, 74 (4): 81–96.

Ilyer, V.M., E.M. Bamber, and R.M. Barefield (1997) "Identification of Accounting Firm Alumni with Their Former Firm: Antecedents and Outcomes", *Accounting Organisations and Society*, 22 (3): 315–336.

Kaufmann, P.J. and J. Stanworth (1995), "The Decision to Become a Franchisee: A Study of Prospective Franchisees", *Journal of Small Business Management*, 33 (4): 22–33.

Keller, K.L. (1993) "Conceptualizing, Measuring, and Managing Customer-Based Brand Equity", *Journal of Marketing*, 57 (1): 1–22.

Kleine, S.S., R.E. Kleine III, and C.T. Allen (1995) "How is a Possession 'Me' or 'Not Me'? Characterizing Types and an Antecedent of Material Possession Attachment", *Journal of Consumer Research*, 22 (3): 327–343.

Lawrence, B. and P.J. Kaufmann (2011) "Identity in Franchise Systems: The Role of Franchisee Associations", *Journal of Retailing*, 87 (3): 285–305.

Lawrence, B. and P.J. Kaufmann (2014) "Strategic Brand Management in Channels", Working Paper.

Love, J.F. (1986) *McDonald's: Behind the Arche.* New York: Bantam.

Mael, F. and B.E. Ashforth (1992) "Alumni and Their Alma Mater: A Partial Test of the Reformulated Model of Organizational Identification", *Journal of Organizational Behavior*, 13 (2): 103–123.

Margulies, W.P. (1977) "Make the Most of Your Corporate Identity", *Harvard Business Review*, 55 (4): 66–74.

McAlexander, J.H., J.W. Schouten, and H.F. Koenig (2002) "Building Brand Community", *Journal of Marketing*, 66 (1): 38–54.

Morgan, R.M. and S.D. Hunt (1994) "The Commitment-Trust Theory of Relationship Marketing", *Journal of Marketing*, 58 (3): 20–38.

Muñiz, A.M. Jr and T. O'Guinn (2001) "Brand Community", *Journal of Consumer Research*, 27 (4): 412–432.

Olins, W. (1992) *Corporate Identity: Making Business Strategy Visible Through Design.* Boston MA: Harvard Business School Press.

Patton, M.Q. (2001) *Qualitative Research & Evaluation Methods*. Thousand Oaks CA: Sage Publications.

Peterson, A. and R.P. Dant (1990) "Perceived Advantages of the Franchise Option from the Franchisee Perspective Empirical Insights from a Service Franchise", *Journal of Small Business Management*, 28 (3): 46–61.

Pfeffer, J. and J.N. Baron (1988) *Taking the Workers Back Out: Recent Trends in the Structuring of Employment*. Stamford, CT: JAI Press.

Pratt, M.G. (1998) "To Be or Not to Be? Central Questions in Organizational Identification", *Identity in Organizations: Building Theory Through Conversations*, ed. D.A. Whetten and P.C. Godfrey. Thousand Oaks, CA: Sage Publications Inc.: 171–207.

Pratt, M.G. (2000) "The Good, the Bad, and the Ambivalent: Managing Identification Among Amway Distributors", *Administrative Science Quarterly*, 45 (3): 456–493.

Pratt, M.G. and P.O. Foreman (2000) "Classifying Managerial Responses to Multiple Organizational Identities", *The Academy of Management Review*, 25 (1): 18–42.

Price, L.L. and E.J. Arnould (1999) "Commercial Friendships: Service Provider-Client Relationships in Context", *Journal of Marketing*, 63 (4): 38–56.

Quinn, R.E. (1988) *Beyond Rational Management: Mastering the Paradoxes and Competing Demands of High Performance*. San Francisco, CA: Jossey-Bass.

Richins, M.L. (1994) "Special Possessions and the Expression of Material Values", *Journal of Consumer Research*, 21 (3): 522–533.

Schmall, E. (2007) "The Cult of Chick-fil-A", *Forbes*, July 23.

Schouten, J.W. and J.H. McAlexander (1995) "Subcultures of Consumption: An Ethnography of the New Bikers", *Journal of Consumer Research*, 22 (1): 43–61.

Stets, J.E. and P.J. Burke (2000) "Identity Theory and Social Identity Theory", *Social Psychology Quarterly*, 63 (3): 224–237.

Stryker, S. (1968) "Identity Salience and Role Performance: The Relevance of Symbolic Interaction Theory for Family Research", *Journal of Marriage and the Family*, 30 (4): 558–564.

Tajfel, H. and J.C. Turner (1979) "An Integrative Theory of Intergroup Conflict", *The Social Psychology of Group Relations*, ed. G.A.S. Worchel. Monterey, CA: Brooks-Cole: 33–47.

Thomson, M., D.J. MacInnis, and C.W. Park (2005) "The Ties that Bind: Measuring the Strength of Consumers' Emotional Attachments to Brands", *Journal of Consumer Psychology*, 15 (1): 77–91.

Tian, K. and R.W. Belk (2005) "Extended Self and Possessions in the Workplace", *Journal of Consumer Research*, 32 (2): 297–310.

Van Riel, C.B.M. and J.M.T. Balmer (1997) "Corporate Identity: The Concept, Its Measurement and Management", *European Journal of Marketing*, 31 (5): 340–355.

Ventura, W.J. (2006) "The Personal Values Communicated by Truett Cathy and Their Effect on the Culture of Chick-fil-A: A Qualitative Study", Unpublished Doctoral Dissertation, Regent University.

Wallendorf, M. and E.J. Arnould (1988) "'My Favorite Things': A Cross-Cultural Inquiry into Object Attachment, Possessiveness, and Social Linkage", *Journal of Consumer Research*, 14 (4): 531–47.

Weaven, S. and L. Frazer (2006) "Investment Incentives for Single and Multiple Unit Franchisees", *Qualitative Market Research: An International Journal*, 9 (3): 225–242.

Weber, M. (2002) *The Protestant Ethic and the "Spirit" of Capitalism and Other Writings*, eds. P.R Baehr and G.C Wells. London: Penguin Classics.

Whetten, D.A. (2006) "Albert and Whetten Revisited: Strengthening the Concept of Organizational Identity", *Journal of Management Inquiry*, 15 (3): 219–234.

22

SUCCESS FACTORS FOR THE IMPLEMENTATION OF AN INTENDED BRAND PERSONALITY

Conceptual framework and insights from the Swiss luxury industry

Wayne D. Hoyer, Harley Krohmer, and Lara Lobschat

Introduction

In today's ever-changing digital and connected world, the importance of brands is more prevalent than ever. Given that consumers nowadays have easy access to a nearly endless assortment of products and services from all over the world, the need for brand managers to differentiate from competing brands and increase customers' brand commitment by carefully establishing compelling brand identities and building close, emotional brand relationships with their customers is steadily increasing (Sweeney and Brandon 2006). Brand personality captures a major component of brand identity and has gained increasing interest both from researchers and managers alike, also due to its important implications for brand performance (e.g., Aaker 1997; Batra *et al.* 2010; Geuens *et al.* 2009; Malär *et al.* 2011; Staplehurst and Charoenwongse 2012).

According to Aaker (1997: 347), brand personality "refers to the set of human characteristics associated with a brand." Existing literature has identified a variety of brand personality dimensions including Aaker's (1997) initial set of dimensions (i.e., sincerity, excitement, competence, sophistication, ruggedness), Geuens *et al.*'s (2009) continuative measurement scale based on personality traits (i.e., responsibility, activity, aggressiveness, simplicity, and emotionality), and brand gender (Grohmann 2009; Lieven *et al.* 2014). For an extensive review, see Geuens *et al.* (2009). While product-related attributes often are becoming increasingly uniform and interchangeable across brands, brand personality serves a symbolic, self-expressive function and, thus, provides a good basis for building and strengthening a brand's competitive advantage (Aaker 1997; Sweeney and Brandon 2006).

The concept of brand personality has received considerable interest in many industries, particularly in those where consumers' brand preferences are closely related to self-expression and self-presentation via a brand with a corresponding brand personality; this is particularly the case in the luxury industry (Wilcox *et al.* 2009). While quality considerations certainly play an important role for consumers of luxury goods and services, they also choose luxury brands because of their specific brand personalities. They prefer and purchase a luxury brand with a specific brand personality that enables them to present themselves to society in a certain intended way, showing their actual or ideal self to others. A luxury brand with such a desired brand personality enables its consumers to maintain or even enhance their self-image among others (Kastanakis and Balabanis 2012; Wilcox *et al.* 2009). For example, the luxury fashion brand Chanel offers "the reflection of an elegant woman, seductive, sophisticated who yet loves to attract attention," whereas Yves Saint Laurent represents an "imperative, provocative, seductive, and inaccessible character" (Kapferer and Bastien 2009: 123). Hence, consumers will choose one of the two luxury brands for the specific brand personality traits with which they are associated.

Brand managers in the luxury industry, therefore, strive to create an appealing brand personality via product design, advertising, and other marketing activities, such as establishing an exciting and sophisticated distribution environment (Perdis 2014). Their clear objective is to make consumers perceive the luxury brand and its brand personality as intended so that it provides self-expression value to them (Keller 2009).

However, such formulation and implementation of an intended brand personality is challenging as "strong brands do not just happen. Rather, they result from the creation of winning brand strategies and brilliant execution from committed, disciplined organizations" (Aaker 1996: 58). A brand's personality is based on the involvement of both brand managers and customers (Johar *et al.* 2005). That is, whereas brand managers intend to convey a certain brand personality through their marketing activities, customers might form different inferences from the marketing stimuli to which they are exposed and, hence, perceive the brand's personality differently than intended, also referred to as "the two different faces of brand personality" (Plummer 1985: 28). Therefore, the successful implementation of an intended brand personality is key for brand managers. However, the scientific literature on drivers of brand personality implementation is still scant, with the notable exception of research from Malär *et al.* (2012). For this reason, this chapter deals with the managerial challenge of implementing an intended brand personality. The key objective is to provide managers with insights on how to be more successful with regard to the implementation of their intended brand personality.

For this purpose, we will first discuss the duality of the brand personality concept by accounting for both the intended and the realized brand personality perspective and factors that influence the fit between both perspectives. Subsequently, we will focus specifically on brand personality implementation strategies that involve the interplay between strategic considerations of brand managers, the corresponding implementation activities, as well as the customer's perspective. We will integrate the results of an exploratory qualitative study that compiled interviews with luxury marketing managers in Switzerland. Putting all this together, we hope to uncover new and important implications for research and practice.

The duality of the brand personality concept

Prior research provides evidence that the creation of brand personality is not the sole achievement of marketing activities implemented by brand managers, but rather "a dynamic process that is not controlled solely by the marketer" (Johar *et al.* 2005: 468). More specifically, Malär *et al.* (2012) distinguish between the brand manager's *intended* brand personality and how brand personality is *perceived* by consumers (i.e., its realized brand personality). The authors further present the calibration process of these two perspectives, and identify factors that influence the fit level that ultimately determines the success of the brand personality implementation. Hence, to accomplish a successful transformation of an intended to a realized brand personality, brand managers not only have to focus on their own considerations and resources, but also need to take other factors into account that influence the fit between the intended and the realized brand personality. Based on Malär *et al.* (2012), we introduce a conceptual framework that depicts the duality of the brand personality concept, as illustrated in Figure 22.1. In addition, we discuss this framework in the context of the luxury goods industry in which, as mentioned previously, brand selection is particularly related to self-expression.

A variety of factors influence the calibration process research that we categorize into the following subgroups: *company-related factors*, *implementation-related factors*, *consumer-related factors*, and factors which deal with the *social relationships among and influence from other consumers*. While we will discuss how companies can actively and successfully implement an intended brand personality, focusing on *implementation-related factors*, our framework also considers factors that influence consumers' perceived brand personality beyond the direct control of companies.

Prior research has shown that *company-related factors*, such as whether a company operates as a for-profit or non-profit organization (Aaker *et al.* 2010), its employees' identities and behavior (Wentzel 2009), as well as the brand's reputation (Veloutsou and Moutinho 2009) impact perceived brand personality. An interesting finding on the influence of product type on perceived brand personality (particularly for the luxury industry) comes from Ang and Lim (2005). The authors find that symbolic brands (i.e., those that provide consumers with added social value beyond a brand's functional attributes) are perceived as more sophisticated and exciting, but less sincere and competent, relative to utilitarian products. Hence, the luxury industry, in general, entails certain perceived brand personality traits that apply to all brands in the category and that have to be taken into account when planning and executing an intended brand personality strategy (Batra *et al.* 2010).

Moreover, *consumer-related factors* influence how consumers perceive a brand's personality. These include the consumer's age (Chaplin and John 2005) and cultural background (Staplehurst and Charoenwongse 2012), his/her individual

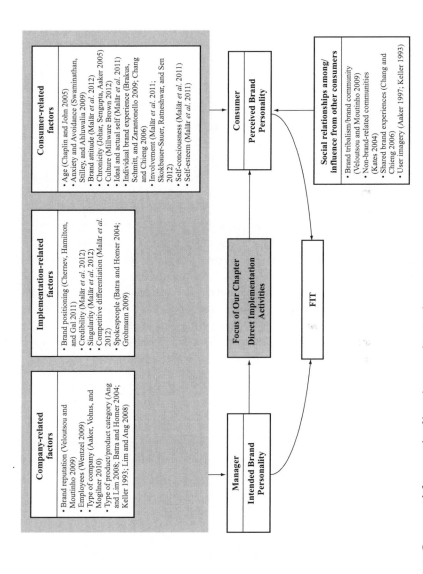

Company-related factors

- Brand reputation (Veloutsou and Moutinho 2009)
- Employees (Wentzel 2009)
- Type of company (Aaker, Vohns, and Mogilner 2010)
- Type of product/product category (Ang and Lim 2008; Batra and Homer 2004; Keller 1993; Lim and Ang 2008)

Implementation-related factors

- Brand positioning (Chernev, Hamilton, and Gal 2011)
- Credibility (Malär et al. 2012)
- Singularity (Malär et al. 2012)
- Competitive differentiation (Malär et al. 2012)
- Spokespeople (Batra and Homer 2004; Grohmann 2009)

Consumer-related factors

- Age (Chaplin and John 2005)
- Anxiety and Avoidance (Swaminathan, Stilley, and Ahluwalia 2009)
- Brand attitude (Malär et al. 2012)
- Chronicity (Johar, Sengupta, Aaker 2005)
- Culture (Millware Brown 2012)
- Ideal and actual self (Malär et al. 2011)
- Individual brand experience (Brakus, Schmitt, and Zarantonello 2009; Chang and Chieng 2006)
- Involvement (Malär et al. 2011; Skokobauer-Sauer, Ratneshwar, and Sen 2012)
- Self-conciousness (Malär et al. 2011)
- Self-esteem (Malär et al. 2011)

Focus of Our Chapter
Direct Implementation Activities

Consumer
Perceived Brand Personality

FIT

Manager
Intended Brand Personality

Social relationships among/ influence from other consumers

- Brand tribalism/brand community (Veloutsou and Moutinho 2009)
- Non-brand-related communities (Kates 2004)
- Shared brand experiences (Chang and Chieng 2006)
- User imagery (Aaker 1997; Keller 1993)

FIGURE 22.1 Conceptual framework of brand personality implementation

brand experiences (Brakus, Schmitt, and Zarantonello 2009), as well as his/her attitude towards the brand (Malär *et al.* 2012). Further, Malär *et al.* (2012: 36) explore the role of consumers' self-concept, namely "the cognitive and affective understanding of who and what we are" in the context of brand personality. Their findings provide support for the notion that brands with actual self-congruence (the fit between the actual self and the perceived brand personality) have a stronger impact on emotional brand attachment than brands with ideal self-congruence do. They also show that this effect is even more pronounced if consumers have a high level of public self-consciousness, a concept which is closely related to the consumption of luxury products. Self-conscious consumers are particularly concerned with the way in which they present themselves to others (Scheier and Carver 1985). Through purchasing and consuming luxury brands in public, consumers can express themselves in line with the luxury brand and, hence, transfer a certain image to society.

Turning to factors that deal with *social relationships among and influence from other consumers*, research provides evidence for the influence of shared brand experiences (Chang and Chieng 2006), brand communities (Veloutsou and Moutinho 2009), and also non brand-related communities (such as the gay community in Kates 2004) on the calibration process of brand personality. The concept of user imagery (i.e., the typical brand user associated with a certain brand) is of specific relevance for the luxury industry. For example, a typical Porsche driver can be identified as a middle-aged man who owns his own business (Winkler 2012). Aaker (1997), as well as Keller (1993), claim that the characteristics of these typical brand users serve as antecedents for perceived brand personality. Hence, given its user imagery, Porsche is likely to be perceived as a middle-aged, sophisticated, and successful male. For luxury brands, aspirational user images play an especially key role (Keller 2009). Thus, brand managers try to implement these types of user images through celebrity endorsements, for example. In the following section, we will go into more detail with respect to brand personality strategies and review how promising they are in translating an intended into a perceived brand personality.

Brand personality implementation activities

Malär *et al.* (2012) focus on specific success factors of brand personality implementation referring to aspects such as the content of communication (e.g., credibility, singularity) and consumer-related variables (e.g., self-consciousness, self-esteem) (see Figure 22.1). Accounting for these factors can facilitate the implementation of an intended brand personality. However, direct implementation activities such as creating a specific organizational design or changing organizational processes have not been addressed. Research examining the role of all marketing mix instruments for the implementation of an intended brand personality is still scant. Against this background, the focus of this chapter is on the direct implementation activities required to implement an intended brand personality; in addition, we illustrate these activities by providing insights from a qualitative study in the Swiss luxury goods industry. In the time between March and September 2014, we conducted 29 interviews with CEOs and chief marketing officers of 24 Swiss and five international luxury brands in Switzerland (from diverse product categories including accessories, alcoholic beverages, fashion, food, handbags, hotel services, jewelry, and watches) in which we discussed the implementation of brand personality, general success factors, and specific marketing capabilities in luxury marketing.

A first category of direct brand implementation activities relates to the design of the organizational structures and processes. A key organizational dimension to be designed in this context is the specialization of the organization. In other words, which organizational unit is responsible for the implementation of an intended brand personality? In the marketing literature, the specialization within marketing and sales units has been discussed. In several studies, it has been shown that, in many companies, particularly in the consumer goods industry, specialized organizational units are assigned to (corporate or product level) brand management (e.g., Günther and Kriegbaum-Kling 2001). In these product and brand management organizational units, product and brand managers are designated direct responsibility for a broad spectrum of tasks related to a certain product or brand, including the development of brand strategies and the corresponding coordination of the implementation activities (cf. Ruekert *et al.* 1985).

In our interviews in the Swiss luxury industry, we found the following with regard to the organizational responsibility for the implementation of an intended brand personality. Similar to the consumer goods industry, in many companies, there are specialized organizational units responsible for the formulation and implementation of the intended brand personality. In addition, for several of our examined luxury companies, we found a highly hierarchical approach. While the dispersion of influence on branding strategy across functional boundaries within the firm and across hierarchical levels has been found in the literature (cf. Krohmer *et al.* 2002), for the luxury industry, we mostly observed a strictly hierarchical responsibility for brand personality definition and implementation. More specifically, in addition to the organizational unit responsible for corporate brand management, top management was highly involved in brand personality implementation. As the CEO of a leading Swiss luxury watch brand put it:

> This is a bit like in religion or a church. I am the high priest of our brand. Our employees finally have to follow "my brand bible." To make sure that they really fully understand the message I have created for our brand, I walk around in our offices and write "commandments" for our brand with a permanent marker directly on the wall – what is the message of our brand and how should it always be implemented? So, the employees actually cannot walk five meters without reading my commandments.

Thus, in addition to a strong specialization, we observed a control-oriented formalization and standardization of the intended brand personality and the corresponding implementation rules. This was especially the case for the highly successful, large luxury companies. In contrast, luxury startups (that were certainly much smaller) seemed to be less hierarchical and much more informal. As the CEO of a young luxury watch brand put it: "When we discuss the brand personality and its implementation, our full team sits together. Even the accountant is invited to join our round table, and sometimes she contributes with great ideas about brand personality implementation." While specialization and formalization certainly is a function of company size, we argue that many successful luxury brands have CEOs and top managers that are highly involved in brand personality formulation and implementation, and often take a high-control and hierarchical approach in which top managers control even the smallest details of brand personality implementation. When asked for the reasons behind such a high-control approach, the CEO of a Swiss luxury hotel company said, for the consumers' perception of his luxury brand, every detail counts in every single customer contact: "We will only be successful, if we can convey the same coherent brand message in every contact with each guest. Our high status image can only be obtained, if we are able to avoid even the smallest mistake or incoherence. Everything must be perfect." The CEO of a Swiss luxury watch agreed:

> The brand message always has to be the same, from product design to print advertising to the consumer's experience in the sales room. Our consumers are not buying a watch, for reading the time they have their smartphones. Instead, our consumers are paying a lot of money for buying a status symbol with a specific story and message to impress others. To make this work, we have to be 100 percent consistent in our message and I am finally responsible for this.

At the same time, several managers warned that too much control and formalization in the context of brand personality implementation proved to not always be beneficial, and, at times, particularly in the context of luxury services, was problematic. As the executive director of a leading Swiss luxury hotel put it:

> In the past, we tried to standardize the customer experience in the direct interaction with our service personnel in order to implement our brand personality strategy. We even gave out handbooks with exact words and phrases to be used when interacting with our guests. We realized that this took away some personal freedom from our employees and reduced their motivation. We now explicitly train our service employees to use their own words and to show their own personality, not just the brand personality of our hotel brand. This is now perceived as much more authentic by our guests. What is more important than perfect and standardized processes is a passion for our brand. That is the most difficult task – to find people who already are and will stay passionate for our brand and show authentic passion during their interaction with guests. Our guests have already seen everything and can afford anything. What makes the difference is the true passion

combined with honest empathy of our personnel. To experience this human factor, our guests will stay loyal to us and will always come back.

This example also clearly illustrates the important role of the customer in generating and maintaining the brand personality. This involves a two-way interaction between the service personnel and customers. Thus, these personnel need to be highly sensitive to and develop a deep understanding of customer perceptions. In addition, management and any other groups within the organization with responsibility for implementation of brand personality need to be sensitive to the customer side of the equation. As we will discuss shortly, this involves the company setting up mechanisms to actively monitor and input customer perceptions into the implementation of brand personality.

A second category of brand personality implementation activities relates to product management as a component of the marketing mix. In the strategy implementation literature, it has been argued that, generally, a key tool for strategy implementation is product management with decisions and activities related to product design, product quality, or product innovation playing a major role (cf. Slater and Olson 2001). This is surely also the case for the context of brand personality implementation, where a consistency of product design, product innovations, and product features with the intended, as well as perceived, brand personality contribute to implementation success. As the CEO of a luxury watch company emphasized,

> The brand's personality and message provide guidance for all decisions related to product innovation. Our key brand message of "fusion" drives the development of all new watches and innovations. The consistency between brand message and product design drives our credibility among our distribution partners and customers."

In our interviews in the context of luxury marketing, we observed an additional phenomenon that goes beyond mere consistency between brand personality and product design. Many respondents emphasized that the product features need to be in line with the brand personality, but, in addition, that the product features not only deliver functional value to the customer but, as the CEO of a Swiss producer of hard liquor stated, "need to tell a story, that the customer then can tell others and actually makes the real difference." This is consistent with a point emphasized by Malär et al. (2011) in their empirical study on brand personality implementation that a successful implementation of an intended brand personality results from the interaction of consumers with the brand. This duality of brand intentions (as formulated by the brand managers) and brand perceptions (as interpreted by the consumers) means that a successful implementation of an intended brand personality is reflected in a good fit between intended and perceived brand personality (see also Figure 22.1), and requires the joint efforts of both brand managers and consumers. In other words, the brand personality is a result of both brand managers' creativity and consumers' imaginations. This concept is in line with the observation that in many industries, consumers become more and more empowered and take an increasingly active role in brand personality creation and interpretation. Concepts and phenomena such as user generated content or crowdsourcing in innovation management support this idea. These activities have proved useful in other areas, such as in new product development where customers are actively involved in the generation of new product ideas through idea generation websites, group discussions, and direct interactions with management. The key point, however, is that companies must actively monitor and measure the brand personality as perceived by consumers in order to determine whether it is consistent with the intended brand personality. This can involve active monitoring of customer conversations in the social media, as well as conducting customer surveys. It is only when this match occurs that implementation is successful. If the intended and perceived personality are inconsistent, corrective action must be taken, which would involve altering either the direct implementation activities or attempting to alter customer perceptions in a direction more consistent with the intended brand personality.

Such joint shaping of brand personality in the context of product management can be illustrated by two examples from our interviews. A first example refers to a Swiss hard liquor brand, which is sold mainly to Chinese customers for around 15,000 USD per bottle. The CEO of this luxury liquor producer claims that:

> This is the most expensive hard liquor in the world. The high price results from the inclusion of a valuable Swiss mountain-shaped berg crystal inside of the bottle. We created this liquor especially for the Chinese market by referring to the Chinese legend in which the hero became extremely rich after he found a well of liquid gold underneath a berg crystal on a mountain at the end of a valley. So, we directly tell our customers that the crystal has not yet been found but that maybe the one who buys the bottle will be the one who found it. So, our brand personality of the mythic dream of affluence and richness is based in our product design. The key point is that our customers do not buy the liquor to really drink it, but to tell their guests in their house bar that they own the most expensive liquor in the world and that they actually are the hero of this legend of unlimited wealth. The beautifully shining berg crystal in the bottle supports this story.

A second example can be found in a Swiss luxury mechanical golf watch, which has special shock protection so that it can be worn while hitting a golf ball. This mechanical watch can also be used for counting the handicap during golf. The CEO told us that:

> We designed the product so that the customer can tell his friends in the golf clubhouse about the functionality of the watch. However, it is not only about the functionality, it is about the status symbol. Many of our customers also

own a Rolex and a Patek, so owning, in addition, our exclusive golf watch is a statement about their status and wealth – they can afford this additional watch. You have to know that "regular" mechanical luxury watches should not be worn during golf. The vibrations of the golf club transfer to the watch and can damage it. As a matter of fact, many of our customers put our watch in their pocket and also do not use it to keep track of their handicap. They rather put it on in the clubhouse after playing golf more or less to show off and to tell an interesting story. Our brand is all about golf and exclusivity, and our customers who tell their friends this story are our best brand ambassadors.

A third category of brand personality implementation activities relates to pricing as a component of the marketing mix. Again, the rationale is that the pricing strategy should be consistent with the intended brand personality. In our interviews among managers in the Swiss luxury industry, we found clear support for this perspective. The Swiss CEO of one the world's leading luxury handbag and fashion brands stated that "our brand is all about exclusivity and superior quality. To realize this brand idea, you have to keep up the prices. You will never ever find a price discount for one of our products. Thus, we need full control of our prices, which we have, since, in Switzerland, we only sell our products via our own luxury boutiques." The importance of such a no-discount policy to implement a brand personality of exclusiveness and luxuriousness was also emphasized by the CEO of a Swiss luxury cosmetics brand that uses caviar as one of its ingredients: "We need to keep up the prices all the time. Otherwise, we are not a luxury brand. We might even attract the 'wrong' customers – bargain shoppers. This might then damage our high-status image among our status-aware heavy users, women who spend about $12,000 a year on our facial creams."

A fourth category of brand personality implementation activities refer to distribution and sales management. Here, our interview partners emphasized the importance of the customers' brand experience in the luxury boutique shop. As the Swiss CEO of an Italian luxury jewelry brand put it,

> The brand personality may be written on paper on a highly abstract level, but what really counts it that our brand's personality comes really alive within our shops. The smell in the shop, the light, the colors, the sounds, the behavior of our sales staff, all this together transfers the brand personality to our customers. They experience in the shops what our brand is all about. In luxury, this sometimes is often more important than print advertising or digital marketing, where you cannot use all of your senses.

Another aspect was the role of the sales staff for the implementation of the brand personality. A marketing director of a Swiss luxury fashion brand said that:

> Our brand is all about authentic luxury and passion. Therefore, it is an absolute must that our sales staff and external distributors fully incorporate

this idea. The CEO has to be 400 percent passionate, then our own sales director will be still 200 percent passionate, so that he can ignite 100 percent passion in the sales personnel of external distributors. Many decisions are made at the point of sale; here, we need the authentic passion of the sales personnel to make sure that our brand idea reaches the consumers.

Given that price plays such an important role in determining the intended brand personality, it is also critical to clearly understand how customers perceive price in relation to the perceived brand personality. Consistent with earlier points, successful brand personality implementation would require a match between the intended price perception and the perceived price perception. Again, this requires that monitoring and measurement systems be established to measure price perceptions.

Conclusion

In conclusion, the goal of this chapter was to highlight important issues in the implementation of a brand personality. In particular, we focused on important direct implementation activities which are needed to ensure the success of the implementation. A key point, however, is that success also depends on a match between the intended brand personality and the brand personality as perceived by the customer. Thus, for each of the direct implementation activities, customer input is important and necessary. We highlighted some key activities that can aid in these efforts; however, this is only a beginning. It is clear that more work is needed to identify strategies for incorporating more customer input into the process. It is our hope that the initial ideas outlined in this chapter provide impetus in this regard.

References

Aaker, D.A. (1996) *Building Strong Brands*. New York: The Free Press.

Aaker, J.L. (1997) "Dimensions of Brand Personality", *Journal of Marketing Research*, 34 (3): 347–356.

Aaker, J.L., K.D. Vohs, and C. Mogilner (2010) "Nonprofits Are Seen as Warm and For-Profits as Competent: Firm Stereotypes Matter", *Journal of Consumer Research*, 37 (2): 224–237.

Ang, S.H. and E.A.C. Lim (2005) "The Influence of Metaphors and Product Type on Brand Personality Perceptions and Attitudes", *Journal of Advertising*, 35 (2): 39–53.

Batra, R. and P.M. Homer (2004) "The Situational Impact of Brand Image Beliefs", *Journal of Consumer Psychology*, 14 (3): 318–330.

Batra, R., P. Lenk, and M. Wedel (2010) "Brand Extension Strategy Planning: Empirical Estimation of Brand-Category Personality Fit and Atypicality", *Journal of Marketing Research*, 47 (2): 335–347.

Brakus, J.J., B.H. Schmitt, and L. Zarantonello (2009) "Brand Experience: What Is It? How Is It Measured? Does It Affect Loyalty?", *Journal of Marketing*, 73 (3): 52–68.

Chang, P.L. and M.H. Chieng (2006) "Building Consumer–Brand Relationship: A Cross-Cultural Experiential View", *Psychology and Marketing*, 23 (1): 927–959.

Chaplin, L.N. and D.R. John (2005) "The Development of Self Brand Connections in Children and Adolescents", *Journal of Consumer Research*, 32 (1): 119–129.

Chernev, A., R. Hamilton, and D. Gal (2011) "Competing for Consumer Identity: Limits to Self-Expression and the Perils of Lifestyle Branding", *Journal of Marketing*, 75 (3): 66–82.

Geuens, M., B. Weijters, and K. De Wulf (2009) "A New Measure of Brand Personality", *International Journal of Research in Marketing*, 26 (2): 97–107.

Grohmann, B. (2009) "Gender Dimensions of Brand Personality", *Journal of Marketing Research*, 46 (1): 105–119.

Günther, T., and C. Kriegbaum-Kling (2001) "Brand Valuation and Control: an Empirical Study", *Schmalenbach Business Review*, 53 (4): 263–294.

Johar, G.V., J. Sengupta, and J.L. Aaker (2005) "Two Roads to Updating Brand Personality Impressions: Trait versus Evaluative Inferencing", *Journal of Marketing Research*, 42 (4): 458–469.

Kapferer, J.N. and V. Bastien (2009) *The Luxury Strategy: Break the Rules of Marketing to Build Luxury*. London: Kogan Page.

Kastanakis, M.N., and G. Balabanis (2012) "Between the Mass and the Class: Antecedents of the 'Bandwagon' Luxury Consumption Behavior", *Journal of Business Research*, 65 (10): 1399–1407.

Kates, S.M. (2004) "The Dynamics of Brand Legitimacy: An Interpretive Study in the Gay Men's Community", *Journal of Consumer Research*, 31 (2): 455–464.

Keller, K.L. (1993) "Conceptualizing, Measuring, and Managing Customer-Based Brand Equity", *Journal of Marketing*, 57 (1): 1–22.

Keller, K.L. (2009) "Managing the Growth Tradeoff: Challenges and Opportunities in Luxury Branding", *Journal of Brand Management*, 16 (5/6): 290–301.

Krohmer, H., C. Homburg, and J.P. Workman (2002) "Should Marketing Be Cross-functional? Conceptual Development and International Empirical Evidence", *Journal of Business Research*, 55 (6): 451–465.

Lieven, T., B. Grohmann, A. Herrmann, J.R. Landwehr, and M. van Tilburg (2014) "The Effect of Brand Gender on Brand Equity", *Psychology and Marketing*, 31 (5): 371–385.

Lim, E.A.C. and S.H. Ang (2008) "Hedonic vs. Utilitarian Consumption: A Cross-Cultural Perspective Based on Cultural Conditioning", *Journal of Business Research*, 61 (3): 225–232.

Malär, L., H. Krohmer, W.D. Hoyer, and B. Nyffenegger (2011) "Emotional Brand Attachment and Brand Personality: The Relative Importance of the Actual and the Ideal Self", *Journal of Marketing*, 75 (4): 35–52.

Malär, L., B. Nyffenegger, H. Krohmer, and W.D. Hoyer (2012) "Implementing an Intended Brand Personality: A Dyadic Perspective", *Journal of the Academy of Marketing Science*, 40 (5): 728–744.

Perdis, N. (2014) "Making the Retail Experience a Luxury in Its Own Right," *Huffington Post*, www.huffingtonpost.com/napoleon-perdis/making-the-retail-experie_b_5398821.html, accessed July 26, 2014.

Plummer, J. (1985) "How Personality Makes the Difference", *Journal of Advertising Research*, 24 (6): 27–31.

Ruekert, R.W., O.C. Walker Jr, and K.J. Roering (1985) "The Organization of Marketing Activities: A Contingency Theory of Structure and Performance", *Journal of Marketing*, 49 (4): 13–25.

Scheier, M.F. and C.S. Carver (1985) "The Self-Consciousness Scale: A Revised Version for Use with General Populations", *Journal of Applied Social Psychology*, 15 (8): 87–99.

Slater, S. and E.M. Olson (2001) "Marketing's Contribution to the Implementation of Business Strategy: An Empirical Analysis", *Strategic Management Journal*, 22 (11): 1055–1068.

Staplehurst, G. and S. Charoenwongse (2012) "Why Brand Personality Matters: Aligning Your Brand to Cultural Drivers of Success", *Millward Brown: Point of View*, www.millwardbrown.com/Libraries/MB_POV_Downloads/Millward_Brown_POV_B rand_Personality.sflb.ashx, accessed July 26, 2014.

Swaminathan, V., K.M. Stilley, and R. Ahluwalia (2009) "When Brand Personality Matters: The Moderating Role of Attachment Styles", *Journal of Consumer Research*, 35 (6): 985–1002.

Sweeney, J. and C. Brandon (2006) "Brand Personality: Exploring the Potential to Move from Factor Analysis to Circumplex Models", *Psychology & Marketing*, 23 (8): 639–663.

Veloutsou, C. and L. Moutinho (2009) "Brand Relationships through Brand Reputation and Brand Tribalism", *Journal of Business Research*, 62 (3): 314–322.

Wentzel, D. (2009) "The Effect of Employee Behavior on Brand Personality Impressions and Brand Attitudes", *Journal of the Academy of Marketing Science*, 37 (3): 359–374.

Wilcox, K., H.M. Kim, and S. Sen (2009) "Why Do Consumers Buy Counterfeit Luxury Brands?", *Journal of Marketing Research*, 46 (2): 247–259.

Winkler, M. (2012) "Cars Says as Much About a Person as Their Clothing and House, Professor Says", *Herald Sun*, www.heraldsun.com.au/news/cars-says-as-much-about-a-person-as-their-clothing-and-house-professor-says/story-e6frf7jo-1226518386974?nk=f 777d28587f13d46b8ce392025f09c34, accessed July 16, 2014.

PART VII

Systems and metrics for measuring brand relationships

23

SECRET RELATIONSHIPS

Understanding consumers' hidden feelings about brands

Chip Walker and Belle Frank

Introduction

Most experienced marketing practitioners have many times observed a focus group in which respondents claimed to do something or believe something that is counter to what real data sources tell us is happening in the marketplace. There isn't a mom today who doesn't say she is watching her family's food intake and yet, as a society, we Americans have never been fatter. If everything said in traditional research were true, we would be a nation of environmentally aware, health-conscious folks who exercise regularly. Marketers uncover disconnects between what people actually do, and what they say they do, over and over again. There has never been as much research fielded and, yet, in some ways, many predictions have never been more *inaccurate*. The marketing business depends on being able to understand what motivates people's brand behavior in order to drive it. Our expectation is that we can predict what people will do based on stimuli we create in order to inspire them to use our brands the way we want them to. Yet, our research often falls short.

Silver (2012) asserts that "data driven predictions can succeed – and they can fail. It is when we deny our role in the process that the odds of failure rise." The marketing research industry is booming. The promise of big data paints a rosy picture and, yet, the more brand research that is conducted, the more its limitations are revealed.

To achieve its objectives, marketing research needs to understand peoples' values and motivations to be able to leverage the learning on behalf of brands. Barden (2013) explains that people's goals and motivations are the fundamental building blocks of marketing because people are intentional (i.e., we are goal-focused; we do stuff to get stuff done), and choose the brand that most helps us get what we need done. He explains that subjective brand value is based on expected goal achievement. Further, he notes that even our attention is goal-focused: we notice things that will help us get done what we want to do. He goes on to assert that solid understanding of motivations is mission critical for marketing: brand relevance is all about aligning with, associating with, and serving people's goals, and marketers create goal-based value propositions. To Barden, conscious goals vary by situation, falling into one of two types: approach goals (wanting something), or avoidance goals (avoiding something). Smart branding should, in his opinion, line up accordingly with these goals. He believes that people share three basic psychological goals across situations that underpin most behavior *even if we aren't aware of them*, specifically security (i.e., being cared for and avoiding fear), autonomy (i.e., power, control, and mastery), and excitement (i.e., stimulation, relief from boredom). While much has been written about values (Maslow first published his classic hierarchy of needs model in 1943) that would support Barden's observation, less has been written about the need to apply multiple types of investigation to really get at the underlying truth of how people feel.

Studies have called for further investigation of the conscious and unconscious motivations of people. To understand consumer attitudes and decisions, emotions, unconscious motives, and automatic processes should be considered (Batra *et al.* 1996; Cohen and Areni 1991; Gorn 1982; Isen 1989; McDonald 1991; Shiv and Fedorkhin 1999). This observation is reasonable based on work in implicit social cognition showing that attitudes can be automatically activated outside conscious awareness (Bargh 1997; Johnson and Weisz 1994).

Additionally, as relates to marketing practice, there is research that suggests the value of better understanding emotional relationships to brands that may not always be obvious when looking at brand usage. Miller, Fournier, and Allen (2012) describe some more complex patterns not typically considered by practitioners. It may be that typical research is not letting marketers discover the truth we need. Additionally, Springfield and Sharma (2012), in a chapter designed to identify a model to help practitioners build differentiated brands based on core principles about how people relate to the brands, further reinforce our belief that we need to research differently in order to get better direction for our strategies and client recommendations.

What we did

At Young & Rubicam, we began to ask ourselves: how can we understand what consumers *aren't* saying, and, in so doing, get better at understanding people and their relationships with brands? Our work surrounding the creation of marketing communications requires us to get at the truth of what will drive people's responses to brands. We need to find some new ways of working to make our creative product stronger.

In search of better answers, we designed and fielded a pilot study to explore both the conscious and unconscious sides of consumer motivation. Our hypothesis was that what people say consciously in response to conventional research questions isn't the whole story and may, in fact, be misleading us. We wanted to learn both about consumer motivations (values) and about their relationships with brands.

Research approach

We decided to partner with noted psychologist Dr Joel Weinberger, an industry expert on understanding how conscious and unconscious brain processes work in marketing. Weinberger is a clinical, personality, and motivation psychologist, partner in Implicit Strategies, and professor at the Derner Institute for Advanced Psychological Studies at Adelphi University. We leveraged his techniques in combination with our individual and personal 20-year expertise with Young & Rubicam's BrandAsset Valuator model (Frank *et al.* 2008) to develop our approach.

Our study was designed to explore two key questions:

1   Are there differences between people's stated important values and values that are unconsciously important to them?
2   What happens to our understanding of brand relationships when we compare assessments collected consciously with those collected unconsciously?

Research design

The pilot study we designed is unusual in its melding of two research approaches: traditional survey research, which reveals what people think consciously, and indirect questioning, using an approach called the Implicit Association Test (IAT) that reveals unconscious motivations – the deep drives that operate outside of our conscious awareness (Greenwald *et al.* 1998). This pilot study was conducted in Spring 2013 online among 900 respondents in the US, Brazil, and China, with representative samples of adults 18+ in the US and A, B, and C social classes ages 18+ in China and Brazil. People were first exposed to an implicit values test, followed by an explicit values test, and then an implicit brands test followed by an explicit brands test. The nature of the implicit collection meant that exposure to it would not influence the explicit responses and the explicit items and brands were rotated to avoid order bias.

Dr Weinberger was responsible for the data collection and analysis of the implicit data. Carbonview Research fielded our explicit study and those findings were analyzed at Young & Rubicam. See Figure 23.1 for our research methodology.

Implicit research methods are designed to uncover unconscious reactions indirectly, e.g., through reaction time (Gibson 2008). The theory (Greenwald *et al.* 1998) is that respondents will react faster to things that are already linked unconsciously in their brains (e.g., in the US, when assessing photos of people, "white = good, black = bad"). Tests like these have been used extensively and reliably in academia in the study of prejudice, psychopathology, and attitudes among other topics (cf. Cunningham *et al.* 2004; De Houwer 2002). They have also

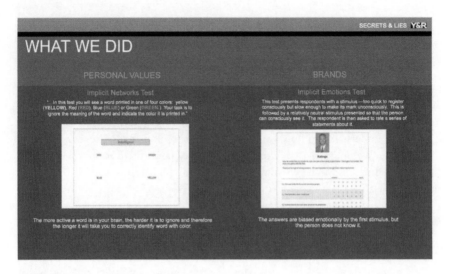

FIGURE 23.1 Research methodology

been used to study brand attitudes (cf. Maison *et al.* 2004; Gibson 2008; Brunel *et al.* 2004).

The two specific tests Dr Weinberger employed in the study were implicit networks and implicit emotions tests. (See Figure 23.1 for more details.)

Pilot study learning: values measurement

The hidden world

We found that some of consumers' most important motivations are hidden from view to the casual observer, and that our consciously stated motives may misstate what lies within. Our personal desires appear to operate on two different planes – the conscious and the unconscious – which turn out to be quite different from one another.

Across all three countries studied (US, China, and Brazil), the #1 most important value consciously was "meaning in life" – whereas, unconsciously measured, it was "sexual fulfillment." The #2 conscious value is "choosing your own path," but #2 unconsciously it's "honoring tradition." According to Dr Weinberger, "What we saw across all the data is that people's unconscious values seem to operate in a world that's independent of what they can readily tell us. This helps explain why we sometime have trouble explaining our actions or sometimes even 'argue with ourselves.'"

Our inner civil war

The study found that not only do consumers' conscious and unconscious values differ – in many cases they actually oppose each other. In all three countries, some values that were highly ranked consciously were ranked much lower unconsciously, and vice versa. For example, the top ranked conscious values in the US (helpfulness, choosing your own path, and meaning in life) seem to channel the voice of talk show host Oprah Winfrey. But, the top unconscious values (maintaining security, sexual fulfillment, and honoring tradition) – suggest we really value someone who may be more reminiscent of television's mobster boss, Tony Soprano.

When we put conscious and unconscious values on a 2 × 2 importance grid (see Figure 23.2) we get a sense of what's truly important, what consumers *say* is important (but isn't), what's secretly important, and what's truly unimportant. As you'll see in Figure 23.2, a complex and contradictory portrait of the US consumer values set emerges.

We applied this same type of quadrant analysis across all three countries to get a sense of commonalities (Figure 23.3). The only common denominator was the secret importance of sexual fulfillment. Perhaps it just goes to show that sex is important, or as we say in the industry, "it sells, but an ad based on it may not score highly in a traditional copy test."

Conscious + Unconscious Portrait: USA

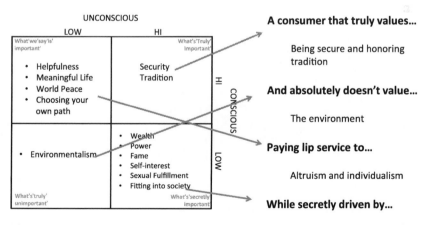

FIGURE 23.2 The four quadrants

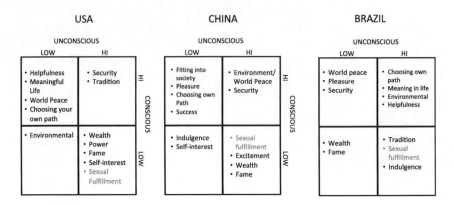

FIGURE 23.3 The importance of sex across markets

Pilot study learning: brand measurement

We measured both conscious and unconscious branding response for 15 brands in the US. The authors selected these particular brands because they were either very prominent (e.g., Apple, McDonalds) or because experience with them suggested that they might have interesting conscious/unconscious tensions (e.g., Playboy, *National Enquirer*.)

The conscious brand ratings (brand liking ratings on a 7–point scale) may not seem surprising: the 'usual suspects' rose to the top (e.g., Amazon, Apple, Google.) However, the top five on unconscious liking included some less expected brands, notably the *National Enquirer*.

Top five conscious liking
1 Amazon
2 Google
3 Apple
4 Microsoft
5 Target

Top five unconscious liking
1 Target
2 Amazon
3 Facebook
4 Whole Foods
5 *National Enquirer*

As we saw with values, conscious and unconscious brand ratings often oppose one another. Brands, such as Google, that were at the top of the conscious list were nearer the bottom of the unconscious list, and brands, such as Exxon, that score poorly on conscious scales moved up considerably when assessed unconsciously (see Figure 23.4).

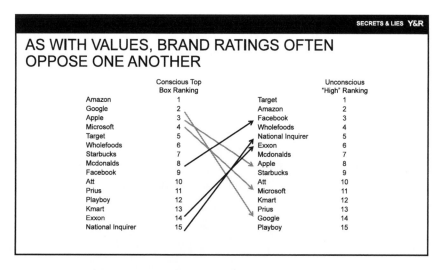

FIGURE 23.4 Brand ratings in opposition

By putting brands on the same type of 2 × 2 grid that we created for values (see Figure 23.5), we see a range of brand relationship types emerge. Two of these are relatively straightforward: brands that have high liking regardless of whether they were consciously or unconsciously assessed (which we refer to as "Truly Liked"), and those that have low liking whether they were consciously or unconsciously assessed (which we call "Truly Disliked").

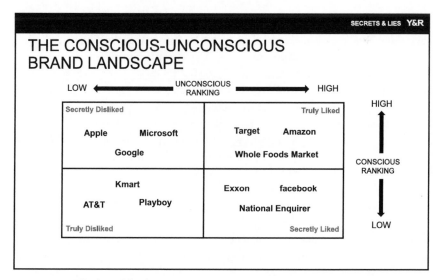

FIGURE 23.5 The brand landscape

But we also saw two types of 'secret relationships' emerge. In the upper left quadrant, where brands are better liked consciously than unconsciously, we find what we're calling "Secretly Disliked" brands. And, in the lower right quadrant, where brands are better liked unconsciously than consciously, we find what we're calling "Secretly Liked" brands.

BAV analysis of "secret relationships"

The pilot study only permitted a very limited amount of brand diagnostic questioning, but we were able to leverage BrandAsset™ Valuator (BAV), the world's largest brand equity database, to understand more about these "secret relationship" types.

The BAV model

At Young & Rubicam, our approach to building brands is inspired by our proprietary BrandAsset™ Valuator (BAV),[1] the world's largest database on brands. Since 1993, Young & Rubicam has surveyed over 500,000 consumers across 44 markets on 35,000 brands. BrandAsset™ Valuator measures the range of brand health dimensions, gauging consumer perceptions on brand health and imagery, as well as brand usage, consideration, and loyalty. BAV has found that brands grow and develop according to the Power Grid (see Figure 23.6), starting out unfocused and unknown, then becoming niche brands as Brand Strength develops, and ultimately leadership brands as Brand Stature increases. The study also measures 48 functional and emotional brand imagery attributes.

Explanatory modeling

Leveraging BAV's consumers' conscious responses, we wanted to understand what the rich and proven measures within the BAV database would reveal about the 'secret relationship' brands uncovered in the pilot study. Using the brand information revealed in our pilot study, we were able to identify how the pilot test brands mapped to the conscious/unconscious brand landscape. Leveraging the wealth of data in BAV, we wanted a better understanding of what kinds of brand pillars and imagery are associated with the different "secrecy" classifications. Further, we were able to query our database to tell us what other brands shared their imagery profile to project the "secrecy" patterns of a broad range of brands. This type of brand imagery "lookalike" modeling is something we have been doing for more than 20 years as a way to help us understand a brand's derived elasticity, or whether a given brand can expand into a new category based on whether it delivers the kind of imagery that is required to succeed in that category.

To place the brands from our pilot study onto the BAV Power Grid, we went into the BAV database (based on 2013 US data) and looked at the average BAV ratings for the brands in each of our relationship types: "Truly Liked" (e.g., Target,

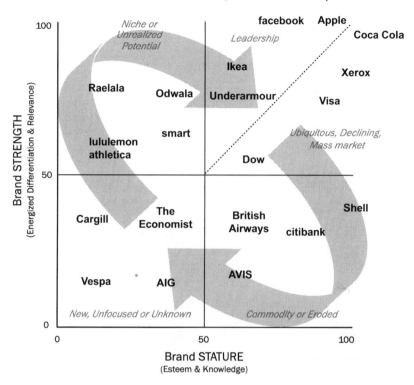

The PowerGrid – How Brands Grow and Develop

FIGURE 23.6 Mapping brands on the power grid

Wholefoods, Amazon), "Secretly Disliked" (e.g., Apple, Google, Microsoft), "Secretly Liked" (e.g., Facebook, Exxon, *National Enquirer*) and "Truly Disliked" (e.g., AT&T, Playboy, K–Mart.)

The two consciously well-liked brand groupings ("Truly Liked" and "Secretly Disliked") are in the leadership quadrant on the Power Grid (see Figure 23.7). This is not surprising, given that BAV measures conscious brand ratings and our pilot study indicated they would perform well consciously. The two consciously less liked brand groups ("Secretly Liked" and "Truly Disliked") are in weaker positions on the Power Grid.

"Secretly disliked" brands

What's a bit surprising on the Power Grid is that the brand grouping with the strongest BAV brand health is actually the "Secretly Disliked" brands, Apple, Google, and Microsoft. This indicates that as iconic and powerful as these brands are, they may well have hidden vulnerabilities. And it raises the question – can a

Power Grid

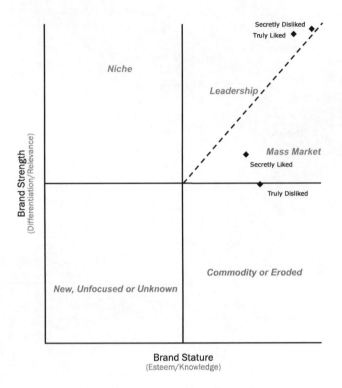

FIGURE 23.7 Unconscious and conscious brand attitudes

brand, like a celebrity, become too popular for its own good, and ultimately be resented for it? These brands are widely used and have millions of fans. Yet, they may be like the prom queen or king in high school – perhaps very popular, but also resented on some level. They are all three technology brands whose popular products may bring with them frustrations, feelings of dependency, and worries about privacy.

It would seem that the power in these "Secretly Disliked" brands comes with great responsibility. When they err, people may be eager to criticize them for overstepping. The secret dislike could easily become more overt.

We also looked within BAV at the imagery attributes associated with each of our 'secret relationship' types (see Figure 23.8). We found that our "Truly Liked" brands' top imagery was very strong overall, emotional in nature (e.g., "cares for customers," "socially responsible"), and that negative imagery ("unapproachable") was at low levels. By contrast, "Secretly Disliked" brands also have strong imagery, but it was less emotional and they had higher "unapproachable" ratings.

BAV Brand Imagery – Brand Relationship Types

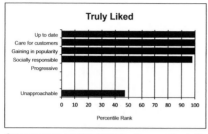

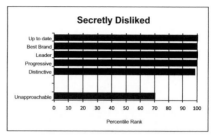

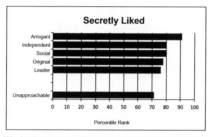

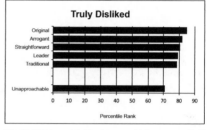

FIGURE 23.8 BAV brand imagery

We also did a 'look-alike' analysis within BAV to see which other brands of the 3,500 in the study had imagery highly correlated to our "Secretly Liked" brand type. Many of the other brands with this imagery pattern were in technology-related categories and include Verizon, Dell, Intel, and LG.

"Secretly liked" brands

When it comes to the "Secretly Liked" relationship quadrant (Figure 23.5), we see that both old and new brands find their way here. *National Enquirer*, Facebook and Exxon seem to be 'guilty pleasure' or embarrassment brands. We may enjoy using them privately, but don't always feel comfortable acknowledging that publicly – and, in fact, we may not even be consciously aware how much we actually like them.

"Secretly Liked" brands had somewhat weaker BAV top imagery (which included a major negative, "Arrogant"), and also had relatively high ranking on "Unapproachable." Other brands with a similar imagery pattern in BAV include a wide range of "guilty pleasure" brands:

Beer: Bud Light
Shopping: HSN
Cable TV: Bravo
Soft Drinks: Mountain Dew
Snack food: Doritos
Gaming: Nintendo

Why are these brands only 'secretly' rather than overtly liked? Just imagine yourself drinking Bud Light which watching HSN and eating a bag of Doritos. You might enjoy doing it, but it's not exactly the image of yourself you'd want to put on your holiday card.

Implications for marketing practice

Few practitioners have access to both conscious and unconscious brand data and, for some, the collection of it seems impractical. We believe that clues that emerged from our BAV analysis may help us identify secret relationships even if we can't measure them specifically. If explicit measures find that you have a strong brand with positive conscious imagery, but also some strong negative imagery (e.g., "arrogant" and "unapproachable"), you may well be at risk of becoming a "Secretly Disliked" brand. That seems especially true if you're in a technology related category. If your brand has some strong conscious negative imagery and is in a "guilty pleasure" category (e.g., fast food), you may be at risk of becoming a "Secretly Liked" brand with a more niche audience.

As practitioners, we appreciate these perspectives. The study suggested two important types of 'secret' relationships that we should consider when we develop strategies. Some brands may be like Facebook (secret crushes) and others may be like Apple (silent grudges). To us, the pilot research is providing useful information about brands and people, above and beyond what we have received in the past from traditional conscious-measure research studies alone. Hence, the real question is what to do if you believe a brand you are managing is living one of these secret relationship types. Depending on your brand's situation, one of the following two strategies may be more appropriate:

1. Embrace your secret relationship

If you have a "Secretly Disliked" brand, one option is to assume that this sometimes just comes with the territory when you're a highly popular brand. Apple, with its closed system and somewhat dictatorial style, may never be warm and approachable – and perhaps that's OK. The question is, given the latent negativity towards the brand, if Apple make a miss-step, (as it has done a few times in recent memory), will consumers desert the brand? Perhaps it is human nature, but many of us seem to enjoy seeing the mighty fall.

If you're "Secretly Liked," it may be that your users crave these kinds of clandestine brand relationships and don't want to give them up. Brands like Kraft Mac & Cheese ("You Know You Love It") and Cheetos, which embraces breaking social conventions, have successfully employed this approach. There is something compelling about having a more private relationship with a brand to which others aren't privy. The only question becomes – will brands like these always remain somewhat niche? Can brands ever become truly mainstream if they are "Secretly Liked"? This has implications for their business models, in terms of share and margin that should be acknowledged.

2. "Fix" your secret relationship

If your brand is "Secretly Disliked," the good news is that there does appear to be at least one pathway to becoming "Truly Liked," and that's adding approachability, humility, and humanity, all characteristics that "Truly Liked" brands in our study seemed to have, but that "Secretly Disliked" brands did not. Microsoft seems to be trying to do that now with its "Honestly" campaign.

If you're a "Secretly Liked" brand in a guilty pleasure category, such as fast food or snack foods, you can try to add new imagery that is more socially acceptable. Burger King recently did an about-face from its approach of targeting non-health conscious young men, and added healthier items to its menu and its advertising. The question for them is will this strategy alienate their core heavy users?

Calls for more learning

We would offer three major observations from the pilot studies and suggest some areas for further study. Practitioners may want to rethink three things:

- **Their reliance on traditional research** – Marketers who rely on direct questioning using traditional surveys and focus groups are probably only getting half the story. We've got to find new, commercially viable ways to hear and understand what consumers aren't saying.
- **Their traditional approach to targeting** – As marketers, we typically put target audiences into distinct segments and expect them to behave in consistent ways (e.g., we look for the soccer mom who drives a minivan and wears mommy jeans.) This research indicates she may be much more complex than that.
- **The way we talk about brand positioning** – We've been programmed to believe that 'single-mindedness' is the foundation of good branding. Yet, this research shows consumers may not be as easy to classify and their brand behavior may not be so predictable. Is it time for brands to move beyond the single-minded proposition and embrace paradox in their marketing approaches?

The Young & Rubicam way

This research reinforces a change in the way we think about research at Young & Rubicam. We expect creative research initiatives to go beyond conscious attitudinal data collection, and we call this approach "Think, Say, Do", reflecting the need for a multi-faceted research approach to get at today's complex consumer who may sometimes be unaware of his or her true motivation. In other words, we will no more rely solely on traditional surveys and focus groups. There are obviously many different ways to implement this policy, including the assessment of implicit associations, the technique we used in the research described above. We also suggest conducting ethnographies; we use a consumer immersion technique called "eXploring," and we are experimenting with neuroscience techniques.

In line with the thinking from the "Secrets and Lies" study, we've been helping clients to go out and find their "Brand Tension." This is the idea that break-away brands – like people – thrive on conflict and polarity (e.g., LandRover = Hardworking AND Luxury.) Brands that are one-note (e.g., K-Mart = Cheap) are simply less interesting to consumers today than those that have more depth of character through embracing a tension (e.g., Target = Cheap + Chic.) Patagonia's new campaign takes this concept to the extreme – by embracing being eco-friendly, while simultaneously acknowledging all the ways they currently harm the environment. It will be interesting to see if this bold approach succeeds.

Final thoughts

As an industry, we are in the early stages of tapping into the unconscious and, thus, still have many unanswered questions. Is there a 'hidden' (unconscious) side of brand equity that is completely unexplored? Can this new side of brand equity help us unlock brands' hidden vulnerabilities and/or potential? Perhaps the frontier for the brand relationship business isn't CRM technology, but rather the unexplored world of the consumer unconscious.

To be clear, this was a pilot study and its purpose was simply to begin to explore questions that will influence the future of marketing. That said, we believe this research reveals there are potentially big rewards for us if we continue delving more deeply into the recesses of the consumer's secret world.

Notes

1   For more detailed information on BAV, see www.bavconsulting.com.

References

Barden, P. (2013) *Decoded – The Science Behind Why We Buy*. New York: Wiley.
Bargh, J.A. (1997) "The Automaticity of Everyday Life", *Advances in Social Cognition* (Vol. 10), ed. R.S. Wyer, Jr. Mahwah, NJ: Erlbaum: 1–61.

Batra, R., J.G. Myers, and D. Aaker (1996) *Advertising Management*. Upper Saddle River, NJ: Prentice Hall.

Brunel, F., B. Tietje, and A.G. Greenwald (2004) "Is the Implicit Association Test a Valid and Valuable Measure of Implicit Consumer Social Cognition?", *Journal of Consumer Psychology*, 14 (4): 385–404.

Cohen, J.B. and C.S. Areni (1991) "Affect and Consumer Behavior", *Handbook of Consumer Behavior*, eds T.S. Robertson and H.H. Kassarjian. Englewood Cliffs, NJ: Prentice Hall: 188–240.

Cunningham, W.A., J.B. Nezlek, and M.R. Banaji (2004) "Implicit and Explicit Ethnocentrism: Revisiting the Ideologies of Prejudice", *Personality and Social Psychology Bulletin*, 30 (10): 1332–1346.

De Houwer, J. (2002) "The Implicit Association Test as a Tool for Studying Dysfunctional Associations in Psychopathology: Strengths and Limitations", *Journal of Behavioral Therapy and Experimental Psychiatry*, 33 (2): 115–133.

Frank, B., M. Sussman, and A. Palkar (2008) "Brand Health Measures Your Mother Would Love", *Admap*, 492 (March): 24–27.

Gibson, B. (2008) "Can Evaluative Conditioning Change Attitudes Towards Mature Brands? New Evidence from the Implicit Association Test", *Journal of Consumer Research*, 35 (1): 178–188.

Gorn, G.J. (1982) "The Effects of Music in Advertising on Choice Behavior: A Classical Conditioning Approach", *Journal of Marketing*, 46 (1): 94–101.

Greenwald, A.G., D.E. McGhee, and J.L.K. Schwartz (1998) "Measuring Individual Differences in Implicit Cognition: The Implicit Association Test", *Journal of Personality and Social Psychology*, 74 (6): 1464–1480.

Isen, A.M. (1989) "Some Ways in which Affect Influences Cognitive Processes: Implications for Advertising and Consumer Behavior", *Cognitive and Affective Responses to Advertising*, eds A. Tybout and P. Cafferata. Lexington, MA: Lexington Books.

Johnson, M.K. and C. Weisz (1994) "Comments on Unconscious Processing: Finding Emotion in the Cognitive Stream", *The Heart's Eye: Emotional Influences in Perception and Attention*, eds P.M. Niedenthal and S. Kitayama. San Diego, CA: Academic Press: 145–164.

Maison, D., A.G. Greenwald, and R.H. Bruin (2004) "Predictive Validity of the Implicit Association Test in Studies of Brands, Consumer Attitudes, and Behavior", *Journal of Consumer Psychology*, 14 (4): 405–415.

McDonald, C. (1991), "Sponsorship and the Image of the Sponsor", *European Journal of Marketing*, 25 (11): 31–38.

Miller, F., S. Fournier, and C. Allen (2012) "Exploring Relationship Analogues in the Brand Space", *Consumer-Brand Relationships: Theory and Practice*, eds S. Fournier, M. Breazeale, and M. Fetscherin. London: Routledge/Taylor & Francis: 30–56.

Shiv, B. and A. Fedorikhin (1999) "Heart and Mind in Conflict: The Interplay of Affect and Cognition in Consumer Decision Making", *Journal of Consumer Research*, 26 (3): 278–292.

Silver, N. (2012) *The Signal and the Noise: Why So Many Predictions Fail but Some Don't*. New York: Penguin Press.

Springfield, S. and P. Sharma (2012) "Brand Humanity: Transforming the Business of Building Brands", *Consumer-Brand Relationships: Theory and Practice*, eds S. Fournier, M. Breazeale and M. Fetscherin. London: Routledge/Taylor & Francis: 382–294.

24

USING RELATIONSHIP METAPHORS TO UNDERSTAND AND TRACK BRANDS

John Wittenbraker, Helen Zeitoun, and Susan Fournier

The practitioner point of view

Theory and research on consumer-brand relationships has grown significantly since the seminal publications in the 1990s (Fournier 1994; 1998), but this growing interest and expanding literature has occurred mainly in the academic community. Despite the rich insights afforded by core concepts in this work, scalable, practical applications have followed, but adoption by practitioners has lagged.

Most managers' understanding of how brands work has been profoundly affected by the widely used AIDA or funnel model. Remarkably, the AIDA concept was originally developed nearly 120 years ago at the end of the industrial revolution, widely attributed to Elias St Elmo Lewis in 1898. This approach persists likely due to the compelling imagery and simplicity of the funnel metaphor.

Marketers find the funnel concept easy to understand and intuitively actionable. Research practitioners also found the funnel compelling because it was easy to measure and respond to marketers' desire for "levers" that they can "pull" to drive demand for their products or services. Funnels and levers may have been useful metaphors for industrial age thinking, but these ideas began to lose relevance, particularly in the advertising community, in the 1980s. More recently, the classic AIDA/funnel model has lost even more ground as evidence builds that it fails to reflect the emotional experience of brands in our more digitally connected and socially networked global culture.

Pine and Gilmore (1998; 1999) capture this evolution in their analysis of the history of economics and marketing that suggests that we have moved well beyond an industrial age economy that was based on *goods*, evolved with increased brand differentiation and potential for premium pricing through the *service* economy, and pushed into what they call the *experience* economy, where brands will succeed in differentiating themselves and generating profits based not on the features and benefits they confer, but rather, by the experiences they create. And now, in the accelerating global expansion of digital life, the distance between brands and people shrinks and we stand at the precipice of what we might call a *relationship* economy, where there is a new appreciation for the emotional forces as well as the social life of brands and their mutual dependence with consumers.

As the new insights and capabilities of consumer-brand relationship research meets the growing demand for a paradigm shift among marketing managers, new approaches to measuring and managing brands become possible. But, these approaches must meet the dual objectives of reflecting the rich realities of brand experience in modern culture, and the need for a simple, clear conceptual model for practical application.

Developments in research on consumer-brand relationships

The development of theory in consumer-brand relationships has been built on deep literatures in social psychology (cf. Rusbult 1983; Rusbult *et al.* 1991), the interdependence theory of Kelley (Kelley and Thibaut 1978; Kelley 1979), developmental psychology (cf. Thompson *et al.* 2005; Park *et al.* 2010), and Bowbly's (1980) attachment theory. These, and other theories of brand relationship quality (BRQ), all use psychometric scales to measure the consumer-brand relationship (Fournier 2009). They tend to be built primarily using deductive methods: positing critical dimensions, measuring them, and building theory based on dependency modeling from the data. This work has been instrumental in advancing the scientific understanding of consumer-brand relationships, but has not resulted in a robust, multidimensional measurement approach that expresses the broad diversity of relationships with which managers have to deal.

An alternative approach is to use a structured, inductive approach to theory build-ing. Rather than pre-specifying theory-based dimensions of consumer-brand relationships, this approach builds a measurement system and theory based on the use of human relationships as metaphors for brand relationships. This approach builds on the work of Wish, Deutsch, and Kaplan (1976) who were focused on inducing the fundamental dimensions of human relationships from ratings of a range of personal relationships (you and your mother, you and your supervisor, etc.) and prototypical or role relationships (close friends, master-slave, etc.). In this work, undergraduate partic-ipants rated 45 different relationship types on 25 bipolar scales. Proximities (Euclidean distances) between the relationship types were computed based on the 25 bipolar scales and the resulting (dis)similarities matrices were used as input for a multidimen-sional scaling (INDSCAL) of the relationship types. The results showed that there were four dimensions underlying the relationship types used in the study: the first dimension was interpreted as cooperative/friendly (e.g., close friends) versus compet-itive/hostile (e.g., personal enemies); the second dimension represented equal (e.g., business partners) versus unequal (e.g., parent-child) relationships; the third dimension reflected intense (e.g., parent-teenager) versus superficial (e.g., casual acquaintances) relationships; and the fourth dimension represented task-oriented/formal (e.g., inter-viewer-applicant) versus socio-emotional/informal (e.g., siblings) relationships.

Iacobucci and Ostrum (1996) extended this work into a marketing context to explore the nature of relationships specifically in *commercial* settings, such as business-to-business marketing, provider-to-customer (as in services marketing), and more classic business-to-consumer marketing. In addition to assessing a range of relationships in each of these three domains, they also included 15 "classical" or prototypical relationships (teammates, divorced couple, neighbors). Student participants rated 30 "real" relationships plus the 15 metaphorical relationships on 18 bipolar scales, 14 from Wish *et al.* (1976) plus four more intended to tap long-term, trust-based relationships versus short-term, risky relationships. Factor analysis of the ratings data across the relationship types resulted in a factor structure that replicated the result from Wish *et al.* (1976). The first factor represented valence (cooperative/positive versus competitive/hostile), the second expressed closeness or intensity, the third reflected formality (work-based versus informal/social), and the fourth factor replicated the symmetry versus asymmetry dimension in the Wish study. Correspondence analysis was used to reveal the overall structure and interdependencies between the relationship types and ratings scales (as columns and rows, respectively, in an aggregate data matrix). The first two dimensions were interpreted and aligned exactly with the first two dimensions of the factor analysis of the attributes alone and with the findings from Wish *et al.* (1976). The first dimension expressed valence and the second dimension expressed intensity.

Fournier (2009) conducted the first inductive relationship structure study that included both brands and prototypical human relationships in the same analysis. This study used 52 bipolar relationship attributes derived from prior research on consumer-brand relationships, 35 national and strong regional brands, and 11 prototypical human relationship types. One sample of student participants rated the 35 brands on the 52 bipolar attributes (each participant provided ratings on only 12 of the 35 attributes to reduce fatigue), while another sample rated the 11 human relationship types on the 52 bipolar attributes (also in subsets to reduce fatigue). Proximities were computed, based on the relationship attributes, to build an aggregate dataset for the brands and another for relationship types. Multidimensional scaling (INDSCAL) of aggregate datasets revealed that the first four dimensions emerged cleanly from both the human relationship and brand data: valence (harmonious versus hostile), arousal (emotional versus functional), potency (strong/deep versus weak/superficial), and equality (equal/balanced versus one-sided/hierarchical). These dimensions generally correspond with the findings of both Wish *et al.* (1976) and Iacobucci and Ostrum (1996).

These studies show that it is possible to develop a consistent analysis of consumer-brand relationships using inductive methods, but they all have some limitations. First, while they each derive a structural analysis of the relationship space from ratings of prototypic relationships, these structures are dependent to some extent on the particular selection of relationship attributes they employ. Both Wish *et al.* (1976) and Iacobucci and Ostrum (1996) rely on highly similar and relatively small inventories of these attributes. Fournier (2009) remedies this, to some extent, by expanding the number of attributes based on a thorough review of prior quantitative and qualitative research. Second, all of these studies relied on students as participants. The findings are compelling and largely consistent, but the generalizability of the results is not guaranteed. Finally, these studies were all conducted in the US and may reflect the specific culture of a western, highly developed culture and brand and marketing environment.

Global system for measuring consumer-brand relationships

Inspired by this research, we set out to build a globally consistent and validated system to measure and track brands that uses human relationships as metaphors for brand relationships. This idea is compelling for several reasons. At their core, relationships provide meaning to people.

They range across several dimensions and take many forms: they can be deep and intense or weak and ephemeral, positive or negative, durable or brittle. They can also evolve and change over a series of experiences or interactions and in response to contextual forces (Fournier 2009). From a practical point of view, human relationship metaphors are intuitive for research respondents and marketers alike, affording a high fidelity transmission of nuanced, complex information from consumers to marketing decision makers. In the end, they are also a system built on an idea as simple as the brand funnel was: that consumers are on a journey with the brands in their life. We can track this journey using human relationship forms as the basis for a rigorous, quantitative approach that is validated to business outcomes.

This work was based on an exhaustive review of the literature and early qualitative research to assay the widest array of relationship forms possible, including forms that signal the absence of a connection with the other (e.g., complete stranger), which is itself a relationship form. We also mined the psychological, sociological, and marketing literatures to identify a wide array of dimensions along which relationships might vary. We undertook a two–part quantitative research program involving over 7,000 interviews in four countries selected to represent a wide range of cultural contexts: US (developed, mature), China (emerging), Spain (representing cultures of growing importance), and Germany (where we have extensive data on the financial performances of brands). Respondents were recruited from Internet access panels, and surveys were conducted using computer-assisted web-based interviewing.

Two parallel studies were conducted: a relationship structure study and a brand study. To ensure that our relationship metaphors cover the entire range of relationship types, the first study was designed to reveal the underlying structure of human relationships, exploring the underlying dimensionality of a large number of cross-culturally relevant, prototypic relationships that might serve as metaphors for brand relationships in global research.

A second study focused on the associations consumers draw between the relationships they have with a large number of brands across a wide range of categories with the same set of human relationship metaphors used in the first study. This study also captured the "usual" set of brand key performance indicators (KPIs) used in contemporary brand and advertising research to provide validation and a basis for establishing the relevance and effectiveness of the new relationship metaphors in a brand context.

Understanding the structure of relationships

As a foundational step in the use of relationship metaphors for brand research, we needed to empirically quantify and understand the structure of human relationship forms so that we could extract clear meaning and implications from the metaphors we ask consumers to use. Thus, a foundational study was designed to reveal the structure of prototypic human relationship forms or relationship types (RTs) across three divergent cultures: US, China, and Spain. Based on an exhaustive review of the literature and results from early qualitative research, a wide-ranging list of 53 prototypic RTs was developed. In addition to the usual candidates (e.g., best friend, enemy), special attention was paid to include more extreme relational forms, ranging from very weak relationships (e.g., strangers, seatmates on a plane) to more extreme relationships (e.g., one-night stand, stalker-prey, star-groupie). A similarly exhaustive list of 48 bipolar relationship attributes (RAs) was culled from research on relationships in the psychological, sociological, and marketing literatures.

Two parallel approaches to measurement and analysis were used to provide convergent validation to our inductive approach to dimension analysis: multiple correspondence analysis (MCA) and multidimensional scaling (MDS). MCA is a more practical approach to dimensional analysis because it simultaneously locates both RTs and RAs in multidimensional space, allowing for direct interpretation of the underlying dimensions. Moreover, the location of brands in space can be established by treating brand profiles on the RTs from the second study as passive or illustrative vectors that can be projected into the dimensional solution. A drawback of MCA is that the solution is dependent on the selection of relationship attributes used to profile each RT. MDS avoids this by directly analyzing direct measures of the similarity between pairs of RTs, unmediated by attributes determined on an a priori basis.

Interviews were conducted via the Internet among a representative sample of 1,000 consumers in each region. For the MCA analysis, respondents rated a random selection of six of the 53 prototypic RTs on 24 of the 48 bipolar RAs. Subsets of RTs and RAs were used to limit respondent fatigue. To accommodate the possibility that the bipolar RAs may not be "perfectly" bipolar, we created (2 × 48) 96 unipolar attributes in the aggregate dataset by splitting at the midpoint the responses provided by each respondent. These data were used to build an aggregate 53 RT × 96 RA matrix for each region. These data were analyzed with multiple correspondence analysis (MCA) to reveal the underlying dimensionality of the RT × RA space.

For the MDS analysis, respondents rated the similarity of a random selection of 18 of the RTs to a single "exemplar" RT, also randomly selected from the six that were used for the attribute rating task. This was repeated three times using different random selections of exemplar RTs and rating RTs. These data were used to build an aggregate 53 RT × 53 RT similarity matrix for each region. Multidimensional scaling (MDS) was used to discover the underlying dimensionality of the RT × RT space. This approach provides a cleaner analysis of the inherent dimensionality of the relationship space, unmediated by the particular attributes that were in the list of RAs used in the first task. This affords an efficient and independent validation test of the dimensionality of the space from the same sample of respondents.

Four dimensions were extracted from the MCA analysis, accounting for 94 percent of the variance in the data. These dimensions can be interpreted as: 1) valence (positive-negative), 2) intensity (intense/strong-weak), 3) arousal/passion (exciting-dull), and 4) equality (equal status-unequal status). Figure 24.1 contains a plot of the RTs on first two dimensions.

The results of the MDS validation analysis aligned very closely with the MCA results. The RT profiles were highly similar to what we found in the multidimensional scaling results. Four dimensions were extracted with goodness of fit of 0.85. Both the content and the order of these dimensions were the same as in the MCA analysis. Observe the similarity of the plot of the first two MDS dimensions in

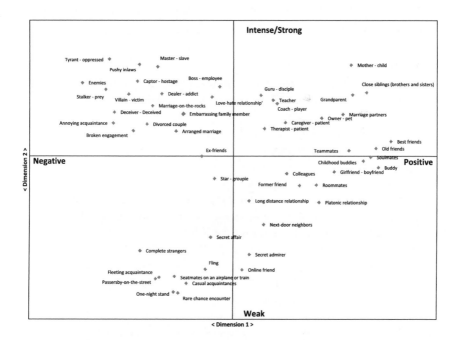

FIGURE 24.1 First two dimensions of a multidimensional scaling analysis of direct similarity ratings of 53 prototypic relationship types, combining data from US, China, and Spain

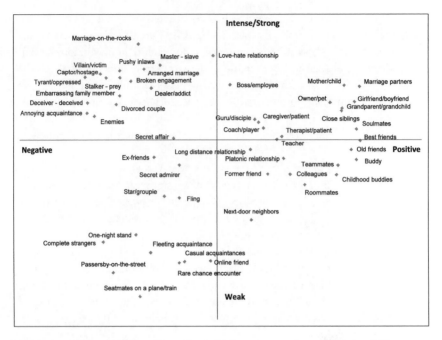

FIGURE 24.2 First two dimensions of a multiple correspondence analysis of 53 prototypic relationship types and 96 relationship attributes (not visible), combining data from US, China, and Spain

Figure 24.2 to the MCA solution in Figure 24.1. This provides compelling evidence for the convergent validity of the four dimensional nature of human relationships.

These two analyses align reasonably well with the results of prior research conducted with different populations and methods summarized in Table 24.1. In all five analyses, valence (positive-negative) was the first dimension, explaining the most variance. Intensity (intense-weak) was the second dimension in three of the five analyses. And equality (equal-unequal status) was replicated in all four analyses, more commonly entering in the third or fourth dimension. Unlike prior research, our study recovered a dimension that represents passion or arousal in both the MCA and MDS analyses. This dimension clearly differentiated a subset of the relationships such as flings, secret affairs, and one-night stands as more exciting, sometimes more hidden, and often less durable in the long-run. Taken as a whole, these studies all align with fundamental dimensionality measures replicated often in psychological research (e.g., the cross-cultural meaning of language illuminated in Osgood *et al.* (1957) and the emotional appraisals of Fountaine *et al.* (2007).

Finally, the dimensionality of the relationship space was replicated across the three divergent cultures included in the study. Figure 24.3 simultaneously shows the location of the relationship types for US, Spain, and China on the first two

TABLE 24.1 Summary of methods and findings of research on the dimensionality of human relationships

	Wish et al. (1976)	Iacobucci and Ostrum (1996)	Fournier (2009)	GfK MCA	GfK MDS
Method	MDS	Factor Analysis/MCA	MDS	MCA	MDS
Data Matrix	Proximities computed from attributes	FA: Attribute ratings MCA: Proximities computed from attributes	Proximities computed from attributes	Proximities computed from attributes	Direct measurement of RT similarities
Relationship Attributes	25*	18*	52	n/a	48 bipolar, split to 96 unipolar
Relationship Types	45	45	46	53	53
Relationship Domains	Personal and prototypic	Business and prototypic	Prototypic	Prototypic	Prototypic
Sample	Students	Students	Students	Consumers (US, China and Spain)	Consumers (US, China and Spain)
Dimensions	1. Valence 2. Equality 3. Intensity 4. Formality	1. Valence** 2. Intensity** 3. Equality** 4. Formality**	1. Valence 2. Intensity 3. Potency 4. Equality	1. Valence 2. Intensity 3. Passion/Arousal 4. Equality	1. Valence 2. Intensity 3. Passion/Arousal 4. Equality

Notes: MDS = Multidimensional Scaling, MCA = Multiple Correspondence Analysis, *14 attributes were common to both studies, **Solution from factor analysis, only DIM 1 and DIM 2 were reported for the MCA solution

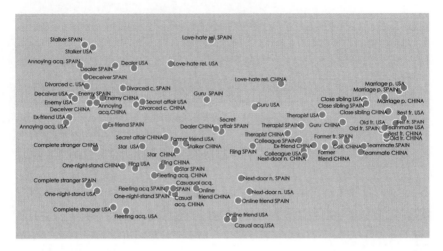

FIGURE 24.3 Multiple correspondence analysis map of the first two dimensions from RT × RA data shows a high degree of similarity in the position of relationship types in US, China, and Spain

dimensions. Not only are the relationships closely adjacent in this joint solution, but when the dimensions were extracted separately for each country, the same four dimensions resulted, and occurred in the same order of descending variance explained.

To summarize, this cross-cultural study of the structure of human relationship forms found that relationship types fall on four dimensions, which were convergently validated with two different methods and replicated across different global cultures. These four dimensions both align with and advance past research on the structure of relationship forms, as well as the broader literature on the structure of language and emotion.

Applying human relationship metaphors to brand relationships

The second study extended these relationship types into the brand and marketing space by asking consumers to use relationship forms that best described the connections they feel with a wide range of 253 brands across eleven product/service categories. The study was conducted in US, Spain, Germany, and China. Both global and regional brands were included from the laundry detergent, automotive, mobile device, shampoo, beverage, fast food restaurant, airline, television/entertainment, fashion, retail, and confection categories. We also included a sampling of non-traditional brands, such as major cities, professional sports teams, and public institutions. Using the same 53 relationship types employed in the first study, respondents (screened for category use) were asked to choose all that would apply to each of the brands in that category. They then selected the single relationship type that *best describes* their connection with the brand. Respondents also rated the brands on a series of more traditional brand metrics, such as consideration, preference, liking, proximity, differentiation, trust, loyalty, word-of-mouth, and recommendation.

These data were also used to understand how consumers use these relationship metaphors to describe brands and the extent to which these metaphor associations provide new insight into brand dynamics. Are there differences in the relevance of various relationship forms for the brand space? Does the nature of brand relationships vary across categories and cultures? What insights could brand relationships add to our understanding of categories and brands?

Narrowing the focus to brand-relevant relationship metaphors

We learned in initial qualitative research that not all human relationship forms may be relevant as metaphors for brand relationships. To produce a system that is practical for brand research, it is important to narrow the focus to a subset of relationship metaphors that 1) fully express the dimensionality of the relationship space, and 2) are relevant for expressing consumer-brand relationships. These requirements were explored by analyzing the frequency with which the 53 relationship types were associated with the brands in the brand study in the context of a cluster analysis of the 53 types. Applying these two criteria, we were able to identify 27 relationship metaphors that had a criterion frequency of brand associations and expressed the breadth of the deeper structure of relationship similarity. To confirm that we retained the structure of the full set of 53 types, we used the clustering of the 53 types to collapse the dimension study data (relationship types × relationship attributes) to the final set of 27 types and re-ran the MCA analysis. The results of this reanalysis replicated the original solution, reconstituting the four-dimensional space and the relative location of the 27 brand-relevant relationship types in the context of the original full set of 53 types.

Sensitivity to category and cultural differences

In order to be useful for applied research, especially for brand strategy, it is critical that a brand measurement system be capable of expressing the wide array of consumer-brand connections, as well as category and cultural commonalities and differences. Data from the brand study were used to identify patterns of brand relationships for each of the categories and countries in the brand study. These patterns of consumer-brand relationships were derived from cluster analysis of the overlapping use of relationship metaphors across the brands in each category. Observe the pattern of brand relationships from the television/entertainment category in the US in Figure 24.4 and the automotive market in Germany in Figure 24.5. In both cases, we can detect and size a critical mass of very ephemeral relationships (strangers and acquaintances). We also gain visibility into both positive and negative relationships (stalker, soured break-up).

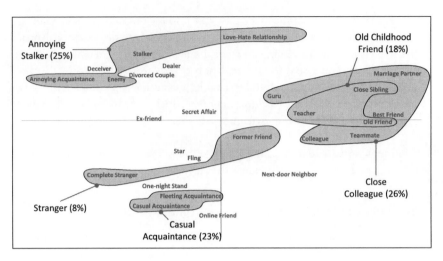

FIGURE 24.4 Cluster analysis of consumer relationships with television/entertainment brands in the US

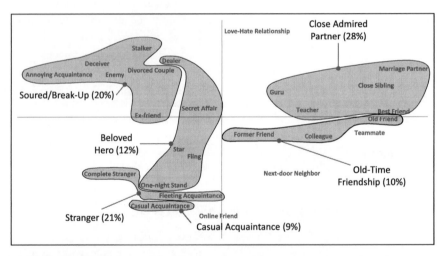

FIGURE 24.5 Cluster analysis of consumer relationships with automotive brands in Germany

Now contrasting the two solutions, category and cultural differences become apparent. The five clusters in the US television/entertainment category reflect the unique brand equities of some of the family/children's programming brands (e.g., Disney and PBS as old childhood friends) versus some of the more politically polarizing cable brands (e.g., Fox News and Comedy Central as annoying stalkers, depending upon your political point of view). In the German auto market, we detect the closely loyal connection consumers feel with iconic German brands (e.g., Mercedes Benz and BMW as close admired partners), the reverence directed toward high performance brands (e.g., Porsche as beloved hero), and the distance and/or antipathy toward some imports (e.g., strangers and soured break-up).

Relevance for business outcomes

These consumer-brand relationships provide deep insight into the emotional and social connections consumers have with brands in their lives. Consumer-brand relationships are also very strongly related to important business outcomes for brands. Figure 24.6 shows the correlations of the prevalence of each relationship type across the brands with market share and price premium data from independent (consumer panel) sources from a database of brand studies conducted using these relationship metaphors.

Brands with a high incidence of warm, enduring relationships (e.g., best friends, marriage partners) have larger market shares, especially compared to those with weaker relationships (e.g., strangers, fleeting acquaintances). Conversely, brands with more exciting, but also more short-lived engagement (e.g., flings, secret affairs) produce higher price premiums compared to those with lower excitement

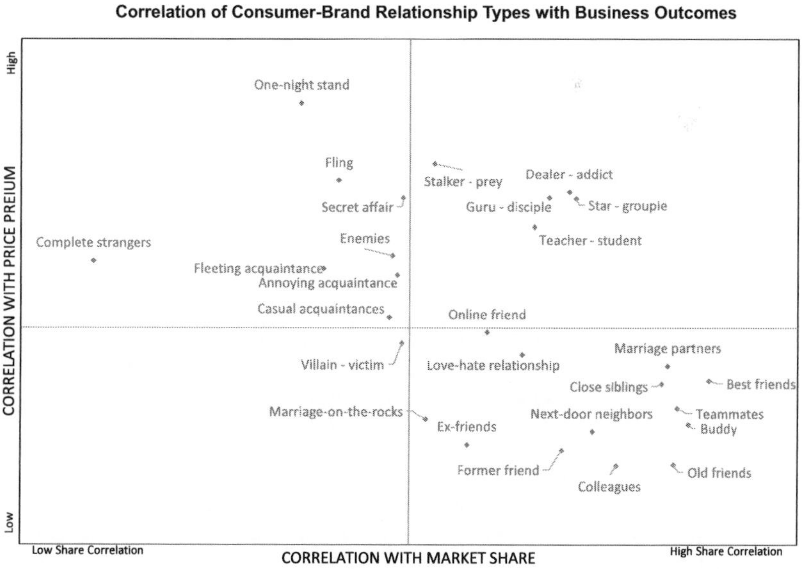

FIGURE 24.6 Correlation of relationship types to market share and price premium from independent (consumer panel) data

(e.g., colleagues, old friends). Finally, relationships that reflect strong status differentials (e.g., gurus, stars, addictions) also can show strength on both market share and price premium.

But, is having a strong consumer-brand relationship enough? To yield positive business outcomes, consumer-brand relationships must be transformed into a consumer's predisposition to act. When a strong relationship is combined with a positive competitive preference for the brand that is activated, strong market shares should result. Conversely, when brands show strong relationships that are based more on positive heritage or brand nostalgia, then the strong relationship will remain unexploited or latent. This idea was validated in a separate study of 109 US brands across a variety of categories. Data were collected in November 2012 and again in August 2014. Figure 24.7 shows a strong correlation between Active Relationship Equity and market share 20 months later.

In this view, latent equity might be interpreted as impairing brand success, but it also can be seen as a reservoir of positive relationship resources, waiting to be activated with the right strategy.

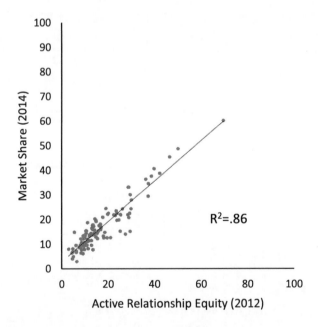

FIGURE 24.7 Correlation between active relationship equity in 2012 and market share in 2014 for 109 US brands across multiple categories (including food, beverage, health and beauty, technology, financial). Active relationship equity is based on consumers who have strong relationships (e.g., close friends or family, social circle, guru, and fling) and positive competitive preference

Implications for marketing practitioners

Understanding and managing brands through the lens of consumer-brand relationships offers unique visibility into how consumers and brands co-create experiences and connections that determine the commercial success of brands over time (Neudecker *et al.* 2013). In fact, the funnel model itself is a sort of rudimentary model of consumer-brand relationships, cobbled together from multiple brand metrics (e.g., awareness, consideration, preference, and loyalty). Yet, the shortcomings of this model are becoming more and more apparent as managers find it increasingly difficult to measure and understand the emotional and social side of brands, just as these factors seem to become more and more important. As a consequence, managers often find that the funnel fails to always reflect a brand's market share dynamics: brands are not always responding to hierarchical patterns. Other, more contemporary approaches that focus on a single outcome measure (e.g., preference) or prescriptive outcome (e.g., relevance or differentiation), also fall short of providing visibility into the interaction effects of consumer-brand relationships. Moreover, practitioners need differential visibility into the aspects of their brand relationships that affect topline performance (e.g., penetration/share) as well as bottom line performance (e.g., value/premium). This approach produces simple, transparent, and intuitive KPIs that achieve both of these objectives.

Brand management is relationship management

Understanding consumer-brand relationships is important because these relationships are functional for consumers, helping them to maintain predictability in their lives by outlining the uses and solutions that brands provide as they navigate the flow of experiences from day to day. These relationships vary in form (Fournier 1998), as demonstrated by the research outlined in this chapter and they evolve over time in response to experience and changes in context. It is this evolution of relationships that managers are trying to affect, aspiring to activate weak relationships, deepen good relationships, and recover from poor relationships. All of these aspirations are made more measureable, predictable and, hence, manageable by using relationship metaphors in consumer research and in brand management. In doing so, we can gain efficient quantitative measure of this deep and complex phenomenon. With relationships quantitatively measured and sorted, we can also discover which brand experiences, features and benefits, and imagery will help accelerate deepening interdependence with the brand and drive pro-brand behavior. Figure 24.8 illustrates the insights from this kind of modeling of the stimulators of relationship evolution for social media brands in the UK.

Each of the nodes in the model represent a constellation of relationship types that commonly co-occur for social media brands in this market. Notations on the pathways between these nodes cite the brand equities (e.g., experiences, imagery, features, and benefits) that differentiate each pair of nodes. This type of analysis

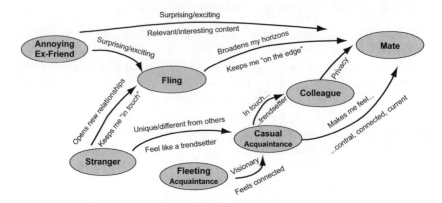

FIGURE 24.8 Better brand management comes from predictive models that show which brand equities and experiences will accelerate the evolution of brand relationships, and hence, long-term behavior

provides managers with clear guidance on how to focus and prioritize marketing and brand management to optimize their portfolio of brand relationships.

This thinking and measurement approach leads to a potential new generation of brand equity policies that managers are starting to operationalize: they can either create a totally new framework of relationship management, or link relationships to the current attitudinal and pre-behavioral performance indicators to transition more smoothly into a relationship-based approach to brand management.

Summary

Relationships are rich and complex; they have vibrant emotional dimensions and they are woven into our personal, social, and cultural lives. They are intuitive for consumers as market research respondents to think about. Relationships are also intuitive for marketers, allowing them to leverage their knowledge of human relationships to better manage brand relationships. Finally, relationship metaphors inherently can carry deep-seated, complex emotional tonality not possible with traditional scalar methods for measuring brands. All these features make relationship types a rich template to evoke insights about brand relationships and a much more suitable foundation for tracking and managing brands.

References

Bowlby, J (1980) *Loss: Sadness and Depression*. New York: Basic Books.

Fountaine, J.R.J, K.R. Scherer, E.B. Roesch, and P.C. Ellsworth (2007) "The World of Emotion is not Two-dimensional", *Psychological Science*, 18 (12): 1050–1057.

Fournier, S. (1994) "A Consumer–Brand Relationship Framework for Strategic Brand Management", PhD Thesis, University of Florida.

Fournier, S. (1998) "Consumers and Their Brands: Developing Relationship Theory", *Journal of Consumer Research*, 24 (3): 343–373.

Fournier, S. (2009) "Lessons Learned about Consumers' Relationships with their Brands", *Handbook of Brand Relationships*, eds J. Priester, D. MacInnis, and C.W. Park. New York: Society for Consumer Psychology and M.E. Sharp: 5–23.

Iacobucci, D. and A. Ostrum (1996) "Commercial and Interpersonal Relationships: Using the Structure of Interpersonal Relationships to Understand Individual-to-Individual, Individual-to-Firm and Firm-to-Firm Relationships in Commerce", *International Journal of Research in Marketing*, 13 (1): 53–72.

Kelley, H.H. (1979) *Personal Relationships: Their Structures and Processes*. Hillsdale, NJ: Lawrence Erlbaum.

Kelley, H.H. and J.W. Thibaut (1978) *Interpersonal Relations: A Theory of Interdependence*. New York: Wiley.

Neudecker, N., O. Hupp, and A. Stein (2013) "Is your Brand a One-Night Stand? Managing Consumer-Brand Relationships", *St. Gallen Marketing Research Review*, 6 (6): 22–33.

Osgood, C.E., G.J. Suci, and P.H. Tannenbaum (1957) *The Measurement of Meaning*. Urbana, IL: University of Illinois Press.

Park, C. W., D.J. MacInnis, J.R. Priester, A.B. Eisingerich, and D. Iacobucci (2010) "Brand Attachment and Brand Attitude Strength: Conceptual and Empirical Differentiation of Two Critical Brand Equity Drivers", *Journal of Marketing*, 74 (6): 1–17.

Pine, J. and J. Gilmore (1998) "Welcome to the Experience Economy", *Harvard Business Review*, 76 (4): 97–105.

Pine, J. and J. Gilmore (1999) *The Experience Economy*. Boston, MA: Harvard Business School Press.

Rusbult, C.E. (1983) "A Longitudinal Test of the Investment Model: The Development (and Deterioration) of Satisfaction and Commitment in Heterosexual Involvements", *Journal of Personality and Social Psychology*, 45 (1): 101–117.

Rusbult, C.E., J. Verette, G.A. Whitney, L.F. Slovik, and I. Lupkis (1991) "Accommodation Processes in Close Relationships: Theory and Preliminary Empirical Evidence", *Journal of Personality and Social Psychology*, 60 (1): 53–78.

Thomson, M., D.J. MacInnis, and C.W. Park (2005) "The Ties that Bind: Measuring the Strength of Consumers' Emotional Attachment to Brands", *Journal of Consumer Research*, 15 (1): 77–91.

Wish, M., M. Deutsch, and S.J. Kaplan (1976) "Perceived Dimensions of Interpersonal Relations", *Journal of Personality and Social Psychology*, 33: 409–420.

25

CONSTRUCTING CONSUMER-BRAND RELATIONSHIPS TO BETTER MARKET AND BUILD BUSINESSES

Max Blackston and Edward Lebar

The term consumer-brand relationship has become so ubiquitous that it now verges on losing any specific meaning. Unheard of 30 years ago when the term was first used in print, it is now used to describe virtually any brand–consumer construct or interaction. With the more universal recognition that the creation of value in brands has something to do with consumers as well as brand owners and managers, *consumer-brand relationship* seems to have replaced *brand equity* as the preferred term at the high ground of branding practice. What does it actually mean? Or, more exactly, what do the people who use the term actually mean?

By default, consumer-brand relationships are assumed to mean something analogous to interpersonal relationships. Although some (cf. Patterson and O'Malley 2006) may have questioned the wholesale appropriation of interpersonal relationships by brands, most users of the term in a specific sense – as opposed to its use as a generic surrogate for the term *brand equity* – are comfortable with the application of the interpersonal relationships (IPR) model to brands. Based on several years of our own experience of attempting to operationalize the IPR approach to identifying and measuring consumer-brand relationships, however, we will make the case that its application leads to limitations that make it a less appropriate model for understanding the relationships consumers have with brands. The more appropriate model is a psychological one, rather than a sociological one, specifically the theory of object-relations, the basis of relational psychology. Before describing this approach, we will briefly review the issues relating to the use of the IPR model.

Interpersonal relationships – the personal brand

There are a number of variations in the specific IPR model that companies adopt and the methods and approaches they employ to measure the constructs in which they are interested in understanding. Several models involve no more than placing a brand on a uni-dimensional scale, which, at its simplest, goes from a bipolar hate/love, to a more articulated semantic scale as used by BERA (Brand Equity Relationship Assessment) (www.berafindlove.com), which attempts to label relationships on a scale from "new" to "divorced" via "dating," "love," and "boredom." Saatchi and Saatchi's "Lovemarks" (Roberts 2005) model measures respect as well as love, which enables them, by crossing the two dimensions, to position brands in a simple four-quadrant chart.

Fournier, Aaker, and other consumer researchers (Fournier 1998; Aaker *et al.* 2004) have used more nuanced IPR models, which have demonstrated that it is possible to use IPR-based taxa to describe various types of relationships that consumers have with brands. That is to say, the qualities that consumers attribute to their relationships with brands are often very similar – if not identical – to the stereotypical qualities of a specific interpersonal relationship.

However, being able to deconstruct the relationship that a specific consumer has with a specific brand and labeling it in IPR terms does not provide a methodology for mapping on to an IPR taxonomy the generality of consumer-brand relationships. In fact, attempts to generalize and quantify the correspondence between consumer-brand relationships and IPR have been less than successful. When, for example, consumers are asked to allocate brands to specific IPR descriptors, their selection is highly idiosyncratic because it is specific to their own personal human relationships and personal brand experiences. The idiosyncratic nature of the ways in which consumers anthropomorphize brands and their relationships with them is illustrated by the following two examples from qualitative explorations of brand relationships.

In a study of auto insurance brands in the US, respondents' preferred brand was anthropomorphized by various consumers in figures as widely different as "A benign king who knows what is best for his subjects" and "my child's pediatrician." The common elements that can be identified in these anthropomorphisms are: a) the perception of an authority figure that has knowledge and expertise that the customer lacks, combined with b) a feeling of confidence in the brand that relies on the inference that the authority figure has the best interests of the customer at heart.

In a study of toilet paper conducted in Israel, a premium brand known for its strength (as opposed to the typical category benefit of softness) was variously described by non-users of the brand as "like Santa Claus" or a "foreign fashion model." What are the common elements here? Here, both figures are perceived as somewhat exotic (Santa Claus was described by an Israeli respondent and was thus foreign in that context), with unique competencies. However, and perhaps as a result of this initial perception, both figures are experienced with a feeling of a lack of intimacy, an indispensable element of a trusting relationship, based on the inference that the brand does not feel involved with the consumer.

What each of these cases illustrates are the diverse ways in which consumers can describe essentially similar relationships with a brand. In the context of qualitative research, these idiosyncratic articulations of brand relationships are definitely susceptible to decoding, or the use of semiotic tools or analysis of archetypes, as they have been here. However, the point is that they have to be skillfully decoded; these anthropomorphisms have no useful meaning if taken literally.

The hope, therefore, that forcing anthropomorphisms in a quantitative research setting (i.e., as probed by researchers using questions such as, "Is this brand like the sister you never had/the partner you wished you'd had/the wife you once had") can reliably identify types of brand relationships is, unfortunately, illusory. The interpersonal relationship model can be used anecdotally, but is not capable of generalization.

Object relations – the relational brand

The key insight of relational psychology is that relationships – with other people and with things – are paralleled by psychic representations of these relationships within the mind. A personality is, in fact, a composite and dynamic structure, which has been formed and built up out of countless never-ending influences and exchanges between ourselves and others. Relationship-forming starts with the mother/infant relationship, and then develops to include relationships with objects, such as an infant's comforter, a special blanket, a favorite doll or toy, and brands. Relationships thus constitute an integral part of the personality of the individual. This stands in stark contrast to traditional Freudian drive theories, that preserve a very fixed and absolutist view of personality attributes. They do not allow for how such attributes may take on other meanings depending on the context or the relationship. Relational psychology, in reformulating the concept of self in personality development, also reformulates the concept of a brand. A Freudian drive-based brand is always the same, irrespective of the nature of its consumer-partner; a relational brand, on the other hand, is a variable outcome of its interactions with its consumers.

The other advantage of relational psychology as a basis for understanding consumer-brand relationships is that it recognizes how inanimate relationship partners, so-called "transitional objects," may be invested with the same type of characteristics (e.g., personality, motivations, etc.), as animate ones. In relational branding, the brand functions as a transitional object, so the model does not depend on an argument by analogy, as the IPR model does. Instead, it is merely a more focused perspective on relational psychology itself. Consumer-brand relationships emerge organically from the relational psychology model, without having to make a special case for them.

Measuring consumer-brand relationships – the parameters of brand relationships

The nature of any relationship can be deduced by observing the attitudes and behaviors to which the relationship gives rise. In a consumer-brand relationship, as in all relationships, there are two participants, two sets of attitudes that are being expressed, and two sets of behaviors that have to be observed before any deductions can be made. We all sit inside our own heads constructing our relationships; our dialogue with the world is all taking place inside our heads. Of course, the outside world (people, advertising, the web) impinge upon our psyche. We are not arguing that the outside world doesn't exist, or that reality is an illusion, but, rather, that the perceptions and projections that form the basis for relational behavior are all internally generated.

Here is a thought experiment concerning a hypothetical relationship between a doctor and a patient:

The Doctor–Patient Relationship
One side of the conversation: "What do you think of the doctor?"
The other side of the conversation: "What does the doctor think of you?"

FIGURE 25.1 Understanding consumer perceptions and projections

If we let the doctor stand in for the brand, the characteristics on the left can be thought of as constituting the patient's attitude towards the doctor, or the patient's *perception* of the doctor's brand personality. He's highly skilled, caring, and funny. Overall, he sounds like a doctor we would all like to have, and we, therefore, would expect the patient to like the doctor.

However, when we uncover the crucial bit of information about what the patient *infers* about the doctor's opinion of him – that he is a hypochondriac – our understanding of the nature of the relationship changes completely. It doesn't matter what the doctor really thinks because, for the patient, the relationship is based on his *projection* of the inferred attitude of the doctor and the doctor's behavior toward him.

Analogously, understanding the relationship between a brand and a consumer requires the observation and analysis of two distinct types of parameters, both of which are recoverable from the consumer: *consumer perceptions* (or the consumer's attitudes and behaviors towards the brand), and *brand projections* (the brand's attitudes towards the consumer as inferred by the consumer through his/her experience of the brand's behaviors).

While consumer perceptions do not require further elucidation on our part, we do need to clarify the less familiar concept of brand projections. Object relations theory informs us how people project onto inanimate relationship partners, such as a brand, the same type of characteristics (e.g., personality, motivations) that they project onto animate ones. We identify two distinct types of brand projection, which, while they parallel the dimensions of consumers' attitudes and behavior, are not identical, for the simple reason that we are not actually interrogating the brand in order to elicit them. As with the examples of the auto insurance and toilet paper brands cited above, they are projections onto the brand made by the consumer.

Some general (i.e., non product category-specific) examples of brand attitudes are shown below. They are statements about the brand that reflect an inference made by the consumer about how the brand perceives him or her:

> The brand cares about me (the brand thinks that my needs are worth caring about)
> The brand cares what I think (the brand values me/my opinion)
> The brand doesn't talk down to me (the brand thinks I am on the same level)
> The brand expects a lot of me (the brand thinks I am capable)
> The brand shares my values (the brand values what I value)
> The brand makes me feel good about myself (the brand likes me)
> The brand helps me to express myself (the brand is interested in me)
> The brand knows me (the brand regards me as an intimate)

In addition to generating brand attitudes in the mind of the consumer, the brand exhibits behaviors, which create brand experiences for the consumer. Here are some examples of brand experiences:

> The brand provides a little treat for me
> The brand inspires me
> The brand connects me with other people
> The brand simplifies my life
> The brand responds to my needs
> The brand brings back good memories
> The brand makes me look good to others

There is a dialogue between the brand and the consumer going on inside the consumer's mind, and that dialogue includes what consumers understand about the brand (brand perceptions), and what the brand tells consumers about themselves (projections). Traditionally, in most consumer research, we elicit and measure only one side of that dialogue: the one that reflects consumers' perceptions of the brand. Using metrics such as those above, we are able to tap into the other side of the dialogue.

Why is that important? Because brand projections can often be the deal-maker or the deal-breaker in the consumer-brand relationship. Brand perceptions have generally been very purposively managed by the brand's managers, but brand projections, particularly brands' attitudes, have not. The right brand attitude can help create a strong relationship, but, if a brand has a bad or inappropriate attitude, then no amount of emphasis on its good image qualities can make up for that, and, in fact, may even make the relationship worse. There are many examples of how bad (or unmanaged) attitudes can undermine the image of a brand and lead to poor consumer-brand relationships.

Emphasis on the separate identification of the two dimensions of the consumer-brand relationship gives a much clearer picture of both the strengths and weaknesses of the brand. Brand attitudes and brand behaviors can be crafted just as readily as brand image and brand personality, thus providing a whole new set of dimensions of positioning space and a new set of tools for marketing management.

Over the last 20 years, many specific product category studies of consumer-brand relationships have been successfully completed using this approach. Here, we report on the first attempt to generalize this approach to consumer-brand relationships via the identification and measurement of a set of brand relationships at a degree of universality sufficient to apply across brands in very different product categories.

Methodology

Following two pilot investigations, a large-scale study involving 48 brands in eight different categories was implemented. This involved an Internet survey of a representative sample of over 1,500 consumers, divided into three cells, each of whom were questioned on 16 brands. Brands were evaluated on the following series of issues:

- Familiarity
- Perceptions of brand image and personality
- Brand experiences and brands' attitudes
- Brand touch points (advertising, websites, social media, etc.)
- Brand usage and consideration
- Overall brand evaluations
- Other brand-related behavior

Thirty of the 48 brands were so-called "mono-brands," brands that are co-identical with their corporate owners, such as Apple, Walmart, or American Express. This allowed us to compile extensive data from public sources relating to the marketplace performance of the brands, including but not limited to market capitalization, sales, operating profit, price/earnings ratio, and operating margin.

Our overall objective was to measure the concomitant influence of consumers' relationships with the brand and the value of the customer franchise on the financial value of these brands, as reflected in the various measures.

Identifying and measuring universal brand relationships

We define a brand relationship as the combination of a specific perception of the brand (brand image, brand personality) and a specific projection, or inference about the brand's attitude and/or brand experience. The strength of the relationship is a function of strength of these individual components, but that function is not a simple additive one.

One key assumption of all additive models is that a brand's strengths can, in theory, compensate for its weaknesses. The relational brand model departs from the additive assumption, because relationships are composed of two essentially different components that interact in a non–compensatory manner. A relationship is more than the sum of its parts; it has emergent properties, so the function relating brand relationship strength to the strength of the two components has to reflect those properties.

In theory, the number of possible brand relationships is determined by the combinatorial possibilities of the two sets of component dimensions: consumer perceptions and brand projections. In practice, not all combinations have a relational logic to them. Beyond that, we further screened possible relationships for emergent properties, i.e., relationships that have properties that neither of the separate components do. In practice, this meant that we were looking for relationships that had incremental predictive power over that of both of the separate components. Screening by this criterion led us to a set of five consumer-brand relationships that we refer to as the five "universal" relationships. Let us take a closer look at them.

1 **Reinforcement:** The brand is seen as having superior performance and providing heightened customer satisfaction (brand perception). Use or purchase of the brand makes the customer feel better and smarter in their own eyes and in those of others (brand experience), thereby strengthening the consumer's attachment to the brand.
2 **Identification:** There is a very strong affection for the brand and (or because) it is experienced as expressing the customer's own values and aspirations.
3 **Role Model:** The brand is admired for its charisma, a standard of leadership and innovation, that the customer is invited to share in by allying themselves with the brand.
4 **Self-differentiating:** The brand is seen as distinctive and unique, but not in a distant or iconoclastic way. The brand's difference is inclusive of the customer, who therefore feels distinctive and unique too.

5 **Playful:** The brand is liked for its relaxed style; it demands nothing of the consumer other than to experience the pleasure it gives.

The following table joins the consumer perception factors and the brand projection factors to summarize the essence of the five Universal Relationships.

Grand Projections–Attitudes/Experiences					
Consumer Perceptions	Self-Esteem • Makes me look good to others • Makes me feel good about myself	Self-Expression • Simplifies my life • Helps me express myself • Frees me to be myself	Mentoring • Challenges me to think differently • Teaches me • Inspires me • Shares my values	There For Me • Appreciates my biz • Recommended by people I care about • Responds to my needs • Has my interests at heart	Pleasure • Brings back good memories • Provides a little treat for me • Excites me
Functionality • Performs well • Satisfaction	**Reinforcement** Your brand of choice makes you look and feel good				
Emotional Attachment • Love it • Fits my life		**Identification** Let the brand you love tell the world who you are			
Charisma • Dynamic • Excitingly innovative • Leader • Progressive			**Role Model** Be empowered by brands that lead the way		
Positive Differentiation • Distinctive • Unique				**Self-Differentiating** Let a brand with a difference make a difference to you	
Relaxed and Stylish • Fun • Friendly • Cool • Stylish • Easy • Different					**Playful** Fun brands that are just to enjoy

FIGURE 25.2 The five Universal Relationships

Brands' scores for each relationship can be represented on a two-dimensional graph that captures the strength of each of the relationship components and identifies the balance between perceptions and experiences. Figure 25.3 compares the two components of the reinforcement relationship; the functional attributes of performance and satisfaction with the experience of self-esteem. Brands in the hair care category deliver highly on the self-esteem component of reinforcement, but are relatively weak on functionality. Brands in retail channels like Amazon and Wal-Mart deliver strong attributes of performance and satisfaction. The corporate brand Johnson & Johnson has built both sides of the relationship.

Conceptually, the key point that the brand relationship space reminds us of is that, unlike in an additive model, point A (i.e., Good Image, Bad Attitude) is not

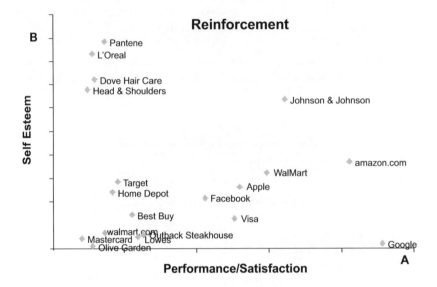

FIGURE 25.3 The dimensions of the reinforcement relationship

equivalent to point B (i.e., Bad Image, Good Attitude). Thus, Google has a very different type of reinforcement relationship than the hair care brands do.

Modeling the impact of brand relationship equity on the market value of branded businesses

In order to test our principal objective, connecting consumer-brand relationship based equity to brand financials, we constructed a brand relationship equity statistic (BRE) based on the predictive equation connecting the five Universal Relationships with a measure of overall brand equity. Figure 25.4 shows the relative weights that each of the five Universal Relationships had in computing BRE.

BRE is clearly not the only variable influencing the market value of a branded business. Two other variables that we include in the model are brand franchise – its size and quality – and operating profit. We have also worked with a number of alternative model specifications involving different definitions of these two variables. In one such specification, we found a significant relationship among ratio variables, as shown in Figure 25.5.

Stable franchise is defined as the percentage of customers saying that they use the brand regularly, less the percentage saying they do so only if there is no alternative.

As shown by the standardized regression coefficients, BRE and stable franchise

Relative Importance of Brand Relationships in determining
Relationship Equity (all categories and brands)

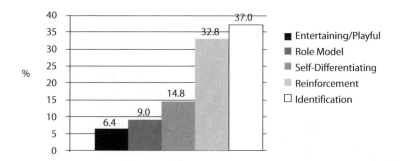

FIGURE 25.4 Relative importance of relationship types to BRE

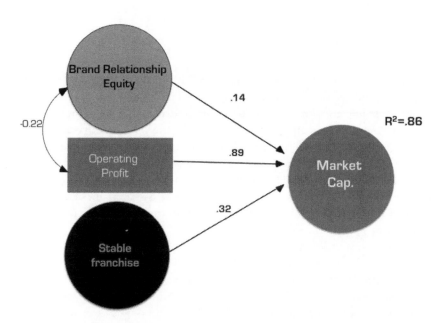

FIGURE 25.5 Determinants of market capitalization

(both normalized for the level of familiarity of the brand) have roughly the same influence on the market capitalization to sales multiple.

Another formulation of the model, shown in Figure 25.6, included the non-normalized values of BRE, stable franchise, and operating profit as explanatory variables of the absolute value of market capitalization.

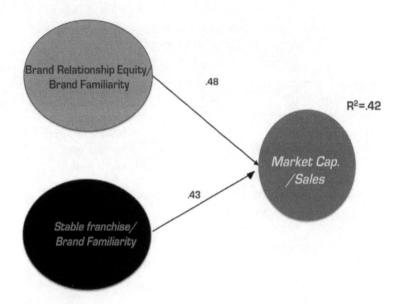

FIGURE 25.6 Determinants of the market capitalization to sales ratio

Not surprisingly, although BRE and the relative size of stable franchise are still significant contributors, the difference in the level of operating profit is clearly the major single influence on variation found within market capitalization.

An interesting observation pertains to the negative correlation between BRE and operating profit. This is not an indication that companies should not invest in relationship equity, but a recognition that investments in the brand must be appropriately paced to avoid overspending and being faced with a reduced operating profit in the short term. There is, as there has always been, a trade-off between investing in building the brand asset and achieving profit targets in the quarterly or yearly earnings statement.

However, this trade-off between BRE and operating profit may be improving. The digital world has opened up new dimensions for unpaid brand support beyond public relations. There are a multitude of new channels (e.g., social media, customer reviews, and digital word of mouth) for consumer communication. Later in the chapter, we will show how consumer-brand relationships are impacting the positive and negative things consumers are saying about brands.

Equally interesting is the apparent lack of correlation between BRE and stable franchise. This is an artifact of the way the BRE and stable franchise variables have been constructed in these model specifications. Both are highly aggregated statistics, with BRE acting as a weighted average of the five Universal Relationship scores, and stable franchise, the net result of movements into, out of, and within the brand franchise. To see the very strong influence of consumer-brand relationships on the development of the customer franchise, both variables need to be unpackaged, which is what we turn to next.

Brand relationships influence customer acquisition and retention

Consumer-brand relationships impact both the acquisition and retention strength of the franchise. However, the role of specific brand relationships is different in each phase of franchise building and maintenance, with each of the five Universal Brand Relationships varying in degree of importance.

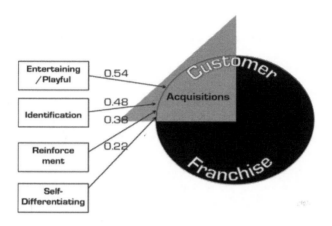

FIGURE 25.7 Relationship types vary in their impact on customer acquisition

Acquisition phase of development

Attraction to the brand that can yield new users for the franchise comes from three key relationships. The most influential on trial consideration is the Playful relationship – liking the brand for its relaxed style and feeling that use of the brand would give pleasure. This is followed by Identification and Reinforcement relationships.

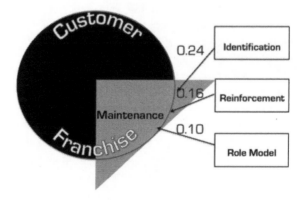

FIGURE 25.8 Relationship types vary in their impact on customer retention

Retention phase of development

Among brand users, the most influential of the relationships on brand loyalty is Identification – loving the brand because in some way it reflects and strengthens the consumers' own values and aspirations.

Brand relationships are thus intimately entwined with the strength of the brand's franchise. As a result, relationships have a dual role in building financial value in branded businesses, both directly via the influence of BRE, and indirectly via the influence of individual relationships on the development of the customer franchise.

Consumer-brand relationships and consumer-brand communication

Along with consumers' roles in creating BRE, we have to acknowledge their role in brand communication too. The voice of the consumer is louder than ever. The new digital channels for consumer communication, like Facebook, Twitter and Yelp!, customer reviews on retail channel websites, and informal recommendations to friends all serve to amplify the voice of the consumer. These channels have laid the foundation of a new brand democracy, in which brand owners now no longer monopolize or even dominate the control of brand messages.

This shared control has brought many new challenges and opportunities for brand managers. While embracing new models and metrics of engagement, advocacy, and sharing of content, they must take into account the interplay between consumer-brand relationships and consumer-brand communication (CBC), how and how much consumers talk about brands. We have talked about the fact that brand experiences, and brands' attitudes in particular, have been largely left unmanaged. It is our contention that better management of these will result in stronger consumer-brand relationships, which will result in more positive CBC via the channels that consumers control.

In order to test this hypothesis, in our study, we included questions about the various media types in which brands had been encountered, and about whether and how consumers had communicated about brands in their own media. The relationship between how/where brand messages are received, and what resulting messages are transmitted is shown in Figure 25.9.

Those exposed to a brand's communications in social media and by word of mouth are more likely to themselves communicate about the brand than those who were exposed to its messages in other types of media. However, communicating more does not mean communicating positively. In fact, in net terms, the additional communication of these two groups is negative. This, perhaps, reflects the lack of control over social media and word of mouth by brand owners, and emphasizes the need to somehow harness these channels. Unlike with owned or bought media, the influence of brand owners in these channels can often only be indirect. Do stronger, better consumer-brand relationships represent the means to that control?

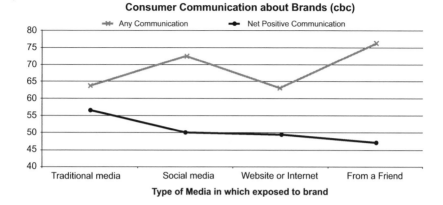

FIGURE 25.9 How brand communications influence consumers to talk about the brand

Figure 25.10 shows the variation in positive CBC by channel for four different levels of BRE. (If communication is not positive, it is coded as negative.)

At the lowest level of BRE, only brands seen in traditional media result in CBC that is more positive than negative. For the second BRE quartile, the situation is very different: the level of positive CBC for brands seen in other media rises dramatically to the same level as for traditional media. In the third BRE quartile, positive communication about brands seen in owned or paid media (traditional and digital) continues to increase at a steeper rate than the increase in positive CBC for

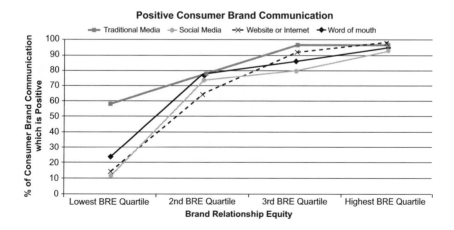

FIGURE 25.10 BRE and positive consumer brand communication

social media and word of mouth. For brands encountered in these uncontrolled media, it is only in the highest BRE quartile that negative CBC virtually disappears.

Thus, stronger consumer-brand relationships result in more positive communication about brands in whatever media they are encountered. They are essential for the digital media (whether owned, such as brand websites, or earned, such as in social media) and for word of mouth.

The relative strength of American Express vs. VISA on consumer-brand relationships and CBC

In the credit card category, there is a strong relationship between consumer-brand relationships and CBC. Consumer-brand relationships explain about 30 percent of the variance in CBC.

Figure 25.11 looks at the way that consumer-brand relationships develop and change for American Express and VISA among two franchise segments with different levels of preference for each brand. The changes in the importance of key brand relationships, between these levels, will help explain the difference in brand preference. Also, the comparative difference between the two brands' relationships impacts the relative strength of net positive CBC as customers move up each brand's funnel.

There are dramatic changes in the relative importance of Identification between VISA and American Express as customers move from "one of the cards I keep in my wallet" to the "the card I prefer to use." Among those who prefer VISA, Identification (driven by self-expression) improves by 18.1 points, but only 4.3 points for American Express. The important build for American Express is significant improvement in Reinforcement (drive by performance), up 13.5 points.

The relative changes between the two brands are shown in Figure 25.12. As the customers of American Express and VISA move to preferring to use the card of one brand, American Express's relative power to generate positive CBC dramatically declines. The advantage drops by 20 percentage points from 139 to 119 percent. This drop can be mostly explained by the significant increase by those preferring VISA feeling more closely identified with the brand.

It appears that the cost of American Express becoming a more mass brand through offering a multiplicity of branded cards and co-branded cards has led those with the highest preference to have a relationship structure that looks more like those who prefer VISA. The risk is that by pushing brand preference via increased functionality (e.g., by giving points, offering revolving credit, etc.), Amex may have made itself more vulnerable to VISA because it sacrificed the relative importance of its Identification and some Self-differentiation (distinction) for stronger Reinforcement (via Performance).

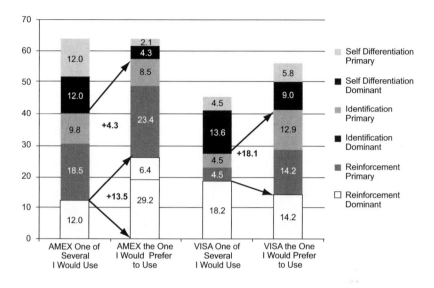

FIGURE 25.11 Changes in principle brand relationship profiles across brands

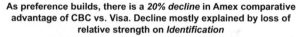

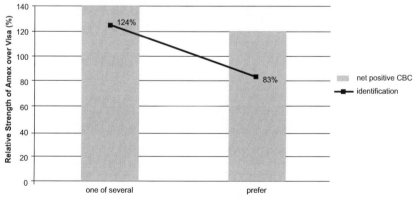

FIGURE 25.12 Relative changes between American Express and VISA brands

Summary

The use of relational psychology (object-relations theory) as a model has the advantage of not requiring special-pleading for its application to consumer-brand relationships. Brands can legitimately be considered as transitional objects, in just the same way we consider all of things that we have interacted with and carry around with us in our heads.

Brand relationships are not readily accessible to consumers when solicited by direct means. Because they are so inextricably linked with the individual's personal relationships and brand experiences, they are often not susceptible either to articulation by analogy with interpersonal relationships or to an unequivocal decoding. The nature of brand relationships – just like any other relationships – can best be deduced from observing the attitudes and behaviors to which they give rise. There are two sets of such attitudes and behaviors that result from the brand relationship: the consumer's and the brand's, both of which may be accessed from the consumer.

Brands' attitudes and consumers' brand experiences provide what has often been the missing link between brand image and a complete definition of consumer-based brand equity. Brand relationship equity, derived from brand image and brand experiences, is a direct influence – along with the size and stability of the brand's customer franchise – on the financial value of a brand.

Consumer-brand relationships are also a significant influence on the development of brand franchises – although the link is partially time-lagged. The acquisition and retention phases of franchise development are impacted by different relationships. Thus, over the long term, brand relationships contribute both directly and indirectly to the financial value of a brand.

Managing brand experiences and brands' attitudes, as well as traditional brand messaging, is an essential part of creating strong consumer-brand relationships. In addition, all of the evidence points to these elements as being the determining influence on the tenor of brand communication by consumers via the increasingly important channels that they control.

References

Aaker, J., S. Fournier, and A. Brasel (2004) "When Good Brands Do Bad", *Journal of Consumer Research*, 31 (1): 1–24.

Fournier, S. (1998) "Consumers and Their Brands: Developing Relationship Theory in Consumer Research", *Journal of Consumer Research*, 24 (4): 343–373.

Patterson, M. and L. O'Malley (2006) "Brands, Consumers and Relationships: A Review", *Irish Marketing Review*, 18 (1/2): 10–20.

Roberts, K. (2005) *Lovemarks: The Future Beyond Brands*. New York: Powerhouse Books.

PART VIII

Contemplating the futures of branding

26

CONTEMPLATING THE FUTURES OF BRANDING

*Michael Breazeale, Susan Fournier, and Jill Avery
with contributions from David Aaker, John Deighton,
Gavan Fitzsimons, Robert V. Kozinets, Deborah MacInnis,
Ann L. McGill, Deborah Roedder John, and
Jonathan Schroeder*

Volumes such as this typically conclude with a wrap-up chapter from the editors that compiles reflections on the included works. We wanted to take a different tack: something that could perhaps deliver better on the goals of capturing state-of-the-art thinking and motivating future branding practice and research. So, we went beyond the editor team and approached some of the brightest and best researchers in our domain – people with foundational contributions to branding – and asked them for help. Each of the thought leaders represented in this chapter was asked to reflect on the future of branding and identify one issue that they found critical to the advance of branding theory and practice. Contributors were encouraged to dig deep and consider the things we are doing well in brand research, the theories and frameworks we are getting wrong, research lenses that are under- or over-utilized, assumptions that should be challenged, forces on the brand landscape in need of exploration, and lost or less-appreciated insights that deserve to be revisited – from within our own disciplines and elsewhere. Four broad themes emerge in these mini-essays. The result is an extensive and dynamic collection of thoughts that encourages the reader to shake loose the dust that has settled on our thinking about the very essence of brands. With these words as inspiration, we can envision a new frontier of research made possible by both evolving technologies and the work of these thought leaders themselves.

Revisiting the essence of brands and branding

This volume is about brands and branding, and two contributors ask us to take pause to consider the meaning of these elemental ideas. Susan Fournier encourages marketers and brand researchers to rethink the frames we implicitly assign to brands, shifting from an understanding of brands as ends to brands as means, from assets to risk control mechanisms, and to idiosyncratic meaning webs versus unique selling propositions. John Deighton urges marketers to reconsider the purpose of brands and their capabilities, and warns of brand overuse that alienates potential customers who are forced to experience brands where they do not want or need them.

Filling the missing gaps in brand theory

Some contributors highlight missing links in our brand research agendas and provide fodder for inspiring work along these lines. Deborah MacInnis posits that our understanding of the phenomena of brands requires a deeper understanding of the processes and phases of brand relationships. Consistent with that viewpoint, Deborah Roedder John explains that researchers have looked long enough at the reasons consumers buy or use brands and should now turn to the after-effects of brands on consumers. She urges examination of whether the accepted reasons that consumers use brands – to enhance feelings of self-worth or to support desired identities, for example – actually produce those psychological effects.

Improving the creation and capture of value through branding

Branding is a pragmatic, managerial discipline, and some of our contributors consider ways we can improve the creation and capture of value through brands and brand relationships. David Aaker reflects on the evolving strategic role of the brand as a platform for creating new categories, and stresses the role of branding as a critical component of firm growth. Jonathan Schroeder considers a key issue in executing branding practice: the under-examined role of photography in brand identity, brand relationships, and brand strategy.

Futuristic contemplations of the power and evolution of branding

Prognosticators contributing to the final theme take us forward to contemplate the power of brands in contemporary and future society. Gavan Fitzsimons describes the ability of brands to morph the very way consumers think, and suggests that their influence is becoming inescapable. Ann McGill extends that thinking to consider a future filled with consumers who are themselves ecosystems composed of branded body enhancements. Robert Kozinets, pointing to the Internet and social media as not only the new brand battleground but also a rich cultural medium for research, highlights how digital technology changes the ways that brands are conceptualized and the roles they play in people's lives.

* * *

Rethinking brands

Susan Fournier

This piece reflects on some essential habits-of-mind that undergird current branding theory and practice and advocates a reframing of brands along three planes: brands as means versus ends; brands as complex signals versus simple selling propositions; and brands not as assets, but rather as risk management tools. By shifting our perspectives on the essence and purpose of brands and branding, we can encourage new frameworks, cultivate new skillsets, and create more value in our brands.

Brands are a means to an end, not ends in themselves

As brand managers and researchers, we put brands at the center of our thoughts and activities, and in doing so, we lose perspective. We have supermarkets brimming with 60,000 SKUs and literally thousands of brands. Every brand manager thinks that their brand plays or could play a big role in people's lives. That is not and cannot be the case.

People are social animals and, at their core, they are all about relationships with others. Our families, our friends, our coworkers – that's what drives us. Brands sometimes play a role in that, but no matter how you slice it, they are the means in people's lives, not the ends.

Brands can serve as a means to express a certain vision of ourselves, an identity that matters to us, or a role we want to perform well. The key word here is "can" and yet 90 percent of our research focuses on the self-expressive functions of brands.

Linda Price's chapter makes very clear that brands are often in the background. Maybe John likes to bike and he is part of a biking club and he goes out every Saturday and participates in races. The bike is there, and he enjoys it, but the point of this brand relationship is the people with whom John rides and not the bike itself. John's Cannondale is a means to that end.

To advance brand strategy, marketers typically execute category studies – mapping the attributes and benefits of, for example, Minute Maid versus Tropicana versus Simply Orange – and they act as if this brand-defined context is what the world is all about. This arrogance distorts reality: it's about the people, not the brands. If we want strong brands, we have to start with a deep understanding of the people and figure out where our brands fit into their lives, if at all.

Ironically, big data can thwart the mission to develop more inspired insights. The IS manager's job is to reduce everything to '0's and '1's; to take out context that can complicate things; to reduce the data to simple empirical relationships and correlations. However, these findings are information without meaning. We are overly enamored of information when we need to be focused on meaning. The quest for meaning complicates things, but no one said it would be easy. We have to bring context back into our branding work, and method barriers cannot get in our way.

From USPs to brand meaning webs: brand meaning is complicated

Marketers engage in much work to figure out a brand's positioning, and then subsequently spend millions of dollars communicating and reinforcing that position. To make things tractable, they circumscribe brand meaning and put it in a box: "This brand is the [blank] among all [blanks] because it [blank]." To capture value, they strive for consistency in brand expression over time. Yet, brands are culture-sensitive, multi-vocal creatures, and this muddles the rhetoric of unique selling propositions that build differentiated brands.

Snapple got this right with an original campaign that embraced Rush Limbaugh, Ivan Lendl, and Wendy from Long Island in a 200+ flavor line. Botox, per Giesler's research (Giesler 2012), mutated constantly in the face of Doppelgängers challenging the brand. Successful brands claim resonant meanings, but those meanings have a shelf life; brands have to transform as their meanings get stale. People change, cultures change, competition changes. Cultures are dynamic and temporality is the rule. Counter to the myth of long-term brand consistency, there is a strong case for time-bound, short-term brands.

Decades of consumer research have taught us that when a brand gets into a person's life, there isn't consensus about what it means. Co-creation is a term that has been used: a brand is heard speaking many voices. Claudio Alvarez reports the empirical reality that brands have less shared meaning than they have idiosyncratic or personalized meaning. Peapod for one person represents the leading edge of technology and for another the nostalgic milkman. Stephen Brown and colleagues (Brown *et al.* 2013) extol the virtues of brand ambiguity; leave meanings open and the brand will thrive. The very architecture supporting our branding practices is founded on the task of finding one unique selling proposition and repeating it until everyone develops shared knowledge of that positioning. Things would change radically if the paradigm were refocused to embrace and encourage idiosyncratic and fluid meanings in our brands.

Everything managers do affects brand meaning, whether it is in the brand strategy or not. Marketers might send out coupons or a survey and their intent is clear – to ignite purchase and solicit feedback – but these are meaning-laden signals and people perhaps interpret these signals in completely different ways. For one person the coupon says, "you don't care about the important things in this relationship;" for another it validates the tit-for-tat nature of a basic exchange. Brands and the managers that represent them leak signals constantly, all of which affect our brands. In work with Giana Eckhardt (Fournier and Eckhardt 2013), we see leakage most vividly in the case of what we call corporeal brands: brands that are at once human beings and marketplace brands. Unintended signals can stand as big statements about what the brand believes in or doesn't believe in. Brand meaning-making is a messy business, and we need models that can capture and acknowledge the signals that brands receive and send.

Risk is elemental to brands

In marketing, we are revenue-centric and top-line oriented, but we don't think a lot about risk to our cash flows. But, risk is the foundation of branding. Brands reduce the risk of making wrong decisions. People stick with a brand to control risk: psychological risk, financial risk, the risk of failure. In brand stewardship, the logic also follows that the manager's job is to understand and manage the risks relating to the brand.

In a project with Shuba Srinivasan and Liwu Hsu (Fournier *et al.* 2011), we analyzed ten years of data on brand architecture strategies – e.g., Fed-Ex and its Branded House structure wherein everything is branded Fed-Ex; Apple's sub-branding strategy with Apple iPod; endorsed branding as with 3M Post-It Notes. We learned that some of these strategies are inherently riskier than others: they are better and worse in managing risks of brand meaning dilution, reputation loss, cannibalization, and financial risk from lost opportunities or competition for management time. When you factor in risk, you actually change standing recommendations for certain brand strategies. Sub-branding, most notably, exacerbates rather than controls risk, and yet, our branding gurus continue to recommend this approach.

Corporeal branding is another interesting context where managing risk – the risk of personal crisis, the risk of mortality, the risk of uncontrolled meaning leakage, the risk of exposure via the celebrity social circle – is more elemental than managing revenues and returns. Brands on social media do not need to be reminded that risk management – risks of transparency, parody, hyper-criticism, and hijacking – is the name of the game.

We could rethink the entire exercise of branding as risk management versus asset management. Here, brand building gives way to brand protection, branding looks more like public relations than marketing, and the CFO cares daily about the risk exposure affected through the company's brand portfolios. To realize this alternate vision, we need a new paradigm, different skill sets, and cross-disciplinary collaborations to guide us through.

* * *

Brands are just nouns

John Deighton

In reading the rich account of brands and relationships with brands laid out in this book, there is a risk of neglecting one banal feature: a brand is a noun. It works, as all nouns do, to do two things. First, it denotes. Second, it connotes.

This fact matters because successful branding is, at bottom, a matter of adding a noun to a language. It is an audacious feat of linguistic engineering. By that I mean that, when marketers do branding, and even more so in the case of sub-branding, they are imposing their wills onto the natural process by which language evolves and words come into being. To be sure, any act of naming, even the naming of a child, is audacious engineering. Parents presume they have the power to decide what proper noun will denote an individual from infancy to adulthood and through all of its relationships. But, you need only name a child Aloysius to discover the limits to that power. Equally, when a brewer proposes that millions of consumers refer to its beer as Bud Lite, the brewer must be confident that the name will stick. This is linguistic engineering on a global scale. It shapes language as surely as road designers engineer the landscape when building roads that will change traffic flows for decades to come, and, just as the civil engineer must account for the natural travel wishes of those who must use the road if it is to be successful, so must the linguistic engineer.

Brands must first denote. They must point to something. In the natural and un-engineered course of events, nouns enter the language when some new feature of discourse presents itself as needing to be marked out. Perhaps the noun is needed because there needs to be talk about a danger such as a tsunami, or a new choice attribute such as keyless ignition. People quickly see that a new noun is needed and fall into line behind the early winner. In the engineered course of events, brands, and particularly sub-brands, face headwind if consumers do not have a compelling need to talk about the distinction to which the brand points. That is the key to imposing a noun on a language. Build a decision tree diagram that maps a consumer choice, and you will reveal the brandable moments in the flow of thought. If consumers want to get to a branch of the decision tree and don't know how, a brand can be built at the fork with no money at all, as Google did when it marked the fork between 'Shall I get the encyclopedia?' and 'Shall I Google it?' If consumers don't feel any need to choose at the point in the flow of thinking that the marketer wishes were a decision fork, then building a brand can be unreasonably expensive as Bing found. Metaphorically, it is a matter of being sure that the destination is attractive before building the signpost.

When a marketer launches a new product, a new choice occasion arises and denotation is welcomed by the consumer as long as the choice object is meaningfully differentiated from others. For example, as the alternative beverage category began to form in the US in 1980s, a plethora of brands emerged to navigate the new space. Snapple, Napa Naturals, Natural Quencher, SoHo, After the Fall, Ginseng Rush, Elliot's Amazing, Old Tyme Soft Drink, Manly Sodas, Syfo, and Original New York Seltzer were some of the many contenders. There were many choice alternatives, so the value of denotation was not in dispute.

But not every fork in the decision tree marks a brandable moment. Sometimes the language has a serviceable word already. Imagine you ask a concierge at a Westin hotel where to find the fitness center, and are told, "Our Westin Wellness Studio is on the rooftop." By choosing to brand its exercise room, Westin is adding a noun phrase to the vocabulary its customers do not to have to learn to navigate its choice environment, and metaphorically erecting a signpost where one already exists. Consumers are perhaps confused: I am not unwell, I am in need of exercise. Conversely, they could be put off: back home we call them fitness centers and you are making me feel like an outsider. They could also be disappointed: if the branded facility contains only a small collection of exercise equipment and no spa services, the redundant brand will not even deliver the connotative value it seems to promise.

And many brands – particularly sub-brands – don't even mark forks in the decision tree. Instead, they mark points where the marketer would like a decision to be made, but the market sees no reason to. Cotton versus wool might be a decision, but sanforized versus mercerized cotton? Dry cleaning or Martinized dry cleaning? If the flow of thought does not want to pause, denotation is in vain.

The essay began by saying that a brand must first denote and second connote. Connotation is a rich and complex topic, and is a well-trodden theme in branding texts. This brief note will not touch on it. The argument here is simply that if there is no pressing need for a brand to denote, then the topic of connotation can be skipped.

* * *

Relationships as processes

Deborah MacInnis

Given the burgeoning nature of the intriguing domain of brand relationships, it is difficult to identify one area that deserves priority. However, I do believe that much can be gained by adopting a process perspective on brand relationships. Brand relationships evolve over time (see Fournier 2009). They are subject to change as brand experiences occur, as consumers themselves change, as the competitive context evolves, as meaning makers imbue additional brand meanings, and as marketers adapt (or fail to do so) to prevailing market conditions. Yet, our understanding of brand relationships from a process perspective is nascent. Whereas a myriad of process issues can be examined, I focus here on a) deepening our understanding of particular relationship phases, and b) studying the evolutionary nature of brand relationships. Each offers a rich set of questions for future research.

Understanding particular relationship phases

At a very simple level, relationships have a beginning, middle, and an end. Focusing on *what precipitates consumers' movement* from one stage to another is a critical piece to understanding brand relationships. The chapters in this volume on relationship termination (cf., McAlexander and DuFault) are noteworthy in delving more deeply into a specific phase of a brand relationship (here, the termination stage). Collectively, they illuminate the multi-determined nature of relationship termination from the brand's search for new targets (cf., Luedicke and Pichler-Luedicke), brand discontinuation (cf., Russell and Schau), firm firing (cf., Mende,

Scott, Lemon, and Thompson), or consumer circumstances (cf., Goode, Khamitov, and Thomson; Long, Yoon, and Friedman). Understanding relationship termination in terms of when it occurs, who initiates it, and how it is enacted offers strong potential to contribute to our understanding of negative (and positive) spillover effects to a parent brand or other brands in the category, carry over effects to new brand relationships, brand forgiveness vs. attempts at brand revenge, and the potential for brand relationships to be revitalized. Moreover, whereas our field has extensively studied consumer dissatisfaction as a driver of relationship termination, dissatisfaction does not appear to capture the more emotional and visceral feelings like betrayal, abandonment, exploitation, neglect, and boredom that can precipitate relationship termination.

Equally important is studying how brand relationships are established in the first place. Clearly, consumers develop relationships with brands for their functional, symbolic and experiential impact. But we need to drill down more deeply to understand the relationship development process. What set of consumer, marketer, social, and contextual influences *move* consumers from a non-relationship to a relationship (or vice versa)? What consumer, marketer, and contextual factors drive some relationships to be characterized as "committed partnerships," while others are "best friends" or "dependencies"? How do these factors impact the various dimensions on which relationships can be described (e.g., their depth, their valence, the extent to which they are "out in the open" vs. "secret", and their prominence in consumers' lives)? Why do some relationships take longer to form (or end) than others? What facilitates the establishment of relationship norms and the extent to which these norms are characterized as communal as opposed to exchange-based?

Knowing whether a consumer is just beginning, in the midst of developing, or in the process of terminating a relationship with a brand can also help us understand whether, when, and why consumers react differently to brand transgressions. In turn, such knowledge could help marketers in identifying repair processes best tailored to a specific relationship phase and when marketers are most vulnerable to relationship transgressions. Understanding where consumers are in their relationship with a brand (formation, development, termination) also has the potential to help firms assess the nature, duration, and value of brand alliances, brand extensions or partnerships from which a given brand relationship can be leveraged.

Understanding relationship evolution over time

In addition to studying *particular phases* of brand relationships (initiation, development, or termination), given the dynamic nature of brand relationships (Fournier 2009) there is much to be gained by considering the *entire brand relationship evolution process* – from start to finish. To illustrate, studying relationship evolution allows us to ask not about whether a consumer's brand relationship is described as a committed partnership, a dependency, a fling or an enmity, but rather to ask how, whether, and why a brand relationship changes from one type to another over time (e.g., from a fling, to a committed partnership, to a dependency or marriage by convenience) over time. Studying relationship evolution helps us identify critical consumer, brand community, cultural, and/or marketplace incidents that precipitate change over time in the nature, type, and depth of consumers' commitment to brands. Such study can help us understand how consumers negotiate (and re-negotiate) brand relationships as relationships evolve. Studying the evolution of a brand relationship also helps us to tie brand relationship changes to broader changes in consumers' lives (Price, this volume; Fournier 2009).

Studying relationship evolution allows us to delve into questions about how marketers can not only deepen bourgeoning brand relationships, but also keep solid brand relationships fresh, or revitalize relationships that are flagging. We might also ask whether all consumers follow a natural evolution in their brand relationships (initiation, development, termination) or whether brand relationship trajectories are more nuanced and complex. By comparing brand relationships with different evolution trajectories, we might better understand why certain brands remain relevant to consumers over time while others cease to remain so.

Studying relationship evolution and relationship trajectories requires research methods that incorporate change and time. Longitudinal research designs, case studies, and long-term ethnographic methods will be particularly useful. Quantitative models that incorporate change elements such as shocks to the system (VAR models) and those that incorporate lagged effects can be equally important. Clearly, this exciting and vibrant research domain remains rich with potential.

* * *

Exploring brand consumption: what really happens when consumers use brands?

Deborah Roedder John

How can we advance branding research into new and interesting directions? I propose that one such direction is examining actual consumption behavior. What happens when consumers use brands – how does it affect their feelings and emotions, attitudes about themselves and others, and behaviors? We know a fair amount about why consumers value brands, and why consumers are motivated to purchase and use brands. However, we know relatively little about how actually consuming brands affects consumers' psychological states and behaviors.

I began pursuing this research direction several years ago. At that time, I was a dissertation advisor for Ji Kyung Park, who was interested in studying impression management and brands. A common theme in existing research was that consumers use brands as a way to signal who they are (or want to be) to themselves and other people. Also emerging was the idea that brands could be used to enhance one's feelings about oneself when aspects of one's self-concept were uncertain or challenged. These insights into consumer motivations for using brands were important. Yet, we noticed a potentially interesting omission: none of the studies observed what happened when consumers actually used brands. As a result, we really did not know whether consumers experienced the intended effects of using brands. For example, did consumers really perceive themselves differently after using a brand?

Finding such a large research gap elicited mixed emotions. On the one hand, there was excitement about new questions that could be posed and new findings that could be uncovered. On the other hand, there were anxious feelings that perhaps other researchers had made attempts in this area and had found it to be intractable or unproductive. We threw caution to the wind, and decided to go ahead with an experiment we planned to conduct in a local shopping mall during the Christmas season. We gave women a branded item to use (a Victoria's Secret shopping bag) in the shopping mall for one hour, after which they returned to answer questions about how they perceived themselves on several personality traits. We found that women who carried the Victoria's Secret shopping bag perceived themselves as more glamorous, feminine, and good looking, which are personality traits associated with the Victoria's Secret brand (Park and Roedder John 2010). Further, we found this effect was not universally experienced, and was only evident for women with a fixed mindset (entity theorists), who believe they cannot change who they are through their own attempts at self-development and self-improvement. Thus, by examining actual brand consumption, we were able to document the self-enhancement effect suggested by prior research, and also identify which type of consumers are most affected by brand use in this way.

Subsequent studies have borne out the promise of studying brand consumption. We have found that using brands can change more than self-perceptions – it can increase one's sense of self-efficacy and actual performance when faced with a challenging task (Park and Roedder John 2014). Gatorade, for example, promises more endurance and better athletic performance, which assures consumers that they can perform better when engaged in a challenging athletic activity *if* they use Gatorade. We found this to be true for consumers who drank plain water from a Gatorade cup, but only for consumers with fixed mindsets (entity theorists). Fixed mindset consumers relied on the Gatorade brand promise to increase their confidence about performing well on a strenuous athletic task, and, as a result, they actually performed better. However, growth mindset consumers (incremental theorists), who derive a sense of self-efficacy through opportunities to learn and develop their skills, did not receive any benefit from using the Gatorade brand.

Currently, I am pursuing a different topic within the realm of brand consumption. Along with Yajin Wang and Vlad Griskevicius, we are examining the consequences of using luxury brands on social behavior (Wang *et al.* 2014). Prior research has shown that consumers often desire luxury goods as a signal of higher social status and power. In our work, we provide participants with luxury products to use and find that using these brands does actually elicit feelings of higher social status. However, we also find that these feelings of higher social status have some unintended consequences. In particular, using luxury brands has a tendency to produce self-interested behavior, resulting in more selfish and less generous behaviors toward others in many situations.

These are but a few of the insights to be gained from examining consumers using brands. Although this research stream is in its infancy, we are beginning to learn much more about the power of brands in our lives, both good and bad. As a field, I believe we have much to gain by stepping away from our conventional methods – including hypothetical purchase and usage scenarios, paper and pencil measures, and a focus on motivations rather than behaviors. You are welcome to join me – it is time to put consuming back into consumer behavior research!

* * *

The new challenge: subcategory branding

David Aaker

The best way to grow, and in many cases, the only way to grow, is to innovate, to create a brand "must have" that defines a new subcategory and renders competitors irrelevant. Such a strategy is being employed by most of the winners in virtually all product categories. It turns out that branding is critical to the implementation of this growth strategy, but a very different branding than the one with which we are all familiar. The branding challenge supporting this growth strategy is to make sure that the subcategory wins and that the brand is the most relevant subcategory entry. That requires a new set of branding skills and a different mindset.

To clarify, a "must have" can be a feature, benefit, appealing design, systems offering, new technology, segment driven offering, or low price point. It can also involve a basis for a customer relationship that a customer segment will insist upon, such as a shared interest (as reflected in Pampers Village, a go-to site for baby care), a personality (the competence of Charles Schwab or the irreverence of Virgin), a passion (Whole Foods Market's focus on organic food), or organizational values (Unilever program on sustainability). It needs to be something that is so compelling to customers that they will have a smaller chance of considering a brand that lacks the "must have," a distinct point of difference, and deliverable by the brand.

Creating a brand "must have" is not easy. It requires deep insight into the customer, the marketing, and the surrounding technology that is not readily available; the ability to employ and evaluate transformational or substantial innovation; and the capability to bringing something new to market. But, branding plays a crucial role in this emerging dynamic marketing place as it addresses three specific challenges.

First, branding needs to change from a focus on "my brand is better than your brand" marketing to framing the subcategory. The task is to make sure that the new subcategory is visible, perceived correctly, and valued by the target segment. Subcategory "branding" is very different than conventional branding task that marketing executives are used to because the measurement and valuation of programs is very different. The task is to build the subcategory and not the offering and brand. The competition is other subcategories rather than other brands.

Second, the brand needs to become the exemplar of the subcategory, its best representative. It does this by becoming the major player, by innovating, by controlling the subcategory perceptions, and by visibly talking about and building the subcategory rather than its own brand. Think of salesforce.com, Prius, Apple stores, Chobani and others that have done just that. They enjoyed huge growth by virtually ignoring competitor brands.

Third, there is a need for brand innovations. The problem with major innovations is that competitors copy or appear to copy them and, as a result, their ability to define subcategories and associate them with the brand fades. If the innovation is branded, no other brands can create an exact copy because they do not have access to the brand. Firms can copy slow churned ice cream, infrared clothing, or a hybrid energy drive, but Dreyer's, Under Armour, and Prius own the branded innovation making everyone else a copy and their firm a follower. A key is to brand only those "big" innovations that will create "must haves" because there is always a temptation to overestimate the potential impact of an innovation. Over-branding and wasting resources on wishful thinking is the result.

In essence, competition is changing from brand preference to brand relevance, with the challenge being to win by making your competitors irrelevant. The alternative, to win by being the preferred brand, is difficult and most often just not fun. This "compete to grow" brand relevance strategy does require a completely different branding set of tools and mindset. Not easy, but the payoff can be huge.

* * *

Brands, photography, and strategy

Jonathan Schroeder

In 2007, Ray-Ban rolled out a $30 million branding effort that relaunched their iconic sunglasses after the Luxottica Group bought the brand. The "Never Hide" campaign, directed by Ray-Ban's creative agency at the time, TBWA/Chiat/Day, involved a pioneering multi-media mix of agency and consumer-generated video and photographic imagery, posted on their corporate website, YouTube, and on a huge screen in New York's Times Square. "Enough of models and celebrities. It's your turn to shine," read their website, as Ray-Ban joined a growing list of brands that employ consumer-generated content for the twin purposes of promotion and building strong relationships with consumers. Ray-Ban's successful campaign underscores what I consider to be a key issue in understanding branding theory and practice: the under-looked role of photography in brand identity, brand relationships, and brand strategy.

It is hard to think about branding without photography. Photography – including digital photography, film and video photography, still photography, and "snapshot" photography permeates contemporary branding strategy. Photography remains a basic method of imaging brands, products, spokespeople, and scenarios in which brands are promoted, including advertising, annual reports, brochures, packaging imagery, point-of-purchase displays, product demonstrations, and websites.

Many leading Internet brands, such as Facebook, Instagram, Pinterest, Snapchat, Tripadvisor, Tumblr, and YouTube, depend upon photography for their core business model. Photography, in the form of uploaded, posted, sent, and commented upon photographs and videos provide the basic content and look of much of their brand. In the meantime, Google's book project is fast at work photographing "all the books," the film and television industry is figuring out more ways to stream its photographed products, and brands, such as Agent Provocateur, BMW, Louis Vuitton, and Porsche, hire well-known photographers and film directors to photograph their products and promote their brands. Additionally, companies, such as General Motors, Doritos, and MasterCard, sponsor contests for the best consumer-generated ads and films.

Consumer-generated photography, which encompasses selfies, uploaded photographs on social media sites, brand websites, and brand community sites, consumer generated advertising (including spoof ads and parody videos), consumer unpacking videos, fashion blogs, and product review sites, has expanded tremendously, punctuated by the incorporation of the camera into the cellphone, and the advent of the web-enabled smartphone. There are now an estimated 400 billion photographs taken every year, and 500 billion photographs exist on Facebook alone. Many are related to brands, and many consumers seem happy to photograph themselves with their brands, consuming their brands, unpacking their brands, sharing their brands, and rating their brands. This complicates how brands are managed, as these images of brands compete for attention with brand identity. This photographic practice makes clear the co-created aspects of brands, as well as the fact that managers do not fully control brand image and brand meaning.

Yet, photography is rarely mentioned in branding and brand strategy books as a key tool of branding. Advertising, packaging, and website design are generally discussed as communicative tools for executing brand strategy. Each of these depends upon photography. However, photography's role in brands and branding goes much deeper than this. Strategy and photography have intertwined histories; the invention of photography in 1839 quickly led to commercial possibilities for the medium; color photography's arrival in the early twentieth century was closely followed by its use for advertising, and digital photography underpins many recent corporate success stories.

Today, we rely on photographic images for so much of our information about brands that they now seem to be a natural, convenient, and accurate way to communicate brand strategy. Photographs seem as if they just *are*; they serve as mere visual records of what has happened, how people appear, or where events took place. This quality is one of the most complicated and powerful properties of photography; it often appears like a transparent window showing what is in front of the lens. However, within branding, photographs and films are often strategic: made by a particular person with special equipment at a specific moment in time, for a specified purpose.

For example, I have written about *snapshot aesthetics* in branding – the use of snapshots or snapshot-like imagery for strategic communication, by both companies and consumers. These are the kind of pictures that dominate social media sites: posed, but trying to look not posed, staged, but not too stagey. Companies such as American Apparel, Apple, Coca-Cola, Ford Motor Company, IKEA, and Volkswagen showcase snapshot-like images – straightforward, generally unposed photographs of everyday life – as a central component of their print, television, and Internet brand communication.

Snapshot aesthetics provide an important strategic resource for branding. These photographs appear authentic, as if they are beyond the artificially constructed world of typical advertising photography. This visual quality can promote brands as authentic by invoking the "average consumer" as a credible product endorser, and also demonstrating how the brand might fit in with the consumer's lifestyle. In this way, we can think about snapshot aesthetics as an important visual aspect of documenting, marketing, and understanding consumer experiences and relationships with brands. It is impossible to think about personal identity – who we are – without photography, and it follows that we cannot imagine brand identity without photography, either. The role of photography for branding deserves a closer look.

* * *

The good, the bad, and the ugly of the new brand

Gavan Fitzsimons

Like it or not, brand names and logos are essentially everywhere one looks or listens in our modern environment. They are under our feet at the supermarket, they serve as props in our favorite movies, and they are displayed on the clothing our friends wear. Recent estimates have documented that a typical consumer is exposed to somewhere between 3,000 and 10,000 brands per day. That's per day!

Brands have come a long way from simple labels on a product to help a shopper pick up another package of a previously enjoyed item. This new omnipresence of brands has led my colleagues and I to investigate the novel ways that consumers interact with brands in the modern world, often without consciously realizing they are doing so. Of course, there are times when we consciously interact with a brand; however, we don't have the capacity to attend to three to ten thousand brand exposures. What is the good, the bad and the ugly of being unconsciously exposed to so many brands on a daily basis?

Let me start by describing work that my colleagues, Keisha Cutright, Tulin Erdem, Ron Shachar, and I (Shachar *et al.* 2011) have performed over the past few years that some feel captures the "bad" or "ugly" side of brands. Since their popular onset some 100 years ago, brands have come to have richer sets of associations and meanings for the typical consumer. When I see a can of "Diet Coke," I think of a physical sense of cold effervescence, an emotional warmth that comes with each sip, Diet Coke's iconic white and red color combo, my friends that are fellow aficionados, Diet Coke's recent "share a can with …" campaign, etc. All of these associations are activated when I see or think of Diet Coke.

The richness of these associative networks suggested to the four of us that brands might have begun to tread on the territory of something with a much longer timeline in the course of human history: namely, organized religion. Just as growing up Irish Catholic for me provided a sense of community, a means of self-worth and self-expression, and a sense of self-identity, so too now does Diet Coke. I am connected to other Diet Coke drinkers, and it says something that I'm a Diet Coke and not a Diet Pepsi person. The consequence of this evolution of brands is that they now provide many of the same functions in the life of the modern human that organized religion has for thousands of years.

In our research, we found that religion and brands substitute for one another, completely outside the consumer's conscious awareness. For example, very subtle activations of brands (versus simply activating unbranded consumer products) lead people to report that it is less important to attend weekly religious services, and to report reduced belief in the existence of a controlling God. Confronting participants with these findings led to numerous upset participants and some of the most impressive steadfast denials I have witnessed in my research career.

However, these rich brand representations can lead to potentially positive behavioral changes outside of consumer awareness. In our first demonstration of the power of the unconscious brand, Grainne Fitzsimons, Tanya Chartrand, and I ran a series of studies examining behavioral shifts in response to nonconscious brand exposure.

In one such study (Fitzsimons *et al.* 2008), we capitalized on the fact that Apple had spent a large amount of money building an association between the Apple brand and the human trait of creativity. We subliminally primed participants (or exposed them extremely quickly, so fast that they could not consciously perceive it) with the Apple logo, the IBM logo, or a neutral pattern. We used the IBM brand as our foil because testing confirmed that although it does not have an association with creativity, it is generally viewed as positively as Apple.

After subliminal exposure to a brand logo, we then tested each participant's creativity using a classic test called the unusual uses task. In this task, participants were asked to list as many alternative uses as they could come up with for a brick (e.g., as a hammer). Participants primed with the Apple logo came up with substantially more uses for the brick than did either the control group or the IBM group. Being exposed to the Apple logo outside of their conscious awareness actually led people to be more creative.

More recently, Danielle Brick, Tanya Chartrand and I explored the interplay between brands and social connection. As brands have evolved to exhibit varied roles in our lives, our belief was that brands might start to potentially serve as proxies for human connection. Recent research suggests that those that are relatively wealthy have weaker social connections than the less wealthy. We tested a slightly more nuanced perspective: greater wealth is associated with reduced closeness with acquaintances and neighbors (i.e., non-significant others), and because these wealthy individuals still have a need to connect, they turn to other sources for connection, namely brands. When consumers feel relatively wealthy, they are more likely to prefer brands to people. Framed more optimistically, when people are not fulfilling a basic need for connection in life through their existing social connections, they can fulfill at least some of this need through brands.

In sum, the ability of brands to influence us via everyday exposures suggests that people are much more affected by brands in the environment than initially thought. We have found that this influence works at a nonconscious level, and as a result can be quite difficult to detect or correct for on the part of the individual.

At times, these effects can be quite positive (e.g., becoming more creative or fulfilling an innate but lacking need for connection), while, at other times, the outcome of exposure to brands may be much less desirable (e.g., shaking a person's belief in God). Given the omnipresence of brands in our modern lives and the fact they are not going anywhere any time soon, we'd best get used to this shift in our lives. To quote the Borg, a favorite "brand" of villain from the Star Trek series, "Resistance is futile."

Rather than attempting to hide from or resist their influence, it is probably sensible to instead embrace it. Consumers can take advantage of the billions spent to build associative networks around brands by surrounding themselves with brands with aspirational traits. At first, of course, one will feel silly to have done so. But, as those brands fade into the background and conscious processing declines, all of a sudden, we may find ourselves more creative, smarter, and more athletic as a result.

* * *

Branded body parts: the extended, embedded, and plural self

Ann L. McGill

I have metal body parts. My left hip was resurfaced years ago and the right one was fully replaced this past year. More relevant to this volume, though, I have *branded* metal body parts. My left side sports the BHR – the Birmingham Hip Resurfacing from Smith and Nephew. I like my BHR. It delivers great performance at (some argue) somewhat higher risk than a standard replacement. It feels sporty and powerful and not too different than having dropped a Porsche 911 into my person. My right side has newer technology, the Mobile Bearing Hip from Stryker. It delivers incredible range of motion, lower risk, and performance close to that of my BHR. I am just getting to know it, but I hope we will have a long happy life together. Experts might dispute my take on these branded products but, hey, they are mine and I have a relationship with them.

These relationships go much deeper, literally, of course, but figuratively as well, than most work on brand–identity connection seems able to explain. My experience is hardly alone. Artificial joints are among the many branded products that might be implanted. People have pacemakers, drug delivery devices, lenses, and, possibly quite soon, monitoring devices (an internal Fitbit perhaps), as well as other internal technology. Frankly, I have always wanted something like Caller ID for handshakes to jog my memory as I greet someone who clearly thinks he or she knows me, and I suspect it could be delivered through a nifty chip in my right hand and a database behind my ear. Google Glass might become Google Lens, implanted and able to correct your cataracts to boot.

Further, while communication about medical devices is heavily regulated and their use largely restricted to correcting maladies, as opposed to improving performance, one can imagine changes in both factors in time. Manufacturers might give these brands the full imagery and personality treatment. I picture the young soccer enthusiast with a poster for the longed-for sport knee, guaranteed to give a leg up in performance, next to the poster for the star goalie.

A critical question is whether people do indeed have special relationships with these branded products – *my BHR is my friend* but in a more intense way than my car is my friend – or whether these products are part of the self – *my BHR is me*. Such products remind us of "possessions and the extended self" (Belk 1988; 2013) but in the case of my hips, I don't feel extended so much as rebuilt or, possibly, reimagined, given that they actually work better than the parts with which I was born. The sense of identity work has grown profoundly intimate for me in selecting these branded products, reflecting questions, literally, about who and what am I. This can only grow more complex as people select health and technology implants that deliver new benefits or enhanced performance. Further, I rather wonder if the sense of self remains unitary such that I have absorbed these products into Brand Ann or if I have become something of a team player – with a very different sense of that term: self as team.

Research in medicine suggests people may be less single organisms than they are ecosystems, for example, relying on gut bacteria to regulate health and weight. Might it be the same with these internal brands? That is, with the potential to give implants full bore brand personalities, are we indeed creating groups more than individuals? Person as brand system? Instead of brand community uniting people around a single brand, are we here single people comprising a community of brands? "Hi, nice to meet you, we are Ann-BHR-Stryker-Google-Apple-Fitbit." And really, what happens if we anthropomorphize a branded body part to the point of thinking it has volition? How does BHR feel about this hike? Do I think of myself as being of sound *minds* and body? Duus (2013) notes that people may treat prosthetics in anthropomorphized terms – "Mr Leg" – laying a foundation for work in this area, and highlights the human–companion relationship. However, this research also raises for me questions about distinctions between internal products and those that attach, and between those that rectify and those that enhance.

Critically, an implant is with us 24/7 and is part of us. Do we absorb it – Ann *with* an implant – or partner with it – Ann *and* the implant? That distinction may suggest a very different self-construal as well as different relationships among and between consumers, brands, and each other. Current models of the self and of self-brand connections seem unable to address these relationships of nearly permanent connection, suggesting an important frontier for future work.

* * *

Digital technologies are creating massive change in the universe of branding

Robert V. Kozinets

When we consider the massive increases in computer power and programming sophistication and link them to the major cultural and social changes wrought by the Internet, we find that we are on the very cusp of evolutionary and revolutionary changes in the way that brands are conceptualized and the ways that they play a part in people's lives. On the frontiers of social branding, examining the rapid transformations technologically transpiring in the world around us, the view has never been more dynamic or thrilling.

The wave that we call social media is already in full development, but is unlikely to crest for at least another decade or two. Let us consider that wave for a moment. We certainly have seen the rapid rise of brands such as Facebook and Twitter, a social networking site and a microblogging service, respectively, that facilitate different kinds of information exchanges between people on a new, largely unfiltered, global platform. Facebook and Twitter themselves have become powerhouse brands, instantly recognizable symbols of a new dotcom boom, a resurgent rise in Silicon Valley, brands that create billions of dollars in value on the stock market. As advertising brands, Facebook and Twitter seek to and sometimes do successfully challenge traditional advertising media such as newspapers, magazines, and television. They have become much more precisely targeted advertising servers, among other things. These social media sites established a form of networked sociality, where established and close relationships can be maintained at the same time as new ones are sought and established. Are there ways to involve brands more directly in new and old friendships than simply sitting as ads to be clicked or pages to be shared or liked? The branding implications of these fifty shades of friendship are ripe and nearly unexplored territory for marketers and academics alike.

Social media also empowers the branding efforts of ordinary people in different ways. Facebook, for instance, is a site that has developed into a place where people can create life narratives for themselves and share them with a group of people, most of whom they presumably know through friend and family personal relationships. Alison Hearn (2008: 205) sees the rise of personal branding as a movement, and links this movement to "neoliberalism, flexible accumulation, and the rise of a culture of promotionalism with the postmodern brand as life-defining resource". This promotionalism is explicit in the occupational social network LinkedIn, which facilitates the act of personal branding for economic purposes. Andrew Wernick (1991: 181), in his book, *Promotional Culture*, explores how many different kinds of communications are now promotional, and how, through them, people seek to develop an edge which he terms a "self-advantaging exchange" that reveals capitalism colonizing social relations and communications. The same could certainly be said of many users of Twitter. The bottom line is that technology in its social media manifestations is not only building massive online advertising and promotions brands that challenge traditional print and broadcast media such as Facebook and Twitter, but it is also facilitating an unprecedented rise in the diffusion, use, and professionalism of personal branding, with potentially major social, economic, and cultural effects.

Digital information and communications technologies are also spawning entirely new ways of producing, co-creating, and consuming. Since the first dotcom boom, it has become incredibly easy for anyone to create an online brand, fueling a branding gold rush. Rubinstein and Griffiths (2001) link the rise of interest in brands and branding to the dotcom boom, and I believe there is little doubt that this enthusiasm is Internet-enhanced. Even online, during fierce price competition, even with the most stringent economic tests, we find that "brand still matters," serving as a proxy for quality and trust, and all the other sources of meaning and value that marketers had always known it stood for. Yet, we are now faced with a myriad of challenges as new forms of brand and branding emerge on an almost-daily basis, a brand proliferation the likes of which marketing and social scientists have never before seen or dreamed. Not only are there many, many more brands, and hence more brand relationships, there are also many more kinds of brands, and thus brand relationships.

In a study of the development of the Apache software brand, Füller, Schroll, and von Hippel (2013) conclude that where once products and brands were expensive to develop and diffuse, with the Internet's low cost communications capabilities, they are now cheap and relatively easy, perhaps even being spawned as natural developments of online social activities. The social and commercial implications of individual, dyadic, small groups, and larger interactions naturally spawning and diffusing brands is almost mind-boggling. Questions regarding how such brands will be managed, defended, and maintained abound. I think there are interesting models and applications of population ecology models to study the Cambrian growth, rapid rises, competitive consolidations, and expansion of ecosystems that we are seeing in the world of Internet branding (cf., Javalgi *et al.* 2004).

Massive brand proliferation at industry and individual levels and brand professionalization at personal levels are only the beginning of the story. For, perhaps the most exciting developments are in the mutations and experimentations that surround what I have recently termed "social brand engagement": the linkage of brand to human relationships. In this emerging field, managers attempt a higher-order level of engagement that transcends individual-brand relationships and extends into active group relations. At that level, with the digital brand autonomously participating in group concerns and conversations, brands will rise to the status of near personhood and an entirely new world of branding will be born.

References

Belk, R.W. (1988) "Possessions and the Extended Self", *Journal of Consumer Research*, 15 (September): 139–168.

Belk, R.W. (2013) "Extended Self in a Digital World", *Journal of Consumer Research*, 40 (October): 477–500.

Brown, S., P. McDonagh, and C.J. Shultz (2013) "Titanic: Consuming the Myths and Meanings of an Ambiguous Brand", *Journal of Consumer Research*, 40 (4): 595–614.

Duus, R. (2013) "Speak to the Leg: A Post-Paralympic Analysis of Consumer-Object Relations", *E – European Advances in Consumer Research*, eds G. Cornelissen, E. Reutskaja, A.Valenzuela. Barcelona: Association for Consumer Research.

Fitzsimons, G., T. Chartrand, and G.J. Fitzsimons (2008) "Automatic Effects of Brand Exposure on Motivated Behavior: How Apple Makes You 'Think Different", *Journal of Consumer Research*, 35 (June): 21–35.

Fournier, S. (2009) "Lessons Learned about Consumers' Relationships with their Brands", *Handbook of Brand Relationships*, eds D.J. MacInnis, C.W. Park, and J. Priester, Society for Consumer Psychology. Armonk, NY: M.E. Sharpe: 5–23.

Fournier, S. and G. Eckhardt (2013) "Managing a Corporeal Brand", Compro Biz Blog Network, September 24, 2013.

Fournier, S., L. Hsu, and S. Srinivasan (2011) "How Brand Portfolio Strategy Affects Firm Value", *Marketing Science Working Paper Series*, Report No. 11–112. Boston MA: Marketing Science Institute.

Füller, J., R. Schroll, and E. von Hippel (2013) "User Generated Brands and their Contribution to the Diffusion of User Innovations", *Research Policy*, 42 (May): 1197–1209.

Giesler, M. (2012) "How Doppelgänger Brand Images Influence the Market Creation Process: Longitudinal Insights from the Rise of Botox Cosmetic", *Journal of Marketing*, 76 (6, November): 55–68.

Hearn, A. (2008) "'Meat, Mask, Burden' Probing the Contours of the Branded 'Self'", *Journal of Consumer Culture*, 8 (2): 197–217.

Javalgi, R., B. Cutler, and P. Todd (2004) "An Application of an Ecological Model to Explain the Growth of Strategies of Internet Firms: The Cases of eBay and Amazon", *European Management Journal*, 22 (August): 464–470.

Park, J.K. and D. Roedder John (2010) "Got to Get You Into My Life: Do Brand Personalities Rub Off on Consumers?", *Journal of Consumer Research*, 37 (December): 655–669.

Park, J.K. and D. Roedder John (2014) "I Think I Can, I Think I Can: Brand Use, Self-efficacy, and Performance", *Journal of Marketing Research*, 51 (April): 233–247.

Rubinstein, H. and C. Griffiths (2001) "Branding Matters More on the Internet", *Journal of Brand Management*, 8 (July): 394–404.

Shachar, R., T. Erdem, K.M. Cutright, and G.J. Fitzsimons (2011) "Brands: The Opiate of the Nonreligious Masses?", *Marketing Science*, 30 (1, January–February): 92–110.

Wang, Y., D. Roedder John, and V. Griskevicius (2014) "The Devil Wears Prada: How Luxury Consumption Influences Social Behavior", working paper, University of Minnesota.

Wernick, A. (1991) *Promotional Culture: Advertising, Ideology and Symbolic Expression*. Thousand Oaks, CA: Sage Publications, Inc.

NAMES INDEX

BRANDS INDEX

GENERAL INDEX

accommodation as loyalty practice 22
actual consumption behavior 403–5
advertising 30, 45, 64, 65, 207, 305, 357,
  364, 379; anthropomorphism 124,
  131–2; celebrities 66, 81–92;
  consumer-generated 407; funnel
  concept 360; luxury industry 66, 331,
  336, 339; photography 406, 407, 408;
  social media 412
AIDA concept 360
alcoholic beverages 335, 337, 338
alliances, brand 402
ambiguous brands 57, 398
anthropomorphism 119–32, 153–4, 155,
  377–8; body parts 411; consumer
  evaluation 124–5; cross-cultural analysis
  135–47; explanations for 121–4;
  humanized brand and branded human
  152–3, 155; implications for brand
  relationships 126–31
apps 161–9
archetypes 149, 153–4, 378
artificial intelligence (AI) 151, 154–5, 157
assembled lives 13–14, 24–5; assemblages
  15–16; assembling loyalties 17–18;
  brands' relational capabilities within
  webs of assembled relations 21–4;
  findings 19–21; imaging consumers'
  14–15; milieus 17; overview of
  informants and data 18–19; territories
  16
associative networks 408–10
athletic shoes and anthropomorphism
  139–44

attachment theory 245–6, 267, 311, 361
attribution theory 234, 245, 246
Austria: immigrant consumers and
  multicultural marketing 203–15
authenticity 180, 182, 291, 292, 336, 408
autonomy 346; or dependence *see* identity
  tensions in business-based brand
  relationships

balance theory 86
bargain shoppers 339
beer 48, 54–6, 57, 65
behavior, actual consumption 403–5
behavioral shifts and nonconscious brand
  exposure 409
belonging, need for 123, 227, 228, 244, 285
bereavement, consumption 263–78;
  continuation 271, 272–3; denial 265,
  268–9, 270; despair/hopelessness 266,
  271, 272; discussion 273–7; findings
  268–73; future research 277–8;
  managerial implications 276–7; method
  267–8; negative emotions 269, 270;
  search 266, 269, 270; social
  embeddedness of consumer-brand
  bonds 273; theoretical framework
  264–7; transference 266–7, 271, 272,
  275, 277
big data 345, 397
big versus small brands 71; competitive
  context *see separate entry*
blogs 156, 166, 167, 168, 407; brand
  building by sharing secrets 172–82
body parts 410–11